KU-607-168

LIVERPOOL JMU LIBRARY

3 1111 01509 4624

How to access the supplemental web resource

We are pleased to provide access to a web resource that supplements your textbook, *Developmental Physical Education for All Children, Fifth Edition.* This resource offers reproducible forms, learning aids from the book, and additional learning activities, some of which are enhanced by video clips that demonstrate concepts in action.

Accessing the web resource is easy!
Follow these steps if you purchased a new book:

1. Visit www.HumanKinetics.com/DevelopmentalPhysicalEducationforAllChildren.

2. Click the fifth edition link next to the corresponding fifth edition book cover.

3. Click the Sign In link on the left or top of the page. If you do not have an account with Human Kinetics, you will be prompted to create one.

4. If the online product you purchased does not appear in the Ancillary Items box on the left of the page, click the Enter Key Code option in that box. Enter the key code that is printed at the right, including all hyphens. Click the Submit button to unlock your online product.

5. After you have entered your key code the first time, you will never have to enter it again to access this product. Once unlocked, a link to your product will permanently appear in the menu on the left. For future visits, all you need to do is sign in to the textbook's website and follow the link that appears in the left menu!

→ Click the Need Help? button on the textbook's website if you need assistance along the way.

How to access the web resource if you purchased a used book:

You may purchase access to the web resource by visiting the text's website, **www.HumanKinetics.com/DevelopmentalPhysicalEducationforAllChildren**, or by calling the following:

800-747-4457 . . . . .U.S. customers
800-465-7301 . . . . .Canadian customers
+44 (0) 113 255 5665 . . . . European customers
08 8372 0999 . . . . Australian customers
0800 222 062 . . . . New Zealand customers
217-351-5076 . . . . International customers

For technical support, send an e-mail to:
support@hkusa.com . . . . U.S. and international customers
info@hkcanada.com . . . . Canadian customers
academic@hkeurope.com . . . . European customers
keycodesupport@hkaustralia.com . . . . . Australian and New Zealand customers

HUMAN KINETICS
The Information Leader in Physical Activity & Health

11-2016

Product: Developmental Physical Education for All Children web resource

Key code: CLELAND-JKUTXL-OSG

This unique code allows you access to the web resource.

Access is provided if you have purchased a new book. Once submitted, the code may not be entered for any other user.

Developmental Physical Education for All Children

Theory Into Practice

FIFTH EDITION

Frances Cleland Donnelly, PED

West Chester University

Suzanne S. Mueller, EdD

Professor Emeritus
East Stroudsburg University

David L. Gallahue, EdD

Dean Emeritus and Professor Emeritus
Indiana University

HUMAN KINETICS

Library of Congress Cataloging-in-Publication Data

Names: Donnelly, Frances Cleland, 1951- author. | Mueller, Suzanne S., 1947-
author. | Gallahue, David L., author. | Gallahue, David L. Developmental
physical education for all children.

Title: Developmental physical education for all children : theory into
practice / Frances Cleland Donnelly, PEd, West Chester University, Suzanne
S. Mueller, EdD, Professor Emeritus, East Stroudsburg University, David L.
Gallahue, EdD, Dean Emeritus and Professor Emeritus, Indiana University.

Description: Fifth Edition. | Champaign : Human Kinetics, [2016] | "This book
is a revised edition of Developmental Physical Education for All Children,
published in 2003 by David L. Gallahue and Frances Cleland Donnelly"--T.p.
verso. | Includes bibliographical references, webography and index.

Identifiers: LCCN 2016017790| ISBN 9781450441575 (print) | ISBN 1492533300
(ebook)

Subjects: LCSH: Physical education for children. | Movement education. |
Motor learning. | Physical education for children--Study and teaching.

Classification: LCC GV443 .G232 2016 | DDC 372.86/044--dc23 LC record available at https://lccn.loc.gov/2016017790

ISBN: 978-1-4504-4157-5 (print)

Copyright © 2017 by Frances Cleland Donnelly, Suzanne Mueller, and David Gallahue
Copyright © 2003 by David L. Gallahue and Frances Cleland Donnelly
Copyright © 1996 by Times Mirror Higher Education Group, Inc.

All rights reserved. Except for use in a review, the reproduction or utilization of this work in any form or by any electronic, mechanical, or other means, now known or hereafter invented, including xerography, photocopying, and recording, and in any information storage and retrieval system, is forbidden without the written permission of the publisher.

This book is a revised edition of *Developmental Physical Education for All Children,* published in 2003 by David L. Gallahue and Frances Cleland Donnelly.

The web addresses cited in this text were current as of March 2016, unless otherwise noted.

Acquisitions Editor: Ray Vallese; **Developmental Editor:** Jacqueline Eaton Blakley; **Managing Editors:** Anne E. Mrozek, Carly S. O'Connor, Karla Walsh, and Nicole Moore; **Copyeditor:** Tom Tiller; **Indexer:** Andrea J. Hepner; **Permissions Manager:** Dalene Reeder; **Senior Graphic Designer:** Joe Buck; **Cover Designer:** Keith Blomberg; **Photograph (cover):** © Human Kinetics; **Photographs (interior):** © Human Kinetics, unless otherwise noted; **Photo Asset Manager:** Laura Fitch; **Photo Production Manager:** Jason Allen; **Art Manager:** Kelly Hendren; **Associate Art Manager:** Alan L. Wilborn; **Illustrations:** © Human Kinetics, unless otherwise noted; **Printer:** Walsworth.

We thank Springton Manor Elementary School in Glenmoore, PA, and Chester County Family Academy (CCFA) in West Chester, PA for assistance in providing the location for the photo and video shoot for this book.

Printed in the United States of America

10 9 8 7 6 5 4 3 2 1

The paper in this book was manufactured using responsible forestry methods.

Human Kinetics
Website: www.HumanKinetics.com

United States: Human Kinetics
P.O. Box 5076
Champaign, IL 61825-5076
800-747-4457
e-mail: info@hkusa.com

Canada: Human Kinetics
475 Devonshire Road Unit 100
Windsor, ON N8Y 2L5
800-465-7301 (in Canada only)
e-mail: info@hkcanada.com

Europe: Human Kinetics
107 Bradford Road
Stanningley
Leeds LS28 6AT, United Kingdom
+44 (0) 113 255 5665
e-mail: hk@hkeurope.com

Australia: Human Kinetics
57A Price Avenue
Lower Mitcham, South Australia 5062
08 8372 0999
e-mail: info@hkaustralia.com

New Zealand: Human Kinetics
P.O. Box 80
Mitcham Shopping Centre, South Australia 5062
0800 222 062
e-mail: info@hknewzealand.com

E5822

I wish to dedicate the fifth edition of *Developmental Physical Education for All Children: Theory Into Practice* to physical educators who touch the lives of children every day (Cathy Hill you rock!) and to future physical educators who will have this amazing opportunity. I also dedicate this textbook to my grandchildren, George Everett Cattell, Max Allen Cattell, Benjamin Joseph Cattell, Brooks Paul King, and Georgia Grace King, in hopes that their physical education teachers will provide them with meaningful and developmentally appropriate movement experiences. A special thanks to a friend and colleague, Jackie Lund, for urging me to pursue this project. I thank my husband Jim Donnelly for his support through the four years it has taken to write this textbook. I also thank my co-author Suzanne Mueller for her amazing depth of knowledge in the field of motor development and motor learning and also for some delicious new recipes! And finally, I thank my mentor, David Gallahue for his support and encouragement throughout my career. - *Fran Cleland*

I dedicate this edition to my grandchildren, Colton Mueller and Jaimie and Angeline Flogel, members of the generation who will benefit from quality developmental physical education and be physically active for life. I am especially grateful to Fran and David for inviting me to join in the creation of the 5th edition. A special thanks to my husband, Norm MacIntyre for always understanding the writing process and to my family and friends for their love and support throughout the journey. – *Suzanne Mueller*

As always, to the *sunshine of my life*: Ellie, and to family, colleagues and friends who have supported our efforts on behalf of children for so many years. Passing the lead authorship torch to such a respected former student and colleague, Fran Cleland Donnelly, and to Suzanne Mueller is a genuine honor and privilege. – *David Gallahue*

Contents

Preface

What do all of the following children have in common?

- Ann chooses to jump rope with her friends during recess.
- Doug and Kaitlin get their parents to help build a backyard obstacle course so they can climb, swing, run, and jump.
- Tasaday enjoys using the community courts to hit balls against the tennis wall.
- Children in Ms. Santiago's math class are more focused after she implements periodic breaks for physical activity.
- Brooks points out to his mom how the midfield players give lead passes to the forwards.
- Ketura helps her younger brother step forward with his opposite foot when throwing.
- Jonathan feels confident enough to join neighborhood friends in a game of four square.
- Kelly and her friends like making up dances to perform for their families.
- Jose uses a pedometer to reach his goal of taking 10,000 steps a day.

All of these children are experiencing the joys and rewards of leading a physically active life. As a result, they are well on their way to developing fitness and movement skills that support academic achievement, confidence to pursue a variety of physical activities, health benefits of an active lifestyle, and social opportunities (e.g., meeting new friends) that are afforded by participating in physical activities.

A quality developmental physical education program lays the foundation for the knowledge, skills, and dispositions that enable children to pursue a physically active life. The importance of quality developmental physical education was emphasized in a recent report by the Institute of Medicine of the National Academies (2013):

> Physical education in school is the only sure opportunity for all school-aged children to access health-enhancing physical activity and the only school subject area that provides education to ensure that students develop knowledge, skill, and motivation to engage in health-enhancing physical activity for life. (p. 2)

Developmental Physical Education for All Children addresses quality physical education from a developmental perspective. The conceptual framework of developmental physical education emphasizes three components: child development, the movement framework (i.e., the vocabulary of movement), and standards-based instruction in physical education. The *child development* component focuses on increased physical competence and the acquisition of movement skills based on the developmental level of learners in pre-K through grade 5 in multiple domains: motor, fitness, cognitive, and affective. The *movement framework* illustrates appropriate movement content for learners' developmental levels (fundamental and specialized phases). The *national standards for physical education* (SHAPE America, 2014) address the developmental phases and provide a framework for designing a physical education program—including activities, instruction, and assessment—that enables children to become physically active for a lifetime.

All three components of the conceptual framework are crucial to any effort to design and implement a quality developmental program. With that fact in mind, *Developmental Physical Education for All Children* is organized into the following sections:

- **Part I—The Learner (chapters 1–4):** Teachers need to thoroughly understand learners in order to "create maximum opportunities for students of all abilities to be successful" (National Association for Sport and Physical Education [NASPE] & American Heart Association [AHA], 2012, p. 6). Teachers can foster success by providing children with learning experiences that reflect their stages of motor development and their levels of motor skill learning. In light of this reality, the chapters included in part I establish the need for quality developmental physical education for all children, highlight national initiatives supporting developmental physical education, and detail the developmental characteristics of learners in pre-K through grade 5 from the perspectives of motor development, movement skill learning, fitness development, cognitive development, and affective (emotional and social) development.

- **Part II—Movement Content and the Learning Environment (chapters 5–7):** The chapters included here introduce the Active Child movement framework to describe the movement content that is developmentally appropriate for learners in pre-K through grade 5. These chapters also explore the learning environment, which includes not only the space and equipment but also the methods used to structure both the movement environment and the movement tasks so that they match learners' developmental needs. To this end, the movement skill learning experiences presented in this textbook are based on a four-part task progression: *preconsistent* (pre-K), *consistent* (K-2), *combination*, and *application* (grades 3 through 5). The goal of *preconsistent* learning activities is to engage pre-K children in movements that support their maturation through the initial and emergent stages of motor skill development. Task progressions for K-2 learners are labeled *consistent* because the goal is to achieve mature performance of the fundamental motor skills. Learning experiences for both pre-K and K-2 learners are based on fundamental movement skill themes and movement concepts.

In grades 3 through 5, students move into the specialized movement skill phase, which consists of the *combination* and *application* progressions. As the name suggests, the goal at the *combination* level is to combine skills into smooth sequences. At the *application* level, the goal is to apply skills in culturally significant movement activities—such as developmental games, dance, and gymnastics—that foster children's achievement of application task progressions. This four-part progression is depicted in the following movement task progression for the skill of kicking (see figure 1).

• **Part III—Instructional Design (chapters 8–12):** These chapters are grounded in the *National Standards and Grade-Level Outcomes for K-12 Physical Education* (SHAPE America, 2014). The national physical education standards and outcomes articulate what students should know and be able to do as a result of a quality K-12 physical education program. The standards-based instruction design process starts with establishing learning goals based on the standards, determining content objec-

Level	Skill	Kicking task progression	
Fundamental	**KICKING**	**Preconsistent** (Immature beginner)	**Consistent** (Beginner)
		Equipment: Stationary, lightweight, and 5˝-7˝ balls and plastic cones. Tasks: Kick a stationary ball from a stance at a wall Kick to large targets • at close to moderate distances • placed low to eye level on wall • that make a sound or move on impact • between cones or through large goals	Equipment: Junior-size, medium-texture balls Tasks: Kick a ball from short to moderate approach Kick ball to short distances that require approach and full windup Kick a ball at or below midline to travel at different levels (along ground or in air) Kick to targets of varying size, height, distance Kick a rolling ball from a stance Kick a rolling ball to different distances Short-tap dribble along ground Start and stop dribbling Dribble on different pathways to avoid obstacles
Specialized		**Combination** (Intermediate)	**Application** (Intermediate)
		Equipment: Soft textured balls varying in size and weight Tasks: Short approach to kick a rolling ball to different levels and locations Trap and kick balls arriving from partner at different distances, directions, levels, and speeds. Kick to moving partner Trap and dribble Dribble and kick to stationary targets Vary pathway and speed of dribble to avoid obstacles Dribble and pass cooperatively with a partner Dribble, pass, and kick to targets or goals cooperatively with a partner	Equipment: Balls of different shapes, sizes, and textures Tasks: Kick a rolling ball to different distances, levels, and locations in fielding games Kick at targets while being defended in 1v1 invasion games. Kick and dribble 2v1 and 3v3 "keep away" games Kick and dribble in small-sided soccer invasion games with tactics of maintaining possession and attacking the goal.

Figure 1 Movement task progression for kicking.

tives and acceptable evidence of students' learning, and designing instructional activities and practices to enable students to achieve the learning goals.

In other words, when we base the instruction design process on standards, we ensure that what we teach, how we teach, and how we assess learning all derive from developmentally appropriate learning goals and content objectives. Helping diverse learners achieve learning goals requires us to understand their unique needs and modify our instruction accordingly. To do so, we acknowledge children's level of motor skill learning in order to provide appropriate practice conditions and feedback.

Part III also addresses the *Spectrum of Teaching Styles* (Mosston & Ashworth, 2008), which provides you with a framework from which to choose styles of teaching informed by awareness of the entire learning process. More specifically, the Spectrum framework enables you to plan and implement instructional strategies that engage your students either in a *reproduction cluster* (in which they duplicate movements or ideas that you explain and demonstrate) or in a *production cluster* (in which they discover movements, concepts, and principles).

All learners need a supportive climate, which you can create through positive classroom management and knowledge of the needs of diverse students and students with disabilities. To help you do so, part III also provides developmentally appropriate protocols, social contracts, and conflict resolution strategies for creating and maintaining an environment that is conducive to both learning and positive behavior; as well as learning experiences for diverse students and students with disabilities.

● **Part IV—Standards-Based Learning Experiences for Pre-K Through Grade 2 (chapters 13–17):** These learning experiences integrate the following elements: knowledge of learners aged 3 to 7; developmentally appropriate content addressing fundamental movement skills; and instruction, practice, and assessment strategies that enable children to achieve grade-level outcomes based on the national standards. We begin with movement activities based on physical education standard 4 in order to lay the foundation for helping children develop behaviors of personal and social responsibility that contribute to a positive learning experience.

Next, developmentally appropriate movement activities address standards 1 and 2 by focusing on fundamental movement skills (locomotor, stability, and manipulative) and movement concepts (body, space, effort, and relationship). Standard 3 is then addressed by engaging children in moderate to vigorous physical activity through participation in fundamental movement skills. For standard 5, K-2 children recognize the value of physical activity by reflecting on how their participation leads to enjoyment and provides a challenge.

● **Part V—Standards-Based Learning Experiences for Grades 3 Through 5 (chapters 18–22):** As in part IV, the learning experiences presented here integrate knowledge of the relevant learners, in this case those aged 8 through 11 years; developmentally appropriate content, in this case involving *specialized* skills; and instruction, practice, and assessment strategies that enable children to achieve grade-level outcomes based on the national standards. And again as in part IV, we begin with movement activities based on physical education standard 4 to lay the foundation for helping children develop behaviors of personal and social responsibility that contribute to a positive learning experience.

Next, developmentally appropriate movement activities address standards 1 and 2, in this case by focusing on *specialized* movement skills and movement concepts in the form of educational games, dance, and gymnastics. Standard 3 is addressed in this section by engaging children in activities that integrate health-related fitness components and the FITT guidelines for frequency, intensity, time, and type of activity. For standard 5, children in grades 3 through 5 recognize the value of physical activity by reflecting on how their participation leads to enjoyment, challenges them, and provides opportunities for positive social interaction.

● **Part VI—Professional Development (chapters 23 and 24):** This section offers a comprehensive view of a 21st-century elementary physical educator who

- uses a conceptual framework to prepare and implement a developmental, standards-based scope and sequence for physical education in pre-K through grade 5;
- stays current in the field;
- is professionally involved; and
- advocates for comprehensive physical activity in school.

UPDATES

The fifth edition of *Developmental Physical Education for All Children* has been thoroughly updated. This edition shows teachers how to incorporate their understanding of motor development and motor learning theory into the design of learning experiences based on the stage characteristics of pre-K through grade 5 children's psychomotor, cognitive, affective, and fitness development. The book is full of sample lessons that are aligned with the new SHAPE America national standards and grade-level outcomes. These movement experiences include tasks and extensions, scaled learning environments, skill cues, practice strategies, teaching style choices, and formative assessments aligned with the outcomes.

We have also added to this edition learning goal blueprints, a tool that integrates fundamental skills (locomotor, stability, and manipulative) with movement concepts (body, space, effort, and relationships) and specialized skills (games, dance, and gymnastics) with movement concepts and game tactics. The fifth edition also provides more depth with respect to fitness education, which is addressed from a developmental perspective. Finally, the fifth edition includes steps for the development of a standards-based curriculum and a chapter about the importance of ongoing professional development, involvement in professional associations such as SHAPE America, and advocacy.

To address the growing trend of schools serving the pre-K population, we have added developmental information about pre-K children along with learning experiences designed for them. Also new to the fifth edition is the application of motor learning theory, including but not limited to, addressing applicable stages of motor learning (cognitive and associative), designing the environment (i.e., equipment, condition and task variables), practice strategies (e.g., constant and variable), and feedback (knowledge of performance and results). This approach helps teacher candidates apply previously learned theory from their motor development and motor learning courses to design and implement learning experiences.

Several learning tools have been included to solidify key points and offer reference points in this comprehensive resource. Each chapter begins with a list of the chapter's objectives and closes with Big Ideas, a thorough summary of important concepts discussed in the chapter. Key terms are highlighted in red when first discussed in the text, and a complete glossary with definitions of these terms is included at the end of the book. A thorough reference list is included at the end as well, along with two appendices: appendix A describes and illustrates the stage characteristics (initial, elemen-

tary, mature) of all fundamental movement skills. Appendix B provides summative assessments for all fundamental movement skills.

ANCILLARIES

Developmental Physical Education for All Children is packaged with several ancillary components to complement the use of the textbook and enhance the teaching and learning processes.

The instructor guide (IG) offers a number of resources instructors can use throughout the semester as they organize and teach their course, including a sample syllabus. The IG includes many sample learning experiences designed for implementation in the gymnasium setting. At first glance some of these activities are similar to activities that appear in the student web resource (WR). However, the IG experiences provide hands-on movement activities engaging teacher candidates in the application of theoretical concepts, whereas the WR activities generally are reinforcing and testing knowledge of content.

For each chapter, the IG includes the following:

- **Chapter objectives** specify the students' learning goals.
- **Chapter summaries** provide a brief overview of chapter content and can serve as a refresher and guide to the major elements of the chapter.
- **Big Ideas** highlight the salient points of the chapter.
- **Learning activities** provide the instructor with several practice learning activities such as:
  - **Sample movement activities** designed for use in a gymnasium setting, stimulating teacher candidates' learning by highlighting theoretical concepts such as "What is quality developmental physical education?"
  - **Worksheets** are provided to challenge teacher candidates to analyze sample learning activities.
  - **Online links** augment students' learning by providing assignments highlighting chapter content.
- **Chapter review questions** challenge teacher candidates to reflect on chapter content.

In addition to the instructor guide we have provided a student web resource (WR) uniquely designed for teacher candidates. The web resource mirrors the instructor guide in many activities, but is designed for teacher candidates to complete either within the context of the classroom setting or independently. The web resource could also be used to "flip" the classroom learning experience. Teacher candidates could complete all or parts of the chapter resource prior to attending class. The instructor could then present additional learning activities to engage teacher candidates in the theoretical content of the chapter. One unique aspect of the web resource for teacher candidates is video footage of the fundamental movement skills and a couple of samples of best teaching practices in action. Worksheets and analysis tools are provided for teacher candidates to use when viewing these video clips. The web resource also includes sample assessments from the book in electronic format as well as both of the book's appendices.

A presentation package and test package are also available to help facilitate teaching this textbook's material. The presentations, delivered via Power-Point, highlight the main concepts of each chapter. The slides can be used as is, or they can be modified by the instructor to better fit the needs of a particular class. The test package contains multiple choice, true/false, fill-in-the-blank, and short-answer questions for each chapter to be used by the instructor to create tests, quizzes, homework assignments, or review sessions. These questions are meant to highlight key concepts from the chapters in order to test the students' knowledge of such concepts.

Quality developmental physical education can change children's lives. With this powerful potential in mind, *Developmental Physical Education for All Children: Theory Into Practice* provides you with a comprehensive approach for preparing programs that enable children to gain the knowledge, skills, and dispositions that are vital to leading a physically active life.

Acknowledgments

The fifth edition of *Developmental Physical Education for All Children: Theory into Practice* has been a challenging and exciting project. We thank Scott Wikgren for his confidence in our vision for this project. Additionally we thank the acquisitions editor, Ray Vallese, for his insight regarding the overall scope of the project but also with details of chapter design, ancillaries, and marketing. When it comes to details Jackie Blakley, our developmental editor, was superb. She made the editing process manageable and enjoyable! Dalene Reeder, our academic permissions editor, kept us on our toes throughout the writing process. Anne Mrozek, our managing editor, brought the project to a new height by facilitating the final edits and design of the textbook. We are also grateful for our two contributing authors, Dr. Debra Ballinger and Dr. Kat Ellis.

We thank Shane Daniels for directing the video and photo shoots, for Caroline Shorey's assistance as the photographer and Joe Watts as the videographer. A special thank you is due to Mr. Mike Petersen, the physical educator at Springton Elementary School in Downingtown, PA. Mike was extremely helpful in organizing all aspects of the photo shoot at his school. In addition, we thank the CEO of Chester County Family Academy (CCFA), Ms. Sue Flynn, and CCFA first and second grade teacher, Ms. Nicky Riess, for expediting the K-2 photo shoot. We also appreciate the assistance of Jayona Allen (West Chester University HPE teacher candidate) and Edgar Packer (West Chester University HPE graduate) who served as the physical educators in the CCFA photo shoot.

Without the pioneering efforts of David Gallahue, as a leader in shaping the theory of developmental physical education, this entire project would not be possible. David's contributions and connections with physical educators and university faculty from around the world are immeasurable.

Finally, we thank our God who sustains us, makes all things possible, and helps us see through new eyes.

PART
I

The Learner

Chapter 1

Quality Developmental Physical Education

Key Concepts

- Providing a rationale for daily quality physical education for children
- Identifying appropriate practices in elementary physical education
- Describing physical activity guidelines for children
- Identifying organizations and national initiatives that promote daily physical activity
- Describing developmental physical education

As a college student, you may be the product of a quality physical education program at the elementary and secondary school levels. On the other hand, you may have participated in physical education programs that were marginal (or worse) in terms of quality, quantity, or both. Take a moment to reflect on your experiences in physical education during your elementary school years. Did these experiences help you learn movement skills, develop fitness, and achieve cognitive and affective growth? Did your physical education take place in an environment conducive to learning about the health benefits of physical activity, developing critical thinking skills, and enjoying your learning? Did the instruction provided in your physical education classes take into account your developmental characteristics, such as your age-related interests, your ability to work productively with others, and your level of skill development?

If you answered yes to each of these questions, then you are one of the many fortunate individuals who benefited from a *quality physical education* program. If, on the other hand, you answered no to one or more of the questions, then you were deprived of a critically important educational experience. This sentiment was emphasized in the 2012 *Shape of the Nation Report* published by the National Association for Sport and Physical Education (NASPE) and the American Heart Association (AHA):

Quality physical education is an essential element in the formative growth of children and adolescents. At a minimum, it assures some degree of regular physical activity for most school-aged students. At its best, however, it creates a framework of life skills, which shape the whole person, encouraging smart choices and influencing a healthy lifestyle. Physical education is, in short, the best hope for the shape of our nation. (p. 4)

The 2016 *Shape of the Nation Report* also conveys the importance of quality physical education:

As our nation strives for school-age children to achieve the recommended 60 minutes of daily physical activity, all schools need to commit to making evidence-based physical education the cornerstone of their comprehensive school physical activity program. Physical education programs are a meaningful contributor to the development of healthy, active children and provide the safe, supervised, structured environment children need to learn and practice physically active behaviors." (p.3)

THE CASE FOR QUALITY PHYSICAL EDUCATION

Never before has the physical education profession been so strategically positioned to make a vital difference in the lives of children. The need is clear, as articulated in a 2013 report, titled *Educating the Student Body: Taking Physical Activity and Physical Education to School*, put forth by the Institute of Medicine of the National Academies:

School districts should provide high-quality curricular physical education during which the students should spend at least half . . . of the class-time engaged in vigorous or moderate-intensity physical activity. All elementary school students should spend an average of 30 minutes per day and all middle and high school students an average of 45 minutes per day in physical education class. (p. 1)

The report also suggests that the U.S. Department of Education designate physical education as a core subject because "physical education in school is the only sure opportunity for all school-aged children to access health-enhancing physical activity and the only school subject area that provides education to ensure that students develop knowledge, skill, and motivation to engage in health-enhancing physical activity for life" (p. 2).

In December 2015, the United States Congress passed the reauthorization of the Elementary and Secondary Education Act, the Every Student Succeeds Act (ESSA). The act replaces *No Child Left Behind* as the federal education legislation that funds and provides the framework for elementary and secondary education in the United States. School health and physical education have been included in ESSA and as a result, states and school districts will have access to significant funding for health education and physical education programs. School health and physical education are now identified as part of a student's "well-rounded" education.

This realization has even reached the White House, as evidenced by the launch of the Let's Move! program in 2013. A part of the First Lady's *Let's Move!* initiative, Let's Move! Active Schools helps schools develop a culture in which physical activity and physical education are foundational to academic success. **Let's Move! Active Schools** addresses five key areas (see figure 1.1):

- Physical education
- Physical activity during school
- Physical activity before and after school
- Family and community involvement
- Staff involvement

To help educators develop, implement, and evaluate comprehensive school physical activity programs, an online guide has been developed by the Centers for Disease Control and Prevention (CDC) and the Society of Health and Physical Educators (SHAPE America) (CDC, 2015). SHAPE America is the premier organization promoting research and advancing professional practice in health and

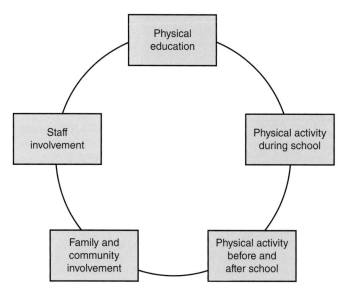

Figure 1.1 Five key areas of the Let's Move! Active Schools program.

physical education. The society collaborates with government agencies, organizations, and companies to sponsor physical activity programs and initiatives conducted in schools.

Parents can also play a key role in helping children get physically active, as indicated in the 2012 **Shape of the Nation Report** (NASPE & AHA). The report highlights ways in which parents can advocate proactively for quality physical education and physical activity programs in schools. Specifically, it suggests that parents ask their child's principal the following questions:

- How much time does my child spend in physical education class each week?
- Is my child taught by a certified physical education teacher?
- Is there enough equipment for all children to participate at the same time?
- Is the class size similar to that of other subject areas to ensure safe, effective instruction?
- Is physical education required for all grade levels from kindergarten through grade 12?
- Do children have other opportunities to be physically active before, during, and after school?

National Reports

The *Shape of the Nation Report* (NASPE & AHA, 2012) has provided alarming statics about the medical status of U.S. children. For example, in 2009-2010, 16.9% of children and adolescents from two

through 19 years of age were obese (Ogden, Carroll, Kit & Flegal, 2012).

It is clear, then, that our children need to get moving, because regular physical activity can serve as a significant preventive measure. With this fact in mind, the U.S. Department of Health and Human Resources published **Physical Activity Guidelines for Americans** in 2008. These guidelines indicate that children and adolescents (those aged 6 to 17 years) should engage in at least one hour of physical activity every day in order to accrue substantial health benefits. In addition, most of this activity time should involve aerobic physical activity of either moderate or vigorous intensity. Furthermore, as part of their daily physical activity, children and adolescents should engage in vigorous activity on at least three days per week. They also should perform muscle- and bone-strengthening activity on at least three days per week.

QPE and Future Physical Activity

Quality physical education (QPE) programs are needed in order to help students increase their physical competence, their health-related fitness, their self-responsibility, and their enjoyment of physical activity so that they can be active for a lifetime (NASPE, 2004, p. 6). Quality physical education classes can engage children in appropriate and meaningful physical activity, help them achieve a portion of the recommended daily physical activity, and provide them with the knowledge and skills necessary to lead a healthy active lifestyle.

Motor **development** scholars generally agree that fundamental movement skills serve as the building blocks for more complex motor skills and movement patterns and enable the underlying performance required for students to participate in many forms of physical activity (Gallahue, Ozmun, & Goodway, 2012; Haywood & Getchell, 2014; Payne & Isaacs, 2008). In fact, "research shows a real link between quality physical education and present and future physical activity participation. One possible reason for this link is that youth choose to participate in physical activities if they have skills that enable them to participate" (NASPE & AHA, 2012, pp. 3–4).

QPE and Health Benefits

When students participate in a quality physical education program and engage in regular physical activity, they experience overall health benefits. In fact, the U.S. Department of Health and Human Services has noted in the *Shape of the Nation Report*

Instant activities engage children in purposeful movement in the first few minutes after entering class.

a *direct correlation* between regular physical activity and health among children and adolescents. More specifically, regular physical activity can help prevent risk factors for various chronic diseases, such as heart disease, high blood pressure, type 2 diabetes, and osteoporosis (NASPE & AHA, 2010, p. 3).

QPE and Academic Performance

Quality physical education has also been associated with a range of academic performance indicators, including cognitive skills (e.g., concentration, creativity), attitude (e.g., self-esteem, motivation), academic behaviors (e.g., conduct), and academic achievement (e.g., GPA, standardized test scores) (Centers for Disease Control and Prevention [CDC], 2010). In addition, increasing one's physical activity can provide more benefits. Ericcson (2008) found that extending physical education from two days per week to daily sessions was associated positively with academic achievement in math, reading, and writing test scores. Furthermore, the increased time devoted to physical education does *not* appear to have negative associations with academic achievement; in fact, the majority of research addressing how physical education affects academic achievement finds a positive relationship (CDC, 2010, p. 18).

QPE Achieved by Appropriate Practices

In 2009, NASPE published a report titled Appropriate Instructional Practice Guidelines for Elementary School Physical Education that laid out best practices with respect to the learning environment, instructional strategies, curriculum, assessment,

and professionalism. Specific practices addressed in each of these categories are covered in the following summary.

- **Lesson content:** SHAPE America's *National Standards and Grade-Level Outcomes for K-12 Physical Education* (2014) is an excellent resource and enables teachers to design standards-based lessons with objectives to address students' developmental status. Lesson objectives should be clearly communicated to the children and be based both on children's stages of motor, cognitive, and affective development and on their level of motor skill learning. Once these objectives are established, all instructional tasks must then be aligned with them. (See chapters 8 through 10 for more on standards-based instruction.)

- **Instant activities:** Instant activities engage children in purposeful movement in the first few minutes after entering physical education class. An instant activity might be based on a review of previously learned movement skills; it might also focus on one or more fitness components or include a cognitive or social focus.

- **Sequential developmental curriculum:** In pre-K through grade 2, units of instruction carefully sequence lessons based on fundamental movement skill themes and movement concepts (see the pre-consistent and consistent skill progressions provided in chapters 13 and 14). In grades 3 through 5, children are engaged in logically sequenced educational games, dance, and gymnastics instructional tasks (see the combination and application skill progressions in chapters 18 through 21). More generally, teachers do not simply choose an activity because they recently learned it at a convention or found it on the Internet! To help you plan purposefully, chapter 23 provides an overview of the process of planning and sequencing a developmental curriculum.

- **Positive learning environment:** Teachers must create a welcoming, encouraging, and stimulating environment in which all children feel safe when learning new motor skills and concepts. Both emotional and physical safety can be fostered when developmentally appropriate rules are used consistently in the classroom. Therefore, teachers must reject practices that are not conducive to learning new movement skills or are otherwise inappropriate—for example, forming groups in a way that singles children out or conducting movement activities (e.g., relays) in a way that puts children "on display." To put it simply, teachers should always strive to preserve the dignity of the children in their care. Children must also learn how to communicate effectively with each other (see chapter 12 for more about developmentally appropriate protocols, rules, and social contracts).

- **Maximizing participation:** A given lesson should provide multiple practice opportunities, and half of the lesson should engage children in moderate to vigorous physical activity (CDC, 2000). Children should not have to wait in line for turns, and all children should be provided with appropriately sized equipment to facilitate practice.

- **Class size:** Physical education class sizes should be the same as for classes conducted in the regular classroom.

- **Differentiated instruction:** When physical educators design instructional tasks modified to address all students' developmental needs (see chapter 6 regarding scaling the environment and equipment; chapter 10 regarding inclusion-style instruction; and chapter 11 regarding differentiated instruction strategies). Meeting the unique needs of each child promotes high rates of success and helps each child build a positive sense of self.

- **Assessment:** Assessment can be either formative or summative. Formative assessment is directly linked to a lesson objective and should be used *during* an instructional unit to determine the effect of instruction on children's learning. The curriculum should also include summative assessments, which evaluate student learning and comprehension *at the end* of an instructional unit. (For more on assessment in physical education, see chapter 9.)

- **Professionalism:** A quality physical education program is taught by a certified physical educator who is a lifelong learner. Teachers grow professionally through getting involved in their district, state, and national profession associations. They keep up to date by reading professional literature, attending workshops, listening to webinars and podcasts, and taking graduate classes. They should also be part of a professional learning community at their school and serve as advocates by keeping administrators, colleagues, and parents informed about the physical education program (see chapter 24 for more on professionalism, leadership, and advocacy).

QPE Benefits

When teachers implement quality physical education practices, students experience the following benefits (National Association for Sport and Physical Education, 2004, pp. 6-7):

- **Skill development:** Physical education develops motor skills that allow for safe, successful, and satisfying participation in physical activities.

- **Regular, healthful physical activity:** Physical education provides a wide range of developmentally appropriate activities for children and youth. It encourages young people to choose to be physically active and aware of the benefits of this choice.

- **Improved physical fitness:** Quality physical education improves cardiorespiratory endurance, muscular strength, flexibility, muscular endurance, and body composition.

- **Self-discipline:** Physical education facilitates development of responsibility for personal health, safety, and fitness.

- **Improved judgment:** Quality physical education influences moral development. Students learn to assume leadership, cooperate with others, and accept responsibility for their own behavior.

- **Stress reduction:** Physical activity becomes an outlet for releasing tension and anxiety and facilitates emotional stability and resilience.

- **Strengthened peer relations:** Physical education is a major force in helping children and youth socialize with others and provides opportunities to learn positive social skills.

- **Improved self-confidence and self-esteem:** Physical education instills a stronger sense of self-worth in young people based on their mastery of skills and concepts in physical activity. They become more confident, assertive, independent, and self-controlled.

- **Goal setting:** Physical education gives children and youth the opportunity to set and strive for achievable personal goals.

OVERVIEW OF DEVELOPMENTAL PHYSICAL EDUCATION

This textbook addresses quality physical education from a developmental perspective. Developmental physical education (DPE) involves both study and application of the ways in which children in pre-K through grade 5 acquire skills in the motor, fitness, cognitive, and affective domains of learning in order to become physically active for a lifetime. When physical educators integrate and apply knowledge about learners, movement content, learning environment, and instructional design, they become highly qualified physical education teachers. Specifically, they do the following:

- Make instructional decisions based on their students' developmental stages and levels of learning.

- Deliver a standards-based curriculum that helps children adopt and maintain healthy lifestyles (NASPE, 2007).

- Implement appropriate instructional practices that embrace the tenets of quality physical education and the approaches indicated in *Appropriate Instructional Practice Guidelines for*

Elementary School Physical Education (NASPE, 2009).

- Plan comprehensive school physical activity programs supported by a standards-based physical education curriculum and led by a developmental physical educator who embodies professionalism.

At the center of developmental physical education is the learner. DPE uses concepts that address child development in the motor, cognitive, fitness, and affective domains to support the design of standards-based, best-practice instruction. In these ways, developmental physical education equips teachers to structure movement experiences that enable children to participate in and value a physically active lifestyle.

The time for quality physical education is now. This sense of urgency is shared by national entities (e.g., the Institute of Medicine of the National Academies and the U.S. Department of Health and Human Services) that recognize the importance QPE and its link to leading a physically active lifestyle. Quality physical education provides several health benefits and is positively associated with academic achievement. With all of this in mind, *Developmental Physical Education for All Children* provides you with a theoretical foundation and with practical applications for offering quality physical education learning experiences for all children.

Big Ideas

- Quality physical education classes enable children to engage in appropriate and meaningful physical activity, achieve a portion of their recommended daily physical activity, and develop the knowledge and skills necessary to lead a healthy active lifestyle.

- Research shows a connection between quality physical education and both present and future participation in physical activity. One possible reason for this link is that youth choose to participate in physical activities if they have skills that enable them to do so successfully.

- The importance of quality physical education and daily physical activity is supported by federal legislation, national reports, and national initiatives.

- Developmentally appropriate practices enable teachers to provide quality physical education.

- Developmental physical education involves study and application of the ways in which children in pre-K through grade 5 acquire skills in the motor, fitness, cognitive, and affective domains of learning in order to become physically active for a lifetime. Developmental physical education provides best-practice, standards-based instruction that enables children to develop the movement skills they need in order to lead a physically active life.

 Visit the web resource for learning activities, video clips, and review questions.

Chapter 2

The Healthy Child

Key Concepts

- Discussing the relationship between physical activity and children's health
- Defining the components of health-related fitness
- Explaining fitness education from a developmental perspective
- Describing developmentally appropriate practices in fitness education and fitness assessment
- Explaining the importance of good nutrition during childhood

A healthy child is one who engages in daily moderate to vigorous physical activity, achieves and maintains a health-enhancing level of physical fitness, and is provided with sound nutrition. Therefore, student health can be greatly improved by a comprehensive school physical education program. This chapter examines three specific, interacting factors that contribute to children's health: physical activity, fitness education, and nutrition education.

PHYSICAL ACTIVITY

This section examines the relationship between physical activity and children's growth patterns, the characteristics of a school physical activity program, and common obstacles that affect children's physical activity patterns.

Recommended Amount of Physical Activity

In 2008, the U.S. Department of Health and Human Services published the *Physical Activity Guidelines for Americans*, which advised that children and adolescents (aged 6 through 17) engage in 60 minutes or more of physical activity every day in order to accrue substantial health benefits. In addition, most of this activity time should involve aerobic physical activity of either moderate or vigorous intensity. Furthermore, as part of their daily physical activity, children and adolescents should engage in vigorous activity on at least three days per week. They also should perform muscle- and bone-strengthening activity on at least three days per week.

Physical activity is critical for childhood growth processes in the brain, in the nerves, in bone and muscle, and in other parts of the body. It also promotes students' health and academic development; in fact, when students spread physical activity throughout their day and limit their daytime *inactivity* to two hours, they are both readier to learn and able to achieve more. The question, then, is how to help students engage in appropriate levels of physical activity. Thankfully, a quality physical education class engages children in appropriate and meaningful physical activity and helps them achieve a portion of their recommended daily physical activity.

School Physical Activity Programs

To address the *Physical Activity Guidelines for Americans* (U.S. Department of Health and Human Services [HHS], 2008), SHAPE America has become a managing organization for the Let's Move! Active Schools (LMAS) campaign. This initiative promotes comprehensive school physical activity programs (CSPAPs) with quality physical education as the foundation. To help schools develop, implement, and evaluate CSPAPs, an online guide has been provided by SHAPE America and the Centers for Disease Control and Prevention (2013). The five components of a CSPAP are as follows:

- The *physical education program* comprises planned, sequential curricula and instruction based on physical education standards (state, national, or both) that enable all students, including those with disability, to develop the knowledge, skills, and confidence needed to adopt and maintain a physically active lifestyle.

- *Physical activity during school* provides opportunities for all students to practice what they have learned in physical education, work toward the nationally recommended 60 minutes or more of daily moderate to vigorous physical activity (MVPA), and prepare their brains for learning through integration of physical activity into classroom lessons, classroom breaks, and recess.

- *Physical activity before and after school* can include a variety of opportunities, such as walking or biking to school; participating in informal recreation or play on school grounds; engaging in physical activity in school-based child care; and taking part in school-based programs, clubs, or intramural sports.

- *Family and community involvement* can support a CSPAP by participating in evening or weekend special events and providing volunteer service to promote physical activity. School–community collaborations can use physical activities to create and enhance positive connections between school and community.

- *Staff involvement* in school-based physical activity provides multiple benefits. It improves staff members' health and provides positive role modeling and increased support for student participation in physical activity (see www.cdc.gov/healthyschools/physicalactivity/cspap.htm).

To help educators master these five components of *Let's Move!* Active Schools, SHAPE America provides toolkits for administrators, parent–teacher organizations, and physical education teachers. It also offers a free webinar series and extensive resources targeting each of the five components (see www.shapeamerica.org/prodev/lmas.cfm).

The goals for children's participation in physical activity are addressed in standard 3 of the national standards for physical education published by SHAPE America (2014): "The physically literate individual demonstrates the knowledge and skills to achieve and maintain a health-enhancing level of

Community fitness events present opportunities for collaboration between schools and the community at large.

physical activity and fitness" (p. 2, emphasis added). Thus standard 3 focuses on tools that enable children to internalize a desire to participate in MVPA on a daily basis. In pre-K through grade 2, the focus is on children participating in unstructured, enjoyable physical activity outside of school. By grades 3 through 5, children are expected to voluntarily choose regular participation in enjoyable, health-enhancing physical activities after school and in the community.

Taken together, then, standard 3 and the LMAS guidelines provide clear direction to help physical educators, families, and community members engage children in regular physical activity. This participation can be assessed through self-report surveys and fitness logs. For children in kindergarten through grade 2, families might be asked to keep a physical activity calendar for a week or more. In grades 3 through 5, children might use logs to record the frequency, duration, and intensity of the types of physical activity in which they participate regularly outside of school.

Obstacles to Physical Activity

A child's level of physical activity is influenced by various factors, including parental habits, socioeconomic status, use of technology, and play patterns. For example, research demonstrates that parental inactivity is a strong and positive predictor of child inactivity and that parent obesity is a strong predictor of child obesity. Thus poor lifestyle choices by parents can put their children's lives at risk (Fogelholm, Nuutinen, Pasanen, Myohanen, & Saatela, 1999).

Data reported on physical activity have also demonstrated that low-income children engage in physical activity less often than do children in higher income groups. In addition, low-income children are less likely than their higher-income counterparts to be involved in a team sport or other physical activity, and they watch significantly more television (Fox & Cole, 2004).

Excessive use of technology such as smartphones, tablets, and video games also leads to inactive lifestyles among children. In a typical day, children consume just over three hours of media (computers, phones, tablets, music, and reading). Two thirds of this time is spent with "screen media" (TV, computers, the Internet, etc.) while reading is less than 20 minutes per day (Conrad, n.d.). Current research is aimed at teaching children healthy lifestyles through active videogames, motor games and gamification of education activities (Gonzalez et al., 2016).

Trends in play patterns indicate that U.S. children have nine hours less free time per week than did children 25 years ago; more specifically, this decline includes a 25 percent decrease in play and a 50 percent decrease in outdoor activity (Gleave & Cole-Hamilton, 2012). Granted, *organized* activities for children contribute to children's physical activity levels, but unorganized activity is also important. Ginsburg states that "play is essential to development because it contributes to the cognitive, physical, social, and emotional well-being of children and youth. Play also offers an ideal opportunity for parents to engage fully with their children" (2007, p. 182). At the expense of recess or free child-centered play, our hurried lifestyles, changes in family structure, and increased attention to academics and enrichment activities contribute to sedentary behavior among children. Finally Ginsburg emphasizes, "Because every child deserves the opportunity to develop to their unique potential, child advocates must consider all factors that interfere with optimal development and press for circumstances that allow each child to fully reap the advantages associated with play (Ginsburg, 2007, p. 182). Thus free play is an important contributor to children's physical activity levels. This is supported by *The 2014 United States Report Card on Physical Activity for Children and Youth*: "Active play is a product of children's natural inclination to be active, creative, and imaginative. It can take many forms, such as using playground equipment at school or parks and playing active games with friends at recess. When children engage in active play they are free to move in ways they select on their own without formal structure from adults. Research provides evidence that children may engage in more moderate-to-vigorous intensity activity during free play than during organized physical activities. One study reported that children's moderate-to-vigorous physical activity levels during outdoor organized activities were, on average, 55% lower than when children were engaged in unorganized outdoor activities" (NPAP, 2014).

Although children may not have direct control over physical activity time at home, the school can play a vital role in three ways:

- Conducting physical education lessons that promote moderate to vigorous physical activity

- Providing opportunities for engagement in physical activity throughout the school day, as well as before and after school

- Offering parent education regarding developmentally appropriate ways to engage children in physical activity

FITNESS EDUCATION

Fitness education should be woven throughout the developmental physical education curriculum, which should teach children fitness concepts so that they can engage in physical activities promoting physical fitness. Children must be competent in performing fundamental movement skills so that they have the confidence, ability, and desire to engage in physical activities that develop fitness.

An active child can make significant health-related fitness gains. To facilitate this process, physical educators must understand the unique characteristics of children's fitness development so that they can design fitness activities that are developmentally appropriate. Appropriately designed fitness activities enhance a child's overall health, help prevent childhood injury, and promote the child's enjoyment of regular participation in physical activity.

Physical fitness comprises the body's ability to function efficiently and effectively in both work and leisure activities, to be healthy, to resist hypokinetic diseases (i.e., diseases tied to physical *inactivity*, such as type 2 diabetes, high blood pressure, and heart disease), and to meet emergency situations (Corbin & Welk, 2008). The components of health-related fitness are as follows:

- Cardiorespiratory endurance
- Muscular strength and endurance
- Flexibility
- Body composition

Cardiorespiratory Endurance

Often referred to as aerobic endurance, **cardiorespiratory endurance** consists of the ability to continue a vigorous activity that places demands on the heart, lungs, and vascular system for an extended period of time without undue fatigue. This capacity differs between children and adults, and research supports the notion that true biological differences exist between children and adults in this area. For example, Strand and Mauch (2008) reported that "children's maximal heart rates are age independent and generally range from 195–205 beats per minute and do not change until the late teens" (p. 19).

More specifically, a child's cardio-respiratory system is generally less efficient than an adult's because it has slower circulation, lower concentrations of hemoglobin (and therefore lower concentration of oxygen in the muscles), and less ability to store glycogen (which the body uses for energy). These factors contribute to early fatigue during endurance activities. This fact does not mean, however, that children are unable to perform endurance exercise or improve their endurance exercise capacity; rather, it means that they cannot be expected to perform and train at adult levels.

Developmental implications for teaching: Graham, Holt/Hale, & Parker suggest that children engage in short bouts of aerobic activity rather than continuous aerobic activity of long duration (2010, p. 52). For example, rather than running laps, a teacher might offer instant activities that engage all children in continuous movement for one or two minutes, such as tag games, builders and bulldozers, rope jumping, and locomotor movements performed to music of varying tempos.

Muscular Strength

Muscular strength consists of the ability to exert maximum force against an object external to the body. For example, children can do much to enhance muscular strength in their legs in the form of jumping and landing activities. They develop arm strength through such activities as lifting and carrying large objects and hanging from and swinging on equipment.

Muscular strength improves progressively during childhood, principally as the result of growth that increases muscle size. It can also be improved through resistance training before puberty in both boys and girls; however, this type of change occurs without substantive increase in muscle size. In other words, increase in muscle size results more from a child's growth than from training.

Developmental implications for teaching: Educators should provide children with activities focused on moving and lifting their own body weight (Graham et al., 2010) or using resistance from gravity. Children can be engaged in building muscular strength through whole-body activities—for example, climbing, hanging, and swinging; pushing and pulling; and jumping onto, over, or off of low equipment.

Muscular Endurance

Muscular endurance consists of the ability to exert force against an object external to the body for several repetitions or for one long continuous period without fatigue. It is similar to muscular strength in terms of the activities performed but differs in emphasis. Two examples of muscular endurance activity are sit-ups and push-ups.

Throughout childhood, both boys and girls tend to make steady year-to-year improvement in most measures of muscular endurance. Boys slightly outperform girls prior to puberty, but girls tend to reach puberty ahead of their male counterparts (generally around age 10 or 11), whereupon they often outperform boys for a short period (Gallahue, Ozmun, & Goodway, 2012, p. 254).

Developmental implications for teaching: Children develop muscular endurance when they are

These students are having fun and developing muscular endurance while climbing a traverse wall.

involved in weight-bearing activities with several repetitions. Age-appropriate examples include performing 5 to 10 inchworms, crab walks, or bear walks, as well as repetitively jumping in and out of a hoop.

Flexibility

Flexibility consists of the ability of various joints to move through their full range of motion; it is joint specific and can be improved with practice. Stretching for flexibility can be performed in various ways. Both static and dynamic stretching through a full range of motion are safe and effective, whereas ballistic stretching may cause injury. Indeed, in order to minimize the risk of injury, even static and dynamic stretches should be performed only after doing an aerobic warm-up.

Children are typically more flexible than adults because their bones have not completely ossified. However, during the prepubescent growth spurt, bone growth precedes muscle and tendon growth; therefore, young performers must engage in a proper stretching program in order to reduce the risk of injury around their joints (Gallahue et al., 2012, p. 258).

Developmental implications for teaching: Flexibility exercises must be modeled carefully so that children use correct form. In addition, stretching should be performed without bouncing and should follow an aerobic instant activity; it can also be done during the lesson closure.

Body Composition

Body composition consists of the proportion of lean body mass to fat body mass; more specifically, it is a person's relative fatness or leanness as adjusted for height. Body composition is an important aspect of overall health and fitness. The issue is overfatness (a condition of having more than a healthy percentage of body fat), not overweight as determined by traditional height-and-weight tables. Childhood obesity contributes to degenerative diseases, other health problems, and reduced longevity. Keys to maintaining a health-enhancing body composition include sound nutrition and daily engagement in MVPA and activities that promote muscular endurance.

Developmental implications for teaching: Children should be engaged in health-related fitness through daily enjoyable physical activity in order to develop a positive attitude toward leading an active lifestyle.

Teaching Fitness Principles

As with the goals for children's participation in physical *activity*, the goals for children's participation in physical *fitness* are addressed in standard 3 of the national standards for physical education published by SHAPE America (2014), which, again, reads as follows: "The physically literate individual demonstrates the knowledge and skills to achieve and maintain a health-enhancing level of physical activity *and fitness*" (p. 2, emphasis added). Thus standard 3 focuses on tools that enable children to gain, improve, maintain, understand, and enjoy the benefits of health-related fitness.

The focus of guidelines (NASPE, 2009a) for pre-K is to engage children in a variety of moderate to vigorous physical activities through daily participation in a structured program. A physical educator who follows these guidelines purposefully designs group activities and movement stations that reinforce the components of health-related fitness.

For example, muscular strength and muscular endurance can be reinforced through climbing, hanging, swinging, and jumping and landing opportunities. Cardiorespiratory endurance can be developed through locomotor activities, the duration of which should be determined by the child's need for rest. Flexibility can be developed and reinforced by assuming positions that mimic animal poses or letters of the alphabet and require stretching through the full range of motion. Along the way, educators can use imagery, music, and storytelling to stimulate children's imagination and interest while they repetitively perform a variety of fitness-enhancing motor skills.

In kindergarten through grade 2, the focus is on helping children to engage in a variety of activities that promote health-related fitness and to recognize the physiological changes associated with their participation in moderate to vigorous activity. This instruction emphasizes activity-based fitness rather than fitness achieved through formalized exercises or calisthenics (Strand & Mauch, 2008, p. 2). In other words, physical educators use the performance of fundamental motor skills as the vehicle for health-related fitness development.

This approach also teaches children to understand FITT guidelines experientially. FITT is an easy-to-remember acronym for frequency, intensity, time, and type of exercise. The concept of frequency is understood by keeping track of how often (how many days per week) children are active, either during recess (after which children report their activity choices to their classroom teacher) or outside of school. Children can also be asked to have their caretakers keep an activity calendar.

The variable of intensity is best understood by K-2 children through comparisons such as the following: "Is my heart beating faster or slower?" "Is my breathing faster or slower?" "Have I worked hard enough that my muscles are getting tired, or can I keep going because my muscles are not tired?" In other words, primary-grade children do not use heart-rate monitors or make abstract comparisons, but they can make concrete comparisons based on their body's response to physical activity.

The variable of time can be taught by having children compare what it feels like to move for a shorter time and to move for a longer time—for example, moving to short and long musical selections. Children can also begin to determine duration by counting; for instance, they might collect a Popsicle stick every time they complete a lap of walking, jogging, skipping, or sliding. Finally, the variable of type can be conveyed easily through the use of the Physical Activity Pyramid (Corbin, 2010, chapter 22), which illustrates how different types of physical activity build different components of fitness.

Children understand health-related fitness terms more readily when they are given age-appropriate definitions and examples. For example, flexibility can be defined as the ability to stretch and lengthen one's muscles like rubber bands. Similarly, strength can be defined as lifting, pushing, or pulling something heavy, and cardiorespiratory endurance can be defined as moving long enough that you breathe hard and your heart beats fast.

By grades 3 through 5, children are expected to understand the components of health-related fitness, interpret fitness test scores, and use the FITT guidelines to engage in a variety of activities that promote and improve fitness. Here are examples of questions they should be able to answer:

- What is the essence of each health-related fitness component?
- What tests are used for each health-related fitness component, and how do I interpret the results?
- How *frequently* (i.e., on how many days per week) do I need to work on each of the components of health-related fitness?
- How do I safely increase the *intensity* (i.e., amount of resistance or number of repetitions) of activities that develop the different health-related fitness components?
- What *time*-related measures (e.g., how much time it takes to cover a specified distance or time spent doing an activity) do I track while engaged in each of the health-related fitness components?
- What specific *types* of activity develop each of the various health-related fitness components?

Physical Activity Pyramid (Corbin & Lindsey, 2007).

Developmentally Appropriate Fitness Instruction Practices

Guidelines for fitness instruction and testing have been published by NASPE (2010) (see table 2.1). Physical educators should follow these best-practice guidelines when designing and implementing health-related fitness activities and assessing children's fitness.

Designing and Implementing Health-Related Fitness Activities

Age-appropriate fitness activities are designed to be relevant to children's interests and level of fitness development. For example, using a theme such as superhero fitness may capture children's attention due to their fascination with the idea of superpowers. Within such a theme, differences in children's levels of fitness development can be addressed by offering choices of intensity for a given fitness activity. Activities should also be designed with the following guidelines in mind:

- Fitness activities should be fun—and they can be, when children are successful and when the learning environment is stimulating (e.g., when music is used or an activity is augmented by equipment). Children enjoy physical activity when a balance is struck between their fitness capacity and the demands of the fitness challenge. If a child's fitness capacity is greater than the fitness challenge, then

Table 2.1 Appropriate and Inappropriate Fitness Instruction Practices

Appropriate Practice	Inappropriate practice
COMPONENT: DEVELOPING HEALTH-RELATED FITNESS	
Fitness activities focus on the health-related component of fitness.	Fitness activities are random and unrelated to lifelong learning benefits. The activities consist of mass exercises in which students follow a designated leader or standard routine.
The physical educator helps students interpret and use assessment data to set goals and develop lifelong fitness plans.	The teacher conducts fitness assessments but never involves students in using the results to set goals or to design a personal fitness plan.
COMPONENT: FITNESS TESTING	
The physical educator uses fitness assessments as part of an ongoing process of helping students understand, enjoy, and maintain or improve their physical fitness and well-being (e.g., students set goals for improvement and revisit them during the school year).	The teacher uses fitness test results to assign a grade.
As part of an ongoing program of physical education, students are physically prepared in each fitness component so that they can safely complete assessments.	Students are required to run a long distance (e.g., a mile) without appropriate conditioning or acclimatization.

the child may get bored; conversely, if the fitness challenge exceeds the child's fitness capacity, then the child may feel anxious or even quit.

• Fitness should be nonthreatening. When fitness activities are both individually appropriate and age appropriate—that is, when the teacher plans for the cognitive, affective, and physical attributes of the children—then the children are more likely to want to participate because they feel more confident that they will succeed. The fitness *environment* should also be nonthreatening, which can be achieved by having children participate simultaneously rather than being put on display; keeping results private rather than publically displaying them or communicating them in front of the class; comparing children's performances with their own previous results rather than with those of their peers; and by providing children with praise, encouragement, and motivation to achieve their personal best.

• Fitness must be progressive. Over time, teachers should strive to increase each child's work capacity through a series of progressively demanding activities (i.e., increasing the duration or intensity of exercise). For example, a teacher might have children walk briskly, jog, or perform other locomotor skills to musical selections of increasing duration.

• Fitness education should promote self-improvement through goal setting, monitoring, and reflection. When children set personally meaningful goals, monitor their progress, and think about how their fitness behaviors have led them to reach their goals, they become confident about their ability to regulate their health-related fitness.

• Fitness should be intrinsically motivating (Kouli et al., 2009).

• Research suggests that, in addition to providing challenge, fitness education must foster children's intrinsic motivation by incorporating choice, engaging curiosity, and inviting creativity and control. In terms of choice, children can be allowed either to choose a fitness task from a set of options or to choose the level of difficulty of a given task. As for curiosity, it is peaked when fitness activities are novel, child centered, and interesting to the intended participants. Creativity is encouraged when children are given the opportunity to design fitness activities based on predetermined criteria. Finally, control is enabled when children are given the opportunity to make decisions about fitness tasks—for example, when to stop and start, how to sequence tasks, and what pace and rhythm to use.

Assessing Fitness

Fitness assessment hinges on measuring changes in a person's body in response to activities that promote physical fitness. Assessment can be compatible with and woven throughout the course of instruction so that students and teachers understand the immediate effect of ongoing participation in fitness activities. This type of assessment is referred to as formative assessment, or assessment *for learning*. It gives students direct feedback (from a teacher or peer) about what they are learning and what can be improved (Strand & Mauch, 2008, p. 5).

Fitness assessment can also be summative—that is, it can involve assessment *of* learning. This type of assessment is conducted by means of a standardized fitness test administered at the end of a predetermined period of time during which students have engaged in activities to improve their fitness. The test results can then be used for goal setting in order to begin another cycle of formative and then summative fitness assessment.

Formative assessment of fitness is best used with children in pre-K through grade 2, for whom the goal is to develop proficient movers who can engage repetitively in physical activity and (because of their competence) perceive it as enjoyable. These formative assessments take the form of self-monitoring by students of their bodily responses to physical activity, such as this: "Am I breathing harder?" "Is my heart beating faster?" "Did I continuously move for a longer period of time?" (In other words: "Did I move to a longer piece of music?" "Did I collect more Popsicle sticks by completing more locomotor laps?")

The use of standardized fitness testing begins in grade 4, when children's movement skills and physical capacity are sufficiently developed to perform testing tasks correctly and safely. Of course, this testing should be preceded by practicing the test items (formative assessment) and participating in instructional activities purposefully designed to develop the components of health-related fitness. The standardized fitness test supported by SHAPE America is Fitnessgram (a summative assessment) (Cooper Institute, 2010, chapters 9 and 22).

NUTRITION EDUCATION

The goal of nutrition education is to teach, encourage, and support healthy eating by students. Poor nutrition leads to obesity and debilitating health conditions (e.g., type 2 diabetes, high blood pressure, cardiovascular disease). On the other hand, *proper* nutrition during childhood is critical for growth processes in the brain, in the nerves, in bone and muscle, and in other body components.

Good nutrition also enhances students' readiness for learning and enables them to achieve more. In fact, nutrition is a modifiable factor that can influence children's cognitive development (Bryan et al., 2004, p. 302). As the brain—in particular, the part of the brain in the frontal lobes (which focus attention, inhibit irrelevant stimulation, and solve problems)—continues to develop during childhood, nutrition is likely to continue affecting cognitive development.

Dietary Guidelines

Dietary Guidelines for Americans (U.S. Department of Agriculture [USDA], 2015) provides authoritative advice about consuming a healthy number of calories; making informed food choices; and being physically active in order to attain and maintain a healthy weight, reduce one's risk of chronic disease, and promote overall health. More specifically, a healthy diet

- emphasizes fruits, vegetables, whole grains, and fat-free or low-fat milk and milk products;
- includes lean meat, poultry, fish, eggs, beans, and nuts; and
- is low in saturated fat, salt, and added sugar.

To help students learn about healthy eating, teachers can create bulletin boards and engage children in discussions about the following messages:

- Enjoy food, but eat it in healthy amounts; avoid oversized portions.
- Fill half of your plate with fruits and vegetables.
- Switch to low-fat (1 percent) or fat-free milk.
- Choose whole grains for at least half of your grains.
- Choose food that is low in sodium.
- Drink water instead of sugary beverages.

MyPlate (USDA, n.d.) provides a graphic depiction of the recommended portion sizes for each food group. For instance, the new icon (figure 2.1) divides the plate into sections to show fruits and vegetables making up half of the food on the plate. Similarly, *Dietary Guidelines for Americans* (USDA, 2010) helps individuals to

- make smart choices from every food group;
- strike a healthy balance between food consumption, inactivity, and physical activity;
- get the most nutrition out of the calories they consume; and
- keep their consumption within their daily caloric needs.

Obstacles to Proper Nutrition

For many people, poor nutritional habits result from falling into a 21st-century lifestyle marked by a demanding and hectic family schedule that leads to eating fewer planned and home-cooked meals and more "fast food." In fact, although 75 percent of U.S. residents typically eat dinner at home, nearly half of their dinners consist of fast food, delivery, or takeout from restaurants or grocery delis (Gillaspy, n.d.).

In a 2005 sample of children in grades 3 through 5, researchers found that their food intake fell far below dietary recommendations for fruits and vegetables but was high in sodium and saturated fat (Vadivello, Zhu, & Quatromoni, 2009). Children who are home alone either before or after school may not have the ability to make healthy snacks; furthermore, even when given a choice, they may opt for snack foods (e.g., cookies, potato chips) rather than healthier choices (e.g., fruits, vegetables).

In addition, lower-income children may consume fewer than three meals a day and are less likely than higher-income children to eat breakfast every day. At the same time, however, their intake of fat, saturated fat, and sodium exceeds the levels recommended in *Dietary Guidelines for Americans* (USDA, 2015). As a result, research found that school-aged children

Figure 2.1 MyPlate.

USDA's Center for Nutrition Policy and Promotion.

in the lowest income group were significantly more likely to be overweight than were school-aged children in higher income groups (Fox & Cole, 2004). "Thus, by choice and by circumstance, many children are the victims of poor nutrition" (Graham et al., 2010, p. 43). However, whereas children may not have direct control over the food that is purchased or prepared at home, the school can play a vital role in three ways: providing nutrition education lessons, modeling healthy food choices in the school cafeteria and vending machines, and educating parents about healthy eating.

Big Ideas

- Low levels of physical activity lead to obesity and debilitating health conditions, whereas an appropriate level of physical activity during childhood is critical for growth processes in the brain, in the nerves, in bone and muscle, and in other body components. Promoting student health and physical activity enhances students' readiness for learning and increases student achievement.

- The U.S. Department of Health and Human Services published *Physical Activity Guidelines for Americans* in 2008. These guidelines advise that children and adolescents (aged 6 to 17) should engage in one hour (60 minutes) or more of physical activity per day in order to experience substantial health benefits.

- The components of health-related fitness are muscular endurance, muscular strength, cardiorespiratory endurance, flexibility, and body composition. When integrating fitness into a developmental physical education lesson, teachers must keep in mind the unique developmental characteristics of children. Verbal explanations must be based on children's stage of cognition, and fitness activities must take into account children's stage of motor development and level of motor skill learning.

- Guidelines for developmentally appropriate practice suggest that fitness should be part of an ongoing program of physical education during which students are physically prepared in each fitness component so that they can safely complete assessments. Fitness education must be fun (i.e., age appropriate), nonthreatening, and progressive; it must also promote self-improvement.

 Visit the web resource for learning activities, video clips, and review questions.

Chapter 3

The Thinking, Feeling, and Socializing Child

Key Concepts

- Describing developmental characteristics—and their implications for teaching children—in each stage of cognitive development

- Explaining the characteristics of children's social and emotional development from pre-K through grade 5

- Defining self-concept and describing how teachers can foster development of a positive self-concept

- Describing strategies for developing children's motivation and perceived competence in physical education settings

- Explaining strategies for developing children's prosocial behaviors

- Discussing Hellison's levels of teaching personal and social responsibility and strategies that teachers can use to reinforce the levels

In order to design and implement developmentally appropriate physical education experiences for children, physical educators must understand the *whole* child—that is, not just the moving child but also the thinking, feeling, and socializing child. For example, using the same lesson for children across grade levels is *not* a best practice and does not consider the unique developmental characteristics of children. Unfortunately, that one-size-fits-all approach is common in some physical education programs. To help you avoid that pitfall, this chapter equips you to consider the unique features of children in pre-K through grade 5 across all three domains of learning: thinking, feeling, and socializing. It also provides instructional guidelines based on children's development across these domains to help you address the whole child as you design and implement standards-based learning experiences in physical education for children in pre-K, K-2, and grades 3 through 5.

THE THINKING CHILD

Renowned Swiss psychologist Jean Piaget (1954) showed that young children think in strikingly different ways than do adults. According to Piaget, children are born with a basic mental structure (genetically inherited and evolved) on which all subsequent learning and knowledge is based. Piaget's theory of cognitive development emerged from observations of his own children in natural environments. Unique to his theory is the notion that movement is intricately related to cognitive development.

One of the strongest tenets of Piaget's theory of development is that the child must have active control of his or her interaction with the environment (Kruger & Kruger, 1989). This need means that teachers must understand Piaget's four stages of intellectual development so that they can structure developmentally appropriate environments that invite children to learn actively. In each of the four stages—sensorimotor, preoperational, concrete operational, and formal operational—children develop structures for thoughts and action. These structures, referred to as *schemes* or *schema*, result from children *actively* constructing understandings of the world based on their experiences (Shaffer, 1999).

Sensorimotor Stage

Cognitive development begins with the **sensorimotor stage**, which lasts from birth to about age 2, during which time "sensory experiences and movement are coordinated to act upon the world and generate knowledge" (Haibach, Reid, & Collier, 2011, p. 145). In this stage, movement is governed initially by primitive reflexes (e.g., sucking, grasping); as the nervous system matures, the child develops postural reflexes (e.g., startle, protective extension). These reflexes build neuromuscular pathways laying the foundation for voluntary movements that enable the child to explore the world. Here's how the process works:

By one month, children learn to self-initiate a movement that is similar to a reflex, for example a sucking action in anticipation of a nipple. This would be referred to as a sucking scheme. By four months, they repeat actions they enjoy, such as bringing their hand into view to watch it. These actions occur very close to the body. In this early developmental period, infants learn

that their actions have an effect on their own bodies. (Haibach et al., p. 145)

By about one year of age, the child develops object permanence—the ability to realize that an object still exists when it is out of sight. For example, the child can now find a toy hidden under a blanket. The child also experiments with a plethora of actions that produce intriguing outcomes. One such pattern involves action and reaction: If I drop an object from my high chair, my caretaker will pick it up for me!

In the last part of the sensorimotor stage—from about 18 to 24 months—another remarkable change begins to take place. The child who previously could think only in the present, in terms of ongoing actions, becomes able to move beyond action and into internal representation. Thinking requires the ability to hold images of the external world inside one's brain. This new ability to build an internal reproduction of the outside world enables the child to proceed with the development of language and deferred imitation. The latter occurs when the child imitates a behavior, perhaps that of a parent, that he or she observed at some earlier time. Such behavior indicates that the child is now able to retain an accurate mental image of an occurrence and recall it later.

Implications for teaching: It is critical for children in the sensorimotor stage to be in an emotionally and physically safe environment that allows them to discover how their actions affect their world. This environment should provide children with various types of toys to manipulate, particularly those designed on the principle of action and reaction, wherein the child can do something (e.g., push a button) that makes the toy do something (e.g., emit a noise).

The environment must also include safe places for children to crawl and climb in order to develop their motor abilities. During the first year of life, a child progresses from lying solely on the back or tummy to rolling over; then to crawling and pulling up to a standing position; and then to cruising (walking while holding onto something) and, ultimately, walking upright.

Another key element in the child's learning is feedback; indeed, Piaget viewed feedback as an essential condition for growth. Feedback is communication from, or the result of, an interaction between the child and the environment of people, things, and events. Feedback may come from the child's senses (i.e., auditory, visual, kinesthetic, or tactile) or as a direct result of something that she or he has done (Kruger & Kruger, 1989). Feedback should be positive, consistent, and gentle. Negative feedback is accepted only if it is balanced with positive feedback; too much negative feedback causes the child to retreat from the learning situation.

Preoperational Stage

The preoperational stage describes the intellectual capabilities of children in pre-K through grade 2 (or about age 2 to 7 years). During this *early childhood* period, children use "elementary logic and reasoning as they learn to use past experiences and the beginning use of symbols to represent objects in their environment. This process leads the way to oral communication" (Nichols, 1994, p. 23). Yes, early in this stage of cognitive development preoperational children begin to express themselves in words! Still, in social situations, children in this stage are often egocentric in their thinking; this tendency does not, however, "imply selfishness, [but] only that they are unable to view the world from another perspective" (Haibach et al., 2011, p. 145).

Imaginative play also takes on a significant role during the preoperational stage, and it is intricately intertwined with cognitive development. Play offers alternatives and choices as the child controls activity and engages in it for the satisfaction it provides to him. Exploratory play is aimed at acquiring information—for example, the properties of an object or whether something can be turned, twisted, sat on, or climbed. In short, the child is curious; she wants to know. When she has exhausted the possibilities that she perceives, she stops and, if attracted elsewhere, repeats the process. Curiosity can also drive three- and four-year-olds to ask a continuing stream of "why" questions.

Preschoolers' vivid imaginations make it possible for them to jump from supposed "great heights," climb "high mountains," leap over "raging rivers," and run "faster" than an assorted variety of "wild beasts." Children of preschool age rapidly expand their horizons, assert their individuality, develop their abilities, and test their limits—as well as the limits of their family and others around them! In short, young children push out into the world in many complex and wondrous ways. It is critical, though, to understand their developmental characteristics and their limitations as well as their potential. Only in this way can we effectively structure movement experiences for young children that truly reflect their needs and interests and fall within their level of ability.

In the preschool years, children's bodies and imaginations are growing rapidly.

Kindergarten is a time of readiness in which children begin making the gradual transition from an egocentric, home-centered play world to the group-oriented world of adult concepts and logic. They learn to participate in class routines, respond to teacher expectations, and navigate socially among peers in a relatively sheltered environment.

Upon entering first grade, children take a big step into their expanding world. For most children, grade 1 represents the first separation from the home for a regularly scheduled, extended block of academic time. It constitutes their first venture out of the secure play environment of the home, day-care center, or kindergarten and into the world of adults, where they experience systematic instruction and are expected to learn. In addition, for many children, grade school marks the first time that they are placed in a group in which they are not the center of attention. Instead, it is a time when they begin to establish sharing, concern for others, and respect for others' rights and responsibilities.

Children in first grade face the first formal demands for cognitive understanding. For both first and second graders, the major cognitive milestone involves learning how to read at a reasonable level. These children are also involved in developing their first real understanding of time and money, as well as concepts of movement (e.g., personal and general space; fast, medium, and slow speeds; following and leading) and numerous other concrete cognitive concepts. By the second grade, children should be well on their way to meeting and surmounting a broadening array of cognitive, affective, and motor tasks.

Implications for teaching: Through the medium of play, pre-K children develop a wide variety of fundamental stability, locomotor, and manipulative movement skills. To facilitate this development, the physical education environment should allow for free play and exploration during early childhood, particularly during the pre-K years.

Toward this end, Kruger and Kruger (1989) describe a "limited-freedom lesson plan." This approach aims to stimulate three- and four-year-olds to initiate their own exploration of movement possibilities at stations designed to elicit stability, locomotor, and manipulative movement skills. These exploratory opportunities offer children the opportunity to choose. While children are exploring, the teacher's role is to ask "who can" questions. These verbal challenges augment the child's exploration, which has already been stimulated by the arrangement of equipment and tasks at each station. Thus a limited-freedom lesson plan encourages children to explore and to expand their movement repertoire in response to the teacher's questions (see chapter 13 for implementation of this concept using exploration tasks).

Children in the primary grades develop increasingly organized logical thought. For example, they can order objects in a logical sequence and engage in concrete problem solving (e.g., sorting shapes by color or size). Therefore, physical education teachers can engage children of this age in logical sequencing of the movements involved in a specific skill by saying, for example, "Show me the beginning, middle, and ending positions for jumping off of the foam shape." Teachers can also engage children in concrete problem solving, such as designing a sequence of locomotor skills that involve changes in direction and speed. Another concrete problem could be posed by asking, "What happens to my heart rate when I move fast for a long time?" To solve this problem, children might feel their heartbeat while resting and then again after dancing vigorously to a song.

Concrete Operational Stage

Between the ages of 7 and 11 years, children progress into the concrete operational stage of cognitive development, which is commonly referred to as later childhood. In this stage, they develop the capacity to mentally organize or modify their thought processes, and they can now mentally represent objects and series of probable events (Nichols, 1994). In these ways, their thinking is now logical, but it still depends on events that are personally experienced, seen, or heard. Children in this stage are also less egocentric than before and realize that they must learn to consider the perspective of others if they want to be understood. As a result, "they consider [both] what they are saying and the needs of the listener" (Haibach et al., 2011, p. 146).

Implications for teaching: Children in second grade are typically seven years old and are refining their fundamental movement skills (see chapter 4); although they still perform closed skills, some may progress to performing open skills. Specific guidelines for appropriate task progressions are provided in chapter 6, but teachers must also differentiate instruction based on their students' skill range during this developmental period. Early in the concrete operational stage, directions should not exceed two or three at a time—for example, "When I say *go*, please get a ball out of your learning team's hoop. Find your own personal space and try using your ball in different ways within your personal space." This example demands that the child remember three directives, and the teacher must reinforce them as the children complete the task.

Later in this stage of cognitive development (ages 8 through 11, or grades 3 to 5), children can complete more directives, and they begin to realize that the rules of games can be changed and modified. They can also begin to develop strategies in activities based on what another team might do (see chapter 19).

Formal Operational Stage

The final stage of cognitive development is the formal operational stage, which begins at about age 11 or 12 and extends into adulthood. In this stage, "thinking is no longer restricted to concrete objects but can deal with abstractions" (Haibach et al., 2011, p. 146).

Some children enter the formal operational stage as early as grade 4 or 5, because the ages associated with Piaget's stages vary among children. During the formal operational stage, children can look systematically at possible solutions to a problem and use rational and abstract reasoning to choose the best option. Thinkers in this stage can also use prediction and planning.

Implications for teaching: Children in this stage of development can strategize during game play and ponder "what if" statements, such as the following: "What if I move here on the playing field? I'll be open to receive a pass." They may also be able to "read a defense" and know how to react on offense based on specific defensive movements that they observe.

Children at this stage can also mentally picture correct performance of a motor skill if they are given a model of it. As a result, they can consider multiple variables when creating dance and gymnastics sequences. For example, a teacher might ask students to create a dance using a certain theme, such as thunderstorms, and the children would then translate the idea into movement by using the movement framework (see chapter 5). The teacher might also require specific choreographic variables, such

as exits and entrances, formation changes, canons, stillness, and movement motifs.

Table 3.1 summarizes the cognitive development stage and learning characteristics of three age groups, as well as the implications for teaching children in those groups.

THE FEELING AND SOCIALIZING CHILD

When children play, their conversations are rich with expressions of feeling ("That makes me so happy!"), outcomes ("It went over the net!"), evaluation ("I played the game well!"), requests ("Let's try this!"), and outreach ("Please come with me!"). These conversations point out how children feel and how social they can be. At the same time, however, children must *learn* emotional and social skills and dispositions, which must be reinforced by caregivers and teachers who serve as positive role models and plan purposefully for children's emotional and social development.

Therefore, enhancing children's emotional and social development is an important aspect of designing and implementing developmentally appropriate

Table 3.1 Cognitive Development of Pre-K Through Grade 5 Children

Age group	Stage of cognitive development and learner characteristics	Implications for teaching
Pre-K	Preoperational stage: Children are egocentric and unable to view the world from another's perspective. Children are curious and imaginative and enjoy exploring their environment and testing their limits.	Simple instructions and task cards with pictures; activities of short duration; a variety of tasks; moving quickly into activity; brief use of whole-class format (3–5 minutes) with small bits of information during this time period; station format, each with a single focus; activities that stimulate imagination and creativity
K-2	Preoperational stage: Children use elementary logic, their reasoning reflects experiences, and symbols are used to represent objects in the environment (they are learning to read). Children begin to develop a movement vocabulary.	Simple instructions; task cards with few words and pictures; use of whole-class format for increasing periods of time; station format with a single focus; activities that stimulate imagination and creativity; engagement of elementary logic, which enables children to look for one movement cue when observing a peer; opportunities to correct their own performance based on feedback; opportunities to design or vary a short movement combination and follow simple rules
Grades 3 through 5	Concrete operational stage: Children can mentally represent objects or a series of probable events; can think logically about events that they have personally experienced; and are less egocentric and more capable than before of considering others' perspectives. Children are able to follow more complex rules, observe and use critical elements of skills, help others, use feedback to improve performance, and understand and apply simple game strategies and principles of movement.	More complex task cards and worksheets to facilitate understanding and acquisition of movement skills; use of whole-class format for entire class period; stations focusing on multiple tasks

physical education experiences for all children. In SHAPE America's (2014) national standards for physical education, standard 4 states that

> a physically literate individual exhibits responsible personal and social behavior that respects self and others.

This standard supports students' practice of self-initiated behaviors that promote personal and group success in activity settings. These behaviors include safe practices, adherence to rules and proper procedures, etiquette, cooperation and teamwork, ethical behavior, and positive social interaction. This standard hinges on respecting both similarities and differences through positive interaction among participants in physical activity. Achievement of this standard in the lower elementary grades begins with helping students recognize classroom rules, procedures, and safety practices. In the upper elementary grades, children learn to work independently, with a partner, and in small groups (National Association for Sport and Physical Education [NASPE], 2004, p. 39).

When physical educators understand social psychology and children's psychosocial development, they can provide movement experiences that help students develop a positive sense of self as well as positive interaction skills. Social psychology "is the study of how the thoughts, feelings, and behaviors of individuals are influenced by the presence of other people" (Mercier & Hutchinson, 2003, p. 246). When students participate in physical activity and physical education, they interact with classmates, teachers, friends, and family—all of whom can influence their behavior.

Of course, the process of developing some sort of sense of self and interacting with others is ever-present when children are engaged in physical education activities. However, in order to gain the knowledge, skills, and dispositions associated with a *positive* sense of self and *positive* interactions with others, children need teachers to provide them with effective environments. Specifically, children need environments that foster success, target the practice of social interaction skills (e.g., sharing, being respectful, cooperating with others), and prompt them to reflect on how their behavior affects both self and others.

Social psychology concepts and principles can be organized around themes focused on gaining a positive sense of self and relating positively with others. In this way, "as students explore selected concepts and principles of social psychology, they will learn strategies for developing positive self-concept, self-esteem, coping skills, and prosocial behaviors" (Mercier & Hutchinson, 2003, p. 250). And this—children's sense of self and relationship with others—is the essence of SHAPE America's physical education standard 4: "responsible personal and social behavior."

Sense of Self: Becoming Personally Responsible

> Children must see themselves as persons who can do things—persons who have skills. Children who like themselves are willing to make positive statements about themselves, to undertake new tasks with the expectation of success, to be active participants in a group, to take risks, and to become doers (Nichols, 1994, p. 224).

Gaining a sense of self involves developing one's self-concept and self-esteem. The importance to children of gaining a sense of self is illuminated by Erik Erikson's stage theory of psychosocial development (Haibach et al., 2011). In this theory, the pre-K child's sense of self is shaped during the "initiative versus guilt" stage of psychosocial development. During this stage, if children have experiences in taking initiative, they can gain a sense of self-confidence.

In terms of physical education, three- to six-year-old children have a strong desire to move and explore, and if they have opportunities to take risks and succeed, they become more confident movers as they grow and mature (Midura & Glover, 1999). They learn their movement capabilities by exploring their environment through climbing, jumping, running, balancing, throwing, kicking, and striking objects. However, if caregivers and teachers limit their exploration, criticize their ideas, or judge them as inadequate, then children feel a sense of guilt, their self-confidence is stifled, and they withdraw from challenges. Happily, caregivers and teachers can facilitate children's sense of initiative by providing safe and developmentally appropriate environments while encouraging and praising children's active exploration.

Children's feelings about themselves affect all domains of learning. Self-concept has been defined as the "accumulation of knowledge about one's self,

Negotiating a climbing wall is a physical challenge that requires some confidence and motivation.

such as beliefs regarding personality traits, physical characteristics, abilities, values, goals and roles" (Alvarez, 2012)—in other words, as a set of self-perceptions. During early childhood, a child's self-concept is less differentiated than it will be later and centers on concrete characteristics, such as physical attributes (e.g., "I am very tall!"), possessions (e.g., "I have a dog!"), and skills (e.g., "I play the piano!"). During later childhood, the self-concept becomes more abstract and based on psychological characteristics (e.g., "I am a happy person!") and feelings of self-worth that are often influenced by one's peers.

A child's self-concept can be influenced by people from many settings, including her or his nuclear family, extended family, teachers, peers, media, church members, neighborhood residents, and organizations. Amidst these various influences, physical educators can foster the development of a positive self-concept in the following ways:

- Providing age-appropriate class rules and consistent consequences so that children feel safe and secure

- Communicating a sense of value to children by being supportive and encouraging so that they feel appreciated and respected

- Providing inclusive environments in which each child is treated as an individual and feels successful in performing challenges at his or her own level of ability

- Providing adequate practice time in developmentally appropriate conditions to ensure learning so that students feel competent

- Providing children with choice and decision-making opportunities so that they learn to self-evaluate and feel confident

As children gain understanding of their abilities and limitations, they develop self-esteem—that is, a positive evaluation of their self-perceptions. Positive concepts of self give children the confidence and motivation to achieve in physical education and physical activity settings. For example, children with good self-esteem try new challenges in physical education class (e.g., throwing farther, jumping higher, solving a movement problem); they also try new playground equipment during recess.

In turn, being motivated to achieve in settings of physical education and physical activity contributes to children's "effort[s] to pursue goals, intensity of effort, and persistence to achieve through challenge and failure" (Mercier & Hutchinson, 2003, p. 260). Teachers can enhance children's motivation by encouraging them to set criterion-referenced, task-oriented goals that focus on personal improvement and mastery of skills. Research has found that "individuals with task-orientation tend to be persistent and unafraid of failure. They pursue mastery and choose moderately difficult challenges" (Mercier & Hutchinson, p. 261).

More specifically, teachers can help children experience success by helping them set and achieve short-term goals prior to pursuing long-term goals. Young children (i.e., K-2) should focus on setting short-term goals that use self-testing activities, such as the following: "How long can I hold a balance?" "How many consecutive jumps can I do with my jump rope?" "How many times can I throw the ball through the target?" Children in grades 3 through 5 can set short-term goals that lead to long-term goals, such as running longer distances, swimming the same distance in a shorter time, increasing one's shot-on-goal percentage, and using a skill progression to accomplish a certain action (e.g., catching a ball on the move, performing a cartwheel, or mastering a jump-rope routine).

Children's motivation to achieve goals is also enhanced when they engage in self-assessment. Doing so can help children keep a concrete record of their progress toward achieving short- or long-term goals. Such a record (i.e., a log) can help children determine whether they have achieved a goal or need to modify the goal. Engaging in self-reflection also helps children develop their self-esteem as they begin to understand how their actions have either led them to achieve their goals or could be modified to do so. In other words, self-assessment helps children know that their *effort* is what makes the difference in achieving their physical education goals. This is perceived competence—the sense that one's accomplishments result from one's efforts.

The ability to use a criterion-referenced mechanism to assess oneself contributes to the development of evaluation skills. Self-evaluation, in turn, provides the basis for developing self-esteem; it gives children a way to evaluate their self-perceptions. Learning to evaluate their self-perceptions *based on evidence* from personal data leads to perceived competence and therefore can decrease children's dependence on social comparisons. Even though comparing their abilities with those of others is a natural part of self-assessment, it should not be the only way in which children know how to evaluate themselves. Therefore, engaging children in well-rounded self-assessment enables them to gain a skill that is important to their development of healthy self-esteem.

Relating to Others: Becoming Socially Responsible

Children aged 6 to 12 are in a stage of psychosocial development that Erikson characterized as hinging on industry versus inferiority. During this stage, children are learning to relate to others; in turn, through social interactions, they begin to develop a sense of pride in their accomplishments and abilities.

In addition, because children in this age range spend a great deal of time in school, teachers and peers serve as important social agents for them. As a result, they must now conform to a set of social expectations beyond the realm of family: "The need to produce mobilizes children beyond play and to acquire cognitive skills such as reading and writing, as well as social skills appropriate to the culture. They learn to cooperate with others to achieve shared goals" (Haibach et al., 2011, p. 166). In this context, teachers facilitate industry by helping children set and attain realistic, criterion-referenced goals using evidence from personal data; they also help children refrain from exclusively using social comparisons that could lead to feelings of inferiority.

Physical education classes are rich in opportunities for developing social competence. In a school physical education setting, children are always participating in relation to one another—for example, sharing space while practicing a motor skill next to a classmate, cooperating to solve a movement problem, or competing against others in a small-sided game. All such activities require children to demonstrate social responsibility.

To make the most of these opportunities, teachers need to plan a sequence of learning experiences that lead children to understand and respond positively to others as they develop the social skills to interact effectively. Responding positively to others depends on feelings of empathy—that is, on identifying with and understanding another person's situation, feelings, and motives (Mercier & Hutchinson, 2003). Learning social skills provides the means for children to interact effectively with others, solve conflicts peacefully, and build the positive feelings that lead to successful performance in pairs, small groups, and teams.

The prosocial behaviors that children need to develop in order to work productively with others include communication, cooperation, and conflict resolution. Communication involves the ability to be courteous, listen, provide constructive feedback, encourage, and compliment others. Cooperation involves being honest, fair, patient, tolerant, and sensitive to others' ideas. Cooperative activities can also facilitate positive interdependence as students take personal responsibility while working as part of a group toward a common goal. During cooperative challenges, students must monitor their interactions and reflect on how they contribute to the outcome.

When a disagreement arises, students need to apply communication and problem-solving skills that lead to a positive resolution. In conflict resolution, students practice active listening with the goal of understanding each other's point of view. Students express rather than act out their feelings, and they share their ideas without blaming others. For example, they use "I" statements, such as, "I feel left out because I did not get to share my ideas." Finally, they work together to brainstorm solutions and select a mutually agreed-upon option.

To foster children's ability to exercise social responsibility and relate positively to others, physical educators can do the following:

- Model and reinforce the social skills they expect students to demonstrate.
- Define and emphasize social skills as learning targets by having children practice prosocial behaviors and avoid, or eliminate, socially unacceptable behaviors.
- Provide students with opportunities to reflect on how their social skills affect others and either contribute to or detract from efforts to attain partner or group goals.
- Place students in heterogeneous groups and target prosocial behaviors that respect individual similarities and differences.
- Engage students in peer teaching and cooperative learning and target prosocial behaviors that involve teamwork and helping one another.

TEACHING PERSONAL AND SOCIAL RESPONSIBILITY

National physical education standard 4 is intended to support students' "achievement of self-initiated behaviors that promote personal and group success in activity settings" (NASPE, 2004, p. 39). Indeed, children in pre-K through grade 5 are developmentally ready to acquire emotional and social skills.

To do so, however, they depend on caregivers and teachers to provide positive learning environments that address individual levels of ability, reinforce socially acceptable behavior, and present developmentally appropriate learning targets.

In 1978, with this need in mind, Don Hellison designed what has become one of the most prominent models for teaching personal and social responsibility (TPSR). Over the years, he and colleagues have refined the model, and countless physical educators and physical activity professionals have used it to empower and encourage their students to act and reflect on smart personal and social choices. As Hellison (2011) indicates, "Personal and social development is not automatic: progress requires responsibility-based goals, strategies, and teacher qualities" (p. 19). To that end, he developed cumulative levels of personal and social responsibility to provide students with specific targets for taking responsibility (see figure 3.1).

Level zero represents the antithesis of responsibility: *irresponsibility*. It describes behaviors related to denying personal responsibility and blaming others. Levels I and II—respect and participation—encompass the beginning of the child's development of responsibility: "Respect can be traced back to the core value of human decency, whereas effort is an important component in improving oneself and others in just about everything" (Hellison, 2011, p. 21). In Level II children begin to willingly cooperate with their peers during physical activity. Level III and IV—self-direction and caring—are the advanced levels. They expand both the child's *personal* responsibility (by encouraging individual work without direct supervision) and the child's *social* responsibility (by engaging students in helping and leadership roles).

Hellison also provides teachers with an "empowering progression" and "embedding strategies" so that they can integrate the responsibility levels into physical activity content and engage students in recognizing and reflecting on their responsibility-related behaviors and dispositions (see table 3.2). The empowerment progression recognizes the critical role played by self-determination in a child's development of self-concept and self-esteem. The progression allows teachers to gradually shift decision making to students by embedding TPSR into daily physical education lessons.

A companion to the empowerment progression is self-reflection: "Making decisions and choices

Level IV: Caring
Students at Level IV, in addition to respecting others, participating, and being self-directed, are motivated to extend their sense of responsibility beyond themselves by cooperating, giving support, showing concern, and helping.
Level III: Self-Direction
Students at Level III not only show respect and participation but also are able to work without direct supervision. They can identify their own needs and begin to plan and carry out their physical education programs.
Level II: Participation
Students at Level II not only show at least minimal respect for others but also willingly play, accept challenges, practice motor skills, and train for fitness under the teacher's supervision.
Level I: Respect
Students at Level I may not participate in daily activities or show much mastery or improvement, but they are able to control their behavior enough that they don't interfere with the other students' right to learn or the teacher's right to teach. They do this without much prompting by the teacher and without constant supervision.
Level ZERO: Irresponsibility
Students who operate at Level Zero make excuses, blame others for their behavior, and deny personal responsibility for what they do or fail to do.

Figure 3.1   Cumulative progression of personal and social responsibility.

Reprinted, by permission, from D. Hellison, 2011, *Teaching personal and social responsibility through physical activity,* 3rd ed. (Champaign, IL: Human Kinetics), 34: Adapted from Hellison 1985.

requires thoughtfulness" (Hellison, 2011, p. 24). To help students engage in self-reflection, teachers can provide strategies that help students examine the motivation for their choices, as well as the consequences for both themselves and others. As a result, students learn to "get inside their own heads" (Hellison, p. 13), take responsibility for their actions, and internalize dispositions that empower them to make personally and socially responsible choices.

The empowerment progression begins with implementing the goals of the first TPSR level: respecting the rights and feelings of others. Here, teachers engage students in the goals of the lesson, reinforce the behaviors and dispositions of self-control and respect, and provide an inclusive learning environment that maximizes student participation. Providing for individual success goes a long way toward deterring the lack of self-control and lack of respect that can stem from boredom when children are faced with waiting for their turn or with unchallenging tasks. It also heads off the anxiety of performing in front of others or being asked to perform tasks that are too challenging.

In other words, when students are engaged in performing at their current level of ability, they are less likely to exhibit off-task behavior. When interpersonal altercations do occur, teachers reinforce the right of individuals to be treated respectfully and then engage children in conflict resolution strategies (e.g., talking bench, sport court); they can also proactively immerse children in self-officiating (Hellison, 2011, pp. 97–98).

The second level of the empowerment progression is congruent with the level of responsibility involving effort and cooperation. Here, teachers engage students in the goals of the lesson, reinforce the behaviors and dispositions of task persistence and getting along with others, and provide students with limited decision-making power regarding how they participate in lesson activities. For instance, students might be given the opportunity to make choices about the following elements (Hellison, 2011, pp. 69–72):

- Setting the order in which to complete a set of tasks
- Choosing the type of equipment that best fits their ability
- Modifying a task to challenge themselves appropriately
- Moving through progressions at their own pace

Table 3.2   The Empowerment Progression

Level	Empowerment progression
1. Respecting the rights and feelings of others	Inclusion strategies Conflict resolution strategies
2. Effort and cooperation	Limited decision making
3. Self-direction	Independent work without supervision Goal setting Personal plan
4. Helping others and providing leadership	Peer assessment Peer teaching and coaching Group goals

Data from Hellison 2011.

- Redefining success outside the norms of winning or being the best
- Using an **intensity scale** to represent the effort they are willing to (or did) give toward accomplishing a task

The process of acting and reflecting on *choices* is a critical step toward self-determination and lays the foundation for self-esteem. Similarly, the process of acting and reflecting on the *behaviors* and *dispositions* of cooperation is an important step toward social responsibility. Teachers can give students opportunities to feel positive about cooperating with others by providing them with tasks that involve sharing equipment and space, providing support and encouragement to classmates, and performing partner and small-group team-building challenges.

Level three of the empowerment progression extends empowerment to self-direction. Here, teachers engage students in the goals of the lesson, reinforce the behaviors and dispositions of on-task independence, and provide differentiated tasks at stations that empower students to work independently and set goals for personal improvement. Self-determination takes a huge leap forward when students learn how to set, act on, and reflect on personal goals—and, ultimately, when they are empowered to design and pursue personal plans to enhance their skills, fitness, knowledge, and dispositions.

The last level of the empowerment progression is congruent with the fourth level of responsibility: helping others and leadership. At this point, teachers engage students in the goals of the lesson and reinforce the behaviors and dispositions of caring about and helping others. They also provide opportunities for students to engage in peer assessment and peer teaching; lead drills and exercises; work in groups to solve movement challenges; and, ultimately, set, act on, and reflect on achieving group goals. When students contribute to the success of a group and make a difference in the learning and success of their peers, they manifest both self-determination and contributing to the well-being of others.

Thus a logical progression exists both for developing *personal* responsibility (from choosing a level of performance to making and fulfilling a personal plan) and for developing *social* responsibility (from self-control and respect for others to helping and leading others). Even so, each level in the empowerment progression—and each level of responsibility—can be implemented with developmental appropriateness for children in grades K through 5. Table 3.3 shows the congruence between the personal and social responsibility levels of Hellison's (2011) TPSR model and the personal and social responsibility goals of the national physical education standard 4 for grades K through 5 (SHAPE America, 2014).

Table 3.4 summarizes children's social development and the implications for teaching.

Table 3.3 Relationship of Hellison's TPSR Levels and Standard 4

TPSR level	National physical education standard 4
1. Respecting the rights and feelings of others	Safe practices Adherence to rules and procedures Etiquette Conflict resolution
2. Effort and cooperation	Tackling challenges Cooperation Prosocial interactions
3. Self-direction	Working independently Working productively with others to achieve a goal
4. Helping others and providing leadership	Respect for similarities and differences Ethical behavior Teamwork

Table 3.4 Social Development of Pre-K Through Grade 5 Children

Age group	Learner characteristics	Implications for teaching
Pre-K	The child's self-concept is highly influenced by the actions, thoughts, and feelings expressed about the child by caregivers. The child is egocentric and engages in solitary play and then parallel play.	Give children opportunities to explore, take risks, and succeed. Encourage and praise active exploration in tasks that have a variety of correct responses. Provide activities that engage children in moving next to others with their own equipment while respecting others' space and equipment.
K-2	The child's self-concept is less differentiated and is centered on concrete characteristics, such as physical attributes, possessions, and skills. The child's self-esteem is influenced by parents and teachers. The child is less egocentric and is able to engage in associative play and some cooperative play.	Provide developmentally appropriate self-testing activities. Help children set short-term goals and engage in simple self-assessment. Model positive social skills and engage children in activities that elicit appropriate social skills, such as courtesy, honesty, kindness, staying on task, following directions, and encouraging others.
Grades 3 through 5	The child's self-concept becomes more abstract and based on internal, psychological characteristics and feelings of self-worth. The child's self-concept can be influenced by peers. Self-esteem is now influenced not only by what others value but also by what the child deems important. The child is more self-directed and begins to develop empathy for others and engage in cooperative and competitive play.	Provide inclusive environments with challenges appropriate for different levels of ability. Have children set short-term goals leading toward accomplishment of long-term goals. Engage children in self-assessment and reflection to help them understand how their actions led to attaining their goals. Establish prosocial skills as learning targets. Have children reflect on how their social skills (e.g., tolerance, fairness, cooperation, perseverance, listening, positive communication, conflict resolution) affect others and contribute to or detract from the attainment of goals.

Big Ideas

- Pre-K children are in the preoperational stage of cognitive development and are often egocentric yet have very vivid imaginations. Children in the preoperational stage of cognitive development learn through play and should be provided with multiple opportunities to explore.

- Primary-grade children are in the concrete operational stage of cognitive development, during which their thinking is logical but still depends on events that are personally experienced, seen, or heard. They should be provided with choices of instructional tasks and opportunities to explore movement possibilities.

- Intermediate-grade children (in grades 3 through 5) are transitioning from the concrete operational stage of cognitive development into the formal operational stage. In the formal operational stage, children can look systematically at possible solutions to a problem and use rational and abstract reasoning to choose the best option. They also have longer attention spans and can work productively in small groups, solve problems, and carry out a series of instructional tasks.

- The pre-K child's sense of self develops during the "initiative versus guilt" stage of Erikson's model of psychosocial development. During this stage, if children have experiences in taking initiative, they can gain a sense of **self-confidence**. Once they reach the three- to six-year age range, children have a strong desire to move and explore, and if they have opportunities to take risks and succeed, they become more confident movers as they grow and mature (Midura & Glover, 1999). Children aged six to twelve years are in the "industry versus inferiority" stage of Erikson's model. In this stage, teachers can facilitate *industry* by helping children set and attain realistic, criterion-referenced goals using evidence from personal data; they can also help children refrain from exclusively using social comparisons that could lead to feelings of *inferiority*.

- Self-concept has been defined as the "accumulation of knowledge about one's self, such as beliefs regarding personality traits, physical characteristics, abilities, values, goals, and roles" (Alvarez, 2012).

- Physical educators can foster the development of a positive self-concept by providing age-appropriate class rules and consistent consequences, designing inclusive environments, and providing adequate practice time for children to gain a sense of competence.

- Teachers can enhance children's motivation by encouraging them to set criterion-referenced, task-oriented goals that focus on personal improvement and mastery of skills.

- Prosocial behaviors can be learned when teachers model and reinforce social skills, offer children opportunities to practice prosocial behaviors, engage students in partner and small-group activities, and provide opportunities for children to reflect on the social skills they exhibit.

- Levels of personal and social responsibility can be understood in terms of Hellison's (2011) TPSR model, in which level 0 is characterized by irresponsibility, level 1 by respecting the rights and feelings of others, level 2 by effort and cooperation, level 3 by self-direction, level 4 by helping others and exhibiting leadership, and level 5 by transferring behaviors outside of the physical education setting.

- Physical educators must employ specific teaching strategies to develop children's personal and social behaviors. For example, when teachers provide instructional tasks of varying levels of difficulty, children can be successful, in which case they are more likely to exhibit on-task behavior and **self-control**. Other examples include designing instructional tasks in which children work with a partner (thus promoting their respect for others); help with equipment (thus promoting individual responsibility); work independently at stations (thus reinforcing self-direction); lead instant activities, design games, or make up dances (thus reinforcing leadership); and engage in peer teaching (thus promoting care for others).

▶ Visit the web resource for learning activities, video clips, and review questions.

Chapter 4

The Moving Child

Key Concepts

- Describing how children's movement abilities are influenced by visual and kinesthetic perceptual development, motor-skill development stages, and motor-skill learning levels

- Explaining the differences in movement goals and teacher roles for children at different levels of movement skill learning

- Describing the connection between children's stages of motor development and their levels of movement skill learning

Child development literature often reminds us that children are not miniature adults, especially in the areas of motor development and motor learning. Of course, none of us would assume that a 6-year-old possesses the same level of motor skill performance as a 12-year-old, let alone that of an adult. Yet it was not so long ago that some physical educators planned the same lessons for children in kindergarten through grade 3 as for those in grades 4 through 6. This practice ignored developmental differences in both motor development and motor learning; as a result, it over-challenged some children and under-challenged others. With that history in mind, this chapter explores how children's movement abilities are influenced by their stages of development and learning and how physical educators can appropriately challenge children at their differing levels of ability.

MOTOR DEVELOPMENT AND MOTOR LEARNING

In order to understand how a child acquires motor skills and becomes a skillful mover, we must integrate knowledge from the fields of motor development and motor learning. The study of motor development focuses on progressive, age-related changes in motor behavior that are attributed to growth, development, and maturation. For instance, you have different expectations about how fast a two-year-old, a four-year-old, and an eight-year-old can run and about how far they can throw. The study of motor learning, in contrast, focuses on the relatively permanent changes in motor behavior brought about by practice and experience. For instance, in any given sport, you have different performance expectations for a beginner, an intermediate performer, and an advanced performer.

The study of motor development and the study of motor learning each contribute to understanding the motor behavior of the moving child; however, it is the relationship between the aspects that provides a truly rich understanding of how children acquire motor skills. In practical application, physical education teachers must use knowledge of motor *development* to design goals that are appropriate for learners' developmental stages and perceptual–motor abilities. At the same time, they must use knowledge of motor *learning* to design appropriate movement tasks and practice conditions for a given type of skill.

The relationship between motor development and motor learning hinges on three interacting factors that influence changes in motor behavior. Newell (1984) identified these factors as constraints that involve either the learner, the task, or the environment. For example, the developmental differences between a 4-year-old learner and a 10-year-old learner affect the goal of receiving a ball, as well as the design of the movement task and the environmental setting. Whereas the 4-year-old might catch soft, textured balls thrown directly into her or his awaiting hands, the 10-year-old might field ground balls coming unpredictably from a variety of directions. When physical educators identify specifics of the interacting constraints of their learners, movement tasks, and environments, they can structure practice to support changes in motor behavior.

The following section of the chapter examines each of the constraints that influence changes in motor behavior. It also addresses how to apply that knowledge to plan and implement practice that supports motor skill learning by children in pre-kindergarten through grade 5.

THE PROCESS OF LEARNING

In order to choose developmentally appropriate learning goals, tasks, and environments, a physical educator must take into account multiple factors. These factors include the process of learning, as well as children's perceptual–motor abilities, phase of motor development, and level of movement skill learning.

One widely accepted way to understand how motor skills are learned is through schema theory (Schmidt, 1975). As learners perform motor skills, they develop schemata or sets of rules that represent the relationship between movement outcomes and other factors, such as the intended goal, the environmental conditions, and details of how they moved. For example, when developing a schema for throwing accuracy, the performer compares where the ball hits the target with where it was supposed to hit; if it missed, the performer considers changes in distance, force, direction, and release point to make the next attempt more successful.

In this way, through accumulated movement experiences, the learner develops schemata for given movement performances, stores them in memory, and uses them to guide future attempts. In the example just given, the schema developed by the performer for throwing accuracy is referred to as a generalized motor program, which consists of both stable and flexible features. The stable features define the motor program and make up the sequence of movements used to execute the overhand throw—in this case, winding up with the arm brought behind the head, rotating the trunk, transferring weight to the opposite foot, rapidly moving the arm forward, and releasing the ball. The flexible features, on the other hand, define the program's *execution* and vary from one performance to the next, depending on the distance, height, and direction of the target (Coker, 2004; Fairbrother, 2010).

When children first learn motor skills, teachers focus the learners' attention on the *stable* features to help them learn to perform the basic movements of the skill. For instance, when throwing, one steps forward with the opposite foot; similarly, when performing a forward roll, one tucks the chin and

A batter must draw on sensory information in order to execute a swing.

rounds the back. Teachers use the *flexible* features to construct the task and environment to match the learner's developmental needs. For example, beginning learners who are focused on acquiring the basic movements of the skill might hit a ball off of a tee or perform a forward roll down an incline. Intermediate learners, in contrast, might hit balls pitched at different speeds or combine a forward roll with a jump.

During the process of learning motor skills, learners may develop generalized motor programs either explicitly or implicitly. Explicit learning often occurs during instruction when children are consciously aware that they are learning motor skills. For example, a teacher might be giving the child verbal performance cues, a sibling might be demonstrating a new skill, or a coach might be providing feedback about improper technique.

Implicit learning, however, occurs unconsciously. For example, when children are engaged in repetitive movement during play, they are often unaware that they are learning motor skills. When learning to ride a bicycle, for instance, children often focus on balancing, pedaling, and steering to avoid objects. In the process, they are unaware that they are implicitly learning to shift their weight on the seat to lean into turns (Fairbrother, 2010). Likewise, as children freely interact with balls and targets in a preschool gym, they are unaware that they are implicitly learning to throw in an underhand pattern with a given force or trajectory in order to hit a target. Eventually, children may become explicitly aware of movements that they learned implicitly at an earlier time if those movements interfere with correct performance or become a focus during instruction. Just as teachers design learning tasks and environments for explicit learning goals, they can also purposefully design enriched play environments to stimulate implicit learning.

PERCEPTUAL–MOTOR DEVELOPMENT

Every motor skill performance is based on perception. To move purposefully, you extract information from the environment and your position in it, process the information in your brain, and then move. More specifically, of course, this sequence applies to movements such as timing the swing of a bat to hit a pitched ball, accurately shooting a basketball, and performing a sequence of dance movements. The process of perception starts with the senses. The batter, for example, uses her kinesthetic sense to position her body in preparation for the pitch, her sense of touch to grip the bat, and her sense of sight to watch the movements of the pitcher and the ball. All of this multisensory information is sent to her brain, where it is perceived (that is, interpreted and integrated), after which she makes a decision (to swing or not) and acts upon it.

The reciprocal relationship between sensory input and motor output means that perceptual and motor ability develop and work together and continuously influence each other (Haibach, Reid, & Collier, 2011). For instance, when comparing the batting skill of a 5-year-old, an 8-year-old, and a 12-year old who have all been involved in summer baseball, you would expect the 12-year-old to be a more proficient batter. All other developmental factors being equal, he has gathered, perceived, and acted on sensory information much more often than have the 5-year-old and the 8-year-old. In other words, he has more experience—and thus a larger store of information with which to compare the sensory input he receives while at bat—and therefore can make a more informed decision, not only about whether to swing but also about *how* to swing in order to hit the ball to a specific location.

When physical educators understand the process of perceptual–motor development, especially in the visual and kinesthetic sensory modalities, they can design tasks and learning environments that both accommodate and expand the child's motor-control capabilities. For example, preparing the task and environment to enable a five-year-old to bat a ball could mean placing the ball on a batting tee. This setup allows the child to focus on a stationary ball and develop a kinesthetic feel for the swing without having to process information about a moving ball; in this way, it allows the child to have a successful batting experience.

The development of the perception–action system requires movement and is enhanced by affordances—that is, flexible features of the task and the environment that teachers can manipulate to fit the learner's size and developmental capabilities. For example, a teacher might provide a child with a ball sized to fit her hand, thus affording her the opportunity to perform a one-handed throw.

Vision

Vision is a key sensory modality for skillful movement performance; as a result, age-related changes in visual acuity and perception affect motor skill development. Visual acuity consists of how clearly one sees, and it improves as children grow. Infants' visual acuity is restricted to 8 to 20 inches (20 to 50 centimeters)—just enough to distinguish the facial features of their caregivers. Though visual acuity improves during childhood, the eyeball does not reach its full size until 10 to 12 years of age. In addition, the macula of the retina is not completely developed until the sixth year, and young children are generally farsighted.

Taken together, these facts of vision development constitute one important reason that young children have difficulty fixating on and intercepting moving objects. To address this challenge, teachers can use fleece balls and Wiffle balls, which travel at slower speeds and therefore give children more time to process visual information and improve their chances of intercepting the ball (Payne & Isaacs, 2008).

Visual perception determines how visual information is interpreted, and it depends on the development of three capacities: figure–ground perception, motion perception, and depth perception. All three improve throughout childhood, and incomplete development can hinder skillful movement until the child reaches mature vision development.

- **Figure–ground perception** is the ability to distinguish an object of interest from its background. This capacity improves between age 4 and age 8 (Haywood & Getchell, 2014), which means that by age 8 children can focus on an increasing number of aspects in their environment. However, this capacity does not reach the adult level until age 18 (Haibach et al., 2011). To avoid compounding a child's limitations in figure–ground perception, use bright-colored equipment that contrasts with colors in the environment (e.g., walls, floor); make your cues to students distinct and few; and decrease nonessential environmental cues.

- **Motion perception** is the ability to detect the direction, location, and speed of an object (Haywood & Getchell, 2014); therefore, it affects a student's ability to track the path and velocity of an oncoming object. By age 5 or 6, children can track objects moving in a horizontal plane; by age 8 or 9, they can track objects moving in an arc (Morris, 1980, as cited in Payne & Isaacs, 2008, p. 224). Objects moving either very slow or very fast cause greater performance errors than do objects moving at moderate speeds (Payne & Isaacs, 2008). By age 9, the speed at which children process sensory information and judge moving objects has improved enough that they can more accurately intercept moving objects. However, the ability to track objects and opponents does not reach an adult level until about age 15 (Haibach et al., 2011).

- **Depth perception** is the ability to detect the distance between oneself and an object or a certain location in the environment. This ability begins to develop early in the first year of life, then develops slowly during the preschool years, and finally matures in the teenage years. Immaturity of depth perception gives rise to safety concerns in the preschool environment, as children often bump into things that they can apparently see. Depth perception depends on both visual acuity and figure–ground discrimination. As a result, teachers must consider providing affordances involving ball color, size, speed, and trajectory (Haibach et al., 2011).

Perceptual abilities become increasingly refined between the ages of 8 and 12. By the end of this period, the sensorimotor apparatus works in greater harmony, thus enabling children to perform numerous sophisticated skills. The ability to strike a pitched ball, for example, typically improves with age and practice because of improved visual acuity, tracking ability, reaction time, movement time, and sensorimotor integration.

Kinesthetic Perception

Kinesthetic perception is an important modality for movement performance because it enables skillful, fluid movements by providing information about the position of the body and body parts in the environment and where the body is moving. As a result, motor skill development in children is affected by age-related changes that occur in body awareness, laterality, and directionality.

- Body awareness is the ability to recognize and identify body parts, body-part relationships, and the body's location in the environment. Children learn body-part recognition based on interaction with adults, and most children can identify the major body parts by age 6.

- Laterality is the ability to recognize spatial concepts in relation to one's own body. By age 2 or 3, most children have a sense of the spatial orientations, starting with up–down, followed by front–back, and then side. At age 4 to 6, children begin to develop the spatial orientations of near and far and distinguish the left and right sides of the body;

by age 10, most can correctly label the left and right sides without hesitation (Haywood & Getchell, 2014). This knowledge can inform physical educators' use of cues. For example, it is helpful to use supporting cues (e.g., "turn to your right to face the bleachers") to orient preschool and primary-grade children to their left and right.

- **Directionality** is the ability to recognize spatial concepts about movement and objects in the environment. Between the ages of 6 and 12, children improve their sense of directionality and become able to locate objects relative to other objects in general space (Haibach et al., 2011). By age 8, they can typically use body references (e.g., "the trapezoid is on my right"); by age 12, they can identify left and right in another person standing opposite them because they now know that left and right are related to the perspective of the viewer (Haywood & Getchell, 2014). To support children's development of directionality, teachers can use matching and mirroring activities, obstacle courses, and other activities that engage children in moving in a variety of ways through general space.

Evidence indicates that the development of perception and the development of movement proceed together and affect the motor performance of pre-K children through 12-year-olds (Haibach, et al., 2011). Teachers can address this reality by using perceptual–motor development information to provide affordances that enable children to perform successfully while developing their perceptual–motor capacities. One key to maximum development of mature growth patterns in children is *utilization*. In other words, as children develop improved perceptual abilities through the normal process of maturation, they must experiment with those abilities and integrate them with motor structures through practice. When children lack abundant opportunities for practice, instruction, and encouragement during this period, they are prevented from acquiring the perceptual and motor information they need in order to perform skillfully.

Figures 4.1 and 4.2 illustrate the development of visual and kinesthetic perception in children aged 3 to 10. Blank boxes indicate that development has not yet started, and arrows indicate that development is ongoing and does not mature completely until an older age.

Motor control

Stages of motor development	Preschool	Grades K-2	Grades 3-5
	Initial–Emerging elementary (EE)	**EE–Mature–Transition**	**Transition–Application**
Visual perceptual development	Difficulty fixating on and intercepting moving objects	Can track objects moving on a horizontal plane	More accuracy in tracking and intercepting moving objects Can track objects moving in an arc ⟶
		Moderate-speed objects cause fewer performance errors.	Can intercept objects arriving at a greater variety of speeds ⟶
		Tends to focus on limited number of cues regardless of importance; needs help focusing on relevant cues	Tends to focus on all cues; needs help focusing on relevant cues; minimize irrelevant cues ⟶
	Can more easily detect brightly colored objects that contrast with the color of the walls and floor	⟶	⟶

Figure 4.1 Visual perceptual development.

Motor control

Stages of motor development	Preschool	Grades K-2	Grades 3-5
	Initial–Emerging elementary (EE)	**EE–Mature–Transition**	**Transition–Application**
Kinesthetic perceptual development	Learning body parts	Can identify major body parts	Can identify all body parts
	Learning up-down, front-back, near-far, and sides in relation to the body	Developing laterality—left and right sides of body	Laterality developed: can label left and right sides of body consistently
		Beginning the development of directionality: locating objects relative to other objects in general space (above, below, over, under near, far...)	Directionality improving: can identify objects to left and right in environment and beginning to develop sense of left and right of others opposite them ⟶

Figure 4.2 Kinesthetic perceptual development.

PHASES AND STAGES OF MOTOR SKILL DEVELOPMENT

The phases of motor development are classified as the reflexive, rudimentary, fundamental, and specialized movement phases (Gallahue, Ozmun, & Goodway, 2012). The reflexive and rudimentary phases, which lie beyond the scope of this textbook, are characteristic of infancy and toddlerhood and form critical building blocks for the fundamental and specialized phases addressed in the following sections.

Fundamental Movement Phase

The fundamental movement phase of development is characterized by a remarkable change in children's abilities to perform fundamental motor skills of stability, locomotion, and manipulation. Children begin this period unable to produce the balance, speed, and ranges of motion that are needed for performing fundamental movement skills. They end the period with the potential to produce biomechanically efficient movement patterns for such actions as running, skipping, rolling, kicking, and catching (Haywood & Getchell, 2014).

This metamorphosis occurs between the ages of two and seven based in part on maturation of the neuromuscular system and on changes in body proportion that accompany physical growth. On average, children grow about 2 inches (5 centimeters) and gain about 5 pounds (2.3 kilograms) per year. The physiques of male and female preschoolers and primary-grade children are remarkably similar when viewed from a posterior position (boys are slightly taller and heavier). Boys and girls at this age have similar amounts of muscle and bone mass and show a gradual decrease in fatty tissue as they progress through the early childhood period. The chest gradually becomes larger than the abdomen, and the stomach gradually protrudes less. By the time children reach their sixth birthday, their body proportions more closely resemble those of older children in elementary school.

Children also develop an increasing amount of myelin, a fatty substance around the neurons, in a process commonly referred to as *myelination*, which permits the transmission of nerve impulses. At birth, many nerves lack myelin, but as the child grows, greater amounts of myelin encase the nerve fibers. Myelination is largely complete by the end of the early childhood period, whereupon it allows for efficient transference of nerve impulses throughout the child's nervous system. Following myelination, children can exhibit increased complexity in their movement skills.

More generally, the attainment of increased complexity in motor performance between the ages of two and seven is based in part on changes brought about through growth and maturation. One key to maximum development is utilization of one's abilities, which is brought about by high-quality instruction, appropriate ecology of the environment, and opportunities for practice and encouragement. Although teachers cannot make children grow and mature faster, they can design enriched, enjoyable play environments by scaling equipment and performance contexts to fit children's sizes and abilities. They can also engage children in repetition of developmentally appropriate movement skills to foster development of their neuromuscular pathways.

During the fundamental movement phase, children progress sequentially through three stages—initial, emerging-elementary, and mature—as they become more biomechanically efficient movers. All three stages are described in the following subsections. In addition, the stages of many fundamental stability, locomotor, and manipulative skills are described and pictured in appendix A.

Initial Stage

In the initial stage of fundamental motor-skill development, children make their first observable and purposeful attempts at performing fundamental motor skills. This is the stage in which two- and three-year-olds typically function. Development through this stage and into the next depends largely on growth and maturation. The child's balance and range of motion are hindered by the disproportionately large head, the short square trunk, and the short limbs that characterize this age. These hindrances limit flexion, extension, and trunk rotation; make it difficult for the child to come to a quick stop; and present challenges in receiving large balls, because balance is easily lost and the ball easily dropped. The child may attempt balancing, throwing, catching, kicking, or jumping; however, since major components of the mature movement pattern are impossible at this point, the movements are uncoordinated and either inhibited or grossly exaggerated.

Emerging-Elementary Stages

The emerging-elementary stages of fundamental movement-skill development are typical of the performance of three- to five-year-old children. Development through these elementary stages and into the mature stage depends partly on growth and maturation and largely on opportunities for practice, encouragement, high-quality instruction, and the environment. During this transitional period between the initial and mature stages, the child's growth-related increase in strength and gradual lengthening of the trunk and limbs allow moderate ranges of flexion, extension, and rotation; at the same time, however, the child's short, stubby fingers still hamper object handling. As a result of these characteristics, performers in the emerging-elementary stage gain greater control of their movements but still appear somewhat awkward and lacking in fluidity. For example, at this stage the child cannot use hands alone to catch the ball or "give in" upon receiving the ball by bending the elbows to absorb force (see photo on page 41).

In summary, the core of the developmental physical education program for preschool children consists of developmentally appropriate movement goals and skills performed with scaled equipment and performance contexts. This approach supports children's progression through the initial and elementary stages and into the mature stage of motor skill development.

Mature Stage

By age 6 or 7, children's slow and steady growth in height, weight, and strength supports their developmental potential to be at the **mature stage** in most fundamental movement skills. The mature stage is characterized by progress toward well-coordinated and biomechanically efficient movement performances. This capacity is made possible by several developments. For one, by age 6, children can move through full ranges of flexion, extension, and rotation because their body proportions are more similar to those of adults. In addition, growth has made them stronger and lengthened their fingers, thus making it easier for them to manipulate objects.

In this stage, children have the potential to improve their performances rapidly. They are now able to throw farther, run faster, and jump higher. However, even though these children have the *potential* to attain the mature stage in most fundamental skills, they get there at varying rates. Their attainment of motor skill proficiency can be enhanced by opportunities (or limited by lack thereof) for practice, encouragement, high-quality instruction, and appropriate ecology of environment. Children who have few opportunities for practice, experience little or no encouragement, or lack instruction in an environment with regulation equipment may be delayed in achieving the mature stage. In contrast, children who have access to developmentally appropriate equipment, practice opportunities, encouragement, and good instruction may reach the mature stage more rapidly. The photo of the child catching with hands only illustrates the mature stage of catching in which the performer consistently catches the ball with hands only and can bend elbows to pull the ball in toward the chest to absorb force. When children have acquired the mature stage practice can be varied as illustrated by a child catching a ball from an arced trajectory.

The core of the developmental physical education program for children in the primary grades (K–2) consists of developmentally appropriate movement goals and skill development using scaled equipment and performance contexts. This approach supports children as they become mature movers by refining, varying, and combining a wide variety of fundamental movement skills.

These general characterizations notwithstanding, some adolescents and adults function only at the elementary stages in fundamental skills such as throwing, striking, and catching. Why? In most cases, it is simply because they progressed to this stage through childhood maturation but lacked sufficient opportunities for practice, encouragement, high-quality instruction, and other empowering conditions in the child-rearing environment. As a result, they failed to become mature movers in one or more fundamental movement skills. Unfortunately, if these experiences are delayed for a period of years, a person may never attain certain skills in mature form without considerable effort and outside influence. This lack can carry a considerable cost because mature fundamental movement skills form the basis for all cultural movement activities. Therefore, one must learn them in order to avoid the cycle of frustration and failure that often leads to an inactive lifestyle and the various negative consequences associated with sedentary behaviors.

Specialized Movement Phase

The **specialized movement phase** of development typically begins around age 7 and lasts through adolescence and beyond. During this time, children progress from performing stability, locomotor, and manipulative skills in the fundamental phase to performing corresponding and culturally appropriate movement activities in the specialized phase. The three stages of the specialized movement phase are transition, application, and lifelong utilization. Development through these stages depends largely on the quality of the movement and practice experiences in which children and youth participate.

The period of later childhood, from about age 8 to age 12, is typified by slow but steady increases in height and weight and by progress toward greater organization of the sensory and motor systems. Changes in body build, however, are slight. Later childhood is more a time of lengthening and filling out before the prepubescent growth spurt, which typically occurs around age 10 for girls and age 12 for boys. Children also make rapid gains in learning during later childhood and are capable of functioning at increasingly sophisticated levels in their performance of movement skills.

This period of continued slow growth in height and weight gives children time to get used to their growing bodies. This opportunity is an important factor in the typically dramatic improvement we see in coordination and motor control in the later childhood years. The gradual change in size and the close relationship maintained between bone and tissue growth both play a role in older children's increased levels of motor functioning. Both boys and girls have greater limb growth than trunk

Catching at the emerging-elementary stage.

Catching at the mature stage: hands only.

Catching at the mature stage with varied practice: catching a ball from an arced trajectory.

growth, but boys tend to have longer legs and arms and greater standing height during this period. Girls tend to have greater hip width and thigh size.

Because relatively little gender difference is exhibited in physique or weight until the onset of the preadolescent period, girls and boys can participate effectively together in most activities at this age. After the relatively stable growth periods of prepubescence, adolescents experience widely variable changes in body proportion and growth during puberty before attaining the stability of postpubescence as growth slows and then stops, thus ushering in the beginning of adulthood.

Although individual differences in growth and maturation require developmentally appropriate accommodations, children's skill acquisition depends greatly on how teachers and coaches design programs and engage learners in practice and authentic cultural movement experiences. For instance, when children engage in an authentic gamelike activity, they can discover the strategies and skills needed for success. Teachers can then match skill practice with the goals of the activity to help students improve skills, understand the relevance of practice, and find motivation to return to the authentic activity with enhanced performance. Although it begins in childhood, skill development in cultural movement activities continues through adolescence and into adulthood.

Transition Stage

The transition stage of specialized movement-skill development occurs from about age 7 to about age 10. During this period of prepubescence, children's slow and steady growth gives them a chance to get used to their more adult-like body proportions, and the completion of myelination affords increased complexity in movement skills. These changes pave the way for children to transition from biomechanically efficient performance of fundamental motor skills to performance of the corresponding specialized skills in cultural games, sports, and dances. For example, the fundamental movement skill of kicking corresponds to the specialized sport skill of the instep kick in soccer. This skill may be introduced as a way to keep possession of the ball in a gamelike activity, practiced in drill situations, and then applied in a lead-up activity, such as multiple-goal soccer or other small-sided soccer games. A student in the transition stage within the specialized movement phase can catch a ball while moving (see photo).

During the transition stage, children should not play the official sport as part of the instructional physical education program. Rather, they should be exposed to the basic skills, rules, and strategies of several sports through gamelike activities, skill drills, and a variety of lead-up activities. Full sport participation requires the ability to attend not only to one's own use of skills and strategy decision-making, but also to one's teammates and opponents. Small-sided gamelike activities narrow children's attention to manageable skill and decision choices providing for greater success and learning.

Catching at the transition stage.

Not all children develop biomechanically efficient performance in the fundamental motor skills by age 7. This variation presents an impediment for an individual (whether child or adult) who is interested in learning sport skills but possesses insufficient maturity in the fundamental movement skills to do so. Therefore, physical education teachers need to recognize children who are age 7 or older with deficits in mature-stage fundamental skill performance. These children have the physical maturity to perform the skills but need appropriate instruction and practice opportunities in order to develop biomechanically efficient performance in fundamental motor skills so that they can transition to the corresponding specialized movement skills.

Application Stage

The application stage of specialized movement-skill development is typical of middle school and junior high school students from about age 11 to age 13. During this stage children use skill combinations in cultural activity settings. In this age range, many girls and some boys enter puberty and experience changes in body proportion, height, and weight that can initially impede motor performance. Girls' hips widen, they develop breasts, and their body weight increases under the influence of hormones. Early-maturing boys may initially experience awkwardness as their legs and arms grow disproportionately to their trunks; however, once they get through the growth spurt, hormonal influences make them stronger and more coordinated than their less-mature

peers of the same chronological age. A child in the application stage within the specialized movement phase can catch a ball within a game situation (see photo).

This variability in maturity requires teachers to design inclusive, developmentally appropriate goals, tasks, environments, and practice opportunities to support children in applying movement skills and knowledge to cultural activities in competitive, recreational, and performance settings. Form, precision, accuracy, and standards of good performance are all especially important to learners in the application stage. Therefore, children practice more complex skills, and strategies and rules take on greater importance.

Children in this stage have also begun to select certain sports that they prefer. Preferences are based primarily on successful experiences; body type; geographic location; and emotional, social, and cultural factors. Some children prefer individual sports, whereas others prefer team sports. Some enjoy contact sports, whereas others prefer noncontact sports. Some particularly enjoy water sports; others prefer court sports or dance activities. This narrowing of interests is accompanied by an increased desire for competence.

The timing indicated here for the transition and application stages is based on generalizations, and, given children's extensive participation throughout North America (and elsewhere) in youth sport programs, these stages may begin at earlier ages. Indeed, many children these days transition from

Catching at the application stage.

fundamental to specialized sport skills at age 6, and they apply their movement skills to organized sport participation at increasingly young ages.

The core of the developmental physical education program for children in the intermediate grades (3–5) consists of developmentally appropriate movement goals and skill development using scaled equipment and performance contexts to support children as they become transition- and application-stage movers. They do so by refining, varying, combining, and applying a wide variety of specialized skills in cultural games, sports, and dances.

Lifelong Utilization Stage

The final stage in the specialized movement phase is the lifelong utilization stage, which begins at about age 14 and continues throughout adolescence and into adulthood. During the early high school years, most boys are navigating the awkwardness of puberty, but they gain the strength and coordination of postpubescence by about age 16. Most girls are postpubescent when they enter high school and therefore have the opportunity to regain confidence in moving their mature bodies throughout those four years.

Variability among students is still the norm in this stage, which requires teachers to design inclusive and developmentally appropriate goals, tasks, environments, and practice opportunities. They must also equip students to create their own high-quality practice and movement experiences to support lifelong activity participation. Therefore, at this stage, individuals are encouraged to select activities that they particularly enjoy and can pursue throughout life for fun, fitness, and fulfillment. High interest in specific activities is evidenced through active participation on a regular basis, whether in a competitive, recreational, or performance setting.

LEARNING NEW MOVEMENT SKILLS

Research supports the idea that movement skills are learned in identifiable stages by both children and adults (Fitts & Posner, 1967; Gentile, 1972, 2000; Gallahue et al., 2012). However, unlike the stages of motor skill *development*, which are age related, the levels of motor skill *learning* depend on practice and experience. The levels described in the following subsections constitute a progression of learning that combines information from all models created by the authors cited above.

Beginner-Level Learners

The movements of beginner level, or *novice-level*, learners are uncoordinated and jerky. Beginners focus on understanding the placement of body parts and the coordination and timing of movements. They pay attention to *all* of the information in the environment, are unable to screen out what is irrelevant, and cannot adapt movements to changing conditions. Gallahue et al. (2012) suggest that beginning learners progress through the following sequence in order to reach the goal of performing movement skills with adequate timing and technique.

- Awareness stage: The learner tries to get an idea of how to perform the skill.
- Exploratory stage: The learner knows what to do but performs inconsistently.
- Discovery stage: The learner attends to skill cues and performs more efficiently.

Fitts and Posner (1967) suggest that beginners are more dependent on teachers to provide instruction and feedback because they are less able to detect the cause of their movement errors and make appropriate adjustments. Gentile (1972) suggests that teachers focus on teaching learners how to perform the movement pattern, emphasize the goal of the movement task, and direct learners' attention to the relevant cues in the environment.

Intermediate-Level Learners

Intermediate level, or *practice-level*, learners perform movements with greater consistency and fewer errors than do beginners. They have a good general understanding of the movement task and are acquiring a feel for the skill with a more highly attuned kinesthetic sensitivity. They pay less conscious attention to the movements of the skill and begin devoting more attention to the goal or product of the skill. They also become more capable of timing their movements with objects and events and adapting their movements to changes in the environment.

Gallahue et al. (2012) suggest that intermediate learners progress through the following sequence to reach the goal of performing movement skills consistently in a variety of movement activities.

- Combination stage: The learner combines skills into fluid sequences and pays less conscious attention to each element.

- Application stage: The learner refines skill performance and uses skill combinations in a variety of movement activities.

Fitts & Posner (1967) suggest that teachers shift attention from single-skill mechanics to skill combinations and to providing authentic practice opportunities and enabling learners to become more capable of detecting and correcting their own errors. Gentile (1972) suggests that teachers focus on teaching learners how to refine a movement pattern and perform more consistently. Once learners perform skills consistently, the teacher can vary the conditions of the task and environment in order to provide authentic practice conditions that approximate the goal of the movement task in cultural movement activities.

Elementary children and most intermediate-grade children, as well as many adults, are in the intermediate level of learning movement skills and do not achieve advanced levels of strategic sport performance. Fortunately, participation at the intermediate level allows people to engage in moderate to vigorous physical activities that benefit health and to enjoy recreation and competitive movement experiences.

Advanced-Level Learners

Advanced level, or *fine-tuning level*, learners perform movements consistently and automatically. Indeed, their movements appear effortless, but, in reality, performing at the advanced level of learning "requires countless hours of practice" (Coker, 2004, p. 99). Advanced learners completely understand the movement task and are able to detect and correct their own errors. Their movements are characterized by consistency, adaptability, and anticipatory adjustments to changing environments.

Gallahue et al. (2012) suggest that advanced learners progress through the following sequence to reach the goal of automatic skill performance:

- **Performance stage:** The learner performs with increased accuracy, control, and movement efficiency.
- **Individualized stage:** The learner fine-tunes and modifies performance to maximize success based on personal attributes and limitations.

Fitts & Posner (1967) suggest that even though learners have reached high levels of performance, there is always room for improvement. Since improvement gains may be small, teachers may need to motivate learners to reach their full potential by designing challenging, authentic, game-like practice sessions. At this level students are challenged by strategic decision-making, simultaneous performance of multiple skills, and prompting in error detection and correction.

To summarize, figure 4.3 illustrates for each level the learner's movement characteristics, the movement goal that learners are trying to achieve by the end of the level, and the focus for instruction and feedback.

MAKING CONNECTIONS

We have examined the process of motor learning based on schema theory, perceptual–motor development, the phases and stages of motor development, and the levels of motor skill learning. How do we make connections between these areas to inform our decision-making as physical educators? For clarity, references to phases and stages of motor development are highlighted in blue and levels of learning a motor skill are highlighted in green.

Preschool children are characterized by what Jean Piaget (1952) referred to as the preoperational phase of cognitive development, wherein they are unable to reconstruct their thoughts and show others how they arrived at their conclusions. Similarly, when they engage in repetitive movement during play, preschool children are often unaware that they are implicitly learning motor skills. Teachers of preschool children can take the following steps to facilitate their progress through the initial stage of the fundamental motor-development phase: designing enriched, enjoyable play environments that stimulate implicit learning; scaling equipment and performance contexts to fit children's sizes and perceptual–motor abilities; encouraging children to engage in repetition of developmentally appropriate movement skills to foster development of their neuromuscular pathways; and praising their engagement.

Children transitioning into the emerging elementary stage of fundamental motor development exhibit movements that are uncoordinated, stiff, and jerky. These movements are characteristic of three- and four-year-olds at the beginner level of learning a new movement skill. Since elementary-grade children are in the concrete phase of cognitive development, they are capable of explicit learning

Level	Learner characteristics	Movement goal	Teacher's role
Beginner	• Inconsistent movement pattern • Concentration on how to perform movements in a stable environment • Inability to adapt movements to changing environment • Inability to detect own errors	To gain greater consistency in performance of movement skills	Instruction and feedback about • movement pattern • goal of skill • cues in environment
Intermediate	• Greater consistency and fewer errors • Concentration on varying and combining skills with less attention to each element • Becoming capable of timing and adapting movements to changing environment • Ability to detect some of own errors	To combine skills in fluid sequences To apply skills in cultural movement activities	Instruction and intermittent feedback about • refining movement pattern • varying skills • fluidly combining skills • adapting skills to authentic, changing environment
Advanced	• Consistency • Concentration on strategic decisions • Adaptation of movements and anticipatory adjustments to changing environments • Ability to detect and correct own errors	Consistent and automatic performance in cultural movement activities	Instruction and occasional feedback about • simultaneous performance of multiple skills • strategic decision making

Figure 4.3   Levels of learning a new movement skill.

and can benefit from instruction focused on understanding the placement of body parts or sequencing the large motor actions of bending and stretching.

As children develop coordination and timing of fundamental movements, they transition into the mature stage of fundamental motor development and become capable of forming a conscious mental plan for their movement skill performances. Since perceptual–motor abilities are still developing throughout the emerging-elementary and mature stages, teachers need to continue designing affordances that scale equipment and conditions to enable children to perform skills successfully. Once children develop adequate fluidity of movement, they cross over to the intermediate level of learning a motor skill and engage in refining, varying, and combining fundamental movement skills.

When elementary-grade children move into the transition stage of the specialized movement phase of motor development, they may return to the beginner level of learning a new movement skill. Therefore, when they first try new specialized sport skills, their movements may be uncoordinated, stiff, and jerky. As a result, they need instruction focused on the placement of body parts and the coordination and timing of movements. Once they develop adequate fluidity of movement, they cross over to the intermediate level of movement skill learning and engage in combining and varying specialized skills in gamelike activities, skill drills, and a variety of lead-up activities.

The characteristics and goals of the application stage of the specialized movement phase overlap with those of the intermediate level of movement-skill learning. Both focus on combining specialized skills and adapting movements to changing environments in order to perform cultural movement activities in competitive, recreational, and performance settings. The narrowing of interests in the application stage—and the accompanying increased desire for competence—could lead some youth sport athletes to practice and participate enough to move into the advanced level of motor skill learning.

Although the lifelong utilization phase of motor development falls outside the purview of this text, suffice it to say that students in this phase could be at any level of motor-skill learning, depending on their degree of experience and competence in a given movement activity. When they learn a new movement activity, as in taking up the sport of golf, they start at the beginner level of learning a motor skill. However, if they become high school varsity athletes, they may progress from the intermediate level to the advanced level of learning a motor skill.

Figure 4.4 reflects both the developmental and learning characteristics of children. It includes a level labeled "**immature beginner**" to highlight the

special learner characteristics, movement goals, and teacher role that must be addressed for preschool children in the initial stage and the early part of the emerging-elementary stage of fundamental motor development. This is a unique time period, in which children's movements are constrained by perception, body proportion, neuromuscular immaturity, and limited ranges of motion. Although teachers cannot make children grow faster, they can foster development of children's neuromuscular pathways by engaging them in developmentally appropriate movement activities.

The beginner level of learning a new motor skill is concurrent with the latter parts of the emerging-elementary stage and the mature stage of fundamental

Learning level	Development stage	Learner characteristics	Movement goal	Teacher role
Immature Beginner	Initial	• Limited–moderate perceptual–motor control • Limited–moderate flexion and extension • Limited–moderate rotation	• To gain neuromuscular control	Instruction and feedback: • Provide affordances that allow for skill success. • Provide encouragement.
Beginner	Emerging-elementary	• Inconsistent-moderate consistent performance • Concentration on how to perform movements • Inability to adapt movements to changing environment • Inability to detect own errors	• To gain greater consistency in performance of movement skills	Instruction and feedback about • goal of the skill • skill cues • cues in environment • skill variations
Intermediate	Mature / Transition	• Greater consistency and fewer errors • Concentration on varying and combining skills with less attention to each element • Becoming capable of timing and adapting movements to changing environment • Ability to detect some of own errors	• To combine skills in fluid sequences • To apply skills in cultural movement activities	Instruction and intermittent feedback about • refining the movement pattern • varying skills • fluidly combining skills • adapting skills to authentic, changing environment
Advanced	Application / Lifelong utilization	• Consistency • Concentration on strategic decisions • Adaptation of movements and anticipatory adjustments to changing environment • Ability to detect and correct own errors	• To achieve consistent and automatic performance in cultural movement activities	Instruction and occasional feedback about • simultaneous performance of multiple skills • strategic decision making

Figure 4.4 Developmental levels of learning a new movement skill.

motor development, as well as the early part of the transition stage of the specialized phase of motor development. In all three developmental stages, the goal is to move from inconsistent to consistent performance; the types of skill change from locomotor, stability, and manipulative to the specialized-phase cultural skills used in educational games, dance, and gymnastics.

The intermediate level of learning a new motor skill is concurrent with all three stages in the specialized phase of motor development. Here, learners progress from combining skills to applying them in cultural activities, some of which may become lifelong pursuits in noncompetitive and recreational settings. Those who pursue movement activities to higher levels of competition and performance for spectators or an audience reach the advanced level of learning a new motor skill.

Big Ideas

- When physical educators are knowledgeable about the process of perceptual–motor development—especially the visual and kinesthetic sensory modalities—they can provide affordances that enable children to more successfully perform motor skills while they are still developing their perceptual–motor capacities.

- Between the ages of two and seven, children progress sequentially through the initial, emerging-elementary, and mature stages of the fundamental movement phase of motor development to become more biomechanically efficient movers. The increased complexity of their motor performance depends in part on changes brought about by growth and maturation but also in large part on high-quality instruction, access to movement environments with appropriately scaled equipment and conditions, and opportunities for practice with encouragement.

- The specialized movement phase of motor development typically begins around age 7 and lasts through adolescence. As children in grades 3 through 5 progress through the transition and application stages, their fundamental skills are transformed into culturally appropriate movement activities. Their development through these stages depends largely on the quality of the movement and practice experiences in which they participate.

- Both children and adults progress through the levels of learning motor skills when acquiring new skills. Unlike the stages of motor skill *development,* which are age related, the levels of motor skill *learning* are based on practice and experience. The beginner level of learning a new motor skill is concurrent with the latter parts of the emerging-elementary stage and the mature stage of fundamental motor development, as well as the early part of the transition stage of the specialized phase of motor development. The intermediate level of learning a new motor skill is concurrent with all three stages of the specialized phase of motor development, as learners progress from combining skills to applying them in cultural activities, some of which may become lifelong pursuits in noncompetitive and recreational settings. Those who pursue movement activities at higher levels of competition and performance for spectators or an audience reach the advanced level of learning a new motor skill.

 Visit the web resource for learning activities, video clips, and review questions.

PART

II

Movement Content and the Learning Environment

Chapter 5

The Movement Framework

Key Concepts

- Using the Active Child diagram to describe the relationships between parts of the movement framework
- Describing the content of the fundamental movement skills and specialized movement activity themes
- Describing the developmental stages of the fundamental movement skills
- Describing the elements of each of the movement concepts
- Describing the purpose of learning goal blueprints

The developmental approach to teaching children's physical education is based on two concepts: instruction should be **individually appropriate**, and it should be **age-appropriate**. To achieve individual and age appropriateness, educators must make instructional decisions with an eye toward children's developmental and learning characteristics across the psychomotor, cognitive, and affective domains (for more on these characteristics, see chapters 3 and 4).

We must now ask, "What constitutes the core content of the developmental physical education curriculum?" The answer to this question is the movement framework, the components of which help us to design instructional tasks that are both individually and age appropriate. This chapter examines those components, or what we refer to as the "language" of developmental physical education. While recognizing children's unique developmental differences, the chapter explores how to apply the movement framework in designing movement experiences for children in pre-K, K-2, and grades 3 through 5.

RATIONALE FOR THE MOVEMENT FRAMEWORK

The success of a developmental physical education program depends on the teacher's knowledge of the vocabulary of movement: "Physical education teachers need a detailed and clear language to both observe and describe movement so that their mental images of students' movement responses are as complete as possible. Helping children improve their movement skills is much easier when the teacher has such a rich descriptive language to use when observing and talking about those skills" (Allison & Barrett, 2000, p. 46).

This vocabulary of movement is commonly referred to as a **movement framework** and consists of two major parts: movement content and movement concepts. **Movement content** is the central part, and it reflects the phases of motor development of children in pre-K through grade 5. More specifically, the movement content for children in pre-K through grade 2 consists of the fundamental locomotor, manipulative, and stability movement skills. The movement content for children in grades 3 through 5 consists of the specialized skills included in games, dance, and gymnastics.

Movement concepts, on the other hand, fall into four categories that describe the multiple ways in which the human body can move. The concepts are based on the work of Rudolf Laban (1879–1958). Laban's students and others, including the authors of this text, have modified his descriptive analysis of human movement for use in educational settings. Here are the movement concept categories:

- Body awareness—*what* the body can do
- Space awareness—*where* the body can move
- Effort awareness—*how* the body can move
- Relationship awareness—*with whom* and *with what* the body can move

The **Active Child** diagram (figure 5.1) represents the movement framework and depicts the relationship between the movement content and movement concepts (see figure 5.2 for a complete description). Highlighted in the star is the movement *content* that is essential to designing meaningful learning experiences in developmental physical education. As Baumgarten & Langton (2006) put it, "The body is the instrument of movement, and the child's exploration of and development of bodily skills is where movement vocabulary is first established" (p. 33).

The burst surrounding the star depicts the movement *concepts*: body, space, effort, and relationship. Concepts enhance skill development because they are used to vary and refine the movement content. This process enables children to become versatile and competent movers. For instance, the fundamental movement skill of bouncing a ball can be experienced through the following movement concept variations:

- Bouncing the ball with each hand (body)
- Bouncing the ball at different levels (space)
- Bouncing the ball at different speeds (effort)
- Bouncing the ball inside a hoop laid on the floor (relationship)

For the pre-K and primary-grade levels, the Active Child represents the fundamental movement phase of motor development; for the intermediate grades (3 through 5), it reflects the specialized movement phase of motor development. As Langton (2007, p. 17) notes, the movement framework as represented by the Active Child permeates and unifies the physical education curriculum.

MOVEMENT CONTENT

Children hurdling over fences, running into and out of the waves at the shore, jumping into piles of leaves or off of snow banks, chasing each other on the playground—their energy is remarkable and at times seems endless. Of course, these scenarios require a safe and perhaps natural environment, which affords such play opportunities. As physi-

Figure 5.1 The Active Child diagram.

cal educators, we must capitalize on the rich array of movement patterns that children naturally display during free play by extending and refining their movement repertoire through standards-based lessons. Whether children are engaged in free play in preschool, individualized and partner practice in the primary grades, or small-group practice or play in the intermediate grades, we can help them become skillful and versatile movers by providing them with lessons focused on the skill themes of locomotion, manipulation, and stability.

Movement content

Fundamental movement skill themes for pre-K through grade 2

Locomotor: walking, running, sliding, galloping, hopping, jumping, skipping, leaping, climbing, and dodging

Manipulative: bouncing, catching, throwing, striking, kicking

Stability: maintaining and gaining equilibrium

Static: balancing on body parts

Dynamic: transfer of weight along the trunk (rolling, rocking) or from hands to feet/feet to hands

Specialized movement activity themes for intermediate grades (3 through 5)

Games: target, striking-and-fielding, net and wall, invasion

Dance: lyric directed, cultural, social, creative

Gymnastics: balancing, body rolling, step-like actions and flight

Movement concepts

Body awareness: what the body can do

Parts of the body: head, neck, shoulders, chest, sides, waist, arms, elbows, hands, fingers, back, stomach, hips, knees, feet, heels, toes

Body actions: curling, bending, stretching, twisting, turning

Body shapes: straight or round, wide or narrow, twisted, symmetrical or asymmetrical

Relationships of body parts to each other: leading, above or below, support or nonsupport, isolated, moving or still, unison, opposition, sequenced

Space awareness: where the body can move

Levels: high, medium, low

Directions: forward, backward, sideways, up and down

Pathways: air (horizontal, vertical, arced), ground (straight, curved, zigzag)

Extensions: small or large, near or far

Effort awareness: how the body can move

Time: fast, medium, slow; sudden; sustained

Weight: strong, firm; light, fine

Flow: free, ongoing, indirect; bound, stoppable, direct

Relationship awareness: with whom and with what the body can move

With objects: in front of, behind, alongside, around, through, over or under, between, on top of, on or off of, in or out of

With others: in front of, behind, alongside, over or under, on or off, meeting or parting, far from or near to, following or leading, mirroring, matching, side by side, unison or canon, supporting or being supported, parallel, cooperatively, competitively

Other relationship elements: poetry, music, sounds, props, nature, art

Figure 5.2   Movement content and movement concepts for the Active Child.

Fundamental Movement Skill Themes

The fundamental movement skill themes include locomotor movements (e.g., walking, running, galloping, jumping, skipping, hopping, leaping, sliding, rolling), stability movements (e.g., bending, stretching, twisting, curling, dodging, turning, balancing, pushing, pulling), and manipulative movements (e.g., throwing, catching, striking, bouncing, kicking). These themes are the fundamental skills that make up the motor development milestones for children in pre-K through grade 2. They also form the foundation for the specialized skills performed by children in grades 3 through 5 in games, dance, and gymnastics. Appendix B includes descriptions and illustrations for each stage of development of the fundamental movement skills.

Locomotor Skills

Locomotor skills move the body through space on the limbs. Traveling locomotor skills are continuous, include a brief flight phase, and take the body from place to place. Examples include walking, running, galloping, sliding, and skipping. Flight locomotor skills involve takeoff, flight, and landing phases; examples include jumping, leaping, and hopping.

Traveling

- Running: transfer of weight from one foot to the other with a short flight phase

- Galloping: step-close-step pattern, moving forward with one foot leading, and a flight phase as the trailing foot lands in the space vacated by the leading foot

- Sideways sliding: step-close-step pattern, moving sideward with one foot leading, and a flight phase as the trailing foot lands in the space vacated by the leading foot

- Skipping: alternating step-hops

- Dodging: quick changes in direction to avoid objects and others

Running.

Galloping.

Sliding.

Skipping.

Dodging.

Flight

- Jumping: takeoff with two feet and land on two feet, takeoff with two feet and land on one foot, or takeoff with one foot and land on two feet

- Leaping: takeoff with one foot and land on opposite foot
- Hopping: takeoff with one foot and land on same foot

Jumping.

Leaping.

Hopping: preparation *(a)*, action *(b)*, and recovery *(c)*.

Stability Skills

Stability involves the ability to sense a shift in the relationship of body parts that alters one's balance, as well as the ability to adjust rapidly and accurately for these changes through appropriate compensating movements. Virtually all movement involves some elements of either static or dynamic balance, but stability skill themes place a particular premium on gaining or maintaining one's equilibrium in either static or dynamic balance situations.

Static balance involves a stationary posture in which the center of gravity remains stationary and the line of gravity falls within the base of support. Examples include balancing on various combinations of body parts, balancing in upright and inverted positions, and balancing on or hanging and swinging from equipment. Static balances with partners can also be performed with the center of gravity either within the partners' bases of support, as in balancing on top of one another, or between the partners' bases of support, as in counterbalances or countertension. In counterbalances, performers lean toward each other and depend on each other's weight to maintain the balance. In countertension, performers lean away from each other—for example, facing each other with toes touching and grasping hands and extending elbows while leaning away from each other.

Dynamic balance involves controlling the body as it moves through space. The center of gravity shifts constantly beyond the base of support and over the base of support in repetitive succession to keep the body moving. Dynamic balance skills can involve transferring weight along the trunk, as in rolling and rocking; transferring weight from the hands to the feet, as in performing a bear walk or cartwheel or climbing on equipment; or transferring weight from the hands to the feet over a low bench.

Static balance.

Counterbalance.

Countertension.

Dynamic balance.

Manipulative Skills

Manipulative skills are gross-body movements in which force is imparted to or received from objects. These skills are categorized by purpose: sending away, receiving, or maintaining possession.

Sending away

- **Kicking**: imparting force to an object with a foot or leg

- **Striking**: imparting force to an object with an upper body part or an implement

- **Throwing**: imparting force to an object by releasing it from the hand(s) into the air

- **Ball rolling**: imparting force to an object by releasing it from the hand(s) along the ground

Kicking.

Striking.

Throwing.

Rolling a ball.

Receiving

- **Catching**: absorbing the force of an object with the hand(s)

- **Trapping**: absorbing the force of an object with the torso, leg, or foot

Catching.

Trapping.

Maintaining possession

- **Bouncing with hands:** sequentially imparting downward force to an object and receiving upward force from it while either stationary or on the move
- **Dribbling with feet:** while moving, repetitively imparting force from a foot to an object so that it moves along the ground
- **Carrying:** holding and protecting an object with the hand(s), arm(s), or body while moving through space

Bouncing with hands.

Dribbling with feet.

Carrying.

LIVERPOOL JOHN MOORES UNIVERSITY
LEARNING SERVICES

Specialized Movement Activity Themes

Specialized movement activity themes involve combining the fundamental movement skills and concepts in movement activities that are characteristic of the culture. The themes provide the focus for developmental physical education in grades 3 through 5 and include developmental games, dance, and gymnastics. The specialized skills used in developmental games emerge chiefly from the fundamental locomotor and manipulative skills. They are combined in sequences and are classified either as outcome-specific closed skills (e.g., in bowling) or as open skills (e.g., in soccer). The specialized skills used in developmental dance and gymnastics emerge chiefly from the fundamental locomotor and stability skills. They are combined in sequences expressed as dances or gymnastics routines and are classified as form-specific closed skills.

Developmental Games

Developmental games are developmentally appropriate activities in which children engage in play, either with or without an object, within a structure of rules and boundaries (Allison & Barrett, 2000). In these gamelike activities, children practice skills and tactics in formats that can be either cooperative or competitive. Children participate by combining specialized skills derived from fundamental manipulative, locomotor, and stability skills with movement concepts and game tactics. Developmental games fall into the following major categories: cooperative, competitive, and child designed.

- Cooperative games involve partner and small-group activities that promote personal and social responsibility. Children's sense of responsibility is fostered by activities that develop trust, communication, teamwork, and leadership through the strategies of challenge by choice, problem solving, goal setting, and reflection on action (Glover & Midura, 1992; Midura & Glover, 1995, 1999; Orlick, 2006).

- In competitive games, children vie to achieve a goal through the use of movement skills, skill combinations, and game tactics. In noninvasive competitive games, children compete in separate spaces; examples include bowling and tennis. In invasive competitive games, students compete in the same space, as in soccer and basketball. Competitive games can be categorized into groups of noninvasive and invasive games with similar tactics (Werner & Almond, 1990; Mitchell, Oslin, & Griffen, 2013).

- Target: These noninvasive competitive games focus on accuracy wherein players perform independently by projecting objects toward a specific target. Examples include bowling, golf, and disc golf.

- Striking-and-fielding: In these noninvasive competitive games, players work independently to send an object into an opponent's territory in order to gain time to run bases and score. Meanwhile, the opponent's players work together to move the object to the base that will halt the runner's progress and prevent scoring. Base runners and infielders are active at the bases simultaneously, usually one on one, as the fielder tries to tag the bag or the runner, who meanwhile tries to touch the bag first and avoid the tag. Striking and fielding games include baseball, softball, cricket, and kickball.

- Net or wall: In these noninvasive competitive games, players remain within their team's boundaries and attack the space of opponents with objects while defending their own space against attack. Net and wall games include the lead-up games of four square, pickleball, and Newcomb and the games of volleyball, badminton, and tennis.

- Invasion: In invasive competitive games, teammates and opponents occupy the same space as they simultaneously try to defend their territory and attack the opponent's goal. Offensive players try to maintain possession in order to advance the game object toward a goal and score. Defensive players try to defend space and others in order to gain possession of the game object. Players' roles switch between offense and defense based on which team possesses the game object.

- In child-designed games, teachers encourage children to change the games they play in order to develop knowledge of game structures and learn how to accommodate different levels of ability to make games fair. Children are gradually given responsibility for changing various aspects of games, such as size of the playing area, equipment, rules, number of players per side, and skills used.

Developmental Dance

Developmental dance is a movement form in which children use the body as an instrument of communication and creative expression. Forms include lyric directed; cultural and social; and creative.

- In lyric-directed dance, music lyrics indicate the movement skills and concepts to be performed.
- Cultural and social dance express cultural norms, traditions, and beliefs as dancers move with others to music.
- Creative dance communicates ideas, feelings, or concepts and can be performed either alone or with others and either with or without music.

Developmental Gymnastics

Developmental gymnastics places a premium on performing a variety of body management skills, skill combinations, and movement sequences, both on the floor and in relationship to equipment. Skill combinations and movement sequences can be performed individually or with others. In developmental gymnastics, children learn body management skills through a thematic approach. Themes are centered on combining gymnastics actions with movement concepts that affect those actions. For instance, the theme of weight transference and flight combinations could lead to combining rolls, jumps, and wheeling actions and using variations in direction, level, speed, and pathway. Here are some descriptions of gymnastics actions:

- **Balancing**: static positions and dynamic movements performed either alone or with others
- **Rolling**: transfer of weight along the trunk
- **Step-like actions**: transfer of weight from feet to hands or from hands to feet
- **Flight**: transfer of weight from feet to hands to feet with a flight phase between takeoff and landing

Rolling.

Static and dynamic balance.

Flight.

MOVEMENT CONCEPTS

Movement concepts help us describe the various ways in which fundamental and specialized movement skills can be performed. They give movement skills character. Picture a child performing a jump with a two-footed takeoff and a two-footed landing. Now, give the jump some character by having the child jump higher or farther, with a half turn or a tuck, with arms spread wide, in combination after a forward roll, or in tandem with a partner. In this way, the four movement-concept categories described in the following subsections help physical educators challenge children to give their movements character by varying and refining what body parts they move, where they move, how they move, and with whom or with what they move. The categories are body awareness, space awareness, effort awareness, and relationship awareness.

Body Awareness

As depicted in the Active Child diagram (figure 5.1), body awareness involves knowledge of what the body can do. With pre-K children, the emphasis is on learning, experiencing, and exploring the elements of body awareness. For primary- and intermediate-grade children, the elements of body awareness are used for two purposes. One purpose is to perform fundamental and specialized movements with biomechanical efficiency, which is often referred to as "elements of correct form" or "movement cues"—for example, "step with the opposite foot" when throwing overhand, and "lead the turn by moving the head." The other purpose of body awareness for children in kindergarten through grade 5 is to explore and create new ways in which the body can perform fundamental and specialized skills. For instance, cues might prompt the child to "use different body parts to lead you through the spaces in the obstacle course" or to "change the shape and actions of your body to express the opposing emotions of joy and grief."

The elements of body awareness include the following:

- **Parts of the body**: head, neck, shoulders, chest, sides, waist, arms, elbows, hands, fingers, back, stomach, hips, knees, feet, heels, toes
- **Body actions**: curling, bending, stretching, twisting, turning
- **Body shapes**: straight or round, angular or bent, wide or narrow, twisted, symmetrical or asymmetrical
- **Relationships of body parts to each other**: leading, above or below, supporting or nonsupporting, isolated, moving or still, unison, opposition, or sequenced

Parts of the Body

It is essential for children across all developmental stages to be able to identify the different parts of the body and how to use them to perform movement skills efficiently. For initial-stage movers, this process may involve learning the names and locations of various body parts. In a pre-K movement experience, a sample instructional task might involve learning to circle one's head, shrug one's shoulders, or tap one's foot to music. In grades K through 2, children learn to balance on different combinations of body parts and come to understand that one's chest should face the target when one performs an underhand toss. In grades 3 through 5, children learn that multiple body parts are used to perform a movement skill—for example, drawing the arm back behind the ear and rotating one's side to the target when performing an overhand throw.

Body Actions

All movement skills involve at least one body action. These actions can be performed either while stationary or while on the move. For example, one twists the trunk during the overhand throw, bends and stretches in order to jump, and keeps the body curled when performing a smooth forward roll.

As Baumgarten and Langton (2006, p. 33) emphasize, body actions are critical to becoming a skillful mover. Children tend to move with a focus on whole-body activity, but the motion of individual parts must become a focus in order to refine skill development. This phenomenon in beginning-level movers is explained by the motor development principle referred to as "undifferentiated movement." It means that because the mover *cannot* isolate individual body segments, all body parts move together and therefore are neither differentiated nor rhythmically sequenced. Thus educators must focus on specific body actions when teaching movement skills. For example, the educator might design instructional tasks to focus on how the arms swing from back to front when performing an underhand toss, how the body twists or rotates when performing an overhand throw, and how the knees bend to prepare for performing a horizontal jump.

Body Shapes

The body's ability to make shapes is essential for developing body awareness; it is also integral to the performance of manipulative, locomotor, and stability skills. Pre-K children respond joyfully to the opportunity to make body shapes when prompted to do so by a teacher who shows them a picture or an object and asks a "who can" question, such as, "Who can make a round shape like this apple?" Primary-grade children learn to make shapes of varying types and sizes and may even create shape sentences! Intermediate-grade children demonstrate specific shapes for successful performance of a variety of games, dances, and gymnastics skills. For instance, a bent shape is used in a tuck jump off of a box, a wide shape is used to defend a goal, and a narrow shape can be used in performing a turning action (e.g., pirouette).

Relationships of Body Parts to Each Other

To become efficient movers, children must become aware of the relationships of body parts to each other. Pre-K children learn to recognize and vary the body parts that support the body or that move while others are still. They also learn that body parts can move in different ways—either in unison, in isolation, in opposition, or in sequence (Nichols, 1994, p. 169). Primary- and intermediate-grade children learn to refine fundamental and specialized movement skills through intentional use of body-part relationships. For example, primary-grade children learn to use their arms and legs in opposition when skipping and throwing, and intermediate-grade children use arm and leg opposition when coordinating arm action with leg action during a leap or a basketball lay-up.

Space Awareness

Space awareness involves knowledge of where the body can move. It includes the following elements: area, direction, pathway, level, and range of movement. Space awareness is essential for success in moving, regardless of "whether the task is creating a dance or outmaneuvering one's opponent on the soccer field" (Nichols, 1994, p. 172) or combining gymnastics skills.

Area

Children must learn to control their bodies as they move, both within their personal space and through general space. One's personal space is the area immediately around one's body in all directions as far as the body can reach. General space is the larger movement area, including the space of other movers. To illustrate personal space, teachers can use the image of a bubble: "Draw a bubble or circle around your body. Stretch your arms out to touch the sides of your bubble. Stretch your legs out to touch the bottom of your bubble. Make sure that your bubble does not touch any of your classmate's bubbles!"

Developmentally, the concept of space awareness begins with defining general and personal space and designing movement experiences that provide visual aids to illustrate these two elements. For example, pre-K children might find a poly spot to stand on and regard as their personal space. They might then be asked to move to a poly spot of a different color, thus moving through general space to get to the new spot. Gradually, children learn to move through general space without specific visual guides and to avoid others as they all move freely through general space. By fifth grade, children can generally apply tactics in order to move through, attack, and defend space in games; they can also create routines and sequences of movement in order to use space purposefully and aesthetically in dance and gymnastics.

Direction of Movement

Going from one point to another specified point involves direction of movement and is usually introduced after children master the concepts of general and personal space. Directions include forward and backward, to the right and to the left, and up and down. The concept of direction is a component of readiness for learning—and an important one for young children to internalize. For example, moving forward through general space while avoiding others is a critical safety skill for young children.

Changes of direction can also be used to vary skill themes and change the degree of difficulty of a movement task for children in kindergarten through grade 5. For example, skipping forward is much easier than skipping backward, sliding sideways is accomplished after learning to gallop forward, and rolling sideways (to the right or left) is typically an easier developmental gymnastics skill to learn than are the forward and backward rolls. Manipulative skills can also be varied by changes in direction—for example, using different parts of the foot to kick a ball forward, upward, backward, or sideward and changing the direction of movement when dribbling.

Pathway of Movement

The body can move in straight, curved, zigzag, diagonal, and twisted pathways of movement. These pathways may be located on a variety of surface areas or in the air. Instructional tasks typically begin by having children learn to perform locomotor skills along straight pathways before performing the quick directional changes needed for traveling along zigzag pathways. The pathways made through the air by balls and other objects are referred to as trajectories, which can be horizontal, vertical, or arced.

Pre-K children cannot intentionally send objects away along specific trajectories until they reach proficient motor-development stages. In kindergarten through grade 2, teachers can use the environment to prompt children to send objects away along various trajectories (e.g., throwing a ball over a rope or at a low target). In grades 3 through 5, individual instructional tasks can be followed by partner activities and eventually by more sophisticated uses of pathways and trajectories in games—for example, throwing a ball along an arced pathway to achieve height and distance or deceiving and avoiding opponents by changing one's pathway on the field of play. Children at this level can also use pathways for expressive effects in dance and gymnastics sequences.

Level of Movement

Level of movement refers to whether the body (or a part of the body) is in a high, medium, or low position. High positions are usually located from the shoulders to above the head, medium positions from the knees to the shoulders, and low positions below the knees. When children discover and explore the myriad of movement possibilities at different levels, they enhance their space awareness. Pre-K children explore levels ranging from high to low by stretching and bending body parts and by jumping off of low equipment. K-2 children can perform fundamental movements (e.g., throwing, catching, jumping, balancing, rolling) at various levels. Children in grades 3 through 5 can move their bodies to different levels in order to block shots, deny space, indicate being open, or score goals in games. The ability to move one's body at different levels also leads to increased amplitude in gymnastics and more variations for expression in dance.

Range of Movement

Range of movement involves the size of a movement and the extent to which the body can reach. Preschool children explore range of movement by performing movements that are big and small, whereas primary-grade children begin to explore

These students are demonstrating different shapes at various levels as they participate in a dance lesson.

range by extending the body into far space and controlling the body in near-reach space. Intermediate-grade children use variations in range to gain or maintain possession of game objects. As with level, range can also be used to exaggerate and vary movements in gymnastics and dance.

Effort Awareness

Effort awareness, or awareness of how the body moves, emphasizes the dynamics and qualities of movement. Laban, cited in Langton (2007), used the word *effort* to refer to purposeful, inner control of three factors: time, force, and flow. We can think of effort in part as the timing aspect that makes movements look coordinated rather than stiff or jerky.

Effort awareness is often difficult for beginning teachers to understand and apply intentionally when designing instructional tasks for a lesson plan. Graham, et al. (2012) suggested a progression that starts with providing experiences to help children understand the contrasts of time (fast and slow), force (strong and light), and flow (bound and free). Next, the concepts are applied to specific skills and situations, and finally children are invited to focus on the "movement possibilities that occur between the extremes—faster, slower, accelerating, decelerating, sudden changes of speed" (Graham, et al., 2012, p. 269). All movements are performed with *some* degree of speed, force, or flow. To perform coordinated movement, children need to produce the *right* amount of each to meet the demands of the desired skill.

Timing of movement involves the speed at which a movement is performed: fast, medium, or slow. A sustained movement is considered a slow effort, whereas a quick and sudden movement is a fast effort. Moving at the right speed—and at the right time—is the hallmark of skilled, coordinated movement performance. Think of a basketball player dribbling slowly in place after receiving a throw-in, then seeing an open space and dribbling quickly through it to convert a lay-up shot. Or consider the difference between the movement speeds required for dancing the waltz and the jive. To perform coordinated movement, children need to produce the right amount of speed for the demands of the skill in question.

Pre-K children tend to move quickly and have difficulty stopping their movements. Therefore, for safety, teachers focus their attention on signals that cue them to slow down and stop. Likewise, to help them vary their speed of movement, teachers use external stimuli, such as slow or fast music or drumbeats. K-2 children are gradually gaining the ability to vary speed and stop safely; as a result, over time, they rely less on teacher prompts and external stimuli. In grades 3 through 5, teachers create tasks and environments that enable children to use the right amount of speed at the right time— for example, first responding to a tennis ball hit to a known location and then progressing to respond to a tennis ball hit to an *unknown* location.

Force of movement involves the strength or power with which a movement is performed. For the element of weight, the movement descriptors are *strong* and *light*. Think of the contrast between the force needed to throw a yarn ball versus the force needed to put a shot, to jump over a narrow stream versus to jump over a wide one, or to perform a push-up from the knees versus to perform one from the feet. To perform coordinated movement, then, children need to produce the right amount of force for the demands of the skill.

Pre-K children can produce force to push and pull light objects; however, they are constrained by their size, strength, and skill levels when trying to produce force for more complex movements, such as jumping and throwing. K-2 children can produce forces commensurate with their gains in strength, size, and skill. For instance, they can throw for different distances and jump onto and off of low equipment. In grades 3 through 5, teachers can create tasks and environments that enable children to use the right amount of force for the demands of the task—for example, producing the needed force to shoot a junior basketball from a specified distance to a specified height.

Flow of movement involves continuity of movement. In both single movements and combinations of movement skills, the goal is to achieve a continuous, smooth, coordinated pattern. Movements can be characterized by either free or bound flow. Free-flow movement is ongoing and unstoppable— for example, a curvy, wiggly, and loose movement that resembles "cooked spaghetti." As Baumgarten & Langton (2006, p. 38) indicate, free flow gives movement a sense of fluency and ongoingness, whereas bound flow can be stopped, checked, or changed. A leap, for example, is a free movement— once you take off, you cannot stop the movement until you have landed. In contrast, a kick or throw is a bound movement because it can be stopped while it is being performed.

Most often, free-flowing movements involve continuous, serial, flight, or swinging skills, whereas bound-flow movements involve discrete skills. In order to perform a coordinated movement, children need to produce the type of flow that is needed for the demands of the particular skill. Furthermore, in order to perform smooth, flowing combinations of skills, children need to use the recovery phase of the first movement as the preparation phase of the next movement.

Relationship Awareness

Relationship awareness—that is, awareness of with whom and with what the body moves—defines interactions with people, objects, and props. These relationships can be described in two ways. They can consist of the spatial positioning or movement between children and objects, props, or each other (as demonstrated when children move alongside a partner, over a box, or through a hoop). They can also consist of a role or a grouping of people (as demonstrated when children follow or lead a partner or move cooperatively in a group to keep a ball in the air).

Typically, relationships focused on spatial positioning are easier for children to understand because the interaction is more concrete—for example, jumping onto equipment or skipping around a partner. In contrast, relationships focused on roles require more interpersonal skills, such as cooperating with a partner to mirror movements or moving with other players and the ball in a small-sided game of soccer or field hockey.

Spatial Positioning

Moving in relationship to objects, props, and other people challenges children to learn the spatial positioning concepts of over and under, in and out, on and off, along, around, through, near and far, in front of, behind, and alongside. Relationship-with-object challenges might include, for example, moving along the top of a gymnastics bench or around a cone, jumping off of a foam shape, hopping in and out of a hoop, or throwing a ball over a net or through a goal. Relationship-with-prop challenges might include moving a scarf around various body parts or making shapes with a streamer in front of the body. Relationship-with-people challenges might include moving behind or alongside a teammate to get open for a pass, stepping toward the center in a circled group to meet and then stepping

back to part, or maintaining control while kicking a ball back and forth with a partner from increasing distances.

Roles and Groupings

When children perform in relationship to others based on roles or groupings, they are challenged to engage in parallel, cooperative, or competitive interactions either on their own, with a partner, in a group, or between groups. Relationship-with-people challenges might include moving alone in a mass by running among others while avoiding contact, leading and following a partner through an obstacle course, cooperating with a partner to create a balance, cooperating with a group to get untangled from a human knot, and competing as part of a group to keep a ball away from another group (i.e., an opponent).

PUTTING IT ALL TOGETHER

To reiterate, the pre-K and primary-grade Active Child represents the *fundamental* movement phase of motor development, and the intermediate-grade (3 through 5) Active Child reflects the *specialized* movement phase of motor development. Therefore, learning experiences for children in pre-K, K-2, and grades 3 through 5 differ distinctly based on the different developmental characteristics and needs of the children. To help you see how to combine the movement skills and concepts represented in the Active Child diagram, we have created learning goal blueprints. The blueprints for the *fundamental* movement phase, presented in tables 5.1 through 5.3, show how locomotor, stability, and manipulative skills are combined with the movement concepts (body, space, effort, and relationship) to vary and refine movement content, thus enabling children to become versatile and competent movers.

The learning goal blueprints presented in tables 5.4 through 5.6 show how the *specialized* movement skills in games, dance, and gymnastics are combined with the movement concepts to design learning experiences for learners in grades 3 through 5. The learning goal blueprint for developmental games (table 5.4) shows how the specialized movement skills, which are grouped by categories of games (target, striking-and-fielding, net and wall, and invasion), are combined with the movement concepts, which are grouped as game components (base, decision making, skill execu-

Table 5.1 Learning Goal Blueprint for Mature and Versatile Performance of Locomotor Skills

Content	Body	Space	Effort	Relationship
Traveling skills: running, galloping, sliding, skipping	Intentionally uses body actions for mature performance. Curls, stretches, bends, twists, and turns body during, into, and out of traveling skills.	Adjusts movements to move safely move through space. Travels on straight, curved, and zigzag pathways in forward, backward, and sideward directions.	Varies speed of traveling skills. Combines traveling skills in smooth sequences.	Uses traveling skills to move around, along, inside, through, and under equipment. Moves in front of, next to, and behind others and in roles of leading, following, mirroring, and matching. Adjusts movements to chase, flee, and dodge others.
Flight: jumping, leaping, hopping	Intentionally uses body actions for mature performance. Moves body into and out of symmetrical shapes (round, narrow, wide) during flight.	Changes level and varies distance and direction of flight movements.	Creates and absorbs force for mature performance. Combines flight and traveling skills smoothly (e.g., running and leaping; galloping and jumping).	Uses flight skills to move over, into, out of, onto, and off of low equipment. Uses flight to move in front of, next to, and behind others and in roles of leading, following, mirroring, and matching. Adjusts movements using flight to dodge others.

Table 5.2 Learning Goal Blueprint for Mature and Versatile Performance of Stability Skills

Content	Body	Space	Effort	Relationship
Static balances: upright, inverted	Intentionally uses body actions for mature performance. Balances by making different body shapes: round, straight, bent, wide, narrow, and twisted. Changes supporting and nonsupporting body parts to vary balance positions.	Balances on high, medium, and low levels. Uses near and far to extend the range of a balance.	Intentionally uses force to maintain balance.	Performs balances inside, on top of, underneath, next to, inside, outside, and through equipment. Performs nonsupport balances with a partner: in front of, next to, behind, over, and under and in roles of mirroring and matching.
Transference of weight by rolls, step-like actions	Intentionally uses body actions for mature performance. Curls, stretches, bends, twists, and turns body segments and parts during, into, and out of transference of weight skills. Changes supporting and nonsupporting body parts to vary transference of weight skills.	Changes level and varies direction and pathway of transference of weight skills.	Varies speed and force while performing transference of weight skills. Smoothly combines transference of weight skills.	Uses transference of weight skills to move over, into, out of, onto, and off of low equipment. Uses transference of weight skills to meet and part and to move next to others and in roles of leading, following, and matching.

Table 5.3 Learning Goal Blueprint for Mature and Versatile Performance of Manipulative Skills

Content	Body	Space	Effort	Relationship
Sending objects away: throwing, kicking, volleying, striking	Intentionally uses body parts in unison, in opposition, and in sequence and uses body actions (curling, stretching, bending, twisting, and turning) for mature performance.	Sends away objects to forward and sideward directions; on the high, medium, and low levels; in arced, vertical, and horizontal trajectories; and at short, medium, and long distances.	Creates and applies force appropriately for sending objects to intended targets or receivers.	Sends objects toward, over, under, and through equipment or targets. Sends objects to partners who are in front of or alongside the sender.
Receiving objects: catching, trapping	Intentionally uses body parts in unison, in opposition, and in sequence and uses body actions (curling, stretching, bending, twisting, and turning) for mature performance.	Receives objects sent from low, medium, and high levels; in horizontal, vertical, and arced trajectories; and at short, medium, and long distances.	Moves at appropriate speeds to approach and receive objects. Absorbs force appropriately to receive and control objects.	Receives objects coming over, under, and through equipment. Receives objects while moving on top of or off of equipment. Receives objects from partners who are in front of or alongside the receiver.
Maintaining possession of objects: bouncing, dribbling with feet, carrying	Intentionally uses body parts in unison, in opposition, and in sequence and uses body actions (curling, stretching, bending, twisting, and turning) for mature performance.	Moves through general space changing direction (forward and sideward) and pathways (straight, curved, and zigzag) while maintaining possession.	Uses different speeds (slow, medium, and fast) and applies appropriate force to maintain possession of objects.	Maintains possession of objects while moving alongside or around equipment or others. Uses roles of leading, following, meeting, and parting while maintaining possession of objects.

Table 5.4 Learning Goal Blueprint for Developmental Games

Game components	Target	Striking-and-fielding	Net and wall	Invasion
Base: position to which players return between skill tries	Starts in a setup or stance position.	Returns to fielding position or base.	Returns to court position between shots or rallies.	Sets up in a position.
Decision making: appropriate decisions about what to do with the ball during a game	Makes decisions using distance and direction for accuracy.	Fielder decides where to move to receive and throw the ball. Batter detects pitch and decides hit placement. Runner decides when to advance.	Positions body to hit to most open place to set up attack or score.	Makes appropriate decisions about passing, dribbling, or shooting on goal.
Skill execution: efficient execution of selected skills	Demonstrates accuracy.	Fielder gets into position to receive ball and accurately sends ball to receiver. Batter accurately hits ball to desired placement. Runner runs through or rounds bases.	Offensive player accurately sends shots to the most open area and varies force and location of shots.	Offensive player accurately shoots on goal when open, passes to open receivers, maintains possession, and fakes. Goalkeeper prevents scoring.
Supporting: moving into position to receive passes from teammates		Fielder moves into position to receive throws from teammates.	Volleyball player moves into position to receive passes from teammates.	Offensive player moves into position to receive passes from teammates.
Covering: backing up a player making a challenge for the ball		Fielder backs up teammates fielding the ball.	Volleyball receiver backs up teammates as ball comes over net.	Defensive player moves into position to help or back up teammate going for ball.
Guarding or marking: defensive maneuvering to deny the offense the ball or prevent scoring				Defense player maneuvers to prevent scoring or block offense and gain possession of ball.
Adjusting: changing position to accommodate game flow				Adjusts from offense to defense and vice versa.

tion, supporting, covering, guarding and marking, and adjusting). Table 5.5 shows how genres of dance are combined with the movement concepts (body, space, effort, and relationship). And table 5.6 shows how gymnastics actions (balancing, rolling, step-like, and flight) are combined with the movement concepts to vary, combine, and perform with partners.

Table 5.5 Learning Goal Blueprint for Developmental Dance

Content	Body	Space	Effort	Relationship
Lyric-directed dance	Intentionally uses body actions and shapes in unison, in opposition, and in sequence as directed by the lyrics, and uses correct technique.	As designated by lyrics, correctly performs dance steps while changing direction, level, pathway, or range of movement.	Performs dance actions to the tempo of the music.	Maintains relationships with others as designated by dance lyrics.
Cultural dance	Intentionally uses body actions and shapes in unison, in opposition, and in designated dance sequences with correct performance technique while expressing desired meaning.	Correctly changes direction, level, pathway, or range of movement in accordance with dance steps.	Performs dance actions to the tempo of the music. Intentionally uses force for correct performance technique while expressing desired meaning.	Uses props, formations, roles, and positions as designated by the dance.
Creative dance	Intentionally uses body actions and shapes in unison, in opposition, and in sequence with correct performance technique while expressing desired meaning.	Performs dance movements by varying direction, level, pathway, or range of movement while expressing desired meaning.	Performs dance actions using appropriate tempo, force (strong, medium, light), and flow (bound or free) to express desired meaning.	Uses props, positions (e.g., in front of, alongside, behind, above), roles, and groupings to express desired meaning.
Social dance	Intentionally uses body actions and shapes in unison, in opposition, and in sequence with correct performance technique.	Correctly performs dance steps while changing direction, level, pathway, or range of movement.	Performs dance actions to the tempo of the music.	Performs dance using correct positions and roles of leading and following.

Table 5.6 Learning Goal Blueprint for Developmental Gymnastics

Content	Skills	Variations	Combinations	Partners
Balance Roll Step-like Flight	Intentionally uses body actions for correct performance technique on mats and equipment.	Performs and creates variations of gymnastics actions on mats and equipment using movement concepts. Body: Varies shapes that are symmetrical or asymmetrical by curling, stretching, and twisting during actions or to get into or come out of actions; varies position of nonsupport body parts. Space: Varies level, range, direction, and pathway of actions or uses variations as transitions between actions. Effort: Varies speed and force of actions or uses variations as transitions between actions.	Combines 3 or 4 gymnastics actions on mats and equipment using variations as transitions. Combines and sequences skills on mats and equipment with few hesitations.	Coordinates movements with partner on mats and equipment for counterbalances, countertensions, and supports. Coordinates combinations of skills in relation to partner on mats and equipment in order to meet and part or to move next to and in roles of leading, following, and matching.

Big Ideas

- The movement framework provides a language for physical educators. Allison and Barrett (2000) suggest that helping children improve their movement skills is much easier when the teacher possesses a rich descriptive language to use when observing and talking about skills. The Active Child diagram depicts the language of physical education for pre-K through grade 5.

- The movement framework has two parts: *movement content,* which consists of the fundamental movement skills (locomotor, manipulative, and stability) and the specialized movement activities (games, dance, and gymnastics); and *movement concepts,* which include body, space, effort, and relationship awareness.

- The fundamental movement skills can be described by the characteristics of the stages—initial, emerging elementary, and mature—that represent the sequence of motor development.

- The learning goal blueprints provide a developmental picture of the movement framework and show how skills can be varied and refined using the movement concepts. Educators can use the blueprints to design developmentally appropriate learning experiences that help learners in kindergarten through grade 5 become skillful and versatile movers.

 Visit the web resource for learning activities, video clips, and review questions.

Chapter 6

The Environment and the Task

Key Concepts

- Identifying the affordances used to scale equipment and conditions in the learning environment
- Differentiating between a movement skill and a task
- Explaining the relationship between biomechanical principles and critical cues
- Defining closed and open skills and describing the task progressions for each
- Identifying the relationships between the constraints of the learner, the environment, and the task
- Describing the four levels of task progression for learning fundamental and specialized motor skills

Developmental physical educators embrace the challenge of designing movement experiences that meet the needs of children at different levels of ability. The goal of physical education is to enhance the motor performance of *all* children, regardless of athletic prowess. Thus it is critical for educators to scale movement tasks and environments to performer size, maturity, and ability. To help you meet that challenge, this chapter explores the effect of environmental variables on the design of instructional tasks. It introduces a four-part task progression, along with instructional cues to promote movement skill learning in both fundamental and specialized movers.

THE ENVIRONMENT

The environment is the setting in which learners perform movement skills. It consists of equipment and condition variables that influence the movement characteristics necessary for skillful performance. For instance, when defending a goal, the goalie must tailor her movements to the size, height, speed, and trajectory of the incoming ball. Physical education teachers purposefully choose equipment and create conditions that are scaled to the learner's body size, perceptual–motor ability, stage of motor development, and level of motor learning. This intentional manipulation of variables affords learners the opportunity to successfully perform skills. More specifically, an affordance is a flexible feature of a task or environment that the teacher manipulates to fit the size and developmental capabilities of the learner in order to promote motor skill acquisition and to simulate performance in an authentic movement setting. Appropriate environmental affordances include providing equipment that fits the child's size and strength and setting up a condition that creates a small challenge.

For example, in a throwing task, choose a size, weight, and texture of ball that fit the child's hand size and strength. When choosing the distance for the throw, start with one that is moderate—neither too near nor too far. If the learner is unable to throw to that distance, then he can shorten it; similarly, if he can easily throw to that distance, then he can start farther away. Thus the affordance continuum related to the environment gives educators an important tool for making choices that affect children's motor performance success and improvement.

Equipment

Regulation equipment that is sized for adults has no place in a gymnasium intended for children in pre-K through elementary school. Such equipment compromises the biomechanical efficiency of children's movement performance because it is too large, too heavy, and too long for their size and strength. Equipment selection should be influenced by the variables of size (length, width, height), weight, texture, surface, and motion. The affordance of each variable can be manipulated to match the size and developmental level of the child.

For example, a learner in the fundamental movement phase can develop a more success-ful sidearm striking pattern when using a lightweight, short-handled foam paddle with a large face than when using a junior tennis racket that is longer and heavier. Similarly, such learners can take a more level swing when using short plastic bats, "fat" bats, and Wiffle bats than when using slimmer or heavier bats. They also find it easier to strike or kick balls and other objects that are stationary, lighter, and somewhat large, and they can make one-handed throws more easily with objects that are softer and fit the size of the hand. In addition, stationary objects afford greater opportunity for pre-K students to make contact—for example, a stationary ball to kick or a ball placed on a tee to bat. It is also easier, of course, to send a ball through a large or wide goal than through a small or narrow one.

Students are also more accurate with stationary *targets* than with ones that are moving. Balloons and scarves that travel slowly and remain aloft afford pre-K students the time necessary to make an interception, and equipment such as Wiffle balls and fleece balls (rather than tennis and playground balls) afford primary-grade students the time to process visual information and improve their chances of intercepting the object (Payne & Isaacs, 2008). Likewise, beach balls and light foam balls are easier to send away with immature hands and finger pads than are regulation volleyballs. And, when moving in relation to large equipment, children find low and wide beams easier to traverse, narrower and lower obstacles easier to get over, wedge mats easier than flat surfaces to roll along, and lower obstacles easier than higher ones to negotiate.

Figure 6.1 shows the affordance continuum, ranging from easy to more difficult, for each of the equipment variables.

Condition

The condition or characteristics of the environment can be modified by spatial, temporal, and relationship variables. Like equipment, the condition of the environment should fit the learner's size, perceptual–motor ability, stage of motor development, and level of motor learning in order to support her or his development of biomechanically efficient performance. Evidence suggests that children can perform challenges featuring spatial variations more easily than those featuring temporal or relationship variations.

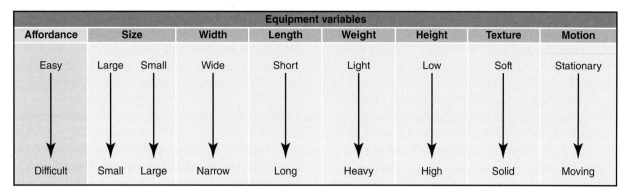

Equipment variables							
Affordance	**Size**		**Width**	**Length**	**Weight**	**Height**	**Texture**	**Motion**
Easy	Large Small	Wide	Short	Light	Low	Soft	Stationary
↓	↓ ↓	↓	↓	↓	↓	↓	↓
Difficult	Small Large	Narrow	Long	Heavy	High	Solid	Moving

Figure 6.1   Affordance continuum for equipment.

Spatial Variables

Spatial variables influence where movement goes. For example, it is often obvious how to modify a movement challenge by shortening the distance or height. It may be less apparent how to modify the other spatial variables—direction, pathway, and trajectory—but they are also important to the developing child.

- **Distance:** Shorter distances, of course, are easier than longer ones when jumping a gap or hitting a target. However, if children are in transition between the emerging-elementary and mature stages of throwing, throwing for a longer distance at a large target affords the greater range of motion that the child needs in order to progress to the mature stage.

- **Direction:** It is easier to receive an object coming from a location in front of the body than to receive one coming from the side or (even more difficult) from behind. It is also easier to kick or volley a ball coming from the front rather than one from the side. However, it is easier to strike a ball with an implement from the side rather than from the front, though a ball arriving from farther away from the side is more difficult to strike than one arriving from closer. For instance, using a groundstroke in tennis is more difficult than hitting a volley.

- **Pathway:** Straight pathways along the floor afford greater dynamic balance for the performance of locomotor skills because no changes in direction are needed. In contrast, curved pathways require slight changes, and zigzag pathways pose the most difficult challenge to dynamic balance because they require quick, sharp changes in direction.

- **Level:** Low levels afford greater stability when balancing than do moderate levels, which in turn are easier than high levels with the center of gravity farther from the base. Locomotor skills (e.g., walking, running, skipping) are easier to perform at one's own height than at lower or higher levels. Locomotor activities requiring takeoff and landing (e.g., jumping, hopping, leaping) are easier to perform to lower heights; in addition, pre-K students may need the affordance of a low step from which to take off in order to get air time.

- **Trajectory:** A horizontal trajectory affords greater opportunity for pre-K and primary-grade learners to intercept incoming objects because they do not have to move their eyes or head in order to track the object. Vertical trajectories are more difficult, and arcs are the most difficult and are usually not mastered until age 8 or 9.

Temporal Variables

Temporal variables influence the speed, rhythm, and timing of movements. Is slower easier than faster? What rhythms provide the greatest challenge? What does predictability have to do with timing?

- **Speed:** When introducing the variable of speed in a reception task (e.g., catching, striking), find a speed that enables success, use it consistently for a short time, and then gradually vary it. Likewise, stability, locomotor, and manipulative skills that require travel (e.g., dribbling) should be performed at moderate speeds, slowed down if coordination poses an issue, and gradually sped up as the learner exhibits skillful performance.

- **Rhythm:** Children find it easier to move to their own internal rhythms than to move to external rhythms. Allowing children to begin by moving to music in their own time affords them the opportunity to "feel" the beat, which can be followed by activities in which the beats are clapped or stomped. When movement to external rhythms is introduced, even beats afford greater success than uneven ones.

- **Timing:** Predictable environments are easiest because they are stable and unchanging—for example, when a learner times her movements to jump for height or perform cartwheels. When timing movements to coincide with the movements of objects or other people, predictable movement of the object or other person affords greater success than unpredictable movement. When a child knows that he will receive a chest pass from a partner, it is easier to succeed than when he receives an unexpected pass. See figure 6.2 for a visual representation of the affordance continuum for spatial and temporal variables.

Relationship Variables

Relationship variables influence the challenge of moving with others. In this area, we must consider how children's movement success is affected not only by the number of people in the environment but also by the nature of the interactions. It is easier for children to perform motor skills by themselves than with others. Performing alone affords the learner the opportunity to move at his or her own time, rhythm, and pace. Children need to learn how to work by themselves, but in the con-

text of a classroom or gymnasium, they are usually in the company of others. Consequently, they must learn how to work alone on a task while not interfering with others and while developing the social skills to interact with others in partners and groups.

The easiest interactions involve parallel relationships, in which children move near each other with low levels of interaction. Cooperative relationships, on the other hand, require the ability to communicate and work together toward a common goal. And the most difficult relationships are competitive ones that require cooperation with teammates in order to vie with opponents.

Parallel relationships afford children the opportunity to engage in movement activities near each other with low levels of interaction. These activities progress from staying in one's own space near others while performing alone (e.g., each person balancing in personal space) to moving alongside each other in the same direction with a destination goal (e.g., skipping to the green line) and eventually to moving among each other in different directions while avoiding contact (e.g., galloping throughout the gym). Activities of parallel interaction require children to stay on task, be aware of each other, and maintain a safe movement environment.

Cooperative relationships afford learners the opportunity to work together and accomplish tasks interdependently. Cooperative activities can take the form of simply sharing equipment, taking turns, or playing follow-the-leader. They can also take a more complex form, such as making shapes and balances with partners, performing locomotor or rhythmic patterns together, or alternating ma-

Affordance	Condition variables							
	Spatial					Temporal		
	Distance	Direction	Pathway	Level	Trajectory	Speed	Rhythm	Timing
Easy	Near	Front	Straight	Low	Horizontal	Slow Moderate	Even	Predictable
↓	↓	Sides	Curved	↓	Vertical	Slow	↓	↓
Difficult	Far	Back	Zigzag	High	Arc	Fast Fast	Uneven	Unpredictable

Figure 6.2 Affordance continuum for spatial and temporal variables.

nipulative skills (e.g., throwing, catching, striking, kicking). Partners and small groups can engage in team-building and problem-solving activities; practice offensive or defensive strategies as teammates; and engage in folk, line, or square dances.

Competitive relationships afford learners the opportunity to work alone, with a partner, or in a small group to vie with an opponent to meet a goal. Game categories (Werner & Almond, 1990; Mitchell et al., 2013) represent several games categorized by similar tactical interactions.

Noninvasive competition is easier than invasive competition because it affords students the opportunity to compete with one another while performing in separate spaces or shared spaces. In the easiest noninvasive games, neither people nor objects come into competitors' spaces. Students typically work independently as individuals, partners, or teams in order to score points or accomplish tasks based on quantity, time, distance, or accuracy. Examples include vying as individuals to outscore others in races, in throwing for distance, and in jumping for height or distance; cooperating with a group to perform a task more often, for more time, or in less time than other groups; engaging in aiming activities, such as throwing, kicking, and striking for accuracy; and playing target games, such as bowling and golf.

Net and wall games provide more difficulty as students work independently, with partners, or in small groups to both protect their own space and attack the opponent's space with objects. Examples include the lead-up games of two square, four square, pickleball, and Newcomb and the games of volleyball, tennis, and badminton. In wall games, opponents share the same space, taking turns and not interfering with the opponent's shot.

In striking-and-fielding games, each team occupies designated spaces. Students work independently to send an object into the opponent's territory in order to gain the most possible time to run the bases, while the opponents work together to move the object to the base that will halt the baserunner's progress. Runners remain within the basepaths and do not try to occupy other sections of the infield or outfield. Fielders and runners do occupy part of the same space as fielders try to get an out by tagging the bag or runner.

Invasive competition affords students the opportunity to compete within the same space. Striking-and-fielding games are the easiest invasive competitive games because each team occupies designated spaces. As described earlier, there is relatively limited action where opponents occupy the same space (fielders getting an out by tagging the runner or bag).

Invasion games (e.g., basketball, soccer, hockey) are the most difficult ones because opponents interact with objects, teammates, and opponents in the same space as they simultaneously try to defend their territory and attack the opponent's goal. In these games, students must be aware not only of the skills and tactics that they and their teammates are using but also of the positions and tactics of their opponents. To afford students the opportunity to progress in learning the skills and tactics of invasion games, educators can use lead-up activities and games that involve fewer opponents, a smaller playing area, or fewer skills and tactics. The easiest options are one-on-one competitions that teach students how to evade opponents. Games can initially be restricted to body-management skills (as in tag) and then progress to include handling a ball (as in dribble tag). Competitive interactions become more difficult with the addition of more teammates, opponents, skills, and tactics. For instance, as application-stage students learn how to attack the goal, they can progress from one-on-one to two-on-one and then two-on-two games. See figure 6.3 for a visual representation of the affordance continuum for relationship variables.

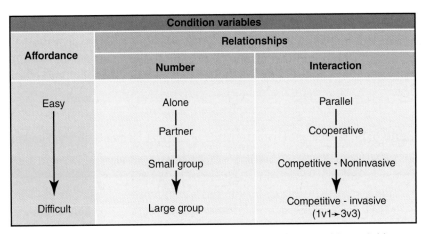

Condition variables		
Relationships		
Affordance	**Number**	**Interaction**
Easy	Alone	Parallel
	Partner	Cooperative
	Small group	Competitive - Noninvasive
Difficult	Large group	Competitive - invasive (1v1→3v3)

Figure 6.3 Affordance continuum for each of the relationship variables.

THE TASK

As physical education teachers design tasks to engage students in learning new movement skills, they must differentiate between a movement skill and a task. A movement *skill* is an action, such as running, throwing, kicking, or balancing. A *task* is a developmentally appropriate experience that a physical educator creates in order to promote learning of the skill. For instance, a movement task for preschool children might involve throwing at a large target, whereas first graders might practice throwing at targets at different heights and fifth graders might throw to teammates in the context of a lead-up game.

In order to design developmentally appropriate movement tasks, educators must possess knowledge of the critical elements and underlying biomechanical principles of motor skills; they must also know how skills are classified. In addition to the affordances based on equipment and conditions of the environment, educators can make affordances based on skill classifications to design developmentally appropriate movement task progressions.

Critical Elements of the Skill

In order to perform a motor skill with biomechanical efficiency, one must know and perform the critical elements of the skill. The goal for children during the fundamental phase of motor development is to achieve biomechanically efficient performance of stability, locomotor, and manipulative skills. Similarly, the goal for all learners in the beginning or novice level of movement skill learning is to perform movement skills with adequate timing and technique.

The critical elements of motor skills are often described sequentially, beginning with preparation movements that get the body ready for the main action; after the main action is performed, the skill is safely ended by means of recovery movements. In the long jump, for example, preparation involves assuming a deep crouch with the arms stretched rearward. The main action involves an explosive extension from the ankles, knees, and hips and a thrust of the arms forward and upward, thus sending the body into the air, followed by a quick flexion of the knees and hips while still airborne. Recovery occurs as the knees extend for a landing on the feet and the body weight is absorbed by another flexion and then an extension of the knees and hips.

As children mature through the fundamental movement phase, they change the extent of their movements and the positioning of their feet. Table 6.1 shows that initial-stage movers exhibit little to no flexion or extension of the limbs and little to no trunk rotation. They also often take a wide stance with their feet side by side. The extent of flexion, extension and rotation and position of the feet change incrementally in emerging elementary and mature stage movers.

The critical elements provide the movement cues used by teachers to describe and demonstrate the actions of skills. They also provide focus for the teacher's observations as students perform the skills, and they form the content of the feedback that teachers give to students in order to help them change or maintain performance technique.

In addition, cognitive learning goals often require students to recognize, identify, or explain critical cues. With these goals in mind, the teacher's consistent use of chosen critical cues focuses learners' attention in order to enhance both motor and cognitive learning. For instance, a teacher could explain and demonstrate how to bounce a ball with the finger pads, observe students' use of finger pads while they practice, and give students feedback that either corrects or supports their use (or lack thereof) of finger pads. The teacher could also expect students to circle the finger pads on an illustration of the hand as a way to demonstrate

Table 6.1 Movement Characteristics of Critical Elements in the Fundamental Phase of Motor Development

Stage of motor development	Flexion and extension	Rotation	Position of feet
Initial	None or limited	None or limited	Parallel
Emerging-elementary	Moderate	Moderate	Ipsilateral
Mature	Full	Full	Contralateral

that they can identify the part of the hand used for bouncing a ball.

An intrinsic part of the critical elements consists of the biomechanical principles that underlie efficient skill performance. Griffey and Housner (2007) identified five "pedagogically relevant" biomechanical principles to help physical educators teach motor skills, and the authors of this textbook have identified a sixth. The six principles address the following areas: maintaining balance, fluidity of movement, generating force, absorbing force, improving accuracy, and sequencing skills. Each principle is described in the following list.

1. Maintaining balance is important in all skills. For an individual to remain balanced, the center of gravity must be over the base of support. This biomechanical principle can be applied when children are learning balances in fundamental stability skills or starting any specialized skill from a stationary position. To become more stable, performers should lower the center of gravity, widen the base, and keep the center of gravity over the base. This principle is relevant during locomotor skills to help children stop moving in a safe manner. It can also be applied in specialized skills to block opponents. To move from a stationary position, performers should shift the center of gravity just outside the base. This principle is also evident when raising the hips and overbalancing to receive weight on the upper back in order to perform the fundamental stability skill of rolling forward and when raising the hips and moving weight forward onto the hands to perform the specialized skill of a track start.

2. Dynamic balance, as in locomotion, requires fluidity of movement. In walking, dynamic balance is achieved by placing the center of gravity over the support foot; pointing the feet straight ahead; swinging the arms close to the sides in opposition to the legs; and alternately flexing and extending at the hip, knee, and ankle. Moving with increased speed, as in running, results in a short flight phase and requires a shift forward in the center of gravity and an increase in step frequency and stride length. Changing direction, as in dodging, requires a shorter stride and a slight lowering of the center of gravity.

3. Force generation occurs during the preparation and main action of the critical elements of most motor skills. For example, winding up to throw or strike—and crouching before a jump—

are preparations that "load" the muscles for action by stretching them in the direction opposite of the main action. Force is generated during the main action through a summation of forces. In the throwing and jumping examples, performers transfer weight in the direction of the movement and sequentially extend and rotate their joints to unwind for the throw or explode upward for the jump, then apply force through the object or against the ground in the intended direction.

4. Force absorption occurs during the recovery part of the critical elements of most motor skills. Examples include following through in throwing and striking, as well as flexing the knees and hips to land a jump or stop momentum from locomotor movements. All of these actions dissipate the force created during the preparation and main action and thus allow the performer to safely end the movement. In the reception skills of catching and trapping, the preparation phase involves reaching toward the ball, the main action involves grasping or coming into contact with the ball, and the recovery involves dissipating the force by flexing the elbows in catching and by giving with body parts in trapping.

5. Accuracy is improved when performers line up their bodies with, and release or strike objects in the direction of, the target. In addition, throwing or striking a ball toward a *moving* target requires the performer to time the release and aim ahead of the receiver so that the receiver's outstretched hands and the object arrive simultaneously. Sometimes the performer must make a speed–accuracy trade-off, in which an increase in speed is associated with a decrease in accuracy, or vice versa. Research reported by Coker (2004) found that emphasizing accuracy when first learning specialized sport skills impeded the development of efficient movement patterns. Therefore, she suggested that in the beginning of specialized skill acquisition, teachers eliminate sending balls to partners (accuracy) and instead have learners throw, kick, or strike balls forcefully to large targets at varying distances, levels, and locations. As the performer's movement pattern becomes more efficient, targets can be made smaller and learners can find the movement speeds that enable them to perform more accurately.

6. Skill sequencing occurs in open- and closed-skill movement activities as learners perform two or more movements consecutively. The movement goal for a sequence is to connect the skills fluently with no breaks or hesitations. The key to fluent performance is to make the recovery phase of the first movement serve as the preparation phase of the next movement. When preparing to sequence fielding and throwing, for example, the recovery movement of absorbing the force of the catch should lead directly into the preparation movement of winding up for the throw. Similarly, when connecting a forward roll and a jump, the recovery crouch of the roll should become the preparation crouch of the jump.

Teachers need to know both the critical elements and the underlying biomechanical principles in order to focus learners' attention on how body parts should be moved to produce efficient performance. Teachers can also enhance learners' movement performance by having them learn and experience the *connection* between the critical cues and the biomechanical principles. For instance, students could experience the fact that stopping quickly is accomplished by lowering the center of gravity, which in turn is done by bending their knees and hips. They could also compare how *raising* the center of gravity by extending the hips and knees does *not* allow them to stop quickly.

Closed and Open Skills

The closed- and open-skill classification system is based on a continuum representing the predictability of events. At one end of the continuum are the closed skills, which are used in stable environments with no interference, as in gymnastics; at the other end are the open skills, which are used in unpredictable environments with interference from other players, as in soccer (see figure 6.4).

Closed Skills

Closed skills are used in predictable and stable environments, and the goal of the skill is consistency of the movement performance. Indeed, many closed-skill movement activities are *form* specific, meaning that proper form is the goal of the performance. For example, dancers, gymnasts, ice skat-

ers, and divers all strive to perform consistently with proper technique. Some other closed skills are outcome specific, meaning that the outcome of the skill (rather than its form) is key to the game. For example, in golf, bowling, archery, basketball free-throw shooting, baseball pitching, and tennis serving, the desired result is to get the object to the designated target.

All closed skills are performed in a stable environment with no interference from competitors. The schemata or rules made by closed-skill performers relate to gaining a consistent kinesthetic feel for where and how they move their body parts in order to perform single movements or to combine movements in sequences or routines. For example, a gymnast aims to perform the forward roll on the beam by consistently imparting the same amount of force, the same tight tucked position, the same placement of her spine along the beam, and the same balanced recovery to her feet in each iteration.

In addition, a skill is easier to coordinate if it requires fewer body parts or smaller ranges of motion; more complex if it involves more body parts and larger ranges of motion; and most complex when combined with other skills. For example, the skill of rocking back and forth along a curled spine requires less range of motion and is therefore easier to coordinate than that of a forward roll. Similarly, performing a single forward roll is easier than the more complex skill of combining two forward rolls in sequence.

Most closed skills are self-paced, meaning that the performer controls when to start and how to time the sequence of movements, as is the case in bowling and diving. Exceptions include dance and gymnastics floor-exercise routines, which involve a series of closed skills that are paced by external rhythms, as well as track and aquatic events that begin with the crack of a starter's pistol.

Designing progressions differs according to the type of closed skill in question: outcome specific or form specific.

- Outcome-specific closed-skill progressions hinge on identifying how skill execution can be simplified, providing timing that is self-paced,

Figure 6.4 Closed- and open-skill continuum.

and scaling equipment and performance conditions to accommodate the performers' stages of motor development and levels of learning. For instance, putting is the simplest golf swing because it uses the smallest range of motion. Teachers can allow learners to putt when they are ready (self-paced), provide them with putters that fit their size, give them instruction and feedback focused on the critical elements, enable them to practice in order to gain performance consistency, and provide task variations that change the distance and size of the target.

- Form-specific closed-skill progressions hinge on identifying how skill execution can be simplified, providing timing that is self-paced, and increasing the difficulty by varying and combining skills in smaller or larger chunks until the sequence or routine is complete. Teachers prepare tasks for form-specific closed skills by providing learners with instruction about the critical elements of the skill and the skill combinations and by scaling equipment and performance conditions to accommodate their stages of motor development and levels of learning. For instance, forward and backward rolls are discrete skills that can be simplified by rolling down an incline. Once the rolls can be performed along the mat, they can be varied with changes in starting and ending positions (e.g., a straddle) or combined with other skills in a sequence (e.g., forward roll, jump half turn, backward roll).

Figure 6.5 illustrates the affordances for each task constraint for closed skills: skill execution, pace, task variation, and skill combination. The

skill execution constraint relates to the fact that the coordination of movements is simpler when it uses fewer body parts and smaller ranges of motion. The pace constraint relates to the fact that skills are easier to perform when they are self-paced—that is, when the performer determines when to start, when to stop, and what rhythm to use. The task variation constraint refers to the fact that the performance of closed skills can be altered by spatial, temporal, relationship, and equipment variables. For instance, after learning to perform a jump by taking off from and landing on two feet, performers could vary the performance by changing the direction, distance, or level; by performing the jump side-by-side with a partner; or by jumping onto and off of a low box. And finally, skill combinations are easier when fewer skills are performed continuously (without a break between them) in a sequence.

The affordances indicated in the figure range from easy to difficult, not only as depicted vertically within each constraint-specific column but also as depicted horizontally from one constraint to the next. For instance, simple, self-paced skills are the easiest, whereas adding a task variation or combining skills increases the difficulty.

Open Skills

Open skills are used in unpredictable and unstable environments. The goal of practicing open skills is to learn a variety of movement patterns in order to develop the schema or rules to respond appropriately to changing environments. In open-skill sports, the outcome of the skill is important. Success in the game is determined not by the form of movement in executing a skill but by the results,

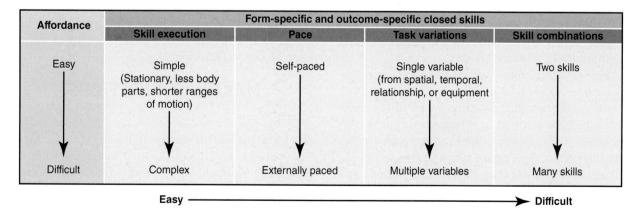

Figure 6.5 Affordance continuum for closed-skill progressions.

such as blocking a shot, receiving a pass, or scoring a goal. As a result, in competitive games composed primarily of open skills, success requires anticipatory skills. Players need to know where to look and what cues to attend to or anticipate; they also need to practice responding with the right skills, speed, and location. For example, successful fielding in softball requires the player to move with the right amount of speed to where the ball is moving, place the glove in line with the ball, catch it, and quickly throw it accurately to the intended player.

Teachers prepare children to perform open skills by providing instruction not only about the critical elements of the skill but also about the environmental cues to which they must attend. Children can then respond with the skills that enable them to move at the right time, in the right way, and at the right speed to meet the demands of the environment and affect the outcome of the game. For instance, students are taught the triple-threat position in basketball so that they can watch opponents and teammates and attend to cues that enable them to respond by either shooting, passing, or dribbling the ball.

When preparing instruction for open skills, teachers identify the critical cues, the complexity of skill coordination (the number of body parts and the ranges of motion), and how to scale equipment and performance contexts to accommodate learners' stages of motor development and levels of learning. Children in the beginning level of motor skill learning concentrate on learning the movements of a skill. Therefore, teachers start with a more closed environment by simplifying skill execution and providing self-paced conditions—for example, batting from a tee. Once students are capable of performing the movements, teachers design progressions using task variations and skill combinations that start in more predictable environments and require limited response choices before advancing to unpredictable environments with multiple response choices.

For example, tennis students are taught the defensive tactic of returning to a spot midway between the sidelines in order to be in the most advantageous position to return strokes from opponents. They are also taught to keep their eyes on their opponent's racket face and then track the tennis ball in order to predict where to move and what stroke to choose. To help children practice moving in the right direction from that defensive spot and choosing the right return, teachers make the task more predictable. For instance, a set number of balls might be sent to the player's dominant side in order to limit the response to a forehand and then sent to the nondominant side for a backhand response. Teachers then choose which variables remain predictable (e.g., forehand stroke) and which become unpredictable (e.g., groundstroke or volley) and ultimately progress to responses requiring more decisions (e.g., forehand or backhand as groundstroke or volley).

Figure 6.6 illustrates the affordances for each task constraint for open skills. The first four constraints are the same as those for closed skills because they focus on performing the skill without interference. The last two constraints address the additional demands of open skills. The attend-and-anticipate constraint—which addresses the questions of where to look and what cues to look for—focuses the learner's attention on the cues in the environment. The response-selection constraint directs the learner's choice to the movement that he or she must use in order to address the cues detected in the environment.

When teaching open skills, as soon as learners are developmentally able to perform the movement responses from which they must select, teachers need to invoke task progressions based on predictability and response selection. Table 6.2 presents a sample progression for learners in the transition stage of motor development who are at the intermediate level of learning the open skill of attacking the goal in a two-on-one game of team handball.

In order to design learning experiences that help students acquire or improve movement skills, teachers must know whether the goal of the skill is consistency of performance or effective response to unpredictable environments. For example, practices intended to prepare students to consistently perform dance sequences should look vastly different from practices intended to prepare students to move in response to unpredictable cues in a two-on-two soccer lead-up game.

MAKING CONNECTIONS

How do teachers make connections between their learners' perceptual–motor ability, motor development stages, and motor learning levels; the factors of skill goals, critical elements, and information processing; and the equipment and performance contexts of the environment that are important when structuring tasks?

To facilitate preschool children's progress through the initial stage and the early part of the emerging-elementary stage of fundamental motor skill development, teachers can design enriched, enjoyable play environments that stimulate implicit learning. The challenge for pre-K teachers is to enable success in motor skill performance for learners who are limited by perception, body structure, and range of motion. To do so, teachers must encourage and praise movement engagement, apply what they know about how initial and emerging-elementary learners perform the critical elements of each fundamental motor skill, and scale equipment and performance conditions to make the repetition of movements fun.

For instance, *initial* performers cannot overcome gravity in order to jump. However, providing them with a low box from which to take off affords them the opportunity to experience the skill. Similarly, using balloons affords emerging-elementary learners the opportunity to experience catching and striking with the hands.

For learners in the *beginning* level of movement skill learning, the goal is to perform movement skills

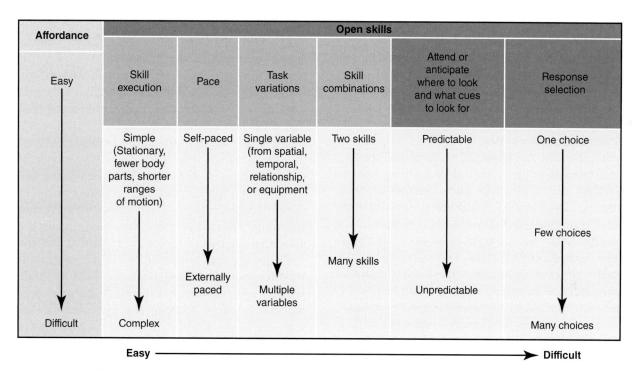

Figure 6.6 Affordance continuum for open-skill progressions.

Table 6.2 Sample Open-Skill Progressions

Constraint	Open-skill progression
a. Task variation	Practice a variety of throws at a team handball goal from different distances and positions within the attack circle and to different parts of the goal.
b. Skill combination	Practice moving into the attack circle, receiving a pass from a teammate, and immediately throwing for the goal.
c. Attend-and-anticipate response selection	1v1 practice: From different distances and positions within the attack circle, choose throws to defeat a *stationary* goalie positioned in different locations.
d. Attend-and-anticipate response selection	1v1 practice: From different distances and positions within the attack circle, choose throws to defeat an *active* goalie.
e. Attend-and-anticipate response selection	2v1 practice: Move into the attack circle, receive a pass from a teammate, and immediately throw for the goal to defeat an *active* goalie.

with adequate timing and technique. Whether they are in the emerging-elementary or the mature stage of the fundamental phase of motor development—or in the specialized phase of learning the stable features of generalized motor programs—learners benefit from teachers who focus performance on the critical elements, draw attention to supporting biomechanical principles, and provide affordances by scaling equipment and performance conditions to fit learners' sizes and abilities.

To design experiences that help students in the *intermediate* level of learning acquire and improve movement skills, teachers must not only provide affordances through scaling equipment and performance conditions but also identify whether the goal of the skill is consistent performance or effective response to unpredictable environments. The schemata or rules made by performers of *closed* skills relate to gaining a consistent kinesthetic feel for where and how they move their body parts to perform single movements or combine movements in sequences or routines.

Learners in the *transition* stage of the specialized movement phase should be learning how to perform simple variations and sequences of form-specific closed skills. They should also be learning how to use force and direction for outcome-based closed skills—for example, to shoot a free throw into the basket or hit a tennis serve into the court. Learners in the *application* stage of the specialized movement phase should be performing more-complex skill variations and combining skills in smaller to larger chunks for the performance of routines. They should also be adjusting force and direction to reach more challenging outcome-based accuracy goals, such as serving to specific places and picking up spares in bowling.

The schemata or rules made by performers of *open* skills depend heavily on integrating stable and flexible features into generalized motor programs in order to respond appropriately to unpredictable environments. Teachers use strategies to help learners speed up their information processing by giving them information about the goal of the skill, relevant cues to attend to, and rules for anticipating the response that will accomplish the goal.

For learners in the *transition* stage of the specialized movement phase, teachers design skill drills and authentic gamelike activities in relatively predictable settings. For *application* stage learners, teachers design skill drills and authentic gamelike

activities in less predictable settings. In addition to providing affordances by scaling equipment, teachers can use the spatial, temporal, and relationship variables to create conditions characterized by either more or less predictability as students learn open skills.

Figure 6.7 illustrates the relationships between the constraints of learner, task, and environment. The learner column represents the phases and stages of motor development and the levels of motor skill learning. For each stage of motor development, the figure indicates the approximate ages of children. During the fundamental phase of motor development, children are in the immature-beginner and beginner levels of motor skill learning. In the specialized phase, they typically progress to the intermediate and advanced levels of learning. However, regardless of age, when students are challenged with learning new motor skills they return to the beginner level of learning until they can perform the skill efficiently.

The task column in the figure represents closed and open skills. The goals for achievement of closed and open skills are the same during the fundamental phase and the beginner level of motor skill learning: achieve correct timing and technique. The goals differ, however, during the specialized phase of motor development and the intermediate and advanced levels of motor skill learning because closed skills are used in stable settings whereas open skills are used in unpredictable settings. Finally, the environment for learners in pre-K through grade 5 must always contain equipment and conditions that are scaled to their size, strength, and capabilities in order to afford skill success throughout the stages of motor development and the levels of motor skill learning.

BUILDING MOVEMENT TASK PROGRESSIONS

The relationships depicted in figure 6.7 can guide teachers in developing movement task progressions for learners in the fundamental and specialized phases of motor skill development. Each phase consists of two task progression levels—specifically, the preconsistent and consistent levels for the fundamental phase and the combination and application levels for the specialized phase. The task progression for kicking is presented in figure 6.8; additional task progressions, for fundamental and specialized skills, appear in part IV and V in the appropriate age-level chapters.

In figure 6.8, the purple band represents the fundamental motor-skill task progressions, which are appropriate for students at the immature-beginner (light purple box) and beginner (dark purple box) levels of motor skill learning. The task progressions for *immature-beginner* learners are labeled *preconsistent* because the goal is to engage in movements that support their maturation through the initial and emerging-elementary stages of motor skill development. In order to provide affordances that allow these learners to experience skill success, teachers scale the equipment and conditions in the environment—for example, by using large and stationary objects and short distances.

The task progressions for *beginner* learners are labeled *consistent* because the goal is to achieve mature performance of the fundamental motor skills. In order for teachers to provide affordances that help these learners achieve correct timing and technique, they can scale the equipment and conditions in the environment by using, for ex-

ample, junior-size balls. They can also provide tasks that occur in predictable environments and are simple, self-paced, and varied by changes in one variable at a time (e.g., kicking to a low level; kicking to a moderate distance; kicking a ball arriving at moderate speed).

The gold band in the figure represents the specialized motor-skill task progressions, which are appropriate for students at the intermediate level of motor skill learning. The task progressions for intermediate learners are divided into two periods: combination (dark gold box) and application (light gold box).

In the combination period, the goal is to combine skills into smooth sequences. More specifically, with closed skills, the aim is to elicit variations in the way the skills are combined by increasing the number of factors used to vary the task and the number of skills combined—for example, combining a roll, jump, and balance using a change in level, speed, and direction. In open skills, the aim is to elicit variations both in the way skills are combined and in the number of skills combined. The particular skills used are based on the variables of the given game or sport environment; refer to table 6.2 (item b), where the skills of receiving a pass and

Learner			Task		Environment
Phases of motor development	Stages of motor development	Stages of learning a motor skill	Closed skill	Open skill	
Fundamental	Initial and emerging elementary (ages 3-4)	Immature beginner	Goal: Provide affordances that allow for skill "success" even though movements are immature	Goal: Provide affordances that allow for skill "success" even though movements are immature	Scale equipment and performance conditions
Fundamental	Mature (ages 5-6)	Beginner	Goal: Achieve correct timing and technique for mature performance	Goal: Achieve correct timing and technique for mature performance in predictable environments	Scale equipment and performance conditions
Specialized	Transition and application (ages 7-13)	Intermediate	*Form-specific or outcome based* Goal: Elicit consistency of performance and variations in skill situations, combinations, and routines	Goal: Elicit responses to a *range of more- to less-predictable environments with fewer or more response choices*	Scale equipment and performance conditions
Specialized	Lifelong utilization (ages 14+)	Advanced	*Form-specific or outcome based* Goal: Elicit consistency of performance and variations in skill situations, combinations, and routines	Goal: Elicit responses to *unpredictable environments with many response choices*	Scale equipment and performance conditions

Figure 6.7   Relationships between constraints of learner, task, and environment.

immediately throwing for goal are combined, and figure 6.8. In order to provide affordances that help learners combine skills, teachers scale the equipment and conditions in the environment by, for example, using cooperative relationships with moving partners and varying distances, levels, and speeds.

In the application period, the goal is to apply skills in cultural movement activities. With closed skills, the aim is to perform sequences of many movements, as in a dance or gymnastics routine. With open skills, the aim is to perform movements in gamelike conditions; refer to table 6.2 (items c through e), where a progression of gamelike conditions from 1v1 to 2v1 is illustrated, and figure 6.8. In order to provide affordances that help learners apply skills in games and sports, teachers scale the equipment and conditions in the environment by, for example, providing noninvasive and invasive competition in environments that are either more or less predictable with either fewer or more movement response choices.

Level	Skill	Kicking task progression	
		Preconsistent (Immature beginner)	**Consistent** (Beginner)

Fundamental	KICKING	Equipment: Stationary, lightweight, and 5″-7″ balls and plastic cones.
		Tasks:
		  Kick a stationary ball from a stance at a wall
		  Kick to large targets
		    • at close to moderate distances
		    • placed low to eye level on wall
		    • that make a sound or move on impact
		    • between cones or through large goals
			Equipment: Junior-size, medium-texture balls
			Tasks:
			  Kick a ball from short to moderate approach
			  Kick ball to short distances that require approach and full windup
			  Kick a ball at or below midline to travel at different levels (along ground or in air)
			  Kick to targets of varying size, height, distance
			  Kick a rolling ball from a stance
			  Kick a rolling ball to different distances
			  Short-tap dribble along ground
			  Start and stop dribbling
			  Dribble on different pathways to avoid obstacles

		Combination (Intermediate)	**Application** (Intermediate)

Specialized		Equipment: Soft textured balls varying in size and weight
		Tasks:
		  Short approach to kick a rolling ball to different levels and locations
		  Trap and kick balls arriving from partner at different distances, directions, levels, and speeds.
		  Kick to moving partner
		  Trap and dribble
		  Dribble and kick to stationary targets
		  Vary pathway and speed of dribble to avoid obstacles
		  Dribble and pass cooperatively with a partner
		  Dribble, pass, and kick to targets or goals cooperatively with a partner
			Equipment: Balls of different shapes, sizes, and textures
			Tasks:
			  Kick a rolling ball to different distances, levels, and locations in fielding games
			  Kick at targets while being defended in 1v1 invasion games.
			  Kick and dribble 2v1 and 3v3 "keep away" games
			  Kick and dribble in small-sided soccer invasion games with tactics of maintaining possession and attacking the goal.

Figure 6.8 Movement task progression for kicking.

Big Ideas

- The two main environmental variables that affect learners' skill acquisition are equipment and condition.

- The variables that affect equipment selection are size (length, width, height), weight, texture, surface, and motion. For each variable, the affordance level (ranging from easy to difficult) can be manipulated to match the size and developmental level of the child.

- The scaling of conditions can involve spatial variables (distance, direction, pathway, level, trajectory), temporal variables (speed, rhythm, timing), and relationship variables (number of individuals and the interaction between them).

- A movement skill is an action (e.g., running, throwing, kicking, balancing), whereas a task is a developmentally appropriate experience that a physical educator creates to promote learning of a skill.

- The critical elements of a skill provide the movement cues used by teachers to describe and demonstrate the skill actions. They also provide focus for teacher observations as students perform the skills, and they structure the content of the feedback that teachers give to students in order to help them maintain or change performance technique.

- Movement skill development is influenced by six biomechanical principles: maintaining balance, fluidity of movement, generating force, absorbing force, improving accuracy, and sequencing skills.

- Closed (static) skills are used in predictable and stable environments; the goal of these skills is consistency of the movement performance. In contrast, open (dynamic) skills are used in unpredictable and unstable environments; the goal of these skills is learning a variety of movement patterns in order to develop the schemata or rules to respond appropriately to changing environments. When designing open-skill task progressions, teachers must consider all of the variables associated with closed skills, as well as where the performer looks (attention) and how the performer selects a response (i.e., the performer's choice of movement to address cues detected in the environment).

- When physical educators design instructional tasks, they should purposefully manipulate facets of the constraints of learner, task, and environment. In figure 6.7, the learner column represents the phases and stages of motor development and the levels of motor skill learning. The task column represents closed and open skills. The environment for learners in pre-K through grade 5 must always contain equipment and conditions that are scaled to their size, strength, and capabilities in order to afford skill success throughout the stages of motor development and the levels of motor skill learning.

 Visit the web resource for learning activities, video clips, and review questions.

Chapter 7

Designing Movement Skill Practice

Key Concepts

- Focusing practice sessions on the goal of the skill
- Distinguishing between constant practice, variable practice, and contextual interference
- Describing the relationships between types of practice and closed and open skills
- Distinguishing between knowledge of results (KR) and knowledge of performance (KP) feedback
- Distinguishing between the uses of prescriptive and descriptive feedback
- Distinguishing between intermittent, faded, and delayed timing of feedback
- Describing the relationships between types of skill, types of practice, and types of feedback

Motor learning specialists agree that practice is the most important factor in learning movement skills and improving one's performance of those skills; they also agree that practice is enhanced when teachers give learners feedback about their performance (Griffey & Housner, 2007; Young, LaCourse, & Husak, 2000; Coker, 2004; Fairbrother, 2010). The success of practice also improves when the type of feedback reinforces learning, the goal of the skill is clear, and the type of practice matches the goal of the skill. In fact, if physical educators mismatch the skill and the type of practice, they can impede learning. One common mismatch occurs when physical educators have students practice game skills in isolation and then expect them to move right into playing the game! Integrating skills in a game requires practice of skills in a sequence of easier to more complex game contexts. This chapter helps you focus practice sessions on the goal of the skill and match types of skill with appropriate types of practice and feedback.

FOCUSING PRACTICE

To prepare learners for skill practice, give them verbal and visual information about the task goal, the movement cues, and the environmental stimuli to which they must attend and respond, as well as feedback that enables them to recognize their own progress. Receiving information about the task goal helps learners understand what is expected of them; in other words, learning is enhanced when students clearly understand the purpose of the learning task. For example, if you want students to focus on how they should move in order to get open to receive a pass, tell and show them; otherwise, when you question them later about how well they "got open," they may be unable to answer. In fact, they might have been thinking not about how they got open but about how fast they were moving or about any number of other parts of the game.

Learners also focus better on the movement goal when they know the movement cues and environmental stimuli to which they must attend and respond. In regard to getting open for a pass, for example, students can be taught faking and quick-movement cues to help them create and move through open space, thus increasing their availability to receive a pass. To reinforce learners' attention to the movement goal, provide feedback as learners compare their own performance results with the expected task outcome. For instance, knowing the goal and the accompanying movement cues helps students focus their internal feedback (e.g., "Yes, the fake got me open!") and prepares them for the focus of external (augmented) feedback from a peer or teacher. There is no better way to reinforce student performance than to help them keep track of their successes and needs for improvement. Students who witness their own progress by recording performance results over time (e.g., "I made four of five fakes today—I'm improving!") can become more goal directed and independent.

As discussed in chapter 6, closed and open skills have different goals. The closed- and open-skill classification system is based on the predictability of events. On one end of the closed-to-open continuum, closed skills are used in stable environments with no interference, as in gymnastics; at the other end, open skills are used in unpredictable environments with interference from other players, as in soccer. Given these differences, table 7.1 presents the implications for closed- and open-skill task design. As you can see, the task goal for each skill determines the focus of the movement cues and environmental stimuli, which in turn determine the focus of feedback and tracking performance success.

CLASSIFYING PRACTICE

Physical practice involves repeating movements in order to learn or improve motor skill performance. Mental practice, on the other hand, involves cognitive rehearsal or visualization of the movement in order to focus attention on the critical aspects of performance. Together, physical and mental practice have been found superior to physical practice alone in acquiring and improving motor skill performance (Young et al., 2000; Coker, 2004). Teachers use physical and mental practice together when they tell students to visualize the sequence of movements for a skill and then engage students in physically practicing the skill (e.g., "step, step,

Table 7.1 Differences Between Closed- and Open-Skill Task Design

	Closed skill: forward roll	Open skill: receiving a pass from a team-mate when guarded
Task goal	Perform a smooth, continuous roll.	Move to get open.
Movement cues and environmental stimuli	From a squat, raise hips, transfer weight to hands, tuck chin, push off feet and bend elbows, take weight onto upper back, keep knees tucked to chest in order to roll on rounded back, take weight on feet, and stand.	Look at position of teammate with ball; quickly respond with fake in opposite direction to out-maneuver opponent; and move to open space in line with teammate.
Feedback	"How smooth did your roll feel? Keep your chin tucked and your knees close to your chest."	"Nice work faking out the opponent and getting to the open space. What helped you decide where to move?"
Tracking success	"Today my rolls were smooth when . . ."	"Today I was able to get open when . . ."

step-hop"). Teachers also use physical and mental practice together when they tell students to rehearse rules for choosing the right motor program before engaging them in an unpredictable physical practice setting. Here is an example: "When my opponent rushes the net, I'll lob the ball behind him."

One time-honored rule for learning is specificity of practice. Specificity means that the practice experience "reflects the movement components and environmental conditions of the target skill and target context" (Haibach, Reid, & Collier, 2011, p. 313). If, for example, you want learners to be able to pass a ball in gamelike conditions, then they must practice passing in the context of a game. This principle holds true especially for intermediate-level learners who can perform the mechanics of the skill. Beginning-level learners, on the other hand, need progressions that enable them to perform the passes in more closed conditions, after which they can work to enhance their performance in more open conditions. For example, you might have them pass to a wall with correct technique, then vary the distance, then have them pass to a partner on the move, and then vary the location of the partner.

Another way to classify practice is to locate it on a continuum of variability. The continuum ranges from constant practice with no variability to variable practice with unpredictable variability. Deciding which type of practice to use depends on the constraints of learner, task, and environment.

Constant Practice

Constant practice involves repeating a skill using the same movement characteristics. Two examples of constant practice are repetitively performing an underhand toss to a target from the same distance and direction and repetitively performing a sequence of dance steps to the same tempo and rhythm. Constant practice is used when learners are at the beginning level and are acquiring the critical elements (stable features) of a motor skill. The repeated performance of motor skills in constant practice enhances the learner's rhythmic coordination of movements.

Most often, constant practice is used only as long as it takes for the learner to complete the beginning level by demonstrating adequate timing and execution of the skill's critical elements—for instance, throwing overhand in the mature stage or punting a ball with correct technique. However,

constant practice is also used in the intermediate and advanced levels of learning when the goal is to consistently perform a sequence of closed skills, as in a dance or gymnastics routine. Since repetition of the sequence leads to consistent performance, constant practice is used for a longer time in these cases.

For learners at the beginning level, constant physical practice can be accompanied by mental practice focused on skill cues (e.g., "step, then throw"). For learners at the intermediate and advanced levels, mental practice that accompanies constant physical practice usually focuses on mentally rehearsing skill connections and visualizing oneself performing skills, sequences, or routines with correct technique and timing.

Variable Practice

Variable practice "involves variability in the parameters of the movement, not different movements" (Haibach et al., 2011, p. 302); for example, an underhand toss could be aimed at targets at different levels, distances, or directions. Whereas constant practice helps learners gain the critical elements, or stable features, of a generalized motor program, variable practice helps them gain the characteristics, or flexible features, that vary skill execution from one performance to the next. The flexible features involve performing skills using different parameters, such as level, direction, distance, speed, trajectory, and relationship (e.g., with a partner).

Practicing a skill using many different movement parameters expands the learner's generalized motor program. In turn, this expansion enables the performer to learn a greater variety of ways to perform closed skills. For instance, dancers might vary turns by the number of revolutions or by the position of nonsupporting body parts, and volleyball players might vary serves by sending them to different locations. For open skills, a generalized motor program with many flexible features enables the performer to respond faster and more accurately to an unpredictable environment. When structuring variable practice for open skills, teachers design progressions that start with more predictable environments and shift to less predictable ones.

Contextual interference is a form of variable practice of open skills that can be used to positively influence retention and transfer by having the student perform multiple skills or variations in the same practice session. Depending on the level of contextual interference, variable practice can fall into any of three categories: blocked, serial, and random. In blocked practice, performers practice two or more skills separately for a specific number of trials—for instance, catching 10 balls arriving above the head, 10 arriving at chest level, and 10 arriving below the knees. In serial practice, the three different types of catching would be repeated 10 times *in sequence*—above the head, chest level, below the knees. In random practice, the three levels of catching would be varied unpredictably in order to simulate gamelike conditions.

For learners at the beginning level, variable practice of open skills consists primarily of predictable schedules of blocked practice because young children can be overwhelmed by random practice due to their limited information-processing capabilities (Haibach et al., 2011, p. 311). Intermediate-level learners, on the other hand, benefit from serial and random practice schedules that engage them in less predictable or unpredictable environments. Advanced-level learners benefit from random practice in authentic, unpredictable environments.

Mental practice that accompanies variable physical practice focuses on rehearsing rules for matching motor programs to identified environmental stimuli; this type of rehearsal improves the learner's anticipation and his or her speed and accuracy in both response selection and performance. For example, in a lesson with the goal of intercepting the game object, the defensive player would mentally rehearse the following rule: If closer to the ball and faster than the offense, go for the ball; if farther from the offense, get in position to block the shot or pass and slow down the offense (Rovegno & Bandhauer, 2013).

FEEDBACK

Feedback is the information that performers receive about their movement responses, and it influences their rate of learning and level of performance (Coker, 2004; Young et al., 2000). As with practice, feedback works best when teachers and coaches match the type and amount of feedback to the learner, the task, and the environment.

Feedback can be either intrinsic or augmented. **Intrinsic feedback** consists of information that comes from the performer's senses: she sees the ball, feels it in her hands, and adjusts her balance to prepare to throw. **Augmented feedback** consists of information that comes from a source other than the performer—for example, a teacher, a heart rate monitor, or a video recording of the performance. Augmented feedback is used to guide, motivate, and reinforce the learner.

Feedback that is used to guide performance points out errors and ways to correct them. Ultimately, the goal is to enable learners to detect and correct their own errors. Feedback is motivating when it informs learners about their progress toward an established goal. To provide motivating feedback, teachers often use statements such as, "Keep trying—you're almost there," which can encourage learners to keep working toward their performance goals. When reinforcing correct performance, describing specific movements makes it more likely that the learner will perform similarly under like circumstances in the future. Two examples of specific reinforcing feedback are, "Nice job—by moving quickly, you were able to intercept the ball" and "Way to go—that tight tuck made your roll smooth."

Augmented feedback to guide stepping with the opposite foot.

Feedback can also be classified according to whether the skill goal is process or outcome oriented. Process goals address the *pattern* and/or *parameters* (direction, level, speed and/or force) of the movement focusing on the biomechanical efficiency of the skill's critical elements. Outcome goals, on the other hand, address the *product* of the movement and focus on end results, such as score or shot percentage or final speed, height, distance or accuracy of performance.

Knowledge of Performance

Knowledge of performance (KP) is provided by augmented feedback about the process or movement pattern of the performance; it includes information about the location, speed, direction, or coordination of body actions. Since the purpose of KP is to reinforce or change the way the performer moves, teachers must be knowledgeable about the critical elements and biomechanical principles that determine correct performance. Here are some examples of KP: "Step forward with the opposite foot." "Keep your knees closer to your chest." "Keep your head still and your eyes on the ball." These KP statements are all **prescriptive feedback (KPp)** because they focus specifically on what the performer needs to do in order to correct her or his movements. These specific, prescriptive KP feedback statements are especially important for beginning-level learners, whose goal is to minimize errors and develop the correct movements of new closed and open skills.

KP feedback about the movement pattern is also important for intermediate-level learners of form-specific closed skills as they learn how to perform skill variations and connect movements in gymnastics and dance sequences; for example, "To make a smoother connection, start your jump from the ending position of the roll." KP feedback for intermediate-level learners of outcome-based closed skills must include information about the parameters (direction, level, speed, or force) used to make the movements fit the environment, for instance, "For serves toward the back of the court, create more force by using a bigger wind-up." To aid intermediate learners in correcting their own errors, teachers can use **descriptive feedback (KPd)** with a prompt for error correction (e.g., "The foul shot was wide. What do you need to change to be more accurate?")

KP feedback for intermediate-level learning of open skills must also pair error information about movement patterns and the parameters (direction, level, speed, or force) used to make the movements fit the environment. The latter is especially important for open skills because the learner is focused on detecting and responding to unpredictable environmental cues. In this example, identify the feedback that is about the movement characteristics and the feedback that is about the parameters. "You moved too slowly to block your opponent. Keep your knees bent and weight forward to move quickly. Watch your opponent's hips to detect the direction to move." Take another look at the feedback. What parts were descriptive (KPd)? What parts prescriptive (KPp)? You are on the right track if you identified:

"You moved too slowly to block your opponent" as descriptive about movement parameters.

"Keep knees bent and weight forward to move quickly" as prescriptive about movement characteristics.

"Watch opponent's hips to detect the direction to move" as prescriptive about movement parameters.

Knowledge of performance feedback is critical for learning. Important for physical education teachers is the ability to match and deliver the right type of feedback for the learning level of the performer (beginning/intermediate) and the type of skill (closed/open).

Knowledge of Results

Knowledge of results (KR) is provided by either intrinsic or augmented feedback about the outcome or end result of a movement performance. Information about goal attainment is critical for acquiring and performing movement skills (Young, et al., 2000). Most often, KR is known intrinsically by performers because, for example, they see the ball hit a target, feel themselves going off balance, or hear the ball hit the sweet spot of the bat. In order to aid goal attainment, teachers and coaches can provide augmented KR that is unknown or less obvious to the learner—for example, "you finished the dash in 10 seconds," "your foot was out of bounds," or "you successfully fielded 40 percent of the ground balls." These KR teacher feedback statements are all **descriptive feedback (KRd)** because they simply describe what happened in the performance.

Timing of Feedback

For learners at the beginning level, KP feedback should be delivered intermittently—after every three to five trials, rather than after every trial—in order to decrease their dependence on the teacher and engage them in attending to their intrinsic feedback responses. At the intermediate level, as learners improve, teachers can use a faded format, in which feedback is given less and less frequently and, eventually, learners decide for themselves when they want to receive augmented feedback (Coker, 2004; Fairbrother, 2010; Young et al., 2000).

Motor learning specialists agree that feedback should be delayed for a few seconds after performance in order to give learners a chance to process their intrinsic feedback. Specialists also suggest that the teacher ask learners to tune in to their intrinsic feedback by estimating their own performance errors before receiving augmented feedback. In addition, the focus on performance errors should be congruent with the goal of the movement performance—that is, movement pattern cues for closed skills, and links between movement pattern and parameter cues for outcome-based closed skills and open skills. Learners at the intermediate level can also be given prompts that ask them to describe how they will change their performance in order to reduce or eliminate errors (Coker, 2004; Fairbrother, 2010; Young, et al., 2000).

Figures 7.1 and 7.2 summarize the relationship between the interacting factors of learner, task, and environment and the types of practice and feedback for both closed skills (figure 7.1) and open skills (figure 7.2). Teachers should structure both the type of practice and the type of feedback based on the learning level of the performer and the goal of the skill. At the same time, one constant need is to provide all learners with an environment that supports their body size and stage of development. Scaling equipment and contexts avoids the pitfall of unnecessarily compromising learners' performance through the use of adult equipment, rules, and boundaries; instead, it enables learners to optimize their performance.

Environment	Stages of learning	Closed skill	Practice	Feedback
Scale equipment and conditions	**Immature beginner**	Goal: Provide affordances that allow for skill "success" even though movements are immature	**Constant** Foster repetition for development of neuromuscular pathways	**Praise and encouragement**
	Beginning	Goal: Achieve correct timing and technique for mature performance	**Constant**	**Knowledge of performance** Intermittent Prescriptive
	Intermediate Combination Application	*Form-specific or outcome-based* Goal: Elicit consistency of performance and variations in skill situations, combinations, and routines	**Variable** *(skill variations)* **Constant** (combinations and routines)	**Knowledge of performance** *(form specific)* Descriptive and/or prescriptive **Knowledge of performance results** *(outcome based)*
	Advanced	*Form-specific or outcome-based* Goal: Elicit consistency of performance and variations in skill situations, combinations, and routines	**Variable** *(skill variations)* **Constant** (combinations and routines)	**Knowledge of performance** *(form specific)* Faded and descriptive **Knowledge of results** *(outcome based)*

Figure 7.1 Relationships between the constraints on closed-skill practice and feedback.

Environment	Stages of learning	Open skill	Practice	Feedback
Scale equipment and conditions	**Immature beginner**	Goal: Provide affordances that allow for skill "success" even though movements are immature	**Constant** Faster repetition for development of neuromuscular pathways	**Praise and encouragement**
	Beginning	**Open** Goal: Achieve correct timing and technique for mature performance in predictable environments.	**Variable** Contextual interference Block	**Knowledge of performance and results** Intermittent and prescriptive
	Intermediate Combination Application	**Open** Goal: Elicit responses to a range of more- to less- unpredictable environments with fewer or more response choices	**Variable** Contextual interference Serial and random	**Knowledge of performance and results** Faded Descriptive and/or prescriptive
	Advanced	**Open** Goal: Elicit responses to unpredictable environments with many response choices	**Variable** Contextual interference Random	**Knowledge results** Faded and descriptive

Figure 7.2   Relationships between the constraints on open-skill practice and feedback.

Big Ideas

- The axiom that practice makes perfect holds true only if one practices appropriately. Specificity of practice means that the practice experience engages the learner, the goal of the skill, in a developmentally appropriate performance context.

- Constant practice has no variability and is used when children at the immature-beginner level are acquiring skills, when beginner-level learners are acquiring closed skills, and when intermediate learners are practicing the form-specific closed skills for dance and gymnastics sequences and routines.

- Variable practice involves using different parameters (level, direction, distance, speed, trajectory, relationship to a partner) to perform closed skills in a variety of ways. When variable practice is used with open skills, it involves a range of predictability referred to as contextual interference. Beginners usually practice with blocked contextual interference (more predictability) and intermediate learners with serial to random contextual interference (less predictability).

- The purpose of knowledge of performance (KP) feedback is to reinforce or change the ways in which performers move their bodies and body parts. In giving this feedback, teachers use critical elements and biomechanical principles to describe correct and incorrect movement patterns and parameters and to prescribe changes that will improve the movement performance. KP feedback about movement patterns is used most often to enhance the learning and performance of closed skills. Linking KP feedback about movement patterns and parameters is used most often to enhance the learning and performance of outcome-based closed skills and open skills.

- Knowledge of results (KR) feedback addresses the outcome or end result of a movement performance. Teachers augment students' perceptions of obvious results (e.g., ball going into basket) with specific information to frame the outcome in relation to performance goals (e.g., shot percentage or degree of height or distance). KR feedback is used most often to enhance the learning and performance of open skills and outcome-based closed skills for learners in intermediate and advanced levels of learning.

- The delivery of KP feedback should be intermittent (every three to five trials) for learners at the beginning level and faded for learners at the intermediate level. Feedback should be delayed for a few seconds after performance in order to give learners a chance to process their intrinsic feedback and consider how to correct their performance if necessary.

 Visit the web resource for learning activities, video clips, and review questions.

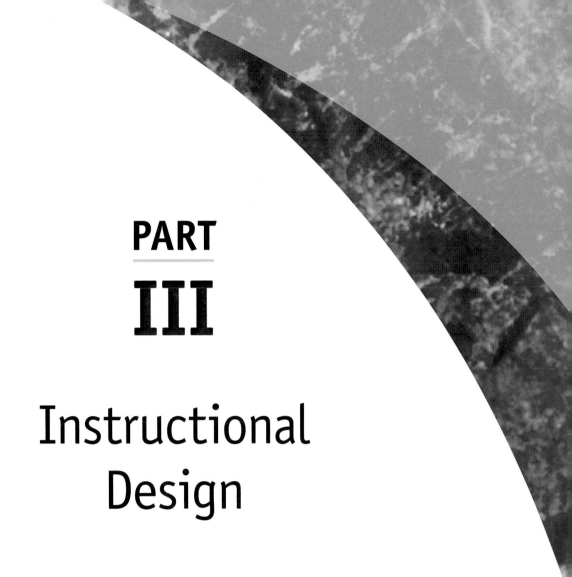

PART
III

Instructional Design

Loan Receipt
Liverpool John Moores University
Library Services

Borrower Name: Rudd, James
EDNJRUDD
Borrower ID: ********

Developmental physical education for all
children : theory into practice /
311115094624
Due Date: 02/05/2019 23:59:00 BST
Total Items: 1
25/04/2019 16:34

Please keep your receipt in case of
dispute.

Standards-Based Physical Education

Key Concepts

- Articulating the five national standards for K-12 physical education
- Explaining the relationship of standard 2 to standards 1, 3, 4, and 5
- Explaining the relationship of standards 1 and 2 to standards 3 through 5
- Describing the rationale for, and the steps in, the backward design process for unpacking standards
- Describing how the physical activity guidelines and the appropriate practices guidelines for preschool children relate to the national standards for K-12 physical education

This chapter provides a framework for making developmentally appropriate curricular decisions for children in pre-K through grade 5 physical education. In establishing this framework, we are fortunate to have SHAPE America's (2014) *National Standards and Grade-Level Outcomes for K-12 Physical Education,* which articulates movement learning outcomes that support the movement framework and the psychomotor, cognitive, fitness, and affective development of K-5 students that you have learned about in preceding chapters. When we combine these national standards with other key SHAPE America documents—*Active Start: A Statement of Physical Activity Guidelines* and the *Opportunity to Learn* series of guidelines (National Association for Sport and Physical Education [NASPE], 2009a, 2010a, 2010b, 2010c)—we are equipped with a framework for making effective curricular choices for **developmental physical education**.

The chapter begins with a history of the development of standards. It then examines the five **content standards for physical education**, explores a backward design process for understanding and implementing the standards, and reviews a translation of guidelines and practices for pre-K that reflect the standards.

DEVELOPMENT OF STANDARDS, OUTCOMES, AND GUIDELINES

In 1995, national standards for physical education were adopted by the National Association for Sport and Physical Education (NASPE), which was one of five national associations under the umbrella of the American Alliance for Health, Physical Education, Recreation and Dance (AAHPERD, now known as SHAPE America). These standards were produced in order to guide educators in developing curricula, instruction, and assessment to reflect what K-12 students should know and be able to do as a result of a quality physical education program. By 2004, sample performance outcomes were added to each standard in order to indicate the levels of achievement that K-12 students were expected to reach in knowledge and ability (NASPE, 2004).

In 2013, NASPE and AAHPERD aligned the goal of physical education with the language of the Common Core initiative to specify developing physically *literate* rather than physically *educated* individuals (Council of Chief State School Officers and National Governor's Association Center for Best Practices [CCSSO & NGACBP], 2010). By 2014, when AAHPERD's name had been changed to SHAPE America, a curriculum framework had been developed to indicate specific student outcomes for each standard at every grade level, as well as a scope and sequence for quality physical education (SHAPE America, 2014a, 2014b).

Along the way, in addition to standards and outcomes for physical education, NASPE was also working to provide physical activity guidelines for children aged 5 to 12 in order to address the obesity epidemic (NASPE, 2004). By 2009, NASPE updated the guidelines to include infants and young children indicating that "all children from birth to age 5 should engage in daily physical activity that promotes movement skillfulness and foundations of health-related fitness" in order to combat the long-term health problems of a physically inactive lifestyle (NASPE, 2009a, p. 23). Building on that foundation, NASPE (2010a, 2010b, 2010c) published the *Opportunity to Learn* documents, which highlight appropriate and inappropriate practices in physical education programs for elementary, middle, and secondary students. These documents demonstrate how developmentally and instructionally appropriate physical education programs should function.

Taken together, the national standards (SHAPE America 2014a, 2014b), the physical activity guidelines (NASPE, 2004, 2009a), and the appropriate practices guidelines (NASPE 2009b, 2010a, 2010b, 2010c) provide physical education professionals with the means to develop programs that promote and foster, at an early age, students' enjoyment of movement, as well as their motor skill confidence and competence. These programs also make students more likely to experience healthy development and commit themselves to lifelong participation in physical activity (NASPE, 2004).

The curricula, assessments, and instruction for developmental physical education should all be guided by SHAPE America documents. The K-5 curricula are based on the national standards for physical education (SHAPE America, 2014a), and embedded in those standards are the physical activity guidelines for children aged 5 to 12, (NASPE, 1998) and developmentally appropriate curricula and practices (NASPE, 2010a). Since national standards do not exist for pre-K physical education programs, the physical activity guidelines and appropriate practice guidelines (NASPE, 2009a, 2009b) were used by the authors to shape curricula for children from age 3 to 5.

In the following sections, you will first be acquainted with the national standards for physical education (SHAPE America, 2014a) and the process for designing curricula based on the standards. Then you will be introduced to the physical activity guidelines (NASPE, 2009a) and the appropriate practices guidelines for children aged 3 to 5 (NASPE, 2009b) and how they relate to the standards and curriculum design.

NATIONAL STANDARDS AND OUTCOMES FOR PHYSICAL EDUCATION

The national standards for physical education (SHAPE America, 2014a) were designed to help teachers develop physically literate individuals who possess the knowledge, skills, and confidence to enjoy a lifetime of healthful physical activity. Physical literacy is the ability to move with competence, confidence, and an understanding of movement concepts in order to purposefully make physical activity an integral part of a healthy lifestyle (SHAPE America, 2014a).

Standards-Based Physical Education

Key Concepts

- Articulating the five national standards for K-12 physical education

- Explaining the relationship of standard 2 to standards 1, 3, 4, and 5

- Explaining the relationship of standards 1 and 2 to standards 3 through 5

- Describing the rationale for, and the steps in, the backward design process for unpacking standards

- Describing how the physical activity guidelines and the appropriate practices guidelines for preschool children relate to the national standards for K-12 physical education

This chapter provides a framework for making developmentally appropriate curricular decisions for children in pre-K through grade 5 physical education. In establishing this framework, we are fortunate to have SHAPE America's (2014) *National Standards and Grade-Level Outcomes for K-12 Physical Education,* which articulates movement learning outcomes that support the movement framework and the psychomotor, cognitive, fitness, and affective development of K-5 students that you have learned about in preceding chapters. When we combine these national standards with other key SHAPE America documents—*Active Start: A Statement of Physical Activity Guidelines* and the *Opportunity to Learn* series of guidelines (National Association for Sport and Physical Education [NASPE], 2009a, 2010a, 2010b, 2010c)—we are equipped with a framework for making effective curricular choices for **developmental physical education**.

The chapter begins with a history of the development of standards. It then examines the five **content standards for physical education**, explores a backward design process for understanding and implementing the standards, and reviews a translation of guidelines and practices for pre-K that reflect the standards.

DEVELOPMENT OF STANDARDS, OUTCOMES, AND GUIDELINES

In 1995, national standards for physical education were adopted by the National Association for Sport and Physical Education (NASPE), which was one of five national associations under the umbrella of the American Alliance for Health, Physical Education, Recreation and Dance (AAHPERD, now known as SHAPE America). These standards were produced in order to guide educators in developing curricula, instruction, and assessment to reflect what K-12 students should know and be able to do as a result of a quality physical education program. By 2004, sample performance outcomes were added to each standard in order to indicate the levels of achievement that K-12 students were expected to reach in knowledge and ability (NASPE, 2004).

In 2013, NASPE and AAHPERD aligned the goal of physical education with the language of the Common Core initiative to specify developing physically *literate* rather than physically *educated* individuals (Council of Chief State School Officers and National Governor's Association Center for Best Practices [CCSSO & NGACBP], 2010). By 2014, when AAHPERD's name had been changed to SHAPE America, a curriculum framework had been developed to indicate specific student outcomes for each standard at every grade level, as well as a scope and sequence for quality physical education (SHAPE America, 2014a, 2014b).

Along the way, in addition to standards and outcomes for physical education, NASPE was also working to provide physical activity guidelines for children aged 5 to 12 in order to address the obesity epidemic (NASPE, 2004). By 2009, NASPE updated the guidelines to include infants and young children indicating that "all children from birth to age 5 should engage in daily physical activity that promotes movement skillfulness and foundations of health-related fitness" in order to combat the long-term health problems of a physically inactive lifestyle (NASPE, 2009a, p. 23). Building on that foundation, NASPE (2010a, 2010b, 2010c) published the *Opportunity to Learn* documents, which highlight appropriate and inappropriate practices in physical education programs for elementary, middle, and secondary students. These documents demonstrate how developmentally and instructionally appropriate physical education programs should function.

Taken together, the national standards (SHAPE America 2014a, 2014b), the physical activity guidelines (NASPE, 2004, 2009a), and the appropriate practices guidelines (NASPE 2009b, 2010a, 2010b, 2010c) provide physical education professionals with the means to develop programs that promote and foster, at an early age, students' enjoyment of movement, as well as their motor skill confidence and competence. These programs also make students more likely to experience healthy development and commit themselves to lifelong participation in physical activity (NASPE, 2004).

The curricula, assessments, and instruction for developmental physical education should all be guided by SHAPE America documents. The K-5 curricula are based on the national standards for physical education (SHAPE America, 2014a), and embedded in those standards are the physical activity guidelines for children aged 5 to 12, (NASPE, 1998) and developmentally appropriate curricula and practices (NASPE, 2010a). Since national standards do not exist for pre-K physical education programs, the physical activity guidelines and appropriate practice guidelines (NASPE, 2009a, 2009b) were used by the authors to shape curricula for children from age 3 to 5.

In the following sections, you will first be acquainted with the national standards for physical education (SHAPE America, 2014a) and the process for designing curricula based on the standards. Then you will be introduced to the physical activity guidelines (NASPE, 2009a) and the appropriate practices guidelines for children aged 3 to 5 (NASPE, 2009b) and how they relate to the standards and curriculum design.

NATIONAL STANDARDS AND OUTCOMES FOR PHYSICAL EDUCATION

The national standards for physical education (SHAPE America, 2014a) were designed to help teachers develop physically literate individuals who possess the knowledge, skills, and confidence to enjoy a lifetime of healthful physical activity. Physical literacy is the ability to move with competence, confidence, and an understanding of movement concepts in order to purposefully make physical activity an integral part of a healthy lifestyle (SHAPE America, 2014a).

Every discipline has knowledge, skills, and dispositions worth learning.

- Knowledge is what people should know.
- Skills are what people should be able to do or perform.
- Dispositions indicate how people should behave.

For each educational discipline—whether it be science, social studies, mathematics, or physical education—standards define the knowledge, skills, and dispositions that make individuals competent, educated, and capable of applying the discipline in order to enhance their lives. In the discipline of physical education, national content standards define what students should know, be able to perform, and behave like in order to achieve and maintain a health-enhancing and physically active lifestyle across the lifespan. Specifically, a **physically literate** person needs to

- know healthy ways of engaging in physical activity;
- possess the movement skills, fitness, and confidence to perform a variety of physical activities; and
- have the disposition and motivation to participate regularly in physical activities throughout life.

National Standards and Grade-Level Outcomes for K-12 Physical Education (SHAPE America, 2014a) includes content standards and **grade-level student outcomes** arranged in a curricular framework to provide physical educators with a common understanding of the knowledge, skills, and dispositions that K-12 students need in order to become physically literate. Physical educators can use the standards and outcomes both to develop learning experiences that help their students attain the needed knowledge, skills, and dispositions and to develop assessments that measure their students' success in this learning.

The five content standards constitute large goals focused broadly on what students should know, be able to do, and behave like as physically literate individuals. The five goals (SHAPE America, 2014a) indicate that a physically literate individual does the following:

1. Demonstrates competency in a variety of motor skills and movement patterns (p. 12).

2. Applies knowledge of concepts, principles, strategies, and tactics related to movement and performance (p. 12).

3. Demonstrates the knowledge and skills to achieve and maintain a health-enhancing level of physical activity and fitness (p. 12).

4. Exhibits responsible personal and social behavior that respects self and others (p. 12).

5. Recognizes the value of physical activity for health, enjoyment, challenge, self-expression, and/or social interaction (p.12).

The field of physical education is distinctive in that its standards contribute to the development of the whole person. Taken collectively, the standards address the cognitive, psychomotor, fitness, and affective domains of learning. The cognitive domain addresses what students should know, the psychomotor and fitness domains address what students should be able to do, and the affective domain addresses how students should behave.

Most of the standards require a performance in order to demonstrate that they have been met, and each involves cognitive concepts that are important for understanding how to engage in the performance. Therefore, standard 2 ("applies knowledge of concepts, principles, strategies, and tactics related to movement and performance") relates to each of the other standards. Figure 8.1 shows the cognitive concepts related to each of the other standards.

Each physical education content standard is associated with certain student outcomes, which constitute broad objectives for achievement in grade-level ranges.

- Elementary: kindergarten through grade 5
- Middle school: grades 6 through 8
- High school: grades 9 through 12

Within these grade ranges, the student outcomes are consistent with children's developmental patterns in the psychomotor, cognitive, fitness, and affective domains (see chapters 2 through 4). You can also see that the physical education outcomes for the elementary grades reflect the skills of the fundamental and specialized phases of the movement framework (chapter 5), as well as the skill progressions (preconsistent, consistent, combination, and application) from chapter 6.

Although all five standards are important for becoming a physically literate person, the student outcomes in the first two standards form the backbone of the K-5 curriculum. These two standards focus on gaining skill competence (standard 1) and knowledge (standard 2) of the fundamental motor skills and skill combinations. Performing and understanding movement skills enables students to become physically active, which in turn is a key factor in attaining standards 3 through 5. Figure 8.2 presents standards 1 and 2 as the foundation for all other standards in grades K through 5.

For instance, becoming skilled enough to run at different speeds and jump rhythmically (standards 1 and 2) leads to a sense of movement competence, which can provide motivation to run for cardiorespiratory fitness benefit (standard 3) or engage in a team-building rope-jumping activity (standard 4). These activities, in turn, can lead a learner to identify running and jumping as enjoyable movement experiences worth repeating (standard 5),

thus perpetuating the cycle of being a physically active person.

The grade-level student outcomes are described as performance outcomes, which must be observable and measurable. They describe behaviors that can be observed in order to determine how well students are progressing in meeting the standards. Teachers can use performance outcomes in three ways, which are illustrated in the following list for the underhand throw.

- To develop specific learning goals: By second grade, learners will throw underhand using a mature pattern (SHAPE America, 2014a, 2014b).

- To design motivating learning experiences that engage students in performing the underhand throw using the correct performance

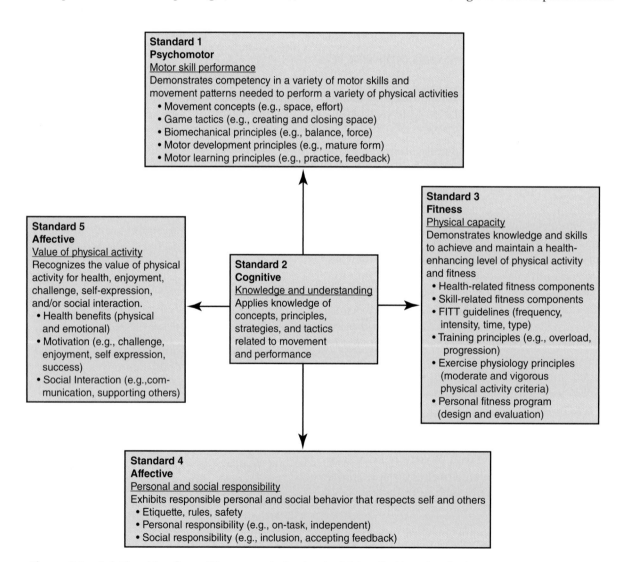

Figure 8.1 Relationship of cognitive concepts in standard 2 to all other standards.

criteria: Provide targets of various colors and types for learners to throw at, over, and into and give visual and auditory reminders about the performance criteria.

- To design assessments that objectively measure student progress: See table 8.1 for a checklist to help you observe how well students are able to use the underhand throw performance criteria.

The content standards and grade-level student outcomes serve as a guide for physical educators in developing curricular experiences and assessments that enable their students to learn effectively. Student achievement of the content standards constitutes a national goal in the United States, and many states have used the national standards as a guide to fashion their own standards for physical education. Some school districts have even designed their own standards based on their state standards and the national standards. Whether you are expected to adhere to national, state, or district standards, you as a physical educator

need to know how to interpret or unpack those standards. Doing so enables you to decide what content, learning experiences, and assessments to use in order to enable your students to learn the knowledge, skills, and dispositions they need for regular participation in health-enhancing physical activities.

UNPACKING STANDARDS

Unpacking standards involves delving into the true meaning of each standard by defining terms and extracting the essential or important content. This understanding can be achieved through a process called backward design, which means starting at the end (Wiggins & McTighe, 1998; Lund & Tannehill, 2010). If you know what the end goal (true meaning) of the standard is, you can plan how to get there. Thus unpacking the standards through backward design is a way to implement Covey's (2004) idea of beginning with the end in mind in order to stay focused on goals.

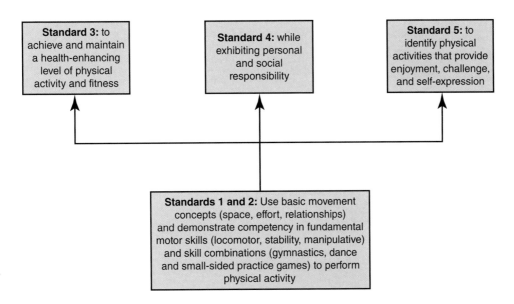

Figure 8.2 Standards 1 and 2 provide the foundation for the other standards in grades K through 5.

Table 8.1 Underhand Throw Performance Assessment Checklist

Performance criteria	Yes	Needs more practice
Arm is back in preparation.		
Opposite foot is forward.		
Ball is released forward toward target.		

One way to think about unpacking the standards is to compare the process with that of attending college in order to become a teacher. In going to college, you begin with the end—that is, your big goal: "My intent is to be a teacher." Then you unpack the goal by considering the smaller goals you must achieve in order to get there: getting into college, getting accepted into a teacher education program, progressing through the program, becoming a student teacher, gaining certification, and graduating from the program.

At the beginning of this journey, you are informed of the acceptable evidence that you must produce along the way in order to reach each small goal: maintaining a certain grade point average, passing increasingly complex courses in a particular sequence, and passing national certification exams, to name only a few. Of course, in order to meet these demands, you must engage in learning and practice experiences in many courses, thereby becoming knowledgeable and skillful enough to achieve your goals. If you follow Covey's advice and keep the end in mind, you'll work hard, stay focused, and be more likely to reach your big goal of becoming a teacher.

Similarly, using backward design to unpack the standards involves clarifying what each standard means, how to measure student success, and how each standard can be achieved. The backward design steps are shown in figure 8.3.

In the first step, clarifying the goal, you extract the enduring understanding and essential content of the standard. The enduring understanding is the big picture—the major intent of the standard, or the goal to be reached by the end of twelfth grade. It is found in the general description of the standard. The essential content, on the other hand, is found in the grade-level outcomes. The student outcomes describe the learning goals at each grade-level range—what students need to know, be able to do, and behave like—that lead to the enduring understanding by the end of twelfth grade.

In the second step, you identify the acceptable evidence for demonstrating that students have achieved the grade-level outcomes. Acceptable evidence determined by teachers often consists of consistent performance of a skill or use of the skill in a dance combination or small-sided game. Acceptable evidence could also consist of a passing score that must be achieved on a test or project. In the third step, you decide the learning experiences that students need to go through in order to become knowledgeable and skilled enough to achieve the learning goals. This part of the process includes making decisions about learning activities, how you'll teach, and how students will practice.

The backward design process can be used to keep the end in mind not only while you plan but also while you teach. To help students become successful learners, focus their attention before they

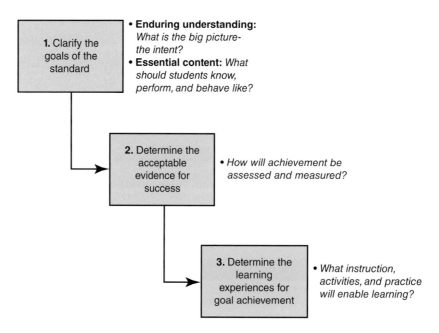

Figure 8.3 Backward design process.

engage in learning activities. You can do so by telling or showing them

- the end learning goal (the essential content) and
- the acceptable evidence they need in order to show achievement of the goal (assessment task and criteria).

If children are aware of the learning goal and what they must do to show that they have achieved it, they are able to focus on the essential content as they engage in learning and practice activities. For example, you might tell second graders that the learning goal is to recognize and perform the critical elements of a forward roll—and that they'll need to show that they recognize the critical elements by pointing to a partner's movements, circling correct body positions on drawings, and stating the performance cues before performing a roll. Since they have this knowledge as they engage in the learning activities, they can concentrate on remembering and practicing the critical elements of the roll.

Now, let's explore the steps of the backward design process in greater detail.

Step 1: Clarifying the Goals

Each of the five national content standards addresses an important part of becoming a physically literate person who establishes and maintains a health-enhancing and physically active lifestyle. To extract the enduring understanding that distinguishes the role of each standard, start by carefully reading its general description and intent. For instance, standard 2 reads as follows: "The physically literate individual applies knowledge of concepts, principles, strategies, and tactics related to movement and performance" (SHAPE America, 2014a, p. 12). The intent of this standard is to facilitate learners' ability to use cognitive information in order to understand and enhance their acquisition and performance of motor skills (NASPE, 2004, p. 21).

People who can use knowledge about movement to perform safely, enhance their fitness, and improve their skills and game play tend to feel competent in physical activity and are more likely to participate throughout their lives. The enduring understanding that standard 2 contributes to becoming a physically literate person is found in the statement of intent: "the ability to use cognitive information to understand and enhance motor

skill acquisition and performance" (NASPE, 2004, p. 21). You can see, then, that standard 2 plays an important role in the goal of becoming a physically literate individual, and the same is true for the other four standards.

Once you are clear about the role of the standard in becoming physically literate, you can start the process of determining its essential content: what students need to know, perform, and behave like in order to achieve the enduring understanding of the standard. The grade-level student outcomes provide key ideas about what students need to know, perform, and behave like on their journey to achieving the standard. The focus for these key ideas draws from many areas of the discipline of physical education.

Indeed, you will find valuable resources for determining the essential content for kindergarten through grade 5 in your studies in biomechanics, exercise physiology, motor development, motor learning, sociology, psychology and philosophy of sport and exercise, and elementary physical education, as well as your study (and performance) of various movement activities and sports and types of dance and exercise. For example, one standard 3 student outcome for grade 3 states that the learner "identifies physical activity benefits as a way to become healthier" (SHAPE America, 2014a, p. 34). For your own part, your studies in exercise physiology support your understanding of the benefits of physical activity for living a healthy life.

To determine the essential content—what students need to know, perform, and behave like in order to achieve a given standard—you must unpack the grade-level student outcomes. This process involves examining the actions (verbs) and the supporting content (nouns and adjectives) required to perform the action. The supporting content provides information about *what* students need to know, perform, and behave like, whereas the actions provide information about *how* students demonstrate what they know, perform what they can, and behave appropriately in given situations.

For instance, one standard 2 student outcome for grade 2 is for the learner to "identify elements of correct form for fundamental motor skills and use them in performance" (NASPE, 2004, p. 22). The content (nouns and adjectives) indicates *what* students need to know and perform: the elements of correct form for fundamental motor skills. The actions (verbs) indicate *how* they know by identifying elements of correct form for fundamental motor skills and *how* they perform by using elements of correct form for fundamental motor skills.

Student outcomes addressing knowledge are demonstrated differently than student outcomes addressing performance and behavior. To determine whether an outcome addresses knowledge, performance, or both, examine the actions (verbs) in the description of the student outcomes. Knowledge outcomes address cognition and use action verbs such as *identify*, *describe*, *explain*, *design*, *apply*, *select*, and *plan*. In contrast, performance and behavior outcomes address how students actively show what they can do or how to behave appropriately. Therefore, these outcomes use action verbs such as *demonstrate*, *perform*, *use*, *achieve*, *engage*, *maintain*, *participate*, and *perform*—or verbs indicating a specific action itself, such as *throw*, *kick*, *balance*, *run*, *persist*, and *cooperate*. For example, consider which type of action (knowledge or performance) is included in the standard 2 student outcome quoted at the start of the preceding paragraph.

This process of identifying the concepts (nouns) and actions (verbs) provides you with initial direction for understanding the focus of a student outcome. To attain a deeper understanding of the focus, it is helpful to *define* the concepts (nouns). For example, take a moment to identify the concepts that you would need to define in order to gain a deeper understanding of the standard 2 student outcome discussed in the preceding two paragraphs. You were correct if you said you would define elements of correct form and fundamental motor skills. Moreover, from your studies in biomechanics, you know that the elements of correct form for movements are composed of three phases: preparation, main action, and recovery. And from your studies in motor behavior, you know that the

fundamental motor skills are basic movements categorized as relating to either stability, locomotion, or manipulation.

To further deepen your understanding and get *specific* about the essential content, you can compose and answer essential questions about the defined concepts. Essential question prompts begin with words such as *what*, *where*, *how*, *when*, *why*, and *who*. The type of question is guided by the action verbs in the student outcome. For instance, returning to that same standard 2 student outcome, the cognitive action (verb) is *identify* and the performance action (verb) is *use*. To arrive at the specific essential content for this student outcome, you can answer the essential question for multiple fundamental motor skills (see table 8.2 for two examples).

This first step of the backward design process (clarifying the goal by determining the enduring understanding and essential content of the standard) serves as the polestar that guides step 2 (how to assess students) and step 3 (how to instruct students). The process of using the focus of the essential content as the focus of assessment and instruction is referred to as alignment. In table 8.2, the elements of correct form for the indicated fundamental motor skills provide the focus of the essential content. That same focus should also be the focus in cognitive assessments, wherein students identify the elements of correct form as depicted in pictures or models of children performing the underhand throw and forward roll in correct and incorrect positions.

Likewise, you can use a checklist in evaluating students' abilities to use the elements of correct form as they perform the underhand throw and forward roll. To continue the alignment process, plan instruction that includes explanations and

Table 8.2 Deriving Essential Content from the Essential Question

Essential question	Essential content
What are the elements of correct form, and how are they performed for the following skills?	The elements of correct form are identified and used by doing the following:
Underhand throw	Preparation—swinging arm back and opposite foot forward
	Main action—swinging arm forward and releasing toward target
	Recovery—following through toward target
Forward roll	Preparation—crouching with chin to chest and palms apart on mat in front of feet
	Main action—raising hips, pushing from feet, and bending elbows to transfer weight from hands to rounded back
	Recovery—rolling to feet

demonstrations of correct form by showing pictures or models and by having children say the elements of correct form and point to or circle them on drawings. You can also create a motivating learning environment to engage children in practicing the underhand throw and the forward roll using the elements of correct form.

Step 2: Choosing Acceptable Evidence

There are two parts in the process of designing assessments to measure acceptable evidence for achieving the standards. First, you must choose or design the method of assessment—skill demonstration, quiz, worksheet—by which students will demonstrate what they know, what they can do, and how they behave. Second, you must choose or design the scoring tool to measure how well students do on the skill demonstration, quiz, or worksheet. A scoring tool typically consists of an answer key (for a quiz, test, or worksheet), a checklist (for a performance or product involving multiple parts), or a rubric (for a performance or product with a range of possible success, from poor to excellent).

In kindergarten through grade 5, when the essential content focuses on having students demonstrate what they *know*, you can use the action (verb) from the grade-level student outcome to design or choose assessment methods that engage students in producing a product that demonstrates their ability to recognize, identify, explain, or describe their knowledge. For instance, students could be asked to produce answers to questions either orally or in writing or by drawing. To evaluate how well students answer the questions, either choose or design a scoring tool in the form of an answer key, checklist, or rubric.

When the essential content focuses on having students demonstrate what they can *do* or how they behave, use the action (verb) from the grade-level student outcome to design or choose assessment methods that engage students in performing, demonstrating, or participating in movement, fitness, or affective skills or activities. For example, depending on the given standard, students could be asked to perform a skip, demonstrate moving to an open space in a game, or demonstrate cooperation with a partner in order to solve a problem. To evaluate how well students perform, use a scoring tool in the form of a checklist or rubric while observing the performance.

Step 3: Designing Appropriate Instruction

As a teacher, you will use the essential content, assessment method, and scoring tool to guide your choice of teaching strategies, movement activities, and practice conditions. When choosing teaching strategies, consider whether to have students *duplicate* the movements or ideas that you explain and demonstrate or to have them *discover* movements, concepts, or principles by solving a problem. When choosing learning activities, consider when to use single skills, skill combinations, and small-sided games. When choosing practice conditions, determine whether repetition of movements under the same or different conditions is better for achieving the learning goal.

There are many "right" ways to reach the outcomes of the standards. The essential content tells you what students should know, be able to do, and behave like. As a teacher, you plan assessments to measure students' achievement of the essential content, and you plan instruction to enable students to learn and demonstrate that content. For instance, one of the outcomes for standard 1 for grade 5 is to throw "with reasonable accuracy in dynamic, small-sided practice tasks" (SHAPE America, 2014a, p. 28). You could use any of a number of sports for teaching and assessing accuracy in small-side practice tasks—for example, basketball, softball, Newcomb, lacrosse, wallball, or netball. Of course, the options may vary from one state or district to another, depending on the designated curriculum. The constant across all of the possible choices, however, lies in the essential content outcome: "throws with reasonable accuracy in dynamic, small-sided practice tasks."

GUIDELINES FOR PRESCHOOL CHILDREN

The physical activity guidelines reflect research in motor development, movement, and exercise physiology regarding young children's physical activity needs. With that grounding, the guidelines support the position that "all children from birth to age five should engage in daily physical activity that promotes movement skillfulness and foundations of health-related fitness" (NASPE, 2009a, p. viii). When children engage in daily physical activity and eat a diet marked by balanced nutritional intake, they are well on their way to maintaining a healthy lifestyle and avoiding childhood obesity.

In summary, the physical activity guidelines for preschoolers aged 3 to 5 (see figure 8.4) call for children to engage in hours of daily structured and unstructured physical activity. The goal for *structured* experiences is to help children develop their skill in performing the fundamental movements with partners and in small groups in environments that are safe, noncompetitive, and developmentally appropriate. The goal for *unstructured* experiences is to give children opportunities to participate both indoors and outdoors in safe, child-initiated movement and physical play for most of the day, with no more than 60 minutes at a time of sedentary activity (except when sleeping). In order to be successful, of course, all of these experiences rely on knowledgeable teachers, caregivers, and parents who value and promote safe and developmentally appropriate physical activity for preschoolers.

The appropriate practice guidelines for preschool children aged 3 to 5 (NASPE, 2009b) were developed in alignment with the national content standards for physical education (SHAPE America, 2014a).These guidelines address the components of quality movement programs that "focus holistically on acquiring fundamental motor skills, learning basic movement concepts, and instilling the joy of moving to assist children's motor, cognitive, emotional, and social development" (NASPE, 2009b, p. 3). The guidelines address developmentally and instructionally appropriate practices that teachers can use in designing learning environments, instructional strategies, curricula, and assessments and in pursuing their work with professionalism.

The sections that address learning environment and curriculum also help teachers glean the content advocated for preschool movement programs (NASPE, 2009b):

- Developing fundamental movement skills (sections 3.3, 3.6, 3.7)
- Gaining a cognitive understanding of movement skills and concepts (3.3.2)
- Developing health-related fitness (3.5.1) and regular participation in a physically active lifestyle outside of school (3.4.1)
- Developing self-control and cooperative behaviors (1.1.7, 1.6.2)
- Expressing a sense of joy when engaged in physical activity (1.2.1)

ALIGNMENT CHARTS

Figures 8.5 through 8.9 present the K-5 alignment charts for each physical education standard and the related physical activity and appropriate practice guidelines for preschoolers. Remember that the first two standards form the backbone of the curriculum, both for preschool and for grades K through 5. Performing and understanding movement skills enables students to become physically active, which is the key to attaining the remaining standards.

The alignment charts separate K-5 student outcomes into two clusters: K-2 and grades 3 through 5. This separation recognizes the typical shift

---

Guideline 1: Preschoolers should accumulate at least 60 minutes of structured physical activity each day.

Guideline 2: Preschoolers should engage in at least 60 minutes—and up to several hours—of unstructured physical activity each day, and should not be sedentary for more than 60 minutes at a time, except when sleeping.

Guideline 3: Preschoolers should be encouraged to develop competence in fundamental motor skills that serve as the building blocks for future motor skillfulness and physical activity.

Guideline 4: Preschoolers should have access to indoor and outdoor areas that meet or exceed recommended safety standards for performing large-muscle activities.

Guideline 5: Caregivers and parents in charge of preschoolers' health and well-being are responsible for understanding the importance of physical activity and for promoting movement skills by providing opportunities for structured and unstructured physical activity.

Figure 8.4 Physical activity guidelines for preschoolers.

Reprinted from NASPE 2009a.

that occurs in psychomotor, cognitive, and affective development around age 7 or 8 as children progress

- from fundamental skills to skill combinations and specialized skills,
- from preoperational to concrete thinking, and
- from associative and cooperative play to cooperative and competitive play.

The alignment charts also represent the three steps in unpacking the standards:

1. **Clarifying the goals:** An abbreviated description of each standard for physical education appears in the box above the relevant chart, and it includes the intent—the enduring understanding—of the standard. The essential content, which appears on the left side of each chart, is derived by extracting key pieces of the grade-level student outcomes for the given standard.

2. **Choosing acceptable evidence:** The measurement of success appears to the right of the essential content in the charts in order to emphasize the alignment between essential content and assessment. When students must demonstrate what they can *do* or behave like, use observational assessment methods.

When students must demonstrate what they *know*, use cognitive assessment methods that match the type of understanding signified by the cognitive action verb (e.g., *identify*, *describe*). Score success with answer keys, checklists, and rubrics. For more information about standards-based assessment, see chapter 9.

3. **Designing appropriate instruction:** Instruction is addressed at the bottom of each chart, thus appearing below and spanning the boxes for essential content and assessment. This placement serves as a reminder that instruction must focus on the essential content and prepare students to succeed on the assessments. As noted earlier, you have many choices in how you design instruction, activities, and practice to help students learn and demonstrate achievement of essential content. For more information about standards-based instruction, see chapter 10.

The alignment charts in figures 8.5-8.9 are organized sequentially by standard. In keeping with the backward design model, we begin with the grade 3-5 outcomes for each standard followed by the K-2 outcomes and then the pre-K guidelines related to the standard.

Standard 1: "The physically literate individual demonstrates competency in a variety of motor skills and movement patterns" (SHAPE America, 2014a, p. 12). "The intent of this standard is development of the movement skills needed to enjoy participation in physical activities" (NASPE, 2004, p. 12). The standard focuses on psychomotor performance of fundamental and specialized motor skills, patterns, and the execution of tactics to engage in a variety of physical activities.

Standard 1 (grades 3–5)

Essential content	Measurement of success
Refines, combines, and varies fundamental movement skills and develops basic specialized movement skills by demonstrating • mature performance in all fundamental movement skills, • skills for performance outcomes (e.g., speed, distance, hitting targets), and • skill combinations in small-sided • practice tasks and games and in gymnastics and dance sequences.	Assess attainment by using answer keys, checklists, or rubrics to score students' levels of success based on • mature movement criteria for all fundamental movement skills, • performance outcome goals, and • criteria for skill combinations performed • in small-sided practice tasks and games and in gymnastics and dance sequences.

Instruction engages children in learning the essential content and successfully demonstrating attainment.

Standard 1 (K-2)

Essential content	Measurement of success
Develops maturity and versatility in fundamental movement skills to be able to demonstrate • mature performance in locomotor, most stability, and some manipulative skills; • versatility in locomotor, stability, and • manipulative skills; and • smooth transitions in sequences of locomotor skills.	Assess attainment by using answer keys, checklists, or rubrics to score students' levels of success based on • mature movement criteria for each fundamental movement skill, • criteria for versatility (body, space, effort, and relationship variables), and • criteria for smooth transitions.

Instruction engages children in learning the essential content and successfully demonstrating attainment.

The preschool guidelines related to standard 1 are physical activity guidelines 1 and 3 and appropriate practice guidelines 3.3, 3.6, and 3.7: "Preschoolers should be encouraged to develop competence in fundamental motor skills that will serve as the building blocks for future motor skillfulness and physical activity" (NASPE, 2009a, p. 15).

Pre-K guideline 1 (ages 3–5) related to Standard 1

Essential content	Measurement of success
Develops emerging elementary stage of fundamental movement skills. • Performs emerging elementary characteristics of locomotor, stability and manipulative skills.	Assess attainment by using checklists to score students' levels of success based on emerging-elementary movement criteria for each fundamental movement skill.

Instruction engages children in learning the essential content and successfully demonstrating attainment.

Figure 8.5 Alignment chart for standard 1.

Standard 2: "The physically literate individual applies knowledge of concepts, principles, strategies, and tactics related to movement and performance" (SHAPE America, 2014a, p. 12). "The intent of this standard is facilitation of learners' ability to use cognitive information to understand and enhance motor skill acquisition and performance. This includes the application of concepts from disciplines such as motor learning and development, sport psychology and sociology, and biomechanics and exercise physiology" (NASPE, 2004, p. 21).

Standard 2 (grades 3–5)

Essential content	Measurement of success
Applies concepts to authentic movement settings by • combining elements of body, space, effort, and relationships with the performance of skills and skill combinations in small-sided practice tasks and games and in gymnastics and dance environments; and • using offensive and defensive strategies and tactics in small-sided practice tasks.	Assess attainment by using answer keys, checklists, or rubrics to score students' levels of success based on • correct performance of movement concepts with skills and combinations in games and gymnastics and dance environments, • use of strategies and tactics in small-sided games, • descriptions and explanations of movement concepts, and • application of concepts from strategies and tactics.

Instruction engages children in learning the essential content and successfully demonstrating attainment.

Standard 2 (K-2)

Essential content	Measurement of success
Establishes a movement vocabulary and applies introductory concepts by • identifying and performing movement • concepts of the body, space, effort, and • relationships in order to vary the quality of movement; and • differentiating between movement concepts.	Assess attainment by using answer keys, checklists, or rubrics to score students' levels of success based on • performance of movement concepts and • identification of and differentiations between movement concepts.

Instruction engages children in learning the essential content and successfully demonstrating attainment.

The preschool guideline related to standard 2 is appropriate practice guideline 3.3.2: "Preschoolers should gain a cognitive understanding of the skills and concepts they are exploring and add to their movement vocabulary" (NASPE, 2009b, p. 15).

Pre-K guideline 2 (ages 3–5) related to Standard 2

Essential content	Measurement of success
Develops a movement vocabulary. Recognizes fundamental movement skills. Recognizes basic movement concepts addressing body, space, effort, and relationship awareness.	Assess attainment by using checklists to score students' levels of success based on • student performance of fundamental movement skills in response to teacher prompts and • student performance of basic movement concepts in response to teacher prompts.

Figure 8.6 Alignment chart for standard 2.

Standard 3: "The physically literate individual demonstrates the knowledge and skills to achieve and maintain a health-enhancing level of physical activity and fitness" (SHAPE America, 2014a, p. 12). The intent of this standard is establishment of patterns of regular participation in physical activity and acquiring the knowledge and skills to achieve and maintain physical fitness (NASPE, 2004).

Standard 3 (grades 3–5)

Essential content	Measurement of success
Uses physical activity knowledge by • charting and analyzing participation in physical activity outside of school for fitness benefit. Uses fitness knowledge by • describing and applying FITT* guidelines to the components of health-related fitness, • identifying the need for warm-up and cooldown in relationship to various physical activities, • monitoring physiological indicators of moderate to vigorous physical activity and adjusting activity levels accordingly, and • interpreting and understanding the significance of fitness test results and designing a fitness plan with help from the teacher.	Assess attainment by using answer keys, checklists, or rubrics to score students' levels of success in terms of knowledge about physical activity and fitness. Evaluate physical activity knowledge by documentation of • regular participation in physical activity with logs such as Activitygram and Activity Log (Fitnessgram) and • Presidential Active Lifestyle Award materials from the President's Challenge youth fitness program. Evaluate fitness knowledge by observation of • safe and correct technique when performing activities for each component of fitness. Evaluate students' ability to • apply FITT guidelines to the components of health-related fitness, • describe the importance of warming up and cooling down, • monitor physiological indicators and adjust moderate to vigorous activity levels, and • interpret test results from Fitnessgram or the President's Challenge and design a fitness plan.

Instruction engages children in learning the essential content and successfully demonstrating attainment.

*FITT guidelines: Frequency (how often), Intensity (how hard), Time (how long) and Type (mode of activity/exercise) are used to improve performance with each of the components of fitness.

Standard 3 (K-2)

Essential content	Measurement of success
Uses physical activity knowledge by • describing and actively engaging in physical activities outside of physical education class. Uses fitness knowledge by • engaging in and identifying moderate to vigorous physical activity (MVPA) and • recognizing the effects of MVPA on the heart and how one's body can be used as resistance to develop muscular strength and endurance.	Assess attainment by using answer keys, checklists, or rubrics to score students' levels of success in terms of knowledge about physical activity and fitness. Evaluate physical activity knowledge by • documentation of students' descriptions of physical activity in physical activity participation. Evaluate fitness knowledge by observation of • safe and correct technique for fitness activities and • students' recognition of physiological signs of MVPA.

Instruction engages children in learning the essential content and successfully demonstrating attainment.

The preschool guidelines related to standard 3 are physical activity guidelines 1, 2, 4, and 5 and appropriate practice guideline 3.4.1 and 3.5.1:

Guideline 1: Preschoolers should accumulate at least 60 minutes of structured physical activity each day (NASPE, 2009a, p. 24).

Guideline 2: Preschoolers should engage in unstructured physical activity for 60 minutes or more each day and should not be sedentary for more than 60 minutes at a time, except when sleeping (NASPE, 2009a, p. 24).

Figure 8.7 Alignment chart for standard 3.

(continued)

Figure 8.7 *(continued)*

Guideline 4: They should have access to safe indoor and outdoor areas for performing large-muscle activity (NASPE, 2009a, p. 24).

Guideline 5: Caregivers and parents should provide opportunities for structured and unstructured physical activity (NASPE, 2009a, p. 24).

Appropriate Practice 3.4: Teachers should foster regular participation by extending in-class activity lessons to community and family activities (NASPE, 2009b p. 15).

Appropriate Practice 3.5: Teachers should provide opportunities for developing health-related fitness (NASPE 2009b p. 16).

Pre-K guideline 3 (ages 3–5) related to Standard 3

Essential content	Measurement of success
Participates in unstructured physical activity by • engaging in enjoyable movement activities intermittently throughout the day, both indoors and outdoors and both during and outside of school. Participates in structured physical activity by • engaging in a variety of moderate to vigorous physical activities sustained for increasing periods of time.	Assess attainment by using checklists to score students' levels of participation based on observation of • voluntary participation in unstructured physical activity during allotted playtime and • sustained participation for longer periods of time during structured activity and by evaluating • classroom teacher's logs of student activity during school and • family reports of regular student participation in physical activity.

Instruction engages children in learning the essential content and successfully demonstrating attainment.

Standard 4: "The physically literate individual exhibits responsible personal and social behavior that respects self and others" (SHAPE America, 2014a, p. 12). "The intent of this standard is achievement of self-initiated behaviors that promote personal and group success with emphasis on developing respect for individual similarities and differences through positive interaction among participants in physical activity" (NASPE, 2004, p. 39).

Standard 4 (grades 3–5)

Essential content	Measurement of success
Works independently, in pairs and small groups, and participates cooperatively in physical activities by • identifying the purpose for and following activity-specific safe practices, rules, procedures, and etiquette; • working independently and productively for longer periods of time; • accepting responsibility for personal and interpersonal behavior in physical activity environments; • working cooperatively and involving others of various skill abilities in physical activities and group projects; and • respectfully listening and giving corrective feedback to peers.	Assess attainment by using answer keys, checklists, or rubrics to score students' levels of success based on observation of • following safe practices, rules, procedures and etiquette; • working independently and productively; • cooperating with others during peer feedback and goal-directed pursuits; • accepting rule-infraction decisions positively; and • assessing and accepting responsibility for their own behavior problems without blaming others and on evaluating student identification of • safe practices, rules, procedures, and etiquette; and • behaviors representing independent and productive work, cooperation, respect, and self-responsibility.

Instruction engages children in learning the essential content and successfully demonstrating attainment.

Standard 4 (K-2)

Essential content	Measurement of success
Recognizes classroom rules, procedures, andsafety; tackles challenges; works independently and builds a foundation for successful interpersonal communication during group activity by • using and recognizing safe practices, rules, and procedures; • working independently with others in partner environments; • cooperating with others by taking turns, assisting when they need help, and sharing (equipment, ideas, and peer feedback); and • staying on task, following directions, and honestly reporting the results of own work.	Assess attainment by using answer keys, checklists, or rubrics to score students' levels of success based on observation of • using safe practices, rules, and procedures; • cooperating with others by taking turns, helping, and sharing; and • staying on task, following directions, and reporting results honestly and on evaluating student recognition of • safe practices, rules, and procedures; and • behaviors representing cooperation, honesty, and on-task participation.

Instruction engages children in learning the essential content and successfully demonstrating attainment.

The preschool guidelines related to standard 4 are appropriate practice guidelines 1.1.7 and 1.6.2: "Preschoolers adhere to fair and simple rules, accept responsibility for their own behavior, (NASPE, 2009b, p. 7) and cooperate with others" (NASPE, 2009b, p. 10).

Pre-K guideline 4 (ages 3–5) related to Standard 4

Essential content	Measurement of success
Behaves and cooperates by • using safe practices and following rules, • staying on task and following directions, and • cooperating with others (i.e., taking turns and sharing equipment).	Assess attainment by using checklists to score students' levels of participation based on observation of • using safe practices and following rules, • staying on task and following directions, and • cooperating with others by taking turns and sharing equipment.

Instruction engages children in learning the essential content and successfully demonstrating attainment.

Figure 8.8 Alignment chart for standard 4.

Standard 5: "The physically literate individual recognizes the value of physical activity for health, enjoyment, challenge, self-expression, and/or social interaction" (SHAPE America, 2014a, p. 12). "The intent of this standard is development of the understanding of the intrinsic values and benefits of participating in physical activity" (NASPE, 2004, p. 45).

Standard 5 (grades 3–5)

Essential content	Measurement of success
Recognizes the value of physical activity by • attributing success and improvement to effort and practice; • choosing appropriate levels of challenge to develop success; • selecting and practicing skills needing improvement; • describing the social benefits gained from participation in physical activity; • explaining the health benefits and positive feelings associated with participation in physical activity; • positively participating with others; and • analyzing physical activities for enjoyment and challenge and identifying reasons for positive and negative responses.	Assess attainment by using answer keys, checklists, or rubrics to score students' levels of success based on observation of • interacting positively with others and • choosing appropriate levels of challenge and evaluation of students' • analysis of reasons for enjoying or not enjoying physical activities, • attribution of success and improvement to effort and practice, • selection and appropriate practice of skills for improvement, and • explanations of the health benefits and positive feelings associated with participation in physical activity.
Instruction that engages children in learning the essential content and successfully demonstrating attainment.	

Standard 5 (K-2)

Essential content	Measurement of success
Recognizes the value of physical activity by • trying new movements and skills, • persisting when not initially successful, • identifying enjoyable movement activities, and • describing the relationship between physical activity and good health.	Assess attainment by using answer keys, checklists, or rubrics to score students' levels of success based on observation of • trying and persisting when learning new skills and on evaluation of students' • descriptions of the relationship between physical activity and good health, • identification of enjoyable physical activities, and • recognition of behaviors that demonstrate trying and persisting to gain new skills.
Instruction engages children in learning the essential content and successfully demonstrating attainment.	

The preschool guideline related to standard 5 is appropriate practice guideline 1.2.1: Preschoolers express a sense of joy when engaged in physical activity (NASPE, 2009b).

Pre-K guideline 5 (ages 3–5) related to Standard 5

Essential content	Measurement of success
Recognizes the value of physical activity by • engaging in repetitive movements, • voluntarily choosing to participate in physical activity, and • expressing enjoyment verbally and nonverbally while participating in physical activity.	Assess attainment by using checklists to score students' levels of participation based on observation of • engagement in repetitive movements, • voluntary choice of participation in physical activity, and • verbal and nonverbal expressions of enjoyment.
Instruction engages children in learning the essential content and successfully demonstrating attainment.	

Figure 8.9 Alignment chart for standard 5.

Big Ideas

- The five national content standards for physical education (SHAPE America, 2014a, p. 12) constitute large goals that focus broadly on what students should know, be able to do, and behave like as physically literate individuals. Those goals are as follows:
  - To demonstrate "competency in a variety of motor skills and movement patterns"
  - To apply "knowledge of concepts, principles, strategies, and tactics related to movement and performance"
  - To demonstrate "the knowledge and skills to achieve and maintain a health-enhancing level of physical activity and fitness"
  - To exhibit "responsible personal and social behavior that respects self and others"
  - To recognize "the value of physical activity for health, enjoyment, challenge, self-expression, and/or social interaction"

  - Unpacking standards is a process of clarifying (1) what each standard means, (2) how student success can be measured, and (3) how each standard can be achieved. The process of using backward design to unpack the standards helps teachers align or make sure all three parts match each other. Step 1 in the process involves determining the intent of the standard so that you know what the goal is (where you're going). Once you know the intent, you can determine the essential content—what students need to know and be able to do in order to reach the goal. Step 2 involves deciding what acceptable and unacceptable performance of the essential content look like and how you will measure performance (e.g., project, test, performance). Step 3 involves designing the learning experiences that will help students learn and practice in order to become knowledgeable and skilled enough to reach the goal (i.e., the standard) at an acceptable level.

  - The physical activity guidelines and appropriate practice guidelines for preschool students (NASPE, 2009a, 2009b) match the national standards for K-12 physical education. These guidelines indicate the amount of structured and unstructured daily physical activity needed for children's fitness and health. They also address the need for children to develop fundamental movement skills, gain cognitive understanding of movement skills and concepts, develop self-control and cooperative behavior, and express a sense of joy when engaged in physical activity.

  Visit the web resource for learning activities, video clips, and review questions.

Chapter 9

Assessing Student Learning

Key Concepts

- Distinguishing between psychomotor, cognitive, fitness, and affective assessments

- Describing the difference between product and process assessments and how they are used to assess progress toward psychomotor and fitness goals

- Distinguishing between methods of assessment and scoring tools and how they are used to assess progress toward psychomotor, cognitive, fitness, and affective goals

- Distinguishing between diagnostic, formative, and summative assessments and how they are used to plan and execute the learning process

- Describing the four-step process for designing summative assessments

- Explaining how to use standards-based grading

Chapter 8 examined the national standards (SHAPE America, 2014) that reflect what K-12 students should know, be able to do, and behave like as a result of a quality physical education program. For each standard, grade-level student outcomes are used to identify the essential content that students need to know and be able to do by grades 2, 5, 8, and 12 in order to become physically literate and adopt a physically active lifestyle. As you know, clarifying student learning goals is a crucial first step in the design of standards-based curricula and learning experiences. You need to know the goal before you can determine how to get there! This chapter focuses on the next step—determining what constitutes acceptable evidence to demonstrate that students have achieved the goal.

UNDERSTANDING ASSESSMENT

Lambert (2007) defines standards-based assessment as "the process of determining whether and to what degree a student can demonstrate, in context, his or her understanding and ability relative to identified standards of learning" (p. 12). Demonstrating learning requires something tangible in the form of a performance that can be observed or a product that can be examined and assessed with predetermined criteria. Demonstrating learning *in context* is referred to as **authentic assessment**, which implies that the performance or product represents the student's understanding and use of learned content in a real-life situation.

For example, one goal for standard 4 (grades 3 through 5) is to give corrective feedback respectfully to peers (SHAPE America, 2014). Assessment for this goal involves having students observe peers performing a skill, compare their movements with teacher-designed critical elements, and provide feedback to the peers about their performances. Concurrently, the teacher uses a scoring tool with specific criteria to assess the observers' ability to detect whether the critical elements were performed correctly and to assess whether the feedback was appropriate and respectful. Thus, in order to determine whether students can meet the learning goal of giving corrective feedback respectfully to peers, the teacher must assess students in the role of observer and supplier of feedback about movement performance. The peer feedback could be structured by use of a rubric, such as the one shown in figure 9.1.

To be sure that assessments measure attainment of the essential content of a specific learning goal, teachers make sure that the evidence collected matches the *focus* of the essential content. As you may recall from chapter 8, alignment is the process of using the focus of the essential content as the focus of assessment and instruction. How do you know that alignment was achieved between the learning goal giving corrective feedback respectfully to peers and the assessment Peer feedback observation form used in the example above?

Alignment helps assure that what teachers measure and how they measure it demonstrate how and what they intended for students to learn. For example, if the learning goal is for students to use the elements of correct form when running, would the teacher observe students' form as they run or time how long they run? Or if the learning goal is for students to choose an open space through which to pass a ball, would the teacher observe students' passing form or their placement of the pass? Be careful with this one. You might want to say, "Both!" And, indeed, teachers may ultimately want both, but measuring correct decision making about passing enables teachers to help students focus on the importance of avoiding an interception by looking for and passing the ball through the open space, even if the pass itself was inaccurate.

To align assessments with learning goals, teachers must focus on what, how, and when to assess.

- **What:** Am I assessing a psychomotor, fitness, cognitive, or affective goal?

Observer _____   Performer _____

Skill	Cue detected	Cue undetected	Feedback respectful and appropriate	Feedback respectful and inappropriate	Feedback disrespectful or absent
Cue 1:					
Cue 2:					
Cue 3:					

Scoring

Proficient = all cues detected, feedback respectful and appropriate

Developing = some cues undetected, some feedback inappropriate

Basic = cues undetected and/or feedback disrespectful or absent

Figure 9.1 Peer feedback observation form.

- **How:** What methods of assessments and scoring tools do I use to determine goal achievement?
  - What developmentally appropriate, authentic types of assessment will enable students to demonstrate what they know or can do?
  - What criteria can be used to score how well students know or can perform the learning goal?
- **When:** What phase of learning am I assessing?
  - Prior to learning (diagnostic assessment)?
  - During the process of learning (formative assessment)?
  - At the end of a unit or period of instruction (summative assessment)?

WHAT TO ASSESS

In physical education, we must identify just what a particular learning goal entails. Specifically, is it psychomotor (motor performance), fitness related (physical capacity), cognitive (knowledge), or affective (personal or social behavior)? The following subsections of the chapter begin with a description of standard 2 learning goals because they influence the learning goals for knowledge and understanding in standard 1 (psychomotor), standard 3 (fitness), standard 4 (personal and social behavior), and standard 5 (the value of physical activity). For instance, psychomotor goals include performance of cues to demonstrate correct movement technique. An accompanying cognitive goal would be recognizing or describing the cues for correct performance of a skill (stepping forward with opposite foot when throwing a ball).

Cognitive Learning Goals and Assessments

Cognitive learning goals address what students need to *know* in order to understand and enhance their acquisition and performance of psychomotor, fitness, and affective skills. Therefore, cognitive assessments measure how well students can demonstrate understanding of movement concepts, principles, strategies, and tactics as applied to the learning and performance of physical activities. The concepts used in physical education derive from the fields of motor behavior, biomechanics, social psychology, and exercise physiology.

Cognitive assessments require students to think about concepts and demonstrate that they have been learned. Bloom (1956) categorized thinking into levels ranging from easiest to most difficult. For example, the easiest level of thinking involves knowledge (i.e., recalling facts), whereas application (using facts in a new situation) is more difficult. For each of Bloom's levels, Lujan (2008) described thinking actions (verbs) and developed prompts to help teachers consistently help students use the lower order or higher order levels of thinking that are appropriate for them.

Table 9.1 defines each level of thinking, indicates the action words associated with each level, and provides examples of learning goals from the fields in physical education for pre-K, K-2, and grades 3 through 5.

Pre-K children are beginning the preoperational stage of cognitive development by using their experiences to come to know their world. To facilitate this process, teachers engage children in exploring the movement environment by using a variety of fundamental movements (e.g., running, skipping, throwing, balancing), movement concepts (e.g., low, over, fast, next to), and affective behaviors (e.g., following simple directions, playing alongside or cooperating with others in simple tasks). In turn, pre-K children demonstrate their knowledge by recognizing, identifying, or responding to teacher prompts in order to perform a skill, movement concept, or affective behavior.

An assessment to determine preschool children's understanding of a movement concept could look something like this: Give each student five flash cards, each of which pictures a child engaged in one of the movement concepts. Position yourself in front of the students, who are facing you, and say, "Show me the card with the child moving at a low level." As students each hold a card up, scan the group and using a list of names, check the names of students whose card choice is incorrect. Have all of the students put their chosen cards back into their piles of five. After completing all five questions, score the results, perhaps using the following system: 4 or more correct = proficient, 2 or 3 correct = developing, 1 correct = beginning, and 0 correct = undeveloped.

K-2 children are advancing through the preoperational stage of cognitive development by using elementary logic and reasoning to frame their movement experiences and by using symbols to represent objects in the environment. To facilitate

Table 9.1 Levels of Thinking

Level of thinking	Action words	Learning goal examples (National Association for Sport and Physical Education [NASPE], 2004)
Knowledge—recalling information in the form in which it was learned	Demonstrate recall by recognizing, recalling, defining, listing, repeating, or identifying who, what, when, where, and how.	Motor behavior (pre-K): Recall by performing or pointing to someone performing each fundamental skill called out by the teacher (walk, gallop, kick, balance on three parts). Motor behavior (K-2): Repeat cue words for the underhand throw and demonstrate or tell what each means. Social psychology (K-2): Identify sharing with a partner as a way to cooperate. Exercise physiology (K-2): Recognize changes in heart and breathing rates during moderate to vigorous physical activity.
Comprehension (prerequisite: knowledge)—using one's own words to describe or summarize facts and main ideas	Demonstrate comprehension by describing, clarifying, reviewing, illustrating, restating, paraphrasing, summarizing, or giving examples.	Biomechanics (grades 3–5): Describe why it is necessary to transfer weight from the back leg to the front leg during actions that send an object forward. Exercise physiology (grades 3–5): Provide examples of physical activities that enhance fitness. Motor behavior (grades 3–5): "Explain two offensive strategies . . . to increase your chance of being successful when participating in . . ." (Giles-Brown, 2006, p. 164).
Application (prerequisites: knowledge and comprehension)—using ideas, facts, rules, principles, procedures, and concepts in new, real-life situations	Demonstrate application by showing, acting out, demonstrating, performing, changing, modifying, solving, constructing, designing, or developing.	Social psychology (grades 3–5): Use ideas about safety to appropriately arrange soccer equipment for a kicking-on-goal task. Exercise physiology (grades 3–5): "Maintain heart rate within the target heart rate zone for a specified length of time during an aerobic activity" (NASPE, 2004, p. 35).
Analysis (prerequisites: knowledge and comprehension)—separating ideas, concepts, principles, and procedures into parts and showing the relationships between the parts	Demonstrate analysis by classifying, categorizing, comparing, contrasting, and making connections between parts.	Exercise physiology (grades 3–5): "Charts and analyzes physical activity outside physical education class for fitness benefits of activities" (SHAPE America, 2014, p. 34).
Evaluation (prerequisites: knowledge, comprehension, application, analysis)—judging the value of ideas and using criteria to support views	Demonstrate evaluation by judging, critiquing, or interpreting the importance, meaning, or significance of something and by showing how the evaluation is informed by the national physical education standards.	Motor behavior (grades 3–5): Use a checklist to interpret the critical elements of a catch made by a peer and provide feedback about correct and incorrect movements.
Synthesis (prerequisites: knowledge, comprehension, application, analysis)—combining concepts, facts, and ideas in order to create something new	Demonstrate creation and synthesis by incorporating, integrating, or combining facts, ideas, or concepts in order to develop, create, or design something new.	Motor behavior (grades 3–5): Combine "locomotor skills and movement concepts to create and perform a dance with a group" (SHAPE America, 2014, p. 28).

this process, you can engage these children in exploring the movement environment by combining fundamental movements and movement concepts (e.g., running along curved pathways, skipping to the beat of the drum, throwing a ball to targets at different heights and distances, balancing to make various body shapes with some parts on equipment), performing and identifying movement cues for fundamental skills (e.g., "step with the opposite foot" and "release toward the target"), and helping them understand the effect of moderate to vigorous physical activity on body systems (e.g., heart and breathing rate increase as physical activity becomes more vigorous).

Since primary-grade children are becoming less egocentric, they can be challenged to stay on task; follow simple rules and procedures; report results honestly; and demonstrate cooperation by sharing, helping others, and resolving conflicts peacefully. They can demonstrate their knowledge by recognizing, identifying, and defining movement skill cues, movement concepts, and appropriate and inappropriate affective behaviors. They can also respond to teacher prompts to perform skill and movement-concept combinations or demonstrate affective behaviors.

For example, you could use a scenario such as the following one to allow a K-2 learner to demonstrate understanding of a physical activity concept, in this case how physical activity affects the body: "Your friend Alex was sitting on a park bench while petting her dog Spot. All of a sudden, a squirrel ran by and Spot ran after it. Alex jumped up and ran after Spot. Alex ran and ran, chasing Spot all over the park until the squirrel ran up a tree and Spot stopped. Describe everything that was happening to Alex's body after all that running." Students should be able to identify various effects of the physical activity, such as faster heart rate, faster breathing (or being out of breath), feeling tired, and sweating. You could score the results as follows: listing three or more effects = advanced, 2 effects = proficient, 1 effect = developing, and 0 effects = undeveloped.

Students in grades 3 through 5 progress into the concrete operational stage of cognitive development, in which they use logic grounded in personal experience and gain the capacity to mentally organize and modify their thoughts; as a result, they can apply movement concepts to real-life physical activity (SHAPE America, 2014). To facilitate this process, you can engage these students in performing and identifying movement cues

for fundamental and specialized skills; observing movement cues and giving feedback to peers; and understanding and applying concepts from biomechanics, exercise physiology, motor behavior, and social psychology. Students who advance into the formal operational stage of cognitive development can also engage in problem solving, planning, and predicting next steps. Therefore, you can challenge students in the formal operational stage to strategize during game play, use problem solving to address team-building challenges, and consider multiple variables in order to create games and dance and gymnastics sequences.

Students in grades 3 through 5 realize that positive interactions require them to consider the perspectives of others, accept responsibility for their actions, treat others with respect, and accept differences. They also know that they need to be able to work independently and productively, set goals, and monitor their pursuit of those goals.

Figure 9.2 presents an assessment that allows children in grades 3 through 5 to demonstrate understanding of a fitness concept.

In summary, cognitive learning goals address what students need to *know* in order to understand and enhance their acquisition and performance of psychomotor, fitness, and affective skills. They provide the focus of standard 2 and are also found in all the standards.

Psychomotor Learning Goals and Assessments

Psychomotor learning goals address movement skill performance, which can provide far-reaching benefits: "Mastering movement fundamentals establishes a foundation to facilitate continued movement skill acquisition and gives students the capacity for successful and advanced levels of performance to further the likelihood of participation on a daily basis" (NASPE, 2004, p. 15). In other words, these goals help learners develop tools that enable them to enjoy a life of healthy physical activity.

Psychomotor assessments, in turn, measure how well students perform motor skills. Psychomotor goals and assessments are focused either on the process or on the product of movement performance. The *process* of performance involves how well the movements are executed—that is, whether they are performed with correct mechanics. Therefore, **process assessments** are most often associated with learners in the beginning levels of learning movement skills, because their goal is to gain consistency in performing movement patterns. Process assessments are also used to evaluate the performance of form-based closed skills, as in gymnastics, dance, and figure skating. Figure 9.3 shows a K-2 process assessment for the underhand throw.

The *product* of performance consists of the outcome of the movement skill performance. **Product assessments** measure such things as how high someone jumped, how far someone threw, how many goals a team scored, how accurate a shot was, and what result a certain game tactic produced. When assessing outcome-specific closed skills (e.g., those used in golf, bowling, archery, shooting basketball free throws, and making pitches and serves), the focus is on getting the object to the designated target. When assessing open skills, the focus is on the series of decisions made and skills performed in order to achieve such outcomes as winning a point, scoring a goal, or outmaneu-

vering an opponent. Figure 9.4 shows a product assessment for game play in grades 3 through 5.

In summary, psychomotor learning goals address movement skill performance, are addressed in standard 1, and call for process or product assessments.

Fitness Learning Goals and Assessments

Fitness learning goals involve attaining and maintaining physical capacity. Therefore, fitness goals and assessments focus on the product of students' use of their physical capacity and the regularity of their participation in physical activity. The product of one's physical capacity is a measurement of his or her strength, endurance, flexibility, or body composition. Fitness goals are designed based on individual needs, and learners' attainment of goals is determined by comparing their physical capacity before and after a designated period of time. The

---

Assessment: Dan needs your help! He wants to set a new goal for improving his cardiorespiratory endurance. He wants to follow the Goldilocks principle by making his new goal "just right"—not too hard and not too easy. Last week, he rode his bicycle on Monday, Wednesday, and Saturday. On each of those days, he rode around the track five times, which took 20 minutes. Give Dan at least two safe choices for setting a new goal for next week. Bonus: For each new goal, circle the part (i.e., the specific letter) of the FIT acronym that is addressed by the goal (F = frequency or how often, I = intensity or how hard, and T = time or how long).

Goal 1:_____ F I T

Goal 2:_____ F I T

Goal 3: _____ F I T

Goal 4: _____ F I T

Answer Key

   Frequency: Add another day.

   Intensity: Add half a lap and ride for 20 minutes.

   Time: Add one lap or ride for up to 25 minutes.

Scoring Checklist

   Advanced: three or more safe choices

   Proficient: two safe choices

   Developing: one safe choice

   Undeveloped: no safe choices

Bonus

   Proficient: all correctly labeled

   Developing: half correctly labeled

   Beginning: fewer than half correctly labeled

Figure 9.2 Sample cognitive assessment for grades 3 through 5.

Skill: throwing a ball underhand using a mature pattern (SHAPE America, 2014, p. 28)

Underhand throw elements	Yes	Needs work
Positions feet together and shoulders square to target.		
Swings throwing arm straight back.		
Steps forward onto opposite foot.		
Swings throwing arm forward.		
Releases with arm outstretched toward target.		

Scoring:

    Proficient: yes for all

    Developing: Needs work for one or more

Figure 9.3   K-2 process assessment for the underhand throw.

Tally checklist: Record a check mark every time your partner performs the skill during the 2v2 game.

Student names	Player moves to get open.	Player passes to open teammate.	Player positions to block the passing lane.
Partner 1			
Partner 2			

Scoring

    5 or more for each skill = great offense and defense (Keep it up!)

    3 or 4 for each skill = good offense and defense (Keep improving!)

    < 3 for any skill = getting started (Keep working!)

Figure 9.4   Product assessment (grades 3 through 5) for player movement during game play.

measurements used depend on the fitness component in question. Cardiorespiratory endurance is determined by measurements of heart rate, time, and distance; flexibility by extent of stretches; strength by quantity of sets and repetitions; and body composition by percent body fat.

Standardized fitness tests are used to measure norm-referenced or criterion-referenced gains over a long period of time, usually annually or semiannually. The recommended fitness-testing program for children aged 10 or older is Fitnessgram (The Cooper Institute, 2010). Children under age 10 are not developmentally ready for fitness testing. "At young ages, physical activity is not strongly linked to physical fitness. Therefore an emphasis on structured fitness testing is not recommended for children in grades K-3. The goal at this age should be to expose children to the different test items and help them learn about the various parts of physical fitness. Self-testing is recommended as the primary means to teach children about these assessments" (The Cooper Institute, 2010, p.11). Students in grades 4 and 5, however, typically understand the components of fitness; therefore, they can use feedback from assessments to help them set and pursue physical fitness goals.

Fitnessgram (The Cooper Institute, 2010) is a physical fitness program developed by the Cooper Institute and based on the latest research in children's physical fitness. Its primary objective is to provide students, teachers, and parents with information about individual students' levels of fitness for the purpose of establishing personal programs for developing and maintaining physical fitness. Fitnessgram is intended to assess the components of health-related fitness from kindergarten through college. A key feature of Fitnessgram is that participants are not compared with each other or with national averages but with minimal health fitness standards established for each age and gender. Therefore, norms are not used for comparison of one child or group with another; instead, each child strives to reach or exceed the minimal health fitness standards, or **Healthy Fitness Zones.**

Fitnessgram addresses the following six areas and corresponding tests:

1. Aerobic capacity: 1-mile (1.6-kilometer) walk/run for time, PACER test for aerobic endurance, walk test (age 13 and older)

2. Body composition: percent body fat as assessed through triceps skinfold thickness, body mass index, and bioelectrical impedance analysis

3. Abdominal strength and endurance: curl-up

4. Trunk extensor strength and flexibility: trunk lift

5. Upper-body strength and endurance: 90-degree push-up, modified pull-up, flexed-arm hang

6. Flexibility: back-saver sit-and-reach, shoulder stretch

Once you have conducted initial fitness assessments, you can print out a Fitnessgram report for each student. The report contains recommendations for physical activity program options to help students make it into the Healthy Fitness Zones in areas where they need to improve. It also includes a section for parents explaining the value of physical activity.

An important complement to Fitnessgram was created in the form of Physical Best (NASPE, 2011a), a complete educational program for teaching health-related fitness concepts. Activity guides are available for both the elementary and secondary levels. These guides include a wealth of instructional activities that are developmentally appropriate, educationally sound, fun, and relevant to today's students. All Physical Best materials meet the requirements of the SHAPE America national standards for physical education (SHAPE America, 2014). A teacher's guide is also available (NASPE, 2011b), and it would be a valuable resource in your personal professional library.

Another useful tool can be found in the **Brockport Physical Fitness Test** (Winnick & Short, 2014), which is a unique health-related, criterion-referenced fitness test for children of age 10 to 17

years with disability. The test consists of 27 potential items—potential because you can customize a test battery for an individual or group depending on particular needs. The test is designed to work in conjunction with the Physical Best educational resources once you have determined your students' levels of fitness and identified their fitness goals, and the Brockport software can be used in conjunction with Fitnessgram software. The Brockport test is adaptable to—and provides fitness parameters for—individuals with mild mental retardation, visual impairment, spinal cord injury, cerebral palsy, congenital anomaly, and amputation.

In addition to using a standardized fitness test (e.g., Fitnessgram), it is also important to conduct formative assessment of children's fitness. Figure 9.5 presents a product assessment for upper-body strength.

Although fitness goals focus primarily on students' capacity, the *process* of their movements matters as well. Indeed, proper technique is critical for safe and optimal movement performance as students repetitively run, stretch, jump rope, or perform push-ups, sit-ups, seal walks, or inchworms. Figure 9.6 shows a process assessment for jogging form in grades 3 through 5.

The regularity of students' participation in fitness activities is measured through a self-report log, such as the Activity Log module available in Fitnessgram/Activitygram 8.0 (The Cooper Institute, 2010). Over a designated period of time, students record some or all of the components of the FITT principle—that is, the frequency, intensity, time (duration), and type of physical activity in which they engaged. Since regular participation in physical activity is a lifetime goal, students' attention is focused on how to monitor their participation outside of school and how participation affects their health.

Figure 9.7 presents the daily self-report log from the *Physical Best Activity Guide* (NASPE, 2011a), in which students record the frequency, intensity, and time of their participation in aerobic activity. The figure also presents the worksheet with which students determine goals using data from the previous week. In addition, the figure includes an assessment and scoring rubric for analyzing the log and worksheet results in order to determine how well students have understood the use of the FITT principle.

Fitness learning goals address attaining and maintaining physical capacity, are usually found in standard 3, and use assessments of the fitness

For each activity completed, record a check mark in the Completed column. If your time or number of reps differ from the challenge, record the information in the Actual column.

Exercise	Challenge	Completed	Actual
Modified push-up	5 reps		
Bent-arm hang	1 minute		
Horizontal ladder	2 crossings		
Medicine-ball catch	10 throws and catches		

Scoring:

Advanced = Challenge was exceeded on two or more and met on all others.

Proficient = Challenge was met on 3 or 4.

Developing = Challenge was not met on 2 of 4.

Beginning = Challenge not met on 3 or 4.

Figure 9.5 Product assessment (grades 3 through 5) for development of upper-body strength.

Adapted from Virgilio 1997

Jogging form elements	Yes	Needs work
Runs tall and leans slightly forward.		
Swings legs from hips with knees bent.		
Lands on heels with weight rolling along the outside portion of foot to toes.		
Points toes straight ahead.		
Swings arms straight forward and backward with hands relaxed.		
Breathes from stomach in an even rhythm.		

Scoring:

Proficient = yes for all

Developing = Needs work for one or more.

Figure 9.6 Process assessment (grades 3 through 5) for jogging form.

Adapted, by permission, from S. Virgilio, 2012, *Fitness education for children: A team approach,* 2nd ed. (Champaign, IL: Human Kinetics), 66.

components and the regularity of participation in physical activity.

Affective Learning Goals and Assessments

Affective learning goals focus on students' personal and social responsibility and their identification of the benefits of physical activity. Affective assessments about personal and social responsibility measure the learner's achievement of self-initiated behaviors related to following rules, playing safely, staying on task, respecting others, and working cooperatively with partners and small groups. These assessments are usually twofold: process oriented and cognitive. The process-oriented portion measures students' demonstration of *behavior* typifying personal or social responsibility in a movement setting, as well as their ability to recognize or reflect on their own or others' use of responsibility-related behaviors. The cognitive portion of the assessment measures students' *knowledge* of how and why behaviors typifying personal and social responsibility are important.

Log

For each day, place a check mark under the F (for frequency) if you participated in your chosen outside-of-school aerobic activity. Under the I (for intensity), write M (for moderate) or V (for vigorous). Under the T (for time), write the number of minutes for which you did the activity.

Week 1			Week 2			Week 3			Week 4		
Monday			Monday			Monday			Monday		
F	I	T	F	I	T	F	I	T	F	I	T
Tuesday			Tuesday			Tuesday			Tuesday		
F	I	T	F	I	T	F	I	T	F	I	T
Wednesday			Wednesday			Wednesday			Wednesday		
F	I	T	F	I	T	F	I	T	F	I	T
Thursday			Thursday			Thursday			Thursday		
F	I	T	F	I	T	F	I	T	F	I	T
Friday			Friday			Friday			Friday		
F	I	T	F	I	T	F	I	T	F	I	T
Saturday			Saturday			Saturday			Saturday		
F	I	T	F	I	T	F	I	T	F	I	T
Sunday			Sunday			Sunday			Sunday		
F	I	T	F	I	T	F	I	T	F	I	T

Worksheet

Record your progress for week 1. Before week 2, set a goal to increase your activity in *one* training area. For example, you could increase the frequency by one day per week, increase the intensity on one day per week, or increase the time each day. By week 3 and 4, you could increase in *two* training areas.

Week 2	Week 3	Week 4
Goal:	Goal:	Goal:

Assessment of Fitness Log and Worksheet Results

1. How were you able to safely build up to a higher frequency, intensity, and time over the course of the month?
2. How might the changes have affected your aerobic fitness?

Scoring

Advanced

- Described a safe build-up of changes throughout the month by appropriately increasing frequency, intensity, or time each week.
- Made increases in all three training areas by the last week.
- Described changes in physical capacity by comparing differences between weeks 1 and 4 in measures of the training principles.
- Related changes to at least five health benefits of aerobic fitness.

Figure 9.7 Self-report fitness log, worksheet, and assessment for aerobics FITT (grades 3 through 5).

Based on NASPE 2011a.

Figure 9.7   *(continued)*

Proficient

- Described a safe build-up of changes throughout the month by appropriately increasing frequency, intensity, or time each week.
- Made increases in two training areas by the last week.
- Described changes in physical capacity by comparing differences between weeks 1 and 4 in measures of the training principles.
- Related changes to at least three health benefits of aerobic fitness.

Developing

- Described safe changes throughout the month by increasing either frequency, intensity, or time.
- Described changes in physical capacity by comparing differences between weeks 1 and 4 in measurement of one training principle.
- Related changes to one or two health benefits of aerobic fitness.

Beginning

- Described changes based on one training principle.
- Described changes in physical capacity as "feeling better," without regard to differences based on measures of training from weeks 1 and 4.

For example, as depicted in figure 9.8, a teacher conducting a process assessment might observe and record students' behaviors of encouraging others and avoidance of put-downs during several team-building activities. After the activities, the teacher might follow up by having students complete a set of partial prompts about how they felt when giving and receiving encouragement and about how positive social interactions affected the class environment (see figure 9.9). In the cognitive assessment, the teacher might have students write or talk about examples of positive and negative interactions and about how positive social interactions are beneficial (see figure 9.10). The process and cognitive assessments are especially important when students are first learning specific behaviors of personal or social responsibility. Reflecting on their feelings and describing the benefits of being socially responsible helps students internalize the notion that, rather than simply reacting negatively without thinking, they can *choose* verbal and nonverbal behaviors to interact positively with others.

Learning goal: Demonstrate acceptance by encouraging others and refraining from put-downs

Observation checklist: Place a check mark in the appropriate box each time that students use either encouraging or put-down behaviors.

Scoring

Advanced: Exclusively used encouraging behaviors as a sincere expression of empathy and support.

Proficient: Used only encouraging behaviors.

Developing: Used more encouraging behaviors than put-down behaviors.

Undeveloped: Used more put-down behaviors than encouraging behaviors.

Student	Encouraging behaviors	Put-down behaviors

Figure 9.8   Observation process assessment for encouraging others (grades 3 through 5).

Learning goal: Demonstrate acceptance by encouraging others and refraining from put-downs.

Complete the following statements:

    During this class, I encouraged my classmates by . . .

    My classmates reacted to my encouragements by . . .

    When I received encouragements, I . . .

    During this class, put-downs were . . . and caused classmates to . . .

    During this class, I did not use encouragements because . . .

    In order to be able to use encouragements, I need . . .

Scoring

Advanced

- Reported the use of verbal and nonverbal encouragements and the perception that self and classmates reacted positively and contributed more to the group when receiving encouragement.
- Accurately reflected the use of put-downs and how they negatively affected classmates, self, progress, or some combination of these.

Proficient

- Reported the use of verbal and nonverbal encouragements and the perception that self and classmates reacted positively when receiving encouragement and negatively when receiving put-downs.

Developing

- Reported the use of verbal and nonverbal encouragements (or of just one of these two).
- Either reported that reactions to encouragements and put-downs were limited to feelings of good and bad, respectively, or reported not using encouragements and what needs to happen to enable self to use them.

Beginning

- Reported the use of verbal and nonverbal encouragements (or of just one of these two) or reported no use of encouraging behaviors and gave no information about how to enable self to use them.

Figure 9.9   Reflection process assessment for encouraging others (grades 3 through 5).

Learning goal: Demonstrate acceptance by encouraging others and refraining from put-downs.

Assessment: Write or speak a story, rap, skit, or poem that helps new fourth graders learn how you and your classmates interact positively during physical education class. Make sure that they also know what *not* to do—and why.

Scoring

    Advanced: Includes verbal and nonverbal positive and negative behaviors. Conveys a clear sense that positive behaviors are appropriate and negative behaviors inappropriate. Addresses why it is important to support and uplift classmates and avoid put-downs.

    Proficient: Includes verbal and nonverbal positive and negative behaviors. Conveys a clear sense that the positive behaviors are appropriate and the negative behaviors inappropriate.

    Developing: Includes verbal and nonverbal positive and negative behaviors.

    Undeveloped: Fails to identify positive and negative behaviors.

Figure 9.10   Cognitive assessment for encouraging others (grades 3 through 5).

When assessing personal and social responsibility, it is critical to identify the positive and negative behaviors that demonstrate the affective goal. Teachers need to know what *specific* behaviors they are observing for personal or social responsibility, just as they need to know what movements to observe when assessing for correct performance of a motor skill. To meet this need, teachers often use a T-chart (see figure 9.11) to clarify personal or social responsibility behaviors by asking what the personal or social responsibility goal looks and sounds like. For example, in the case of encouragement and put-downs, you could ask, "What do encouraging behaviors and put-down behaviors look and sound like?" Identifying specific personal or social responsibility behaviors enables you to align assessment criteria with the essential content goal and then align learning activities that help students demonstrate the behaviors in physical activity settings.

Affective assessments related to awareness of the value and benefits of physical activity measure students' expressions of enjoyment when engaged in physical activity, their perseverance when learning new skills, their association of positive feelings with participation, and their identification of benefits of participation. These assessments are usually twofold: process oriented and cognitive. The process-oriented portion measures behaviors that demonstrate valuing physical activity in a movement setting. The cognitive portion measures students' ability to recognize and reflect on the benefits of physical activity and on the cause of their enjoyment: health, skill mastery, social interaction, self-expression, or personal meaning. For example, in a process assessment, you might observe and record students' perseverance and success in a multi-level movement challenge. In a cognitive assessment, you might have students write or speak about how they determined the level of challenge appropriate for them and persevered to accomplish the challenge.

In assessing for the valuing of physical activity, it is critical to identify the positive and negative behaviors that demonstrate valuing. As with personal and social responsibility, you need to know what specific behaviors you are observing for in order to detect students valuing physical activity. You can identify valuing behaviors by asking, "What does the valuing goal look and sound like?" In pre-K, children experience joy as they participate in movement activities; in K-2, they persist in trying new skills and express joy as they gain competence; and in grades 3 through 5, they identify positive feelings with participation in physical activity. Of course, you must set the scene for enjoyment and positive feelings by differentiating tasks in the movement environment to match the learners' levels of ability.

Affective learning goals address students' personal and social responsibility as indicated by standard 4 and their identification of the benefits

Encouraging Others

Looks like	Sounds like
Thumbs-up	"Way to go."
Pat on the back	"You're getting it."
Nodding	"Keep trying."
Index finger raised for "one more try"	"Give it another shot."
	"How can I help?"

Put-Downs

Looks like	Sounds like
Negative facial expression	"You're stupid."
Mocking gesture	"You're doing it wrong."
Pointing and derisive laughter	"Get out of the way."
	"Huh!" (exasperation)

Figure 9.11   T-chart assessment for identifying encouragement and put-downs.

of physical activity as indicated by standard 5. Assessments are twofold—process oriented in order to examine students' use of and reflection on their affective behaviors, and cognitive in order to determine their understanding of the effect of their behavior on themselves, others, and the achievement of group goals.

HOW TO ASSESS

There are two parts in the process of designing assessments to measure acceptable evidence for achievement of grade-level standards. First, you must choose or design the **method of assessment**—for example, quiz, exit ticket, skill demonstration, or summary of journal reflections. In other words, how will students demonstrate what they know, can do, and behave like? Second, you must choose or design the **scoring tool** to measure how well students did on the chosen assessment. Scoring tools typically take the form of an answer key (for a quiz, exit ticket, or worksheet), checklist (for a performance or product with parts), or rubric (for a performance or product with a range of possible success from poor to excellent).

When the essential content in grades K through 5 involves students in demonstrating what they *know*, use *verbs* from the grade-level student outcomes to choose or design assessment methods in which students demonstrate their ability to recognize, identify, describe, or apply what they know. For instance, students could be asked to recognize, identify, or apply a concept orally, in writing, or by drawing a picture or filling in a chart. Use the *nouns* in the grade-level student outcomes for the content—for example, effects of exercise on the body or critical elements of an underhand throw. To evaluate how well students do on the assessment, choose or design a scoring tool in the form of an answer key, checklist, or rubric.

The scoring tool contains the critical elements of the concept and indicates the quality of performance that demonstrates proficiency (mastery). When an answer key or checklist is used, the scoring is usually based on attaining some percentage of the answers correctly (e.g., 80 percent). A rubric, on the other hand, describes a range of answers presented in different levels:

- Advanced: Demonstrates in-depth knowledge or high level of skill performance.
- Proficient: Demonstrates satisfactory knowledge and adequate use of skills. Reaching this level demonstrates achievement of the standard.
- Developing: Demonstrates partial understanding and limited skill performance. The student is approaching proficiency but needs additional instruction and practice opportunities, as well as a commitment to achieving the proficient level.
- Beginning: Demonstrates little understanding and displays minimal skill. The student has a major need for additional instruction and practice opportunities.
- Undeveloped: Demonstrates no understanding and no skill elements. The child may be too immature for the outcome or need instruction and practice in prerequisite levels of skill or thinking.

The cognitive assessment chart presented in figure 9.12 illustrates assessment methods that are appropriate for the level of thinking represented by the verbs in the student outcomes, as well as the type of scoring tool that matches the level of thinking.

When the essential content involves students in demonstrating what they can *do* and *behave* like, use the action *verb* from the grade-level student outcome to design or choose process (movement form) or product (movement outcome) assessment methods that engage students in performing, demonstrating, or participating in movement, fitness, or affective skills or activities. For example, depending on the given standard, students might be asked to perform a skip, demonstrate moving to the open space in a game, or demonstrate cooperating with a partner in order to solve a problem. To evaluate how well students perform, observe the performance and use a scoring tool in the form of a process or product checklist or rubric. The performance assessment chart presented in figure 9.13 indicates assessment methods and scoring tools that match the process and product performance demands of the given skill. For each skill, the scoring tool addresses the content and level of performance necessary to reach a proficient level of achievement.

WHEN TO ASSESS

Student learning is assessed throughout the learning process. Indeed, the main purpose of assessment is to provide learners and teachers with information about where learners are in their journey toward mastery of the knowledge, skills, and dispositions designated by learning goals and standards. Aguilar (2012) referred to the embedding of assessments throughout the learning process as "creating experiences of flow" for students (p. 2). She described a synergy that develops between teachers and students when teachers create—and students engage in—instructional experiences with clear, challenging goals matched to students' abilities and accompanied by immediate feedback. More specifically, students get into a "zone of flow" and accomplish learning goals when teachers provide developmentally and individually appropriate challenges, monitor their progress, give feedback,

Assessment verb and method	Scoring tool	Assessment method and scoring tool examples
Recognize a concept by circling, checking, underlining or pointing.	Answer key	K-2: Draw an arrow to the part of the ball that you kick to make it go *high*. Answer: below the midline
Identify a concept by matching, listing, or sequencing.	Answer key	K-2: Draw a line to match the word with the pathway. C .... Zigzag —— .... Curved Z .... Straight Answer key: C .... Curved —— .... Straight Z .... Zigzag Scoring: Proficient = all correct Developing = < all correct
Describe a concept by • speaking or writing a paragraph, story, poem, rap, or newsletter; • drawing a picture, model, comic strip, or collage; • or creating a skit or kinesthetic representation.	Rubric	Grades 3–5: Write or record a story in which you describe to an alien how to move your body in order to throw a ball to hit a target. Rubric: Proficient = Describes most of the movements accurately and in the correct order. Developing = Describes some of the movements accurately and puts some in the correct order. Beginning = Describes few of the movements accurately with no regard for order.
Apply a concept by • completing a scenario, • completing a graphic organizer, • summarizing journal entries, or • logging data.	Rubric or checklist	Grades 3–5: Janice is a really good throw-tennis player. She is able to score more points than most of her opponents. Write or record an explanation of how Janice uses game tactics to win. Checklist for tactics explained: ___ Returns to base position between catches. ___ Moves opponents around court by throwing to open spaces. ___ Moves opponent to end line and then throws to front of court. ___ Throws ball quickly after catching. Scoring: Advanced = explaining 4 tactics Proficient = 3 tactics Developing = 2 tactics Beginning = 1 tactic

Figure 9.12 Cognitive assessment chart.

Assessment verb and method	Scoring tool	Assessment method and scoring tool examples
Demonstrate or perform	Observation checklist and scoring rubric	Assessment and scoring tool
Demonstrate or perform • proficient pattern in fundamental movement skills and • critical elements of specialized movement skills.	Observation checklist and scoring rubric for critical elements of movement pattern	K-2: Perform vertical jump. Cues checklist: Y N Crouch Y N Forceful extension Y N Landing on two feet Y N Bending of knees Scoring: ❏ Proficient = all yes ❏ Developing = 2 or 3 yes ❏ Undeveloped = 0 or 1 yes
Demonstrate or perform • combinations of movement concepts and fundamental movement skills.	Observation checklist and scoring rubric for critical elements of movement concepts combined with movement pattern	K-2: Perform locomotor movements and change direction on the drumbeat. Criteria for changes of direction: ❏ Quickly ❏ Smoothly ❏ Slowly ❏ Awkwardly ❏ Not at all Scoring: ❏ Proficient = quickly *and* smoothly ❏ Developing = quickly *or* smoothly ❏ Undeveloped = slowly, awkwardly, or not at all
Demonstrate or perform • combinations and sequences of form-based closed skills (dance and gymnastics).	Observation checklist and scoring rubric for critical elements of combining skills	Grades 3–5: Perform forward roll, jump with half turn, and backward roll. Criteria: 1. Crouch at end of roll becomes takeoff position for jump. ❏ Smooth and flowing ❏ Hesitant ❏ Off balance 2. Crouch at end of jump becomes starting position for backward roll. ❏ Smooth and flowing ❏ Hesitant ❏ Off balance Scoring: ❏ Proficient = all smooth and flowing ❏ Developing = 1 smooth and flowing, 1 hesitant or off balance ❏ Undeveloped = 2 hesitant or off balance
Demonstrate or perform: • accuracy in performance of outcome-specific closed skills.	Observation checklist and scoring rubric for percent, quantity, or consecutive successes	K–2: Find the farthest distance and smallest hoop through which you can make at least 5 of 8 underhand throws. Distance: Size of hoop: ____ 5 feet ____ Large ____ 10 feet ____ Medium ____ 15 feet ____ Small Quantity ___/8 Scoring: ❏ Advanced = >5/8 at 10–15 feet through small or medium hoop ❏ Proficient = 5/8 at 10–15 feet through small or medium hoop ❏ Developing = 5/8 at 5 feet through large hoop ❏ Undeveloped = <5/8 at 5 feet through large hoop

Figure 9.13   Performance assessment chart.

Figure 9.13 *(continued)*

Assessment verb and method	Scoring tool	Assessment method and scoring tool examples

Demonstrate or perform
 	
• correct movement responses during open-skill progressions.
	Observation checklist and scoring rubric for appropriate and consistent attending, anticipation, and response selection	Grades 3–5: Move to catch balls arriving from different levels and directions.
		Criteria:
		❑ Attends to direction of thrower's step and torso and to ball speed, tracks ball, and responds by aligning body with ball.
		❑ Attends to release point, tracks ball, and responds with appropriate hand placement.
		❑ Catches at least 60 percent of balls.
		   ____ Above head ____ Center
		   ____ At chest ____ Left
		   ____ Along ground ____ Right
		Scoring:
		❑ Advanced = Attends to direction and release point and attains 60 percent accuracy for all types of catches.
		❑ Proficient = Attends to direction and release point and attains 60 percent accuracy for all levels of catches and two of three directions.
		❑ Developing = Attends to direction or release point and attains 40 percent to 50 percent accuracy for some levels and directions.
		❑ Undeveloped = Gives erratic attention to direction and release point and attains <40 percent accuracy for most levels and directions.

Demonstrate or perform • application of game tactics.	Observation checklist and scoring rubric for appropriate decision making and performance of game tactics	Grades 3–5: Set up to attack in throw tennis. Criteria: *Skill execution* ❑ Underhand throw over net from where ball was caught ❑ Moving to catch within one bounce *Decision making* ❑ Moving opponent around the court ❑ When opponent is back, throwing ball to front of court Scoring: ❑ Proficient = all checked ❑ Developing = 1 of 2 per category ❑ Undeveloped: 0 or 1 in a category

Demonstrate or perform
 	
• application of concepts from personal and social responsibility, exercise physiology, biomechanics, or motor behavior.
	Observation checklist and scoring rubric for appropriate decision making and performance	Grades 3–5 (personal and social responsibility): Demonstrate honesty during game play.
		Criteria:
		*Calls "out on me" for own boundary violations.
		   _____ Mostly _____ Sometimes _____ Never
		*Calls "you got me" when tagged.
		   _____ Mostly _____ Sometimes _____ Never
		Scoring:
		❑ Proficient = mostly for all
		❑ Developing = sometimes or a combination of frequencies
		❑ Undeveloped = never for all

and make adjustments during the learning process to meet their needs. Figure 9.14 illustrates the process of using embedded assessments to create flow.

Assessments come in various forms. Diagnostic assessments are used before a unit or period of instruction to help teachers understand what their students already know and can do. Teachers can then match students' levels of knowledge and performance to appropriately challenging tasks. As students engage in the learning process, teachers periodically use formative assessments to see how students are progressing and to adjust challenges that are too difficult or too easy. As Aguilar observes, this process should be used frequently: "We need to check students' understanding every 10 minutes and use a range of formative assessment strategies so then we can adjust course and ensure that they'll be successful with the task" (Aguilar, 2012, p. 2). Summative assessments are administered at the end of a unit or period of instruction in order to determine how well students have mastered the learning goals.

Diagnostic assessment occurs first, as teachers engage students in the learning process, but summative assessments are the first to be designed in planning the learning process. Recall the backward design model: start with the end in mind. In physical education, begin with the learning goal—what students need to know, be able to do, and behave like. Next, choose or design summative assessments to determine how students will demonstrate that they have the knowledge, skills, and dispositions to reach the learning goal. Diagnostic assessments are then culled from the summative assessments in order to determine how much students already know and can perform in relation to the learning goal. You can then plan developmentally and individually appropriate learning experiences that enable students to reach the goal, as well as the formative assessments that show how well students are progressing toward the goal. Figure 9.15 illustrates how to use the backward design model to plan for embedding assessments in the learning process.

Embedding assessment into the lesson can fully engage students in their own learning. Right from the beginning of a unit of instruction, you can help students see their learning destination by telling or showing them the learning goal and the summative assessment. You can then administer the *diagnostic* assessment so that students know where they are and how far they have to go in order to reach the destination. Students engage more readily in learning activities when they perceive the activities and associated feedback as a means to reach the destination.

Along the way, *formative* assessments provide information about how well students are progress-

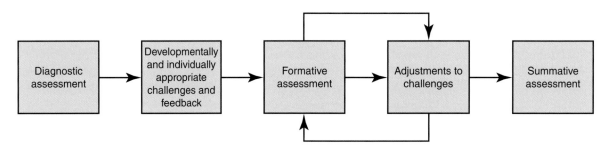

Figure 9.14 Executing the learning process with embedded assessments.

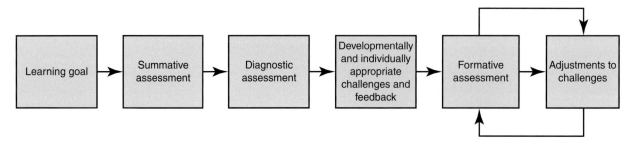

Figure 9.15 Planning the learning process with embedded assessments.

ing and whether or not they need to take a detour, slow down, or speed up their journey in order to reach the learning destination. The entire process is synergistic because students and teachers alike are fully engaged in the learning process: Students see the progress they are making; the teacher provides feedback and makes changes to further facilitate students' progress; and, in turn, students feel fully supported by the teacher as they pursue learning goals. See figure 9.16 for an example of embedded assessment.

Assessments that support standards are referred to as criterion referenced. In other words, student performance on an assessment is compared with criteria that assign a rating based on level of achievement. For instance, many of the assess-

ment examples presented here describe different levels of achievement and corresponding ratings: advanced, proficient, developing, and beginning or undeveloped. All of the criteria used in these descriptions refer to performance of the learning goal; thus students' capabilities are gauged not in comparison to those of other students but in terms of how well they met the learning goal.

Summative Assessment

Summative assessments are used at the end of a unit or period of instruction. They bring learning goals to life by clarifying what goal achievement looks like, and they can be used as a basis for both diagnostic assessment (what students already know or can do) and formative assessment (how

---

Standard 1: Demonstrate competency in motor skills.

Learning goal (grades 3 through 5): Consistently catch balls thrown to different levels.

Summative assessment: For proficiency, catch at least 60 percent of balls thrown randomly to each level—above the head, at the chest, and along the ground.

Diagnostic assessment: Determine the percentage of balls caught at each level when thrown randomly—above the head, at the chest, and along the ground.

Challenges: Choose the tier with stations that are developmentally and individually appropriate based on diagnostic results.

Tier 1: stations with movement cues to work on catching separately at each level

Feedback: visual cues (release point, ball tracking) and movement cues (moving to ball, keeping arms and hands in line with ball, assuming ready position for next catch)

Formative assessment: After practicing, catch a set of five throws each from each level—above the head, at the chest, and along the ground—and record the percentage of catches made for each.

Adjustments: ball size, distance, and self-talk of visual and movement cues before each level of throw

Tier 2: stations with movement cues to work on catching balls thrown in predetermined sequences: above the head, at the chest, along the ground; chest, above head, ground; ground, chest, above head; above head, ground, chest; chest, ground, above head; and ground, above head, chest

Feedback: visual cues (release point, ball tracking) and movement cues (moving to ball, keeping arms and hands in line with ball, assuming ready position for next catch)

Formative assessment: After practicing, record the percentage of catches made for each level in five different predetermined sets.

Adjustments: ball size, distance, time between throws, and self-talk of visual and movement cues before each sequence

Tier 3: stations with movement cues to work on catching balls thrown randomly

Feedback: visual cues (release point, ball tracking) and movement cues (moving to ball, keeping arms and hands in line with ball, assuming ready position for next catch)

Formative assessment: After practicing, determine the percentage of balls caught at each level when thrown randomly (five above head, five at chest level, five along the ground).

Adjustments: ball size, distance, time between throws

Figure 9.16   Embedded assessment.

well students are progressing toward the learning goal). To be effective, summative assessments must match the level of thinking and performance of the learning goals; provide criteria for measuring how well students have learned, and use a scoring system that supports grading and class evaluation.

When designing summative assessments, use criteria from learning goal blueprints (Moss & Brookhart, 2012), which describe proficient (competent or target) performance of the learning goal. Next, design a scoring tool by describing what student performance looks like at various levels, from undeveloped to advanced. Then design assessment methods (e.g., skill performance, test, project) for using the criteria to rate student achievement. If achievement of the criteria will be used to determine numerical grades and whole-class evaluation, assign points to the ratings. Thus, the process for designing summative assessments includes the following elements:

1. Refer to learning goal blueprints for proficient performance criteria.

2. Design or choose a scoring tool and that includes descriptions of ratings above and below the proficient level.

3. Design or choose an assessment method and data collection tool.

4. Quantify ratings, as necessary, for the purposes of grading and whole-class evaluation.

Here is an example of the four-step process for designing summative assessments.

1. The learning goal blueprint presented in figure 9.17 describes versatile performance of locomotor skills at the proficient level. To design or choose a summative-assessment scoring tool for one or more of the locomotor skills, refer to the descriptors for body, space, effort, and relationship and to the mature-stage characteristics of the skill (see chapter 5). See summative assessments for fundamental motor skills in appendix B.)

2. Use information from the blueprint to fill in specifics for the proficient level on the scoring tool for the chosen locomotor skill, then complete descriptions of the other levels (see figure 9.18). See the section above on How to Assess for a general description of advanced, developing, and beginning performance.

3. Use the descriptors from the proficient level to design or choose an assessment method that engages children in performing the learning goal. For example, activities for the jumping assessment stations presented in

Content	Body	Space	Effort	Relationship
Traveling skills: running, galloping, sliding, skipping	Intentionally uses body actions for mature performance. Curls, stretches, bends, twists, and turns body during, into, and out of traveling skills.	Adjusts movements to move safely through space. Travels on straight, curved, and zigzag pathways in forward, backward, and sideward directions.	Varies speed of traveling skills. Moves rhythmically to beats and music. Combines traveling skills in smooth sequences.	Uses traveling skills to move around, along, inside, through, and under equipment. Moves in front of, next to, and behind others and in roles of leading, following, mirroring, and matching. Adjusts movements to chase, flee, and dodge others.
Flight: jumping, leaping, hopping	Intentionally uses body actions for mature performance. Moves body into and out of symmetrical shapes (round, narrow, wide) during flight.	Changes level and varies distance and direction of flight movements.	Moves rhythmically to beats and music. Combines flight and traveling skills in smooth sequences.	Uses flight skills to move, over, into, out of, onto, and off of low equipment. Uses flight to move in front of, next to, and behind others and in roles of leading, following, mirroring, and matching. Adjusts movements using flight to dodge others.

Figure 9.17 Learning goal blueprint for mature and versatile performance of locomotor skills.

Rating	Body	Space	Effort	Relationship
Advanced	Proficient performance: Moves body quickly into and out of symmetrical and asymmetrical (twisted) shapes.	Jumps over high levels and wide distances and performs at least a half change of direction in the air.	Makes smooth, effortless transitions between three or more traveling and flight skills.	Makes smooth transitions between combinations of flight skills in low obstacle courses and with others.
Proficient	Consistent proficient performance: Jumps in a coordinated, rhythmical pattern. Preparation—takeoff crouch and arm position appropriate for height and distance of jump (two feet to two feet or one foot to two feet) Main action—quick extension of legs and arms Recovery—landing on balls of feet with crouch appropriate to absorb height and distance of jump Moves body into and out of symmetrical shapes at height (round, narrow, and wide) of flight movement.	Achieves jumps to medium and low levels. Jumps forward across moderate and short distances. Performs a quarter to a half change of direction in air.	Consistently jumps rhythmically to beats and music. Makes smooth transitions between combinations of jumps with other flight or traveling skills (e.g., run and jump, gallop to jump, jump to jump).	Uses flight skills to adeptly move over, into, out of, onto, and off of low equipment. Adeptly uses flight to move in front of, next to, and behind others and in roles of leading, following, mirroring, and matching.
Developing	Inconsistent proficient performance: Jumps are somewhat coordinated. Preparation—takeoff crouch and arm position somewhat appropriate for height and distance of jump (two feet to two feet or one foot to two feet) Main action—legs and arms extended Recovery: landing on balls of feet (sometimes flat-footed) with moderate to appropriate crouch to absorb height and distance of jump Uses inconsistent timing of movement into symmetrical shapes (starting to take shape early or late or releasing shape late).	Jumps to small heights and distances.	Times some jumps to beats and music. Combines jumps with other flight or traveling skills with some hesitation (e.g., run and jump, gallop to jump, jump to jump).	Uses flight skills to move over, into, and out of lines, hoops, or ropes on the floor. Can jump off of (not onto) low equipment. Uses flight to move in front of, next to, and behind others; may have trouble keeping up with others.
Beginning	Emerging elementary performance: Performs preparation, main action, and/or recovery with moderate degrees of flexion and/or extension; timing is somewhat coordinated.	Performs inconsistently in jumping for height and distance.	Performs inconsistently in timing jumps rhythmically. Combines jumps and other traveling skills but is hesitant, stiff, or off balance.	Jumps off of (not onto) low equipment. Inconsistently achieves flight to move over, into, and out of lines, hoops, or ropes on the floor and when moving in front of, next to, or behind others; has trouble keeping up with others.

Figure 9.18 Summative assessment rubric for mature and versatile performance of jumping.

figure 9.19 derive from the proficient-level performance expectations presented in figure 9.18. The chosen assessment activities allow students to demonstrate consistency and versatility.

4. Design a means for recording data that provides for individual and class evaluation. Use the data collection instrument in (see figure 9.20) to record observation ratings from scoring rubrics. Individual and class evalu-

ation ratings can be quantified for individual and class evaluation reports.

Diagnostic Assessment

Diagnostic assessments are used before teaching a unit of instruction in order to determine what students already know and can do in relation to the new content. Diagnostic performance assessments that address psychomotor skills, fitness development, and prosocial behaviors typically mirror

Body	Performs long jumps and vertical jumps with mature form. Jumps off of low boxes and make symmetrical shapes in the air.
Space	Jumps over low and medium obstacles (up to 1/4 of child's height). Jumps short to moderate distances (up to 1/4 of child's height). Jump over lines with quarter or half turn in the air.
Effort	Performs jumps as designated in a song (e.g., "Pop Goes the Weasel"). Runs and jumps over low objects and short spaces. Performs smooth combinations of three jumps.
Relationship	Jumps over, onto, off of, into, and out of low equipment (e.g., box, hoop, rope, or line shape). Leads a partner through low obstacle courses using at least three jumps.

Figure 9.19 Jumping assessment stations.

Directions: Indicate a rating of A (advanced), P (proficient), D (developing), or B (beginning) for each student. Tally and calculate the percentage for each rating.

Student	Proficient form	Shapes	Levels	Distances	Direction	Rhythm	Running and jumping	Combination	Equipment	Partner	Total A	P	D	B	Percent A	P	D	B
Class																		

Individual scoring (by grade 2): Outstanding performance consists of 75 percent of scores in A and 25 percent in P. Satisfactory performance consists of 80 percent of scores in A or P and no scores in B.

Class evaluation: Satisfactory performance consists of 80 percent of scores in A or P and no scores in B.

Figure 9.20 Collection of assessment data for jumping.

some or all of the summative assessment criteria. This alignment allows you to compare changes in skill level or fitness development from the time of the diagnostic assessment to the time of the summative assessment. Along the way, you can track student progress through formative assessment.

You are probably familiar with the fitness testing used at the beginning and end of a period of time in order to determine what gains have been made in flexibility, cardiorespiratory endurance, body composition, and strength. Knowing students' fitness capacities before instruction can help both teachers and students set and track appropriate individual goals. Similarly, you can use a variety of established motor-skill tests to diagnose children's stage of fundamental motor-skill development. Two such tests are the Fundamental Movement Pattern Assessment Instrument (FMPAI; figure 9.21) developed by Gallahue and Cleland Donnelly (2003) and the Test of Gross Motor Development (Second Edition; TGMD-2) developed by Ulrich (2000).

Both of these tests contain valid items, are highly reliable across trained observers, and are easy to administer. For each fundamental movement skill, the TGMD-2 provides both norm-referenced interpretations (i.e., comparing scores with a statistical sample) and criterion-referenced interpretation (i.e., comparing scores with a preestablished standard). It can be used for between-individual, between-group, and within-individual comparisons. The FMPAI contains a physical education progress report (figure 9.22) to facilitate record keeping and parent reports. Whether you choose the FMPAI, the TGMD-2, or another diagnostic assessment instrument, you can use the results to diversify instruction, track progress through formative assessment, and compare diagnostic with summative observation data in order to measure students' gains.

Diagnostic assessments can also be derived from summative assessments for specialized movement skills, tactics, and prosocial behaviors in grades 3 through 5. For example, you might engage fourth-grade students in playing a game before they learn the skills and tactics or the prosocial behaviors. You would use the summative-assessment scoring rubric to gather diagnostic (baseline) data; track progress through formative

Class_____ Grade _____ Observer _____

Directions: Mark the proper stage (I, E, M) for each skill.

  I = initial stage

  E = elementary stage

  M = mature stage

Name	Stability skills								Locomotor skills										Manipulative skills							
	Static balance	Dynamic balance	Body rolling	Dodging	Springing and landing	Axial movements	Inverted supports	Transitional supports	Running	Jump for distance	Jump for height	Jump from height	Hopping	Skipping	Sliding	Galloping	Leaping	Climbing	Throwing	Catching	Kicking	Trapping	Dribbling	Volleying	Striking	Ball rolling

Figure 9.21   Sample total-body and group observational assessment chart.

In this report, your child's progress is indicated for selected skills throughout all four quarters of this semester. Please refer to the following key for stages of development. These represent developmental stages, which are partially dependent on maturation. For instance, 2-3 year olds are I to E and 5-6 year olds are E to M:

I = initial stage

E = elementary stage

M = mature stage

	Quarter 1	Quarter 2	Quarter 3	Quarter 4	Comments
STABILITY SKILLS: MAINTAINING BALANCE IN STATIC AND DYNAMIC SITUATIONS					
One-footed balance					
Beam walk					
Body rolling					
Dodging					
Landing					
LOCOMOTOR SKILLS: GIVING FORCE TO THE BODY THROUGH SPACE					
Running					
Jumping					
Hopping					
Skipping					
Leaping					
MANIPULATIVE SKILLS: GIVING FORCE TO AND RECEIVING FORCE FROM OBJECTS					
Throwing					
Catching					
Kicking					
Dribbling					
Striking					

Parent or guardian signature:_____Date:_____

Comments:

Parent or guardian signature:_____Date:_____

Comments:

Parent or guardian signature:_____Date:_____

Comments:

Figure 9.22 Sample progress report for fundamental movement skills

assessment; and compare student performance of skills, tactics, or prosocial behaviors at the end of instruction with the baseline data in order to determine learning gains.

Diagnostic assessments for knowledge are often referred to as "accessing prior knowledge" (Pollock, 2007). In the beginning of a unit of instruction—and at the beginning of individual lessons—engage students in answering questions or responding to scenarios in order to determine their levels of understanding in relation to what they must demonstrate to reach the cognitive learning goal. You can use the information from "accessing prior knowledge" to determine the depth and breadth of students' gains in knowledge from the time of diagnostic assessment to the time of summative assessment. You can also use track students' progress in the meantime through formative assessment.

Formative Assessment

The primary purpose of formative assessment is to improve learning. This type of testing is "an active and intentional process that partners the teacher and the students to continuously and systematically gather evidence of learning with the express goal of improving student achievement" (Moss & Brookhart, 2009, p. 6). As discussed by Heritage (2010, citing a synthesis of research findings by Black & William, 1998) formative assessments were found to trigger the largest student gains ever reported for an educational intervention. Black and William proposed that effective formative assessment involves the following elements:

teachers making adjustments to teaching and learning in response to assessment evidence;

students receiving feedback about their learning with advice on what they can do to improve; and

students' participating in the process through self-assessment (Heritage, 2010, p. 2) and peer assessment (McManus, 2008, p. 5).

Teachers strive to create a class climate that welcomes formative assessment because it informs learners about how well they are progressing and how to improve. It also helps teachers make necessary adjustments to support student attainment of learning goals. Assessing progress toward learning goals becomes routine with the use of formative assessments and is always disconnected from grades (Andrade, 2007/2008).

As you embed formative assessment into the learning process, you play multiple roles. One role is to gather and interpret group data in order to determine how well the class or specific parts of the class are progressing toward learning goals. Group data helps inform you about whether adjustments need to made in teaching and learning. For instance, if you scan the class halfway through a lesson and see that one-third of the students are unsuccessful at the learning goal, you may need to change something in the learning environment to remove an impedance (e.g., add a softer ball, shorten the distance, use a blocked practice format). Similarly, if, during closure, you find that many students are confused about the meanings of terms in the FITT principle, you can give homework to help clarify the terms and then reteach the content in a different way during the next class.

Another role that you play during formative assessment is that of providing individual students with feedback about their progress toward the learning goal—specifically, what they're doing well and how they can improve. When you provide individual students with formative assessment, they use the criteria to describe what they're doing well and what and how to improve; it also encourages students to keep trying. Taking the time to use this three-part "feedback sandwich" (figure 9.23) helps students become more knowledgeable about how assessment works. It reinforces their understanding of how assessment aids improvement and how persistence helps them reach their learning goals.

A third role of formative assessment is to engage students in self-assessment and peer assessment. Both of these forms of formative assessment can be very instructive because they engage students repeatedly in using, and thus reinforcing, the criteria for success. Self-assessment (figure 9.24) is a valuable way to help students learn how to learn. In this approach, students engage in first drafts or first skill attempts with the understanding that they will use criteria to examine and then revise their work or performance. When you expect students to self-assess before turning in a rough draft, or before observing a "novice" performance, you gain valuable information not only about where students are on their learning goal journey but also about how well students understand the criteria for success. When students engage in self-assessment, your teacher feedback needs to address students' understanding of these criteria. In other words, the initial focus is on how well students use the criteria to self-assess.

In peer assessment (figure 9.25), students use the criteria to observe each other. Observing each other with the criteria for success in mind reinforces what the skill or product is supposed to look like. It also engages students in interpreting and comparing what they see their partner doing with the performance or product expected for achieving a proficient level. For peer feedback to succeed, teachers must help students learn how to observe appropriately and how to give appropriate feedback. The teacher's role during peer feedback is to focus on and support student observers in order to help them really see their partner's performance, accurately compare what they see with the proper criteria, and give helpful feedback.

In the benchmark years (grades 2, 5, 8, and 12), teachers assess how well students have achieved grade-level outcomes by means of summative assessments that sample students' knowledge and performance of key components of SHAPE America's (2014) five national standards for physical education. NASPE (2010) developed PE Metrics, a collection of reliable and valid standards-based assessments for addressing the national standards in grades 1 through 6. The assessments are provided both as examples for measuring student achievement of the standards and for use as formative and summative assessments during units of instruction.

GRADING

Grades are used to report the status of student learning. They typically take the form of ratings: letters (e.g., A, B), numbers (e.g., 100, 85), or descriptors (e.g., satisfactory, unsatisfactory). When used on a report card, the letters, numbers, or descriptors represent an aggregated score from a variety of tests, projects, and performances depicting students' progress for the quarter, semester, or academic year.

Traditionally, report-card grades in physical education have consisted of an aggregation of scores from categories such as participation, attendance, effort, attitude, knowledge, and skill performance. However, in standards-based physical education, the elements of participation, attendance, effort, and attitude are simply expected. Students need to be in class, dressed, and willing and ready to participate in instructional activities and assessments that lead to reaching performance outcomes. As a result, grades are based not on these factors but on students' progress toward and achievement of standards-based learning goals—mature form in

fundamental skills, knowledge and use of game tactics, use of the FITT principle to improve fitness, and cooperation with others to solve movement challenges. If teachers also want to report on behaviors that reflect readiness and willingness to learn, they can do so in a separate section of the report card.

As you may recall, alignment is the process of using the focus of the essential content as the focus of assessment and instruction. Since grading is an extension of (summative) assessment, it too must be aligned with the standards. Guidelines for standards-based grading include the following:

- Connect grades directly to standards. The basis for grades should be the achievement of learning goals or performance outcomes—that is, demonstrations of what students know and can do for each standard (Fox, 2012; O'Connor & Wormeli, 2011; Melagrano, 2007).

- Choose criterion-referenced performance outcomes for grading. Students' grades should represent *not* how well they performed as compared with others (e.g., bell curve, normative scale) but their level of achievement (e.g., advanced, proficient, developing) of standards-based goals (Melagrano, 2007).

- Use only summative assessments for determining grades. Summative assessments are those conducted at the end of a period of instruction and learning. They represent how well students have achieved the learning goals or performance outcomes. In contrast, formative assessments are used for feedback during the learning process; in other words, they are used to determine areas for improvement—not as part of grades (O'Connor & Wormeli, 2011; Melagrano, 2007).

- Analyze a *body of evidence* when determining grades. Use a collection of results from a variety of summative assessments to determine grades and place emphasis on the most consistent and recent scores. Since learning is an ongoing process and students learn at different rates, keep records of students' progress on summative assessments that can be updated without difficulty (Marzano & Heflebower, 2011; Melagrano, 2007).

Figure 9.26 presents an example of a standards-based report card for grade 2 that is patterned after recommendations by Melagrano (2007). The standards indicated in the left column and the specific

Learning goal (grades 3 through 5): Perform a smooth sequence of forward roll, jump with a half turn, and backward roll.

Scoring checklist results	Teacher feedback
Checklist: **1.** Crouch at end of roll becomes takeoff position for jump. ❏ Smooth and flowing ❏ Hesitant ❏ Off-balance **2.** Crouch at end of jump becomes starting position for backward roll. ❏ Smooth and flowing ❏ Hesitant ❏ Off-balance Score: ❏ Proficient = all smooth and flowing ❏ Developing = 1 smooth and flowing, 1 hesitant or off-balance ❏ Undeveloped = 2 hesitant or off-balance	"Alex, take a look at the checklist." Good: "As you can see, your connection from the crouch of the roll to the jump was smooth—as soon as your weight was moving to the balls of your feet, you exploded upward." Improvement: "The next connection needs work. You landed the jump turn with your weight to one side. Work on looking over your shoulder more quickly to get a faster turn. Then you can have a more balanced landing and go right into the crouch." Encouragement: "Look quickly—I know you'll get it!"

Figure 9.23 "Feedback sandwich" for formative assessment.

Assess yourself by placing a check mark along the learning line.

1. Before I roll, I stand still, in line with the pin, and hold the ball in both hands.

Never...Some of the time.....................................✔...............Most of the time

2. As I roll, I have a smooth delivery (swinging back, stepping long and low, and swinging forward).

Never...Some of the time.............................✔...................Most of the time

3. I release the ball low and toward the pin.

Never...✔.....Some of the time...Most of the time

4. I knock the pin down.

Never...✔..........Some of the time...Most of the time

Teacher feedback: "From your marks, it looks like you're starting in a good position. What do you think happens during the release that prevents you from knocking down the pin more often?" (Student and teacher can verify the cause and decide what can be done to improve.)

Figure 9.24 Bowling self-assessment.

Assess the player by placing a check mark along the learning line.

1. Makes underhand throw from where the ball was caught.

Never...Some of the time..✔......Most of the time

2. Moves to catch the ball.

Never...Some of the time.............................✔...................Most of the time

3. Throws ball to open spaces, which moves opponent around the court.

Never...✔......Some of the time...Most of the time

Before delivering teacher feedback, observe both the student observer and the player, then provide feedback to the student observer. Start by asking questions to elicit information from the student observer: "How is the player doing?" "What is she doing well?" "What does she need to improve?" "What have you said to let her know?" You can then address what the observer saw or said well. If you observe something different from what the student observer reports, you can tell the observer to look again and focus his or her attention on the appropriate action.

Figure 9.25 Peer assessment for throw tennis.

Student name: _____ Teacher: _____

School: _____ School year: _____

Rating Scale for Achievement of Grade-Level Expectations

4 = Exceeded expectation of grade-level indicator.

3 = Met expectation of grade-level indicator.

2 = Made progress toward expectation of grade-level indicator.

1 = Made limited progress toward expectation of grade-level indicator.

0 = Not assessed at this time

Standard	Performance outcome	Quarter			
		1	2	3	4
1. Demonstrates competency in a variety of motor skills and movement patterns.	Achieves mature performance in running, galloping, sliding, hopping, and skipping.				
	Demonstrates 4 of 5 critical elements in horizontal and vertical jumps.				
	Performs rhythmic activity with correct response to simple rhythm.				
	Balances on different bases of support, combining level and shape.				
	Balances in an inverted position.				
	Transfers weight from feet to different body parts for balance or travel.				
	Rolls in different directions with a narrow or curled body shape.				
	Combines balances and transfers into a 3-part sequence (dance or gymnastics).				
	Throws underhand using a mature pattern.				
	Throws overarm using 2 of 5 critical elements.				
	Catches large, light, self-tossed or quality-thrown ball with hands.				
	Dribbles in self-space and while walking in general space with mature pattern.				
	Uses running approach and kicks moving ball using 3 of 5 cues for mature pattern.				
	Volleys object upward with consecutive hits.				
	Strikes object with short-handled implement upward with consecutive hits.				
	Strikes a ball off a cone or tee with a bat using side orientation.				
2. Applies knowledge of concepts, principles, strategies, and tactics related to movement and performance.	2.1 Combines locomotor skills in general space to a rhythm.				
	2.2 Combines shape, levels, direction, and pathways into simple travel, dance, and gymnastics sequences.	_			
	2.3 Demonstrates gradual increases and decreases in time and force.				

Figure 9.26 Physical Education Report Card (Grade 2)

(continued)

Figure 9.26 *(continued)*

Standard	Performance outcome	Quarter			
		1	2	3	4
3. Demonstrates the knowledge and skills to achieve and maintain a health-enhancing level of physical activity and fitness.	3.1 Describes physical activities for participation outside of physical education class, before and after school, in the community, etc.				
	3.2 Actively engages in physical activities outside of physical education class, before and after school, in the community, etc.				
	3.3 Engages in and recognizes physiological signs associated with participation in moderate to vigorous physical activity.				
	3.4 Uses own body resistance for developing strength.				
4. Exhibits responsible personal and social behavior that respects self and others.	1.1 Practices skills with minimal teacher prompting.				
	1.2 Demonstrates responsibility for class protocols.				
	1.3 Accepts corrective feedback from the teacher.				
	4.4 Works independently with partner.				
	4.5 Recognizes the role of rules and etiquette in physical education class.				
	4.6 Works safely in class and with equipment.				
5. Recognizes the value of physical activity for health, enjoyment, challenge, self-expression, and/or social interaction.	5.1 Recognizes the value of "good health balance."				
	5.2 Compares physical activities that bring confidence and challenge.				
	5.3 Identifies physical activities that provide self-expression.				

"Grading and report cards for standards-based physical education," V. Melagraono, *JOPERD* 78 (6), 45-53, Taylor and Francis, adapted by permission of the publisher (Taylor & Francis Ltd, http://www.tandfonline.com).

performance outcomes for grade 2 indicated in the middle column are derived from the K-12 national standards and grade-level outcomes (SHAPE America, 2014, pp. 26–36). The third (right) column provides four spaces for the teacher to enter the rating that indicates the student's level of achievement for each outcome during each marking period.

To determine the rating or grade for each performance outcome, the teacher aggregates scores or evidence from a variety of summative assessments. For instance, for performance outcome 1.1, the teacher reviews student levels of achievement toward mature performance of fundamental motor skills. For performance outcome 5.3, the teacher reviews a set of scores from observations of students' cooperative behaviors, as well as students' reflections on or descriptions of cooperation with others.

Big Ideas

- Standards-based assessment is used to determine whether and to what degree students can demonstrate, in context, what they know and can perform relative to identified standards of learning. Demonstrating learning requires something tangible in the form of a performance that can be observed or a product that can be examined and assessed with predetermined criteria.

- Physical education assessments address standards from four domains:

  - Cognitive assessments measure how well students can demonstrate an understanding of movement concepts, principles, strategies, and tactics as applied to the learning and performance of physical activities. Cognitive assessments are differentiated based on levels of thinking and stages of cognitive development.

  - Psychomotor assessments measure how well students can perform motor skills, movement concepts, strategies, and tactics. More specifically, process assessments focus on describing how well students execute the movements of a skill, whereas product assessments focus on the outcome of the skill (e.g., how far, how high, how well a game tactic worked). Psychomotor assessments are differentiated based on stages of motor development and learning.

  - Fitness assessments measure students' regularity of participation in physical activity and how well they have achieved and maintained health-related fitness. Fitness assessments are specific to the component of fitness being measured (e.g., muscular endurance, flexibility) and differ based on maturation of children's body systems.

  - Affective assessments measure students' personal and social responsibility and their identification of the benefits of physical activity. More specifically, process assessments are used to measure student performance of personal and social responsibility, whereas cognitive assessments are used to determine students' ability to describe and reflect on their responsibility behaviors and on the feelings and benefits that they associate with participation in physical activity. Affective assessments are differentiated based on children's levels of social and cognitive development.

- Psychomotor, cognitive, fitness, and affective goals are measured by means of various assessment methods and scoring tools. Assessment methods include, among other options, skill demonstration, game and movement sequence performance, quizzes, and reflection summaries. Assessment provides a way for children to demonstrate what they have learned. Scoring tools can take various forms, including answer keys, checklists, and rubrics—all of which are used to measure how well students perform on a given assessment.

- Student assessment occurs throughout the learning process, in which it is embedded from beginning to end. It can be diagnostic, formative, or summative.

- Diagnostic assessments, in the form of pretests, give teachers information about how well prepared students are to engage with new content. Formative assessments, on the other hand, are used periodically to determine students' progress toward learning the new content. Teachers use evidence from diagnostic and formative assessments to differentiate and individualize learning experiences.

- Summative assessment is used at the end of a designated learning period (i.e., unit of instruction or marking period) to determine how well students have mastered the learning goal. Planning learning requires starting with the end in mind. Thus, summative assessments are designed first, so that the diagnostic and formative assessments and the learning experiences can be designed with an eye toward helping students prepare to reach the learning goal.

- Grades are based on students' progress toward and achievement of standards-based learning goals. It is expected as a matter of course that students will be prepared for and participate in learning activities.

 Visit the web resource for learning activities, video clips, and review questions.

Chapter 10

Designing and Implementing Learning Experiences

Key Concepts

- Describing the process of instructional alignment
- Explaining how movement activities, practice conditions, and feedback are chosen
- Defining the term *instructional strategies* and describing how the Spectrum of Teaching Styles provides choices for planning and delivering instruction
- Describing the purpose and types of homework in physical education
- Describing the core principles of universal design and its relationship to the Spectrum of Teaching Styles

In standards-based instructional design, the key is alignment. In chapter 9, you learned how to align *assessment* with a psychomotor, cognitive, fitness, or affective learning goal. In this chapter, you will learn how to align *instruction* with assessment and with the learning goal. As a reminder, here are the steps in the alignment process (Wiggins & McTighe, 1998; Lund & Tannehill, 2010):

1. Clarify the goals of the standard.
   - Enduring understanding: What is the big picture—the intent?
   - Essential content: What should students know, perform, and behave like?
2. Determine the acceptable evidence for success. How will achievement be assessed and measured?
3. Determine the learning experiences for goal achievement. What instruction, activities, and practice will enable learning?

To guide your choice of movement activities, practice conditions, feedback, and teaching strategies, use the essential content from the selected physical education standard (SHAPE America, 2014) and the assessment method and scoring tool. When choosing movement activities, refer to skill progression charts to determine when to use single skills, skill combinations, and small-sided games or dance or gymnastics sequences. When choosing practice conditions, refer to the charts for structuring closed- and open-skill practice and feedback (see chapter 7, figures 7.1 and 7.2) to determine whether repetition of movements under the same or different conditions is better for achieving the learning goal. When choosing instructional strategies, consider whether students will duplicate the movements or ideas you explain and demonstrate or discover movements, concepts, or principles through problem solving (you will learn how to choose instructional strategies in this chapter).

Figure 10.1 summarizes all of the parts to consider when performing instructional alignment for physical education. This chapter addresses choosing movement activities, practice conditions, and instructional strategies.

CHOOSING MOVEMENT ACTIVITIES

As discussed in chapter 8, physical education content standards 1 and 2 lay the foundation for achieving standards 3 through 5. The first two standards focus on gaining skill competence and knowledge about the fundamental and specialized movement skills. Performing and understanding movement skills enables students to become physically active, which is the key ingredient for attaining standards 3 through 5. For instance, becoming skilled enough to run and jump leads to a sense of competence, which could provide the motivation to participate in running and jumping activities outside of school, run for cardiorespiratory fitness, or engage in a team-building rope-jumping activity. More generally, it can enable a person to have fun while moving, which perpetuates the cycle of being a physically active person.

The physical education content standards also identify the phase of motor development (chapter 4) that is appropriate for the maturity of the learner. In addition, movement skills specific to the phases of motor development are described in the movement framework (chapter 5). For instance, in kindergarten through grade 2, the expectation or goal of standard 1 is to demonstrate versatility in locomotor and stability skills. The teacher must consult the movement framework to identify the appropriate locomotor skills (e.g., running, jumping) and stability skills (e.g., balancing on different body parts), as well as the movement concepts (body, space, effort, relationship) that are appro-

priate for developing the versatility of those skills.

In order to help students progress toward the versatility of performance called for in standard 1, a teacher might set up a K-2 instructional task that calls for students to walk, gallop, skip, or slide sideways along different pathways. Similarly, in grades 3 through 5, standard 1 includes an expectation of performing skill combinations in dynamic environments learned in the specialized movement phase of motor development. Activities might include playing keep-away within a bounded space (which involves moving to open space, catching, and passing); moving to maintain a rally with a partner using a short-handled racket; performing a forward roll into a jump turn; or performing a three-step turn followed by a grapevine step to music.

CHOOSING PRACTICE CONDITIONS AND FEEDBACK

Practice conditions are based on children's stage of motor skill learning, the type of skill (closed or open), and the parameters of scaling the environment to fit the learner, as illustrated in figures 7.1 and 7.2 in chapter 7. For example, suppose that you want to help kindergarteners at the beginning level of learning achieve correct timing and form for the closed skills of walking, galloping, skipping, and sliding sideways along different pathways. You could use floor paint, tape, or jump ropes to create straight, zigzag, and curved pathways on the floor. These pathways could be

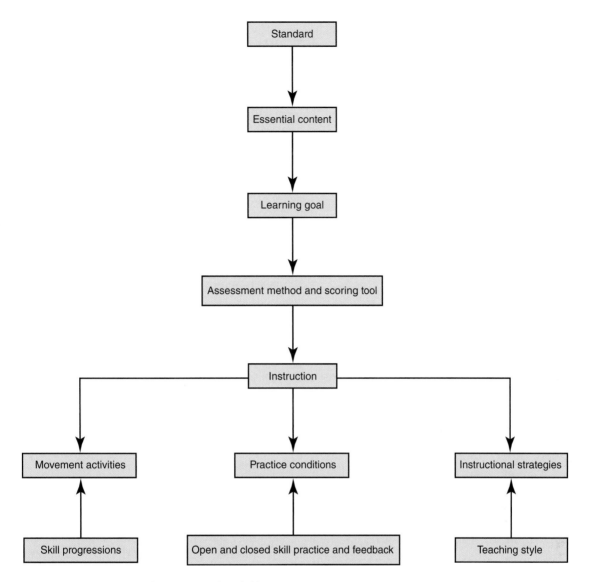

Figure 10.1   Summary of the instructional alignment process.

scaled for the learners by using different widths or degrees of sharpness (e.g., series of S curves versus series of sharp zigzags).

Constant practice can be achieved by having children move along the pathways multiple times. As children repeat their practice along different pathways, you can provide intermittent and prescriptive feedback to help them improve the timing and form of their locomotor skill performance. For instance, "Step quickly and sharply toward the new direction to move on the zigzag pathway."

The goal for third graders at the intermediate level of learning is to perform open skills in predictable environments. For example, one prerequisite for playing keep-away is to throw a series of

catchable passes to a moving partner, then move to an open space in order to receive a pass. This learning environment can be scaled by using cones to manipulate the size of the bounded space, the distance between poly spots to which the students must move in order to receive the game object, and the size and texture of the game object based on students' catching capabilities (e.g., rubber chicken, gator-skin ball).

Variable practice is achieved by having children catch from varying distances and angles, as determined by placement of the poly spots within the bounded space. While children engage in a series of throwing, moving, and catching actions, you should provide faded descriptive or prescriptive feedback to improve children's timing and placement of catchable passes, their quickness in moving to a poly spot after a throw, and their body positioning to enable successful receiving of a pass.

CHOOSING INSTRUCTIONAL STRATEGIES

Instructional strategies provide teachers with a means of delivering lesson content. They connect the activities and practice conditions that enable children to meet assessment criteria in order to achieve the learning goal. The Spectrum of Teaching Styles (or, simply, the Spectrum), originally conceived by Muska Mosston (Mosston, 1966), is a framework of 11 teaching styles that enable teachers to plan and implement instruction that either engages students in duplicating movements or ideas explained and demonstrated by the teacher (this is the reproduction cluster: Styles A-E) or foster students' discovery of movements, concepts, or principles (this is the production cluster: Styles F-K).

Suppose, for example, that you want to help kindergarteners at the beginning level of learning achieve correct timing and form for the closed skills of walking, galloping, skipping, and sliding along different pathways. You could choose a style from the reproduction cluster to engage students in duplicating movements that you explain and demonstrate. On the other hand, if you want children to design a dance sequence that uses elements related to body, space, effort, and relationship, then a production teaching style would be appropriate.

The Spectrum provides teachers with a framework from which to choose styles of teaching as a result of examining the entire learning process. In fact, "the fundamental proposition of the Spectrum is that teaching is governed by a single unifying process: decision making" (Mosston & Ashworth, 2008, p. 8). Teaching behavior consists of a chain of decision making grouped into three sets: pre-impact (i.e., planning), impact (i.e., implementation), and post-impact (i.e., feedback given to learners about their performance during impact).

Both teachers and students can make decisions within any of the three sets, and the decisions made in each set should reflect the psychomotor, cognitive, affective, and fitness characteristics of the learner. For example, the criteria for self-assessment by a first grader call for an illustration, whereas for a fifth grader the illustration is accompanied by a written description. Similarly, stopping and starting cues for kindergarten might consist of a red stop sign for stop and a green light for go, whereas the corresponding cues for fifth graders might consist of hand signals.

Addressing each decision in the pre-impact, impact, and post-impact decision sets can help you examine the whole picture of a lesson. As a result, you can create instruction that addresses students' development and is congruent, from objectives to teaching styles to assessment. Below are the lists of decisions that must be made to plan a lesson (pre-impact), to implement the lesson (impact), and to provide feedback to students (post-impact) (Mosston & Ashworth, 2008, pp. 21–25).

Pre-Impact (Planning) Set Decisions

- Learning objectives: based on grade-level standard, essential content, and diagnostic assessment results

- Assessment procedures and materials: differentiated to accommodate individual learning differences; summative assessment linked to essential content; formative assessment linked to lesson objective; forms of feedback related to type of practice and teaching style used for the lesson

- Selection of teaching styles: based on lesson objective(s)

- Lesson content: differentiated to accommodate individual learning differences, quantity of tasks, quality of performance expected, order of performance based on stages of motor development and learning

- Time decisions: starting and stopping cues, pace and rhythm, duration (time spent on each task depending on children's cognitive and fitness development), termination (ending lesson)

- Modes of communication:
  - Audio: brief explanations using age-appropriate vocabulary with clear cues
  - Visual: demonstration of whole skill, then parts; more than once; under actual practice conditions; from different angles; at correct speed; and with and without verbal cues
  - Tactile: touching of student by teacher or peer to facilitate correct movement performance (e.g., spotting a gymnastic movement)

- Questions: teacher-planned questions based on teaching style and children's stage of cognitive development
- Learning environment: logistics and management of materials, space, and children to maximize participation (all students productively engaged during instructional task); organization of individuals, partners, or small groups based on children's social development and level of personal responsibility; spatial boundaries distinctly marked; colorful equipment standing out from the background; materials and equipment placed in multiple areas and accessible containers (e.g., plastic bins, crates, hoops); teacher movement maximizing ability to see as many children as possible at one time

Impact (Implementation) Set

- Implementing and adhering to pre-impact decisions
- Maintaining a positive learning environment: prompting children to reinforce logistics (e.g., when to get equipment, where to stand), behavior (e.g., staying on task), and content (e.g., providing performance cues)—for example, "Be sure you have enough distance between you and others for a safe personal space" (logistics prompt).
- Adjustment of decisions to address observed learner needs: identifying pre-impact decisions that are not working and correcting them—for example, task order, practice duration, type of equipment, formations of students, size of movement area

Post-Impact Set

- Assessing learner performance and selecting and delivering appropriate feedback about behavior and content—for example, "I like the way you are working together" (approving feedback about behavior) or "Step forward on your opposite foot" (prescriptive knowledge-of-performance feedback about content)
- Using management protocols to consistently respond to learner actions regarding logistics and behavior (see chapter 12)
- Treatment of students' answers to teacher-generated questions (i.e., feedback) and student-initiated questions
- Adjustment of learning activities based on assessment data gathered

(Mosston & Ashworth, 2008, pp. 21–25)

The order of the Spectrum of 11 teaching styles is based on who is responsible (teacher or learner) for making the decisions described in the preceding list. Each successive style along the Spectrum gives students more decision-making responsibility. For our purposes, in elementary physical education, only the first eight styles (A-H) are used: all styles in the reproduction cluster and the first three styles in the production cluster. Style I is more appropriate for middle school and above and Styles J and K are self-teaching styles used outside a school setting.

Teachers of developmental physical education use a variety of teaching styles in order to address the diversity of learning goals and students. Figure 10.2 illustrates the clusters of teaching styles, described in the following sections, from which teachers make choices (Mosston & Ashworth, 2008, p. 11). The discovery threshold represents the line of demarcation between the replication thinking required by the reproduction cluster of styles and the discovery thinking (convergent and divergent) required by the production cluster of styles.

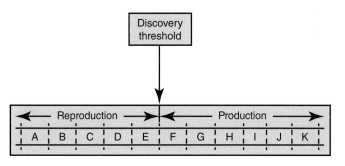

Figure 10.2 The clusters of teaching styles.

Mosston, M. & Ashworth, S. (2008). *Teaching physical education.* (6th ed.). First online version. www.spectrumofteachingstyles.org.

REPRODUCTION CLUSTER

Reproduction teaching styles focus on replication of *known* ideas, movements, and rules. The purpose of using reproduction styles is for students to duplicate movement skills—that is, fundamental movement skills or specialized game, dance, or gymnastic skills. In this cluster of styles, the teacher provides a model of correct performance and the practice conditions that enable students to perform the skill. Teachers can also use reproduction teaching styles in order to reinforce the idea of critical elements of movement skills. The hallmark of reproduction styles is to provide opportunities for correct practice and frequent feedback.

The reproduction cluster includes the following styles: A - command, B - practice, C - reciprocal, D - self-check, and E - inclusion. Each of the reproduction styles is presented here with a statement of purpose; a designation of who makes the pre-impact, impact and post-impact decisions; developmental considerations about using the style with children of different ages; and the critical impact and post-impact teaching behaviors that characterize implementation of the style.

Command Style (A)

The **command style** of teaching is a time-honored method of teaching movement skills. Its primary purpose is to promote active participation and accurate performance of skills in compliance with the teacher's cues. The essence of this style involves immediate response to a stimulus. It is a process of replication, reproduction, and duplication of correct performance.

In command style, the teacher makes all pre-impact, impact, and post-impact decisions. In other words, the teacher controls what is to be practiced, how it is to be done, when the activity should begin and end, and when to give feedback. Therefore, this approach emphasizes uniformity, conformity, and replication. The command style can be used effectively to teach, for example, a folk dance step, correct overhand throwing technique, or a step-aerobics routine.

Developmental Considerations

Pre-K children should engage in very brief command-style learning experiences. For example, at the beginning of a lesson, you might have a "circle time" during which children replicate rhythmic body movements to music. Children in kindergarten through grade 2 can participate in command episodes of longer duration; however, the duration of any given episode should not exceed children's ability to attend to the same task. For example, command style could be used to teach the skill cues for the underhand toss or for a short lyric-directed dance. In grades 3 through 5, command episodes can be of even longer duration and address more complex material—for example, a folk or line dance or the skill cues for a specialized sport skill.

This teacher is using the command style to demonstrate part of an urban folk dance for students to replicate.

Teaching Behaviors

Impact: Implement teaching behaviors decided on in the pre-impact set.

- Explain the objective and assessment method for the lesson.
- Briefly explain and demonstrate the skill(s) to be performed.
- Implement the chosen organizational arrangement.
- Provide stopping, starting, and cadence cues for the practice of the movement skills.

Post-impact: Implement teaching behaviors related to student performance during the lesson.

- Give the learners descriptive or prescriptive feedback about their performance and adjust learning activities if necessary.
- Provide a closure that assesses the degree to which student learning met the objective.

Practice Style (B)

Research has shown that practice style (B) is the most widely used teaching style in the Spectrum (Hasty, 1997; Kulinna et al., 2000; Cothran et al., 2000). This style is appropriate for teaching children to perform skills or movement activities in a prescriptive manner. It offers students time to work individually to complete a specified number of skill repetitions described on teacher-designed task sheets or posted on a whiteboard. It also shifts some decisions from the teacher to the learner. For example, students make decisions about location (where they practice the task), the order of the task(s), starting and stopping times, pace and rhythm, interval of practice, and questions for clarification. Shifting these impact decisions to students also gives the teacher time to move among the learners and offer private, individual feedback.

Developmental Considerations

Pre-K children are engaged in practice-style instruction when they explore movement in learning environments designed by the teacher to elicit fundamental movement skills and concepts. Children choose how long they stay at a task and their pace and rhythm. In kindergarten through grade 5, the teacher can gradually give children the opportunity to make an increasing number of practice-style decisions, including choosing the order of tasks,

and by grades 3 through 5 recording the quantity of tasks performed.

Teaching Behaviors

Impact: Implement teaching behaviors decided in the pre-impact set.

- Explain the objective and assessment method for the lesson.
- Explain and demonstrate the task using a task sheet in written or pictorial form.
- Implement the chosen organizational arrangement.
- Give students time to practice the designated tasks.

Post-impact: Implement teaching behaviors related to student performance during the lesson.

- Offer descriptive feedback, prescriptive feedback, or both and stay with learners to verify the corrected or reinforced behavior.
- Offer specific, skill-related, approving feedback to learners who perform correctly and make decisions appropriately.
- Provide a closure that assesses the degree to which student learning met the objective.

The task sheet used in the practice style of teaching guides student practice and holds learners responsible for recording the quantity of practice trials completed (see figure 10.3).

Reciprocal Style (C)

The reciprocal style (C) provides students with immediate feedback about performance. This style is sometimes referred to as "peer teaching," because students work with a partner, use specific criteria established by the teacher to assess partner performance, and offer peer feedback. Thus the reciprocal style promotes cooperation between peers for mutual improvement as students reciprocate by taking turns in the role of observer or performer. As a result, this style shifts to the student observer the post-impact decisions of assessing learner performance and selecting and delivering appropriate feedback. The teacher's role, in turn, is to observe both learners but to provide feedback *only to the peer observer*. This feedback pertains to the accuracy of the observer's conclusions and the appropriateness of the feedback given to the partner. If the teacher were to provide the performer with

Student: _____ Classroom teacher: _____ Date: _____

Practice each of the jumps described below. Try each jump

- on a mat,
- off of a low foam shape, and
- off of a high foam shape.

Place a check mark next to each completed task.

Stretched body shape jump from two feet to two feet

____ On a mat

____ Off of a low foam shape

____ Off of a high foam shape

Jump from two feet to two feet while bringing knees up toward chest (tuck)

____ On a mat

____ Off of a low foam shape

____ Off of a high foam shape

Jump from two feet to two feet with arms and legs wide (star jump)

____ On a mat

____ Off of a low foam shape

____ Off of a high foam shape

Teacher's comments:

Figure 10.3   Practice-style task card for jumping variations.

prescriptive feedback, it would undermine the observer's role. However, when the teacher speaks directly to the observer, it reinforces the importance of his or her role as a peer teacher. Refer to the reciprocal-style task card for the overhand throw shown in figure 10.4 to see the teacher-designed criteria used by the peer observer.

In some cases, skill practice requires a third person, whose responsibility is to act as a feeder or a retriever of equipment. For catching, as an example, one student serves as the performer, a second as the observer, and a third as the tosser or feeder. The performer executes the specific task of, say, catching a 6-inch (15-centimeter) playground ball from a specified trajectory and distance. The observer refers to the catching cues on the teacher-designed task card; watches to see if the performer uses the criteria (moves to get "square" or behind the ball, extends the arms outward, reaches for the ball, uses only the hands to catch, and bends the elbows upon catching to absorb force); gives the performer approving or corrective feedback; and marks down whether each cue was performed correctly or needs more work. Meanwhile, the teacher circulates, asking peer observers about specific aspects of the performers' movements and about the peer feedback they have given; the teacher also gives observers prescriptive or approving feedback about their own observations and peer feedback.

Developmental Considerations

Pre-K children do not have the social or observational skills to participate in reciprocal-style learning episodes. K-2 children can do so, provided that they receive instruction and practice about how to observe and provide helpful feedback to a partner. For instance, a teacher might provide a demonstration and post illustrations of a given movement. Student observation should be restricted to movement of one body part or segment—for example, bending the knees upon landing. By grades 3 through 5, children are able to perform an observation, give feedback, and use a reciprocal task card to record how well the partner performed in terms of as many as three criteria.

Teaching Behaviors

Impact: Implement teaching behaviors decided on in the pre-impact set.

- Explain the objective and assessment method for the lesson.
- Demonstrate the skill or activity, the roles of the performer and observer, and the use of the task card.
- Implement the chosen organizational arrangement.
- Give students time to practice the designated tasks.

Post-impact: Implement teaching behaviors related to student performance during the lesson.

- Observe the performer and the observer and provide feedback to the observer about his or her role.
- Provide a closure that assesses the degree to which student learning met the objective.

Self-Check Style (D)

The **self-check style (D)** promotes self-reliance by shifting to the performer the post-impact decisions of assessing performance. This style should be used only when the learner is ready to use it with a given task: "The criterion for task selection is that learners must have some proficiency in performing the task before they can engage in post-impact self-assessment" (Mosston & Ashworth, 2008, p. 145). The self-check style is applicable to tasks that focus not on the movement itself but on the result of the movement and in which the end results are external to the body.

Once the learner is aware of performance results, the teacher should pose questions prompting the performer to analyze how he or she moved the body to achieve those results. For example, if the task is to kick the ball to a high target and the ball does not fly accordingly, then the learner knows that something is incorrect in the kick. The learner then refers to the relevant part of the criteria—in

---

Performer: Throw a tennis ball toward a target on the wall. You will throw nine times.

Observer: Watch the thrower and give help when needed. Remind the thrower to do the following:

- Begin with side to target.
- Begin with throwing hand behind ear.
- Step forward onto opposite foot.
- Throwing with release toward target.

On the first three throws, watch for the thrower to begin with the side toward the target and the throwing hand behind the ear. On the next three throws, watch for the thrower to step forward onto the opposite foot. For the final three throws, watch for follow-through across the body. For each of the nine throws, check *Yes* or *No* to indicate whether the thrower performed the phase accurately.

Throws 1–3: side toward target, hand behind ear

1. Yes _____ No _____

2. Yes _____ No _____

3. Yes _____ No _____

Throws 4–6: stepping forward onto opposite foot

1. Yes _____ No _____

2. Yes _____ No _____

3. Yes _____ No _____

Throws 7–9: throwing with release toward target

1. Yes _____ No _____

2. Yes _____ No _____

3. Yes _____ No _____

Teacher's comments: _____

_____

_____

Figure 10.4 Reciprocal-style task card for the overhand throw.

this case, the details of placing one's foot under the lower part of the ball—and uses that information to correct the performance.

In self-check teaching, the teacher provides a task sheet that describes the task, the skill cues, the results of performing the cues (e.g., contacting the ball below its center with the shoelaces makes the ball go high), and common errors. The role of learners is to detect whether or not they are doing the task correctly by linking the actions of their bodies with the results of their performances. The role of the teacher is to question learners about the results of their performances. If learners cannot accurately compare their performances with the provided criteria, the teacher asks questions to lead them to see any discrepancies; if the learner cannot identify the discrepancies, then the teacher identifies them. Figure 10.5 presents a self-check task card for kicking to different levels.

Developmental Considerations

This style is most appropriate for children in grades 3 through 5 because self-checking requires the ability to explain the results of one's performance based on the critical cues provided on the task card. In other words, children must "diagnose according to the prepared criteria, identify errors, and correct them" (Mosston & Ashworth, 2008, p. 149).

Teaching Behaviors

Impact: Implement teaching behaviors decided in the pre-impact set.

- Explain the objective and assessment method for the lesson.
- Demonstrate the skill or activity and the role of the learner as self-assessor.
- Implement the chosen organizational arrangement.
- Give students time to practice the designated tasks.

Post-impact: Implement teaching behaviors related to student performance during the lesson.

- Observe the performer and provide feedback that addresses her or his self-assessment.
- Provide a closure that assesses the degree to which student learning met the objective.

Inclusion Style (E)

The inclusion style (E) introduces a different concept of task design—multiple levels of performance in the same task. This style is consistent with the intent of universal design, which is to differentiate the design of instructional tasks in order to meet children's various needs and abilities. In the inclusion style, another major decision is shifted to children: "What level of performance fits my level of ability?" Students also retain the responsibility of self-assessment (using teacher-provided criteria) from the two previous styles. The teacher designs a task card containing the task, number of repetitions, different performance levels, and criteria for self-assessment (see figure 10.6).

Student: _____   Date: _____

Task: Kick a stationary ball with force so that it travels up in the air.

Directions: Kick the ball up in the air toward the wall six times. Place a check mark in the column that indicates where the ball went after each kick. If the ball went up in the air, give yourself a thumbs-up and kick again! If not, look at what you should do and then try again.

Self Check Style Task Card: Kicking a ball up in the air

Kick	Up in the air	Along the ground	Why?	What should I do?
1				
2				
3				
4				
5				
6				

Figure 10.5   Self-check task card.

These boys are completing self-check task cards in soccer.

For example, in an educational gymnastics lesson based on jumping and landing, the teacher may say, "Boys and girls, practice jumping from one to two feet 20 times. You may jump on a mat, off the low foam shape [12 inches, or 30 centimeters] onto a mat, or from the higher foam shape [24 inches, or 60 centimeters] onto a mat. After you try your chosen level, if it is too easy or too difficult for you, change to a more appropriate level for your performance. Remember to take a step and swing your arms up as you take off; land on both feet and absorb the jump with a knee bend." The children then decide which of the three jumping tasks they think they cay can perform and start practicing. The teacher circulates, asking children questions about whether the level they chose was appropriate ("How are you doing with that level?") and whether they are performing the skill according to the criteria ("Are your knees bending enough to absorb force for the level you chose?")

Developmental Considerations

When using the inclusion style, teachers must prepare children to perform both a pre-performance and a post-performance self-assessment. In addition, as teachers design the levels of the movement task and self-assessment criteria, they must be mindful of children's stages of cognitive understanding. Pre-K and primary-grade children may be able to select a task that they can successfully

---

Student: _____ Date: _____

Choose the level of cartwheel that you can perform but need to refine. If the level you choose is too easy, switch to a more difficult one. If the level you choose is too difficult, switch to an easier one. For each time that you practice a given type of cartwheel demonstrating most of the skill cues, place a check mark in a box on the appropriate line.

Cartwheel skill cues: hand, hand, foot, foot; straight legs in V above head

Level 1—cartwheel on a mat	❏	❏	❏	❏	❏	❏	❏	❏	❏	❏
Level 2—cartwheel over a foam shape	❏	❏	❏	❏	❏	❏	❏	❏	❏	❏
Level 3—cartwheel on a line	❏	❏	❏	❏	❏	❏	❏	❏	❏	❏
Level 4—cartwheel on a bench	❏	❏	❏	❏	❏	❏	❏	❏	❏	❏
Level 5—cartwheel on a low beam	❏	❏	❏	❏	❏	❏	❏	❏	❏	❏

Figure 10.6 Inclusion-style task card.

perform from an array of options (ranging from easy to more difficult) presented by the teacher. However, they most likely are *not* able to engage in the self-assessment aspect of inclusion style. The ability to assess the quality of one's movement performance according to established criteria typically begins in grade 3 and progresses through grade 5.

Teaching Behaviors

Impact: Implement teaching behaviors decided on in the pre-impact set.

- Explain the objective and assessment method for the lesson.
- Demonstrate the skill; the levels; and the roles of the learner in choosing a level, staying with or changing the level, and comparing personal performance with the relevant criteria.
- Implement the chosen organizational arrangement.
- Give students time to practice the designated tasks.

Post-impact: Implement teaching behaviors related to student performance during the lesson.

- Observe the performer and provide feedback that addresses his or her choice of skill level and self-assessment.
- Provide a closure that assesses the degree to which student learning met the objective.

PRODUCTION CLUSTER

The second cluster of teaching styles is the production cluster, which invites learners to discover new movements and engage in cognitive operations other than memory and recall. Children may be challenged to solve problems, create, compare and contrast, categorize, and apply. The discovery process can result in either divergent or convergent thinking. Convergent thinking involves discovering a specific movement or idea through what are referred to as the guided discovery and convergent discovery styles of instruction. Divergent thinking, in contrast, involves discovering or creating multiple movements or ideas in what is referred to as the divergent discovery style. All of these production teaching styles focus on the discovery or creation of ideas, movements, and rules previously unknown to the learner.

One purpose of using production styles is for students to *discover* movement concepts (e.g., shapes the body can make; different ways to move in relationship to a partner), tactics (e.g., ways to maintain possession of an object in response to an opponent's movement), and principles (e.g., relationship of range of motion to force production; release point and trajectory of an object). Another purpose is for students to *create* a new game, new movement, or new sequence in dance or gymnastics. The hallmarks of these styles include opportunities for self-worth, self-expression, and self-evaluation.

The production styles include, but are not limited to, the three styles mentioned a moment ago: guided discovery, convergent discovery, and divergent discovery. For each of these styles, the following subsections present a description, a statement of purpose, a designation of who makes the decisions (pre-impact, impact, and post-impact), developmental considerations for using the style with children of various ages, and the critical impact and post-impact teaching behaviors that characterize implementation of the style.

Guided Discovery Style (F)

The purpose of the guided discovery style (F) is to guide learners in the process of discovering a predetermined concept by answering a sequence of teacher-designed questions. Each question elicits a single, correct response by the learner, thus leading eventually to the discovery of a content target. During the discovery process, the teacher provides feedback to students about their answers and acknowledges their discovery of the content target. The questions must take into account children's stages of cognitive and motor development by using age-appropriate vocabulary and content targets that children can physically achieve. For instance, K-2 learners might move in response to a series of questions in order to discover that when they are balancing, a wider base provides more stability.

To begin, set the scene: "Children, we are going to discover what we need to do with our bodies to be more balanced."

1. "Balance on your hands and knees. Good! Now try balancing in a narrower shape by lifting one hand and one knee. Which balance was easier to hold and control—the wide balance on four body parts or the narrower balance on two body parts?"

2. "Now try standing in a straddle position on two feet. Excellent! Now lift one foot. Which

balance was easier to hold and control—the wide balance on two feet or the narrower balance on one foot?"

3. "Which balances are easier to hold and control? Wide or narrow?"

Some kinds of information cannot be discovered, including facts such as dates, the names of specific movement skills, how points are scored in a game, or the number of players on a regulation team. Content targets that *can* be discovered include movement concepts, principles, and game tactics unknown to the learner. For instance, learners might discover the importance of moving to open space in order to gain possession of a game object. Children can then build on this learning in other ways: "Once the principles, concepts, or relationships are discovered, the learners move to a different teaching–learning style [e.g., practice style] to apply the principles discovered" (Mosston & Ashworth, 2008, p. 220).

Developmental Considerations

As illustrated in the preceding example about balance, children in kindergarten through grade 5 can use elementary logic and think about events that they have personally experienced. In the balance example, the teacher provides a series of questions that logically guide learners to use their movement experiences to discover the principle of base of support and its relationship to balance. As children in grades 4 and 5 enter into the formal operational stage of cognitive development, they are more capable of discovering abstract concepts related to game tactics, application of fitness principles, and more complex biomechanical principles.

Teaching Behaviors

Impact: Implement teaching behaviors decided on in the pre-impact set.

- Explain the objective and assessment method for the episode.
- Explain the roles of the teacher and the learner (the learner answers each question posed by the teacher).
- Implement the chosen organizational arrangement.
- Ask the questions, one at a time. Give learners time to discover the answer to the question. Reinforce the correct answer before moving on to the next question.

Post-impact: Implement teaching behaviors related to student performance during the lesson.

- Observe learners and provide approving feedback about correct responses to the questions.
- Modify questions when learners are confused or giving incorrect answers (do not give answers).
- Acknowledge learners' discovery of the content target.
- Provide a closure that assesses the degree to which student learning met the objective.

Convergent Discovery Style (G)

In the convergent discovery style (G), children are again challenged to proceed through the discovery process in order to discover a content target—but this time to do so *without* the series of questions from the teacher. Instead of responding to questions, the learner in this style "*produces* the questions and arranges the logical sequence that ultimately leads to discovery of the anticipated response. Although learners may use different approaches to solve the problem, they will each converge on the same response using logic and reasoning" (Mosston & Ashworth, 2008, pp. 237–238, emphasis added).

For example, if your content target is for fourth or fifth graders to discover the relationship between heart rate and intensity of exercise, you can have them record their heart rate as they engage in a series of exercises that are more or less intense in terms of speed or resistance. After performing the exercises and analyzing their heart rate data, students can draw conclusions about the relationship between heart rate and intensity of exercise. As students use trial and error to discover the content target, you can ask questions, if necessary, to facilitate the discovery process without providing the solution.

Developmental Considerations

Again, children in kindergarten through grade 5 can use elementary logic and think about events that they have personally experienced. Accordingly, the use of movement experiences to discover concepts is especially important in convergent discovery because students generate their own trial-and-error steps to find the solution (no steps are guided by the teacher). When this teaching style is used with a group working to solve a challenge, it is important for the children to have developed the requisite social skills—for example, a disposition of willingness to listen to others' ideas and to take risks in offering ideas.

Teaching Behaviors

Impact: Implement teaching behaviors decided on in pre-impact set.

- Explain the objective and assessment method for the episode.
- Pose the movement challenge and state the expectation that learners will use trial and error to solve the movement challenge.
- Implement the chosen organizational arrangement.
- Ask questions, if necessary, to facilitate the discovery process without providing the solution.

Post-impact: Implement teaching behaviors related to student performance during the lesson.

- Teacher and learners acknowledge discovery of the content target.
- Provide a closure that assesses the degree to which student learning met the objective.

Divergent Discovery Style (H)

The purpose of the **divergent discovery style (H)** is for the student to discover multiple responses to a single question and to "expand the imagination of learners in physical performance. For the first time, learners are engaged in discovering and producing options within the subject matter. Until now, the teacher has made decisions about the specific tasks in the subject matter—the role of the learners has been either to replicate and perform or to discover the specific target" (Mosston & Ashworth, 2008, p. 248).

In the divergent discovery style, the teacher decides the subject matter and designs the movement problems. The problems must be developmentally appropriate, taking into account children's levels of skill proficiency, cognitive understanding, and emotional maturity—as well as, ultimately, their safety. Time must be allotted for children to inquire, explore, and design movement solutions. The teacher's role during the discovery process is to accept students' responses and verify that they are indeed solving the problem. It is also important to remember that what may be new to children may *not* be new to the teacher.

In convergent discovery students generate their own trial-and-error steps to find a solution without guidance from the teachers.

Feedback should generally be descriptive, acknowledging the learner's response to the problem but not judging its quality or correcting it. Corrective feedback should be used sparingly: "The only time corrective feedback is given is when responses do not conform to the original question, for example, 'that design develops flexibility; this question seeks designs that develop strength'" (Mosston & Ashworth, 2008, p. 250). For example, if the movement problem is for children to create different balances at different levels, an example of appropriate feedback would be, "I see that you have created three different balances using different levels." An example of inappropriate feedback would be, "Wow, that is such a creative balance." Value-laden feedback such as this may stop children from continuing to create new balances, because they may think that they have already satisfied the teacher. This type of feedback may also imply that one student's responses are better than another's and therefore may shut down the creative process.

A divergent discovery episode could be intended solely for students to discover multiple responses to a movement challenge. It could also be intended,

In divergent discovery, students discover multiple solutions to a movement challenge.

however, for students to select a few responses from multiple available solutions and use them in a specific context. For instance, students could discover multiple turns and shapes with the intent of selecting a few to incorporate into a movement sequence.

Developmental Considerations

Although children in kindergarten through grade 5 can use elementary logic and think about events that they have personally experienced, divergent discovery requires learners to go beyond what they can already physically perform (i.e., do) and cognitively recall (i.e., know). Therefore, teachers need to provide children with the opportunity to respond to a divergent challenge first by performing what they already know and *then* prompt them to go beyond their knowns, thus moving into the unknown, which is to say the creative process. As children progress into the formal operational stage of cognitive development, they can use the movement concepts as a catalyst for finding multiple responses. Pre-K children explore their movement potential within teacher-designed learning environments; however, they do not typically engage in finding multiple responses to a movement challenge.

Teaching Behaviors

Impact: Implement teaching behaviors decided on in the pre-impact set.

- Explain the objective and assessment method for the episode.

- Pose the movement challenge and state the expectation that learners will seek multiple solutions.
- Implement the chosen organizational arrangement.
- Ask questions, if necessary, to facilitate the discovery process without providing the solution.

Post-impact: Implement teaching behaviors related to student performance during the lesson.

- Generally, give descriptive feedback; offer corrective feedback only when the responses are not addressing the movement challenge.
- Teacher and learners acknowledge discovery of multiple responses.
- Provide a closure that assesses the degree to which student learning met the objective.

For each teaching style, table 10.1 provides a quick view of the purpose, student expectations, task card design, and feedback.

MOBILITY ABILITY

Mobility ability is the capacity to plan lessons that incorporate two or more teaching styles. In doing so, teachers can either plan lessons with two or more styles from the same cluster (either reproduction or production) or plan episodes with one or more styles from each cluster. Remember, the choice of

Table 10.1 Quick View of the Spectrum of Teaching Styles

Reproduction styles	Purpose	Student expectations	Task card design	Feedback
A. Command	To learn to do tasks accurately within a short period of time by moving to a cadence or set of commands	Students move in assigned spaces to the cadence or command given by the teacher (or by a recording).	Skill cues or sequence of skills posted for all to see	Teacher gives descriptive and prescriptive feedback to the group.
B. Practice	To learn to work independently by repetitively performing a set of skills To give the teacher time to circulate among students and provide individual feedback	Students work independently in their own space or at stations and make decisions about the pace and order of skill performance.	Description of skills and tasks, number of repetitions expected, and space to record quantity completed (may also include illustrations and criteria)	Teacher gives descriptive and prescriptive feedback to individual.
C. Reciprocal	To learn to work with a partner, assess his or her performance, and offer feedback to help partner maintain or change performance	Students work in pairs in their own space or at stations, taking turns as performer and observer. Observer compares partner's performance with teacher-designed criteria, gives feedback, and records findings.	Description of task, number of repetitions, and illustration of skill Checklist of criteria and samples of descriptive feedback statements	Teacher observes the performer and the feedback interaction between performer and observer. Teacher gives feedback to observer about accuracy of observations and appropriateness of feedback given to performer.
D. Self-check	To learn self-sufficiency by assessing the results of one's own performance and whether and how to change movements for improvement	Students work independently in their own space or at stations, using a checklist to compare results of performance with teacher-designed criteria.	Description of task, number of repetitions, illustration of skill, checklist of cues, results of cues (e.g., if you contact the ball below its center with your shoelaces, the ball goes high), common errors, and space to record results	Teacher observes performer and asks questions about self-assessment. If learner cannot accurately contrast own performance with provided criteria, teacher either asks questions to lead learner to see the discrepancy or identifies the discrepancies if the learner cannot see them.
E. Inclusion	To learn to choose, from a variety of task levels, the level that fits one's ability To learn to make adjustments, if necessary, and self-assess using teacher-provided criteria	Students work independently in their own space or at stations to choose task level, perform repetitions, make adjustments if necessary, and use a checklist to compare performance results with teacher-designed criteria.	Description of task, number of repetitions, illustration of skill, description of skill performance levels, and criteria for self-assessment	Teacher observes performer and asks questions about whether the level chosen was appropriate and whether performer is performing the skill according to the criteria.
Production styles	**Purpose**	**Student expectations**	**Task card**	**Feedback**
F. Guided discovery	To discover a concept by answering a sequence of teacher-designed questions, each of which elicits a single correct response, thus leading to the discovery of a concept, principle, or tactic	Students work independently to answer and confirm the answer to each question before addressing the next question in the sequence.	Description of task goal, list of questions, and space to record answers	Teacher provides approving feedback about correct responses, modifies questions when learners are confused or give incorrect answers (but does not give answers), and acknowledges discovery of the concept, principle, or tactic.
G. Convergent discovery	To discover a single solution to a question or problem by using their own trial-and-error procedure	Students work independently or in small groups to seek the answer to a challenge.	Description of task goal, description of challenge, and space to record answer	Teacher asks questions if necessary to facilitate the discovery process without providing the solution and acknowledges discovery of the concept, principle, or tactic.
H. Divergent discovery	To discover multiple responses to a single challenge	Students work independently or in small groups to generate multiple responses that fit the parameters of the challenge.	Description of the challenge and space to record multiple answers	Teacher gives descriptive feedback, acknowledging responses to the problem but not judging or making corrections unless the response is outside the parameters of the problem.

teaching styles always depends on the lesson objectives and formative assessments. Choose styles that engage students in learning and practice activities that enable them to achieve the learning objective.

Figure 10.7 illustrates the use of mobility ability between three teaching styles. To help students reach the learning objective of knowing the criteria for catching balls arriving from different levels, the teacher starts with the guided-discovery production style. In this approach, students are asked a series of questions about the different ways in which they must position their hands in order to catch a ball arriving above the head, at the midsection, or below the waist. Once the students discover the right answers, the teacher uses the practice reproduction style to engage them in blocked and serial practice that enables them to become consistent in using the skills. Then, to reinforce students' knowledge and performance of the criteria, the teacher uses the reciprocal reproduction style. To check students' understanding, the teacher also uses a formative assessment that allows students to describe, demonstrate, or draw a picture of the correct criteria in response to two of three situations.

UNIVERSAL DESIGN FOR LEARNING

Universal Design for Learning (UDL) is a framework that guides the development of curriculum and instruction to accommodate individual learning differences. The core principles (Rose & Meyer, 2002; National Center on Universal Design for Learning, 2014) reflect inclusionary practices and include the need for

- *multiple means of engagement* to tap into learners' interests, challenge them appropriately, and motivate them to learn;
- *multiple means of representation* to give learners various ways of acquiring information and knowledge; and
- *multiple means of expression* to provide learners alternatives for demonstrating what they know.

The purpose of UDL is to provide full access to learning goals for all. Full access requires that content, instruction, and assessment be differentiated based on need and ability. The framework of standards-based instruction is congruent with UDL because it provides benchmarks that enable progression toward meeting the standards, assessments that provide clear descriptors of learning at different levels, and instructional strategies that provide for individual differences. Common components of UDL and standards-based instruction include using diagnostic assessment to assess the functional abilities of all students; providing multiple means for learners to acquire, demonstrate, and engage in learning; and using formative assessments to modify and adjust instruction.

However, to be fully compliant with UDL, standards-based instruction must reflect a greater range of benchmarks and achievement levels, as well as a wider array of instructional strategies tailored for the unique learning needs of a wider diversity of students. What have you learned thus far in this book that would help you incorporate UDL into physical education learning experiences?

- Standards are chunked by developmentally appropriate grade-level student expectations and performance outcomes.
- Summative assessment uses rubrics that describe criteria for different performance levels.
- Learning tasks are differentiated to meet students' stages of motor development and learning.
- Learning environments are scaled to match learner needs.
- Teaching and practice strategies are matched to learning targets and differentiated based on learner needs.

HOMEWORK

The value of homework lies in the fact that it enables continued student engagement in learning. More specifically, homework can be assigned either to engage students in practice and application of content already learned in class or to introduce them to new concepts. The first of these purposes is the most common use of homework because it gives students a chance to practice what they already know and understand. This type of homework should be tied directly to the learning goals and performance outcomes that students engaged and practiced during the lesson.

Homework also gives students another opportunity to learn from formative assessment conducted by teachers, parents, or themselves. This form of assessment is an integral part of the learning process: "It's not about homework's value for the grade, but homework's value for learning" (Vatterott, 2011, p. 63). Homework should not, however, be based on practicing something with which students are struggling. If they can't do the work under your guidance, then practicing it wrongly at home will only impede the learning process (Moss & Brookhart, 2012).

Using homework for the second purpose—as a way to introduce students to new concepts before covering them in the classroom—is known as "flipping" the classroom (Bergman & Sams, 2012; Hertz, 2012). In this approach, teachers prepare materials about the new content for students

---

Grade 3 learning target: Know and perform criteria for catching balls arriving from different levels.

Objectives

- Discover that catching balls arriving from different levels requires pointing fingers in the direction of flight: pointing fingers up (thumbs together) to receive a ball coming from above the head, pointing fingers horizontally (palms facing) for a ball coming toward the midsection, and pointing fingers down (pinkies together) to receive a ball coming below the waist.
- Consistently catch balls arriving from different levels using correct technique.
- Identify the correct technique for catching balls arriving from different levels.

Episode 1: Guided Discovery

Students answer a series of questions leading to the discovery that catching balls arriving from different levels requires pointing the fingers in the direction of the ball's flight.

Episode 2: Practice Style

Students circle the number of times they correctly performed each skill.

Catch 10 balls arriving toward midsection. 1   5   10   Catch 10 balls arriving above head. 1   5   10

Catch 10 balls arriving below waist. 1   5   10

Repeat each series three times:

Catch a ball arriving below the waist, one at the midsection, and one above the head.	1 2 3
Catch a ball arriving at the midsection, one above the head, and one below the waist.	1 2 3
Catch a ball arriving above the head, one below the waist, and one at the midsection.	1 2 3

Episode 3: Reciprocal Style

Observe a partner catching balls that arrive from different levels. Record the results and give feedback about her or his performance of the cues.

Performer: Catch three balls arriving from each level.

Observer: Observe, record results, and give feedback using performance cues.

Skill	Criteria	Circle successful catches using criteria.
Ball arrives at midsection.	Pointing fingers horizontally (palms facing)	0 1 2 3
Ball arrives above head.	Pointing fingers up (thumbs together)	0 1 2 3
Ball arrives below waist.	Pointing fingers down (pinkies together)	0 1 2 3

Formative Assessment

Answer any two of the following items.

1. Amy must catch a ball coming in overhead. Tell her, show her, or draw a picture of how she should position her hands for a successful catch.
2. Bruce wants to catch a ground ball. Tell him, show him, or draw a picture of how he should position his hands for a successful catch.
3. Joaquin wants to catch a ball coming toward his chest. Tell him, show him, or draw a picture of how he should position his hands for a successful catch.

Figure 10.7   Mobility ability example.

to view and answer questions about at home. The idea is that when they come to school, the teacher does not have to take lesson time to introduce the new material; instead, that time can be used to engage students in practice with feedback.

The bottom line is that homework in physical education is needed because schools often allot very limited time for instruction. However, teachers can continue student engagement in learning outside of school by assigning homework such as the following: watching a video and answering questions about muscular endurance, practicing an appropriate physical skill at home, tracking one's moderate to vigorous physical activity, applying concepts learned in class, and reflecting on how one's class participation is socially responsible.

Big Ideas

- Instructional alignment ensures that the essential content and the content standard of the lesson are addressed in the learning objective (or target or goal), the assessment method, and the instructional content (i.e., movement activities).

- The choice of movement activities to achieve the learning objective is based on the movement framework (see chapter 5) and on task progressions (chapter 6). Both the movement framework and task progressions are based on children's phase and stage of motor development and level of movement skill learning.

- Practice conditions are based on children's level of movement skill learning. The choice of constant or variable practice conditions depends on whether children are at the beginning, intermediate, or advanced level of movement skill learning and on whether they are learning a closed or open movement skill.

- Environment scaling and type of feedback also reflect children's level of movement skill learning (see chapter 7).

- Instructional strategies provide teachers with a means of delivering lesson content. They connect the activities and practice conditions that enable children to meet the assessment criteria in order to achieve the learning goal.

- The Spectrum of Teaching Styles (i.e., Spectrum) is a framework enabling teachers to plan and implement instructional strategies that either engage students in duplicating movements or ideas explained and demonstrated by the teacher (reproduction cluster) or foster students' discovery of movements, concepts, or principles (production cluster). The Spectrum is based on the proposition that teaching consists of a chain of decision making. These decisions can be categorized into the three phases of teaching: pre-impact (planning), impact (implementation), and post-impact (feedback).

- Mobility ability is the capacity to plan lessons that incorporate two or more teaching styles. Teachers can either plan lessons with two or more styles from the same cluster (i.e., reproduction or production) or plan episodes with one or more styles from each cluster. The choice of teaching styles always depends on the lesson objectives and formative assessments.

- Universal Design for Learning involves differentiating instruction so that all learners have full access to achieving the learning goal. Full access requires that content, instruction, and assessment be differentiated based on learner need and ability.

- Homework in physical education can be used either to reinforce a previously taught concept or to introduce a new concept that will be addressed in an upcoming lesson (i.e., to "flip" the classroom).

 Visit the web resource for learning activities, video clips, and review questions.

Chapter **11**

Diverse Learners

Marjorie Ellis

Key Concepts

- Recognizing the aspects of diversity that may be represented in a general physical education class
- Identifying essential aspects of federal laws affecting the quality of education for students with disability and implications of these laws for teaching physical education
- Identifying federal special education programs available for children with disability and the responsibilities of physical education teachers
- Becoming familiar with the concept of "differentiated instruction" and its use in high-quality programs for students with diverse needs
- Identifying disabilities represented in federal law, as well as specific needs in physical education programs
- Identifying the diverse populations often represented in physical education classes and the unique characteristics and needs of each

In contemporary society, diversity plays a large role in instructional decision making and the development of effective instructional practices. There is no longer a single, clear-cut expectation for the student body as a whole that applies to the typical classroom environment. Some years ago, recognized categories of diversity addressed race, gender, ethnicity, and national origin. Diversity initiatives in education today, however, address a wider range of categories and practices, and instructional focus has been expanded to include such categories as sexual orientation, ability, and learning styles. Teachers have focused on revising instructional strategies to be more inclusive and on addressing the various needs and learning styles of diverse students in the same curriculum.

One effective means of serving students with diverse needs and learning styles in the classroom is to incorporate differentiated instructional strategies. However, in order for any instructional strategy or curriculum modification to be effective, the educator must have a clear understanding and a sharp awareness of diversity. This chapter focuses on diverse learners from two perspectives: students with disability and students who come from diverse backgrounds in terms of gender, race, socioeconomic status, sexual orientation, and other underrepresented groups. Students with disability receive greater attention in the chapter because their needs often affect physical performance in a physical education setting and because ways of addressing their specific needs are often less well known.

WHAT'S IN A NAME?

Before discussing inclusive practices in the physical education setting, let's establish a clear understanding of the possible effects of the terminology used in describing individuals and characteristics. As a present or future educator, it is essential for you to practice the use of *person-first* terminology. Historically, it's been a common practice to do the opposite—that is, to refer to a characteristic, disability, or other label as the primary identification of a person. Here are some examples of language that focuses on a *characteristic* first:

- A cerebral palsied person
- That blind boy
- The Hispanic child
- A wheelchair-bound child
- That gay student

Rather than using a characteristic to define an individual, use person-first terminology to respect the person and deflect attention away from a particular characteristic or source of differentness. By using person-first language, we place the focus *not* on a disability or other characteristic but on the person as a whole. This practice reminds us that, as educators, we are working with someone who is not defined by an aspect of diversity but who is a whole person with feelings, dignity, and rights. Here are some examples of person-first terminology:

- A person with cerebral palsy (or John, who has cerebral palsy)
- The boy who is blind or (Mike, who is blind)
- The child who is Hispanic (or Anna, who is Hispanic)
- A child who is a wheelchair user (or Melanie, who uses a wheelchair)

- A student who is gay, lesbian, bisexual, or transgendered (or Sean, who is gay)

Making it a practice to use person-first language ensures that the focus is on the individual that we are accountable for educating, regardless of any particular characteristics. It also models the behavior expected of others, including students, teachers, and administrators alike. This practice of using person-first language has become more popular over the years and has led to advocacy aimed at removing popular but derogatory terms from everyday use. A prime example can be found in the international push to stamp out the "R-word," or *retard(ed)*, by raising awareness and eradicating the term from the vocabularies of younger and older people alike.

DIFFERENTIATED INSTRUCTION

Every student has specific needs related to success in the educational environment. One of the most effective strategies that a teacher can use to meet the needs of all students is to incorporate differentiated instruction into the curriculum. **Differentiated instruction** is an effective and successful strategy for educating students from diverse populations in the same educational setting. In order to effectively use differentiated instruction, teachers must be experts in the content in which they teach, as well as experts in the diversity of learners. Differentiated instruction is not a "one size fits all" concept but rather includes *responsive teaching*. Responsive teaching is responding to student needs and involves in-depth proactive and collaborative planning of not only meaningful, but important, learning opportunities. With responsive teaching, a backward lesson design approach is incorporated first analyzing student needs, collaborating with multiple professionals and other educators, and planning learning opportunities prior to students undertaking lessons in the content area of interest.

Developmentally based differentiated instruction is designed to incorporate various strategies for individual students while focusing on a common outcome. In other words, the students are all learning similar content, but the strategy for reaching the shared goal depends on individual development levels and student learning styles (Ellis, Lieberman, & LeRoux, 2010). In differentiated instruction, three elements of the curriculum can be differentiated based on student needs: content, process, and product (figure 11.1).

The content of the curriculum consists of exactly what is to be taught. It is based on curriculum guidelines set by the state or school district, standards, and benchmarks that students are expected to accomplish. The content may vary by state and grade level. Where applicable, it is also affected by a student's Individualized Education Program or IEP (discussed later in this chapter).

Inclusive practices used to make curricular content available to all learners may include various instructional strategies for delivering content, such as verbal instruction, demonstration, tactile modeling, video demonstration, peer tutoring, and partner and small-group activities (Tomlinson, 2001). In addition, both objectives and tasks should be connected to content goals in that each objective represents an incremental step in a skill-building activity. This connection allows for clear instructional steps and outcomes at various levels of the skill, thus simplifying decisions made by learners at different levels of skill attainment. Finally, and most important from a developmental perspective, the instructional content should address the same concepts with all students, but the degree of difficulty should be appropriate for the individual learner.

The process consists of planning and implementing instruction so that learning occurs within diverse populations. One of the critical aspects of the instructional process involves grouping students for learning. Students can be grouped in a multitude of ways, including on the basis of their readiness to learn certain skills or content, their knowledge of content, their ability to perform the task or skill at hand, the use of cooperative group learning (in which learners work toward a common goal), age and ability levels, areas of interest, and peer tutoring (Gregory & Chapman, 2007). In addition, various curricular approaches are used in order to meet the unique needs of diverse learners, including such strategies as learning stations, learning contracts, choice boards, problem-based learning, and the incorporation of projects to enhance content learning. In making such choices, the teacher must have a clear understanding of individual students' developmental needs, abilities, interests, motivations, and learning styles.

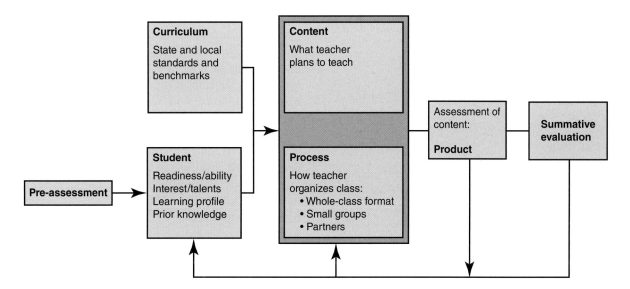

Figure 11.1   Learning cycle and decision factors used in planning and implementing differentiated instruction.

Reprinted from T. Hall, N. Strangman, and A. Meyer, *Differentiated instruction and implications for UDL implementation* (National Center on Accessing the General Curriculum), 3.

The product, or analysis of student proficiency outcomes, in differentiated instruction depends on using inclusive strategies for determining how students demonstrate that they have learned a skill and how they are assessed and graded (Thousand, Villa, & Nevin, 2007). Differentiated instruction does not succeed without pre-assessment to determine exactly how and what an individual learner needs. Assessment, both formal and informal, is also ongoing throughout the differentiated instruction process, and it enables the teacher to identify any changes that need to be made in order to ensure continued student success and development. Throughout differentiated instruction, the learner should be appropriately challenged in order to foster interest, motivation, and engagement in skill learning and understanding. Student assessment should also allow for a variety of outcomes, depending on level of ability, task difficulty, and initial baseline performance (Hall, Strangman, & Meyer, 2009).

Developmentally based differentiated instruction is valuable in all educational settings, including physical education. Its success depends on using inclusive instructional strategies focused on individual student learning styles and needs. Another way to look at it is to view differentiated instruction in physical education as constituting adapted physical education for all learners in an inclusive classroom setting.

Differentiated instruction depends on several key factors that are critical to its success as a pedagogical strategy for meeting the educational needs of diverse learners in an inclusive setting. The major focus is to determine what each learner requires from the educational environment in order to feel comfortable, motivated, and, most important, confident and successful. In addition, differentiated instruction helps teachers accomplish the following goals (Thousand, Villa, & Nevin, 2007):

- Meeting the needs of diverse learners
- Meeting legal mandates established by federal education laws (e.g., the Individuals With Disabilities Education Improvement Act, or IDEIA)
- Challenging stigmas and dispelling myths that persist in education relating to diverse populations
- Following ethical practices in applying curricular standards within diverse populations

- Enhancing overall effectiveness in educating all students

Differentiated instruction follows two approaches. The first is known as retrofitting, which is a reactive approach used when a mismatch is recognized between the content or learning activity and an individual student's learning needs *during* the course of instruction. The second is Universal Design for Learning (UDL), which is a proactive approach in which the teacher gathers information about diverse learners *before* instruction so that the content, lesson process, and expected product or outcome matches individual learner needs. Thus the UDL approach minimizes the need for retrofitting.

IMPACT OF FEDERAL LAWS ON PHYSICAL EDUCATION FOR STUDENTS WITH DISABILITY

Historically, students with disability have been the one group whose education has been protected by a series of federal education laws. The first major U.S. education law addressing disability in education, the Education for All Handicapped Children Act of 1975 (EHA; Public Law 94-142), ensured that children with disability between the ages of 3 and 21 would receive a free, appropriate public education. In 1986, the Education for the Handicapped Act Amendments (EHAA; Public Law 99-457) were enacted and included extensive changes to PL 94-142 in that they required the inclusion of infants and preschoolers up to five years of age in the form of early intervention services (Sass-Lehrer & Bodner-Johnson, 1989). The Education for All Handicapped Children Act (EHA) was later revised and renamed the Individuals With Disabilities Education Act (IDEA) in 1990 (Public Law 101-476). However, throughout multiple revisions, one standard persisted which mandated that all children with diagnosed disability be provided with an appropriate educational program in the "least restrictive environment"—a requirement that all children with disability be educated with their peers who do not have disability unless a student's needs could be met only through specially designed programs as determined through his or her IEP (Davis & Davis, 1994).

Before the passage of EHA, EHAA, and IDEA, children with disability were routinely denied early intervention, educational access, and the opportunity to learn in the public education system. In fact, prior to the passage of EHA, only one in every five students with disability was educated in the public school system. In fact, many states had policies and laws *against* allowing public education for students with specific disabilities, including intellectual disability, emotional disturbance, blindness, deafness, and several other disabling conditions (U.S. Office of Special Education Programs, 2001). Today, however, more than six million children with disability are receiving a free, appropriate public education as defined by IDEA, and about 95 percent of them are educated in general classroom environments with their peers who do not have disability (National Center for Education Statistics [NCES], 2012).

This change affects teachers who are responsible for educating students with disability alongside their peers without disability in the general physical education setting. Under IDEA, physical educators are responsible for providing eligible children who have a disability with instruction specifically designed to meet their unique needs, adapting or modifying lessons, and providing supports or supplementary aids required for the child to fully participate and learn effectively. In addition, in 2013, a report released by the U.S. Department of Education's Office of Civil Rights clarified that the law also allows qualified students with disability to take part in extracurricular athletic programs. This civil rights law ensures quality physical education programs for students with disability, which is critical to their development and their potential future involvement in extracurricular programs (U.S. Department of Education, 2013a, 2013b). Therefore, physical educators and coaches must also ensure equal opportunity for students with disability to participate in extracurricular programs, including athletics.

Because of teachers' intricate responsibilities in providing the most effective opportunities for students with disability, IDEA requires several programs to ensure that students with disability are allowed the most effective educational plan possible. Such opportunities have the intention of ensuring equality for students with disability in multiple environments, whether it be in the classroom setting, gymnasium, or sports/physical activity environment.

Ensuring Educational Opportunities for Students With Disability

U.S. education law includes programs designed specifically to ensure that students with disability receive the most appropriate educational opportunities possible. Each program is designed for a specific purpose, and physical educators must not only be aware of these programs but also understand how to make them an integral part of their daily planning. Table 11.1 presents the programs that most commonly involve educators, including physical education teachers: the Individualized Family Service Plan, the Individualized Education Program, and the Individual Transition Plan.

These three programs are intended to provide a seamless transition from one environment to the next. The Individualized Family Service Plan (IFSP) provides an interdisciplinary approach to supports and services with the intent of preventing further developmental delays. It is also intended to help very young children achieve age-level developmental stages before entering school. When the child reaches age 3, an Individualized Education Program (IEP) is developed based on the child's unique preschool needs and the progress experienced through the IFSP.

The IEP provides the foundation for a high-quality education for a child with disability. It guides the delivery of special education services and supports

Table 11.1 Programs under IDEA

Program	Ages	Purpose
Individualized Family Service Plan (IFSP)	Birth to 3 years	This program focuses on the needs of the child and family to enhance the child's development; is better known as "early intervention."
Individualized Education Program (IEP)	3 to 21 years	This program focuses specifically on the child's educational needs, including special education and related services in the school setting.
Individual Transition Plan (ITP)	16 to 21 years (planning starts at 14 years)	This section of the IEP focuses on transition goals and services designed to lead to positive postsecondary and long-term adult outcomes.

provided to the student in the school setting. As a result, creating an IEP for individual children with disability in the physical education classroom is a critically important part of a physical educator's responsibilities. The IEP requires the physical educator to use formative assessment in order to evaluate the child's progress in class.

One component of the IEP is the Individual Transition Plan (ITP), which focuses on the student's education, training, and employment objectives for transition into the postsecondary world. The ITP is preplanned beginning at age 14 and then implemented at age 16. The ITP includes lifetime physical activities that the physical educator can help the student incorporate into daily life beyond the school years. Even though this time line involves students at the middle school level, the foundation for the ITP planning process is often laid during the elementary school years.

Each IEP includes the following critical information related to the child and his or her unique needs:

- The student's present level of academic achievement based on physical education standards and curriculum objectives

- The student's present level of functional performance (i.e., ability to perform successfully in the physical education environment with peers)

- The annual goals and short-term objectives toward which the student will work

- Details about how progress will be measured, including how often and using what means of assessment

- Details about special education, related services, and supplementary aids and services that will be provided, which may include modifications in curriculum, instruction, equipment, or environment; involvement in adapted physical education; use of a paraeducator or other professional during instruction; use of peer tutoring; or other specific methods for ensuring full success and participation in physical education classes

- Explanation of the extent (if appropriate) to which the child will *not* participate in physical education class with peers who do not have a disability

- Modifications or adaptations that will be incorporated when undertaking state- or districtwide physical education assessment

- When the specific program will begin, how long it will be used, and how often and where will it be conducted

- How information in the IEP, including progress toward goals and short-term objectives, will be communicated to the child's parents

Definition of Physical Education Under IDEA

Physical education is the only subject area that is specifically defined within the definition of a special education service under IDEA. As defined by IDEA, physical education is "the development of (a) physical and motor fitness; (b) fundamental motor skills and patterns; and (c) skills in aquatics, dance, and individual and group games and sports (including intramural and lifetime sports)" (U.S. Department of Education, 1998). Thus physical education contributes to the growth and development of children with disability through the medium of movement.

As noted earlier, IDEA mandates that all children with diagnosed disability must be provided with an appropriate physical education program and that this program must be offered in the "least restrictive environment." This provision means that children with special physical, intellectual, or emotional or behavioral needs must be given the opportunity to take part in the general physical education program unless their needs can be met only through a specially designed program as prescribed by an IEP. In this way, IDEA mandates a policy of inclusion—that is, educating children with disability in the same environment as their peers who do not have disability—whenever and wherever possible.

Inclusion

As an outgrowth of IDEA, the philosophy of inclusion of children with disability has gained popularity in the United States. Full inclusion refers to educating a student with any disability, whether mild or profound, in the same educational environment as the child's peers who do not have disability. Inclusion in physical education, then, takes place in the general physical education classroom. Schools that practice a philosophy of full inclusion involve children with a wide range of disabilities not just as participants in certain aspects of the program but in *all* aspects. As a result, full inclusion places special demands on the physical education teacher and is viewed by many as a very difficult task. Indeed, it is by no means easy, especially when it involves severe disability. However, by incorporating differentiated instruction, teachers can achieve successful inclusion in any classroom setting.

CATEGORIES OF DISABILITY, CHARACTERISTICS, AND NEEDS

IDEA identifies 13 categories of disability covered under the federal law, and educators should become knowledgeable of specific disability characteristics that may present challenges in the physical education environment. It is also critical to understand that these disability characteristics serve only as a general guide, because unique individual differences exist within each disability category. The categories are presented in table 11.2.

In reviewing table 11.2, please note that in many instances it is currently viewed as more appropriate to use an alternative term than to use the original term. For example, educators have moved away from using the term *mental retardation* and toward using *intellectual disability* or *cognitive impairment* in an effort to be more respectful of individuals who have special needs. Therefore, when discussing disabilities in this chapter, the alternative term will sometimes be used to address a specific disability population.

In the public school setting, students with disability may be educated either in a general classroom with their peers who do not have disability, in a special education classroom, or in both. More than six million school-aged children in the United States receive special education services due to a specific disability that adversely affects their educational performance; of these, more than half

Table 11.2 Disability Categories

Federal disability term	Alternative terms	Brief description
Learning disability (LD)	Specific learning disability (based on type and focus – example: dyslexia)	Disorder related to processing information that leads to difficulties in reading, writing, and computing; the most common disability, accounting for half of all students who receive special education
Speech or language impairment	Communication disorder (CD)	Disorder related to accurately producing the sounds of language or using language meaningfully to communicate
Mental retardation (MR)	Intellectual disability, cognitive impairment	Significant limitations, occurring across a range of severity, in intellectual ability and adaptive behavior
Emotional disturbance (ED)	Behavior disorder (BD), emotional disability	Significant problems in the social-emotional area to a degree that learning is negatively affected
Autism	Autism spectrum disorder (ASD)	Disorder, occurring in many forms from mild to severe, characterized by extraordinary difficulty in social responsiveness
Hearing impairment	Deaf or hard of hearing (DHH)	Partial or complete loss of hearing
Visual impairment	Low vision, blind	Partial or complete loss of vision
Deaf-blindness		Simultaneous significant hearing loss and significant vision loss
Orthopedic impairment (OI)	Physical disability	Significant physical limitation that impairs the ability to move or complete motor activities
Traumatic brain injury (TBI)		Medical condition that involves serious brain injury resulting from accident or injury; varies widely; and may affect learning, behavior, social skills, and language
Other health impairment (OHI)		Disease or health disorder so significant that it negatively affects learning (e.g., cancer, sickle cell anemia, diabetes)
Multiple disabilities		Presence of two or more disabilities such that none can be identified as the primary disability, manifesting most commonly as mental retardation and physical disability
Developmental delay (DD)		Nonspecific disability category that states may use as an alternative to specific disability labels for identifying students up to age 9 who need special education

From Friend and Bursuck 2011.

(59 percent) are categorized as having either a specific learning disability (about 37 percent) or a communication disorder (about 22 percent) (National Center for Education Statistics [NCES], 2012). Students categorized as having a form of "other health impairment" (OHI) account for about 11 percent, followed by those with intellectual disability (about 7 percent), autism (about 6 percent), a behavioral disorder (about 6 percent), a developmental disability (about 6 percent), and multiple disabilities (about 2 percent). A much smaller group of students is categorized as deaf or hard of hearing (about 1 percent); physically disabled (about 1 percent); or traumatically brain injured, blind or having low vision, or deaf-blind (each less than 1 percent).

Regardless of percentages, however, teachers must be familiar with how to incorporate differentiated instruction so that *any* child with disability in their classroom can be successful. This is especially true given that about 95 percent of school-aged children served under IDEA are enrolled in regular public schools, meaning that they are most likely to be placed in a general physical education class (NCES, 2012).

In adapted physical education, the focus is on adapting or modifying the instruction, curriculum, activities, or environment to meet the needs of learners with disability. Differentiated instruction, in contrast, focuses on modifying the content, learning activities, outcomes, and environment in order to meet the needs of *all* learners. The strate-gies are similar to each other with one focused on a specific population and the other on the complete student body population.

The following sections address diverse populations and introduce differentiated instructional strategies to provide you with the tools for understanding how to incorporate UDL based on individual student needs.

Specific Learning Disability

A specific learning disability leads to difficulties in one or more of the basic psychological processes involved in understanding and using spoken or written language. This difficulty in language understanding and use may lead to difficulty in reading, writing, spelling, speaking, listening, and completing mathematical calculations.

It is often thought that students with a specific learning disability have problems only in reading, writing, spelling, or math—and not in other academic areas, such as physical education. In reality, however, a learning disability may affect a child's performance in the physical education environment in a number of ways. Many students with a learning disability have both lower self-esteem and lower self-concept, both of which may affect their performance in physical education due to the desire to avoid participation or performance in front of their peers (Elbaum & Vaughn, 2001). Furthermore, in many cases, students with a learning disability are instructed in small-group settings in the

---

Teaching Tips for Children With Specific Learning Disability

Some children with a specific learning disability may require modifications or adaptations in the general physical education classroom. Here are some specific strategies:

- For students with low self-esteem or low self-concept, give positive feedback and praise during their participation in activities.
- Post and frequently review key information (e.g., skill cues, critical elements of movement skills, the order of a gymnastics sequence) in order to increase the chances that the student will remember it.
- Keep an open line of communication with the student's general or special education teacher and inform him or her of the activities planned for the day so that they can be reviewed with the student before physical education class.
- Allow the student to watch a video of the fundamental movement skill, game progression, dance, or gymnastics activity in order to gain a visual understanding before coming to class and participating in it.
- Teach fundamental movement skills and game, dance, and gymnastics skill progressions in a small-group setting.

classroom and may be unprepared to participate in the large-group setting typically found in physical education. In addition, many physical education concepts require memorization and recall of information—for example, skill cues for fundamental movement skills, rules associated with game progression, and sequencing of gymnastics skills or dance steps. These cognitive functions may be challenging for students with a learning disability.

Communication Disorders

Communication disorders include issues related to auditory processing, speech, and language. They range from stuttering to misarticulation of words to complete inability to use speech and language for communicative purposes (Owens, Metz, & Farinella, 2010). Although communication disorders can be connected with such disabilities as developmental disorders, autism, hearing loss, intellectual disability, and neurological disorders (to name a few), the cause is usually unknown.

Students who have a specific learning disability or communication disorder typically develop physical and motor skills at an age-appropriate level. Therefore, in working with these students, physical educators most likely will not need to make ad-aptations or modifications in the physical education content per se. However, when working with students who have a communication disorder, concerns may arise in regard to a student's social development, communication with the teacher to express understanding of class requirements, and communication with peers during activity (Heward, 2006). In years past, these difficulties with language and communication often led educators to mistakenly classify students with a communication disorder as having an intellectual disability, behavioral disorder, or hearing loss.

Students with communication disorders might be more comfortable learning new skills with the assistance of a trusted peer.

Teaching Tips for Children With a Communication Disorder

Most often, children with a communication disorder can be fully included in the general physical education setting without modifications or adaptations. In some cases, however, specific adjustments are required when incorporating differentiated instruction, and they may include the following:

- Allow students to work with peers with whom they are comfortable when learning new skills.
- Allow students to use alternative means of communication (e.g., sign language, voice box, iPad, gesturing) to interact with their peers
- Encourage an accepting learning environment in which the child feels comfortable regardless of communication differences, especially for students who stutter or misarticulate words and therefore may be the focus of teasing and bullying.
- Encourage students to develop nonverbal communication with their peers in order to enhance a team atmosphere in which a common goal and outcome is shared.

Intellectual or Cognitive Disability

The American Association on Intellectual and Developmental Disabilities (2010) defines an **intellectual disability** as one "characterized by significant limitations both in intellectual functioning and in adaptive behavior, which covers many everyday social and practical skills. This disability originates before the age of 18." This was the first definition of the term *intellectual disability* which replaced the previous label of "mental retardation" (now viewed as inappropriate and not to be used).

Determinations of intellectual functioning are typically based on the outcome of an IQ test, and scores of 75 or lower are held to indicate intellectual disability. In order to be classified as having intellectual disability, however, a student must also exhibit deficiency in adaptive behaviors. These behaviors involve practical, social, and conceptual skills and relate to forms of daily activity, such as problem solving, personal care, and recognizing important aspects of time and money. Therefore, a determination of intellectual disability is based not only on a child's intellectual functioning but also on the amount of support needed in various environments. With this in mind, teachers must take into account the amount of support needed to implement differentiated instruction in the general physical education classroom.

Individuals who require only limited or intermittent support are viewed as having a **mild intellectual disability**. Such a student is likely to succeed in a general physical education class when differentiated instruction is implemented in relation to her or his intellectual level and required support. Students who have a more severe intellectual disability are likely to require more extensive and continuous support and are most likely to be educated in a more adapted physical education environment. These children may require one-on-one instruction and focus on activities that lead to enhancement of practical skills and adaptive behaviors. Of all children with intellectual disability, about 95 percent are in the mild range and therefore can be expected to take part in general physical education activities with the benefit of differentiated instructional strategies focused on specially designed instruction and content adapted to their particular needs.

An intellectual or cognitive disability generally results in significantly sub-average intellectual functioning, affecting both motor and cognitive development. The lag in motor development

---

Teaching Tips for Children With Intellectual Disability

Although children with intellectual disability have the potential to attain levels of motor skill and physical fitness similar to those of their peers without disability, they may need more time to do so. Here are some suggestions for enhancing the general physical education experience for students with mild intellectual disability.

- Permit ample time for learning—even extending the time allocation, if required.
- Keep instruction short, use shorter sentences and fewer verbal cues, use more visual and tactile cues, and repeat instruction frequently.
- Provide instructional support for only one skill at a time and allow the student time to become familiar with the skill before moving to the next skill in a sequence.
- Reinforce and praise all attempts and accomplishments, no matter how small.
- Use frequent demonstrations of the task to be learned, as well as hands-on physical manipulation through the skill, if necessary.
- Ask the student to demonstrate the skill in order to check for understanding.
- Use visual prompts and color coding as learning tools.
- Regularly review and stress compliance with basic safety rules.
- Treat the student based on chronological age rather than cognitive age.
- Teach all students as equals.

results in part from problems with cognition (an intrinsic condition) and often from lack of opportunity for activity (an extrinsic condition). This dynamic means that children with an intellectual disability have the ability to achieve motor skill levels similar to those of their peers, but the lack of structured learning and participation opportunities leads these children to have skills lower than those expected for their age and gender.

Indeed, what can be expected if a person's life is spent in endless hours of sedentary activities that do nothing to promote the development of motor skills and physical fitness? Human beings need physical activity in order to function at their optimal level, and this is true regardless of intellectual capability. Therefore, children with intellectual disability cannot be expected to succeed at the same level as their chronological counterparts do in terms of physical functioning if they lack sufficient movement experiences and sound guidance in their motor development. Although a child's intellectual functioning may affect the outer limits for his or her physical functioning, this fact must not prevent physical educators from striving for maximal performance. Regardless of the severity of a child's intellectual disability, it is not the child's *overall* ability to develop motor skills that is affected, but rather the *rate* at which he or she can learn these skills.

With these realities in mind, we can recognize that a child with intellectual disability must be helped to learn the movement skills needed for a physically active life rather than the sedentary lifestyle so common among those with this type of disability. This need is especially pressing among children with Down syndrome, where multiple disabilities are common, including metabolism and heart issues that may directly affect physical fitness and activity levels, as well as muscle issues that affect proficient performance of motor skills.

Emotional/Behavioral Disorders

Ask teachers about the make-up of their classrooms and you will likely hear most of them mention of at least one or two students with behaviors that the teacher refers to as "challenging." One of the challenges faced by the educational system lies in the way that emotional/behavioral disorders (EBDs) have been defined by IDEA. The definition of EBDs according to IDEA applies to only 1 percent or 2 percent of the student population and focuses on students who are oppositional, aggressive toward

For students with a mild intellectual disability, hands-on instruction can facilitate skill learning.

others, and have difficulty with following directions (Kauffman, 2001). In contrast, starting with the fourth edition of the *Diagnostic and Statistical Manual of Mental Disorders* (DSM-IV; American Psychiatric Association, 2000) describes both internalized EBDs (e.g., depression, bipolar disorder, anxiety) and externalized EBDs (e.g., oppositional defiant disorder, conduct disorder, ADHD) that may affect 15 percent to 20 percent of the total student population (Kauffman, 2001; Shaffer et al, 1996). Due to these incongruent definitions, teachers may have students in their classrooms who are affected by an EBD but are neither diagnosed nor receiving appropriate special education or support services.

Regardless of the definition used, however, the bottom line is that EBDs not only pose a challenge to educators but also influence the educational performance of students with an EBD, as well as their peers' enjoyment and success in the physical education environment. The academic performance of a student with an EBD is adversely affected by the student's emotional or behavioral problems, such as inappropriate behavior that detracts from learning and performing physical education content. In addition, the time and focus that the educator puts toward controlling negative behavior reduces the time and focus that he or she can devote to providing instruction, feedback, and activities for the class as a whole.

Here are some ways in which EBDs affect performance across the board in inclusive settings:

- Students with an EBD may demonstrate behavioral traits that interfere with high-quality instruction by educators and learning by the student and his or her peers due to disruption of the classroom environment that leads the teacher to focus on behavior control.

- Students with an EBD may influence the teacher's behavior in ways that lead to decreased instruction time, a less challenging curriculum (to placate inappropriate behaviors), and greater enforcement of such behavioral management strategies as time-outs.

- Teachers of students with an EBD may feel overwhelmingly unprepared to provide an effective learning environment for these students due to lack of preparation in regard to behavioral and classroom management strategies specifically for this population.

- Teachers need more information based on empirical research about effective strategies for addressing an EBD in the physical education environment.

(Wehby, Lane, & Falk 2003)

In the midst of these concerns, the main issue remains that the education of students with an EBD is affected both by their demonstration of inappropriate behaviors and by teachers' lack of the experience and understanding needed to ensure that these students receive the best possible physical education program.

The critical first step in ensuring a positive learning environment is to identify students who may have an EBD. The following common characteristics may be demonstrated over several interdisciplinary settings (Kamps, Wendland, & Culpepper, 2006).

- Little understanding or consideration of social, cultural, and classroom rules
- Impulsiveness
- Poor concentration or focus
- Resistance to changes and transitions in academic content and settings

- High absenteeism
- Difficulty working in groups
- Regular disruption of classroom activities
- Seeming preoccupation, distractibility, and inattention
- Possible demonstration of aggressive behavior, as well as intimidation and a tendency to bully

Though school is not the only factor affecting a child's EBD, teachers can exert great influence on students. This influence can be seen in the expectations that teachers have for individual students, the questions they ask of students and how they ask them, the feedback and reinforcement they provide, and the interactions they have with students. In all of these ways, what teachers do can make a difference—for better or for worse.

For example, suppose that a teacher has not received appropriate preparation in behavioral or classroom management or disability awareness. As a result, this teacher may be unaware of or insensitive to students' individual differences and therefore contribute inadvertently to an environment where frustration, aggression, and disrespect are common responses. In contrast, consider a teacher who has received appropriate preprofessional preparation in both behavioral and classroom management, as well as awareness of disabilities. The difference between these two teachers—and their classroom—may be like night and day, as the teacher who is better prepared provides a learning environment based on consistent and appropriate educational experiences and interventions that match individual students and behaviors.

Effective educators consistently use strategies geared toward ensuring a welcoming and effective learning environment for all students by incorporating elements such as the following:

- Acceptance of and sensitivity to cultural diversity
- Schoolwide strategies for conflict resolution
- High student involvement in all classroom activities
- Strong, positive interactions with students that lead to empowerment in the physical education environment
- Consistent expectations, rules, and consequences across the school to ensure greater understanding of and expectations for all students

Teaching Tips for Children With an EBD

No research indicates that students with an EBD lack the capability to achieve movement skills and fitness at levels similar to those of their peers. However, both internalized and externalized disorders can create concerns in educational settings, and educators can address them by means of several strategies for preventing or reducing issues associated with EBD in the general physical education setting. Here are some suggestions for enhancing the experience of students with EBD and their classroom peers (Gunter, Coutinho, & Cade, 2002; Kamps, Kravits, Stolze, & Swaggart, 1999):

- **Consistent standards:** Be sure that all educational and administrative staff members use the same standards for acceptable and unacceptable behavior and for consequences attached to undesirable behaviors.
- **Peer involvement:** Use a peer reminder system to have peers reinforce each other's understanding of expectations and appropriate behavior practices.
- **Systematic intervention plans:** Use different and appropriate tactics, depending on the type and severity of student behavior.
- **Behavior management:** To facilitate appropriate behavior and task completion, use a point system in which positive student behaviors are visibly charted and rewarded, thus allowing students to see how their behavior influences outcomes involving desirable rewards.
- **Classroom structure:** For transitions between activities, use well-organized or guided transitions.
- **Supervision of free periods:** Make sure that unstructured activities (e.g., hall changes, lunch, recess) are monitored by adults who are well aware of the consistent behavioral standards.
- **Home–school communication:** Ensure clear communication between teachers and parents about behavioral standards and point systems and encourage home-based reward systems to enhance student consistency in behavior.

- An educational climate that encourages and reinforces learning
- Effective use of space to avoid overcrowding and overwhelming students
- Early identification of students who exhibit behaviors that are often predictive of future EBD problems

Autism Spectrum Disorder

Autism spectrum disorder (ASD) is the fastest-growing developmental disability in the United States, where it is increasing at an annual rate of 10 percent to 17 percent (Centers for Disease Control and Prevention (CDC), 2012). Approximately 1 in 88 school-aged children in the United States has been diagnosed with ASD, and the figure is about five times higher among males (1 in 54 children) than among females (1 in 253 children). In about 10 percent of children with ASD, autism is part of a dual diagnosis along with a specific genetic or chromosomal disorder, such as Down syndrome, tuberous sclerosis, or fragile X syndrome (Kim, et al., 2011).

In earlier versions of federal education law in the United States, autism was classified as an emotional disturbance (i.e., what is now referred to as a behavioral disorder). Presently, however, it has its own diagnostic category under IDEA (U.S. Department of Education, 1998). Even so, children with autism are often grouped generally with children who are classified as having a behavioral disorder and those who have significant problems requiring behavioral management.

In 2013, the American Psychiatric Association published the fifth edition of its *Diagnostic and Statistical Manual of Mental Disorders* (DSM-5), which includes a drastic new definition of ASD. This updated definition includes the following five major changes:

Provide equipment with a variety of color and texture and let students choose the equipment they prefer.

- The definition eliminates and combines under the ASD umbrella a number of subcategories that were previously grouped under the label of pervasive developmental disorder (PDD), including autism, Asperger syndrome, Childhood Disintegrative Disorder (CDD), Rett syndrome, and pervasive developmental disorder not otherwise specified (PDD-NOS).

- Previously, autism symptoms were classified into three domains: impairment in language and communication, impairment in social interaction, and repetitive or restrictive behavior. The new definition, in contrast, includes just two main symptom categories: (1) restricted interests and repetitive behaviors and (2) social communication impairment. For each area, the definition lists characteristics that a child may demonstrate; in order to be diagnosed, a child must exhibit at least two symptoms in the category of restricted interests and repetitive behaviors and three symptoms in the category of social communication. When determining a diagnosis of autism, symptoms demonstrated by the child can be from past reports or present behavior.

- Any related conditions are attached to the autism diagnosis—specifically, any genetic cause (e.g., fragile X syndrome), any language deficit or intellectual disability, and any other related medical condition (e.g., seizures, gastrointestinal problems).

- A new category under the ASD umbrella— social communication disorder (SCD)—has been created to allow for diagnosis specifically in regard to social communication without the presence of repetitive behavior.

Children with autism are frequently included in general physical education classes, but autism can have a large effect on a student's participation. Students with autism may exhibit difficulty with social interaction; withdrawal behaviors; inappropriate responses to stimuli due to issues with sensory integration; repetitive behaviors; and differences in communication, which can range from advanced use of language to echolalia (involuntary repetition of others' words) to no use of verbal language. In addition to these diagnostic characteristics, many children with autism also experience delays in developing fundamental motor skills. In one study, 83 percent of children with ASD scored below average on movement skill performance (Hilton, Zhang, White, Klohr, & Constantino, 2012). The study also found a connection between lower skill levels, greater impairment in social communication, and severity of ASD. Although children with ASD generally display deficits in movement skills and social behavior, the majority (more than 60 percent) do not have any form of intellectual deficiency (CDC, 2012).

Communication challenges associated with ASD may take various forms. Children with ASD may "hear in pictures" and have difficulty with

Teaching Tips for Children With Autism Spectrum Disorder

In working with children who have ASD, it is important to be familiar not only with any motor delays that they may demonstrate but also with their level of communication and social ability. In addition, the following guidelines can be incorporated to ensure the most effective program for these students.

- Establish clear channels of communication with all professionals who are involved in the child's education, including special and general education teachers, related service providers, behavioral specialists, school nurses, and **paraprofessionals**.
- Include illustrations of movements, directions, vocabulary, and game plays. Use gestures to supplement starting and stopping signals, as well as approving feedback (e.g., thumbs-up) and corrections (e.g., pointing in the other direction).
- Allow the student to work with peer tutors or partners on specific content.
- If the student has a paraprofessional, make sure that the paraprofessional is aware of and understands the physical education content and your expectations for the individual student.
- As much as possible, reduce or eliminate sensory stimulation and distractions. Do not leave unnecessary equipment around that may catch the student's attention.
- In some cases, the student has difficulty and even experiences sensory overload when confronted with large spaces (e.g., open gymnasium), echoes and acoustics, glares from the floor or ground surface, mercury-vapor or fluorescent lights, or cars passing by. If such factors cause a problem in the learning environment, communicate with the interdisciplinary team about possible solutions, such as having the student wear headphones or sunglasses, allowing the student to use a personal CD player with his or her choice of calming music, or using a mat wall to separate the learning area into multiple spaces.
- Allow the student to use his or her choice of equipment color or texture.
- Use the student's restrictive interests to advantage in the learning environment; for example, if a student is focused on squeezable things, use yarn, foam balls, or other squeezable equipment.
- Use creative, engaging equipment to facilitate interaction and learning such as a spider ball or rubber chicken.
- Teach age-appropriate movement skills.
- Use peer tutors, who are trained by the physical educator, to help the child develop skills in social interaction.
- Emphasize individual or partner activities and games over group activities wherever possible to minimize disruption due to difficulty with social interaction; individual and partner activities do include social situations but do not require a great deal of social interaction.
- If a team game is taught, focus on instruction regarding skill development and lead-up activities in small groups.
- Develop and stick to a class routine that is constant and predictable.
- Keep all directions short and to the point, including demonstrations, and allow the student to model the skill.
- Use progressive skill teaching, with small steps, to help the student be successful at all times.
- Use a communication board or motivation chart to take advantage of the student's strong visual skills.
- When using stations, incorporate task cards or cards picturing the skill being performed.
- Use video modeling (showing either the student or an expert performing the skill) to enhance skill learning and understanding.
- Give a verbal and/or visual alert when a change in activity is approaching in order to help the student know what to expect—for example, "In three minutes, we will move to the next station."
- Teach skills in various settings (e.g., in physical education, during school recess, at home, or in a community setting) to enhance transfer of skills from school to home and community.
- Create a positive learning environment and a safe climate in which the student feels secure and unthreatened when performing.

processing oral directions and feedback, as well as auditory information received from the environment. In addition, the impairment in social communication that characterizes ASD can involve not only receptive but also expressive communication skills. As a result, children with autism may have difficulty communicating their thoughts, feelings, needs, wants, ideas, and desires. Therefore, teachers must be prepared to alter their instructions and feedback to include visuals that a child with ASD can see rather than hear.

Due to the child's restrictive interests and repetitive behaviors, the teacher must also provide a structured educational environment with clear routines. This approach allows students with ASD to become familiar with class content without unexpected surprises that could cause them to display behavioral patterns, sometimes aggressive, brought on by their inability to communicate clearly about an unknown environment or activity. In summary, to enhance the child's success, the teacher should ensure that he or she is provided with a structured environment, clear routines, and supplemental visual communication (Zhang & Griffin, 2007).

Deafness and Hardness of Hearing

Children who are deaf or hard of hearing make up about 1 percent of the school-aged population receiving special education services in the United States (CDC, 2012). The effect of hearing loss on a child's education depends on the type of loss, its severity, and its impact on communication. There are three main types of hearing loss: conductive, sensorineural, and mixed. Children with conductive hearing loss most likely use either a hearing aid or an FM system to amplify sound so that it can be transmitted through the auditory canal and into the inner ear before being converted to a sound wave sent to the brain for interpretation. Children with sensorineural hearing loss most likely use a hearing aid, a cochlear implant, or a sign language interpreter. In sensorineural hearing loss, sound is not effectively transmitted to the brain due to damage to either the cochlea, the auditory nerve, or both. Teachers must be aware of the type of hearing loss affecting a child in order to identify and incorporate the most effective communication strategy.

Depending on the activity, children who use hearing aids or cochlear implants may be unable to wear them at certain times during physical education. For example, cochlear implants cannot be worn during any activity in which static electricity may occur—such as activities using plastic equipment, trampolines, balloons, or ball pits, all which may cause electrostatic discharge and thereby interfere with the audio external processor.

Teaching Tips for Children With a Hearing Impairment

- Learn sign language and teach all students how to communicate by means of this method.
- When giving instructions, directly face the student with a hearing loss and make sure that *you* are facing any light, including the sun.
- Use a variety of visual cues and signals for gaining attention, starting and stopping activities, and ensuring that the student understands expectations.
- Teach movement activities, especially in music and dance, using high bass so the student can feel the beat and incorporating signs to enhance expressiveness of performance.
- Assess children on various motor skills, including balance, and physical fitness components in order to ensure that their development and fitness is on par with recommended levels.
- When checking for student understanding, beware of the "deaf nod"; many children who are deaf or hard of hearing get into the habit of nodding affirmatively when asked questions, regardless of whether they understand.
- Incorporate rhythmic activities, such as dance or gymnastics, into your curriculum to allow the child to work on balance skills.

Rhythmic activities can help children work on balance skills.

Children with cochlear implants should also avoid contact sports and other activities that could lead to a blow to the head. In addition, both cochlear implants and hearing aids must be removed before a student participates in aquatic activities. In these situations, the child is put into a situation where communication must be supported through other means, most likely a sign language interpreter. Therefore, it is very important for children who are deaf or hard of hearing to learn sign language, if only as a back-up measure.

In the United States, American Sign Language (ASL) is the fourth most common language overall and the third most common studied at the post-secondary level. However, less than 10 percent of all hearing parents with deaf children know how to use ASL. Still, as a teacher, you can incorporate ASL into your curriculum and encourage all students to learn it and use it to communicate with their deaf peer. Then perhaps they will take these skills home and teach their parents (Mellon, et al., 2015).

Research has reported conflicting outcomes with respect to motor development and physical fitness levels among children who are deaf or hard of hearing (Ellis, et al., 2005; Ellis, Lieberman, & Dummer, 2013; Gheysen, Loots, &Van Waelvelde, 2008; Hartman, Houwen, & Visscher, 2011; Rajendran & Roy, 2011; Zwierzchowska, Gawlik, & Grabara, 2008). In some cases, delays were related to balance deficiencies that can accompany hearing loss, especially of the sensorineural type.

Therefore, physical education teachers should be diligent in conducting assessment in order to identify any deficiencies. They can then develop the physical education program as needed in order to allow the child to address any delay in motor skills or physical fitness that would affect performance in the physical education curriculum.

Blindness and Low Vision

Low vision and blindness are found in about 1 percent of children (i.e., a total of about 416,000 children) between the ages of 5 and 15 years who receive special services in public schools in the United States (Erickson, Lee, & von Schrader, 2013). The terms *blindness* and *low vision* have a variety of meanings, depending on the defining organization. Educational definitions describe blindness and low vision as any loss or change in vision that requires corrective lenses or other aids (i.e., braille, auditory support) to engage in activities in the school environment (National Eye Institute, 2013). Physical educators must understand both the type and the severity of a child's vision loss in order to plan the most effective educational experience for the child.

There are a number of common types of vision loss in children. The most common types involve simple refractive errors, which can be treated through the use of corrective lenses. Some other types, of course, are more serious. Here are some common eye conditions:

Stand close to the student with blindness or low vision and allow the student to be positioned where she or he can make best use of any residual vision.

- Astigmatism—inability to focus on objects that are either near or far due to an error preventing appropriate focusing of light within the retina.

- Hyperopia—difficulty with focusing on objects that are close; also known as farsightedness.

- Myopia—difficulty with focusing on objects that are far away; also known as nearsightedness.

- Amblyopia—reduced visual acuity (clarity) due to weak muscles and poor eye positioning (also known as lazy eye); the most common cause of low vision in children.

- Cortical visual impairment—damage in the pathways that transport visual information to the brain, thus preventing the brain from receiving the information. This condition may cause fluctuating vision and is common in children with seizure disorder, cerebral palsy, and some developmental delays. Children with this condition may choose to explore objects through touch rather than vision.

- Retinitis pigmentosa—inherited, degenerative condition that leads to loss of peripheral vision and, over time, more severe loss of vision.

- Retinopathy of prematurity—detachment or scarring of the retina resulting from loss of oxygen during premature birth and possibly leading to loss of vision.

- Strabismus—condition caused by muscle imbalance that prevents the eyes from focusing on an object at the same time.

- Congenital blindness—Loss of vision at or before birth due to any of multiple potential causes, including maternal injury or infection during pregnancy, prematurity, and accident during childbirth.

- Albinism—Inherited condition in which certain genes do not allow the body to produce the correct amount of melanin, which can cause blindness or low vision and which also causes light or white hair, reddish eyes, and pale skin.

Vision gives human beings a tremendous amount of information about the immediate environment and the larger world. It is one of the most highly used of the five senses, and it contributes heavily to both incidental and direct learning. Even so, children with blindness or low vision are still able to achieve the same skills as their peers, but they may require more time and modified instruction in order to do so. Because they lack the easy visual access to learning that sighted children have, they must adapt to using other senses and methods in order to accomplish the learning that their sighted peers accomplish through vision. As a result, their learning depends more heavily on listening, tasting, smelling, touching, and using any level of

Teaching Tips for Children With Blindness or Low Vision

- Be aware of the student's level of vision loss, as well as what usable vision he or she possesses.
- Ask students what they are able to see, which conditions and objects present issues, and at what distance they are able to see the relevant game object.
- Ensure that areas of activity are well lit or, in some cases, that lights are dimmed, according to student preference.
- Be consistent with equipment and activity setup and make sure that the activity area is free of obstacles and is as uncluttered as possible
- When giving instructions, stand close to the student with blindness or low vision and allow the student to be positioned where she or he can make best use of any residual vision.
- Use equipment of light color (e.g., white, yellow, orange) and sharp contrast (e.g., bright ball on dark floor, colored tape to identify playing area on wall or floor).
- When setting the boundaries or location of activities, change the texture of the boundary or other marker in order to make it readily identifiable. For example, use mats or carpet runners to identify the outermost portion of the playing area or areas where certain activities are to be performed (i.e., warm-ups on the mats).
- When necessary, modify activities and equipment—for example, use a buddy system, audible or larger equipment, tethers, or ropes or guide runners.
- Use tactile modeling when demonstrating skills and physically move the student through the skill progression when necessary.
- For activities requiring balance (e.g., jumping), provide the student with something to use as a support (e.g., your outstretched arm).
- Independence is critical. Ensure that the student has ample opportunity to perform skills independently in order to avoid being put in a position of "learned helplessness."
- Allow the student to explore the physical education environment in order to become familiar with the surroundings; make good use of an orientation and mobility specialist (OMS).
- As with all children, move from less challenging skills to more challenging ones. Break skills down into their component parts to enhance the student's learning of each skill component, thus leading up to whole-skill performance. For example, when teaching how to strike a ball, start with a larger ball on a tee and then a smaller ball on a tee before tossing a larger auditory ball and then tossing a smaller auditory ball.
- Enhance the student's involvement by limiting the playing space or slowing the action (e.g., using a balloon or slower ball).
- Always keep in contact verbally with the student.
- If using an unfamiliar environment, give the student time to get oriented to the new surroundings in order to prevent disorientation and loss of confidence; use techniques introduced by the OMS.
- Remember that cloudy and very sunny days may affect the student's visual functioning.

vision that they may have. In particular, their hands serve as primary tools for information gathering, and they learn what an object or environment "looks like" through exploration using their hands as their guide.

This tactile exploration can be supplemented by auditory descriptions, as well as any associated smells or tastes that are unique to the situation, especially for nutrition topics. Multisensory learning allows a student with blindness or low vision to develop a rich understanding of the materials and the performance environment. In one example of sensory learning, a student could explore the dimensions of a playing area identified by raised tape on the gymnasium floor, thus creating a tactile cue regarding location. When instructing students with blindness or low vision, use descriptive verbal instruction by narrating exactly what you are doing in language that describes body orientation. For example, when teaching how to hop, instruct the student by saying, "Stand on your right foot, raise your left foot off of the ground, push off of your right foot, and land only on your right foot." When working with this population, remember that tactile instruction is critical to learning new skills.

Because blindness and low vision reduce the opportunities for a child to be active, many children with vision loss have lower levels of fitness and motor development than do their sighted peers. Lieberman and McHugh (2001) reported that less than 20 percent of children with blindness or low vision passed at least four Fitnessgram items, as compared with 50 percent to 70 percent of children who were sighted. Other studies have found that even when they followed the same developmental process, children with blindness or low vision were delayed in developing many motor skills, as well as static and dynamic balance, and were of course limited in participation in sports that involve visually following a moving object (Bouchard & Tetreault, 2000).

Studies have also found that motor development, performance, and physical fitness are all greater when children possess a greater degree of usable vision (Lieberman & McHugh, 2001). Because of the demands and energy cost of performing everyday tasks, it is critical for children with blindness or low vision to maintain an appropriate level of fitness (Nakamura, 1997). Lower fitness levels may be related directly to the lower physical activity levels reported in this population. They may result from parental overprotectiveness and lower expecta-

tions, liability concerns, lack of appropriate teacher preparation, and lack of opportunities and programs for participation (Skaggs & Hopper, 1996).

These studies highlight the importance of taking advantage of a child's usable vision as a means to enhance his or her learning experience. In addition, with adaptations, modifications, and opportunities to practice and build their base of experience, children with blindness or low vision may be able to succeed in the general physical education environment.

Physical Disability

Students with **physical disability** account for about 1 percent of school-aged children in the United States (NCES, 2012), and most of these students are educated in general education classrooms for the majority of the school day. As a result, physical educators who are responsible for inclusive settings are likely to work with children who have some degree of physical disability.

There are two categories of physical disability: neurological and orthopedic. Neurological conditions are commonly caused by incomplete development of, or damage to, the brain and spinal cord. The most common conditions in this category are cerebral palsy, spina bifida, **traumatic brain injury**, and epilepsy. Orthopedic conditions, on the other hand, are associated with lack of development of, damage to, or disease of the bones, joints, or muscles. They include such conditions as absence or loss of part or all of a limb, osteogenesis imperfecta, juvenile rheumatoid arthritis, and muscular dystrophy. Physical disability may be present at birth (due to a birth defect, prematurity, or trauma) or may be caused by disease, accident, or the aging process.

Physical disability often causes mobility difficulties due to weakness, paralysis, poor muscle coordination or control, or abnormal muscle movements. These effects are not limited to the large muscles of the body; they can also affect smaller muscles, such as those controlling the tongue, throat, and face. As a result, the student may have difficulty with speech, swallowing, and expressing emotions. Students who are unable to produce speech sounds for effective communication commonly experience difficulty with peer interactions and social relationships. However, not all students in this situation have intellectual disability but rather have average or above average intelligence.

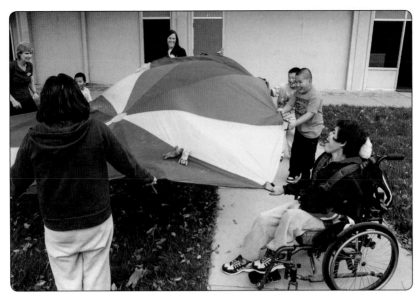

With planning on the teacher's part, students who use assistive devices can be included in physical education activities.

In these cases, students may use alternative methods to communicate with teachers and peers, such as picture boards and synthetic speech systems.

Students with movement and mobility limitations due to physical disability may find it difficult to participate when faced with physical or social barriers unless they have access to a program or opportunity designed for their success. In addition, students' emotional and social development may be affected if treatment or hospitalizations cause them to be away from their peers or if physical differences and side effects (e.g., incontinence, drooling) prevent them being easily accepted by peers. Physical educators need to ensure a safe environment for students with physical disability so that they can feel comfortable being themselves and performing at their level of capability without peer judgment. Doing so may help students with physical disability develop emotional well-being based on confidence in their skills and acceptance by their community of peers, thus reducing their risk of becoming both socially isolated and physically sedentary. In fact, one of the major concerns for physical educators is the effect of physical disability on a student's physical and motor skills and therefore on his or her physical fitness.

The most common physical disability among school-aged children is **cerebral palsy** (Rosenbaum, 2003. Cerebral palsy (CP) is a nonprogressive impairment of motor functioning due to an injury (e.g., lack of oxygen) in the motor control areas of the brain. The word *cerebral* refers to the brain, and *palsy* indicates a lack of or change in motor control. Congenital CP occurs once in about every 500 births, other, less common instances result from postpartum trauma or accident (CDC, 2013). There are three types of cerebral palsy, depending on which part of the brain's motor control area is affected:

- **Spastic CP** is the most common type, accounting for about 80 percent of all cases. It involves muscle hypertonicity and jerky movements. Students with spastic CP have difficulty attempting purposeful movement due to tense or contracted muscles; they may have a hard time moving from one position to another or controlling motor movements. In many cases, physical therapists work with these students on passive movements, where the therapist moves the student's limbs to engage muscle contractions, in order to prevent increased muscle tone. Spastic CP is usually described in terms of the part of the body that is affected; for example, a student with spastic hemiplegia CP is affected on one side of the body, and the arm is affected more than the leg.

- **Athetoid CP** is characterized by slow, uncontrolled movements and low or fluctuating muscle tone. When the student moves the limbs and trunk, shaking prevents the movements from being smooth and controllable. Students with athetoid CP may have problems with walking or sitting. If the face and tongue are affected, they may also have slurred speech, drooling, and trouble with swallowing.

- **Ataxic CP** is characterized mainly by difficulty with balance and coordination. Students with this condition may exhibit an awkward or unsteady gait and may have difficulty with movements that are quick or require a high level of control (i.e., fine motor skills).

Depending on the type of cerebral palsy, some very specific recommendations can be made for the physical education environment:

- For a student with spastic CP, avoid activities that involve pointing the toes or walking on tiptoe. Recommended activities for spastic CP include swimming in warm water (the most preferable activity), horseback riding, dances emphasizing good posture, and walking up inclined surfaces.

- Students with athetoid CP should not perform the skill of bridging in a supine position, because it can be counterproductive and lead to injury. Preferable activities for athetoid CP include ones that reinforce midline control and trunk strength, especially activities requiring balance (e.g., bicycle riding). Any activity is best performed with rest and relaxation between motor movements.

- Many students with ataxic CP do not perform well on skills requiring kinesthesis and balance. A good strategy for decelerating unwanted movement and enabling performance is to use light wrist weights with hook-and-loop (e.g., Velcro) fasteners.

- There are many ways to creatively adapt skills (e.g., manipulative skills) so that a student with CP can demonstrate successful performance. For example, if the student has difficulty in throwing a ball, use a more graspable object (e.g., beanbag, soft foam ball) to make it easier

Teaching Tips for Children With Physical Disability

- Always respect the person first and encourage the student to reach her or his potential.
- Treat all students the same with respect to expectations to achievement, including those with CP.
- Adapt situations to help students maintain self-respect and to promote independence. Avoid situations that may lead to embarrassment or fear of failure.
- Sit or kneel so that you are talking to the student at eye level.
- Treat the individual based on chronological age, both in activity selection and in communication.
- Be prepared to include students with physical disability who may use wheelchairs, braces, prostheses, crutches, or other assistive devices (and, in some cases, service animals).
- Do not assume that the student wants or needs assistance. It is preferable to ask if the student needs or desires help before giving it, especially for students who are adamant about their independence.
- Some students with CP also have difficulty with verbal communication. Incorporate augmentative communication systems (e.g., picture boards, sign language) into your classroom and teach the student's peers how to use them.
- Be aware that students with CP have higher incidences of seizure. Ensure that a seizure plan is in place before the student participates in physical education.
- Be familiar with how to perform transfers (e.g., proper technique for physically lifting and moving a child from a wheelchair into a swimming pool, onto a floor mat, or to any other environment either solo or in tandem) in the event that the student requires assistance.

to grip or have the student work on dropping the ball instead. When working on kicking activities, use larger or lighter balls (e.g., tetherball) or allow the student to "kick" with a crutch or other sticklike object.

- Students with CP expend more energy when performing fitness movements and may need more rest and water breaks to relax their muscles.

Cerebral palsy is not a disease. Though there is no cure for it, it is not progressive; nor is it hereditary, contagious, or life threatening. About 85 percent to 90 percent of all cases of CP are congenital, meaning that they occurred before or during birth (Pellegrino, 2007). The severity of CP ranges from very mild (minimally noticeable) to severe (requiring a motorized wheelchair to move about). There is also a great deal of variability among individuals within a given classification of cerebral palsy. Regardless of type and severity, it is critical that a student with CP be as physically active as possible in order to prevent joint contractures, muscle wasting, and sedentary lifestyle.

Other Health Impairment

This section provides basic information about working with students who have what is referred to as "other health impairment" (OHI). Many of these conditions are specific to individual students, who demonstrate various signs and symptoms at various levels of severity. Therefore, only preliminary recommendations can be provided, and physical educators should communicate with school administrators, the school nurse or other medical practitioner, parents and guardians, and students themselves in order to gain a clear picture of the student and the condition. As a physical education teacher, you are more likely than any other educator to see OHI. Thus it is crucial to be aware of the various chronic health issues that may affect a child's performance in physical education.

Students with OHI provide physical educators with unique challenges. IDEA defines OHI as involving "limited strength, vitality, or alertness, including a heightened alertness of environmental stimuli, that results in limited alertness with respect to the educational environment, that – (i) is due to chronic or acute health problems such as asthma, attention deficit disorder or attention deficit hyperactivity disorder, diabetes, epilepsy, a heart condition, hemophilia, lead poisoning, leukemia, nephritis, rheumatic fever, sickle cell anemia, and Tourette syndrome; and (ii) adversely affects a child's educational performance" (U.S. Department of Education, 1998, Sec. 300.8).

About 11 percent of all school-aged children in the United States are classified as having an OHI (NCES, 2012). The main determining condition for a student to be classified as having an OHI is whether or not the student meets the requirement of having "limited strength, vitality, or alertness" that "adversely affects . . . educational performance." For example, a child diagnosed with Tourette's syndrome may not have limitations with respect to physical activity. In that case, the student is not categorized as having an OHI because the condition does not adversely affect educational performance in this environment.

The following subsections address the forms of OHI that most often affect performance in the physical education environment: attention-deficit/hyperactivity disorder, asthma, and diabetes.

Attention-Deficit/Hyperactivity Disorder

One of the most common OHI conditions is attention-deficit/hyperactivity disorder (ADHD) (NCES, 2012). Males are three times more likely than girls to be diagnosed with ADHD. This condition is associated with academic difficulties and with three main behavioral issues: hyperactivity, difficulty with paying attention, and impulsivity. Other characteristics that may be present include disruptiveness and lack of responsiveness to instruction and direction.

Students with ADHD may have difficulty in the physical education environment due to being unable to follow directions or remain focused on the task at hand. As a result, they may miss out on how and when to perform a skill or a skill progression; they may also miss feedback given during or after a skill performance. Students with ADHD also have difficulty with following through on instructions and focusing on specific skill sequences, which can lead to problems with whole-skill performance. In addition, though students with ADHD tend to be very active, they may not always demonstrate proficient skill levels due to inattention and lack of focus, which reduce their time spent on task. Students may be more interested in moving in *any* fashion than in concentrating to make sure that they are performing motor skills with correct technique. However, if the teacher uses well-planned strategies for managing student behavior, attention, and focus, students with ADHD can engage in a successful physical education experience.

Asthma

Students with **asthma** account for slightly less than 10 percent of school-aged children in the United States (Bloom, Cohen & Freeman, 2012). Asthma involves chronic inflammation of the airways that hinders oxygen from getting to the lungs and causes any number of respiratory symptoms, including chest tightness, coughing, wheezing, and shortness of breath. It can vary in severity and follow an unpredictable pattern of recessions and flare-ups. In many cases, the students take medicines to control asthma and may also require rescue inhalers in the event of an acute attack.

For many children, physical activity is a common trigger for their asthma—thus the term *exercise-induced asthma*. In some cases, physical education at school is the only regular physical activity in which the child participates, which makes it critical for teachers to be aware of the student's asthma action plan. In most school districts, the school nurse must manage the student's inhaler and therefore must be aware of when and where the student participates in physical education. Some students visit the nurse to use the inhaler immediately before coming to physical education class. Students with well-controlled asthma can participate at the same levels in physical education as students without asthma.

Several important steps can be taken to reduce the chances that a student with asthma will have problems during physical education class. In addition, some activities may be more suitable than others for students with asthma. Here are some general considerations for physical educators:

- Consult the student's parent or guardian and the school nurse to discuss the student's asthma management plan and any limitations that the student may have in relation to physical activity.

- Monitor the environment for potential asthma-triggering irritants or allergens, such as a recently varnished gymnasium floor, weather changes, mowed grass, or even the chlorine in the pool. If you find an allergen known to trigger a student's asthma, consider a temporary change in location.

- Make any program modifications necessary to allow the student appropriate time on task and appropriate participation levels. For example, if a high-aerobic activity is scheduled, modify the activity to include intermittent high-an-

Warming up and cooling down are always good practice, especially for students with exercise-induced asthma.

aerobic activity (e.g., station work), which is less likely to cause asthma symptoms.

- Lead-up games are suitable for students with asthma because they provide intermittent activities. When activities are prolonged and of high aerobic nature, modifications may be required to incorporate more intermittent low-aerobic activities and reduce the duration of the aerobic component.

When planning lessons and physical activities for classes that include students with asthma, physical educators should take into account the following considerations related to the type and duration of exercise:

- Always include appropriate warm-up and cool-down sessions to help prevent exercise-induced asthma.

- Incorporate interval training or intermittent activities as much as possible.

- Start with low-intensity activities and increase the intensity gradually in order to improve exercise tolerance.
- Put a plan in place for the eventuality of a student demonstrating symptoms of asthma.

Unless a student is directly exempted by a medical professional, there is no reason for a student with asthma not to be fully included in the physical education environment. Some modifications may be warranted in the intensity of exercise, but this does not exclude the student from participating to his or her fullest potential.

Diabetes

Diabetes is a chronic condition that continues to rise in incidence; recent estimates indicate that 1 of every 400 school-aged children in the United States has been diagnosed (Bloom et al., 2012). In diabetes, the body either does not produce insulin (type 1) or does not properly use insulin (type 2). Diabetes may lead to either hyperglycemia (high blood sugar) or hypoglycemia (low blood sugar). In children with type 1 diabetes, physical activity typically causes hypoglycemia due to increased insulin sensitivity and reduced blood glucose during exercise. Therefore, a student with type 1 diabetes should monitor glucose levels before and after physical activity to determine whether insulin is required or should be adjusted and whether the student would benefit from eating a snack. If a student with type 2 diabetes demonstrates symptoms of hypoglycemia, such as pale skin, dizziness, sweating, headache, clumsy/jerky movements, or behavioral changes, it is important to have a carbohydrate based snack on hand for them to ingest (Sigal, et al., 2004). Physical activity is critically important for students with diabetes because it has a positive effect on diabetes symptoms by reducing blood glucose levels, improving sensitivity to insulin, and reducing the likelihood of future negative health situations such as coronary heart disease (CHD) (Kollipara & Warren-Boulton, 2004).

As with asthma, all teachers should be provided with an action plan for managing changes in blood glucose levels in students with diabetes. The plan should include not only the action steps to take in the event of low or high blood glucose but also the common signs and symptoms that the student displays when blood glucose levels become too high or too low.

Physical education teachers should be aware of strategies for helping a student with diabetes succeed in the physical education environment, as well as ways to help the student manage his or her diabetes. These strategies are student focused and include the following:

- Develop a clear understanding of how exercise can affect blood glucose levels, thus causing hypoglycemia.
- Students with type 1 diabetes may need to adjust their insulin and food consumption and check blood glucose levels when engaging in physical activity in order to prevent hypoglycemia.
- Be aware of and prepared to respond to signs and symptoms of both hyperglycemia and hypoglycemia.
- Establish a clear plan of action that includes details about when to contact the school nurse, parents or guardians, and emergency personnel.
- Consider taping a fast-acting form of glucose (e.g., hard candy that is *not* sugar free) to a clipboard or including it in a first-aid fanny pack that is available wherever physical education activities are performed.
- Make sure that the student drinks extra water to remain fully hydrated. Dehydration causes a drastic change in blood glucose, which can speed the onset of hypoglycemia.
- Physical activity is critical for students with diabetes because it not only helps reduce the prevalence of type 2 diabetes but also helps manage the drastic changes in blood glucose that lead to hypoglycemia.

As with any other OHI, students with diabetes can benefit tremendously from regular physical activity. In some cases, physical education classes may be the only regular activity that a child receives, making it critically important for students with an OHI to be fully involved. At the same time, physical educators must remember that one of the main differences between OHI and other disabilities is that many children with an OHI take some form of medication for their condition (e.g., inhalers for asthma, insulin for type 1 diabetes, stimulant-type medications for ADD and ADHD), and some of these medicines may have side effects that affect a student's performance in physical education. Therefore, physical educators must be aware of and familiar with the medications and their possible effects.

Teaching Tips for Children With an OHI

- Treat all students the same with respect to achievement expectations, including those with an OHI.
- Encourage all students to exercise and participate in physical activities and sports regardless of any disability.
- Stress quality rather than quantity of work so as not to overwhelm or discourage the student.
- Keep directions and feedback simple and to the point, emphasizing important concepts or outcomes.
- Use different colors of equipment to represent an activity or emphasis in the instructions.
- Use frequent short activities rather than a few longer activities that require greater focus and attention.
- If the student's confidence is an issue, allow her or him to demonstrate performance in a private location without an audience.
- For students who have issues with strength and vitality, allow frequent water and rest breaks in order to optimize performance.
- Provide support and intervention before a behavioral problem or disruption becomes an issue; communicate with other teachers and parents to ensure consistency between home and various classrooms.
- Make sure that comprehensive information is documented and provided to substitute teachers in order to communicate the needs of students with an OHI.
- If a student experiences excessive absenteeism, revise the curriculum so that there is still a high chance for success; in addition, develop a program that the student can complete at home.
- Never make the student feel guilty or ashamed about having an OHI.

In addition, many students with an OHI also have self-esteem and confidence issues that affect their overall quality of life and can lead to social isolation, absenteeism, and decreased school performance (Diette et al., 2000; Klassen, Miller, & Fine, 2004; Vetiska et al., 2000). As a result, physical educators may need to revise the content and curriculum to allow the student to succeed even with a reduced number of days in attendance or reduced time on task to master a skill. It may also be beneficial to develop a series of assignments related to the course content for the student to complete at home, thus preventing him or her from falling behind. Finally, physical education class may become a safe haven for students with an OHI, where students may feel more comfortable and able to be themselves regardless of their disability, so physical education teachers should ensure that the environment is conductive to acceptance of all students regardless of the OHI.

Obesity

Over the past few years, much debate has focused on whether students who are overweight or obese should be classified as having a disability—specifically, one that would fit under the diagnosis of "other health impairment" (OHI). Doing so would be a critical and long-reaching decision, given that childhood obesity affects almost one in five school-aged children in the United States, a number that has increased drastically since the 1980s (NCHS, 2012). This increase is particularly concerning for physical educators, who are focused on lifelong health and wellness. Childhood obesity has both immediate and long-term detrimental effects, including increased risk factors for cardiovascular

Unhealthy snack foods are cheap and abundantly available to children. Over-consumption of such snacks is a major lifestyle cause of obesity.

disease, diabetes, and bone and joint problems. In addition, students who are obese are more likely to be the victim of bullying and may experience "fat shaming," both of which can lead to reductions in self-confidence, self-esteem, and overall quality of life (Janssen, Craig, Boyce, & Pickett, 2004; Kolotkin, Crosby, & Williams, 2002).

Most obesity results from one or more of three main causes: lifestyle, disability, and medical issues. For the vast majority of children, obesity results from an unhealthy lifestyle that includes excessive or unhealthy consumption of food and a lack of sufficient physical activity for the body to use the calories consumed. Thus the rise in childhood obesity is the result of various trends, including the increase in fast-food restaurants; the increase in "screen time" in the form of video games, computer use, and television viewing; and the ready availability of soft drinks, unhealthy snack foods, and sugar-sweetened drinks. However, though lifestyle is the most common cause of obesity, physical educators must also be familiar with disability-related and medical causes.

- **Lifestyle causes:** This is the most common cause of obesity and is often related to poor eating habits and poor exercise choices. It may also involve environmental factors, such as socioeconomic status, cultural practices, lack of physical activity opportunities, and lack of qualified individuals to ensure that appropri-

ate steps or programs are followed to combat obesity.

- **Disability-related causes:** Some disabilities (e.g., Down syndrome, Prader-Willi syndrome) have higher incidences of obesity than do others. This discrepancy may be due to metabolic and endocrine differences in disabilities that lead to higher obesity rates. Children with disability have a higher overall percentage of obesity (about 22 percent) than do children without disability (about 18 percent) (Child and Adolescent Health Measurement Initiative, 2007).

- **Medical causes:** Some medicines can lead to uncontrollable weight gain. For example, Depakote, a common epilepsy drug, alters the proteins involved in appetite control and metabolism, which can lead to weight gain, mainly in females. In addition, oral corticosteroids, such as Deltasone (generic name: prednisone), carry a high risk of weight gain with long-term use. Corticosteroids are taken by individuals with asthma, inflammatory bowel disease, and rheumatoid arthritis due to their anti-inflammatory properties.

Regardless of the cause of obesity, physical educators must be prepared to adapt the curriculum in order to encourage complete participation by all students. In many cases, the most important focus should be on the student's psychological and social well-being. Too often, children who are obese find themselves on the receiving end of bullying or teasing behaviors, which can lead to issues with self-esteem, self-confidence, self-concept, and social isolation. In addition, in some cases, increased absenteeism occurs when the student attempts to remove her- or himself from an undesirable situation due to psychological and social issues (Griffiths, Parsons, & Hill, 2010). Physical educators must provide students who are obese with programs that are well rounded and focused

---

Teaching Tips for Children Who Are Obese

- Children who are obese can participate in the physical education curriculum with some simple modifications. Allow frequent water and rest breaks as needed, but make sure that the student completes all of the required curriculum content.

- Some movement skills may be difficult for students who are obese. For example, due to their weight, students who are obese may have difficulty in performing fundamental movement skills such as jumping and hopping, as well as gymnastics movements that involve specific body movements (e.g., forward roll) or supporting body weight (e.g., headstand). As needed, allow students to perform a modified version of fundamental motor skills and use a incline mat to assist with specific gymnastics movements. It may also be feasible to substitute a log roll for a somersault.

- For fitness activities, especially during assessment, allow students to walk rather than run (if necessary—many obese children can run), perform wall push-ups rather than modified push-ups, and do alternative forms of core abdominal exercises such as "dead bugs."

- When evaluating cardiorespiratory endurance, determine how long the student can continue moving without stopping and use this result as a baseline for future evaluations.

- Be sensitive about weight with a child who is overweight or obese; he or she may be self-conscious and have low confidence.

- Remember that students who are overweight or obese carry an amount of weight that makes movement more difficult. A good way to remain mindful of this reality is to consider the fact that a child who is, say, 40 pounds overweight is in effect exercising with a 40-pound weight vest.

- Do not push the child to exercise, even with the noble intention of getting her or him active in order to lose weight. Students who are obese find exercising difficult, and forcing them to perform exercise places undue stress on them, which can lead them to dislike exercising and prefer a more sedentary, and safe-feeling, lifestyle.

- Promote a climate of respect and acceptance in order to increase understanding and awareness of obesity in the class culture and thereby minimize occurrences of bias or stigmatizing.

- Take steps to get parents involved. In many cases, the parents themselves are overweight or obese, and the children are following in their footsteps. Encouraging parents to help their children get the activity they need may lead to parental participation as well.

on improving all areas in which the student is affected—not solely weight loss.

DIMENSIONS OF DIVERSITY

Students with disability account for approximately 13 percent of all school-aged children in the United States (NCES, 2012). In comparison, students from other diverse populations make up a much greater percentage of the school-aged population. In its entirety, diversity is made up of various characteristics, among which are sex, race, ethnicity, culture, and socioeconomic status. Each dimension of diversity has its own unique effect on an individual's performance and success in physical education and also raises specific considerations that teachers must take into account in order to provide the most effective program for all students.

Sex

Sex differences are common, of course, at all grade levels, and the general make-up of the U.S. student population is estimated at 51 percent male and 49 percent female (NCES, 2012). Research has found that both male and female teachers have often treated boys and girls differently because of gender role expectations; fortunately, research findings documenting the negative effect of these discrepancies on girls' physical performance have led the way for the establishment of equitable learning environments by teachers (Ambrose, 1996; Brown, Brown, & Hussey, 1996; Davis, 2003; Weiller & Doyle, 2000; Wellhousen & Yin, 1997).

More specifically, research found that teachers were more likely to interact both verbally and nonverbally with male students and to ask questions more often of male students than of female students (Dunbar & O'Sullivan, 1986; Napper-Owen, Kovar, Ermler, & Mehrhof, 1999; Wellhousen & Yin, 1997). In addition, research found that teachers acknowledged males more often for good performance and gave them feedback about physical skills and abilities while praising females for effort (Dunbar & O'Sullivan, 1986; MacDonald, 1990). Teachers also requested skill demonstrations by male students more often than by female students and disregarded inappropriate gender-patterned behaviors between male students (Lock, Minarik, & Omata, 1999; Cheptayor-Thomson & Ennis, 1997). It was also found that during problem-solving activities, teachers were more likely to give girls who were struggling the answer, whereas they would prompt boys to "figure it out" with encouraging statements like, "I know you can do it!" (Sadker & Zittleman, 2009).

Similarly, Hansen, Walker, and Flom (1995) indicated that physical education teachers had different expectations of physical ability between males and females; specifically, males were praised for their physical performance and females for their effort regardless of performance. This outcome derived in part from misconceptions, developed over time, that females demonstrate physical performance at a lower skill level and are unable to succeed in highly competitive situations (Davis, 2003).

During the prepuberty years, both males and females seem to have similar potential for physical

---

Teaching Tips for Avoiding Gender Stereotypes

- Employ a gender-inclusive curriculum with a variety of activities in cooperative and competitive games, dance, gymnastics, and fitness.

- Consciously use inclusive classroom practices, including inclusive, gender-neutral language; materials that show female as well as male athletes and performers; sharing of roles by boys and girls during demonstrations; equal questioning of both sexes; opportunities for both sexes to figure out solutions to problems; and specific feedback about skill performance with the expectation that all students can improve through effort and practice.

- Present activities as gender neutral and open to anyone who has the interest to participate; provide differentiated participation opportunities based not on sex but on student ability.

Cooperative activities tend to negate differences between boys and girls and allow for more equitable participation.

and psychomotor growth (Ormrod, 2010). However, males tend to develop their physical and motor skills in more depth during this time period than do females, due in part to greater participation in organized sport. In physical education, it has been reported that males are more likely to participate in class, whereas females tend to require more motivation to fully participate at the same levels as males (Dowling, 2001; Penney, 2002; Rink, 2005). As children get older and experience puberty, males also have a biological advantage over females in both height and muscular strength due to increased levels of testosterone (Halpern, 2006; Hyde, 2005).

However, physical education is the environment in which all students are gaining the skills, knowledge, and dispositions to stay physically active for life. Therefore, it is incumbent upon physical educators to provide inclusive movement environments that support the efforts and achievements of both boys and girls. All students should have opportunities to explore and excel in a variety of physical activities. To this end, physical educators should use inclusive, gender-neutral language—for example, "player-to-player defense" rather than "man-to-man" and "third-base player" rather than "third baseman"—to reinforce the fact that both sexes are represented on the court and field. Equal

representation should also be practiced in images of male and female athletes and performers used in learning materials, including pictures depicting how to perform skills and literature about sport and physical activity participants.

Race and Ethnicity

Of the roughly 50 million elementary and secondary school students in public schools in the United States, about 52 percent are Caucasian, 23 percent Hispanic, 16 percent African American, 5 percent Asian/Pacific Islander, 1 percent American Indian/Alaskan Native, and 2 percent identifying as two or more races (NCES, 2012). It is projected that by 2021 these percentages will have changed to 53.1 million school-aged children, 48 percent Caucasian, 27 percent Hispanic, 16 percent African American, 6 percent Asian or Pacific Islander, 1 percent American Indian or Alaskan Native, and 3 percent identifying as two or more races. Of these children, more than 4.7 million (almost 10 percent) are in English Language Learner (ELL) programs, which indicates that English is not their first or most proficient language.

Historically, as with disparities between males and females based on gender expectations, many teachers have treated racial minorities inappro-

---

Teaching Tips for Racially and Ethnically Diverse Classrooms

- Respect and have high expectations of all students.
- Respect that some ethnic minorities are part of a culture that may view physical activity differently than you do.
- Educate yourself about diverse races, ethnicities, and cultures.
- Hold "culture days" in your classroom and introduce activities that are specific to particular cultures, such as different types of dance.
- When your class includes students whose first language is not English, use more visual ways to explain how to perform skills and connect each movement with an English word or phrase to help students learn the language.

---

priately. Teachers need to become aware of and confront their own biases about racial minorities, including expectations of greater or lesser ability in physical activities (e.g., the idea that African Americans excel in basketball and track but do not swim well); assumptions about African Americans having lower cognitive abilities; and assumptions that African American boys have greater proclivity for disruptive behavior (Sadker and Zittleman, 2009).

A child's use of ethnically or culturally specific language can affect his or her success at using language in an educational setting. According to the U.S. Census Bureau (2012), more than 20 percent of the school-age population speaks a language other than English at home, with the most common being Spanish (72 percent), followed by Indo European languages (13 percent), Asian or Pacific Islander languages (11 percent), and various other languages (4 percent). Of these children, 24 percent have difficulty with speaking, reading, and writing in English.

Socioeconomic Status

According to the NCES (2012), more than 21 percent of all school-aged children in the United States come from households with low socioeconomic status (SES), or families who were at or below the poverty level. The percentage of students from low-SES backgrounds varies by state, ranging from about 30 percent in Washington, D.C., to 9 percent in North Dakota. Socioeconomic status also varies by race and ethnicity, with the highest level of poverty occurring among African Americans (39 percent),

followed by American Indians and Alaskan Natives (36 percent), Hispanics (34 percent), Native Hawaiians and Pacific Islanders (30 percent), those who identify as biracial (22 percent), and Asian Americans and Caucasians (13 percent each).

Of the roughly 98,000 public schools in the United States, 25 percent are located in a city or urban area, where 37 percent of schools are considered high-poverty. In comparison, 33 percent of all schools are located in a rural area, where only 10 percent of schools are considered high-poverty (NCES, 2012). A high-poverty school is defined as having more than 75 percent of students eligible for free or reduced-price lunch (FRPL).

Educating diverse populations requires teachers to develop a deeper understanding of diversity and how a student's background and characteristics may directly affect his or her ability to participate in physical education to the fullest extent possible. When developing instructional programs for students from diverse populations in the physical education environment, teachers should examine a wide array of characteristics, including physical and gross motor development, academic and intellectual functioning, emotional and behavioral characteristics, and social behaviors in relation to peer interaction. Entrenched in these individual student characteristics may lie such elements as differences or deficits in social skills, speech and language delays, and issues involving teasing and bullying.

When educating *any* student, physical educators must examine all of these aspects related to individual characteristics. However, they should pay close attention to each area when educating a student who brings diversity to an inclusive setting. It is critical for teachers to understand how a student's disability or background can affect his or her success in the physical education setting, as well as how individual differences can affect the development of instruction and specific modifications. Students can have different needs and requirements in the same setting, and successful educators and learning experiences meet the diverse needs of all students.

Teaching Tips for Economically Diverse Schools

- Remember that a child from a low-SES household may not have had the opportunity to be involved in many different physical activities, especially if he or she comes from a single-parent household. Give the child an opportunity to learn activities that she or her can participate in outside of school.
- Some children's families may not have the finances to afford clothing intended specifically for physical education. Have extra pairs of sneakers, shorts, and T-shirts available for students who need them.

Teaching Tips for Diverse Population Groups

Here are some teaching tips that are effective for all diverse populations:

- Make sure that the physical education climate is safe, respectful, and inclusive of all students, regardless of their diversity.
- Encourage students to share ways in which they can be respectful, cooperative, and helpful with each other; use this sharing to make class rules.
- Take charge of dividing teams and use creative approaches, such as birthday month, shirt or sneaker color, first letter of last name, or favorite color.
- Teach personal and social responsibility in instructional activities so that everyone can learn and enjoy physical activity skills; teach good sporting behavior whether winning or losing.
- Intervene and teach respectful and caring behaviors to put a stop to name calling, teasing, and bullying.
- Diversify the physical education curriculum by including a broad spectrum of activities in which diverse students have the opportunity to succeed, as well as activities specific to diverse groups (e.g., culturally specific dances) and disability activities that can be used as teachable moments. Disability activities are those specific for individuals with disability, such as sit volleyball, goalball, or wheelchair sports.
- Provide instruction and skill practice that meet students' different ability levels.
- Serve as a role model for the acceptance of diversity.

Big Ideas

- Diverse learners include every individual student who may be a part of your educational environment.

- All children have a right to a physical education program geared toward their physical, motor, affective, and intellectual levels.

- In many cases, physical education teachers must advocate to get the physical education curriculum into the student's Individualized Education Plan (IEP).

- In public schools, children with disability must be integrated into a physical education program in the least restrictive environment possible.

- Teachers need to know and incorporate the teaching tips presented in this chapter for working with students with specific disabilities in order to ensure equal learning opportunities for all children in the physical education environment. Teachers should also use appropriate terminology for the 13 categories of disability identified by IDEA.

- It is not unusual to have students with disability in your general physical education classroom without knowing it. Some common disabilities (e.g., learning disability, speech disorders) may have little effect on physical education performance.

- An essential tenet of differentiated instruction is to provide responsive teaching rather than following a one-size-fits-all method.

- Teachers must be aware of and avoid acting on cultural biases regarding factors such as gender, race, ethnicity, and socioeconomic status.

 Visit the web resource for learning activities, video clips, and review questions.

Chapter 12

Classroom Management

Key Concepts

- Describing strategies for addressing discipline issues based on Hellison's model
- Listing the steps for conflict resolution and how strategies differ in pre-K through grade 2 and grades 3 through 5
- Describing the teacher attributes that foster positive behavior and strengthen the teacher–student relationship
- Explaining how learning outcomes and response strategies in social contracts differ based on the developmental characteristics of children in pre-K, K-2, and grades 3 through 5
- Discussing how each of the following components helps maintain a positive learning environment:
  - Physical environment
  - Developmentally appropriate protocols
  - Management practices

In working to create and maintain an environment that is conducive to learning and positive behavior, teachers face a multidimensional task. To accomplish it, they must possess the knowledge and skills necessary to promote responsible behavior and motivate children to succeed (Lavay, French, & Henderson, 2006; Hellison, 2011). Key strategies include expecting specific behaviors of personal and social responsibility, implementing social contracts, and developing classroom protocols. To use these strategies effectively, teachers must understand children's cognitive and social development (see chapter 3). Children cannot comply with what they do not understand, nor can they exhibit behaviors that are not relevant or age appropriate for them.

A positive classroom environment is a prerequisite to learning: "Learning cannot take place in an atmosphere of chaos. The ideal learning environment must be safe, structured, consistent, and motivating" (Lavay et al., 2006, p. 7). With this need in mind, this chapter addresses knowledge and skills you should strive continually to achieve and improve on as you plan and manage physical education environments that help children learn.

TEACHING PERSONAL AND SOCIAL RESPONSIBILITY

An environment conducive to learning and positive behavior is built on helping children develop self-responsibility and acquire the social skills they need in order to interact appropriately with others. The physical education setting is rich with opportunities for children to demonstrate responsibility for self, respect the rights of others, and, ultimately, demonstrate empathy for others.

Hellison's (2011) model of **teaching personal and social responsibility (TPSR)** highlights the importance of creating opportunities for children to reflect on their own behavior in order to develop self-awareness. Hellison's model also offers strategies for helping children learn to care for others. The model articulates five levels of personal and social responsibility. The teacher facilitates students' attainment of the levels by integrating responsibility-based strategies and an empowerment progression within the physical education learning environment. Students learn the levels and the respective behaviors associated with each level and are held accountable for demonstrating and reflecting on their behavior.

Chapter 3 provided an overview of the TPSR framework as it relates to building children's self-esteem and developing self-determination (see the empowerment progression in table 3.2). This chapter addresses how the TPSR framework contributes to effective **classroom management** and positive student behavior. Specifically, it addresses the following topics:

- How teachers use the levels of individual accountability
- Strategies for addressing discipline issues
- Conflict resolution strategies

Student Accountability

Two overarching goals of TPSR are for children to take responsibility for their own actions and well-being and to take responsibility for contributing to the well-being of others. Self-control, self-motivation, and self-direction are the students' responsibilities (Hellison, 2011, p. 22). The five levels of personal and social responsibility (see table 12.1) provide children with descriptive guidelines for their behavior. The numbered levels and the descriptors for each level help children examine and reflect on their behavior in physical education class. Although students don't always progress in a linear fashion (i.e., from level 0 to level 1, then to level 2, and so on), the levels provide specific steps to keep in mind when planning lessons and making personal plans for individual students (Hellison, 2011, p. 21).

You can use the five levels as presented here or modify the structure to fit your students' specific needs. Either way, you can use several methods to hold students accountable for exhibiting behaviors that are congruent with each level and for reflecting on their own behavior. Here are some examples.

High five: Display the numbers vertically on the wall next to the gymnasium door. As children exit, have children "high-five" the number that represented their level of personal and social responsibility for the day's class.

Hand signal: During a lesson, have children hold up the number of fingers that represents their level of personal and social responsibility.

Token box: Provide variously colored tokens that represent the various levels. Have children choose a token of the color that represents their level of personal and social responsibility

Table 12.1 Components of the Levels of Responsibility

Level	Components
0. Irresponsibility	Blaming others
	Making excuses
	Denying personal responsibility
1. Respecting the rights and feelings of others	Self-control
	Right to peaceful conflict resolution
	Right to be included and have cooperative peers
2. Effort and cooperation	Self-motivation
	Exploration of effort and new tasks
	Getting along with others
3. Self-direction	On-task independence
	Goal-setting progression
	Courage to resist peer pressure
4. Helping others and exercising leadership	Caring and compassion
	Sensitivity and responsiveness
	Inner strength
5. Transfer outside the gym	Trying these ideas in other areas of life
	Being a positive role model for others, especially younger kids

Adapted, by permission, from D. Hellison, 2011, *Teaching personal and social responsibility through physical activity,* 3rd ed. (Champaign, IL: Human Kinetics), 21 and 34.

for the day's class and put it into a box (e.g., shoebox with slot on top). Use a visual aid to remind students what color each token represents. Your responsibility is to count the tokens for each color and debrief the class regarding the results during the following class (you could even graph the results).

Journals: Children in grades 3 through 5 can use journals to record both fitness data and their level of personal and social responsibility for a given day in physical education class. Ask the children to write the number of the level at which they performed on that day and to provide a reason for choosing that level. Then read the journal entries and provide feedback about their self-reflection.

The choice of which accountability measure to use should be based on children's stage of cognitive and social development. Of course, the choice must be made before the lesson is conducted; in other words, it is a pre-impact decision (see chapter 10).

Strategies for Addressing Discipline Issues

As noted by Pastor (2002), "Discipline is not a matter of keeping things under control by making choices for students. . . [but] of helping students learn to make good choices and to be responsible for those choices" (p. 659). This is, of course, a process; it takes time for students to learn how to be good citizens in class. The literature offers several reasons that students may not adhere to classroom rules. These reasons include both out-of-school and in-school causes that can contribute to a lack of self-control and lack of respect for self and others.

One out-of-school cause involves the fact that some children do not have a secure family environment. As a result, the children may lack the values necessary for success at school because, in their experience, those values are either untaught or, more important, unlived. Jensen's research has demonstrated a correlation between socioeconomic status and success in school; more specifically, poverty negatively affects academic achievement and behavior (Jensen, 2009). Students from families of lower socioeconomic status are also more likely to live in a culture that does not value academic achievement (Kerri, T., 2016).

Another out-of-school cause for children lacking self-control and respect for classroom rules can be found in the media (e.g., movies, music, and video games). By the age of 18 years, children in the U.S. typically see 200,000 acts of violence on television (both fictional and real-life) (Media Education Foundation, 2005). In addition, a 2000 report by the U.S. Federal Trade Commission showed that children under age 17 were the target market of 80 percent of R-rated movies, 70 percent of restricted video games, and 100 percent of music with "explicit content" warning labels. In fact, 75 percent of fourth-grade children have watched an R-rated movie, and 65 percent have played a violent video game (see Curwin, Mendler, & Mendler, 2008, p. 13). These out-of-school factors collectively contribute to children's lack of self-control and respect for classroom rules.

In-school causes may include boredom, unclear limits (i.e., when the teacher does not specifically state what children should and should not do; such as stating how many times a child can go to the drinking fountain during physical education class), and powerlessness. Boredom can result from poor lesson design or lack of differentiated instruction. Powerlessness can play out in the classroom in the following manner: "When one group (adults) develops rules and procedures that define behavioral standards for another group (students) that has had little or no input, a conflict of control and power can result" (Curwin et al., 2008 p. 19).

For all of these reasons and others, children need to have a positive set of explicitly laid out classroom rules with an array of consequences. However, one size does *not* fit all, and the social contracts described later in this chapter offer several teacher-response strategies (consequences). At the same time, other consequences may be needed for individual children and specific circumstances. In addition to the response strategies provided in the social contracts, Hellison (2011) offers several strategies and consequences for addressing students who exhibit level 1 discipline problems. The choice of which strategy to employ is a post-impact decision (see chapter 10); that is, it is made in response to students' behavior during a lesson. Hellison's strategies include the following:

- **Accordion principle:** Expand or reduce the time allotted for an activity depending on the amount of disruptive behavior.

- **Negotiation:** This multistep approach involves addressing the issue, agreeing on a plan (suggested by students or teacher) to solve the problem, following up to ensure compliance with the plan, and monitoring to see if the plan helps the student make better choices. The extent and complexity of the plan depend on the child's age.

- **Grandma's law:** This approach can be used when children show lack of interest or refuse to participate. "Grandma's law states that the kids must eat dinner before going out to play" (Hellison, 2011, p. 94). Similarly, a physical education teacher might suggest that if a student tries five jump-rope progressions, then she or he can choose from other activity options for the next three minutes of class.

- **Teacher-directed group:** In this strategy, the teacher directs a group consisting of students who need more structure, while other students engage self-directed activities (e.g., station work).

- **Five clean days:** The essence of this approach is to devise and carry out a plan for a specified time period, during which the child is expected to be at level 1 or 2.

- **Sitting out:** This strategy does take a child out of the lesson; however, it can be used by asking the child to sit out when he or she cannot exhibit self-control (i.e., level 1 behavior). In this "sit" or "time-out" approach, the child may choose to rejoin class when he or she feels ready to re-enter the activity at level 1. However, if the student opts out of an activity because he or she simply does not like it or perceives it as too difficult, then the teacher needs to provide developmentally appropriate choices that address the student's interests.

If you are unable to bring a disruptive student under control through the aforementioned strategies, then it is sometimes appropriate to provide a time-out space. This space should be a predesignated spot in the gymnasium or on the playground that is removed from the class but in clear view of the teacher at all times. According to Henderson, French, Fritsch, and Lerner (2000), the idea is to send the student "to a safe, easy-to-monitor, nonreinforcing area each time he or she exhibits an undesirable behavior" (p. 31). The physical educator may ask the child to re-enter the lesson when they feel they can demonstrate appropriate behaviors or it may solely be the decision of the teacher as to when the child rejoins the lesson.

Removing a disruptive child from the class for a portion of the lesson gives both the student and the teacher time to regroup and refocus. Be sure, however, not to overuse this technique and not to exclude the child for too long. Exclusion for longer than 5 minutes tends to be less effective than exclusion for shorter periods (French, Silliman, & Henderson, 1990). Also, be certain to talk privately with the child before it is time to reenter the class, asking questions such as the following: "What did you do that caused you to be removed from class?" "How should you have behaved, or how can you prevent this from happening again?" "What behaviors will you use to show that you're ready to rejoin the class?" If the problem exists between two students (e.g., name calling, pushing, fighting) and they have been removed for time-out, be certain that they talk over the problem and work it out together before returning to class.

Time-outs offer the advantages of being simple and quick to implement; however, they also carry disadvantages:

- When used exclusively, time-outs teach the student which behaviors are unacceptable but not which behaviors are desirable.

- A time-out takes away the student's opportunity to participate in physical activity during that period of time.

- Students may misbehave purposefully in order to be assigned to a time-out. If this is the case the physical educator should try to determine the reason and subsequently address it with the child.

Given these disadvantages, teachers should document their use of time-out with students. When possible, avoid excluding students from an entire class or sending them to the principal's office. Handling your own discipline problems whenever possible conveys a message to the children that you are in control. In fact, teachers who routinely send disruptive students to the principal's office invite further difficulty because they are viewed by students and fellow teachers alike as ineffective leaders who are unable to manage their own class-

rooms. In addition, it is less likely that a third party will effectively solve a behavioral problem since they were not first-hand witness to the situation nor may they have an extensive understanding of the history of the child's behavior in the physical education setting. However, if a student engages in a *pattern* of level 0 behavior and is unable to gain the self-control to function at level 1, then the appropriate school authority should be contacted.

Conflict Resolution Strategies

Conflict resolution is a specific problem-solving technique. It entails a process of communication and problem solving that leads to resolution among two or more students. Conflict resolution helps turn conflicts into win-win situations. Teaching children to use positive strategies to resolve conflicts empowers them to employ these techniques to handle problems on their own (Nelson, 2006). When children are in conflict, the way in which the teacher frames the issue provides them with cues about the goals for the interaction. The following approach encourages children to listen to one another and offer acceptable solutions to a problem.

1. A supportive teacher first asks about the situation: "Let's talk about what is going on and see if we can find a solution." This cue is aimed at helping children view the solution to the problem as one that must be arrived at together. It is a positive alternative to something like, "How would you like it if . . . ?" because it does not focus blame or exclude any person from responsibility. Starting the conversation by looking for a solution together validates the opportunity for learning (Shidler, 2009, p. 89).

2. Listen as each child recounts his or her version.

3. Have each child offer an acceptable (as determined with the teacher's guidance) solution.

The process used by physical educators to help children resolve conflicts should also be based on children's cognitive and social development. Pre-K children need the teacher to serve as a mediator and help them recount their version of the problem situation. Primary-grade (K-2) children may be able to offer their version of a situation with only minimal prompts by the teacher. The teacher, or mediator, should strive to help the children frame their stories in their own words without inflicting blame on each other. For example, let's say that two children bump into each other while playing at a station designed for jumping in and out of a hoop, off of a foam shape, and over low obstacles. The children get loud and blame each other for the bumping. Here is a potential dialogue:

Teacher: "I hear that the two of you have a problem. Let's see if we can discuss what the problem is and find a solution together."

Andrea: "I was jumping off of the foam shape and when I landed Susie got in my way and pushed me."

Susie: "I didn't see Andrea because I was jumping over the foam noodle. It was an accident."

Andrea: "Maybe I need to look where others are before I jump."

Susie: "I accidentally moved the foam noodle on the floor too close to where Andrea was jumping. We need to have the foam noodles far away from that mat."

Teacher: "Thank you both for offering your ideas. I think your ideas will work. Let's put the foam noodles farther away, and I can tape them down to the floor. Will that help?"

For students in grades 3 through 5, a more formal process can be used to resolve conflicts. Here is a possible approach:

1. Participants gather information about the conflict.
2. They work to clarify the conflict as seen from each person's point of view.
3. They identify common interests among the people involved.
4. They brainstorm options for a solution to the conflict.

5. Students write out an agreement or complete and sign a contract provided by the teacher.
6. The contract is sealed with a high five or handshke.

A sample conflict resolution contract is shown in figure 12.1. Hellison (2011) also offers useful conflict resolution strategies.

• **Talking bench:** The students go to a designated bench, where they must "come up with one story of what happened"; as Hellison notes, the teacher should not take part in this process because doing so removes the responsibility from the students for solving their problem (p. 97). When the two students have resolved the conflict, they rejoin the physical education class.

• **Sport court:** A group of students collectively attempts to discuss an issue and devise an acceptable solution for the entire class. This strategy is appropriate for children in grades 3 through 5. Hellison suggests that students elect the sport court group; however, at an elementary level, we suggest that the teacher appoint the members.

Children must practice the steps involved in the conflict resolution process. The teacher can facilitate their learning by having two children model a hypothetical situation.

POSITIVE TEACHER ATTRIBUTES

Sometimes teachers, especially new teachers, assume that their position of authority ensures that students will respect both them and other students. Not so. In reality, what goes around comes around. In other words, if you treat students with respect and model positive behaviors, then your students

Sit together at the talking bench and share each of your accounts of the problem situation. Then describe the problem here: _____

After both of you have discussed several options, offer a solution here: _____
_____
_____

Sign your names here: _____

Teacher comments: _____
_____
_____

Figure 12.1 Sample conflict resolution contract.

will tend to reflect many of the same behaviors.

Unfortunately, some teachers show little respect for their students; in turn, they receive little respect from them. Sarcastic remarks such as, "How stupid," "You never listen," and "You've got to be kidding" have no place in the vocabulary of teachers who are intent on serving as good role models. So too, demands such as, "Get over here" and "Shut up" are without justification. Children and adults alike have a tendency to treat others similarly to how they are treated. Serving as a positive role model in your actions and being respectful of students in your words will rub off on your students.

What attributes and teaching behaviors do you possess that contribute to building positive relationships with your students—that is, to what Hellison (2011) describes as "being relational with kids" (p. 103)? There is no exact "set of implements or place setting" (p. 103) to bring to the table. However, scholars suggest that excellent professionals possess numerous helpful attributes, including the following: passion (a vibrant, animated approach), enthusiasm, optimism, respect for students as human beings, the ability to establish clear rules and expectations, approachability, and the ability to create a safe and supportive environment (Williams, Alley, & Henson, 1999).

Establishing a good relationship with students lays the foundation for a positive class atmosphere: "The teacher-student relationship is at the heart of this notion of classroom management/atmosphere that supports student learning" (Graham, Holt/Hale, & Parker, 2013, p. 105). In the following pages, we suggest some teaching behaviors to develop and consider bringing to the table; all are aimed at strengthening the student–teacher relationship.

Have a sense of purpose. The teaching profession is challenging, children are challenging, and school politics are challenging. Given these challenges, do you really have a sense of purpose? Does teaching children provide you with fulfillment and a sense of satisfaction? Hellison (2011, p. 107) suggests that teachers must have a sense of purpose and that their purpose is, in fact, what matters the most. Your sense of purpose reflects your vision, your primary values, and your beliefs. We hope that your vision is to become a knowledgeable and skillful teacher, that you value learning and helping others learn, and that you believe all children can learn. If, on the other hand, your vision is to roll out the ball, supervise large-group games, and help only the best-behaved and most skillful chil-

dren, then we respectfully suggest that you question your sense of purpose as a future teacher.

Listen to students. Hellison (2011) also suggests that in order to "be relational with kids," teachers need to respect children and understand that they are unique individuals who have their own values, perceptions, fears, and aspirations; who deserve to be acknowledged, listened to, and negotiated with; and, in short, who deserve to be cared about and treated with dignity (p. 108). Hellison also reminds us that children should "have a voice to tell their side and be part of finding a solution" (p. 105).

In an attempt to really listen to children and hear their voices, teachers can pose questions that prompt children to reflect on their own behavior. For example, if a child is off task—for example, using equipment unsafely or disrespecting a classmate, and thus operating at level 0—the following process allows the child to offer her or his thoughts and opinions:

1. Assess the situation and ask the child a question about the behavior that is specific to the situation.

2. Involve the child in helping to resolve the situation and come to a reasonable solution.

Consider some examples:

Off-Task Behavior

1. What choice are you making right now?

2. Is this choice consistent with our acceptable classroom behaviors?

3. What acceptable classroom behaviors are you using when you make this choice?

4. What choice or choices might you make that are acceptable?

Unsafe or Improper Use of Equipment

1. Do you remember how to use the equipment safely?

2. Are you using the equipment in the same way that I demonstrated earlier?

3. Would you please show me how to safely use the equipment (within your personal space or as you move through general space)?

Demonstrate trust. Show children that you have faith in them through the developmentally appropriate responsibility that you give them. If you have taught children how to demonstrate behaviors consistent with the levels of personal and social responsibility, then they are more likely to demonstrate the responsibility that you expect. To reinforce your trust in them, acknowledge their success. In addition, if you trust that children can complete a task and they do *not* succeed, you must help them recognize that they are not meeting the expectation and then either reteach or remind them of the appropriate behaviors to demonstrate.

Use praise. Praise often and appropriately. Praise effort as well as performance, because trying hard shows responsibility even when the results are not perfect. Be sure, however, that your praise is sincere. General praise (e.g., "Great!" or "Good job!") should be followed by the specific reason. Praising children's steps (effort) toward accomplishing the final goal (performance) is sincere and enhances their learning.

Be enthusiastic. Your voice, physical posture, facial expressions, and overall excitement all affect how your students respond to you and whether they feel that you care about them. You don't have to be "over the top" or giddy all the time. However, given that your job is to motivate children to move and feel a sense of belonging, you must communicate with a sense of genuineness and zest for what you do.

Preservice teachers sometimes exhibit behaviors that are less than enthusiastic when teaching children who come to campus for weekly physical education instruction. In some cases, this behavior may be attributable to fear and lack of confidence, since, for many, this is their first time teaching young children. More generally, however, beginning teachers often demonstrate a lack of intonation, poor volume and poor projection, lack of eye contact, physical distance from students, and a scarcity of prompting and praising—all of which indirectly reflect one's enthusiasm. Fortunately, all of these attributes can be learned; for some beginning teachers, they must also be practiced, which is time well spent because expressions of enthusiasm are a critical component in creating an environment that is conducive to learning.

Enthusiasm is also indirectly conveyed through lesson preparation. A carefully planned lesson is evident when the gymnasium is preset, equipment is readily available, instructional tasks are developmentally appropriate, and the sequence and pace of the lesson maintains students' attention. All of these components of an effective lesson suggest that the teacher is enthusiastic about the subject matter and cares about providing children with a relevant and engaging lesson. Best practices in lesson planning are discussed further in chapter 10.

Be assertive but keep your cool. Distinguish between the terms *assertive* and *aggressive* as applied to behavioral control. Teachers who nag, accuse, argue, speak in anger, get into power struggles, and use harsh punishment are displaying **aggressive behavior. Assertive behavior,** on the other hand, is apparent in teachers who make clear, direct requests; reveal honest feelings; persist; listen to children's points of view; give brief reasons; and carry out reasonable consequences for misbehavior.

Curwin et al. (2008) offer two interventions to employ when misbehavior occurs: stabilizing and reframing. When students misbehave, teachers must first stabilize things in order to avoid confrontation, escalation, and generally making matters worse. "Stabilizing involves reducing anger, avoiding power struggles, and lowering the noise that can increase hostility to the point where interventions cannot work" (Curwin et al., 2008, p. 110). Here is an example of stabilization:

> A student confronts a teacher in front of classmates by saying, "This task is boring." The teacher asks, "Can you help me understand why you feel what you are practicing is boring?" The teacher then gives the child time to respond.
>
> Possible student response: "I already know how to do this task."
>
> Teacher's reply: "Thank you for being honest. It's important to me that everyone in our class feels as if they are successful and what they are practicing is useful. Take a look at the list of tasks on the whiteboard and choose two new tasks to practice. Would that work for you?

This teacher's response did not make matters worse; instead, it stabilized the situation.

Reframing involves understanding a situation in a way that provides the best chance for a positive outcome (Molnar & Linquist, 1990). When teachers reframe, they engage students in reviewing the situation through the lens of personal and social responsibility. As a result, the issue is not about making excuses for or ignoring behavior. For example, imagine that a student is arguing with a peer over the rules of a game. Consider the difference between reframing and blaming:

Cooperative activities encourage students to get to know each other, which can help to develop respect for varying cultural backgrounds in your class.

- Reframing: The teacher says, "I see that you two have a difference of opinion. Let's look at the whiteboard and review the rules we established for this game. Tell me how the rules apply to your game situation." If students are still in disagreement, the teacher can have each student describe his or her interpretation of the rule and then ask, "How does your interpretation agree with the rules we established for the game?"

- Blaming: The teacher says, "You are so stubborn and rude. I have told you and the entire class not to argue over rules in a game. When are you going to listen to me?"

How do you think students might respond differently to these two teacher responses?

Respect children's cultural differences. As shown by the 2010 census, the United States is more ethnically, racially, culturally, and linguistically diverse than ever before (Graham et al., 2013, p. 642). As a result, a monolingual physical education teacher is increasingly likely to face the challenge of teaching young children whose languages and backgrounds are completely unfamiliar (Harrison, Russell, & Burden, 2010). In the 21st-century, teachers must be culturally responsive and must aspire to understand the cultural traditions observed by members of their student population.

This work may include learning how different cultures communicate and what social values they hold. To do so, Graham et al. (2013) suggest making home visits, learning greetings in different languages, and asking children how to say basic expressions in their language. Cruz and Peterson (2011, p. 23) describe culturally responsive teachers as individuals who "ask questions and take the time to learn about the culture of their school, their students as individuals, the students' families, and the communities they live in. They understand culturally and ethnically congruent forms of communication and demonstrate respect for all despite cultural differences." Cruz and Peterson also offer the following specific teaching strategies for interacting with children of different races and ethnicities (p. 23):

- Do not assume racial identity based on physical characteristics alone (e.g., not all dark-skinned people are African American).

- If necessary, ask students how to pronounce their names and practice saying them until you pronounce them correctly.

- Do not make assumptions about a student based on race or ethnicity; not all Asian students are good at math, not all African American students play basketball, and not all Hispanic students speak Spanish.

- Get to know students as individuals and encourage them to get to know one another during class activities.

- Use visual aids and demonstrations of skills and class organization to help non-English speakers understand what they should do.

- Ensure that posters and other visual aids depict cultural diversity and do not stereotype; for example, not all basketball players are African American, and not all tennis players are Caucasian.

In addition, the following strategies are offered for interacting with students who are economically disadvantaged (Cruz & Peterson, 2011, pp. 23–24):

- Keep extra supplies (e.g., sneakers, socks, shorts, and T-shirts) available for students who may need them. Offer them discretely to students in need, or offer them to the entire class without mention of financial need.

- If assigning computer-based homework, be sure that students have access to a school or library computer in case they do not have one at home.

- If suggesting fun, active things to do outside of school, include some free activities, since not all families have the resources to pay for recreation.

- Do not make assumptions about students' (or their parents') intelligence, values, or other attributes based on their socioeconomic status.

- Provide adequate opportunities for both organized and unorganized physical activity before and after school so that students who lack access to a YMCA, fitness club, or youth sport team have a chance to participate in physical activity.

Respect children's religious differences. U.S. citizens are granted First Amendment rights—that is, freedom of religion. These days, schools are not only culturally diverse but also religiously diverse. With this reality in mind, physical educators should communicate with administrators to learn about school policies that enable them to recognize and respect the religious rights of all children. They also need to understand current law with respect to how religion is addressed in the physical education curriculum. As Kahan (2003) reminds teachers, religious symbols (e.g., cross, menorah) may be used as teaching aids but not as seasonal decorations. In addition, the music, art, and dance traditions associated with specific religions can be incorporated into physical education instruction

as long as they are presented in a religiously neutral manner. With respect to dress, students whose clothing reflects their religion's views or laws must be permitted to wear it (e.g., long pants under shorts, hijab over hair, yarmulke, turban).

To summarize, teachers should be effective instructors, and they should be friendly, helpful, and congenial in the process. Teachers should empathize with students, understand their world, and listen to them. However, good teachers are not uncertain, undecided, or confusing in the way that they communicate with students. Nor are they grouchy, gloomy, dissatisfied, aggressive, sarcastic, or quick tempered. They should set standards and maintain control while still allowing students the responsibility and freedom to learn (Wubbels, Brekelmans, van Tartwijk, & Admiral, 1999, p. 167).

THE SOCIAL CONTRACT

Like Hellison's model, the use of social contracts is a way for teachers to hold students accountable for their behavior in the physical education setting. A social contract is just what its name suggests: "an agreement between teacher and students about the values, rules, and consequences for classroom behavior" (Curwin et al., 2008, p. 68). In the following discussion about social contracts, *rule* refers to a learning outcome, *behavior* refers to actions that meet the desired outcome, and *consequence* refers to response strategies based on the expectations for personal and social responsibility in standard 4 of the national physical education standards (SHAPE America, 2014).

A social contract adheres to the following guiding principles:

- Connect rules (learning outcomes) to values (standard 4 expectations).

- Identify rules (learning outcomes) and acceptable behaviors needed to run an effective classroom.

- Involve students in developing the acceptable behaviors they need in order to meet the learning outcomes.

- Make response strategies (consequences) relate as directly as possible to the rule (learning outcome).

- In developing a response strategy (consequence), be guided primarily by what the student is likely to learn in order to improve behavior.

- Develop a predictable range of response strategies (consequences) for unacceptable behaviors.

- If a parent thinks a different response strategy (consequence) would be more effective in changing a student's behavior, consider how consistent that strategy is with your classroom learning outcomes and protocols.

Based on these guiding principles, Curwin et al. (2008) suggest that teachers use the following process for developing a social contract:

1. Establish values (standard 4 expectations for personal and social responsibility).
2. Create and use rules (learning outcomes).
3. Create a range of consequences (response strategies) for each rule.
4. Use student input about acceptable behaviors.
5. Invest the time needed to discuss and practice the acceptable behaviors associated with the learning outcomes.
6. Administer a test about the acceptable behaviors to determine whether students understand them.

Using this process, step 1 in developing a social contract involves establishing values guided by the expectations for personal and social responsibility provided in national physical education standard 4. The expectations provide the reasons for rules (learning outcomes) and place acceptable behaviors in a larger context. This framing helps students understand the need for the learning outcomes and behaviors.

Step 2 in developing a social contract is to establish rules, or learning outcomes, which are behavioral expressions of standard 4 expectations. Rules should define clearly what is acceptable in the physical education classroom—and what is not. Children are generally more secure when they know what is expected of them; they are also more likely to succeed. As Curwin et al. (2008) state, "The importance of specific and predictable rules is directly related to developing responsibility. The more understandable the expectations, the better the students' chances of meeting them" (p. 72).

When establishing guidelines for acceptable behavior, it is wise to limit the number of *don'ts* because, in its own way, that word reinforces unacceptable behavior. Instead, address behaviors from a positive standpoint. For example, rather than saying, "Don't run," "Don't talk," or "Don't get out of line," it is usually better to say, "Walk quietly," "Remain silent," or "Stay in line." Emphasizing the positive gives students clear expectations and often exerts a positive influence.

Here are some guidelines for developing and using learning outcomes for standard 4:

- Involve students in the process of establishing acceptable behaviors that meet the outcomes. This approach fosters ownership.
- State acceptable behaviors in positive terms.
- Develop an appropriate number of learning outcomes for the children's age.
- Develop and use learning outcomes and acceptable behaviors that cover various class situations.

As noted by Curwin et al. (2008), teachers can empower children and help them feel a sense of ownership by involving them in the process of creating rule-following behaviors in class. Doing so enables students to "feel that the plan is part of them" (p. 75). If children are part of the process, they are more likely to use the behaviors that meet the learning outcomes; in turn, they are more likely to achieve the goal of engaging in self-discipline.

Step 3 in the process of creating a social contract is to develop response strategies (consequences). Response strategies should *not* be punishments, threats, or rewards; instead, they should offer an array of developmentally appropriate choices. "Good consequences [response strategies] are clear and specific, have a range of alternatives, are designed to teach improved behavioral choices, are natural and logical, and are related to the rule" (Curwin et al., 2008, pp. 74–75). In addition, response strategies should always preserve students' dignity, attempt to increase students' internal locus of control, and, ultimately, increase students' motivation to succeed.

Classroom learning outcomes related to standard 4 should be posted, which can be done in various captivating ways. One appealing option is to collaborate with the art or classroom teacher to have children design acceptable-behavior posters. Some physical educators also choose an acronym, such as RESPECT, in which each letter represents a classroom rule (learning outcome); for an example, see figure 12.2.

Recognition gained properly by raising your hand, listening to the teacher, and following instructions.
Equipment used on the teacher's signal. The equipment is for you; treat it carefully.
Stay on task to have a safe and positive class.
Practice skills as best you can to become skillful movers.
Encourage each other to do your best and support each other with positive statements.
Considerate of others' feelings through good sportsmanship.
Together we learn and become our best.

Figure 12.2   RESPECT rules.

From T. Moone, 1997, "Teaching students with respect." *Teaching Elementary Physical Education* 8(5): 16-18.

After you determine the learning outcomes, acceptable behaviors, and response strategies for personal and social responsibility, you must teach students *how* to use the acceptable behaviors. To help children learn and practice, you can use role-playing activities and games. In this manner, children can experience, both physically and cognitively, the acceptable personal and social responsibility behaviors.

All of the learning outcomes described in the following social contracts help children become better people in terms of both holistic self-development and human decency. Holistic self-development involves children in persevering, trying their best, working with others, making good choices, and being safe. Human decency, of course, involves

cultivating positive relationships with others in the following ways (Hellison, 2011, pp. 18–19):

Respecting others

Respecting the learning environment

Demonstrating self-control

Showing acts of kindness

Engaging in peaceful conflict resolution

In order to be developmentally appropriate, the learning outcomes, behaviors, and response strategies addressed in the social contract must reflect children's cognitive and social development (see chapter 3). Therefore, examples of age-appropriate social contracts are shown in tables 12.2 through 12.4 for children in pre-K through grade 5.

Table 12.2   Social Contract for Pre-K Children

Learning outcome	Behaviors	Response strategies
Play nicely.	We are nice to our friends by sharing equipment. We say nice words to our friends, such as, "You are doing a great job bouncing the ball."	Child has these choices: • Take a time-out and determine when to rejoin. • Practice saying a nice statement to a friend.
Make good choices.	We choose stations to play at that have smiley-face tokens. If there is not a token, we choose a new station.	Child has these choices: • Change playing area or station. • Let teacher choose where he or she should play or practice.
Be safe.	We try to stay far away from others when they use equipment. We avoid others while moving. We move at a safe speed.	Child has these choices: • Voluntarily move farther away from friend or equipment. • Have the teacher provide a clearer area for the child to play in by using cones, poly spots, or other markers. • Have the teacher or a classmate show how to move at a safer speed and then practice with the teacher or classmate.
Listen to the teacher.	When the teacher says "bus stop" we stop moving and cross our arms and legs like we are waiting for the bus to come!	Child has these choices: • Have the teacher use touch to help him or her freeze in "bus stop" position. • Mirror a classmate to learn how to do bus stop.
Try my best.	Keep playing at your station/play area. Don't stop until the music stops playing.	Child has these choices: • Have the teacher examine how the task needs to be changed to be either more or less difficult. • Have the teacher provide a partner who is staying on task.

Table 12.3 Social Contract for K-2 Children

Learning outcomes	Behaviors	Response strategies
Be attentive. Exhibit personal responsibility during class activities. (SHAPE America, 2014).	Know and perform the listening position for the day, such as "bus stop." Listen to the teacher's signal to start and stop play.	Proximity control: If a student is continually off task, have him or her practice in a specific bounded area where you can model the "freeze" and the student can mirror you. Provide a peer tutor to help the student stay on task and freeze when signaled.
Respect equipment. Take responsibility for class protocols (SHAPE America, 2014).	Place equipment gently on the floor and carefully in bins.	Have the student model a classmate's actions of appropriate equipment use. Use peer tutoring.
Try your best. Practice with minimal teacher prompting (SHAPE America, 2014).	Practice all skills—those you are already good at and those you still need to learn!	Student and teacher examine how the task needs to be changed in order to be either more or less difficult. Have the student use a practice task card to record information about each practice trial (see the Practice Style [B] task card in chapter 10) in order to see how practicing improves performance.
Praise and encourage. Praise movement performance of others (SHAPE America, 2014).	Say "magic words" to each other: "Keep trying!" "Way to go!" "You are awesome!" "Super job"!	Have the student practice writing "magic words" with a partner on a handout or on a whiteboard and use them during a partner activity. Keep a record of the student's encouraging statements during a span of lessons.
Work with others (SHAPE America, 2014).	Share equipment and space and work together both independently and cooperatively.	Say, "It looks like you are unable to share the equipment. Is that true?" If the child says yes, ask why. Then restate the rule about sharing equipment and say, "You have a choice—share your equipment or sit out and think about why sharing is important." If the child chooses to sit out, say, "When you can explain to me why sharing is important, you may rejoin the class activity."

Table 12.4 Social Contract for Children in Grades 3 Through 5

Learning outcome	Behaviors	Response strategies
Persevere. Exhibit personal responsibility (SHAPE America, 2014).	Keep practicing to improve motor skills; don't give up! Seek opportunities to learn.	Student and teacher examine how the task or environment need to be changed to become either more or less difficult.
Accept, implement, and respectfully give feedback (SHAPE America, 2014).	Listen to teacher and peer feedback and try to use it to change behavior or improve motor skills. Provide approving and corrective feedback in a helpful way.	If a student is having trouble accepting advice, hold a conference with the student to discuss the purpose of feedback, how to use it, and how to accept it positively; then have the student make a journal entry about how they have changed their behavior with respect to accepting feedback. Hold a conference to discuss the purpose of feedback and how to provide feedback in a helpful way; then have the student make a journal entry or do a role-play about giving appropriate feedback to a peer.
Practice cooperative interdependence. Work with others (SHAPE America, 2014).	Show commitment to the group as follows: • Using positive statements • Encouraging others • Demonstrating patience • Taking responsibility for one's role • Offering ideas • Accepting others' ideas	Have the student observers take responsibility for their designated roles and describe how he or she could also engage in such behaviors. Have the student complete a behavior ticket stating what she or he said that was not positive and what should have been said instead.
Exhibit application of rules, etiquette, and safety (SHAPE America, 2014, p. 36).	Adhere to etiquette and rules. Design appropriate etiquette and rules for created games. Apply safety principles in activity settings.	Say, "It looks like you are not adhering to rules." If the child agrees, ask, "What should you be doing? Let me see you do that." If the student does not admit to breaking rules, state the purpose of the rule and ask, "If you were to follow the rule, what would it look or sound like?" If the student provides a reasonable answer, have him or her commit to the behavior and rejoin the class. If not, state your expectations, ask if the student can comply, and say that you want to see him or her follow the rule. If the student continues to break the rules, use a time-out with a focus question that must be answered before the student rejoins the class.

THE PHYSICAL ENVIRONMENT

The physical appearance of the gymnasium matters because an atmosphere that is bright, cheery, and generally appealing is conducive to positive behavior and student learning. Neat bulletin boards, posters, painted murals, activity charts, and photographs of students—which should be changed frequently—all promote interest and give students a sense that you care. You can also display student-designed posters and other work to instill a sense of pride in your students. And bulletin boards designed by you and your students can reinforce concepts taught in class and help create a stimulating overall environment.

In addition, the facilities and equipment used by your students must be developmentally appropriate, accessible, and safe. The following facility and equipment concerns are addressed by pre-impact decisions (see chapter 10), meaning that they should be made before you teach a physical education lesson.

Facilities

• Is your gymnasium well organized? If it doubles as a lunchroom, are the tables adequately secured so that they are do not interfere with instruction or, more specifically, children's movement through space? If not, can you discuss this safety issue with your administration and come to an agreeable solution?

• Are large pieces of equipment (e.g., foam vaulting blocks, balance boards or beams) adequately stored away from the general flow of movement in your class?

• Do you have appropriate floor markings? These markings can be used to indicate such areas as meeting spots for learning teams; boundaries for game play; and locations for listening and demonstrations. Help children learn where these markings are and what purpose they serve. At the same time, keep in mind that having too many lines or other markings on the floor can cause students to experience spatial confusion.

• Is your outdoor space adequately maintained (e.g., grass mowed, debris cleared)? You may need to speak with your administrator to clarify your areas of responsibility in maintaining the outdoor space used for physical education. Hopefully, you have the support of school maintenance staff in mowing the grass and removing debris. On the other hand, it may be your responsibility to handle tasks such as putting down line markings for small-sided game play.

Equipment

• Equipment room: Is your equipment room organized logically and safely? It should be organized so that older children can help you get out equipment and put it away, thus communicating to your students that they can be trusted. Caveat: Children should *always* be supervised if permitted to assist

A well-organized equipment room facilitates set up of equipment for lessons.

in getting out and putting away equipment. In addition, some equipment may simply be too large or be positioned too high for children to handle.

- Setup: Do you have your equipment preset so that class can begin with instant activity rather than having students wait for you to complete the setup? Do you put the equipment to be used during the lesson in multiple places within the gymnasium, field, or movement area in order to facilitate easy distribution and collection?

- Quantity and type: Do you have enough equipment available to maximize participation? Is the type of equipment (e.g., size, weight, texture) varied to enable scaling (chapter 6) and differentiated instruction?

For more help in establishing an effective learning environment, see table 12.5 for a set of guidelines provided by the National Association for Sport and Physical Education (2009).

ESTABLISHING DEVELOPMENTALLY APPROPRIATE PROTOCOLS

Class protocols involve "predetermined ways of handling situations that frequently occur in the physical education setting" (Lavay et al., 1997, p.

25). The following situations demand a routine or protocol in order for your classroom to run smoothly! Do you have a set procedure for each one?

- Using the rest room (e.g., taking a brightly painted stick that is kept in a particular location)
- Taking attendance (e.g., scanning the class during an instant activity)
- Getting drinks from a water fountain located in the gymnasium or a nearby hallway
- Knowing where to place clothing taken off before, during, or after an activity (e.g., bin or crate placed at side of gymnasium)
- Handling minor and major injuries
- Starting and stopping an activity
- Getting out and putting away equipment
- Establishing partners or small groups (teams)

Some protocols, or classroom routines, should be communicated at the start of the school year, whereas others need to be reinforced throughout the year. To help you organize your handling of these issues, table 12.6 presents a checklist for the beginning of school originally created by Evertson, Emmer, & Worsham (2009), then adapted by Graham et al. (2013, p.114), and further modified by the authors of this textbook.

Table 12.5 Guidelines for Establishing the Learning Environment

Appropriate practice	Inappropriate practice
1.1.1 The teacher systematically plans for, develops, and maintains a positive learning environment that is focused on maximizing learning and participation, in an atmosphere of respect and support from the teacher and the child's peers.	1.1.1 The environment is not supportive or safe (e.g., teacher makes degrading or sarcastic remarks). As a result, some children feel embarrassed, humiliated, and generally uncomfortable in physical education class.
1.1.2 The environment is supportive of all children and promotes development of a positive self-concept. Children are allowed to try, to fail, and to try again, free of criticism or harassment from the teacher or other students.	1.1.2 Only the highly skilled or physically fit children are viewed as successful learners. The teacher and peers overlook and/or ignore students who are not highly skilled or physically fit.
1.1.3 Programs are designed to guide children to take responsibility for their own behavior and learning. Emphasis is on intrinsic, rather than extrinsic, incentives.	1.1.3 Children behave appropriately because they are fearful of receiving a poor grade or other "punishment" if they don't follow the teacher's rules.
1.1.4 Fair and consistent classroom management practices encourage student responsibility for positive behavior. Students are included in the process of developing class rules/agreements.	1.1.4 The rules are unclear and can vary from day to day.
1.1.5 Bullying, taunting, and inappropriate student remarks and behaviors are dealt with immediately and firmly.	1.1.5 Verbal or nonverbal behavior that is hurtful to other children is overlooked and ignored.

Reprinted with permission from SHAPE America – Society of Health and Physical Educators, 2009, 1900 Association Drive, Reston, VA 20191, www.shapeamerica.org.

As physical educators, part of our goal in establishing class protocols is to appreciate the developmental differences between children ranging from pre-K to grade 5. For example, fifth graders certainly do not need as much guidance as pre-K children do with respect to using the bathroom, responding to an injury, or getting out or putting away equipment. With such differences in mind, the following sections provide developmentally appropriate variations for some of the most frequently used protocols. These protocols should be determined before you teach a lesson and are therefore categorized as pre-impact decisions (see chapter 10).

Entering and Exiting

Every teacher needs to follow general school guidelines regarding how children are escorted to the gymnasium and how they enter and exit the gymnasium. Here are some suggestions!

Entering

Pre-K

- Greet each child by name and perhaps give a pat on the shoulder or a high five.
- Remind children that you always begin class with "circle time at the class circle"; this area can also be referred to as the Calling All Kids Area.
- Play a drumbeat or music for children and ask them to skip to the class circle area and freeze in a shape. To mark the circle area, laminate stars and secure them with clear tape to form a circle in the middle of the gymnasium floor; the circle could also be painted on the floor.
- Perform quick, rhythmic, call-and-response activities. For example, say, "1-2-3 eyes on me!" Children respond, "1-2 eyes on you!" Then you say, "Let's hear three claps if you're ready to begin moving today!"

Table 12.6 Checklist for the Beginning of School

Item	Date completed	Notes
Have you inspected outdoor and indoor facilities for safety?		
Is your physical education equipment organized and ready?		
Are you familiar with the parts of the school that you may use (e.g., halls, cafeteria, multipurpose room, lobby)?		
Do you have permission to use alternative areas if the gymnasium is unavailable?		
Do you have pertinent information about students' medical history and current needs (e.g., asthma allergies)?		
If any students have an IEP, do you know their physical education goals? In addition, what specific modifications do you need to consider to accommodate any students with disability?		
Have you established classroom protocols?		
What are your procedures for attending to student injuries? Have you communicated with the school nurse to determine what these procedures should be?		
Do you know how to obtain assistance from school staff members (e.g., custodian, nurse, counselor, office personnel)?		
Advocacy: Do you have a letter ready to include in the school mailing or to put on the physical education website about the school year and your expectations for students in physical education?		

Adapted from Evertson, Emmer, and Worsham 2009; Graham, Holt/Hale, and Parker 2013.

- Briefly review learning stations for the day and dismiss children to play areas by the color of their learning team.
- Other options for entering might include:
  - Having children go to learning stations according to a designated color for their learning group, whereupon the children explore ways to use the equipment at that station
  - Having children report to the Calling All Kids Area, where the teacher conducts a lyric-directed dance or exercise routine to music
  - Having children complete an age-appropriate instant activity

K-2

- Greet each child by name and perhaps give a pat on the shoulder or a high five.
- Ask children to walk carefully, skip, gallop, or slow-jog to the learning area (K-2 students can be previously organized into learning teams).
- Begin an instant activity in the learning area.
- Take attendance during the instant activity.

Grades 3 Through 5

- Greet each child by name and perhaps give a high five.
- Have students move to a pedometer or heart monitor, put on the device, and then begin "racetrack fitness."
- Once all students have put on a device and are participating in racetrack fitness, interact with them to check in and see how they are doing that day or to remind a student of a specific behavior that you would like him or her to focus on during the day's lesson. You may also need to take attendance during the instant activity.
- Begin a whole-class instant activity.
- Have learning teams go to specified areas to perform skills previously learned while the teacher administers a skill assessment.

Exiting

Pre-K

- End with "circle time." Provide lesson closure by reviewing one aspect of the lesson related to the lesson objective—for example, the critical cues of a specific skill, a social behavior

concept, or a review of ways that children discovered to use a specific piece of equipment. This review should be visual and auditory and may involve the children physically.

- Dismiss the children in a manner similar to that used for their entrance. For example, play music and have them gallop to the door with a friend, side by side, and then stand next to the friend at the door, where perhaps you have posted on the wall an image of the school mascot, a cartoon character, or the alphabet letter of the week. You can also paint a line on the floor where the children are to stand with their partners. This line could be dashed or have a dramatic color or be distinctive in some other manner.

K-2

- Children help clean up equipment, after which you call them to the Calling All Kids Area.
- Provide closure by (a) reviewing key aspects of the lesson objective, (b) prompting some student demonstrations, and (c) conducting an assessment aligned with the lesson objective.
- Preview the next class.
- Dismiss the children in learning teams to the exit area, where they form a line.

Grades 3 Through 5

- Have leaders of learning teams gather formative assessments.
- Provide closure by reviewing key aspects of the lesson objective and conducting an assessment aligned with the lesson objective.
- Distribute any homework assignment.
- Preview the next class.
- Dismiss the children by learning teams to the exit area, where they form a line.

Stopping and Starting

Physical educators often use a whistle to stop or start an activity. However, we believe that whistles should be used sparingly—for example, when you are outdoors and need a very loud signal to freeze, gather, or dismiss students. At other times, you can gain children's attention by using various distinctive sounds created by tonal or percussion instruments (e.g., a train whistle, bird sounds, honking noises). Alternatively, electronic push-button whistles offer better hygiene for multiple users and provide a consistent sound every time! Here are a few more options:

- Hand gestures
- Body positions (e.g., bus stop)
- Holding up a piece of equipment (e.g., lollipop paddle)

Given these various options, your starting and stopping signals should respect children's developmental status. For example, a whistle might frighten a pre-K child, and a drumbeat might "turn off" a fifth grader.

Equipment

Equipment should be placed in secure, safe areas of the gymnasium. In general, equipment setup should be handled by the teacher for all lessons, though on special occasions (and based on lesson objectives) the teacher may involve students in the setup. It is our opinion that physical educators should strive to engage students as much as possible in the distribution and collection of equipment. Here are some considerations for distributing, arranging, and collecting equipment for each grade level.

Pre-K

- **Arranging:** Play or learning stations should be set up before class. Balls and any other type of equipment that can roll on the floor should be placed inside of hoops or crates at each station.

- **Distributing:** Because pre-K children are primarily involved in exploring movement skills at predesigned stations, they should have easy access to the equipment at these stations. In addition, task cards with words and pictures can be used to remind children what movement task they are exploring at each station.

- **Distributing:** If a whole-class activity is being taught, equipment should be kept in hoops or crates off to the sides of the movement space. Children can be dismissed by the color of their learning team or some other simple designation to get a piece of equipment, find their own personal space, and use the equipment in any way they choose

within their space. Pre-K children should *not* be expected to wait to use their equipment until all children have secured a piece of equipment.

- **Collecting:** Children should be responsible for cleaning up their station when the teacher gives a designated signal.

K-5

- **Arranging:** Equipment should be prepositioned for easy access. In grades 3 through 5, if your students are designing an obstacle course or participating in an adventure-based initiative, the relevant equipment should be gathered in a specific area for small groups of students to use.

- **Distributing:** Learning-team leaders can be asked to get small equipment (e.g., six beanbags) for all team members; alternatively, learning teams can be dismissed to get equipment placed in team areas.

- **Collecting:** Learning teams or individual students can help collect equipment and place it back into the learning team areas or into crates, hoops, or other containers (e.g., wheeled garbage cans).

Establishing Partners and Groups

Children in pre-K are egocentric beings, and their social skills are quite immature. Because these children are in the midst of learning how to communicate, cooperate, and solve conflicts, teachers should not expect them to voluntarily form partner groups or play effectively in small groups. Instead, if children are exploring movement skills at stations, they may simply play side by side, as in parallel play, while occasionally sharing ideas or expressions of joy or inviting a friend to play with them: "Let's try jumping off the foam block!" Later in the pre-K years, children can be asked to share equipment with a partner, to choose a new partner, and to play in small groups for brief periods of time.

K-2 children should be expected gradually to play with different partners determined by random methods, such as finding a friend who has a ball of the same color or whose first name starts with the same letter. In grades 3 through 5, children begin to play effectively in small groups but may be reluctant to partner with someone of the opposite sex. It may be necessary to engage in frank discussions about willingness to partner with others and accept differences. Here are some techniques for partnering and grouping:

Partnering Techniques

- Find a classmate who has the same card number as you.
- Find a classmate whose puzzle piece fits with your puzzle piece.
- Find a classmate whose birthday is in the same month as yours.
- Find a classmate whose card has the answer to the question on your card.
- Find a classmate who is the same height as you are.

Grouping Techniques

- As students jog in general space, play a drum and have children form groups according to the number of drumbeats played. For example, children are jogging in general space. The teacher beats the drum three times, therefore, children should get into groups of three.
- Form learning teams at the beginning of the school year or marking period. This can be done by having students number off—one through five, for example—and gather according to number (i.e., all ones get together, and so on).
- Group students by using playing cards. For example, all students who have a three card get together in a group.

EFFECTIVE MANAGEMENT PRACTICES

Physical educators should be proactive in using various management strategies to foster appropriate behavior in the physical activity setting. The following strategies offer ways to monitor children and prompt them to be successful throughout the physical education lesson.

- **Proximity control:** Move closer to a child who is displaying inappropriate behavior. Entering the student's space often helps a child refocus and reengage. The decision to use this strategy is a post-impact decision (see chapter 10) because it is made in response to a student's behavior.
- **Back to the wall:** Throughout a lesson, strive to scan the entire classroom by keeping your back toward a gymnasium wall or, if teaching outdoors, toward the outer perimeter of the activity space. This practice enables you to view overall performance and assess the "big picture." However, it is not a management strategy that you should expect to use all the time, because of course you also need to walk through the middle of the learning space. Still, it is important to keep yourself positioned to maximize your ability to see as many children as possible at a time. This is a pre-impact decision because you make it before teaching the lesson.
- **Selective ignoring:** Children sometimes exhibit behaviors that are distracting or slightly inappropriate. If a child seems to be acting out temporarily, perhaps to get your attention or that of a peer, it may be wise to simply ignore the behavior. To make this judgment call effectively, you must have adequate knowledge of the child and his or her typical pattern of behavior; of course, a teacher should *not* ignore repeated inappropriate behavior. The use of selective ignoring results from a post-impact decision, since it is made in response to a student's behavior.
- **Positive pinpointing:** Rather than pointing out misbehavior, you will generally be more successful in keeping a positive learning environment if you point out what a child is doing correctly. For example, to reinforce a rule about the safe level at which to use a stick, you could use positive pinpointing by saying, "I like that you're keeping the stick low to the ground." This strategy results from a pre-impact decision because it is chosen before teaching the lesson.

Big Ideas

- Hellison's model of personal and social responsibility articulates five levels of personal and social responsibility. The teacher facilitates students' attainment of the levels by integrating responsibility-based strategies and an empowerment progression within the physical education learning environment. Students learn the levels and the respective behaviors associated with each level and are held accountable for demonstrating these behaviors and for reflecting on their behavior.

- Discipline has been defined as the process of helping students learn to make good choices and to be responsible for their choices. Hellison (2011) offers the following strategies for addressing discipline issues: the accordion principle, negotiation, Grandma's law, teacher-directed groups, five clean days, and sitting out.

- Conflict resolution involves three main steps: (1) Ask about the situation. (2) Listen as each child recounts his or her version. (3) Have each child offer a solution.

- Strengthening the student–teacher relationship fosters positive behaviors by students. Scholars suggest that excellent professionals possess numerous attributes, including passion (a vibrant animated approach), enthusiasm, optimism, respect for students as human beings, the ability to establish clear rules and expectations, approachability, and the ability to create a safe and supportive environment (Williams et al., 1999).

- Two intervention strategies for addressing misbehavior are stabilization and reframing. Stabilizing involves reducing anger, avoiding power struggles, and lowering the "noise" that can increase hostility to the point where interventions cannot work (Curwin et al., 2008, p. 110). Reframing involves engaging students in reviewing the situation through the lens of personal and social responsibility.

- Social contracts can be developed through following the process: (1) using expectations from national physical education standard 4 for personal and social responsibility, (2) establishing and using learning outcomes, (3) creating a range of response strategies for each learning outcome, (4) using student input about acceptable behaviors, (5) making time to discuss and practice the acceptable behaviors, and (6) administering a test addressing the acceptable behaviors to determine whether students understand them.

- Establishing the physical environment involves being sure that the facility (e.g., gymnasium) is organized and safe and that it provides a cheery and motivating environment by displaying students' works (e.g., on bulletin boards). The equipment room should be safe and accessible. Equipment should be preset so that class can begin quickly, and all equipment should be scaled to children's size and ability.

- Class protocols are predetermined ways of handling situations that occur frequently in the physical education setting. Some protocols, or classroom routines, should be communicated at the start of the school year, whereas others need to be reinforced throughout the year. Common protocols address using the restroom (e.g., take a brightly painted stick kept in a particular location); taking attendance (e.g., scan the class during an instant activity); getting drinks from a water fountain located in the gymnasium or a nearby hallway; knowing where to place clothing taken off before, during, or after an activity (e.g., in a bin or crate placed at side of the gymnasium); handling minor and major injuries; starting and stopping activity; getting out and putting away equipment; and establishing partners or small groups (teams).

- Effective management practices for teaching include positive pinpointing, proximity control, selective ignoring, and back to the wall.

 Visit the web resource for learning activities, video clips, and review questions.

PART

IV

Standards-Based Learning Experiences for Pre-K Through Grade 2

Chapter 13

Designing Learning Experiences for Pre-K Students

Key Concepts

- Learning the relationship between stage of motor development, level of movement skill learning, and design of movement activities for pre-K children

- Designing movement activities that align pre-K guidelines for national physical education content standards, pre-K appropriate practices, pre-K values, Hellison's levels of personal and social responsibility, and pre-K assessment and feedback

This chapter provides a developmental overview of pre-K learners and sample learning experiences that facilitate children's progress through the initial stage and the early part of the emerging-elementary stage of fundamental motor skill development. The importance of designing the movement environment using affordances that promote pre-K children's movement exploration is emphasized. Each learning experience is based on a pre-K guideline and highlights a skill theme and movement concept(s) through sequential movement tasks. Relevant feedback and assessment ideas are also provided.

DEVELOPMENT OF PRE-K LEARNERS

In working with pre-K learners, it is critical to understand their developmental characteristics, their limitations, and their potential. Only in this way can we effectively structure movement experiences for young children that truly reflect their needs and interests and fall within their level of ability. Chapters 3 and 4 provide an in-depth review of pre-K children's cognitive, social, and motor development, and that information is summarized here in the developmental overview provided in table 13.1.

Pre-K children are at the beginning or novice level of learning new movement skills; therefore, we label the skill progressions for pre-K learners as preconsistent (see chapter 6). The preconsistent skill progressions are highlighted in table 13.2.

In addition, a pre-K movement lesson can be designed to address one or more of the pre-K guidelines (NASPE, 2009) related to the national physical education standards (see table 13.3). More specifically, just as physical educators design the movement task and environment to foster fundamental movement skills and movement concepts, they can also purposefully design circle time activities and movement environments (e.g., stations) that implicitly reinforce the health-related fitness components (see chapter 2 for an in-depth review of fitness education for pre-K children).

Similarly, the promotion of personal and social responsibility must be intentionally planned in a pre-K movement experience. To that end, table 13.4 aligns Hellison's levels of personal and

Table 13.1   Pre-K Developmental Overview

Category	Learner characteristics	Teaching implications
Visual	Difficulty focusing on moving objects and relevant cues in the environment	Provide brightly colored objects that contrast with wall and floor coloring.
Kinesthetic	Learning body parts and laterality cues	Provide movement challenges that elicit exploration of location and movements of body parts.
Motor development	Undifferentiated movement Limited flexion, extension, and rotation of body parts	Provide a safe environment with body-scaled equipment and a variety of developmentally appropriate movement challenges. Foster exploration to facilitate development of fundamental movement skills.
Cardiorespiratory endurance	Inability to sustain aerobic activity: hypokinetic circulation, low concentration of hemoglobin, higher respiration, shallower breathing, and less ability to store glycogen Movements using fast, quick bursts of energy	Intentional engagement in exercise is not appropriate for pre-K children, but health-related fitness is implicitly developed through activities fostering development of fundamental movement skills.
Body composition	Dependent on multiple variables, including genetics, maturation, nutrition, and activity level	
Stage of cognitive development	Preoperational stage, during which children are egocentric and unable to view the world from another's perspective Curious, imaginative, and inclined to explore the environment and test own limits	Use simple instructions and task cards with pictures. Move into activity quickly, make only brief use of whole-class format (3–5 minutes), provide small bits of information at a time. Use a station format in which each has a single focus. Use activities that stimulate imagination and creativity.
Self-concept	Highly influenced by the actions, thoughts, and feelings expressed about them by caregivers	Give children opportunities to explore, take risks, and succeed. Encourage and praise children's active exploration.
Personal and social responsibility	Egocentric and engaging in solitary, parallel, and associative play	Provide activities that engage children in moving next to others while respecting others' space and equipment.

Table 13.2 Preconsistent Level Skill Progressions

Traveling	Equipment: taped pathways on floor, cones, props, drums (or musical instruments)
	Learning outcome: Develop traveling on feet through the emerging-elementary stage.
	• Traveling through general space
	  • Walking
	  • Running
	  • Galloping
	  • Sliding
	  • Skipping
	• Traveling and stopping with control
	• Traveling along predefined pathways
	• Traveling around and between obstacles
	• Traveling using imagery and props
	• Traveling at moderate to fast speed
	• Leading and following a partner

Flight	Equipment: low boxes, benches, foam shapes, poly spots, ropes, hoops, tires Learning outcome: Develop taking off and landing on feet through the emerging-elementary stage. • Jumping off of low equipment • Jumping onto and into equipment placed flat on floor • Jumping or leaping over lines, poly spots, and ropes on floor
Balancing	Equipment: low boxes, benches, foam shapes, ropes, hoops Learning outcome: Perform static balances. • Balancing on wide to moderate-sized bases \tab\ • Balancing in different shapes • Balance on different levels • Balance inside and outside of hoops • Balancing on low equipment • Balancing next to or facing a partner

Transferring weight	Equipment: trestles, ladders, foam shapes, tires, ropes, cones, refrigerator boxes, tunnels, arches
	Learning outcome: Perform step-like actions taking weight on hands and feet.
	• Step-like actions using different combinations of body parts under and through equipment
	  • Moving on hands and knees (or feet)
	  • Moving on tummy and using forearms to pull
	  • Moving on bottom by pushing or pulling with feet
	• Step-like actions on different combinations of hands and feet
	  • Animal walks: seal walk, bear walk, puppy walk, crab walk
	    ◦ Along varied pathways
	    ◦ On top of, over, under, and through obstacles
	    ◦ Leading and following a partner
	  • Climbing low trestles and ladders

Throwing	Equipment: soft, textured balls that fit size of hand
	Learning outcome: Develop throwing through the emerging-elementary stage.
	• Throwing at wall
	• Throwing at large targets
	  • Targets at close or moderate distances
	  • Low targets (eye level)
	  • Targets that make a sound or move on impact
	  • Freestanding targets to throw over, under, through

(continued)

Table 13.2 *(continued)*

Catching	Equipment: lightweight, soft-textured balls; balloons; rope balls Learning outcome: Develop catching through the emerging-elementary stage. • Catching balls rolled on floor • Catching balloons hit to waiting arms • Catching soft-textured balls dropped from above or rolled down a chute • Catching soft-textured and rope balls thrown lightly from horizontal trajectory at near or moderate distances • Catching balloons hit from different trajectories • Catching a ball rebounding from a self-drop
Rolling	Equipment: lightweight balls that fit the size of both hands Learning outcome: Develop rolling through the emerging-elementary stage. • Rolling ball to a wall • Rolling ball to and through large targets

Kicking	Equipment: lightweight balls (5–7 in, or 13–18 cm); large targets
	Learning outcome: Develop kicking through the emerging elementary stage.
	• Kicking stationary balls to large targets
	  ◦ Targets at close or moderate distances
	  ◦ Low targets (eye level)
	  ◦ Targets that make a sound or move on impact
	  ◦ Kicks between cones or through large goals

Bouncing	Equipment: 8 in (20 cm) playground balls and light balls that fit the size of both hands
	Learning outcome: Develop bouncing skills through the emerging-elementary stage.
	• Stationary
	  ◦ Bouncing from self-drop to catch
	  ◦ Bouncing repetitively with two hands
	  ◦ Bouncing repetitively with one hand
	• Walking
	  ◦ Series: bounce, catch, walk

Striking with body parts	Equipment: balloons and punch balloons Learning outcome: Develop striking with body parts through the emerging-elementary stage. • Striking with different body parts • Striking with open palms (underhand) • Striking with one hand and then the other • Striking a suspended balloon with two hands (overhead)
Striking with paddles	Equipment: lollipop paddles (polystyrene foam), balloons, foam balls Learning outcome: Develop striking with paddles through the emerging-elementary stage. • Striking balloons noncontinuously • Striking suspended objects using a sidearm pattern • Striking a foam ball off of a cone or tee

Table 13.3 Pre-K Movement Experiences Based on Appropriate Practice Guidelines

PRE-K GUIDELINE 1: DEMONSTRATE COMPETENCE IN FUNDAMENTAL MOTOR SKILLS.	
Essential content	**Measurement of success**
Develop emerging-elementary stage of fundamental movement skills. • Perform emerging-elementary characteristics of locomotor, stability, and manipulative skills.	Assess attainment by using checklists to score students' levels of success from observations of emerging-elementary movement criteria for each fundamental movement skill.

PRE-K GUIDELINE 2: DEVELOP A MOVEMENT VOCABULARY USING BASIC MOVEMENT CONCEPTS.	
Essential content	**Measurement of success**
Develop a movement vocabulary. • Recognize fundamental movement skills. • Recognize basic movement concepts related to body, space, effort, and relationship awareness.	Assess attainment by using checklists to score students' levels of success from observations of • student performance of fundamental movement *skills* in response to teacher prompts and • student performance of basic movement *concepts* in response to teacher prompts.

PRE-K GUIDELINE 3: DEVELOP HEALTH-RELATED FITNESS.	
Essential content	**Measurement of success**

Unstructured physical activity participation: Engage in enjoyable movement activities intermittently throughout the day, both indoors and outdoors, during and outside of school.
Structured physical activity participation: Engage in a variety of moderate to vigorous physical activities sustained for increasingly longer periods of time.
	Assess attainment by using checklists to score students' levels of participation:
	• Observation
	  ◦ Unstructured: Voluntary participation in physical activity during allotted playtime
	  ◦ Structured: Sustaining activity levels for longer periods of time.
	• Evaluation
	  ◦ Classroom teachers' logs of student activity during school time
	  ◦ Family reports of students' regular participation in physical activity

PRE-K GUIDELINE 4: EXHIBIT ACCEPTANCE OF SELF AND OTHERS IN PHYSICAL ACTIVITIES.	
Essential content	**Measurement of success**
Follow rules, behave, and cooperate by • using safe practices and following rules, • staying on task and following directions, and • cooperating with others by taking turns and sharing equipment.	Assess attainment by using checklists to score students' levels of participation from observation of • using safe practices and following rules, • staying on task and following directions, and • cooperating with others by taking turns and sharing equipment.

PRE-K GUIDELINE 5: ENJOY PHYSICAL ACTIVITY.	
Essential content	**Measurement of success**
Recognize the value of physical activity by • engaging in repetitive movements, • voluntarily choosing to participate in physical activity, and • verbally and nonverbally expressing enjoyment while participating in physical activity.	Assess attainment by using checklists to score students' levels of participation from observation of • engagement in repetitive movements, • voluntary choice to participate in physical activity, and • verbal and nonverbal expressions of enjoyment.

social responsibility with the pre-K values and rules described in chapter 12. In addition, five sample activities that reinforce personal and social responsibility are provided later in this chapter; each activity corresponds to a different level of table 13.4. These activities should be conducted before engaging children in the movement stations.

DESIGNING INSTRUCTION

The framework for designing instruction is provided by the pre-K guidelines based on the national physical education standards and grade-level outcomes (SHAPE America, 2014). Let's now review the focus and expectations for each pre-K guideline.

• Pre-K guideline 1 is addressed by engaging children in the fundamental movement skills and movement concepts (body, space, effort, relationship) with the expectation that most children will

perform these skills at the emerging-elementary stage. The developmental assessment rubrics provided in appendix B can be used to determine whether children display the beginning or developing level of movement performance.

• Pre-K guideline 2 is addressed when the teacher helps children acquire a movement vocabulary by verbally prompting them to perform specific movement skills and movement concepts (body, space, effort, relationship). In this manner, children develop the ability to recall and recognize the fundamental movement skills. The expectation is that children will be able to perform a designated traveling skill or movement concept or identify the teacher's demonstration of a hop, jump, skip, gallop, slide, or leap.

• Pre-K guideline 3 is addressed when the teacher intentionally engages children in longer bouts of physical activity or more repetitions of a

Table 13.4 Pre-K Personal and Social Responsibility and Physical Education Guideline 4

Hellison's level of personal and social responsibility	Components	Pre-K learning outcomes (see chapter 12)	Behaviors
0. Irresponsibility	Blaming others		Cannot play safely in movement or play area; interferes or endangers others' play; does not stay on task at any movement or play area; handles equipment unsafely.
	Making excuses		
	Denying personal responsibility		
1. Respecting the rights and feelings of others	Self-control	Move safely. Respect others.	Try to stay at a safe distance from others when they use equipment.
	Right to peaceful conflict resolution		Avoid others while moving.
	Right to be included and have cooperative peers		Move at a safe speed. Don't interfere with others while they are playing.
2. Effort and cooperation	Self-motivation	Listen to the teacher. Try your best!	When the teacher says "bus stop," you stop moving and cross your arms and legs like you are waiting for the bus to come.
	Exploration of effort and new tasks		
	Getting along with others		Keep playing at your station or play area. Don't stop until the music stops playing.
3. Self-direction	On-task independence	Make good choices.	Choose stations to play at that have smiley-face tokens. If there is no token, you choose a new station.
	Goal-setting progression		
	Courage to resist peer pressure		
4. Helping others and exercising leadership	Caring and compassion	Play nicely. Help others.	Say nice words to your friends, such as, "You are doing a great job bouncing the ball."
	Sensitivity and responsiveness		Help by getting or returning equipment for each other and setting equipment back up (e.g., target that has been knocked over).
	Inner strength		
5. Transfer outside the gym	Trying these ideas in other areas of life		Children learn to make good choices on the playground; children compliment each other during play in the classroom.

fundamental movement skill. The expectation is that, over time, children will be able to sustain cardiorespiratory activity for longer periods of time and perform more repetitions of muscular endurance activity.

• Pre-K guideline 4 is addressed when the teacher focuses the movement activity on personal and social responsibility behaviors. The expectation is that children will increasingly display the values of moving safely, respecting others, listening to the teacher, trying their best, cooperating with others, making good choices, and playing nicely.

• Pre-K guideline 5 is addressed when the teacher focuses on children's voluntary participation and verbal and nonverbal expressions of enjoyment in order to determine whether the children value engaging in physical activity.

When designing pre-K learning experiences, you can scale equipment and condition variables to provide affordances that allow for children to succeed at performing skills (see chapter 6). The learning environment must be purposefully designed to elicit specific fundamental movement skills and movement concepts (this is the pre-impact phase of instruction; see chapter 10). In addition, learning environments should be made stimulating by means of colorful equipment and educational materials that bring a lesson to life. For example, providing bubble wrapping material for children to jump on gives them both tactile and auditory sensations and encourages repetitive jumping from

two feet to two feet. For a list of equipment that is useful for designing pre-K movement experiences, please refer to table 13.5.

During learning experiences, teachers should reinforce children's engagement by encouraging repetition and exploration (this is the post-impact phase of instruction; see chapter 10). Some parts of instruction are teacher initiated, but "the majority of time is spent in informal free play and on exploratory projects involving large muscle activity" (Logsdon, Alleman, Straits, Belka, & Clark, 1997, p. xviii). Therefore, although a movement lesson for pre-K children might include embedded whole-group activities led by the teacher, these activities will be very brief. One type of whole-group activity involves gathering the children together for what is often referred to as "circle time" (for a sample circle-time activity, see figure 13.1).

The majority of time in a pre-K movement lesson should involve children in exploring and playing at carefully designed movement stations. Implicit learning is facilitated not only by the design of the movement station and the affordances created by the task design but also by the teacher's feedback. While children are exploring, you can comment on their discoveries to help them become aware of the movement skills and concepts they are performing, thus reinforcing pre-K guideline 2: developing a movement vocabulary. For example, you might comment on a child's discovery by saying, "You just jumped in and out of the hoop from two to two feet—excellent jumping!" Explicit learning is

---

Place a small parachute in the center of the movement area. As children enter according to established protocol, ask them to choose a colored space on the edge of the parachute. After all children have found a space, model how to hold the parachute with two hands in an overhand grip. Then guide the children in a series of locomotor skills while music is played. Here is a sample progression:

• Step side-to-side as you travel in a circular pathway holding onto the parachute (to the left side and to the right side).

• Lower the parachute to your feet; raise the parachute as high as you can while keeping a tight grip with your hands.

• Turn sideways and hold the parachute with one hand (right or left); extend your opposite arm to the side.

• Walk to the tempo of the music.

• Turn in the opposite direction, switching which hand holds the parachute and extending the opposite arm out to the side.

• Turn once again with your tummy toward the parachute and grasp the parachute with two hands; slide sideways, to the right and to the left, to the tempo of the music

Figure 13.1 Sample pre-K circle-time activity: playing with the parachute!

facilitated when children perform a series of movement tasks explained and demonstrated by the teacher. Explicit instruction is often used during circle time, but overall it is used less frequently in a preschool lesson.

ASSESSING LEARNING

Sample learning experiences described later in this chapter address the pre-K guidelines and the national content standards in physical education

Table 13.5 Equipment for Designing Pre-K Movement Experiences

Equipment Type	Fundamental movement skill promoted
Climbing equipment	• Climbing • Hanging • Jumping • Balancing on body parts • Traveling
Foam trapezoid shapes	• Climbing • Jumping • Transferring weight from hands to feet • Balancing
Tall cones	• Marking play areas • Supporting ropes for leaping or jumping
Poly spots (different shapes: hands, feet, round, square)	• Animal walks • Marking pathways for traveling skills • Transferring weight from hands to feet
Balls: yarn, bean bag, playground, slo-mo, geometric, spider, beach	• Catching • Tossing to self
Rackets: foam paddles with short handles	• Striking
Bats: short handles, larger in size	• Striking
Foam hockey sticks (very short handles)	• Striking
Scooters	• Traveling
Ropes	• Jumping • Leaping over • Moving under • Moving along a pathway
Scoops made from gallon jugs	• Catching objects
Balance Board: small platform raised off the ground with a 2-inch by 10-inch narrow base of support that children can stand on	• Balancing
Launch boards	• Catching
Carpet squares	• Personal space • Jumping across
Tunnels	• Crawling through
Parachute	• Cooperative activities
Jump ball	• Dynamic stability • Muscular endurance
Rhythm sticks	• Eye–hand coordination
Scarves	• Tossing and catching
Large targets: sheets, inflatables, targets that can be knocked over and bounce back up	• Throwing at

by providing experiences that intentionally engage students in the essential content and assessment criteria for specific standards. In addition, appendix B provides detailed developmental rubrics for the fundamental movement skills and concepts (standards 1 and 2). These assessments describe the quality of performance at the beginning, developing, proficient, and advanced levels. Most pre-K children are at the beginning or developing level of movement performance on these assessments because they are at the initial and emerging-elementary stages of motor development.

PROVIDING FEEDBACK

The types of feedback appropriate for pre-K children depends largely on their stage of motor skill development. Praise and encouraging feedback is most helpful when children are in the emerging elementary stage. During this stage, children are not capable of biomechanically correct (mature) performance. As children are engaging in environments constructed by the teacher to elicit fundamental motor skills (balloons to catch, low boxes to come off of for "jumps") teachers use praise and encouragement to provide a positive and motivating learning environment. As children transition into the mature stage, provide them with knowledge of performance (KP) feedback which describes the fundamental movement skills and movement concepts they are performing (KPd). This feedback helps children acquire a movement vocabulary and learn how their bodies can move, especially in terms of the fundamental movement skills and movement concepts. For example, when a child jumps off of a low foam shape, you might say, "Shaheem, I see you jumping off with two feet and landing on two feet. Great jump!" Later, when Shaheem repeats the jump off of the low foam shape, you can ask, "Shaheem, what movement did you just do off of the foam shape? Yes, a jump, and you moved off the low foam shape!"

Helping children recognize what movement skill or movement concept they are performing reinforces pre-K guideline 2 (see table 13.3). You should also foster correct performance by focusing on developmentally appropriate skill cues—for example, "Be sure to bend your knees when you land on both feet!" Doing so reinforces pre-K guideline 1. Prescriptive knowledge of performance feedback

(KPp) used for the purpose of correcting children's movement performance, is most helpful when children are transitioning from the emerging-elementary stage to the mature stage of motor skill development. Since mature performance is erratic during transition, children can benefit from KPp to focus efforts on correct movements (e.g.,"You need to bend your knees more in order to safely land."). For mature-stage movers, knowledge of performance feedback can be descriptive (KPd) using skill cues to reinforce correct technique (e.g., "You used your finger pads, nice going.").

In summary, teacher feedback must be congruent with the intent of the movement activity. If the focus is pre-K guideline 1 or 2, feedback is focused on movement skill and concept cues as in the examples above. If the focus is pre-K guideline 3, then your feedback should be consistent with sustaining physical activity or performing more repetitions of an activity. Similarly, if the focus of the activity is pre-K guideline 4, then your feedback may address moving safely through space, cooperating with others, or staying on task. After you provide feedback, you can observe how or whether the child uses it and thereby determine its effectiveness.

The following sections provide movement experiences for pre-K guideline 4 (standard 4), which addresses personal and social responsibility behaviors, as well as skill progressions addressing pre-K guidelines 1 and 2 (standards 1 and 2) for preconsistent movers (see table 13.2).

The personal and social responsibility behaviors that are important for pre-K learners to demonstrate in the physical education setting include the following: moving safely, respecting others, listening to the teacher, trying one's best, making good choices, and playing nicely. Children's development of these behaviors can be enhanced by the creation of a physically and emotionally safe learning environment, which also helps them establish a positive sense of self. Therefore, we suggest having children practice demonstrating the behaviors associated with the pre-K personal and social responsibility values *before* they engage in movement activities for the purpose of addressing pre-K guidelines 1 and 2 (standards 1 and 2).

The following six sample activities reinforce personal and social responsibility as derived from the pre-K values, as well as the pre-K behaviors presented in table 13.4.

Activities to Reinforce Personal and Social Responsibility

BEING SAFE (LEVEL 1)

Tape pictures of children, adolescents, and adults to a set of cones spread out in a designated play area in order to represent a crowded city block; alternatively, make outlines of various sizes of people from the cardboard of old boxes. Invite the children to travel in any way they would like in order to move around the cones in the designated space. Their goal is avoid bumping into a pedestrian! This activity can be revisited as children learn different movement skills (e.g., skipping, hopping, moving on scooters) and movement concepts (e.g., directions, pathways, levels). To augment the practice of these locomotor skills pathways can be taped or painted on the floor for the children to follow; and red stop signs and yellow yield signs could be added to emphasize safety.

LISTENING TO THE TEACHER (LEVEL 2)

While children are playing at various movement or play stations, you can use a visual, verbal, or auditory signal to gain their attention or signify a movement challenge. For example, you might say, "Bus stop!" to indicate that all children should stop what they are doing and assume the "bus stop" position (arms crossed over chest and legs crossed, as if waiting for the school bus to come). Another fun listening position for young children is to kneel and raise one hand in the air like a superhero.

COOPERATING WITH OTHERS (LEVEL 2)

Inform children that at any time during the lesson you might beat the drum a specific numbers of times. If you beat the drum twice, they are to find a nearby classmate with whom to stand side by side to form a pair. After forming their pairs, the children can be asked to move alongside or to lead and follow their partner. Similarly, if you beat the drum three times, the children form groups of three and hold hands to make a circle. Both of these activities can be practiced during circle time at the beginning of class. Pairs and groups of three are most appropriate sizes to use because at this age children are best able to interact and cooperate in small groups.

TRYING YOUR BEST (LEVEL 2)

While children are engaged in circle-time activities or at movement stations, encourage them to keep trying. This effort can be facilitated by using musical selections of increasing length. After children have made a choice to play at a specific station, begin to play the musical selection and encourage the children to keep practicing until the selection ends.

MAKING GOOD CHOICES AND BEING SELF-DIRECTED (LEVEL 3)

Attach four apple tokens to a large picture of a tree (taped to a cone). When children choose to play at this station, they pick an apple off of the tree and put it in a basket by the tree. When they are finished playing at the station, they put the apple back on the tree. If a child comes to play at a station that does not have an apple on the tree, then that child must make a choice to play at a different station. This method promotes self-direction and willingness to make a different choice.

PLAYING NICELY AND HELPING EACH OTHER (LEVEL 4)

During circle time, children can play Beanbag Thank You. In this activity, each child is given one beanbag to place on her or his head. The children then walk around in general space (designate the area with cones). When a beanbag falls off of a child's head, the child is directed to freeze. When another child sees a frozen classmate, he or she is asked to help by picking up the classmate's beanbag. Afterward, the child who had dropped the beanbag says, "Thank you!" Similarly, if children are each rolling a ball toward a wall target, they can help each other by retrieving equipment (i.e., the ball) if it accidentally rolls into someone else's play space. The children are each encouraged to stay in their own "rolling lane" and to ask a classmate to get their ball if they lose it.

Movement Activities

LOCOMOTOR SKILLS: TRAVELING

Pre-K Guidelines
- Guideline 1: Perform emerging-elementary characteristics of locomotor skills.
- Guideline 2: Recognize and respond to skill and movement concept prompts.

Skill Theme
Traveling through general space and stopping with control

Movement Concepts
- Space awareness: general space, pathways
- Effort awareness: changing speeds, stopping with control
- Relationship awareness: in, out, and around obstacles and props; next to, in front of, behind, leading, and following others

Tasks
Task: Children walk through general space while avoiding others and stopping with control. Music can be used as the signal to start or stop traveling.

Environment: general space bounded by cones

Skill cue for stopping with control: Slow down and bend knees.

Task: Children demonstrate locomotor skills for children to replicate. Musical accompaniment can be used to indicate when to start and stop traveling.

Environment: general space

Skill Cues for Running
- Use continuous sequence of pushing off on one foot and landing on opposite foot with flight phase between push-off and landing.
- Land on balls of feet.
- Bend arms at right angles and swing them in opposition.
- Coordinate arms and legs rhythmically.

Skill Cues for Galloping
- Move with one foot forward and one foot back.
- Step with front foot, bring back foot forward to touch heel of front foot, then step with front foot (step, together, step).
- Face tummy forward.
- Swing arms simultaneously forward and back in the same direction.

Skill Cues for Sliding
- Step together with slight flight phase when feet are together.
- Side leads action.
- Arms can be extended.

Skill Cues for Skipping
- Alternate step-hops.
- Face tummy forward.
- Swing arms in opposition to legs.

Task: Children travel through the movement area along pathways and patterns. This activity can be accompanied by music.

Environment: pathways of various patterns, such as square, circle, triangle, spiral, or S curves leading up to zigzags

Skill Cues for Pathways

- Straight: Maintain balance while traveling on pathway.
- Curved: Make gradual changes of direction with control.
- Zigzag: Change direction quickly with control.

Task: Children travel around and between obstacles. This activity can be accompanied by music.

Environment: cones with decorations (e.g., trees, letters, cartoon characters), hoops, poly spots, blow-up characters (e.g., "bop dolls"), trestles, crates, foam shapes

Skill Cues

- Stay close and circle the obstacle.
- Move between obstacles without touching equipment.
- Move along different pathways between equipment.

Task: Children travel using imagery and props (e.g., as if flying like a bird or airplane around the clouds).

Environment: white pillow-type stuffing (available at fabric stores) in low mounds on the floor to simulate clouds

Task: Children travel using imagery. Have them listen to the lyrics of a song—for example, "Walk the Lonesome Trail" (Campbell-Towell & Murray, 2016)—and act them out.

Environment: general space

Task: Children travel at moderate or fast speed. Have them begin by traveling through general space, then along a tracklike pathway, then along varied pathways, and finally around and between obstacles. Musical accompaniment may be used.

Environment: general space, tracklike pathway, varied pathways, obstacles separated by varied distances

Task: Children travel side by side and at a safe distance while leading and following one another. Musical accompaniment may be used.

Environment: general space

Skill Cues

- When side by side, maintain pace with partner.
- When following, stay a safe distance (two giant steps) behind your leader so that you don't bump.
- When leading, move at a speed that allows your partner to stay within two giant steps.
- Look out as you move through general space so that you don't bump into others.

Feedback

Provide knowledge of performance using skill and safety cues.

Assessments

- Pre-K guideline 1: Use observation checklists of skill and safety cues.
- Pre-K guideline 2: Record the child's correct or incorrect movement response to the skill prompt.
- Pre-K guideline 3: Engage children in bouts of moderate to vigorous physical activity of various durations through continuous movement in general space and along pathways. Measure how long each child sustains activity.

LOCOMOTOR SKILLS: FLIGHT

Pre-K Guidelines

- Guideline 1: Perform emerging-elementary characteristics of flight skills.
- Guideline 2: Recognize and respond to skill and movement concept prompts.
- Guideline 3: Engage in moderate to vigorous physical activity.

Skill Theme

Taking off from low equipment and landing on the feet

Movement Concepts

Relationship awareness: off of, over, alongside, in and out

Tasks

Task: Prompt children to move onto and off of equipment.
Environment: foam trapezoid shapes, bench, low boxes

Task: Children jump off of low equipment.
Environment: foam trapezoid shapes, bench, low boxes

Task: Children jump onto or into equipment, going either from one foot to both feet or from both feet to both feet.
Environment: hoops, poly spots, other decorative objects (e.g., smiley faces or flowers laminated and taped to floor)

Task: Children jump over low objects on the floor or at mat, going either from one foot to both feet or from both feet to both feet.
Environment: jump ropes on floor, foam noodles, poly-spot shapes (e.g., stars, triangles, rectangles, circles), dome cones

Skill Cues for Jumping from One Foot to Both Feet

- Bend both knees slightly.
- Use one-foot takeoff.
- Use two-foot landing with knees bent and arms out for balance.

Skill Cues for Jumping from Both Feet to Both Feet

- Bend knees and swing arms back.
- Extend knees during flight and reach arms up and forward.
- Bend knees on landing and hold arms out for balance.

Feedback

Provide knowledge of performance using skill cues.

Assessments

- Pre-K guideline 1: Use observation checklists of skill cues.
- Pre-K guideline 2: Record the child's correct or incorrect movement response to the skill prompt.
- Pre-K guideline 3: Engage children in bouts of moderate to vigorous physical activity of various durations through continuous jumping onto, into, or over low objects on the floor. Measure how long each child sustains activity.

STABILITY SKILLS: BALANCE

Pre-K Guidelines
- Guideline 1: Perform static balance.
- Guideline 2: Recognize and respond to skill and movement-concept prompts.
- Guideline 4: Cooperate with others.

Skill Theme
Balancing on body parts and combinations of body parts

Movement Concepts
- Body awareness: shapes, wide to moderate bases of support
- Space awareness: levels
- Relationship awareness: next to or facing a partner, inside or outside of floor equipment, on low equipment

Tasks
Task: Children balance on wide or moderate bases using different body parts and combinations of body parts.
Environment: mat or floor in personal space

Task: Children balance in different shapes (straight and narrow; wide; twisted; round) on different body parts and combinations of body parts.
Environment: mat or floor in personal space

Task: Children balance at different levels using different body parts and combinations of body parts.
Environment: mat or floor in personal space

Task: Children balance inside or outside a hoop using different body parts and combinations of body parts.
Environment: hoop on mat or floor

Task: Children balance on low equipment using different body parts and combinations of body parts.
Environment: foam trapezoid shapes, low bench, foam beams, sturdy rubber domes

Task: Children balance next to or facing a partner using different body parts and combinations of body parts.
Environment: mat or floor

Skill Cues
- Keep center of gravity (i.e., belly button) over or between base of support.
- Keep body still.

Feedback
Provide knowledge of performance using skill cues.

Assessments
- Pre-K guideline 1: Use an observation checklist of skill and safety cues.
- Pre-K guideline 2: Record the child's correct or incorrect movement response to the skill prompt.
- Pre-K guideline 4: Use an observation checklist for cooperative behaviors when working with a partner.

STABILITY SKILLS: TRANSFERRING WEIGHT

Pre-K Guidelines

- Guideline 1: Perform step-like actions.
- Guideline 2: Recognize and respond to skill and movement concept prompts.
- Guideline 3: Engage in moderate to vigorous physical activity.
- Guideline 4: Use safe practices.

Skill Theme

Transferring weight—step-like actions using different combinations of body parts under and through equipment

Movement Concepts

- Space awareness: low level
- Relationship awareness: over, under, through

Tasks

Task: Prompt children to move under, over, or through equipment in any way they choose. Remind them to be safe by sharing space and not bumping into others. Provide movement prompts such as, "Be safe by sharing space as you . . ." while children perform the following actions:

- Finding objects to move through
- Moving over objects
- Traveling at a low level
- Moving under a piece of equipment (e.g., arch)
- Moving on hands and knees (or feet)
- Moving on tummy by using forearms to pull
- Moving on bottom by pushing or pulling with feet

Environment: obstacle course that elicits moving under, over, or through equipment at a low level—for example, tunnels, refrigerator boxes (perhaps painted by children or decorated with the alphabet or numbers), arches, polystyrene shapes, ropes or crepe paper suspended from cones

Feedback

- KPd: "I see you moving under the rope. Good job!"
- KPd: "You chose the tunnel to move through."
- KPd: "I like how you are sharing space with others as you move under the ropes."
- KP: "Are you moving over or under the rope?"
- KP: "What body parts are you moving on?"

Assessments

- Pre-K guidelines 1, 2, and 4: Use observation checklist of children's ability to perform as prompted.
- Pre-K guideline 2: Provide two or three pictures from which children can identify the correct choice. For example, "Circle the picture of the child moving under equipment" or "Circle the picture of the child moving over the equipment."
- Pre-K guideline 3: Engage children in moderate to vigorous physical activity by creating a pathway along which they can move continuously from one piece of equipment to another. The pathway can be indicated by footprints or arrows for the children to follow. Measure how long each child sustains activity.

STABILITY SKILLS: TRANSFERRING WEIGHT

Pre-K Guidelines
- Guideline 1: Perform step-like actions.
- Guideline 2: Recognize and respond to skill and movement concept prompts.

Skill Theme
Transferring of weight: step-like actions on various combinations of hands and feet

Movement Concepts
- Body awareness: moving body parts above and below each other; identifying and changing supporting and nonsupporting body parts
- Space awareness: pathways
- Relationship awareness: over, under, through; leading and following

Tasks
Task: Prompt children to move through general space while imitating various animals. Foster exploration by reading a story, showing a video of animals moving in their natural habitats, or taking children to a zoo.
Environment: general space

Task: Children perform animal walks (e.g., seal, puppy, bear, crab) through general space while emphasizing skill and body-awareness cues.
Environment: general space

Skill Cues for Seal Walk
- Lie prone with hands flat on floor, elbows extended, and chest lifted.
- Move forward on hands, pulling body behind with legs extended.

Skill Cues for Puppy Walk
- Move forward, alternating hands and feet, with bottom up in the air.

Skill Cues for Bear Walk
- Keep hands flat on floor.
- Keep bottom high.
- Transfer weight simultaneously from left foot and left hand to right foot and right hand.

Skill Cues for Crab Walk
- Keep hands flat on floor and point fingers toward feet.
- Keep tummy high and body in supine position.
- Keep bottom off of ground.
- Alternate hands and feet to move backward or forward.

Task: Children perform animal walks along various pathways or lanes.
Environment: pathways of various configurations (e.g., straight, curved, zigzag, geometrically shaped) marked by floor paint, tape, poly spots, or cones to create lanes of different lengths and widths

Task: Children perform animal walks on top of, over, under, and through obstacles.
Environment: Obstacles may include refrigerator boxes, arches, polystyrene shapes, ropes, cones, tires, hula hoops.

Task: Children do all of the following:
- Leading and following a partner while performing animal walks in general space
- Leading and following a partner while performing animal walks along pathways or in lanes
- Leading and following a partner while performing animal walks on top of, over, under, and through obstacles

Environment: general space with pathways, lanes, and obstacles

Skill Cues

- When following, stay a safe distance (two giant steps) behind your leader so that you don't bump and they don't kick you.
- When leading, move at a speed that allows your partner to stay within two giant steps.
- When leading, look out as you move through general space so that you don't bump into others.

Task: Prompt children to climb on the equipment and be safe by sharing space. Children will climb up, down, on top of, and through low trestles, ladders, wide planks, and arched ladders.

Environment: mats with single pieces and two-piece combinations of trestles, ladders, wide planks, and arched ladders

Skill Cues

- Alternate hands and feet.
- To descend, turn around so that feet lead action.
- Always keep one hand and one foot in contact with equipment.

Feedback

Provide knowledge of performance using the skill and safety cues.

Assessments

- Pre-K guideline 1: Use an observation checklist of skill cues
- Pre-K guideline 2: Record the child's correct or incorrect movement response to the skill prompt.

MANIPULATIVE SKILLS: ROLLING

Pre-K Guidelines

- Guideline 1: Perform emerging-elementary characteristics of rolling skills.
- Guideline 2: Recognize and respond to skill and movement concept prompts.

Skill Theme

Rolling to large targets

Movement Concepts

- Body awareness: moving and identifying body parts used in manipulative skills
- Space awareness: low level
- Relationship awareness: to a wall, through large targets, toward objects that will fall over

Tasks

Task: Children roll a ball using two hands, either between the legs or alongside the body, toward a large target projected on the wall.

Environment: A very large, developmentally appropriate cartoon or picture is projected on the wall low enough that the picture begins at floor level. Poly spots are placed at varying distances to mark where children stand in order to roll a 6-inch (15-centimeter) playground ball. Several balls are kept in bins behind the poly spots. Children do not retrieve balls until told to do so by the teacher.

Task: Children roll a ball through a goal with two hands.

Environment: cones, large arch, shapes made from refrigerator boxes, a suspended rope

Task: Children roll a ball with two hands to knock down oversized objects grouped to make a large target.

Environment: groups of large bowling pins, Lilliputian characters, or empty milk cartons; bowling pin corrals behind groups of object to stop objects and ball

Skill cues

- Grasp ball with both hands.
- Swim arms back in preparation while bending at knees and hips.
- Swing arms forward toward target and release ball on floor in front of feet.

Feedback

Provide knowledge of performance using skill cues.

Assessments

- Pre-K guideline 1: Use an observation checklist of skill cues
- Pre-K guideline 2: Record the child's correct or incorrect movement response to the skill prompt.

MANIPULATIVE SKILLS: THROWING

Pre-K Guidelines

- Guideline 1: Perform emerging-elementary characteristics of throwing skills.
- Guideline 2: Recognize and respond to skill and movement concept prompts.
- Guideline 4: Stay on task and follow directions.

Skill Theme

Throwing to large targets

Movement Concepts

- Body awareness: moving and identifying body parts used in manipulative skills
- Space awareness: eye level, distance
- Relationship awareness: toward targets

Tasks

Task: Children explore ways to send objects toward targets (e.g., sidearm, overhand, underhand) both with one hand and with two hands. Cooperation and staying on task are emphasized because after throwing the objects, the children are asked to work together to collect them and put them back into the bins.

Environment: Use cones to create a bounded area for throwing. Only two or three children will play at a given area or station at the same time. Place poly spots of various colors on the floor to mark where children should stand when throwing the objects; the poly spots should be placed at close to moderate distances from the targets—about 7 to 10 feet (2 to 3 meters) away. Behind the throwing spots, set up bins or hoops containing beanbags, yarn balls, small rubber animals, or other appropriate objects small enough to fit into a child's hand for throwing. Targets may include the following items:

- Very large, developmentally appropriate cartoon or picture projected onto the wall low enough that it begins at floor level
- Large sheets
- Large nylon targets (perhaps adorned with numbers or letters)
- Thematically decorated targets made from refrigerator boxes
- Large hanging targets that move on impact
- Hanging hoops modified with brown-roll paper (decorated by children), tinfoil, or tissue paper taped tautly across the diameter so that the target moves when hit
- Large, colorful T-shirts (like clothes hanging from a drying line)

Skill Theme

Throwing under and through large targets

Movement Concepts

- Body awareness: moving and identifying body parts used in manipulative skills
- Space awareness: eye level
- Relationship awareness: under or through targets

Tasks

Task: Children explore ways to send objects under or though targets (e.g., sidearm, overhand, underhand) both with one hand and with two hands.

Environment: Set up freestanding targets using polystyrene or cardboard shapes or arches. Mark throwing locations with poly spots, footprints, floor tape, or floor paint. At each throwing location, place bins or hoops containing beanbags, yarn balls, small rubber animals, or other appropriate objects small enough to fit into a child's hand for throwing.

Feedback

- Provide knowledge of performance regarding the ways that children discover to send the objects toward, under, or through the targets. For example, say,
- KPd:"I see that you threw the beanbag from low to high."
- KP: "What other ways did you find to send your objects toward the targets?"

Assessments

- Pre-K guideline 1: Use an observation checklist of different ways that children found to send the objects toward the targets. Possibilities include the following:

    _____ Sent object using two hands from low to a higher level.

    _____ Sent object with two hands using a sidearm pattern.

    _____ Sent object using one hand from low to a higher level.

- Pre-K guideline 2: Check for children's ability to identify the action of using the hands to send a ball toward a target as a throw.
- Pre-K guideline 4: Use an observation checklist of children's following through to stay on task, collect objects only after all have been sent toward the targets, and comply with putting them back into the bins.

MANIPULATIVE SKILLS: CATCHING

Pre-K Guidelines

- Guideline 1: Perform emerging-elementary characteristics of catching skills.
- Guideline 2: Recognize and respond to skill and movement concept prompts.

Skill Theme

Catching balls rolled on the floor

Movement Concepts

- Body awareness: how to reach out and prepare the arms and hands to catch a ball
- Space awareness: low level
- Relationship awareness: facing a playmate

Tasks

Task: Children catch a ball rolled on the floor by a partner, the teacher, or a classroom assistant.

Environment: Use small cones to create lanes that are 10 feet (3 meters) long and 5 feet (1.5 meters) wide. At one end of each lane, place a playground ball. A piece of floor tape could be placed in the middle of the lane to provide extrinsic feedback about the direction of the roll. One child stands at one end of the lane and rolls a ball (which is waiting in a crate or hoop) to a playmate, who stands at the opposite end of the lane. The child catching the ball waits for it with outstretched arms and open hands.

Skill Cues for Catching

- Turn chest toward oncoming ball.
- Reach out arms toward oncoming ball.
- Bend at knees and waist to lower the body to ball level.
- Grasp ball with both hands while bending elbows to pull ball into chest.

Feedback

Provide knowledge of performance using skill cues.

Assessments

- Pre-K guideline 1: Use an observation checklist of skill cues
- Pre-K guideline 2: Record the child's correct or incorrect movement response to the skill prompt.

Skill Theme

Catching balls rolled down a chute

Movement Concepts

- Body awareness: how to reach out and prepare the arms and hands to catch a ball
- Space awareness: chest level
- Relationship awareness: to the chute and rolled ball

Tasks

Task: Children wait at the end of a chute with arms outstretched in order to catch a ball at chest level with only the hands.

Environment: Position a chute made of PVC pipe at an angle so that a ball can be rolled into a child's waiting arms. Position a set of foam steps so that they lead up to the elevated end of the chute. Place several foam or gator-skin balls (6- to 8-inch, or 15- to 20-centimeter) in a bin at the bottom of the steps. One child acts as the feeder by taking a ball and rolling it down the chute to the waiting partner.

Feedback

Provide knowledge of performance using skill cues.

Assessments

- Pre-K guideline 1: Use an observation checklist of skill cues
- Pre-K guideline 2: Record the child's correct or incorrect movement response to the skill prompt.

Skill Theme

Catching objects in the air

Movement Concepts

- Body awareness: how to reach out and prepare the arms and hands to catch a ball
- Space awareness: high trajectory (level), horizontal trajectory (level)
- Relationship awareness: to object

Tasks

Task: Children catch an object in the air using only the hands.

Environment: With a parent helper or classroom assistant, toss in one of the following ways:

- Toss balloons from a medium or high trajectory toward children's waiting arms (some children may be able to toss a balloon into the air for themselves and catch it).
- Toss soft gator-skin balls or rope balls to children using a horizontal trajectory.

Feedback

Provide knowledge of performance using skill cues.

Assessments

- Pre-K guideline 1: Use an observation checklist of skill cues
- Pre-K guideline 2: Record the child's correct or incorrect movement response to the skill prompt.

Skill Theme

Catching a ball rebounding from a self-drop

Movement Concepts

- Body awareness: how to reach out and prepare the arms and hands to catch a ball
- Space awareness: medium level
- Relationship awareness: to object

Tasks

Task: Children drop a playground ball measuring 6 to 8 inches (15 to 20 centimeters) in self-space and catch it with the hands at tummy or chest level.

Environment: bounded area marked by cones; playground balls contained in hoops or bins

Skill Cues

- Stretch out arms in preparation to catch ball.
- Catch ball with hands only (some children may use forearms or upper arms and chest).
- Bend elbows to absorb force of oncoming ball.

Feedback

Provide knowledge of performance using skill cues.

Assessments

- Pre-K guideline 1: Use an observation checklist of skill cues
- Pre-K guideline 2: Record the child's correct or incorrect movement response to the skill prompt.

MANIPULATIVE SKILLS: KICKING

Pre-K Guidelines

- Guideline 1: Perform emerging-elementary characteristics of kicking skills.
- Guideline 2: Recognize and respond to skill and movement concept prompts.
- Guideline 4: Stay on task and follow directions.

Skill Theme

Kicking toward large targets

Movement Concepts

- Body awareness: use of different parts of foot to kick
- Space awareness: low or medium level (determined by targets); close and moderate distances
- Relationship awareness: toward large targets or between two poles or through a large goal

Tasks

Task: Children explore ways to use either foot to send a playground ball toward a target.

Environment: Next to a wall, suspend a rope between two volleyball-type poles at a height of about 3 feet (1 meter); strips of crepe paper may be suspended from the rope. Place slightly deflated playground balls (6 to 8 inches, or 15 to 20 centimeters) on carpet squares about 10 feet (3 meters) from the target. The target can represent grass or a car wash! Other decorative targets (e.g., smiley faces) could also be suspended from the rope. Alternatively, the target could consist of a large, developmentally appropriate cartoon or picture projected onto the wall low enough that it begins at floor level, or thematically decorated targets made from refrigerator boxes through which to kick the ball. To elicit the skill of kicking, you can provide an iPad video or a picture (taped to a cone) of a child kicking with the shoelaces (instep). However, children should be permitted to explore various ways to send the ball under the rope with the foot before specific skill cues are provided. Children would be taught to wait until all balls have been kicked prior to going beyond the rope to retrieve them.

Feedback

Provide knowledge of performance regarding ways that children discover to send the objects toward the target using the foot. For example, say,

KPd: "I see that you used your shoelaces to kick the ball."

KP: "What other ways did you find to kick the ball through the target?"

Assessments

- Pre-K guideline 1: Use an observation checklist of different ways that children found to use the foot to kick the ball through the target.

    _____ Kicking ball with shoelaces

    _____ Kicking with inside of foot

    _____ Kicking with outside of foot

    _____ Kicking from a stationary position

    _____ Kicking after running up to a stationary ball

- Pre-K guideline 2: Children should be able to identify the action of sending a ball toward a target with the foot as a kick.

- Pre-K guideline 4: Use an observation checklist regarding children's following through to stay on task, collect playground balls only after all are sent to the target, and comply with putting them back in the bins.

MANIPULATIVE SKILLS: BOUNCING

Pre-K Guidelines

- Guideline 1: Perform emerging-elementary characteristics of bouncing skills.
- Guideline 2: Recognize and respond to skill and movement concept prompts.

Skill Theme

Bouncing a ball in the following ways:

- From a self-drop to a catch using two hands, then walking to a new space and repeating
- Bouncing repetitively with two hands in self-space and moving to a new space between bounces
- Bouncing repetitively with one hand, then walking and repeating

Movement Concepts

- Body awareness: using only the hands to bounce the ball
- Space awareness: medium level, general space
- Effort awareness: learning to push to create force
- Relationship awareness: to poly spots or hoops placed on the floor

Tasks

Task: Children choose how to bounce their ball (see above types of bouncing)

Environment: Create a variety of bouncing environments/stations with a movement area. Playground balls can be kept in a separate hoop or crate for children to use. Children choose which station or option to practice.

- Station Option 1: Spread five numbered cones (1 through 5) around a general area (the number can be taped onto each cone). Have children bounce playground balls from cone to cone, starting at number 1 and going through number 5. Footprints can be put on the floor to encourage children to move to the next number (figure 13.2). Technology can assist children at this station in the form of an iPad for reviewing video footage of how to perform this task.
- Station Option 2: Cones and ropes can be used to mark pathways. To create a stimulating environment, cones can be decorated by cartoon characters, alphabet letters, or shapes that are taped to them.

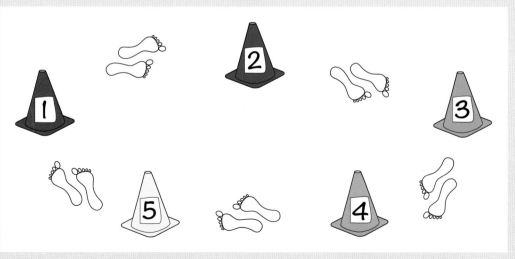

Figure 13.2   Setup for station option 1.

Skill Cues for Bouncing From Self-Drop to Catch

- Hold ball with hands only.
- Extend arms to hold ball slightly in front of body.
- Drop ball to floor.
- Reach for ball with arms as it rebounds up from floor.
- Catch with hands only.

Skill Cues for Bouncing Repetitively With Two Hands

- Hold ball in front of body with arms slightly extended.
- Push ball down toward floor with finger pads.
- Push with enough force to make ball bounce tummy high.
- Repeat.

Skill Cues for Bouncing Repetitively With One Hand

- Hold ball slightly in front of and to side of body with arms slightly extended.
- Push ball down with finger pads of one hand.
- Try to push ball with enough force to make it rebound to waist height.
- Repeat, pushing with finger pads.

Feedback

Provide knowledge of performance using skill cues.

Assessments

- Pre-K guideline 1: Use an observation checklist of skill cues
- Pre-K guideline 2: Record the child's correct or incorrect movement response to the skill prompt.

MANIPULATIVE SKILLS: STRIKING WITH BODY PARTS

Pre-K Guidelines

- Guideline 1: Perform emerging-elementary characteristics of striking-with-body-parts skills.
- Guideline 2: Recognize and respond to skill and movement concept prompts.

Skill Theme

Striking with body parts

Movement Concepts

- Body awareness: using different body parts
- Space awareness: low, medium, and high levels
- Effort awareness: creating force with the arms and hands
- Relationship awareness: to striking object

Tasks

Task: Children find ways to strike a balloon with different body parts.

Environment: Balloons are placed inside of bins for children to use. Cones mark a large movement area.

Feedback

Describe the different ways in which children strike the balloon. For example, say, KPd: "Great job! I see you using your head to strike the balloon up into the air!"

Assessments

- Pre-K guideline 1: Note the different body parts used to strike the balloon (e.g., low level with one hand; low level with two hands).
- Pre-K guideline 2: Ask children to identify what striking is: "When you use your hands to hit the balloon into the air, what are you doing? Yes, striking the balloon!"

Skill Theme

Striking with the hands

Movement Concepts

- Body awareness: using hands only
- Space awareness: low to medium level
- Effort awareness: creating force with the arms and hands
- Relationship awareness: to striking object

Tasks

Task: Children repeat teacher's demonstration of striking a balloon underhand with open palms.

Environment: Balloons are placed inside of bins for children to use. Cones mark a large movement area.

Feedback

Provide knowledge of performance using skill cues for striking a balloon underhand with open palms.

Assessments

Pre-K guideline 1: Use an observation checklist of skill cues for striking underhand with the palms.

Pre-K guideline 2: Record the child's correct or incorrect movement response to the skill prompt.

Skill Theme

Striking with alternating hands

Movement Concepts

- Body awareness: alternating use of the hands
- Space awareness: low to medium level
- Effort awareness: creating force with the hands
- Relationship awareness: to striking object

Tasks

Task: Children repeat the teacher's demonstration of using one palm and then the other to strike the balloon in underhand fashion.

Environment: Balloons are placed inside of bins for children to use. Cones mark a large movement area.

Feedback

Provide knowledge of performance using skill cues for alternating underhand palm strikes.

Assessments

- Pre-K guideline 1: Use an observation checklist of skill cues for striking with the hands.
- Pre-K guideline 2: Record the child's correct or incorrect movement response to the skill prompt.

Skill Theme

Striking with hands upward and forward

Movement Concepts

- Body awareness: using hands only
- Space awareness: medium to high level
- Effort awareness: medium force
- Relationship awareness: to striking object

Tasks

Task: Children strike the balloon with two hands in an upward and forward motion (consider modeling this task).

Environment: A rope is suspended from a pole designed for batting a hanging ball; alternatively, balloons are hanging from a rope that is suspended horizontally between two poles.

Skill Cues

- Stretch arms vertically.
- Prepare by bending elbows at the beginning of the striking action; extend elbows at the end of the striking action.
- Use finger pads to strike balloon with both hands.

Feedback

Provide knowledge of performance using skill cues.

Assessments

- Pre-K guideline 1: Use observation checklist of skill cues
- Pre-K guideline 2: Record the child's correct or incorrect movement response to the skill prompt.

MANIPULATIVE SKILLS: STRIKING WITH A PADDLE

Pre-K Guidelines

- Guideline 1: Perform emerging-elementary characteristics of striking-with-paddle skills.
- Guideline 2: Recognize and respond to skill and movement concept prompts.

Skill Theme

Striking with a paddle

Movement Concepts

- Space awareness: low to medium level
- Relationship awareness: to paddle object

Tasks

Task: Explore different ways to use a polystyrene (lollipop) paddle to strike a balloon.

Environment: Balloons are placed inside of bins for children to use. Short-handled polystyrene paddles are also provided and are placed inside of hoops. Cones mark a large movement area.

Feedback

Describe different ways in which children might use a paddle to strike a balloon. For example, say, "I see that you are using the paddle to strike the balloon from low to high. Great job!" (KPd).

Assessments

- Pre-K guideline 1: Record the ways in which the child uses the paddle to strike the balloon.

  _____ Underhand (low to high)

  _____ Sideways (around the waist)

  _____ Overhand (high to low)

- Pre-K guideline 2: Model a striking pattern with a paddle and balloon. Ask the child what this motion is called. If the child says "striking," this is an indication that he or she has learned to identify this fundamental movement skill.

Skill Theme

Striking sidearm with a paddle

Movement Concepts

- Space awareness: medium level
- Relationship awareness: to suspended Wiffle ball

Tasks

Task: Children repeat the teacher's demonstration of striking a suspended ball using a sidearm pattern.

Environment: Hollow plastic balls are suspended from a rope. Polystyrene paddles are placed inside of hoops at the side of the movement area.

Skill Cues

- Hold paddle at end with one hand.
- Take paddle back behind your side.
- Swing from low to high.

Feedback

Provide knowledge of performance using skill cues.

Assessments

- Pre-K guideline 1: Use an observation checklist of skill cues
- Pre-K guideline 2: Record the child's correct or incorrect movement response to the skill prompt.

Skill Theme

Striking with a paddle off of a tee

Movement Concepts

- Space awareness: medium level
- Relationship awareness: to ball on cone or tee

Tasks

Task: Children repeat the teacher's demonstration of using a sidearm striking pattern to strike a ball off of a tee.

Environment: Yarn balls are placed on tees, and a lollipop paddle is placed at the base of each tee. Additional yarn balls are placed in bins behind the tees. The tees should be three or four feet from a wall so that children strike the balls into the wall. Children are instructed not to retrieve balls until all balls in the bin have been used.

Skill Cues

- Hold paddle at end with one hand.
- Take paddle back behind your side.
- Swing from low to high.
- Finish with arms extended out toward wall.

Feedback

Provide knowledge of performance using skill cues.

Assessments

- Pre-K guideline 1: Use an observation checklist of skill cues
- Pre-K guideline 2: Record the child's correct or incorrect movement response to the skill prompt.

 Visit the web resource for learning activities, video clips, and review questions.

Chapter 14

Designing Learning Experiences for K-2 Students

Key Concepts

- Designing learning experiences for K-2 children based on stages of development and levels of motor skill learning
- Implementing standards-based instruction for K-2 children
- Designing learning experiences to develop personal and social responsibility in K-2 children

This chapter provides a developmental overview of K-2 learners and sample activities for personal and social responsibility to prepare children to work safely and cooperatively with others. Specifically, the chapter provides fundamental movement skill progressions for consistent-level learners; national content standards and K-2 grade-level outcomes and assessment options; and developmentally appropriate guidelines for designing instruction, practice, feedback, and assessment.

DEVELOPMENT OF K-2 LEARNERS

Chapters 15 through 17 provide sample learning experiences that facilitate K-2 children's progress toward the mature stage of fundamental motor skill development. Those learning experiences are based on a rich understanding of how K-2 learners develop, which is the focus of this section. During the mature stage, children progress toward movement performance that is well coordinated and biomechanically efficient. However, reaching the mature stage of any fundamental movement skill requires opportunities for practice, encouragement, and quality instruction. Motor skill proficiency also depends on the ecology of the environment—that is, equipment and condition variables (see chapter 6)—which can either limit or enhance a child's attainment of proficiency. In addition, physical educators must consider K-2 children's cognitive, social, and perceptual-motor development in order to design movement activities that are relevant and developmentally appropriate. A developmental overview of K-2 children is provided in table 14.1.

K-2 children are generally at the beginner level of movement skill learning. At this level, children must concentrate on how to perform movements, are unable to adapt movement to a changing environment, and are also unable to detect errors in their own performance. Table 14.2 presents consistent skill progressions based on K-2 children's stage of motor development and movement skill learning for the locomotor, manipulative, and stability movement skills; activities based on the consistent skill progressions are provided in chapters 15 through 17.

STANDARDS-BASED LEARNING

The national physical education standards and elementary school outcomes (SHAPE America, 2014) provide the basis for K-2 learning experiences. Since the national standards are based on developmentally appropriate content, it is not surprising that the consistent-level skill progressions derived from children's stages of motor development and movement skill learning (table 14.2) inform standards 1 and 2 for K-2 learners.

Table 14.3 presents grade-level outcomes and assessment options for K-2 learners aligned with the national standards. Standards 1 and 2 serve as the foundation for the movement activities described in chapters 15 through 17. Standards 3 through 5 are included as modifications to the movement activities to reinforce the essential content of these standards.

ASSESSING LEARNING

The assessment options presented in table 14.3 address the use of *observation* as a way for teachers to assess what students can *do* (e.g., performance of movement, fitness, and affective skills) and the use of *evaluation* to assess what students *know* (e.g., cognitive skills of recognizing, identifying, and describing). In addition, appendix B provides detailed developmental rubrics for the fundamental movement skills and concepts (standards 1 and 2). These rubrics describe quality of performance at the beginning, developing, proficient, and advanced levels. Most children in kindergarten and grade 1 are at the developing level; by grade 2, most children are at the proficient level. In addition, ideas for formative assessment are provided in each of the sample movement activities presented in chapters 15 through 17.

DESIGNING INSTRUCTION

Consistent movers need repetition in order to reach the mature stage of fundamental movement skill performance. This need can be addressed by instructional strategies found in the *reproduction cluster* of the spectrum of teaching styles (see chapter 10). More specifically, to foster skill development, teachers most often use the practice style (which focuses on repetition of skills) and the inclusion style (which offers varying levels of task difficulty so that students can work on skill repetition at their own level of ability). As students reach grade 2, they become more capable of observing performance cues, and teachers can introduce a limited version (observing one movement cue) of the reciprocal style.

In contrast, in the *production cluster* of teaching styles, the divergent discovery style engages students in creating *new* ways to use the movement concepts with the fundamental movement skills (e.g., Teachers could pose a task: "Discover five different ways to use changes of direction in a locomotor skill sequence"). Two other production-cluster styles—the guided and convergent discovery styles—are used to engage students in discovering the use of movement concepts or principles from

Table 14.1 K-2 Developmental Overview

Category	Learner characteristics	Teaching implications
Visual	Ability to track moderate-speed objects on the horizontal plane and focus on one aspect of the environment	Provide brightly colored objects that contrast with wall and floor coloring.
Kinesthetic	Ability to identify major body parts Learning left and right sides of body and directionality cues	Provide movement challenges to elicit exploration of location and movements of body parts. Provide simple manipulative challenges involving equipment that varies in size, shape, and weight. Provide activities that elicit use of laterality and directionality.
Motor development	Emergence of differentiated movement Moderate to complete flexion, extension, and rotation when performing fundamental movement skills	Provide a variety of developmentally appropriate instructional tasks that develop consistency in performance of fundamental movement skills. Provide simple task variations (e.g., self-paced; focused on a single variable from space, effort, or relationship).
Motor learning	Inconsistent performance (concentration on how to perform movements) Inability to adapt to changing environments Inability to detect one's own errors in performance	Instructional tasks can combine two fundamental movement skills. Intermittent, prescriptive feedback
Cardiorespiratory endurance	Immature aerobic system Beginning to move for longer duration Limited ability to self-regulate energy expenditure	Provide short bouts of aerobic activity rather than continuous aerobic activity of long duration.
Flexibility	Joint specific More flexible than adults because bones have not completely ossified	Static and dynamic stretches through a full range of motion are safe and effective.
Muscular strength and muscular endurance	Progressive improvement in muscle strength and muscular endurance during childhood, due primarily to growth	Children should develop muscular strength and muscular endurance using the resistance of body weight against gravity.
Body composition	Dependent on multiple variables, including genetics, maturation, nutrition, and activity level	Provide activity-based fitness rather than fitness through formalized exercise or calisthenics.
Stage of cognitive development	Preoperational stage, during which children use elementary logic, reasoning reflects experiences, and symbols are used to represent objects in the environment (i.e., learning to read)	Use simple instructions and task cards with pictures and few words. Whole-class format can be used for increasing periods of time. Use a station format in which each has a single focus. Use activities that stimulate imagination and creativity. Elementary logic enables children to look for one movement cue when observing a peer; they can also follow simple rules, correct their own performance based on feedback, and design or vary a short movement combination. Children begin to develop a movement vocabulary.
Self-concept	Centered on concrete characteristics (e.g., physical attributes, possessions, skills)	Provide developmentally appropriate self-testing activities. Help children set short-term goals and engage in simple self-assessment.
Personal and social responsibility	Less egocentric and more able to engage in associative and some cooperative play	Model positive social skills and engage children in activities that elicit appropriate social skills (e.g., courtesy, honesty, kindness, staying on task, following directions, and encouraging others).

In an interdisciplinary lesson based on Dr. Seuss, this child balances his "green eggs and ham" on a paper plate as he performs a consistent-level dynamic balance while walking forward across a wooden bench.

standards 2 and 3 (e.g., Teachers could pose a task: "Try aiming at all the different levels of targets to discover how your release point changes").

When designing K-2 learning experiences, you can provide affordances to allow for skill success by scaling equipment and condition variables (see chapter 6). When you employ various appropriate equipment and environmental conditions, you can address the unique needs of all children and thus achieve differentiated instruction. To ensure that all children can engage in purposeful learning and achieve success, offer various equipment choices (e.g., different sizes, lengths, and widths) and environmental conditions (e.g., spatial [distance], trajectory, temporal [speed]). For more information about scaling, see chapter 6.

The sample movement activities described in chapters 15 through 17 can be conducted in various formats: (1) single task, single station; (2) single task, multiple stations; (3) multiple tasks, single station; and (4) multiple tasks, multiple stations. In the single-task, single-station format, all children practice the same fundamental movement skill, and equipment and condition choices are embedded in the activity. For example, children might use an underhand toss to send an object (e.g., beanbag, yarn ball, small foam tennis ball) toward a target consisting of a stationary hoop placed vertically in a hoop holder or flat on the floor in front of a wall from distances of 10, 12, and 15 feet (about 3, 3.5, and 4.5 meters).

The second format—single task, multiple stations—uses different stations, each of which involves one task. For instance, one station might involve throwing for distance, another throwing at moving targets, and yet another throwing to a partner. Each station contains equipment and condition choices to fit varying levels of student ability. In contrast, in the third format—multiple tasks, single stations—many different tasks are performed in the student's self-space or partner space. For instance, 10 gymnastics balances could be indicated on a task card or whiteboard for students to practice.

As for the fourth format—multiple tasks, multiple stations—we suggest using it after children have achieved the mature stage of movement skill performance. The reason? If a class of 25 to 30 learners in the initial and emerging-elementary stages were to perform different fundamental movement skills at different stations, you would find it difficult to provide them with useful intermittent and prescriptive feedback. For these learners, correct practice is best facilitated when the movement activity is focused on one fundamental movement skill and limited skill cues.

PRACTICE AND FEEDBACK

Constant and blocked practice (see chapter 7) can be provided when teachers employ the reproduction teaching styles (see chapter 10). Provide chil-

Table 14.2 Consistent-Level Skill Progressions (K-2)

Locomotor skills

Traveling

Equipment: hoops, ropes, poly spots, cones

Learning outcome: Gain greater consistency in performance of mature traveling patterns and variations.

Traveling Through General Space
- Running
- Galloping
- Sliding
- Hopping
- Skipping

Traveling Variations
- Space: directions, pathways
- Effort: traveling to rhythms and musical accompaniment; increasing intensity
- Relationship to equipment: around, alongside, on top of, underneath, in and out of
- Cooperative relationships with others: following and leading; matching; meeting and parting
- Adding traveling and flight skills
- Competitive relationships with others: chasing and fleeing; dodging
  - On offense: using fakes, changes of direction, and jump spins to avoid defense
  - On defense: "reading" and anticipating movement of offense to cut off running angles

Flight

Equipment: low boxes, benches, foam shapes; poly spots, ropes, hoops, tires, springboard

Learning outcome: Gain greater consistency in performance of mature flight patterns and variations.

Flight
- Jumping (one foot to both feet; both feet to both feet)
- Leaping

Flight Variations
- Body awareness: body shapes
- Space: levels, distances, directions, pathways
- Effort: force, rhythms
- Relationship to equipment: over, on and off, in and out
- Relationships with others: leading and following, matching and mirroring

Adding traveling and flight skills

Stability skills

Balancing

Equipment: low boxes, benches, foam shapes; ropes, hoops, tires

Learning outcome: Gain greater consistency in performance of balances, variations, and combinations.
- Balancing on different bases of support
- Balance variations
  - Body awareness: shapes
  - Space: levels
  - Effort: intentional use of time to hold balance
  - Relationship to equipment: on, beside, inside of
  - Relationships with others: nonsupport partner balances
- Adding one balance to another
- Adding locomotor and balancing skills

Step-like actions

Equipment: low boxes, benches, foam shapes; ropes, hoops, tires

Learning outcome: Gain greater consistency in performance of step-like actions and variations.
- Step-like actions from feet to momentary weight on hands
  - Animal walks and variations (e.g., bunny, mule kick)
  - Wheels and variations
  - Vaults and variations
- Step-like action variations
  - Body awareness: shapes, body part relationships
  - Space: levels, directions
  - Effort: use of force to propel lower body upward
  - Relationship to equipment: onto, off of, over

(continued)

Table 14.2 *(continued)*

	Stability skills *(continued)*
Rolling	Equipment: low boxes, benches, foam shapes; ropes, hoops, tires Learning outcome: Gain greater consistency in performance of mature rolling actions, variations, and combinations. • Rolling • Sideward (pencil and egg) • Forward • Backward • Adding rolls and balances • Traveling into and out of rolls • Adding jumps and rolls • Adding one roll to another
	Manipulative skills
Throwing	Equipment: balls that fit size of one hand and of two hands Learning outcome: Gain greater consistency in mature throwing patterns and variations. **Throwing Underhand** • To stationary large targets at distances that require full backswing • To varied heights, distances, and directions for purposeful release • To moving targets **Throwing Overhand** • To large targets at distances that require full wind-up (for force) • To varied heights, distances, and directions for purposeful release • To moving targets
Catching	Equipment: balls and other objects of soft or medium texture that are sized for two-handed catching Learning outcome: Gain greater consistency in mature catching patterns and variations. • Catching a bounced ball • Catching a self-toss • Self-tossing to different places around the body and catching • Catching a ball rebounding from a wall at moderate distances • Catching balls thrown to different heights for purposeful reach (chest, above head, below waist) • Catching and throwing with a partner with variation in distance, direction, trajectory, and speed of throw
Rolling	Equipment: plastic pins, lightweight balls that fit the size of both hands Learning outcome: Gain greater consistency in mature ball-rolling patterns and variations. • Stepping and rolling ball through cones set at far to close distances • Stepping and rolling ball from 10 to 15 feet (about 3 to 4.5 meters) toward at least three pins arranged in a V formation
Kicking and dribbling	Equipment: foam balls and #4 soccer balls Learning outcome: Gain greater consistency in mature kicking and dribbling patterns and variations. • Kicking a ball with instep (shoelaces) from short to moderate approach • Kicking a ball to distances that require approach and full wind-up • Kicking a ball at or below midline to travel at different levels (along the ground or in the air) • Kicking to targets of varying size, height, and distance • Kicking a rolling ball from a stance to different distances • Kicking a rolling ball using an approach to different distances • Short-tap dribbling along the ground • Start-and-stop dribbling • Dribbling on different pathways and to avoid obstacles

Table 14.2 *(continued)*

	Manipulative skills *(continued)*
Bouncing	Equipment: 8-inch (20-centimeter) playground balls and junior-size basketballs Learning outcome: Gain greater consistency in mature bouncing patterns and variations. • Bouncing with each hand while stationary • Bouncing with different forces and to different levels while stationary • Bouncing to the front and sides of the body while stationary • Bouncing with each hand while moving • Start-and-stop bouncing. • Bouncing while looking up intermittently • Bouncing on different pathways and to avoid obstacles • Bouncing while following another

Striking with body parts	Equipment: punch balloons and balls with a balloon bladder
	
	Learning outcome: Gain greater consistency in mature striking with body parts (volleying)—patterns and variations.
	
	• Continuously striking a punch balloon underhand and overhead with open palms
	• Striking a balloon or butyl bladder ball noncontinuously from self- and partner tosses: to a wall or targets; to a partner (catching after bounce) over a line, suspended rope, or low net
	  • Underhand with palms and forearms
	  • Underhand, overhand, and sidearm with one hand
	  • Overhead with two hands

Striking with paddles	Equipment: lollipop (polystyrene) paddles, balloons, foam balls
	
	Learning outcome: Gain greater consistency in mature striking with paddles (patterns and variations).
	
	• Striking balloons upward continuously
	• Striking balloons back and forth with a partner
	• Striking a ball from a bounce to the wall or targets at different levels, directions, and distances
	• Striking a ball over a line, suspended rope, or low net
	  • From a self-drop to a partner
	  • After a bounce from an underhand toss from partner and back to partner

Striking with bats and polo sticks	Equipment: lollipop paddles (polystyrene), polo sticks, floor-hockey sticks, oversized plastic bats, foam balls, plastic pucks Learning outcome: Gain greater consistency in mature striking with bats and polo sticks (patterns and variations). • Striking ball off of a tee to different distances and directions • Striking a ball off of a tee and running to a base • Striking a ball or puck with a polo or hockey stick for distance • Striking a ball or puck with a polo or hockey stick through cones to a partner at varying distances • Striking a ball or puck continuously along the ground with a polo or hockey stick in different pathways and directions

Table 14.3 National Content Standards and K-2 Grade-Level Outcomes and Assessment Options

STANDARD 1: DEMONSTRATE COMPETENCE IN A VARIETY OF MOTOR SKILLS AND MOVEMENT PATTERNS.	
Outcomes and essential content	**Assessment options**
Develop maturity and versatility in fundamental movement skills to be able to demonstrate • mature performance in locomotor, most stability, and some manipulative skills; • versatility in locomotor, stability, and manipulative skills; and • smooth transitions in sequences of locomotor skills.	Assess attainment by using answer keys, checklists, or rubrics to score students' levels of success from observations of • mature movement criteria for each fundamental movement skill, • criteria for versatility (body, space, effort, relationship variables), and • criteria for smooth transitions.

STANDARD 2: APPLY KNOWLEDGE OF CONCEPTS, PRINCIPLES, STRATEGIES, AND TACTICS RELATED TO MOVEMENT AND PERFORMANCE.	
Outcomes and essential content	**Assessment options**
Establish a movement vocabulary and apply introductory concepts by • identifying and performing movement concepts of body, space, effort, and relationship to vary the quality of movement; and • differentiating between movement concepts.	Assess attainment by using answer keys, checklists, or rubrics to score students' levels of success from • observations of performance of movement concepts and • evaluation of students' identification of and differentiation between movement concepts.

STANDARD 3: DEMONSTRATE THE KNOWLEDGE AND SKILLS TO ACHIEVE AND MAINTAIN A HEALTH-ENHANCING LEVEL OF PHYSICAL ACTIVITY AND FITNESS.	
Outcomes and essential content	**Assessment options**

Use physical activity knowledge by
 	
• describing and actively engaging in physical activities outside of physical education class.
 	
Use fitness knowledge by
 	
• engaging in and identifying moderate to vigorous physical activity (MVPA),
• recognizing how MVPA affects the heart, and
• recognizing how the use of one's body for resistance develops muscular strength and muscular endurance.
	Assess attainment by using answer keys, checklists, or rubrics to score students' levels of knowledge about physical activity and fitness.
	
	• Evaluate physical activity knowledge in terms of students' descriptions of physical activity during physical activity participation.
	• Evaluate fitness knowledge by
	  ◦ observing for safe and correct technique for fitness activities and
	  ◦ checking students' recognition of physiological signs of moderate to vigorous physical activity.

STANDARD 4: EXHIBIT RESPONSIBLE PERSONAL AND SOCIAL BEHAVIOR THAT RESPECTS SELF AND OTHERS.	
Outcomes and essential content	**Assessment options**
Recognize classroom rules, procedures, and safety practices. Tackle challenges and work independently. Build a foundation for successful interpersonal communication during group activity by • using and recognizing rules, procedures, and safety practices; • working independently with others in partner environments; • cooperating with others by taking turns, assisting when they need help, and sharing (equipment, ideas, and peer feedback); and • staying on task, following directions, and honestly reporting the results of own work.	Assess attainment by using answer keys, checklists, or rubrics to score students' levels of success based on observation of students • using safe practices, rules, and procedures; cooperating with others by taking turns, helping, and sharing; • staying on task, following directions, and reporting results honestly, and based on evaluation of students' • recognition of safe practices, rules, and procedures; and • recognition of behaviors representing cooperation, honesty, and on-task participation.

STANDARD 5: RECOGNIZE THE VALUE OF PHYSICAL ACTIVITY FOR HEALTH, ENJOYMENT, CHALLENGE, SELF-EXPRESSION, AND/OR SOCIAL INTERACTION.	
Outcomes and essential content	**Assessment options**

Demonstrate recognition of the value of physical activity by
 	
• trying new movements and skills,
• persisting when not initially successful,
• identifying enjoyable movement activities, and
• describing the relationship between physical activity and good health.
	Assess attainment by using answer keys, checklists, or rubrics to score students' levels of success based on
	
	• observation of students trying and persisting when learning new skills and
	• evaluation of students doing the following:
	  ◦ describing the relationship between physical activity and good health,
	  ◦ identifying enjoyable physical activities,
	  ◦ recognizing behaviors that represent trying, and persisting in order to gain new skills.

dren with knowledge of performance descriptive (KPd) feedback about how they have performed and knowledge of performance prescriptive (KPp) feedback about what changes should be made. Feedback that is intermittent and prescriptive also facilitates children's progress toward achieving correct technique and timing, or mature performance of the fundamental movement skills. The sample learning activities presented in chapters 15 through 17 indicate the type of practice and feedback that should be used, as well as sample feedback statements.

Activities to Reinforce Personal and Social Responsibility

In physical education settings, K-2 learners should demonstrate the following behaviors for personal and social responsibility: being attentive, trying one's best, respecting equipment, sharing with others, and encouraging others. These behaviors help create a physically and emotionally safe learning environment, which in turn contributes to children's development of a positive sense of self and enhances their learning. Therefore, we suggest having K-2 children practice the behaviors associated with standard 4 for values of personal and social responsibility *before* engaging them in movement activities addressing standards 1 and 2. Sample movement activities designed to address standard 4 are provided in table 14.4.

Table 14.4   K-2 Social Contract

Learning outcomes	Behaviors	Response strategies
Be attentive. Exhibit personal responsibility (SHAPE America, 2014).	Know and perform the listening position for the day, such as "bus stop." Listen to the teacher's signal to start and stop play.	Proximity control: If a student is continually off task, have him or her practice in a specific bounded area where you can model the "freeze" and the student can mirror you. Provide a peer tutor to help the student stay on task and freeze when signaled.
Respect equipment. Take responsibility for class protocols (SHAPE America, 2014).	Place equipment gently on the floor and carefully in bins.	Have the student model a classmate's actions of appropriate equipment use. Use peer tutoring.
Try your best. Practice with minimal teacher prompting (SHAPE America, 2014).	Practice all skills—those you are already good at and those you still need to learn!	Student and teacher examine how the task needs to be changed in order to be either more or less difficult. Have the student use a practice task card to record information about each practice trial (see the Practice Style [B] task card in chapter 10) in order to see how practicing improves performance.
Praise and encourage. Praise movement performance of others (SHAPE America, 2014).	Say "magic words" to each other: "Keep trying!" "Way to go!" "You are awesome!" "Super job!"	Have the student practice writing "magic words" with a partner on a handout or whiteboard and use them during a partner activity. Keep a record of the student's encouraging statements during a span of lessons.
Work with others (SHAPE America, 2014).	Share equipment and space and work together independently and cooperatively.	Say, "It looks like you are unable to share the equipment. Is that true?" If the child says yes, ask why. Then restate the rule about sharing equipment and say, "You have a choice—share your equipment or sit out and think about why sharing is important." If the child chooses to sit out, say, "When you can explain to me why sharing is important, you may rejoin the class activity."

Each standard 4 activity includes a T-chart indicating the positive and negative behaviors of the personal or social responsibility, thus making clear what the learning outcome looks and sounds like. You can share the positive behavior expectations from the T-chart with students as goals for the activity, reinforce the behaviors through specific feedback, and assess student performance of the behaviors through observation checklists and student reflection prompts.

BE ATTENTIVE

Learning Outcome

Exhibit personal responsibility by being attentive (SHAPE America, 2014). See chart in the following assessment section for examples of correct and incorrect behavior for attentiveness.

Assessment

BEING ATTENTIVE LOOKS AND SOUNDS LIKE...	
Correct behavior 🙂	**Incorrect behavior** ☹
Listening to the teacher	Not paying attention (talking or listening to others)
Responding correctly to cues	Responding incorrectly, or not responding, to cues
Watching others to gain understanding of cues	
Asking for help if cues are misunderstood	

DRUMBEAT!

Children are spread out in general space. In response to a music cue, children travel through general space. While children are traveling, beat the drum a specific number of times to represent the number of students per group. Children must be attentive in order to form groups of the proper size!

Feedback

KPd: "I like the way you are listening! You changed from two to three with the drumbeat."

PARACHUTE

In order for children to succeed as a group during parachute activities, they must work together. The goal is for all to listen and respond promptly and accurately to movement cues. Smaller parachutes require fewer children to work together, but larger ones create the most excitement because the results of the group's efforts are much more pronounced.

- **Around and Around:** All students grip the edge of the parachute with the same hand while standing sideways in relation to the parachute. On a signal, they walk forward in a circle. The activity can also include holding with the other hand and introduce different locomotor skills and directions of travel.

- **Mountain:** All students get on their knees, face the center of the parachute, and grip the edge of the chute with both hands. On the signal "up," they all raise their arms above their heads and hold onto the chute as it domes. On the signal "down," they lower their hands to the ground, move their knees onto the edge of the chute, and pat the chute until it deflates.

- **Fly Away:** All students stand facing the center of the parachute, bend and grip the edge of the chute with both hands, and stand up while raising the chute to hip height. On the signal "up," they all raise their arms above their heads and hold onto the chute as it domes. On the signal "fly away," they release the chute and watch it soar.
- **Cave It:** All students stand facing the center of the parachute, bend and grip the edge of the chute with both hands, and stand up while raising it to hip height. On the signal "up," they all raise their arms above their heads and hold onto the chute as it domes. On the signal "cave it," they all bring the parachute behind their heads, squat, and then sit down on the edge of the chute to experience being inside the resulting parachute cave.
- **Popcorn:** Several light balls or balloons are placed on the parachute. All students stand facing the center of the chute, bend and grip the edge of the parachute with both hands, and stand up while raising it to hip height. On the signal "popcorn," they all shake the chute by rapidly moving their hands up and down in front of their chests.
- **Overboard:** Four to eight light balls of two different colors—say, red and yellow—are placed on the parachute. The children around the edge of half of the chute are designated as Starboard Red, and those around the other half are designated as Port Yellow. All students stand facing the center, bend and grip the edge of the parachute with both hands, and stand up while raising it to hip height. On the signal "overboard," they all shake the chute, trying to send all of the other team's balls off of the chute.

Feedback

KPp: "I see you standing and not moving your arms. Remember that 'up' means to raise your arms above your head."

RESPECT EQUIPMENT

Learning Outcome

Accept responsibility for class protocols by respecting equipment (SHAPE America, 2014). See the chart in the following assessment section for examples of correct and incorrect behavior in respecting equipment.

RESPECTING EQUIPMENT LOOKS AND SOUNDS LIKE . . .	
Correct behavior 🙂	**Incorrect behavior** 🙁
Using equipment safely	Unsafe use of equipment (endangering self or others)
Using equipment in the manner designated by the teacher	
	Taking others' equipment
Carefully getting out and putting away equipment	Carelessly getting out or putting away equipment (e.g., throwing, dropping, yanking)

USE IT WISELY!

Place a variety of pieces of equipment (e.g., hoops, cones, ropes, scooters) around the periphery of the movement space. Children are assigned partners (or, for children in grade 2, groups of three or four); in the case of an odd number of students, one group of three can be formed. Explain that the goal of the activity is for the children to safely retrieve equipment, place it in their movement space, use it, and then carefully put it away when asked. Here are some sample activities:

HOOPS

Dismiss the learning teams one at a time by color. Then say, "If you are on the red learning team, please go get a red hoop and take it to your movement space. Carry the hoop to your movement space and then place it on the floor." Once the hoop is placed on the floor, ask the children either to practice jumping in and out of it from both feet to both feet or to move in and out of the hoop in any way that they choose. After all children are moving in and out of their hoops, change the movement task (e.g., "Now circle the hoop around your waist"). After a brief activity time (3 to 5 minutes), have children carefully return their hoops to the sideline in "stacks" according to color. Then dismiss children again by the color of their learning team or hoop.

CONES AND ROPES

Place cones in several stacks on the sideline and hang ropes from a cart so that K-2 children can reach them. For managerial purposes, use color-coded learning teams again; this time, however, each partner group retrieves two cones and one rope. They are asked to put the rope into the top of the cones and travel over the rope in as many different ways as possible within their designated movement areas. After the activity, ask color-specific learning teams to carefully restack their cones and hang their ropes back on the cart.

SCOOTERS

Place scooters on the sidelines with the wheels up so that the scooters are flat on the floor. One partner from each team of children gets one scooter and carries it flat against their chest to their movement space and place it on the floor. One partner sits on the scooter and holds the handles. The other partner stands behind the first student and places his or her hands on the rider's shoulders. On a signal, the standing partner slowly pushes the sitting partner along curvy pathways in general space. Provide starting and stopping signals. After the activity, dismiss partner groups and have them carry their scooter properly to the sideline and place it flat on the floor with the wheels up.

Assessment

See table 14.5 for an observation checklist.

Table 14.5   Standard 4 Observation Checklist

Student	Safe use of equipment	Proper use of equipment	Carefully getting out and putting back the equipment

A check indicates that the student achieved the criterion.

TRY YOUR BEST

Learning Outcome

Try your best by practicing skills with minimal teacher prompting (SHAPE America, 2014). See the chart in the following assessment section for examples of correct and incorrect behavior in trying your best.

TRYING YOUR BEST LOOKS AND SOUNDS LIKE . . .	
Correct behavior 🙂	**Incorrect behavior** 🙁
Continuing to try	Giving up
Trying different levels	"I can't!"
Working at a challenging level	"I quit!"
Staying on task	Being off task
"I did it!"	

BOUNCIN' BOOGIE!

Provide a series of movement tasks on a whiteboard or task card. For children who cannot read, provide a series of photos or illustrations. The movement tasks get progressively more difficult, and the goal is to try one's best to accomplish levels at which one was initially unsuccessful. Children may start with any task in the series. As children attempt different tasks, praise them for trying their best!

KINDERGARTEN

Task 1: dropping a ball and catching it in self-space

Task 2: pushing a ball down with the finger pads of both hands in self-space

Task 3: pushing a ball down with the finger pads of one hand

Task 4: pushing a ball down with the finger pads of one hand while moving around the outside of a hoop

GRADE 1

Task 1: bouncing a ball with the finger pads of one hand

Task 2: bouncing a ball with the finger pads of one hand while moving around the outside of a hoop

Task 3: bouncing a ball with the finger pads of one hand while moving around hoops positioned in general space and avoiding other children

Task 4: bouncing a ball with the finger pads of one hand while moving around hoops positioned in general space, avoiding others, and moving slowly when the music is slow and at medium speed when the music has a medium tempo

GRADE 2

Task 1: bouncing a ball with the finger pads of one hand while moving around hoops positioned in general space and avoiding others

Task 2: bouncing a ball with the finger pads of one hand while moving around hoops positioned in general space, avoiding others, and moving slowly when the music is slow and at medium speed when the music has a medium tempo

Task 3: bouncing a ball with alternating hands while moving around hoops positioned in general space

Task 4: bouncing a ball with alternating hands while moving around hoops positioned in general space, avoiding others, and moving slowly when the music is slow and at medium speed when the music has a medium tempo

PRAISE AND ENCOURAGE

Learning Outcome

Praise and encourage others (SHAPE America, 2014). See the chart in the following assessment section for correct and incorrect behavior in praising and encouraging others.

PRAISING AND ENCOURAGING LOOKS AND SOUNDS LIKE . . .	
Correct behavior 🙂	Incorrect behavior 🙁
"Keep trying!"	"That was awful!"
"You're getting it!"	"Loser!"
"Great job!"	Thumbs-down
Thumbs-up	Expression of exasperation
High five	

COLLECTIVE SCORE HOOPIN'

Children are assigned partners, or you can use a novel way to create partner groups (e.g., matching shapes in kindergarten or matching puzzle pieces in grades 1 and 2). Each group has a small hoop and objects to throw underhand or overhand (e.g., rubber chickens, beanbags, or geometric open-matrix balls). Instruct children to choose an object to throw to a partner who holds the hoop and tries to "catch" the object in the hoop.

The thrower's distance from the hoop can be varied according to skill level—for example, 5, 7, or 10 feet (about 1.5, 2, or 3 meters). In addition, you can give the catcher the option to take a giant step back, away from the thrower, after each successful catch. Signal when the children should switch roles (e.g., after five turns). Children should keep a collective score of the number of times they are successful getting the ball through the hoop. Before children change to work with a new partner, prompt them to give their partner a bit of verbal or nonverbal praise (e.g., thumbs-up, high five, "Good job!") or encouragement (e.g., "Keep trying!" or "You're getting it!").

Adapted, by permission, from T. Orlick, 2006, *Cooperative games and sports: Joyful activities for everyone*, 2nd ed. (Champaign, IL: Human Kinetics), 18-19.

WORK WITH OTHERS

Learning Outcome

Work independently with others (SHAPE America, 2014). See the following chart for correct and incorrect behavior when working with others.

WORKING WITH OTHERS LOOKS AND SOUNDS LIKE . . .	
Correct behavior 🙂	**Incorrect behavior** 🙁
Sharing space to include others	Blocking space to exclude others
Taking turns	Keeping equipment to oneself
Counting for one's partner	Counting only for oneself
Moving the hoop to help others score	Moving the hoop to make others miss
Moving or adjusting pace to keep up with a partner	Moving at own pace without regard for partner

MUSICAL HOOPS

This is a cooperative game of musical chairs with the goal of including everyone as the number of hoops diminishes. Groups of six to eight students stand outside a row of five to seven small hoops. As the music plays, they circle the row of hoops. When the music stops, they must quickly get into a hoop and, as the number of hoops goes down, provide space for others who are without a hoop of their own. You can vary the body parts used to support the body or to demonstrate that one is "inside" the hoop.

Adapted, by permission, from T. Orlick, 2006, *Cooperative games and sports: Joyful activities for everyone*, 2nd ed. (Champaign, IL: Human Kinetics), 21-22.

KEEP IT UP!

Children are partnered using matching numbers or colors. Each pair is given a large balloon (punch balloons are a bit heavier and have more predictable flight paths). The idea is to work together by taking turns and to reach the common goal of increasing the number of consecutive hits while keeping the balloon in the air. On a signal from the teacher, everyone freezes and gives their partner a piece of praise or encouragement. The partner holding the balloon then finds a new partner who has no balloon. The activity can proceed in the following ways:

- Partners take turns working individually to hit the balloon up in the air to themselves. The observing partner counts the number of consecutive hits. The hits by the second partner continue the collective score count (e.g., partner 1 makes hits 1, 2, 3, and 4, after which partner 2 makes hits 5, 6, 7, and so on).

- Partners hit the balloon back and forth to each other, counting the consecutive hits.

- One pair joins another pair, and one of the pairs trades its balloon for a large hoop. Together, they hold the hoop high while the other pair hits the balloon back and forth through the hoop. The hoop holders move the hoop to help the balloon go through. The group of four uses collective scoring to count the number of hits made through the hoop.

Adapted, by permission, from T. Orlick, 2006, *Cooperative games and sports: Joyful activities for everyone*, 2nd ed. (Champaign, IL: Human Kinetics), 15-16.

HOOPING TOGETHER

Children are partnered using matching pictures. Each pair stands together outside a large hoop that has been placed on the floor. On a signal, they each grab a section of the hoop and raise it to hip height. At this point, music begins, and the children must move together throughout the gym while avoiding other pairs. The goal is to work together by moving in the same direction and at the same speed. Partners can find different relationships to each other by holding the hoop with one in front and one in back or by moving side by side. Here are two variations:

- Partners can be challenged to stand inside their hoop and move together.
- Partners can join another pair, stack one hoop on top of the other, and have all four children hold a portion of the hoops and move together throughout the gym. More partners can be added to increase the challenge—and the success of working together!

Adapted, by permission, from T. Orlick, 2006, *Cooperative games and sports: Joyful activities for everyone*, 2nd ed. (Champaign, IL: Human Kinetics), 19-20.

 Visit the web resource for learning activities, video clips, and review questions.

K-2 Learning Experiences for Locomotor Skills

Key Concepts

- Describing the relationship between stage of motor development, level of movement skill learning, and the design of locomotor-skill learning experiences for K-2 children

- Designing locomotor skill learning experiences that align:
  - K-2 national standards for physical education (SHAPE America, 2014)
  - Instructional practices
  - Assessment and feedback

This chapter provides progressive learning experiences for the consistent mover in each locomotor skill theme. Locomotor skills move the body through space on the limbs. **Traveling locomotor skills** are continuous, involve a brief flight phase, and take the body from place to place; examples include walking, running, galloping, sliding, and skipping. **Flight locomotor skills** involve takeoff, flight, and landing phases; examples include jumping, leaping, and hopping. Developing mature-stage locomotor skills in grades K-2 establishes a foundation for children to use when they engage in specialized skill performance in grades 3 through 5 as part of developmental dance, gymnastics, and games.

The movement framework categories depicted in the Active Child diagram (figure 15.1) include the locomotor skill categories (traveling and flight) in the trunk of the child and the movement concepts (body, space, effort, and relationship) in the limbs. The learning goal blueprint for locomotor skills presented in table 15.1 illustrates how locomotor actions and movement concepts can be combined to vary skills.

LIVERPOOL JOHN MOORES UNIVERSITY
LEARNING SERVICES

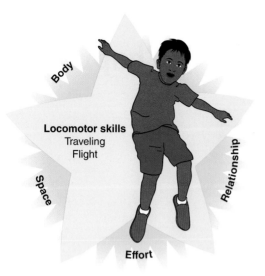

Figure 15.1 The Active Child: locomotor skills.

Each locomotor learning experience can be used over the course of many lessons because children need multiple practice opportunities in order to become consistent. Conversely, a given lesson can consist of multiple learning experiences. For each learning experience, the *task* represents a specific skill progression and the *environment* describes not only the setup of the gymnasium or movement area but also the scaling of equipment and conditions to be appropriate for the performers (see chapter

6). For each learning experience presented in this chapter, the description indicates the relevant national standard(s) and grade 2 outcome, as well as assessment options aligned with the standard(s) (see figure 14.3 in chapter 14).

Standards 1 and 2 are addressed in each of the locomotor skill themes because K-2 children are developmentally ready to achieve the mature stage of the fundamental movement skills and become knowledgeable about movement concepts. Standard 1 can be assessed through observation checklists of skill and safety cues, and an assessment rubric for each locomotor skill appears in appendix B. Standard 2 can be assessed by recording information about children's ability to identify skill cues through pictures, teacher demonstrations, or video clips. For children who can read, you can also use exit tickets or other age-appropriate assessment sheets that address correct skill cues.

Locomotor skills can be either closed or open. They are *closed* when performed in stable, unchanging environments (e.g., moving along designated pathways, jumping off of equipment). They are *open* when performed in unpredictable environments (e.g., tag games in which children chase, flee, and dodge each other).

You can use both constant and variable practice with the learning experiences presented in this chapter. Constant practice is used to help consistent movers achieve mature form. Variable

Table 15.1 Learning Goal Blueprint for Mature and Versatile Performance of Locomotor Skills

Content	Body	Space	Effort	Relationship
Traveling skills: running, galloping, sliding, skipping	Intentionally uses body actions for mature performance. Curls, stretches, bends, twists, and turns body during, into, and out of traveling skills.	Adjusts movements to move safely through space. Travels on straight, curved, and zigzag pathways in forward, backward, and sideward directions.	Varies speed of traveling skills. Moves rhythmically to beats and music. Combines traveling skills in smooth sequences.	Uses traveling skills to move around, along, inside, through, and under equipment. Moves in front of, next to, and behind others and in roles of leading, following, mirroring, and matching. Adjusts movements to chase, flee, and dodge others.
Flight: jumping, leaping, hopping	Intentionally uses body actions for mature performance. Moves body into and out of symmetrical shapes (round, narrow, wide) during flight.	Changes level and varies distance and direction of flight movements.	Moves rhythmically to beats and music. Combines flight and traveling skills in smooth sequences.	Uses flight skills to move over, into, out of, onto, and off of low equipment. Uses flight to move in front of, next to, and behind others and in roles of leading, following, mirroring, and matching. Adjusts movements using flight to dodge others.

practice is used for learning skill variations for closed skills, such as performing locomotor skills to the tempo of a musical selection or drumbeat (to promote effort awareness) or while matching a partner (to promote relationship awareness). Variable practice is also used for making the environment either more or less predictable when practicing the open skills of chasing, fleeing, and dodging.

You can also use both descriptive and prescriptive feedback. When instruction of consistent movers is focused on knowledge and performance of skill cues and performance of *closed* skills, provide children with knowledge of performance descriptive feedback (KPd) about how they have performed and knowledge of performance prescriptive feedback (KPp) about what changes should be made. When instruction is focused on *open* skills, provide descriptive and prescriptive feedback about the results of the student's chasing, fleeing, and dodging actions: "You were able to stay with and tag your opponent because you watched her hips and changed direction with her."

Performance of locomotor skills relates directly to the health-related fitness components of cardiorespiratory endurance and muscular endurance. Therefore, you address standard 3 for physical education (achieving and maintaining health-enhancing levels of activity and fitness) when you purposefully engage and assess your students' ability to perform locomotor skills for increasing periods of time.

Personal and social responsibility are expected throughout the learning experiences and are articulated in the essential content of K-2 standard 4: recognizing classroom rules, procedures, and safety practices; tackling challenges; and building a foundation for successful interpersonal communication during group activity. You can record information about students' adherence to personal and social responsibility on observation checklists. In addition, children can demonstrate their knowledge of responsibility behaviors through age-appropriate assessment sheets.

In standard 5, children are asked to recognize the value of physical activity. In kindergarten through grade 2, children recognize which physical activities are enjoyable to them and which ones they feel most confident about performing. You can use exit tickets to assess students' feelings about the locomotor activities addressed in a given day's lesson and help them recognize that physical activity participation can both bring enjoyment and provide challenge. Figure 15.2 presents sample exit tickets for assessing enjoyment and challenge; you can use information from the tickets to address students' needs and interests.

I like/dislike 😊 ☹ _____ [name of locomotor activity].

It is fun to do _____ [name of locomotor activity].

Today's Activities

_____ [Name of activity]

_____ [Name of activity]

_____ [Name of activity]

Put a check mark by the activities that you need to work harder to perform.
Put an X by the activity that you performed the best.

Figure 15.2 Sample exit tickets for enjoyment (top) and for confidence and challenge (bottom).

LOCOMOTOR SKILLS: TRAVELING

Use table 15.2 as a resource for designing traveling skill challenges. Examples are provided below the table.

Table 15.2 Progression for K-2 Consistent-Level Traveling Skills

Traveling	
	Learning outcome: Gain greater consistency in performance of mature traveling patterns and variations.
	Traveling Through General Space
	• Running
	• Galloping
	• Sliding
	• Hopping
	• Skipping
	Traveling Variations
	• Space awareness: directions, pathways
	• Effort awareness: traveling to rhythms and musical accompaniment; increasing intensity
	• Relationship to equipment: around, alongside, on top of, underneath, in and out of
	• Cooperative relationships with others: following and leading; matching; meeting and parting
	• Adding traveling and flight skills
	• Competitive relationships with others: chasing, fleeing, dodging
	○ On offense, using fakes, changes of direction, and jump spins to avoid defense
	○ On defense, "reading" and anticipating movement of offense to cut off running angles

Learning Outcome

Gain greater consistency in performance of mature traveling patterns and variations.

- Standard 1: Travel through general space using mature traveling patterns.

Movement Concepts

- Body awareness: intentional use of body parts in unison, opposition, and sequence for mature performance of traveling skills
- Space awareness: general space

Teaching Style

Reproduction: practice

Tasks

Task: Lots of Locomotors—Children are spread out in general space and, when prompted, travel through general space using a specified locomotor skill. Announce to children which locomotor skill they should perform (i.e., walking fast, running, sliding, galloping, hopping, or skipping). Music can be played; however, the instructional task does *not* emphasize moving to the tempo of the music or rhythmically to a beat.

Environment: Define a gymnasium space or large outdoor space bounded by cones, perhaps with poly spots designating where children move while performing the locomotor skill, thus enabling instruction such as, "Skip to five different poly spots."

Skill cues:

Running

- Preparation: Push off of one foot; swing arm in opposition.
- Main action: Execute definite flight phase; maximize stride length; completely extend support leg; bend arms at right angle; kick buttocks with heels.

- Recovery: Recovery thigh is parallel to ground; land on ball of foot; bend arms at right angle at sides; body is balanced.

Galloping

- Preparation: Step forward on lead foot; arms begin back and bent at elbows.
- Main action: Step-together with trailing foot touching heel of lead foot; push off of trailing foot is forceful enough to achieve flight phase with feet; arms swing forward in coordination with legs to achieve distance and height.
- Recovery: Land on ball of lead foot with trailing foot behind lead foot; thus entire action is step, together, step with flight phase during together portion.

Sliding

- Preparation: Turn body so side leads action; extend arms at shoulder level.
- Main action: Step to side with lead foot; step-together with opposite (trailing) foot, pushing off of ground with lead foot and trailing foot to attain flight phase; step on lead foot; arms stay extended out to sides.
- Recovery: Land on lead foot with knee slightly bent; body stays upright.

Hopping

- Preparation: Bend nonhopping leg at 90 degrees.
- Main action: Swing nonhopping leg in pendular fashion to produce upward and forward force and distance; bend arms at elbows and swing from back to front to produce a rhythmically coordinated hopping action
- Recovery: Land on hopping leg with bent knee and overall body control.

Skipping

- Preparation: Step on one foot and raise opposite knee.
- Main action: Alternate stepping and hopping and right and left feet, lifting knees to waist height; alternate arms and swing them up and forward (left arm forward when right knee is up).
- Recovery: Bend knee slightly on landing leg.

Learning Outcome

Gain greater consistency in performance of mature traveling patterns and variations.

- Standard 1: Travel through general space using mature traveling patterns.
- Standard 2: Recognize different traveling skills.
- Standard 3: Recognize that when you move for longer periods of time, you breathe faster.
- Standard 4: Work independently with others.

Movement Concepts

- Body awareness: intentional use of body parts in unison, opposition, and sequence for mature performance of traveling skills
- Space awareness: general space
- Effort awareness: intensity of activity
- Relationship awareness: to others in space

Teaching Style

Practice: constant

Tasks

Task: Zone Travel—This task focuses on moving through general space in relationship to others. When prompted by the teacher, children avoid others while running between zones and share space with others once inside a zone.

Enrichment (addressing standard 4): Put enough hoops in each zone for each child to stand in one upon entering that zone. As the activity progresses, on a signal from the teacher, have children remove one hoop at a time from the zone so that children in a given zone must share a hoop. To help children become aware of whether or not they are exhibiting behaviors of personal and social responsibility, ask them these questions:

- "How are you being careful when moving close to others?"
- "How are you sharing space?"

Environment: Use tall cones to divide an outdoor area into numbered zones (see figure 15.3). Use a whistle, drum, or any novel sound to signal children to change zones. Children are spread out in assigned zones. Initially they move to different numbered zones by going from zone 1 to 2, 2 to 3, 3 to 4, 4 to 5, 5 to 6, and 6 to 1. Then randomly choose numbers and create a different order by drawing two numbers at a time from cards numbered 1 through 6.

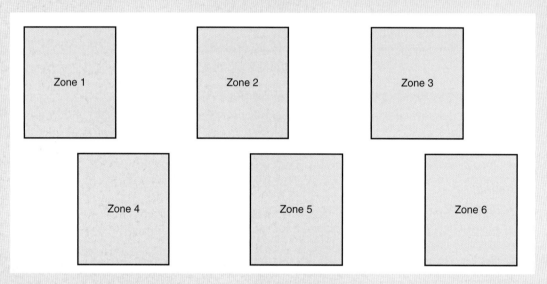

Figure 15.3   Setup for zone travel.

Task: Cone Travel—This task focuses on intensity of activity. Children use various locomotor skills, as designated by the teacher, to travel from cone to cone, each according to the order of the numbers in his or her telephone number. Students can travel with stops or on a more continuous basis to enhance the intensity of their locomotor performance. For instance, students can run and stop after each number of their phone number, after the performance of the first three numbers, after the performance of the entire number, or after the performance of their phone number three consecutive times. During this activity, you can prompt children to monitor their breathing patterns:

- Breathing normally: Shallow, slow breaths through the nose
- A little faster than normal: Deeper, faster breaths through the nose
- Breathing very hard and fast: Deeper, faster breaths through the nose and mouth

Environment: 10 cones numbered 0-9 are positioned randomly in an outdoor space. Place the cones several yards apart from each other. Children begin at the first number of their telephone number (excluding area code).

Enrichment: Cone Consonants, Vowels, and Blends—This activity integrates content from language arts. Children use various locomotor skills, as designated by the teacher, to travel to cones in order to obtain consonants, vowels, or letter blends hidden under the cones. Children then travel back to their learning team area and place the consonant, vowel, or letter blend in the correctly labeled consonant, vowel, or letter blend hoop. At the conclusion of the activity, groups check their hoops to determine whether they have the letters in correct hoops. You can provide each group with a handout or poster (or use a wall projection) showing consonants, vowels, and letter blends. Then groups can be challenged to form a word containing a certain consonant, vowel, or blend.

Environment: Spread cones out in a large rectangular space. Form five groups of five children each and provide each group with three hoops, each hoop labeled as vowel, consonant, or letter blend.

Feedback

Provide knowledge of performance descriptive (KPd) and prescriptive (KPp) feedback using skill cues. For example, you might use the running skill cues to offer the following feedback:

- KPd: "You really used your arms to pump and create energy while you were running."
- KPp: "Try to make your stride a bit larger by pushing harder off of the ground."

Assessment

- Standard 1: Use a running observation checklist (see sample in figure 15.4) with a check mark indicating that the student achieved the criterion.
- Standard 2: Demonstrate skipping, hopping, and galloping and have students circle the correct locomotor skill for each on a worksheet.
- Standard 3: Use the "How's my breathing?" handout with smiley faces (figure 15.5).
- Standard 4: Use a teacher observation checklist of safety and sharing cues (see sample in figure 15.6) with a check mark in the appropriate column for each student's performance.

Student	Arms in opposition?		Definite flight phase?		Heels kick buttocks?	
	Yes	No	Yes	No	Yes	No

Figure 15.4   Observation checklist for running cues.

Name:_____

Circle *one* smiley face if you were breathing normally.

Circle *two* smiley faces if you were breathing a little faster than normal.

Circle *three* smiley faces if you were breathing very hard and fast.

Figure 15.5   Assessment: How's my breathing?

C = consistently

S = sometimes

ND = not demonstrated

Student	Controls body and speed during all activities.	Shares space.

Figure 15.6 Teacher observation checklist for safety and sharing.

Learning Outcome

Gain greater consistency in performance of mature traveling patterns and variations.

- Standards 1 and 2: Travel in different pathways and directions.

Movement Concepts

- Body awareness: intentional use of body parts in unison, opposition, and sequence for mature performance of traveling skills
- Space awareness: direction

Teaching Style

Reproduction: practice

Tasks

Task: Children travel through general space using a designated locomotor skill and in a designated direction as you call out a skill and direction. You can use a drum to accompany their traveling. Tasks may include the following:

- Forward walking
- Backward walking
- Sideways walking
- Forward galloping
- Forward skipping
- Forward hopping
- Forward jumping
- Backward jumping
- Sideways jumping

Enrichment: Position cones throughout general space. An arrow designating forward, sideways, or backward is taped to each cone. Children travel between cones using the locomotor skill that you designate; when they come to an arrow, they perform the designated locomotor skill in the direction indicated by the arrow, requiring greater independence.

Environment: general space

Practice: variable

Skill cues:

- Forward: Tummy leads action.
- Sideways: Side leads action.
- Backward: Bottom or back leads action.

Children travel with a designated locomotor skill through designated pathways.

Feedback

- KPd: "Your side is leading as you jump sideways. Great job!"
- KPp: "Try to look over your shoulder when going backward and leading with your back and bottom."

Assessment

- Standards 1 and 2: Use a teacher observation checklist of movement in different directions (figure 15.7).

Name:_____

	Forward	Sideways	Backward
Walking			
Hopping			
Galloping			
Skipping			

Place a check mark in the appropriate space if the child can execute the indicated locomotor skill in the indicated direction.

Figure 15.7   Teacher observation checklist for moving in different directions.

Learning Outcome

Gain greater consistency in performance of mature traveling patterns and variations.

- Standards 1 and 2: Travel along pathways and in different directions.
- Standard 2: Identify different pathways.

Movement Concepts

- Body awareness: intentional use of body parts in unison, opposition, and sequence for mature performance of traveling skills
- Space awareness: pathways, direction

Teaching Style

Reproduction: practice

Tasks

Task: Children follow straight, curved, and zigzag pathways on the gymnasium floor and change direction on your cue to move forward, sideways, or backward (only walking should be done backward). Provide verbal cues for what type of locomotor skill to use and what direction to travel (e.g., "slide sideways," "gallop forward"). Intermittently ask children to identify the shape of the pathway on which they are moving.

Environment: Use colored tape, floor paint, or poly spots to create several different pathways.

Practice: variable

Skill cues:

- Curvy pathway: Lean slightly in direction of curve and maintain balance over feet to control body.
- Zigzag pathway: Pivot sharply to control body while changing direction quickly at V of zigzag.

Feedback

- KPd: "I like how you quickly changed direction to move along the zigzag pathway."
- KPd: "You did a good job leaning into the curve while sliding sideways along the curvy pathways."

Assessment

- Standard 1: Observe whether child can control body while moving.
  - _____ On curvy pathway
  - _____ On zigzag pathway
  - _____ On straight pathway
- Standard 2: Use a matching worksheet (figure 15.8) to determine whether the student can identify correct pathways.

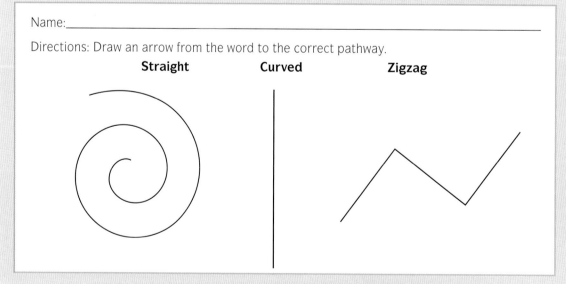

Name:_____

Directions: Draw an arrow from the word to the correct pathway.

Straight   **Curved**   **Zigzag**

Figure 15.8 Pathways worksheet.

Learning Outcome

Gain greater consistency in performance of mature traveling patterns and variations.

- Standard 2: Travel to rhythms and musical accompaniment.

Movement Concepts

- Body awareness: intentional use of body parts in unison, opposition, and sequence for mature performance of traveling skills
- Effort awareness: tempo and rhythm

Teaching Style

Reproduction: practice

Tasks

Task: Use music that elicits skipping, hopping, galloping, and sliding sideways. One good resource for such music is Aventurine Music by Eric Chappelle (www.aventurinemusic.com/about-eric-chappelle.html). You can also use percussion instruments (e.g., tambourine, drum) to provide rhythm and tempo changes. Children can clap hands to learn rhythm and tempo before performing each locomotor skill.

Environment: large general space bounded by colored cones

Practice: variable

Skill cues: Provide verbal cues in time with the rhythm and tempo of music (e.g., "step, together, step").

Feedback

- KPd: "You were able to skip to the fast tempo and rhythm of the music!"
- KPp: "Listen to the music and see if you can perform your gallop to the tempo of the music."

Assessment

Standard 2: Use the rhythm and tempo rubric in figure 15.9 to observe and then rate the child's performance.

Name:_____

	Consistently performs loco-motor skill to the rhythm and tempo of the music.	Sometimes performs locomotor skill to the rhythm and tempo of the music.	Does not yet perform locomotor skill to the rhythm and tempo of the music.
Skipping			
Galloping			
Hopping			
Sliding			

Figure 15.9 Rhythm and tempo rubric for locomotor skills.

Learning Outcome

Gain greater consistency in performance of mature traveling patterns and variations.

- Standard 1: Travel in relationship to equipment.

Movement Concepts

- Body awareness: intentional use of body parts in unison, opposition, and sequence for mature performance of traveling skills
- Relationship awareness: around, alongside, on top of, underneath, and in and out of equipment

Teaching Style

Reproduction: practice

Tasks

Task: Children practice locomotor skills around hoops or cones; alongside jump ropes; on top of wooden benches, low beams, or foam shapes; underneath a net suspended from tall cones; and in and out of tires. Stop and start the practice at each station and have children rotate on cue. Remind children to respect each other's space.

Environment: Set up stations to elicit each type of locomotor skill. Assign five or six children to each station.

- Station 1: Children move around hoops or cones. The cones can be decorated on one side with pictures depicting performance of locomotor skills and on the other side with descriptive words (e.g., fast, slowly, silly, loosely, tightly, lightly, wiggly). As children go around a cone, they perform the designated locomotor skill as indicated by the descriptor: skip silly, walk loosely, gallop slowly, walk wiggly, slide lightly, and so on.
- Station 2: Children move alongside or underneath elements in the environment—alongside ropes, tape, or paint on the ground and under ropes suspended from cones. Cue cards listing the locomotor skills are posted on a tall cone to remind students what skills to practice. This station can be accompanied by music.
- Station 3: Children move on top of wooden benches, foam trapezoid shapes, low beams, or tires that create a mini obstacle course. Children are challenged to walk "on top of" both forward and sideways.
- Station 4: Children move in and out of hoops, tires, and agility ladders that create an obstacle course.

Practice: variable

Feedback

- KPd: "You are running very quickly in and out of the tires and lifting your knees high!" "You are galloping by kicking your front foot out of place as you travel around the cones!" "You are moving carefully underneath the ropes without touching them—great job!" "When you skip around the hoops, you are keeping your knees high and swinging your arms at shoulder level—great job!"
- KPp: "For better balance, focus your eyes a few feet in front of you as you walk across the bench."

Assessment

Standard 1: Create a teacher observation sheet using skill cues.

Learning Outcome

Gain greater consistency in performance of mature traveling patterns and variations.

- Standard 1: Travel in relationship to others.
- Standard 4: Work independently with others in partner relationships.

Movement Concepts

- Body awareness: intentional use of body parts in unison, opposition, and sequence for mature performance of traveling skills
- Relationship awareness: following and leading; meeting and parting; matching

Teaching Style

Reproduction: practice

Tasks

Task: This is a teacher-directed activity in which children perform various locomotor skills while changing partners frequently. Here are some examples of things to say:

- "I expect you to work together to accomplish these partner movement tasks."
- "Keep safe distances between each other when following and meeting."
- "Work cooperatively by giving each other "put-ups" (e.g., praise, thumbs-up, high five) to celebrate your successes and encouragements when you're working out how to meet the challenge."

Present a series of instructional tasks to elicit the partner relationship and desired locomotor skill. Here are some examples of things to say:

- "Walk (or skip, hop, gallop, slide, run) following your partner through general space."
- "Face your partner. Take five giant steps away from them. Meet them by skipping toward them. Give your partner a 'high 10' and move away or part by sliding sideways."
- "Face your partner one step away from them. See if you can move sideways by sliding three times to your right and then three times to your left. Remember that one partner will be moving to their left while the other partner is moving to their right so that you can mirror each other's movement!"
- "Stand beside your partner. Travel forward by skipping six times. When you travel together, you are matching your partner!"

Environment: open space

Practice: variable

Feedback

- KPd: "I like that you each chose a different locomotor skill to perform when meeting and parting!"
- KPp: "I think you need to be sure you have enough space between you when you are meeting so that you don't run into each other!"

Assessment

Standards 1 and 4: Use the moving in relationship to partners rubric in figure 15.10 to observe and then rate each child's performance.

Student could perform the relationship, use adequate space, cooperate with partner, and avoid interfering with others.

C = Consistently

S = Sometimes

N = Not yet developed

Student	Meeting and parting	Mirroring	Following and leading

Figure 15.10   Assessment rubric for moving in relationship to partners.

Learning Outcome

Gain greater consistency in performance of mature traveling patterns and variations.

- Standard 1: Add traveling and flight skills.

Movement Concepts

Body awareness: intentional use of body parts in unison, opposition, and sequence for mature performance of traveling skills

Teaching Style

Reproduction: practice

Tasks

Task: Perform a sequence of locomotor skills, such as the following:

- Galloping, skipping, and sliding sideways
- Running, sliding, hopping
- Hopping, skipping, galloping

Children are challenged to perform a series of each locomotor skill and then transition to performing a new locomotor skill. Teacher can verbally prompt the next skill.

Enrichment: Specify the number of times that children should perform each locomotor skill; add a rhythmic component; or, for children who can read, distribute locomotor word cards and ask children to arrange and then perform them in a locomotor sentence.

Environment: open space

Practice: variable

Skill cues:

- Transition smoothly from one locomotor skill to next by starting new pattern immediately with the next footstep (e.g., left step, right step, left step-hop, right step-hop, left gallop, and so on).
- Do not walk between locomotor skills.

Feedback

- KPd: "You are changing from one skill to the next very smoothly—great job!"
- KPp: "Think about the way to step for the next skill as you're finishing the first skill so that you won't have to stop or walk when you change from one skill to another."

Assessment

Standard 1: Use an observation checklist of skill cues and smooth transitions from one skill to the next.

Learning Outcome

Gain greater consistency in performance of mature traveling patterns and variations.

- Standard 1: Move competitively to avoid and chase others.
- Standard 2: Identify movements that aid avoiding and chasing.

Movement Concepts

- Body awareness: intentional use of body parts in unison, opposition, and sequence for mature performance of traveling skills
- Space awareness: direction
- Relationship awareness: avoiding and chasing others

Teaching Style

Reproduction: practice

Tasks

Task: Children play the following variations of partner tag games.

- **Knee tag:** Each pair gets four poly spots to create a square area measuring about 4 by 4 feet (1.25 by 1.25 meters). The two players face each other in ready position, then try to move quickly to touch the side of each other's knees or avoid having knees touched. The challenge is to see how many times they can touch their partner's knees within 20 seconds. Have the children change partners frequently.
- **Flag tag:** Each pair gets four poly spots to create a square area measuring about 6 by 6 feet (1.75 by 1.75 meters). Each player wears a flag belt with two flags. The two players face each other in ready position, then try to pull the flags off of each other's waist.
- **Lane tag:** Cones are used to create lanes that are 5 feet (1.5 meters) wide; the lanes can be made wider and either longer or shorter as needed. One poly spot is positioned in the middle of the lane. One player begins at one end of the lane and tries to fake out the tagger in order to get to the opposite end. The tagger is in the middle of the lane and must keep one foot on the poly spot while trying to tag the opponent.

Skill cues:

Ready Position

- Bend knees.
- Bend elbows and extend arms out to sides.
- Hold weight on balls of feet.

Tagging Knee

- Maintain ready position.
- Reach quickly with palm of hand to tap opponent's knee.
- Use fakes (e.g., pretending to tap one knee but going toward opposite knee).

Avoiding Knee Tag

- Maintain ready position.
- Watch opponent's hands.
- Pivot torso and feet to twist away from opponent's hand.

Flag Tag

- Maintain ready position.
- Reach quickly with hand to grasp flag off of opponent's belt.
- Use fakes with quick, short movements while pretending to go for one flag but moving toward opposite flag.

Avoiding Defender in Flag Tag

- Maintain ready position.
- Watch opponent's hands.
- Back away, shuffle quickly to side, or twist body to keep flag from being grabbed.

V-Cut

- In flag tag and lane tag, offensive player fakes in one direction, then steps quickly to move in another direction in order to avoid tagger.

Assessment

- Standard 1: Use an observation checklist of skill cues.
- Standard 2: Use a picture worksheet asking children to circle the player who is in the correct ready position for moving quickly to tag or avoid being tagged.

Task: Children move in designated space in groups of four (one versus three). The tagger can be designated by a number, color, or some other method. Within a 30-second time frame, the tagger chases the other players in an attempt to tag them on the upper body. Thus the tagger tries to change direction quickly in response to the movements of the other players while the fleers try to use fakes and quick movements to avoid the tagger.

Environment: gymnasium divided into six sections

Practice: variable

Skill cues:

Chaser

- Use ready position.
- Watch opponents' hips.
- Know positions of runners (e.g., how far, angle, in front of or behind) and choose to pursue opponent who is easiest to tag.
- Change speed and direction quickly.

Runner

- Keep eyes on chaser.
- Change direction quickly by bending knees, pivoting, and twisting to avoid tagger.
- Run backward and forward to avoid tagger.
- Fake in one direction and move in another direction to avoid tagger.
- Change speed and direction quickly to dodge chaser.

Feedback

- KPd: "You are using fakes by moving your body in one direction and then going in another direction—awesome!"
- KPp: "Try to make your movements a bit smaller and quicker in order to get away from your chaser!"

Assessment

- Standard 1: Use the assessment checklist for dodging and fleeing depicted in figure 15.11 to observe and then rate each child's performance.

Student	Changes speed and direction quickly.		Uses fakes.		Responds to movements of others to either tag or avoid.	
	Yes	No	Yes	No	Yes	No

Figure 15.11   Assessment checklist for dodging and fleeing.

LOCOMOTOR SKILLS: FLIGHT

Use table 15.3 as a resource for designing flight skill challenges. Examples are provided after the table.

Table 15.3   Progression for K-2 Consistent-Level Flight Skills

Flight	Equipment: low boxes, benches, foam shapes; poly spots, ropes, hoops, tires, springboard Learning outcome: Gain greater consistency in performance of mature flight patterns and variations. **Flight**<ul><li>Jumping (one foot to both feet; both feet to both feet)</li><li>Leaping</li></ul>**Flight Variations**<ul><li>Body awareness: body shapes</li><li>Space awareness: levels, distances, directions, pathways</li><li>Effort awareness: force, rhythms</li><li>Relationship to equipment: over; on and off; in and out</li><li>Relationship with others: leading and following; matching; mirroring</li></ul>Adding traveling and flight skills

Learning Outcome

Gain greater consistency in performance of mature flight patterns and variations.

- Standard 1: Use mature flight patterns when jumping.

Movement Concepts

- Body awareness: intentional use of body parts in unison, opposition, and sequence for mature performance of traveling skills
- Space awareness: direction, pathway
- Relationship awareness: to equipment (over)

Teaching Style

Reproduction: practice, reciprocal (grade 2), inclusion

Tasks

Task: After you demonstrate, students practice jumping from one foot to both feet using a walking approach and from both feet to both feet from a stationary position. As students progress, they may practice jumping from one foot to both feet using a running approach. Try the following variations:

- Place ropes on the floor in a V shape so that children can choose the distance that they try to jump.
- Suspend ropes from low cones for children to jump over.
- Swim noodles (1-2-3) placed next to each other for children to approach and jump over
- Poly spots placed randomly for children to approach and jump over
- Developmental hurdles for children to approach and jump over

Environment: Students are spread out in general space all facing either north/south or east/west. Students practice individually to jump from one foot to both feet after a walking approach. The students take off from lines or circles indicated by poly spots. If students use a running approach to jump from one foot to both feet, they should land on gymnastics panel mats or landing mats. Depending on the number of mats available, small groups may need to be formed. If using the reciprocal teaching style, have students form partner groups (pairs). The activity also requires clipboards, observations sheets, and pencils.

Practice: constant

Skill cues:

Jumping From Both Feet to Both Feet

- Preparation: Use takeoff crouch and appropriate arm positioning for height and distance of the jump. Swing arms back.
- Main action: Quickly extend legs and arms.
- Recovery: Land on balls of feet with crouch appropriate to absorb force from height and distance of jump. Reach arms out in front for balance.

Jumping from both feet to both feet: preparation *(a)*, action *(b)*, recovery *(c)*.

Jumping From One Foot to Both Feet

- Preparation: Step and push off of one foot with slight knee bend.
- Main action: Push off by extending knee and swinging other foot forward. Bring push-off foot to meet front foot.
- Recovery: land on both feet simultaneously with slight knee bend to absorb force.

Jumping from one foot to both feet: preparation *(a)*, action *(b)*, recovery *(c)*.

Feedback

- KPd: "You are swinging your arms from low to high to help you cover more distance on your jump—great job!"
- KPp: "Bend your knees a bit more on your takeoff."

Assessment

- Standard 1: Use an observation checklist of skill cues (figure 15.12). Second grade readers can use a reciprocal task card.

Performer:_____

Observer:_____

Directions: Watch your partner perform three jumps and check the yes or no column to show whether he or she demonstrates the skill cues. Watch and then check one skill cue at a time.

	Try 1		Try 2		Try 3	
	Yes	No	Yes	No	Yes	No
Takes off from two feet.						
Swings arms from low to high.						
Bends knees on landing.						

Figure 15.12 Observation checklist of skill cues for jumping.

Task: Children engage in continuous jumping from both feet to both feet.
- Forward
- Side to side
- Forward and back

Environment: hoops, ropes, poly spots, ladders, pathways on floor, music to elicit jumping patterns

Skill cues:
- Push off of both feet and land simultaneously on both feet. Stay on balls of feet.
- Use landing as preparation for next jump.
- Pump arms slightly while holding them at sides.

Feedback

- KPd: "You stayed on the balls of your feet. That helped you to jump continuously."
- KPp: "Use a short knee bend to keep your jump going."

Assessment

- Standard 1: Use an observation checklist of skill cues for continuous jumping.

Learning Outcome

Gain greater consistency in performance of mature flight patterns and variations.
- Standard 1: Use mature flight patterns when leaping.

Movement Concepts

- Body awareness: intentional use of body parts in unison, opposition, and sequence for mature performance of traveling skills
- Relationship awareness: to equipment (over)

Teaching Style

Reproduction: practice; reciprocal for readers

Tasks

Task: Children leap over low obstacles, such as lines on the floor, swim noodles, or ropes placed on the floor or held by low cones. As students progress, they may do two or three consecutive leaps with running between leaps.

Environment: Students are spread out in general space all facing either north/south or east/west. Students take a short running approach and leap over the obstacles.

Practice: constant

Skill cues:

- Preparation: Run with forceful push-off from one foot and forward extension of free leg.
- Main action: Legs are fully extended, and arms are stretched out for balance. Fully extend legs during flight. Use forward trunk lean.
- Recovery: Land on ball of lead foot and bend knee slightly to absorb force. You can recover and step out of leap into standing position.

Feedback

- KPd: "You pushed off of one foot and landed on the other with your legs almost getting straight while you were in the air—great job!"
- KPp: "You need to run a little faster and push off of the ground with more force."

Assessment

- Standard 1: Use an observation checklist of skill cues. If the children can read, you can use a reciprocal task card (see figure 15.13).

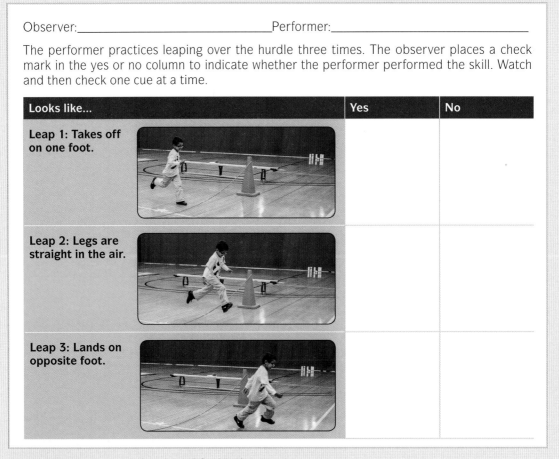

Observer:_____Performer:_____

The performer practices leaping over the hurdle three times. The observer places a check mark in the yes or no column to indicate whether the performer performed the skill. Watch and then check one cue at a time.

Looks like...		Yes	No
Leap 1: Takes off on one foot.			
Leap 2: Legs are straight in the air.			
Leap 3: Lands on opposite foot.			

Figure 15.13 Reciprocal task card for leaping.

Learning Outcome

Gain greater consistency in performance of mature flight patterns and variations.

- Standards 1 and 2: Combine changing shape with jumping.

Movement Concepts

- Body awareness: intentional use of body parts in unison, opposition, and sequence for mature performance of traveling skills
- Space awareness: medium and high levels
- Effort awareness: to a rhythm
- Relationship awareness: mirroring or matching a partner; off of equipment

Teaching Style

Reproduction: practice

Tasks

Task: Model the following jumps and emphasize that a shape should be made quickly at the height of the jump, then quickly released in order to prepare for landing. Children practice combining shapes with jumps off panel mats and trapezoids onto mats.

- Pencil
- Tuck
- Seat kicker
- Star

Enrichment: Have students do more difficult shape jumps, such as the following:

- Off trapezoid shapes
- Mirroring or matching a partner
- Off a vaulting board
- Four pencil jumps in a row on a panel mat, to a drumbeat
- Different types of jumps in sequence, to a drumbeat

Environment: Panel mats can be used for performing jumps on the floor; foam trapezoid shapes can be used to jump off of with 4-inch (10-centimeter) landing mats. Children are organized into small groups (three or four per mat). When mirroring a partner and jumping off of low foam trapezoid shapes, the shapes should be at least 5 feet (1.5 meters) apart so that performers can land safely on a panel mat or landing mat without colliding.

Practice: variable

Skill cues:

Pencil

- Preparation: Use takeoff crouch and appropriate arm position for height and distance of jump (from both feet to both feet or from one foot to both feet). Swing arms back.
- Main action: Fully extend arms and legs to form straight, narrow shape.
- Recovery: Land on balls of feet with appropriate crouch to absorb force of jump. Reach arms out in front for balance.

Tuck

- Preparation: Use takeoff crouch and appropriate arm position for height and distance of jump (from both feet to both feet or from one foot to both feet). Swing arms back.
- Main action: Bend knees and tuck up to chest while extending arms overhead. The shape is made quickly at height of jump, then quickly released to prepare for landing.
- Recovery: Land on balls of feet with appropriate crouch to absorb force of jump. Reach arms out in front for balance.

Seat Kicker

- Preparation: Use takeoff crouch and appropriate arm position for height and distance of jump (from both feet to both feet or from one foot to both feet). Swing arms back.
- Main action: Extend arms overhead. Bend knees and touch buttocks with heels. Make shape quickly at height of jump, then quickly release it to prepare for landing.
- Recovery: Land on balls of feet with appropriate crouch to absorb force of jump. Reach arms out in front for balance.

Star Jump

- Preparation: Bend knees on takeoff; keep arms down at sides.
- Main action: Push off and extend legs out into space in straddle or V. Swing arms up along sides in vertical plane to extend overhead (so that body makes X shape). Make shape quickly at height of jump, then quickly release it to prepare for landing.
- Recovery: Arms come down to sides. Feet come together for landing on both feet with bent knees.

Feedback

- KPd: "You stretched your body out long and narrow during your pencil jump—great job!"
- KPp: "Swing your arms back and up into the air with more energy or force to obtain more height on your pencil jump."
- KPd: "You quickly brought your legs together to land safely on the star jump."

Assessment

- Standards 1 and 2: Use an observation checklist of skill cues (figure 15.14).

When the student is able to perform the skill, place the symbol for the type of jump in the appropriate column, e.g., when a student can make the tuck jump shape quickly and clearly place an O in the first column, and when the student can release the shape quickly and land safely, place an O in the second column.

Jump Key

Tuck = O

Seat kicker = V

Star jump = X

Pencil jump = I

Student	Makes shape quickly and clearly.	Releases shape quickly and lands safely on two feet with bent knees.

Figure 15.14 Observation checklist of skill cues for making shapes.

Learning Outcome

Gain greater consistency in performance of mature flight patterns and variations.

- Standard 1: Add traveling and flight skills.

Movement Concepts

- Body awareness: intentional use of body parts in unison, opposition, and sequence for mature performance of traveling skills; formation of body shapes
- Space awareness: low, medium, high levels
- Relationship awareness: around, over, in and out, and off of equipment

Teaching Style

Reproduction: practice

Tasks

Task: Students move through an obstacle course: run and leap over a swim noodle; jump in and out of hoops placed on the floor; jump side to side over a rope placed on the floor; run and jump off of a vaulting board and land on a panel mat; and jump off of a low- or medium-level trapezoid foam shape. Students try to keep moving from one obstacle to the next throughout the course.

Environment: multiple obstacle courses with small groups of students at each course

Practice: variable

Skill cues:

Running to Take Off From Vaulting Board

- Approach vaulting board in a run.
- Take off on one foot and bring feet together low in air.
- Punch off of board with balls of feet.

Moving Through the Course

- Use landing position for one movement as starting position for next movement.

Feedback

- KPd: "You landed with bent knees on all of your jumps as you performed the obstacle course."
- KPd: "You jumped smoothly from one foot to both feet off of the incline mat—excellent job!"
- KPp: "Try to push off of your back foot with more force during your leap. This will help you straighten your back leg."

Assessment

Standard 1: Use an observation checklist of skill cues.

 Visit the web resource for learning activities, video clips, and review questions.

K-2 Learning Experiences for Stability Skills

Key Concepts

- Designing stability-skill learning experiences for K-2 children based on stages of development and levels of motor skill learning

- Designing stability-skill learning experiences that align the following:
  - K-2 national physical education standards (SHAPE America, 2014)
  - Instructional practices
  - Assessment and feedback

This chapter provides progressive learning experiences for consistent movers in each **stability skill theme**. The themes engage children in both static and dynamic body-control activities. Skillful movement performance requires controlling the muscles in order to hold static balance positions, knowing where body parts are located during balance positions, distributing weight appropriately over the center of balance on the supporting body parts, and positioning nonsupporting body parts to help maintain balance. Skillful dynamic balance requires controlling the muscles in order to shift weight between limbs or along the spine, keeping the center of balance between or over the body parts receiving the weight, and positioning nonsupporting body parts to help maintain balance.

Practicing stability skills provides multiple benefits. It helps children develop core strength and endurance, move safely on uneven surfaces, roll safely to absorb momentum during a fall, and skillfully perform other fundamental skills and specialized skills. However, the most obvious extension of the stability skills learned in kindergarten through grade 2 is to support specialized skill performance in grades 3 through 5 in developmental gymnastics and dance.

STABILITY MOVEMENT SKILLS

The movement framework categories depicted in the Active Child diagram (figure 16.1) contain the stability skill categories (balance, rolling, and step-like actions) in the star and the movement concepts (body, space, effort, relationship) between the points of the star. The learning goal blueprint for stability skills presented in table 16.1 illustrates how stability actions and movement concepts can be combined to vary skills.

Each stability-skill learning experience can be used over the course of many lessons because children need multiple practice opportunities in order to become consistent; conversely, a given lesson might consist of multiple learning experiences. For each learning experience, the *task* represents a specific skill progression and the *environment* describes not only the setup of the gymnasium or movement area but also the scaling of equipment and conditions to fit the performers (see chapter 6). For each learning experience presented in this chapter, the description indicates the relevant national standard(s) and grade 2 outcome, as well as assessment options aligned with the standard(s) (see figure 14.3 in chapter 14).

Standards 1 and 2 are addressed in each of the stability learning outcomes because K-2 children are developmentally ready to achieve the mature stage of the fundamental movement skills and become knowledgeable about movement concepts. Standard 1 can be assessed through observation checklists of skill and safety cues, and an assessment rubric for each stability skill appears in appendix B. Standard 2 can be assessed by recording information about children's ability to use and identify movement concepts (body, space, effort, and relationship) and to identify skill cues through pictures, teacher demonstrations, or video clips. For children who can read, you can also use exit tickets or other age-appropriate assessment sheets that address correct skill cues.

Stability skills are closed skills performed in stable, unchanging environments. The emphasis is on constant practice to enable the consistent mover to gain mature form. A shift to variable practice occurs as the consistent mover learns skill variations (i.e., from body, space, effort, and relationship awareness). In short, constant practice is used to help children achieve mature form, and variable practice is used for learning skill variations.

Because the instruction focuses on knowledge and performance of skill cues, you should provide knowledge of performance descriptive feedback (KPd) about how the student performed and knowledge of performance prescriptive feedback (KPp) about what changes should be made. Examples of congruent feedback and assessments are provided for a sampling of the learning experiences presented in this chapter.

Practicing stability skills is directly related to the health-related fitness components of muscular strength and muscular endurance. Therefore, you address standard 3 for physical education (achieving and maintaining health-enhancing levels of activity and fitness) when you purposefully engage and assess your students' ability to increase the intensity of their movements, either iso-metrically (holding the body in a weight-bearing position for greater duration) or isotonically (performing more repetitions of weight-bearing movements).

Personal and social responsibility are expected throughout the learning experiences and are articulated in the essential content of K-2 standard 4: recognizing classroom rules, procedures, and safety practices; tackling challenges; and building a foundation for successful interpersonal communication during group activity. You address standard 4 for physical education when you purposefully engage and assess students' ability to work toward meeting a challenge (e.g., seal-walking farther than last time) and working cooperatively with others (e.g., working in a trio to balance on a total of four body parts). You can record information about students' adherence to personal and social responsibility on observation checklists. In addition, children can demonstrate their knowledge of responsibility behaviors through age-appropriate assessment sheets.

In standard 5, children are asked to recognize the value of physical activity. In kindergarten through grade 2, children recognize which physical activities are enjoyable to them and which ones they feel most confident about performing. You can use exit tickets to assess students' feelings about the stability activities addressed in a given day's lesson and help them recognize that physical activity participation can bring enjoyment and provide challenge. Figure 16.2 presents sample exit tickets for assessing enjoyment and challenge; you can use information from the tickets to address students' needs and interests.

Figure 16.1   The Active Child: stability skills.

Table 16.1   Learning Goal Blueprint for Mature and Versatile Performance of Stability Skills

Content	Body	Space	Effort	Relationship
Static balances: upright, inverted	Intentionally uses body actions for mature performance. Balances by making different body shapes: round, straight, bent, wide, narrow, and twisted. Changes supporting and nonsupporting body parts to vary balance positions.	Balances on high, medium, and low levels. Uses near and far to extend the range of a balance.	Intentionally uses force to maintain balance.	Performs balances inside, on top of, underneath, next to, inside, outside, and through equipment. Performs nonsupport balances with a partner: in front of, next to, behind, over, and under and in the roles of mirroring and matching.
Transfer of weight: rolls, step-like actions	Intentionally uses body actions for mature performance. Curls, stretches, bends, twists, and turns body segments and parts during, into, and out of transference of weight skills. Changes supporting and nonsupporting body parts to vary transference of weight skills.	Changes level and varies direction and pathway of transference of weight skills.	Varies speed and force while performing transference of weight skills. Smoothly combines transference of weight skills.	Uses transference of weight skills to move over, into, out of, onto, and off of low equipment. With others, uses transference of weight skills to meet, part, and move next to and in roles of leading, following, and matching.

I like/dislike 😊 ☹ _____ [name of stability activity].

It is fun to do 😊 _____ [name of stability activity].

Today's Activities:

_____ [Name of activity]

_____ [Name of activity]

_____ [Name of activity]

Put a check mark by the activities that you need to work harder to perform.

Put an X by the activity that you performed the best.

Figure 16.2   Sample exit tickets for enjoyment (top) and for confidence and challenge (bottom).

STABILITY SKILLS: BALANCE

Use Table 16.2 as a resource for designing balance skill challenges. Examples are provided after the table.

Table 16.2   Progression for K-2 Consistent-Level Balance Skills

Balance	Equipment: low boxes, benches, foam shapes, ropes, hoops, tires
	Learning outcome: Gain greater consistency in performance of balances, variations, and combinations.
	• Balancing on different bases of support
	• Balance variations
	  • Body awareness: shapes
	  • Space awareness: levels
	  • Effort awareness: intentional use of time to hold balance
	  • Relationship to equipment: on, beside, inside of
	  • Relationship with others: nonsupport partner balances
	• Adding one balance to another
	• Adding locomotor and balancing skills

Learning Outcome

Gain greater consistency in performance of balances.
- Standard 1: Balance on different bases of support.
- Standard 2: Recognize that larger bases of support are more stable than smaller bases.

Movement Concepts

Body awareness: body parts, body-part combinations, and bases of different sizes

Teaching Styles

- Reproduction: practice style for practice with feedback
- Production: guided discovery for discovering that wide bases are steadier than small bases

Tasks

Task: Children balance on different bases. Present a series of instructional tasks to elicit the desired stability skill. Here are some examples of things to say:

- "To balance, you must keep your body still in a pose. To hold the pose, tighten your muscles and keep your center of balance (i.e., belly button) over or between your base of support (i.e., body part or parts holding you up)."
- "Try balancing on two feet, holding very still, and squeezing your muscles tight. Then try balancing on two feet and one hand, on your tummy, and on one foot."
- "Sometimes you need to use your "free" body parts to help you hold your balance still. Try balancing on one foot and using "free" body parts to help keep you steady."
- "Think of and try holding five more balances. What body parts did you use to hold you up? What 'free' body parts did you use to help you hold the balance?"
- "Use the body part balance card (figure 16.3) to try at least 10 more balances."

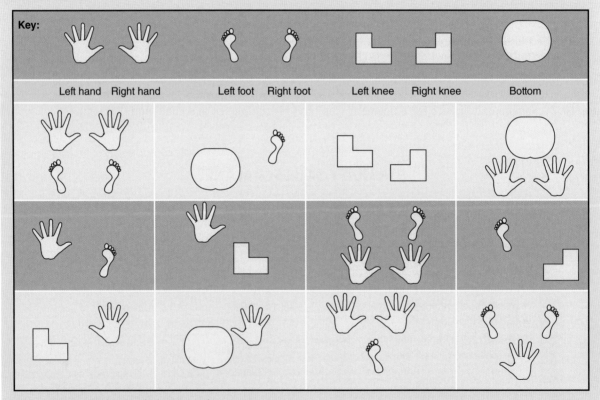

Figure 16.3 Body part balance card.

Adapted from Werner, Williams, and Hall 2012.

- "With a partner, take turns choosing a body part balance card, making a balance, and copying your partner's balance. Try using the same card and making your balance look different from your partner's. How did you use "free" body parts to make your balance different from your partner's?"

Environment: Use a single-station, single-task setup. Students work in personal space in the gym, listening and responding to your cues. Sets of body part balance cards are located under cones distributed throughout the gym; alternatively, a large version of each card is posted on the walls. Mats are distributed throughout the gym for use when needed.

Practice: constant practice to hold balance positions

Skill cues:

- Squeeze muscles tight.
- Keep center of balance over or between base of support.
- Use free body parts to help maintain balance.

Feedback

- KPd: "You are squeezing your muscles tight and your balance is steady."
- KPp: "Use your free body parts to help you hold your balance."
- KPd: "I like the way you are working together: watching and listening to each other and then trying your partner's balance."

Assessment

- Standard 1: Verify students' use of the self-checklist (see figure 16.4) by selecting a sample of balances to check.
- Standard 2: Use the "What holds you up?" assessment card (figure 16.5).

I can balance on different bases of support! Name _____		
Student check	Balance	Teacher check
	2 hands and 2 feet	
	1 foot	
	2 feet and 1 hand	
	Bottom	
	1 hand and 1 knee	
	Bottom and 1 hand	

Figure 16.4 Standard 1: self-assessment balance card.

What holds you up?
Draw a line from the word to the balance.

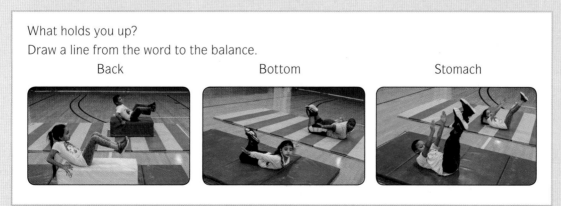

Back   Bottom   Stomach

Figure 16.5 Standard 2: balance assessment card.

Task: Children discover that large bases make more steady balances than small bases. Present a series of instructional tasks to elicit the desired stability skill. Here are some examples of things to say:

- "Perform the balances depicted on the task cards. See if you can hold each balance for a count of 5."
- "Your base of support is what holds you up. Choose and perform four balances, each of which has a different base of support."
- "Some bases of support are wide—they take up a lot of space. Choose and perform four balances that have a wide base of support."
- "Some bases of support are narrow—they take up a small amount of space. Choose and perform four balances that each have a narrow base of support."
- "Now go back and forth, trying a balance with a wide base and then a balance with a narrow base. Which base—wide or narrow—makes you feel steadier, as if it would be hard to fall over?"

Environment: Use a single-station, single-task setup. Students work in personal space in the gym, listening and responding to your cues. Task cards or posters along each of four walls show pictures of children balancing; blue cards or posters depict large bases of support, and red cards or posters depict small bases of support.

Practice: constant practice to hold balance positions

Skill cues:

- Large bases take up lots of space.
- Small bases take up small amounts of space.
- Larger bases make more stable balances than small bases.

Feedback

- KPd: "You have chosen small bases—nice work!"
- KPp: "Some of your choices are large and some are small. Look again at the ones that take up a small amount of space."

Assessment

Standard 2: Use the Bases of Support assessment (figure 16.6).

Name_____

Circle the children who have a *large* base of support.

Are *large* bases of support steadier than small bases? (Circle one.) Yes No

Figure 16.6 Bases of Support assessment

Learning Outcome

Gain greater consistency in performance of balances and variations.

- Standard 1: Balance in different shapes at different levels in relationship to equipment and others.
- Standard 2: Identify body shapes, levels, and relationships with equipment and others.
- Standard 4: Work independently with others in a partner environment. (SHAPE America, 2014, p. 18)

Movement Concepts

- Body awareness: different shapes
- Space awareness: different levels
- Effort awareness: intentional use of time to hold balances
- Relationship to equipment: on, beside, inside of
- Relationship with others: nonsupport partner balances

Teaching Styles

Reproduction: practice and reciprocal

Tasks

Task: Children practice identifying and balancing in different shapes.

- Show the children pictures of objects or symbols that are wide, narrow, round, or twisted and ask them to find at least five ways to make each shape with their bodies. Use word cues to engage children in performing different shape balances.
- Show the children illustrations (or pictures of class members making shape balances) and have them mimic and identify the shapes.

Environment: Use a single-station, single-task setup. Students work in personal space in the gym, listening and responding to your cues.

Practice: constant practice to hold balance positions

Skill cues:

- Squeeze muscles and keep center of balance over base.
- Wide shapes: Spread out arms and legs (cheerleader).
- Narrow shapes: Hold arms close to trunk and legs together (pencil).
- Curled shapes: Round and tuck body (ball).
- Twisted shapes: Rotate trunk or limbs (pretzel).

Task: Children practice identifying and balancing at different levels using different shape balances.

- Show the children pictures of balances at high, medium, and low levels and ask them to perform at least five different balances at each level. Use the cue of squeezing the muscles to hold balances.
- Inverted high balances include the following:
  - Shoulder stand
  - Modified headstand with four points of contact (head, two hands, one foot)
  - Three-point balance (two hands and one foot) with one leg extended high
  - Not included are headstands and handstands, which are developmentally appropriate after second grade.
- Students try to find out which shape balances can be made at each level.

- High, medium, and low cones are arranged in the middle of the gym. Students are partnered, and one partner in each pair is given balance cards each of which depicts a high, medium, or low balance. The partner with the cards chooses a balance to perform. The other partner must then place the cone that identifies the right height (low, medium, or high) of the balance to place next to the performer. Together, the partners name the shape of the balance. Students use equipment to balance at different levels in different shapes.

Environment:

- Single-station, single-task setup: Students work in personal space in the gym, listening and responding to your cues. Lines are marked on the walls at three heights, and groups of three different-height cones are spread out around the gym.
- Multiple-stations, single-task setup: Foam shapes, benches, and hoops of different heights on floor and balanced horizontally across two cones are grouped in stations for children to explore balancing at different levels and in different shapes.

Practice: constant practice to hold balance positions

Skill cues:

- Low balances: Position body below knee height.
- Medium balances: Position trunk between knee height and belly button.
- High balances: Position trunk and arms, or hips and legs, above height of belly button.
- Shoulder stand (Werner, 2004)
    - Put weight on shoulders and upper arms to elbows (no weight on head or neck); support hips by lower arms to hands.
    - Align hips, knees, and feet vertically over shoulder–elbow base.
- Modified headstand
    - Use triangle position for head and hands.
    - Support weight with head, hands, and foot.
    - Extend free leg high.

Assessment

Standards 1 and 2: As children practice, circulate among them and privately ask them to identify the shape and level of their balance; alternatively, designate a balance shape and level for the student to demonstrate (see figure 16.7).

Place a check mark in the column if the correct shape or level is performed.

Name	Wide	Narrow	Curled	Twisted	High	Medium	Low

Figure 16.7 Assessment card for balance shape and level

Task: Children practice balancing in relationship to (on, beside, inside of) equipment.

- Students balance on, beside, and inside of equipment as designated at each station. Before the activity, create cards showing one balance per card, then put the cards in a box for each station. Students choose a card from a box at each station and perform a balance in that shape in the appropriate relationship to the equipment (on, beside, or inside of). Students choose the piece of equipment and create balances in different shapes and levels.

Environment: Use a multiple-stations, single-task setup. Low boxes, benches, foam shapes, hoops and tires are grouped around the gym appropriately for each relationship theme. Balance cards are placed in three boxes, each of which is positioned at a station.

Practice: Constant practice to hold balance positions

Skill cues:

- *On* indicates balancing on top of equipment.
- *Beside* indicates balancing next to the equipment.
- *Inside* indicates balancing while surrounded by the piece of equipment.

Assessment

- Standard 1: Use an observation checklist of balances in appropriate relationship to the equipment.
- Standard 2: Use the assessment for relationship to equipment (figure 16.8).

Name _____

Place a circle to show where you would balance *on* the equipment, an arrow pointing to where you would balance *beside* the equipment, and an X to show where you would balance *inside* the equipment.

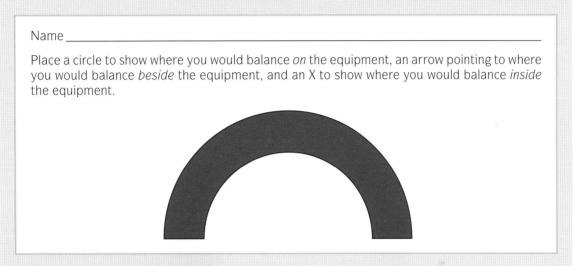

Figure 16.8   Assessment for relationship to equipment.

Task: Children practice balancing in relationship with others. Nonsupport partner balances are performed next to a partner—side to side, facing, back to back, front to back, and above and below.

- Students are given cards that each picture a wide, narrow, curled, or twisted shape balance. Students must choose a partner with a different shape balance and then perform their own balance next to the partner. Together, they hold their "partner balance" for three seconds. They then exchange cards and, on your signal, find a new partner with a different shape and repeat the activity. Alternatively, you can use cards that designate each of the different shapes (wide, narrow, curled, twisted) and have students design a balance representing the indicated shape.
- Students choose one of the balance symbols on the body part balance card (figure 16.3) and find a partner who has chosen a different symbol. The partners then perform their balances next to each other and, together, hold their "partner balance" for three seconds. They then try their balances while relating to each other in different ways: side to side, facing, back to back, and front to back. The partners then exchange symbols and, on your signal, find a new partner with a different symbol and repeat the activity.
- Assign one-third of students in the class to each level: high (raise both hands above head), medium (raise arms out to sides), or low (keep arms at sides). Students think of

and practice a balance to perform at their designated level. On a signal from you, each student places his or her arms in the position that indicates the assigned level and finds a partner with a different level. The partners then perform their balances beside each other. The partners remain together, changing the shape of their balances. On a signal from you, students place their arms in the position that depicts their partner's level, find a new partner at a different level, and repeat the balancing task.

Environment: Use a single-station, single-task setup. Students work with a partner in personal space in the gym to create balances. Provide enough balance shape cards and body part balance cards for each student.

Practice: Constant practice to hold balance positions

Skill cues:

- Nonsupport partner balances are performed next to a partner without touching.
- Body parts may be extended over, under, or through spaces or "holes" created by partner's body or particular parts of body.
- Listen and share ideas as you decide together how to create your "partner balance."

Feedback

- KPd: "You and your partner are close and not touching each other."
- KPp: "Remember to share ideas—you should each give a way to create the partner balance, try each way, and then decide together to practice one or both."

Assessment

Standard 4: Use a student self-assessment for working with a partner (figure 16.9).

When I make balances with my partner . . .	Yes	I need to work on this.
I listen to my partner's ideas.		
I watch my partner's balance ideas.		
I show my balance ideas.		
I work with my partner to use both of our balance ideas.		

Name: _____

Figure 16.9 Self-assessment for working with a partner.

Learning Outcome

Gain greater consistency in performance of balance variations and combinations.

- Standard 1: Add one balance to another.
- Standard 2: Use movement concepts of shape, level, and relationship to equipment and others for balance combinations.

Movement Concepts

- Body awareness: different shapes
- Space awareness: different levels
- Relationship to equipment: on, beside, inside of
- Relationship with others: nonsupport partner balances

Teaching Styles

- Production: Divergent—Students design many different ways to add one balance to another.
- Reproduction: Practice—Students practice specific balance combinations that they or others have designed.

Tasks

Task: Children add one balance to another by holding each balance for a count of three before moving into a different balance. Add one balance to another using the following elements:

- Different bases of support
- The same shape or different shapes
- The same level or different levels
- Different mixes of shape and level
- Different relationships to equipment—on, beside, inside
- Different nonsupport partner balances—side to side, facing, back to back, front to back, above, and below

Environment: Students work in personal space in the gym, listening and responding to your cues or using task cards to choose or design different ways to add balances. The format may vary depending on how tasks and students are grouped (i.e., single station, multiple tasks; multiple stations, single task; multiple stations, multiple tasks).

Equipment: low boxes, benches, foam shapes, ropes, hoops, tires

Practice: constant practice to hold balance positions, variable practice when trying different balance ideas

Skill cues:

- Hold balance for count of three.
  - Keep center of balance over base of support.
  - Squeeze muscles tight.
- Add balances.
  - Move to new balance from position of former balance.
  - Keep core muscles tight.

Assessment

Standard 1: Use an observation checklist of skill cues for adding balances (figure 16.10).

Place a check mark in the box if performed.

Name	Held balances for a count of three.	Performed one new balance from the position of the former balance.

Figure 16.10   Observation checklist for adding balances.

Learning Outcome

Gain greater consistency in performance of balance variations and combinations.

- Standard 1: Transfer weight from feet to different body parts or bases of support for balances or travel (SHAPE America, 2014, p. 4).
- Standard 2: Combine shapes, levels, directions, and pathways into stability sequences (SHAPE America, 2014).

Movement Concepts

- Body awareness: different shapes and weight transfer to different body parts
- Space awareness: different levels, directions, and pathways
- Relationship to equipment: on, beside, inside of, around, and in and out

Teaching Style

Reproduction: practice style with feedback about balance principles

Tasks

Task: Children practice adding locomotor skills and balance skills. For safety, instruct children by saying, "When starting with a balance, move to an upright position and begin the locomotor skill. When starting with a locomotor skill, stop and then move into and hold the balance." Prepare cards with words and illustrations of locomotor skills, balance skills, and movement concept ideas and have children create a variety of ways to add skills together. A sample card is shown in figure 16.11. Here are some instructions that could be derived from the sample card:

- Combine balancing in a curled shape at a medium level with galloping forward.
- Combine skipping on a curved pathway with balancing on two feet in a wide shape.
- Combine walking on the equipment and balancing on one foot and one hand.

Environment: Use a single-station, single-task setup. Students work in personal space in the gym by listening, observing, and responding to your cues. They can work alone, with a partner, or in a small group.

Equipment: low boxes, benches, foam shapes, ropes, hoops, tires

Practice: constant practice to hold balance positions

Skill cues:

- Hold balance for count of three.
  - Keep center of balance over base of support.
  - Squeeze muscles tight.
- Add skills.
  - Balance to locomotor: Perform balance, move to upright position, and begin locomotor skill.
  - Locomotor to balance: Perform locomotor skill, stop, and move into and hold balance.
  - Keep core muscles tight.

Assessment

Standards 1 and 2: Use an observation checklist of skill cues for combining balances and locomotor skills and for correct responses to movement concept cues (body shapes, levels, directions, pathways, etc.).

Balance	Concept		Locomotor	Concept
2 feet	Wide shape		Walking	Pathways
1 foot	Narrow shape		Galloping	Directions
2 feet and 2 hands	Curled shape	**COMBINE WITH**	Sliding	Rhythms
Bottom and 1 foot	Twisted shape		Skipping	On equipment
1 foot and 1 hand	Low level		Hopping	In or out of equipment
	Medium level			Around equipment
	High level			

Figure 16.11   Sample card for adding locomotor and balancing skills.

STABILITY SKILLS: ROLLING

Use Table 16.3 as a resource for designing transference of weight–rolling skill challenges. Examples are provided below the table.

Table 16.3   Progression for K-2 Consistent-Level Transfer of Weight (Rolling Skills)

Rolling	Equipment: low boxes, benches, foam shapes, ropes, hoops, tires Learning outcome: Gain greater consistency in performance of mature rolling actions, variations, and combinations. Rolling • Sideward (pencil, egg) • Forward • Backward Adding rolls and balances Traveling into and out of rolls Adding jumps and rolls Adding one roll to another

For safety, children should participate in rolling activities for only short periods of time or with adequate recovery after a maximum of three attempts to prevent dizziness. Rolling can be done at one station among other stability or locomotor themes. Inclined mats and benches should be available for children who need help with raising the hips above the head.

Learning Outcome

Gain greater consistency in performance of mature rolling actions, variations, and combinations.

- Standard 1: Roll in different directions with either a narrow or curled body shape (SHAPE America, 2014, p. 4).
- Standard 2: Recognize skill cues for rolls.

Movement Concepts

- Body awareness: shapes
- Space awareness: direction

Teaching Style

Reproduction: practice style with feedback about rolling cues

Tasks

Task: Children perform sideward, forward, and backward rolls. They start by rolling down inclines (i.e., forward rolls from a bench) and progress to rolling on mats.

Environment: inclined mats, low benches

Practice: Use constant practice of each roll with few repetitions. Vary practice across types of rolls and other skills.

Skill cues:

- Sideward pencil roll: From stretched position with arms overhead, initiate sideward roll with hips, rolling over from back to stomach to back.
- Sideward egg roll: Roll sideways from tucked position with chin tucked and knees hugged to chest by arms.
- Forward roll:
  - From a bench, kneel on one shin and position other foot on bench with knee bent. Place hands on floor, tuck chin, raise hips, round back, and push off of bench to roll forward along rounded spine.
  - Preparation: Crouch with hands flat on mat. Extend knees to raise hips. Weight moves forward onto hands as head is tucked (chin to chest).
  - Action: Bend elbows and push off of feet to take weight onto upper back. Tuck knees to chest and take weight along rounded spine.
  - Recovery: Reach forward with arms as weight is transferred to feet, then stand.
- Backward roll:
  - Preparation: Crouch with back rounded, chin tucked to chest, and hands positioned by ears with fingers spread out (thumbs pointed toward ears—"elephant ears").
  - Action: Stay tucked, overbalance to take weight onto lower spine, and roll along rounded back. As hands contact mat, forcefully push up and extend hips.
  - Recovery: Land on both feet simultaneously, push off of floor with hands, and extend legs to standing position.

Pencil roll.

Egg roll.

Forward roll: preparation *(a)*, action *(b, c, d)*, recovery *(e)*.

Backward roll.

Feedback

- KPd: "You raised your hips high to get a good start."
- KPd: "Your back was flat."
- KPp: "You opened your tuck too soon. Push off of your feet to get momentum and keep your knees to your chest to remain rounded."

Assessment

- Standard 1: Use an observation checklist of skill cues.
- Standard 2: Provide images of children with hips in different positions in a forward roll. Ask students to circle the picture of the child whose hips are in a good position for performing a smooth forward roll.

Learning Outcome

Gain greater consistency in performance of rolling actions, variations, and combinations.

- Standard 1: Transfer weight to add rolls and balances.

Movement Concepts

- Body awareness: shapes, body part combinations
- Space awareness: direction, level

Teaching Style

Reproduction: practice style with feedback about skill cues

Tasks

Task: Children add rolls and balances. For safety, instruct children by saying, "When adding a roll to a balance, start by holding the balance and then moving the body to a safe position from which to roll" and "When adding a balance after a roll, come to a stop before moving into the balance position." You can designate or model the rolls and balances to be added or use cards with illustrations of rolls and balances for students to add together. For example, if you gave the instruction "Perform forward rolls from different balances," some of the following combinations might result:

- From a balance on two feet with the body piked, reach forward, place the hands on the mat, and roll forward, ending in crouch.
- From a balance on two feet with the legs straddled and the body piked, reach forward, place the hands on the mat, and roll forward, ending in crouch.
- From a balance on one foot, step forward, bring the feet together, and perform a forward roll, ending in crouch.
- Starting from a balance, roll and end in a balance.

Environment: multiple-station, single-task set up with mats, inclined mats, and low benches

Practice: Use constant practice of combinations with few repetitions. Vary practice among types of combinations and other skills.

Skill cues:

- Balance to roll: Hold balance, then move body to safe position from which to roll.
- Roll to balance: Come to stop after roll before moving into balance position.

Assessment

Standard 1: Use an observation checklist of skill cues.

Learning Outcome

Gain greater consistency in performance of rolling actions, variations, and combinations.

- Standard 1: Transfer weight to add locomotor skills and rolls.
- Standard 4: Work independently with others in a partner environment (SHAPE America, 2014, p. 18).

Movement Concepts

- Body awareness: body part combinations
- Space awareness: direction, level
- Relationship to others: beside, front to back

Teaching Style

Reproduction: practice style with feedback about skill cues

Tasks

Task: Children add locomotor and rolling skills. For safety, instruct children by saying, "Place feet together after a locomotor skill to begin a roll" and "Step out of a roll to begin a locomotor skill." Some examples of performing locomotor skills at the end of rolls include the following:

- Step out of a forward roll and walk, gallop, or skip forward.
- Step out of a backward roll and walk, gallop, or skip forward.
- Perform locomotor skills at the beginning of rolls: Walk, gallop, or skip forward and lower the body into a forward roll.
- Perform locomotor and rolling skills in relationship to partners.
- Perform next to a partner (matching).
- Perform at the same time, starting face to face or back to back and moving away from the partner.

Environment: Use a single-station, single-task setup or a multiple-station, single-task setup. Students work in personal space, either responding to your cues or completing tasks on cards.

Equipment: mats, incline mats, low benches, trapezoids

Skill cues:

- Place feet together after a locomotor skill to begin a roll.
- Step out of a roll to begin a locomotor skill.
- With a partner:
  - Choose a starting signal.
  - Work with partner to adjust to each other's stride lengths and speed of travel.
  - Choose an ending and end at the same time.

Practice: Use constant practice of combinations with few repetitions. Vary practice among types of combinations and other skills.

Feedback

KPp: "Try to end your forward roll by stepping from one foot to the other so you can begin walking right away."

Assessment

- Standard 1: Use an observation checklist of skill cues for adding locomotor and rolling skills.
- Standard 4: Use an observation checklist of partner cooperation (figure 16.12).

	Yes	We need to work on this.
We started at the same time. Our starting signal was _____.		
We moved at the same pace.		
We ended together. Our ending position was _____.		

Partner 1: _____ Partner 2: _____
Answer the following questions about your partner sequence.

Figure 16.12 Checklist for partner cooperation.

Learning Outcome

Gain greater consistency in performance of rolling actions, variations, and combinations.

- Standard 1: Transfer weight to add jumps and rolls.
- Standard 2: Use movement concepts of direction, level, and relationship (to partner and equipment) with rolls.

Movement Concepts

- Body awareness: body part combinations
- Space awareness: direction, level
- Relationship to equipment: off of
- Relationship to partner: beside

Teaching Style

Reproduction: practice style with feedback about skill cues

Tasks

Task: Children add jumping and rolling.

Roll and Jump

- Perform a forward roll into a pencil, tuck, or star jump.
- Perform a backward roll to a pencil jump.

Jump, Land, and Roll

- Jump off of a low piece of equipment into a *yielding* landing and transfer weight into a forward roll from the crouch position.
- Walk forward, jump from one foot to both feet, land in a crouch, and transfer weight into a forward or backward roll.

Environment: Use a single-station, single-task setup or a multiple-station, single-task setup. Students work in personal space, either responding to your cues or completing tasks on cards.

Equipment: mats, incline mats, low benches, trapezoids

Practice: Use constant practice of combinations with few repetitions. Vary practice among types of combinations and other skills.

Skill cues:

- Roll and jump: Recover to two feet from roll, push off of both feet, and swing arms up to perform desired jump.
- Jump and roll: Recover to two feet from jump, then crouch and roll.

Feedback

KPp: "Make the crouch from your roll serve as the explosion position of your jump."

Assessments

Standard 1: Use an observation checklist of skill cues for adding jumps and rolls.

Learning Outcome

Gain greater consistency in performance of rolling actions, variations, and combinations.

- Standard 1: Perform consecutive rolls.

Movement Concepts

- Body awareness: body shape
- Space awareness: direction
- Relationship to a partner: beside

Teaching Style

Reproduction: practice style with feedback about skill cues

Tasks

Task: Children perform two forward rolls consecutively.

- Tuck to tuck
- Straddle to tuck
- Tuck to stand and stretch to tuck

Environment: Use a single-station, single-task setup or a multiple-station, single-task setup. Students work in personal space, either responding to your cues or completing tasks on cards.

Equipment: mats, incline mats, low benches, trapezoids

Practice: Use constant practice of combinations with few repetitions. Vary practice among types of combinations and other skills.

Skill cues: Start second roll from balanced position on two feet.

Feedback

KPp: "Remember to raise your hips as you come out of the first roll and go into the second roll."

Assessment

Standard 1: Use an observation checklist for smooth combinations of rolling skills.

STABILITY SKILLS: STEP-LIKE ACTIONS

Use Table 16.4 as a resource for designing transference of weight – step-like action skill challenges. Examples are provided below the table.

Table 16.4 Progression for K-2 Consistent-Level Transfer of Weight (Step-Like Action Skills)

Step-like actions	Equipment: low boxes, benches, foam shapes, ropes, hoops, tires Learning outcome: Gain greater consistency in performance of step-like actions and variations. **Step-Like Actions From Feet to Momentary Weight on Hands** • Animal walks and variations (e.g., 3-legged dog, bunny, mule kick) • Wheels and variations • Vaults and variations • Step-like action variations • Body awareness: shapes, body part relationships • Space: levels, directions • Effort: use of force to propel lower body upward • Relationship to equipment: onto, off of, over

The learning outcomes in step-like actions all help develop upper-body strength. Specifically, weight is transferred momentarily from the feet and hands to the arms, which strengthens the muscles in the back, trunk, and arms. Learning to perform the step-like movements is the goal of national physical education standard 1, and engaging in several repetitions in order to develop strength is the goal of standard 3. Assessments that address each goal appear throughout the tasks.

Learning Outcome

Gain greater consistency in the performance of step-like actions and variations.

- Standard 1: Transfer weight from the feet to different body parts and bases of support for travel (SHAPE America, 2014, p. 4)
- Standard 3: Use own body as resistance for developing strength (SHAPE America, 2014, p. 16).

Movement Concepts

- Body awareness: body part combinations
- Space awareness: level, pathway, distance

Teaching Styles

Reproduction: practice style with feedback about skill cues

Tasks

Task: Children perform the 3-legged dog walk, the bunny jump, and the mule kick to experience transferring weight momentarily from the feet and hands to only the hands and bringing the feet back to the starting position. In all skills, the emphasis is on moving the shoulders over the hands, keeping the arms *straight*, and transferring weight to the hands.

- Perform the 3-legged dog walk by raising one leg in the air from a starting position on two feet and two hands. Step forward on the hands and hop on the foot to travel as follows:
  - For short to longer distances
  - Along straight and curved pathways
  - Along a bench or low beam

- Perform the bunny jump by starting from a crouch on two feet, reaching forward to place the hands on the mat, and jumping forward with the feet toward the hands. Continue the action as follows:
  - For short to longer distances
  - From poly spot to poly spot
  - Along straight and curved pathways
  - Along a low bench or beam
- Perform the mule kick by starting from a position on all fours with the hips raised, shifting the shoulders directly over the hands, keeping the arms straight as one leg swings up, then pushing off of the floor with the remaining foot to raise both feet above the hips with the knees bent. Bring the legs down together and land on both feet. Alternatively, first lowering the swing leg and then lowering the push-off leg, thus landing on one foot at a time so that both end up on the ground together.

Mule kick.

Environment: Use a single-station, single-task setup or a multiple-station, single-task setup. Students work in personal space, either responding to your cues or completing tasks on cards.

Equipment: mats, poly spots, hoops, ropes, floor tape

Practice: Use constant practice of skills, increasing the number of repetitions as strength develops. Vary practice among types of skills.

Skill cues:

3-legged Dog Walk (Continuous Action)

- Raise one leg high.
- Hand-step, hand-step, hop; repeat.

Bunny Jump (Continuous Action)

- Crouch.
- Put weight on hands.
- Jump toward hands.

Mule Kick

- From a crouch, raise hips.
- Position shoulders over hands.
- Swing one leg up.
- Push off and raise second leg.
- Land on both feet or on one foot and then other foot (swing foot comes down first).

Feedback

KPp: "Keep your elbows locked to make a solid base for taking weight."

Assessment

Standard 1: Use an observation checklist of skill cues for each animal walk (figure 16.13).

Standard 3: Keep records of traveling for longer periods of time, longer distances, or more repetitions.

Name _____

Make a check mark to indicate your strength. Keep track of changes each time we work at the animal walk stations.

I can perform the 3-legged dog walk without stopping all around the pathway...	_____ 1 time _____ 2 times _____ 3 times
I can perform the bunny jump without stopping to the...	_____ 1st cone _____ 2nd cone _____ 3rd cone
I can perform the mule kick...	_____ 3 times _____ 7 times _____ 10 times

---

Figure 16.13   Strength improvement self-assessment.

Learning Outcome

Gain greater consistency in the performance of step-like actions and variations.

- Standard 1: Transfer weight from feet to hands to feet by wheeling.
- Standard 3: Use own body as resistance for developing strength (SHAPE America, 2014, p. 16).

Movement Concepts

- Body awareness: body part combinations
- Space awareness: level
- Relationship to equipment: over, onto, off of

Teaching Style

Reproduction: practice style with feedback about skill cues

Tasks

Task: Children perform wheel-like actions over low boxes, benches, and beams. For safety, instruct children by saying, "Start standing parallel to the equipment (e.g., bench). Place the hands on the bench, raise the hips, and cross over the bench by swinging the inside leg up and pushing off of the outside leg. Land on the first leg over, then the second." The progression is as follows:

- Place the hands on the bench and step over the bench.
- Place the hands on the bench and push off of the ground to get the hips high with the knees bent.
- Place the hands on the bench and push off of the ground to kick the legs higher than the hips.

- Place one hand and then the other on the bench, pushing off of the ground to kick the legs higher than the hips.

Wheeling over a foam shape.

Environment: Use a single-station, single-task setup or a multiple-station, single-task setup. Students work in personal space, either responding to your cues or completing tasks on cards.

Equipment: mats, low boxes, benches, beams, ropes

Skill cues:

- Put weight on hands on bench with shoulders over hands and arms *straight*.
- Swing inside leg up.
- Push off and raise second leg.
- Land on first leg over, then second leg.

Task: Children perform wheel actions over low ropes. For safety, instruct children by saying, "Stand parallel to the rope. Place the hands on the floor on the opposite side of the rope, raise the hips, and cross over the rope by swinging the inside leg up and pushing off of the outside leg. Land on the first leg over, then the second." The progression is as follows:

- Place the hands on the floor and push off of the ground to get the hips high with the knees bent.
- Place the hands on the floor and push off of the ground to kick the legs higher than the hips.
- Place one hand and then the other on the floor and push off of the ground to kick the legs higher than the hips. Order of limbs over the rope is hand, hand, foot, foot: *wheeling*.
- Wheel over a slanted rope, going over the highest spot possible. Start by facing the low part of the rope so that the legs must go over the higher part of the rope.

Environment: Use a single-station, single-task setup or a multiple-station, single-task setup. Students work in personal space, either responding to your cues or completing tasks on cards.

Equipment: mats, low boxes, benches, beams, ropes (suspended between cones or standards or held by two students)

Practice: Use constant practice of skills, increasing the number of repetitions as strength develops. Vary practice among types of skills.

Skill cues:

- Start in standing position, facing rope with arms raised above head and one foot in front of the other.
- As weight is taken on first hand, swing back leg up.
- As weight is taken on second hand, push off of front leg.
- As weight comes off of first hand, swing leg lands.
- Push off of second hand, raise trunk, and step down on second leg.

Feedback

- KPp: "Keep your elbows *locked* to make a solid base for taking weight."
- KPd: "Good strong swing up and push-off to get your legs high."

Assessments

Standards 1 and 3: Use an observation checklist of skill cues for wheeling (gaining more height indicates an increase in strength). An example is shown in figure 16.14.

Place a check mark or date in a box to indicate progress.

Name	Over box, bench, or beam		Over rope		
	Hips high, knees bent	Legs higher than hips	Hips high, knees bent	Legs higher than hips	Legs higher than hips; one hand, then other

Figure 16.14 Observation checklist skill cues for wheeling.

Learning Outcome

Gain greater consistency in the performance of step-like actions and variations.

- Standard 1: Transfer weight from feet to hands to feet to vault.

Movement Concepts

- Body awareness: body part combinations
- Space awareness: level
- Effort awareness: creating force for takeoff
- Relationship to equipment: onto, off of, over

Teaching Styles

Reproduction: practice style with feedback about skill cues

Tasks

Task: Children perform a tuck front vault over a knee-high bench, box, or beam. For safety, instruct children by saying, "Start in a standing position with your side to the equipment. Place the hands on the bench, raise the hips, and cross over the bench by jumping off of two feet. Tuck the body and land on the other side of the bench on two feet." The progression is as follows:

- Place the hands on the bench, jump to land with two feet on the bench, keep hands on the bench, and jump off to land on two feet.
- Place the hands on the bench and jump off with two feet; tuck the body and land on the other side of the bench on two feet.
- Place the hands on the beam at one end of the beam. Jump back and forth over the beam while moving toward the other end.

Environment: Use a multiple-station, single-task setup with task cards at each station. Equipment includes mats, knee-high benches and boxes, and hip-high sets of boxes.

Skill cues:

- Put weight on hands on bench with shoulders over hands and arms *straight*.
- Take off with two feet.
- Stay tucked.
- Land on two feet on floor or mat on the other side of the bench.

Task: Children perform a pike front vault over a hip-high set of boxes from a vaulting board. To get the feel of taking off from the vaulting board, students can stand on the vaulting board facing the box, place their hands sideways on the box, and jump up and down repeatedly. Some students may need to use two or more jumps to get the hips high enough to perform the progression. The progression is as follows:

- Stand on the vaulting board facing the box and place the hands sideways on the box. Jump off with two feet and land on the box in a crouch. Jump down onto two feet to land with the side to the box.
- Stand on the vaulting board and place the hands sideways on the box. Jump off with two feet and go over the box in tuck position. Land on two feet with the side to the box.
- Stand on the vaulting board and place the hands sideways on the box. Jump off with two feet and go over the box in pike position. Land on two feet with the side to the box.

Skill cues:

- Put weight on hands on bench with shoulders over hands and arms *straight*.
- Take off with two feet.
- Assume pike position by raising hips and extending legs down.
- Land on two feet on floor or mat on the other side of the bench

Task: Children perform a squat onto a knee-high bench or box. For safety, instruct children by saying, "Start by facing the equipment. Place both hands on the bench shoulder-width apart. Keep the arms straight and jump off with two feet, raising hips and landing with both feet between the arms in a tuck position. Raise the arms and jump forward off of the bench to land on the floor on two feet."

Skill cues:

- Put weight on hands on bench with shoulders over hands and arms *straight*.
- Take off with both feet.
- Tuck knees to chest and land with feet between arms.
- Jump off of bench to land with both feet on floor.

Squat onto bench.

Task: Children perform a straddle onto a knee-high bench or box. For safety, instruct children by saying, "Start by facing the equipment. Place both hands on the bench shoulder-width apart. Keep the arms straight and jump off with both feet, raising the hips, spreading the legs, and landing with the feet outside of the arms in a straddle position. Raise the arms and jump forward off of the bench, bringing the legs together in the air to land on the floor on both feet."

Skill cues:

- Put weight on hands on bench with shoulders over hands and arms *straight*.
- Take off with both feet.
- Straddle legs and land with feet outside arms.
- Jump off of bench and bring legs together.
- Land with both feet on floor.

Straddle onto bench.

Practice: Use constant practice of skills, increasing the number of repetitions as strength develops. Vary practice among types of skills.

Feedback

KPp: "Jump up from the vaulting board to raise your hips high enough to get your legs in the desired position—squat or straddle."

Assessment

Standard 1: Use an observation checklist of skill cues (see figure 16.15).

Place a check mark or date in a box to indicate progress.

| Name | OVER BOXES | | | | ONTO AND OFF OF BOXES | | | |
| | Side squat | | Pike front | | Squat | | Straddle | |
	Arms straight	Tuck over box	Arms straight	Pike over box	Arms straight	Tuck onto box	Arms straight	Straddle onto box

Figure 16.15 Assessment checklist for vaulting

  Visit the web resource for learning activities, video clips, and review questions.

K-2 Learning Experiences for Manipulative Skills

Key Concepts

- Designing manipulative-skill learning experiences for K-2 children based on stages of development and levels of motor skill learning
- Designing manipulative-skill learning experiences that align the following:
  - K-2 national physical education standards (SHAPE America, 2014)
  - Instructional practices
  - Assessment and feedback

This chapter provides progressive learning experiences for consistent movers in each manipulative skill theme. Each learning experience can be used over the course of many lessons because children need multiple practice opportunities in order to become consistent; conversely, a given lesson can consist of multiple learning experiences. For each learning experience, the *task* represents a specific skill progression and the *environment* describes not only the setup of the gymnasium or movement area but also the scaling of equipment and conditions to fit the performers (see chapter 6).

MANIPULATIVE SKILLS

The movement framework categories depicted in the Active Child diagram (figure 17.1) include the manipulative skill categories (throwing, catching, rolling, kicking, bouncing, and striking) in the trunk of the child and the movement concepts (body, space, effort, relationship) in the limbs. The learning goal blueprint for manipulative skills presented in table 17.1 illustrates how manipulative actions and movement concepts can be combined to vary skills.

For each learning experience presented in this chapter, the description includes the relevant national standard(s) and grade 2 outcome, as well as assessment options aligned with the standard(s) (see figure 14.3 in chapter 14).

Standards 1 and 2 are addressed in each of the manipulative learning outcomes because K-2 children are developmentally ready to achieve the mature stage of the fundamental movement skills and become knowledgeable about movement concepts. Standard 1 can be assessed through observation checklists of skill and safety cues, and an assessment rubric for each manipulative skill appears in appendix B. Standard 2 can be assessed by recording information about children's ability to use and identify movement concepts (body, space, effort, and relationship) and to identify skill cues through pictures, teacher demonstrations, or video clips. For children who can read, you can also use exit tickets or other age-appropriate assessment sheets that address correct skills cues.

Manipulative skills are usually performed in changing environments. However, the consistent mover needs a stable environment in order to attain the mature form of the skill and a predictable environment for learning skill variations (i.e., from body, space, effort, and relationship awareness). Therefore, constant practice is used to help children achieve mature form, and blocked practice is used for learning skill variations.

Because the instruction focuses on knowledge and performance of skill cues, you should provide knowledge of performance descriptive feedback (KPd) about how the student performed and knowledge of performance prescriptive feedback (KPp) about what changes should be made. Ex-

amples of congruent feedback and assessments are provided for a sampling of the learning experiences presented in this chapter.

Personal and social responsibility are expected throughout the learning experiences and are articulated in the essential content of K-2 standard 4: recognizing classroom rules, procedures, and safety practices; tackling challenges; and building a foundation for successful interpersonal communication during group activity. You can record information about students' adherence to personal and social responsibility on observation checklists. In addition, children can demonstrate their knowledge of responsibility behaviors through age-appropriate assessment sheets.

In standard 5, children are asked to recognize the value of physical activity. In kindergarten through grade 2, children recognize which physical activities are enjoyable to them and which ones they feel most confident about performing. You can use exit tickets to assess students' feelings about the manipulative activities addressed in a given day's lesson and help them recognize that physical activity participation can bring enjoyment and provide challenge. Figure 17.2 presents sample exit tickets for assessing enjoyment and challenge; you can use information from the tickets to address students' needs and interests.

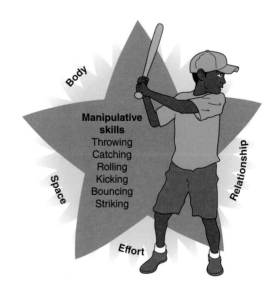

Figure 17.1   The Active Child: manipulative skills.

Table 17.1 Learning Goal Blueprint for Mature and Versatile Performance of Manipulative Skills

Content	Body	Space	Effort	Relationship
Sending objects away: throwing, kicking, volleying, striking	Intentionally uses body parts in unison, opposition, and sequence and uses body actions (curling, stretching, bending, twisting, turning) for mature performance.	Sends objects away to forward and sideward directions; at high, medium, and low levels; in arced, vertical, and horizontal trajectories; and for short, medium, and long distances.	Creates and applies force appropriately for sending objects to intended targets or receivers.	Sends objects toward, over, under, and through equipment or targets. Sends objects to partners who are in front of or alongside the sender.
Receiving objects: catching, trapping	Intentionally uses body parts in unison, opposition, and sequence and uses body actions (curling, stretching, bending, twisting, turning) for mature performance.	Receives objects sent from low, medium, and high levels; in horizontal, vertical, and arced trajectories; and for short, medium, and long distances.	Moves at appropriate speeds to approach and receive objects. Absorbs force appropriately to receive and control objects.	Receives objects coming over, under, and through equipment. Receives objects while moving on top of or off of equipment. Receives objects from partners who are in front of or alongside the receiver.
Maintaining possession of objects: bouncing, dribbling with feet, carrying	Intentionally uses body parts in unison, opposition, and sequence and uses body actions (curling, stretching, bending, twisting, turning) for mature performance.	Moves through general space while changing direction (forward and sideward) and pathway (straight, curved, or zigzag) and maintaining possession.	Uses different speeds (slow, medium, fast) and applies appropriate force to maintain possession of objects.	Maintains possession of objects while moving alongside or around equipment or others. Uses roles of leading, following, meeting, and parting while maintaining possession of objects.

I like/dislike 🙂 🙁 _____ [name of manipulative activity].

It is fun to do 🙂 _____ [name of manipulative activity].

Today's Activities:

_____ [Name of activity]

_____ [Name of activity]

_____ [Name of activity]

Put a check mark by the activities that you need to work harder to perform.

Put an X by the activity that you performed the best.

Figure 17.2 Sample exit tickets for enjoyment (top) and for confidence and challenge (bottom).

MANIPULATIVE SKILLS: THROWING

Use table 17.2 as a resource for designing throwing skill challenges. Examples are provided below the table.

Table 17.2 Progression for K-2 Consistent-Level Throwing Skills

Throwing	Equipment: balls that fit the size of one hand and of two hands
	Learning outcome: Gain greater consistency in mature throwing patterns and variations.
	Underhand Throw
	• To stationary large targets at distances that require full backswing
	• To varied heights, distances, and directions for purposeful release
	• To moving targets
	Overhand Throw
	• To large targets at distances that require full wind-up (for force)
	• To varied heights, distances, and directions for purposeful release
	• To moving targets

Learning Outcome

Gain greater consistency in mature throwing patterns and variations.

- Standard 1: Throw underhand and overhand using elements of a mature pattern in non-dynamic environments (SHAPE America, 2014).
- Standard 2: Identify skill cues for throwing.
- Standard 4: Work independently with others in partner environments (SHAPE America, 2014, p. 18).

Movement Concepts

- Body awareness: intentional sequencing of body parts for mature performance of manipulative skills
- Space awareness: distances, levels, directions
- Effort awareness: force related to distance
- Relationship awareness: to stationary and moving targets

Skill Cues

Underhand Throw

- Preparation
  - Turn chest toward target.
  - Hold ball in both hands at waist level and off center toward throwing side.
- Execution
  - Swing throwing arm back behind bottom.
  - Reach nonthrowing arm toward target.
  - As throwing arm swings forward, step toward target with opposite foot.
  - Release ball at level of target.
- Follow-through
  - Extend throwing arm toward target.

Overhand Throw

- Preparation
  - Turn side to target.
  - Hold ball in both hands at waist level and off center toward throwing side.

- Execution
  - Wind up, bringing throwing arm back behind head with elbow bent at 90-degree angle (in L shape).
  - Step toward target on opposite foot.
  - Rotate chest and hips toward target as throwing arm is extended toward target.
- Follow-through
  - Follow through with throwing arm across body.

Teaching Styles

Reproduction: practice, reciprocal (grade 2), inclusion

Production: guided discovery

Tasks

Task: Children throw to zones or walls to find the distance that requires a full backswing. All children throw simultaneously from behind a throwing line. Balls are retrieved on a signal from you.

Environment: Divide the gym into three to five zones marked with cones. Wall targets can include large projected images or targets drawn on sheets. Throwing objects are placed in bins located behind the throwing line. The objects might be 3- to 4-inch (7.5- to 10-centimeter) plastic balls with holes, foam balls, yarn balls, or beanbags.

Practice: blocked (e.g., five repetitions to each zone from throwing line or to wall from each distance)

Feedback:

- KPd (underhand throw): "You performed a full backswing by bringing your arm back behind your bottom."
- KPp (overhand throw): "To achieve a full backswing, you need to twist more so that your side faces your target."

Task: Throw to different levels.

Environment: large and medium hoops, large pictures (4 feet by 4 feet or about 1.25 by 1.25 meters) taped to wall (e.g., ice cream cone with three scoops; barn with roof, windows, and doors for levels; traffic light; sight words), throwing objects in bins behind throwing line (e.g., 3-inch or 4-inch [7.5 or 10 centimeter]) Wiffle balls, foam balls, yarn balls, beanbags)

Practice: blocked (at least five repetitions for each level)

Assessment

Standard 1: Use an observation checklist (figure 17.3).

A check mark indicates that the student achieved the criterion.

Student	High release	Medium release	Low release

Figure 17.3 Observation checklist for throwing to different levels.

Task: Children throw to large targets from different directions.

Environment: Position large targets on the wall and 3 or 4 poly spots 4 feet (1.25 meter) apart and 15 feet (4.5 meters) from the targets (the distance can be varied to meet children's skill level). Place throwing objects in bins behind the throwing line marked by the poly spots. Objects might include 3-inch or 4-inch (7.5- or 10-centimeter) Wiffle balls, foam balls, yarn balls, or beanbags.

Practice: Blocked (at least five repetitions from each poly spot)

Assessment

Standard 2: Use an exit ticket (figure 17.4).

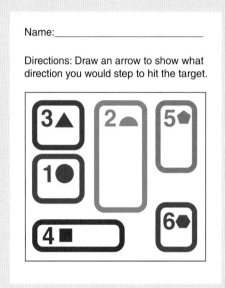

Figure 17.4   Exit ticket for throwing to large targets from different directions.

Task: Children throw for force to knock over a target using a full wind-up and work cooperatively to calculate a collective score in a group of three. Group members work simultaneously, each throwing six beanbags to a personal target and tallying their successful attempts. Group members then total the collective number of times they knocked over their targets and try to better the group score in each trial. Encourage the children to give "put-ups" as group members try hard to help the team.

Environment: Provide each group with three objects to knock over (e.g., blow-up clown punching bags). Mark throwing lines at different distances with poly spots or floor tape. Place throwing objects (e.g., beanbags of different sizes) in bins behind the throwing lines; the objects need to be heavy enough to knock over the targets.

Practice: Blocked

Assessment

Standard 4: The throwing scorecard (figure 17.5) awards one point each time a target is knocked over. Students track on their scorecard the number of times they knock over the target. Each performer throws six beanbags per trial. Students are encouraged to give each other "put ups."

Name:

Group members: _____

Trial 1 group score: _____

Trial 2 group score: _____

Trial 3 group score: _____

Put-ups I gave my teammates:

❏ "Great job!"   ❏ "Way to go!"   ❏ "Keep trying!"   ❏ "Great hit!"

❏ Other _____

Put-ups I received:

❏ "Great job!"   ❏ "Way to go!"   ❏ "Keep trying!"   ❏ "Great hit!"

❏ Other _____

Figure 17.5   Throwing scorecard.

Task: Children throw underhand into or onto large targets placed in various areas in the gym. They throw from a line that is at least 15 feet (4.5 meters) from the nearest target.

Environment: Create a number of round targets positioned in various areas of the gym. Options include two or three gymnastics mats placed on their sides; refrigerator boxes; archery targets; and floor targets marked by ropes, cones, or poly spots. Children are partnered and spread out along two or three throwing lines marked in different positions so that the children do not all throw from the same place. Throwing objects are placed in hoops behind the throwing lines. Children take turns acting as either the observer or the thrower. The observing partner looks at the thrower's arm and stepping action to see if it matches the cues on the reciprocal task card and gives helpful feedback. The throwing partner throws five times and acknowledges partner feedback. You check observers' comments to see if they accurately assess skill cue performance.

Practice: Blocked

Assessment

Standard 2: Use the reciprocal task card for the underhand throw (figure 17.6).

Directions: Watch your partner throw five times. If they perform the skill cue, check the "Yes" box and tell them they did well! If they do not perform the skill cue, check the "Needs work" box and tell them what they need to correct. Here is an example: "You need to swing your arm farther back."

Skill cues	Yes	Needs work
PARTNER 1		
Swings throwing arm back behind bottom.		
Steps toward target with opposite foot.		
PARTNER		
Swings throwing arm back behind bottom.		
Steps toward target with opposite foot.		

Figure 17.6   Reciprocal task card for the underhand throw.

Task: Children throw underhand or overhand to a moving target; specifically, they aim ahead of the target by stepping and releasing toward the stars at the end of a guidance arc provided in the environment.

Environment: A hoop is suspended from a basketball goal, and an arc (figure 17.7) with stars is taped on the wall just behind the target. Place the throwing line close enough for students to reach target from a full wind-up.

Practice: Blocked

Skill cue modifications for throwing toward a moving target:

Underhand Throw Execution

- As throwing arm swings forward, step toward space ahead of target with opposite foot.
- Release ball ahead of target and at level of target.

Overhand Throw Execution

- Rotate chest and hips toward target as throwing arm is extended ahead of target.
- Step toward space ahead of target with opposite foot.

Figure 17.7 Children use the stars at the end of each arc to aim at the moving target.

Feedback

KPp: "Watch the pathway of the swinging hoop. Step and throw your beanbag toward the space just ahead of the hoop (toward a star)."

MANIPULATIVE SKILLS: CATCHING

Use table 17.3 as a resource for designing catching skill challenges. Examples are provided below the table.

Table 17.3   Progression for K-2 Consistent-Level Catching Skills

	Equipment: soft- or medium-texture balls and other objects sized for two-handed catching Learning outcome: Gain greater consistency in mature catching patterns and variations.
Catching	• Catching a bounced ball • Catching a self-toss • Self-tossing to different places around the body and catching • Catching a ball that rebounds from a wall at moderate distances • Catching balls thrown to different heights for purposeful reaching (chest, above head, below waist) • Catching and throwing with a partner with variation in distance, direction, trajectory, and speed of throws

Learning Outcome

Gain greater consistency in mature catching patterns and variations.

- Standard 1: Catch with two hands using mature form.
- Standard 2: Catch using movement concepts of level, distance, direction, speed, and partner.

Movement Concepts

- Body awareness: intentional use and adjustment of body actions (curling, stretching, bending, twisting, and turning) for mature performance
- Space awareness: levels and heights; distance; direction
- Effort awareness: speed
- Relationship awareness: to wall, to partner

Teaching Styles

Reproduction: practice, reciprocal (grade 2), inclusion

Skill Cues

- Move to get behind oncoming ball or anticipate ball position.
- Keep eyes on ball.
- Reach out for ball with hands.
- Put thumbs together to catch above head.
- Put pinkies together to catch below waist.
- Catch with hands only.
- Give with body.

Tasks

Task: Children catch a bounced ball. Each child tosses a playground ball up in the air just above head level and permits the ball to drop and bounce on the floor. The child then catches the ball on the first, second, or third bounce.

Environment: Children are spread out in general space and attempt to toss and catch within their own personal space.

Equipment: Medium sized balls that can be grasped in two hands can be placed in multiple bins or hoops on the periphery of the gymnasium.

Practice: Blocked

Task: Children catch a self-toss. Each child throws the ball from low to high as follows:

- Throw just above head level, then catch the ball in front of the body at chest or waist level.
- Throw three or four feet (about a meter) above head level, then catch the ball in front of the body at chest or waist level.

Environment: Children each have an 8-inch (20-centimeter) playground ball, gator-skin ball, beanbag, or geometric open-matrix ball. Children are spread out in the general movement area and try to stay in their own personal space.

Practice: Blocked

Task: Children catch a ball rebounding from a wall at moderate distances.

Environment: The child stands 10 to 15 feet (3 to 4.5 meters) from the wall and throws a 6- to 7-inch (about 15- to 18-centimeter) playground ball to the wall at a height of 3 feet (1 meter); a target line can be taped on the wall. When the ball rebounds off of the wall, the child catches it after one bounce on the floor, trying to catch it with the hands only.

Practice: Blocked

Task: Children self-toss to different places around the body and catch the object. For example, they might self-toss above the head but off to the right side of the body, then reach to catch the object along the right side of the body. Another example is to toss above the head but catch the object at knee level.

Environment: Children each have an 6-7-inch (about 15- to 18-centimeter) playground ball, gator-skin ball, beanbag, or geometric open-matrix ball. Children are spread out in a general movement area and try to stay in their own personal space.

Practice: Blocked (five times at each place)

Task: Children catch balls thrown by a partner to different heights for purposeful reaching (chest, above head, below waist).

Environment: In pairs, children use an 6-7-inch (about 15- to 18-centimeter) playground ball, gator-skin ball, or geometric open-matrix ball. One child tries to use an underhand toss to throw the ball to the partner at chest level, above the head, and then below waist level. The catching partner moves behind the object to catch it with two hands at the appropriate level.

Practice: Blocked (five to seven times at each height)

Task: Children catch and throw with a partner with variations in distance, direction, trajectory, and speed.

Environment: Put students in pairs or trios, depending on the number of children in the class. Position all children facing each other either east–west or north–south for managerial purposes. Consider using poly spots to mark each group's space and to help each pair or trio maintain a safe distance from others. Provide a variety of throwing objects in bins or hoops on the periphery of the gymnasium. Throwing objects that do not roll readily should be used when children first attempt this skill progression (e.g., beanbags, geometric open-matrix balls). Instruct the children to choose a throwing object. After you demonstrate the activity, instruct the throwing students to toss to their partners from varying distances and directions. They should use high, medium, and low trajectories (i.e., levels).

Feedback

- KPd: "You reached for the ball with both hands—good work!"
- KPp: "Try to move a little quicker to get behind the ball."
- KR: "How did you decide where to move to catch the ball?"

Assessment

Standard 2: Use the self-check task card (figure 17.8).

Name:_____

Write check marks to show which parts of catching you were able to do.

_____ Catch the ball above my head with my thumbs together.

_____ Catch the ball below my waist with my pinkies together.

_____ Move quickly to get behind the ball.

Figure 17.8   Self-check task card for catching.

MANIPULATIVE SKILLS: ROLLING

Use table 17.4 as a resource for designing ball rolling skill challenges. Examples are provided below the table.

Table 17.4   Progression for K-2 Consistent-Level Rolling Skills

Rolling	Equipment: plastic pins, lightweight balls that fit the size of both hands
	Learning outcome: Gain greater consistency in mature rolling patterns and variations.
	• Step and roll a ball through cones set at far to close distances.
	• Step and roll a ball from 10 to 15 feet (3 to 4.5 meters) toward at least three pins in V formation.

Learning Outcome

Gain greater consistency in mature ball-rolling patterns and variations.

- Standard 1: Roll balls with mature form.
- Standard 2: Roll balls using moving concepts of distance and direction.
- Standard 4: Work independently with others in partner environments (SHAPE America, 2014, p. 18).

Movement Concepts

- Space awareness: distance
- Effort awareness: force
- Relationship awareness: to targets

Skill Cues

Preparation

- Place nondominant hand in middle and front of ball.
- Place dominant (rolling) hand in middle and back of ball.
- Swing arms back along dominant side of body to behind bottom.

Execution

- Swing arms forward while stepping and shifting weight forward on foot opposite the side of the rolling hand.
- Bend knee of opposite leg to lower body toward floor level.
- Release ball at low level while taking nondominant hand off of ball.

Follow-Through

- Reach toward target with dominant (rolling) hand and arm.
- Keep weight forward on opposite foot.

Teaching Styles

Reproduction: practice, reciprocal (grade 2), inclusion

Tasks

Task: Children step and roll a ball through cones set at far to close distances.

Environment: Cones are set up along the walls; poly spots are positioned in the middle of the gymnasium at 7, 10, and 15 feet (about 2, 3, and 4.5 meters); see figure 17.9. Children roll a 6- to 8-inch (about 15- to 20-centimeter) playground ball, aiming between two cones. Pairs can be used so that one child acts as the performer and the other as the retriever; the retriever stands near the wall. Balls are placed in bins or hoops in the middle of the gymnasium. All sides of the gymnasium can be used.

Practice: Blocked

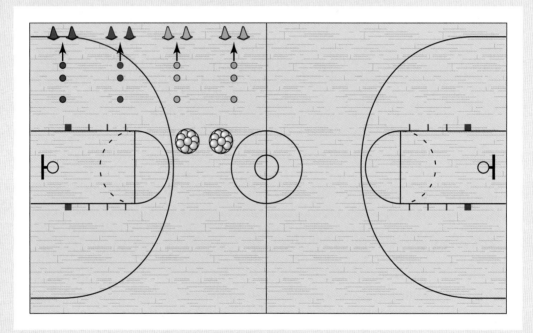

Figure 17.9 Setup for rolling balls through cones.

Assessment

Standards 1 and 2: Use an observation checklist of skill cues.

Task: Children cooperate with a partner to roll three balls toward six pins arranged in a V formation. After each ball is rolled, the helping partner retrieves the ball and sets up any pins knocked over. Instruct students to work nicely together by rolling the retrieved ball back to their partner, quickly setting up pins, and use encouraging words, such as "I hope to see you work nicely together and use encouraging words to compliment your partner."

Environment: Set up six pins in a V formation about 10 to 15 feet (3 to 4.5 meters) from a poly spot (can be set at different distances from target). Use bowling pins or polystyrene cylinders.

Practice: Blocked

Feedback

KPd: "Nice job rolling the ball back quickly to your partner."

Assessment

Standard 4: Use an affective T-chart (figure 17.10). Inform the children that you will be watching and listening for the physical and verbal behaviors indicated in the chart as they perform the rolling task.

See	Hear
• Helping partner rolls ball nicely back to performing partner. • Helping partner quickly sets up pins for performing partner.	• "Nice try!" • "Wow! You knocked over all six pins!" • "Keep trying!"

Figure 17.10   Affective T-chart.

MANIPULATIVE SKILLS: KICKING AND DRIBBLING

Use table 17.5 as a resource for designing kicking and dribbling skill challenges. Examples are provided below the table.

Table 17.5   Progression for K-2 Consistent-Level Kicking and Dribbling Skills

Kicking and dribbling	Equipment: foam and #4 soccer balls Learning outcome: Gain greater consistency in mature kicking and dribbling patterns and variations. • Kicking a ball with the instep (shoelaces) from a short to moderate approach • Kicking a ball to distances requiring an approach and full wind-up • Kicking a ball at or below midline to travel at different levels (along the ground or in the air) • Kicking to targets of varying size, height, and distance • Kicking a rolling ball from a stance to different distances • Kicking a rolling ball using an approach to different distances • Short-tap dribbling along the ground • Start-and-stop dribbling • Dribbling on different pathways and to avoid obstacles

Learning Outcome

Gain greater consistency in mature kicking and dribbling patterns and variations.

- Standard 1: Kick a ball using mature form.
- Standard 2: Kick a ball using moving concepts of distance, level, and force.
- Standard 1: Dribble a ball through general space with control of ball and body (SHAPE America, 2014, p. 7).
- Standard 2: Dribble a ball using movement concepts of pathway, force, and moving around obstacles.

Movement Concepts

- Space awareness: distance, levels, pathways
- Effort awareness: creating (kicking) and controlling (dribbling) force
- Relationship awareness: to targets, around obstacles, avoiding others

Skill Cues: Instep Kick

Preparation

- Focus eyes on ball.
- Use two- or three-step approach with last step on nonkicking foot.
- Place nonkicking foot beside and slightly behind ball.
- Nonkicking foot points toward target.

Execution

- Leg action is from knee down.
- Contact ball with shoelaces.
- Contact middle of ball for low kick (with trunk leaning forward).
- Contact bottom of ball for lofted kick (with trunk leaning backward).
- Put body weight forward over ball.

Follow-Through

- Extend leg toward target at low level.

Teaching Styles

Command, practice (K-2), reciprocal (grade 2), inclusion

Tasks

Task: Children kick a ball with the instep (shoelaces) from a short to moderate approach (one or two steps).

Environment: Use "half cones" to position 6- to 8-inch (15- to 20-centimeter) playground balls for stationary kicking. Place the cones 5 to 10 feet (about 2 to 3 meters) from the wall. Kicks are directed toward the wall. The balls should be slightly deflated and kept inside of bins or hoops positioned in the middle of the gymnasium. Students are organized into partner pairs, with one partner acting as the performer and the other as the retriever.

Feedback

KPd: "You contacted the ball with your shoelaces—awesome!"

KPp: "Be sure to point your nonkicking foot toward your target."

KR: "What do you think made the ball go high off of the floor?"

Assessment

Standard 2: Use a task sheet for correct foot placement when kicking (figure 17.11).

Name:_____

Directions: Draw an X to show where your non-kicking foot should be placed when you kick the ball toward the wall.

Figure 17.11 Task sheet for correct foot placement when kicking.

Task: Children kick a ball to distances requiring an approach and full wind-up.

Environment: This activity is best conducted outside. Children kick into zones marked by tall cones (figure 17.12). To maximize practice time, create four or five zones with about 4 or 5 feet (1.25 to 1.5 meters) between zones. Playground balls (6- to 8-inch, or 15- to 20-centimeter) can be placed on the ground along a kicking line. The distance from the kicking line to the zones can be varied based on the skill level of the children. Provide starting and stopping cues for retrieving balls. Organize the children into partner groups (pairs). One partner serves as a retriever and stands at the far end of the zone. On your signal, retrievers get the balls kicked by their partners and roll them back.

Practice: Blocked (5 times to each zone)

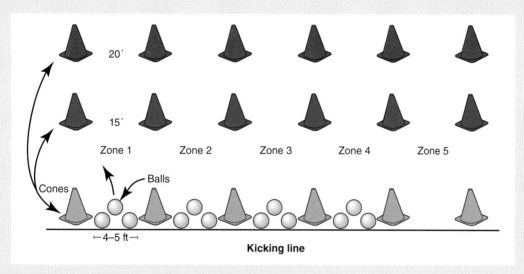

Figure 17.12   Zone setup for kicking activity.

Task: Children kick a ball at or below midline to travel at different levels (along the ground or in the air).

Environment: Use poly spots or floor tape to designate a kicking line. Use standards and ropes for kicking under and over; alternatively, tape lines or targets to a wall at different levels. To help children kick the ball low, tape or mark a small X on the middle or midline of each ball to designate the contact point for kicking a low ball. Similarly, tape or mark an X at the bottom of each ball to designate the contact point for lofting the ball. Consistent with the practice (B) teaching style (see chapter 10), you can model kicking the midline X on the ball and leaning forward to kick the ball at a low level and kicking the X at the bottom of the ball and leaning backward to loft the ball.

Task: Children kick to targets of various sizes, heights, and distances

Environment: Stations can be created featuring different types of targets. Poly spots are placed on the floor at two or three different distances. Here are some target options:

- Polystyrene arches (to kick under)
- Hoops positioned vertically in hoop holders
- Cones to kick between
- Ropes with crepe paper or smiley faces hanging from rope (to kick under or over)
- Hoops taped on walls
- Large alphabet letters, cartoon characters, or other thematic items taped to walls
- Cartoon figures projected on walls
- Refrigerator boxes with holes cut out (to kick through or under)

Practice: blocked (five times to each type of target)

Task: Children kick a rolling ball from a stance to different distances.

Environment: Children are organized into trios, in which one child acts as the roller, another as the kicker, and the third as the retriever. The roller is positioned about 10 feet (3 meters) from the kicker. If indoors, this task should be one of five or six kicking stations, with students kicking toward one of the corners of the gymnasium. Mark distances with floor tape. If the activity is conducted outdoors, then all children can practice the same skill progression at the same time (see figure 17.13), with kickers located in a middle, rollers 10 feet from that circle, and retrievers in an outer circle. Mark distances with cones using a different color for each area. You can use the command (A) teaching style to designate when rollers should roll to the kickers and when retrievers should return the ball to the rollers.

Practice: Blocked (five times from each distance)

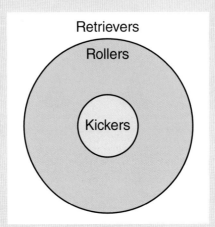

Figure 17.13 Placement of retrievers, rollers, and kickers.

Task: Children kick a rolling ball using an approach to different distances. They take a running or three-step approach before positioning the nonkicking foot beside and slightly behind the ball.

Environment: same as for preceding skill progression (kicking a rolling ball from a stance to different distances)

Practice: Blocked

Feedback
- KPd: "Your three-step approach was done very smoothly."
- KPp: "Contact the ball with your shoelaces."
- KR: "What do you do to keep the kick low to the ground?"

Assessment

Standard 1: Use a teacher observation checklist of skill cues (figure 17.14).

Criteria	Try 1		Try 2		Try 3	
	Yes	No	Yes	No	Yes	No
Use a smooth three-step approach.						
Correctly position nonkicking foot.						
Kick with shoelaces.						

Figure 17.14 Observation checklist of skill cues for kicking.

Skill Cues for Dribbling

- Keep ball one or two steps in front of body.
- Use inside of foot (big-toe area) to tap ball forward.
- Walk briskly or jog while continuously tapping ball forward.
- Stop ball with sole of foot or with knee.

Task: Children perform short-tap dribbling along the ground while alternating left foot and right foot.

Environment: Each child has a #4 soccer ball or a 5- to 6-inch (12.5- to 15-centimeter) playground ball. A general movement area is designated (e.g., by cones). Children dribble around the movement area while avoiding others. Each child determines when to stop or trap the ball.

Task: Children perform start-and-stop dribbling.

Environment: Create a general movement area, in which children use a #4 soccer ball to dribble around in general space. Children start and stop (trapping with the sole of the foot) when indicated by musical cues, drumbeats, or a whistle.

Task: Children dribble on various pathways and avoid obstacles.

Environment: Obstacles can be made with colored cones (decorated cones are especially stimulating). Children dribble through general space, changing pathways to avoid obstacles. If you do not have enough soccer balls for all children, you can also use 5- to 6-inch (12.5- to 15-centimeter) playground balls or foam balls. If this progression is conducted indoors, soccer balls and playground balls should be slightly deflated. Pathways can be created on the floor using floor tape. An obstacle course can be created as suggested in figure 17.15; children would start at different places along the course.

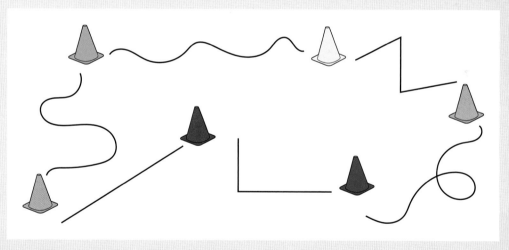

Figure 17.15 Setup for dribbling activity.

Feedback

- KPd: "You kept the ball close to your body as you moved along the pathways."
- KPp: "You need to look up from the ball occasionally so that you can follow the pathway."
- KR: "Did you need to dribble differently to stay on any of the pathways?"

Assessment

Standard 1: Use a peer task card (figure 17.16).

Criteria	Try 1		Try 2		Try 3	
	Yes	No	Yes	No	Yes	No
Uses big-toe area to tap the ball.						
Keeps the ball within one or two steps of the body.						
Follows the pathway.						

Figure 17.16 Peer task card for dribbling.

MANIPULATIVE SKILLS: BOUNCING

Use table 17.6 as a resource for designing bouncing skill challenges. Examples are provided below the table.

Table 17.6 Progression for K-2 Consistent-Level Bouncing Skills

<table>
<tr><td rowspan="2">Bouncing</td><td>Equipment: 8-inch (20-centimeter) playground balls and junior-size basketballs
Learning outcome: Gain greater consistency in mature bouncing patterns and variations.
<ul>
<li>Bouncing with each hand while stationary</li>
<li>Bouncing with different forces and to different levels while stationary</li>
<li>Bouncing to the front and to the sides of the body while stationary</li>
<li>Bouncing with each hand while moving</li>
<li>Start-and-stop bouncing</li>
<li>Bouncing while looking up intermittently</li>
<li>Bouncing on different pathways and to avoid obstacles</li>
<li>Bouncing while following another</li>
</ul></td></tr>
</table>

Learning Outcome

Gain greater consistency in mature bouncing patterns and variations.

- Standard 1: Bounce a ball with mature form while stationary and while walking (SHAPE America, 2014).
- Standard 2: Bounce a ball using movement concepts of level direction, pathway, force, and avoiding obstacles.

Movement Concepts

- Body awareness: selecting appropriate body parts for performing manipulative skills
- Space awareness: levels, pathways
- Effort awareness: varying force
- Relationship awareness: in relationship to body, following, avoiding obstacles

Skill cues

Bouncing

- Use finger pads to push ball down.
- Keep ball in front of and slightly to the side of the body (to the right if bouncing with right hand, to the left if bouncing with left hand).
- Keep elbow of bouncing arm flexed.
- Keep wrist firm.

- Bounce ball waist high.
- Keep chest and head up.

Teaching Styles

Reproduction: practice, reciprocal (grade 2), inclusion

Tasks

Task: Children bounce with each hand while stationary.

Environment: Create a general movement area by using cones or other markers (e.g., lines on floor). Equipment is kept in bins or hoops along the sidelines or end lines of the gymnasium. Children bounce continuously in their personal space.

Task: Children bounce with different forces and to different levels while stationary. Provide children with starting and stopping cues.

Environment: Children spread out in general space at least 3 feet (1 meter) away from each other. Equipment is provided in bins or hoops on the sidelines or end lines of the gymnasium.

Practice: Blocked with 5 repetitions for each of the forces/levels

Task: Children bounce to the front and sides of the body while stationary. Provide starting and stopping cues. You may also need to mirror children by bouncing on their left side when children try to bounce the ball along their right side and vice versa.

Environment: Children spread out in general space and a minimum of 3 feet (about 1 meter) from each other. Balls are provided in bins or hoops along the sidelines or end lines of the gymnasium.

Practice: Blocked with 5 repetitions for each position (front and sides)

Task: Children bounce with each hand while moving.

Environment: Create a general movement area in which children can dribble. Children are prompted to dribble continuously and stop when they think they are about to lose control. Establish a class protocol for what to do when a child loses his or her ball. For example, the child could look to see where classmates are dribbling in order to avoid them while carefully moving to retrieve the ball.

Practice: Blocked with at least 5 repetitive bounces before switching to the other hand

Task: Children perform start-and-stop bouncing.

Environment: Create a general movement area in which children can dribble. When children see you hold up a designated visual aid (e.g., a high-five hand), they give a designated response (e.g., "High five!") and stop bouncing. You can also use musical cues to prompt starting and stopping. Alternatively, you can place red poly spots or cones decorated with stop signs around the movement area. Whenever a child comes close to one, he or she stops bouncing.

Practice: Blocked; repetitions determined by teacher

Task: Children bounce on different pathways and avoid obstacles.

Environment: Pathways are taped or painted on the floor. Obstacles are positioned in general space (e.g., cones, half cones, polystyrene shapes, cardboard cartoon characters).

Practice: Blocked

Task: Children bounce while following another child.

Environment: Children are organized into pairs (or trios), and they decide who serves first as the leader. Each child has a ball. Leaders move through general space, and followers stay within a giant step of their leader. Signal when the children should change leaders or pairs (or trios).

Practice: Blocked

Feedback

- KPd: "You kept the ball tummy high by pushing with enough force—great job!"
- KPp: "Keep the ball a little more in front of your feet and off to the side of your body so the ball doesn't hit your feet and roll away!"
- KR: "What helps you keep the ball tummy high?"

Assessment

- Standard 1: Use a teacher observation checklist of skill cues.
- Standard 2: Use the bouncing self-assessment in figure 17.17.

Name:_____

Directions: Look at the picture below. Draw an arrow to the part of the child's body showing how high the ball should be bounced.

Figure 17.17 Bouncing self-assessment.

MANIPULATIVE SKILLS: STRIKING WITH BODY PARTS

Use table 17.7 as a resource for designing striking with body parts skill challenges. Examples are provided below the table.

Table 17.7   Progression for K-2 Consistent-Level Skills for Striking with Body Parts

Striking with body parts	Equipment: punch balloons, balls with balloon or butyl bladders
	Learning outcome: Gain greater consistency in mature striking with body parts (volleying) patterns and variations.
	• Striking a punch balloon underhand and overhead with open palms continuously
	• Striking a balloon or butyl bladder ball noncontinuously from self- and partner tosses to a wall or targets; to a partner (catching after a bounce); or over a line, suspended rope, or low net
	   • Underhand with palms or forearms
	   • Underhand, overhand, or sidearm with one hand
	   • Overhead with two hands

Learning Outcome

Gain greater consistency in mature striking with body parts (volleying) patterns and variations.

- Standard 1: Strike (volley) an object upward with open palms continuously.
- Standard 2: Strike (volley) an object using movement concepts of level and force with a partner and over objects.

Movement Concepts

- Body awareness: intentional use of body parts in unison and sequence for mature performance of manipulative skills
- Space awareness: levels
- Effort awareness: creating force
- Relationship awareness: to self, to partner, over a line, over a rope

Skill Cues: Striking Underhand

Preparation

- Put pinkies close together.
- Spread out fingers.
- Position hands below waist and extend arms in front of body.

Execution

- Contact ball with pads of all fingers.
- Lift arms from low to high (to chest or face level).

Follow-Through

- Extend hands and arms toward target.

Skill Cues: Striking Overhead

Preparation

- Put thumbs close together.
- Spread out fingers.
- Position hands above head.
- Bend elbows.

Execution

- Contact ball with pads of all fingers.
- Extend arms upward and straighten your elbows.

Follow-Through

- Extend hands and arms toward target.

Teaching Styles

Reproduction: practice, reciprocal (grade 2), inclusion

Tasks

Task: Children strike a punch balloon underhand and overhead with open palms continuously.

Environment: Children work in personal space within a general movement area. Punch balloons are provided in bins along the sidelines or end lines of the gymnasium.

Task: Children strike a balloon or butyl bladder ball noncontinuously from self- and partner tosses.

- Self-toss and hit to a wall or target either underhand or overhand (with one hand or two hands) or sidearm (with one hand).
- Self-toss and hit to a partner either underhand or overhand (with one hand or two hands) or sidearm (with one hand); partner catches after at least one bounce in general space.
- Self-toss and hit to a partner either underhand or overhand (with one hand or two hands) or sidearm (with one hand) over a line, suspended rope, or low net.
- Hit a partner-tossed ball either underhand or overhand (with one hand or two hands) or sidearm (with one hand) back to the partner in general space.
- Hit a partner-tossed ball either underhand or overhand (with one hand or two hands) or sidearm (with one hand) back to the partner over a line, suspended rope, or low net; partner catches after at least one bounce.

Environment: Children are organized in pairs. They first self-toss to a large wall target positioned 5 feet (1.5 meters) high on a wall. The targets might consist of pictures of a variety of stimulating cartoon characters. Provide a general space in which partners can hit the ball to each other after self-tosses and partner feeds. Set up "courts" marked by poly spots and a "net" made with a rope and two cones (see figure 17.18). All children should face either east–west or north–south for ease of classroom management and observation.

Practice: Blocked (10 times for each condition)

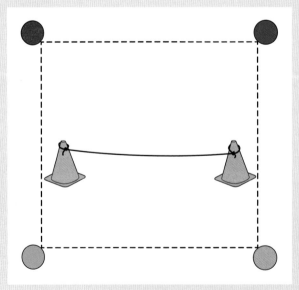

Figure 17.18 Setup for partner toss "court."

Feedback

- KPd: "I like how you are using both hands to strike the ball from low to high."
- KPp: "Try to reach more toward your target with your arms."
- KR: "What helps you to hit the ball high enough for your partner to catch it?"

Assessment

- Standard 1: Use a teacher observation checklist of skill cues.
- Children use figure 17.19 to self-assess by placing a check next to the tasks they were able to perform.

Name: _____

What were you able to do? Check the tasks that you completed:

_____ Self-toss and hit to a wall or target.

_____ Self-toss and hit to a partner in general space.

_____ Self-toss and hit underhand or overhand over a rope or low net.

_____ Hit the ball after partner tosses it to you in general space.

_____ Hit the ball back over a low net to your partner after your partner tosses it to you.

Figure 17.19 Self-assessment for self-toss and partner toss.

MANIPULATIVE SKILLS: STRIKING WITH PADDLES

Use table 17.8 as a resource for designing striking with paddles skill challenges. Examples are provided below the table.

Table 17.8 Progression for K-2 Consistent-Level Skills for Striking With Paddles

Striking with paddles	Equipment: lollipop (polystyrene) paddles, balloons, foam balls
	Learning outcome: Gain greater consistency in mature striking with paddles (patterns and variations).
	• Striking balloons upward continuously
	• Striking balloons back and forth with a partner
	• Striking a ball from a bounce to a wall or target at different levels, directions, and distances
	• Striking a ball over a line, suspended rope, or low net
	◦ From a drop to a partner
	◦ Back to a partner after a bounce from an underhand toss by the partner

Learning Outcome

Gain greater consistency in mature striking with paddles (patterns and variations).

- Standard 1: Strike objects upward and forward with paddles (SHAPE America, 2014).
- Standard 2:
    - Strike objects with paddles using movement concepts of level, direction, distance, force, with a partner, and over objects.
    - Recognize skill cues.

Movement Concepts

- Body awareness: intentional use of body parts in unison and sequence for mature performance of manipulative skills
- Space awareness: levels, direction, distance
- Effort awareness: creating force
- Relationship awareness: to self, to partner, over line, over rope

Skill Cues

Preparation

- Turn side to target.
- Start by bringing paddle or racket back behind bottom.
- Keep wrist and elbow firm.

Execution

- Extend racket arm and swing slightly from low to high.
- Step with opposite foot as you swing.

Follow-Through

- Extend racket arm toward target.

Teaching Styles

Command, practice (K-2), reciprocal (grade 2), inclusion

Tasks

Task: Children strike balloons upward continuously with a racket held in the dominant hand.

Environment: Each child has a balloon and a lollipop (polystyrene) paddle of appropriate shaft length. Children are spread out in general space. Balloons can be kept in garbage bags at the side of the gymnasium. Be aware of any children with latex allergies and use non-latex balloons if necessary.

Practice: Blocked; 3 sets of at least 5 repetitions

Task: Children strike balloons back and forth with a partner.

Environment: Pairs are positioned in general space facing either east–west or north–south. Balloons can be kept in garbage bags at the side of the gymnasium. Children should be approximately 5 or 10 feet (1.5 to 3 meters) apart.

Practice: Blocked – 3 sets of at least 5 repetitions

Task: Children strike a ball from a bounce to a wall or target at different levels, directions, and distances.

Environment: Provide a variety of large targets taped or projected on the wall at a height of 3, 4, and 5 feet (about 1, 1.25, and 1.5 meters). Position poly spots in a semicircle at different distances from the targets (see figure 17.20). Children strike from different poly spots so that they experience striking in different directions and at different distances from the targets. They use 4- to 6-inch (about 10- to 15-centimeter) foam tennis balls, which are kept in bins or hoops behind the poly spots.

Practice: blocked (five times from three different poly spots)

Task: From a drop, children strike a ball to a partner over a line, suspended rope, or low net.

Environment: A rope is suspended from tall cones, and poly spots are used to create a rectangular court (see sample court diagram in striking with body parts, figure 17.18).

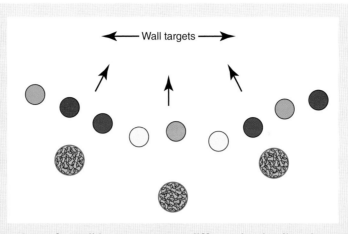

Figure 17.20   Setup for striking to targets at different levels, directions, and distances.

Task: From an underhand toss by a partner, children strike a ball back to the partner over a line, suspended rope, or low net after the ball bounces on the performer's side; the partner then catches the struck ball.

Environment: A rope is suspended from tall cones, and poly spots are used to create a rectangular court (see figure 17.18).

Feedback

- KPd: "You are preparing your racket nicely by bringing your paddle back behind your bottom."
- KPp: "Try to step and swing toward the ball at the same time."
- KR: "Why do you think the ball is not going over the rope?"

Assessment

- Standard 1: Use teacher observation checklist of skill cues.
- Standard 2: Skill cue identification (figure 17.21)

Figure 17.21   Identification of skill cue for striking.

MANIPULATIVE SKILLS: STRIKING WITH BATS AND POLO STICKS

Use table 17.9 as a resource for designing striking with bats and polo sticks skill challenges. Examples are provided below the table.

Table 17.9 Progression for K-2 Consistent-Level Skills for Striking with Bats and Polo Sticks

Striking with bats and polo sticks	Equipment: lollipop (polystyrene) paddles, polo sticks, oversized plastic bats, foam balls, plastic pucks Learning outcome: Gain greater consistency in mature striking with bats and polo sticks (patterns and variations). • Striking a ball off of a tee to different distances and directions • Striking a ball off of a tee and running to a base • Striking a ball or puck with a polo or hockey stick for distance • Striking a ball or puck with a polo or hockey stick through cones to a partner at various distances • Striking a ball or puck continuously along the ground with a polo or hockey stick in different pathways and directions

Learning Outcome

Gain greater consistency in mature striking with bats and polo sticks (patterns and variations).

- Standard 1: Use a bat to strike a ball off of a tee with mature form
- Standard 1: Use a polo stick to strike objects along the ground with mature form.
- Standard 2: Strike objects with paddles using movement concepts of level, direction, distance, force, with a partner, and over objects.

Movement Concepts

- Body awareness: intentional use of body parts in unison and sequence for mature performance of manipulative skills
- Space awareness: distance, direction, pathways
- Effort awareness: creating force
- Relationship awareness: to self, to partner, over line, over rope

Skill Cues for Striking With a Bat

Preparation

- Grip with dominant hand on top.
- Prepare bat over back shoulder, behind ear.
- Hold front elbow level with shoulder.
- Place feet in a side-to-side stance.
- Point side toward pitcher or tee.
- Put weight on back foot.
- Keep eye on ball.

Execution

- Make level swing.
- Shift weight forward during swing.

Follow-Through

- Follow through across body.

Teaching Styles

Reproduction: practice, reciprocal (grade 2), inclusion

Tasks (Striking With a Bat)

Task: Children strike a ball off of a tee to different distances and directions.

Environment: If outdoors, organize tees in a circle and group children in pairs or trios. Position yourself inside the tee circle to manage and observe the children's performance. Balls are kept in bins or hoops inside the tee circle. Each pair or trio has about five balls (heavy foam softball-size balls). Children strike out into general space toward their partners, who field all balls and then take them back to the tee. The partners then switch roles. If indoors, children work at a station on their own. Position the tees along the sidelines so that the children strike 5 balls toward a side wall. Children retrieve 5 balls on a signal from the teacher. Balls can be kept in bins or hoops behind the tees.

Practice: Blocked

Task: Children strike a ball off of a tee and run to a base.

Environment: Use the same organization described for the preceding task with the addition of a base added to the right of the batter's tee. After the child bats the ball off of the tee, he or she runs through first base, then returns to bat.

Practice: Blocked

Feedback

- KPd: "Excellent level swing. You are doing great!"
- KPp: "Get your bat back over your shoulder."

Assessment

Standard 1: Use a teacher observation checklist of skill cues (figure 17.22)

Student	Prepares bat over shoulder.	Uses level swing.	Shifts weight forward during swing.	Follows through across body.

Figure 17.22   Teacher observation checklist of skill cues for striking with a bat.

Skill Cues for Striking With a Polo Stick

Preparation

- Grip end of stick with dominant hand on bottom.
- Swing stick back low to floor.
- Point side to target.

Execution

- Swing stick low to ground.
- Strike ball in middle of polo stick face.
- Step toward target as you swing stick.

Follow-Through

- Extend stick toward target.
- Keep stick low to ground (below knees).

Tasks (Striking With a Polo Stick)

Task: Children strike a ball with a polo stick for distance.

Environment: Use colored cones to create four or five zones in the gymnasium (figure 17.23). Organize students into groups by learning-team colors. Position a bin with balls or pucks along the wall for each group. Each learning team stands behind its color-coordinated line and tries to strike a ball into its color-coordinated zone.

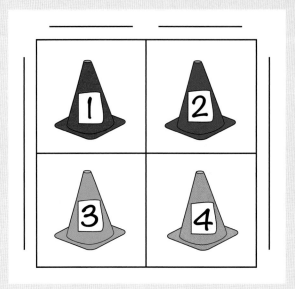

Figure 17.23   Setup for striking with a stick for distance.

Task: Children strike a ball with a polo stick through cones to a partner at various distances.

Environment: Children are organized into pairs or trios (if the class has an odd number of students). The distance between children can vary from 7 to 15 feet (about 2 to 4.5 meters). All children should face either east–west or north–south.

Feedback

- KPd: "You are keeping the stick low to the ground—excellent job!"
- KPp: "Be sure to step toward your target as you swing your stick."
- KR: "Why do you think the ball is not going in the direction you want it to?"

Skill Cues for Striking Continuously With a Polo Stick

Preparation

- Grip end of stick with dominant hand on bottom.
- Swing stick back low to floor.
- Point side in direction of travel of ball.

Execution

- Tap ball with middle of round part of stick.
- Keep ball within one or two steps of body.
- Push ball along ground using quick taps.
- Look up when you can to stay on pathway.

Follow-Through

- Keep stick low to ground.
- Point stick in direction of pathway.

Tasks (Striking Continuously With a Polo Stick)

Task: Children strike a ball continuously along the ground with a polo stick in different pathways and directions.

Environment: Balls and sticks are kept in each learning-team area. Pathways are designated by poly spots or floor tape. Children start on different pathways and strike the ball along the pathway.

Feedback

- KPd: "You are using quick taps that keep the ball close to your body—good job!"
- KPp: "Try to keep walking as you dribble the ball along the ground."

Assessment

Standard 1:

- Use teacher observation of skill cues.
- Children use figure 17.24 to self-assess by placing a check mark next to the tasks they were able to perform.

Name: _____

What were you able to do? Check the tasks that you completed:

_____ Tap the ball with the middle of the round part of the polo stick.

_____ Keep the ball within one or two steps of your body.

_____ Push the ball along the ground using quick taps.

_____ Look up when you can to stay on the pathway.

Figure 17.24 Self-check for striking continuously in different pathways and directions.

 Visit the web resource for learning activities, video clips, and review questions.

PART
V

Standards-Based Learning Experiences for Grades 3 Through 5

Designing Learning Experiences for Students in Grades 3 Through 5

Key Concepts

- Designing learning experiences for children in grades 3 through 5 based on stages of development and levels of motor skill learning
- Implementing standards-based instruction for children in grades 3 through 5
- Designing learning experiences about personal and social responsibility for children in grades 3 through 5

This chapter provides a developmental overview of learners in grades 3 through 5, as well as sample activities addressing personal and social responsibility to prepare children for working both independently and cooperatively as part of a team. The chapter also provides specialized movement-skill progressions in developmental games, dance, and gymnastics for learners at the combination and application levels. In addition, it addresses fitness education; national physical education standards, outcomes for grades 3 through 5, and assessment options; and developmentally appropriate guidelines for designing instruction, practice, feedback, and assessment.

DEVELOPMENT OF LEARNERS IN GRADES 3 THROUGH 5

Chapters 19 through 21 provide sample learning experiences that help children in grades 3 through 5 progress through the specialized phase of motor skill development. Those learning experiences are based on a rich understanding of how learners in grades 3 through 5 develop, which is the focus of this section. Mature-stage fundamental movement skills are now combined with the movement concepts of space, effort, and relationship to form specialized movement skills. Children use these skills to engage in cooperative and competitive practice of skills and tactics in gamelike activities, as well as developmental dance, gymnastics, and fitness-based activities. A developmental overview of children in grades 3 through 5 is provided in table 18.1.

Children in grades 3 through 5 are at the intermediate level of movement skill learning. At this level, children perform movements with greater consistency and fewer errors than before. They have developed a good general understanding of the movement task and possess greater kinesthetic sensitivity and are therefore acquiring a feel for skills. As a result, they begin to pay less attention to skill movements and more attention to the goal or product of a skill. They also become more capable of timing their movements with objects and events and of adapting their movements to changing environments.

Instructional activities described by skill progressions for intermediate learners are divided into two sublevels: combination and application. In the combination sublevel, the goal is to combine skills into smooth sequences. Closed skills within the combination skill progressions aim to elicit variety in the way the skills are combined by increasing the number of variables used to vary the task and the number of skills combined in gymnastics and dance sequences (e.g., walk, skip, schottische). Open skills within the combination level are varied by the way skills are combined and the number of skills combined in gamelike contexts (e.g., catch, immediate throw to a partner). In the application sublevel, the goal is to apply skills in cultural movement activities. When performing closed skills in this sublevel, the aim is to perform longer skill sequences, as in a dance or gymnastics routine. With open skills, the aim is to perform movements in gamelike conditions with offense and defense.

STANDARDS-BASED LEARNING

The national physical education standards and grade-level outcomes (SHAPE America, 2014) provide the basis for the learning experiences for grades 3 through 5. Since the national standards are based on developmentally appropriate content, it is not surprising that the combination- and application-level skill progressions derived from children's stages of motor development and movement skill learning inform national standards 1 and 2 for learners in grades 3 through 5.

Table 18.2 presents grade-level outcomes and assessment options for learners in grades 3 through 5 that are aligned with the national standards. Standards 1 and 2 serve as the foundation for the instructional activities described in chapters 19 through 21. Standard 3 is the focus for the activities reinforcing fitness education concepts in chapter 22, and standard 4 activities appear in this chapter. However, standards 3 through 5 outcomes can also be addressed as you redirect the focus of a game, dance, or gymnastics movement activity to include a goal addressing fitness, social responsibility, or the value of physical activity.

ASSESSING LEARNING

The assessment options presented in table 18.2 address the use of *observations* as a way for teachers to assess what students can *do* (e.g., performance of movement, fitness, and affective skills) and the use of *evaluation* to assess what students *know* (e.g., cognitive skills of describing, explaining, interpreting, and applying). Blueprints and sample summative rubrics for standards 1 and 2 are provided in chapters 19 through 21, which address, respectively, developmental games, developmental dance, and developmental gymnastics. The rubrics provided there describe the quality of performance at the beginning, developing, proficient, and advanced levels. These chapters also provide formative assessment ideas for each of the sample movement activities.

DESIGNING INSTRUCTION

Intermediate-level learners are acquiring new specialized movement skills. The goal of their movement

Table 18.1   Developmental Overview for Grades 3 Through 5

Category	Learner characteristics	Teaching implications
Visual	Ability to intercept objects at a variety of speeds and trajectories; ability to focus on an increasing number of aspects in the environment	Provide brightly colored objects that contrast with wall and floor coloring. Provide increasingly complex manipulative challenges.
Kinesthetic	Ability to identify all body parts; consistent laterality and improving directionality	Provide activities that challenge directionality.
Motor development	Differentiated movement Consistent performance of complete flexion, extension, and rotation of fundamental movement skills Development of specialized skills and application in cultural activities	Provide opportunities for refining and varying form-specific and outcome-specific closed skills through external pacing, multiple variables (space, effort, relationship, equipment), and combining three or more skills.
Motor learning	Greater consistency and fewer errors (concentration on varying and combining skills with less attention to critical elements of skill) Becoming capable of adapting to changing environments Ability to detect some errors in own performance	Provide opportunities for refining and adapting open skills in more to less predictable environments.
Cardiorespiratory endurance	Inability to sustain aerobic activity; hypokinetic circulation, low concentration of hemoglobin, higher respiration, shallower breathing, less ability to store glycogen) Ability to self-regulate energy expenditure and perform aerobic activity for longer periods of time	Provide opportunities for children to engage in aerobic activity of longer duration but have children determine duration for themselves.
Flexibility	Joint specific More flexible than adults because bones have not completely ossified	To minimize the possibility of injury (from prepubescent growth spurts), static and dynamic stretching should follow an aerobic warm-up.
Muscular strength and muscular endurance	Increase in muscle size resulting more from growth than from training	Children can develop muscular strength and muscular endurance through supervised training with high repetition and low resistance using exercise bands, body weight, and light hand weights and weight bars.
Body composition	Dependent on multiple variables, including genetics, maturation, nutrition, and activity level Increase in proportion of body fat during onset of puberty among girls	Promote sound nutrition and daily engagement in moderate to vigorous physical activity and in activities promoting muscular endurance in order to maintain a health-enhancing body composition.
Stage of cognitive development	Concrete operational stage, during which children can mentally represent objects or a series of probable events, can think logically about events that they have personally experienced, and are less egocentric and more able to consider others' perspectives	Use more complex task cards and worksheets to facilitate children's understanding and acquisition of movement skills. Whole-class format can be used for an entire class period. Stations can focus on multiple tasks. Students can follow more complex rules, observe and use critical elements to help others, use feedback to improve performance, and understand and apply simple game strategies and principles of movement.
Self-concept	More abstract and based on internal psychological characteristics and feelings of self-worth Influenced by one's peers	Provide inclusive environments with challenges appropriate for different levels of ability. Have children set short-term goals leading to accomplishment of long-term goals.
Self-esteem	Influenced not only by what others value but also by what the child deems important	Engage children in self-assessment and reflection to help them understand how their actions lead to attaining their goals.
Personal and social responsibility	More self-directed and beginning to develop empathy for others Inclined to engage in cooperative and competitive play	Establish prosocial skills as learning targets. Have children reflect on how their social skills (tolerance, fairness, cooperation, perseverance, listening, positive communication, conflict resolution) affect others and contribute to or detract from the attainment of goals.

Table 18.2   National Content Standards, Grade-Level Outcomes for Grades 3 Through 5, and Assessment Options

STANDARD 1: DEMONSTRATE COMPETENCE IN A VARIETY OF MOTOR SKILLS AND MOVEMENT PATTERNS.	
Outcomes and essential content	**Assessment options**
Refine, combine, and vary fundamental movement skills and develop basic specialized movement skills to be able to demonstrate • mature performance in all fundamental movement skills, • skills for performance outcomes (e.g., accuracy, speed, distance), and • skill combinations in small-sided practice tasks and games and dance and gymnastics sequences.	Assess attainment by using answer keys, checklists, or rubrics to score students' levels of success from observations of • mature movement criteria for all fundamental movement skills, • performance outcome goals, and • criteria for skill combinations performed in small-sided practice tasks and games and dance and gymnastics sequences.

STANDARD 2: APPLY KNOWLEDGE OF CONCEPTS, PRINCIPLES, STRATEGIES, AND TACTICS RELATED TO MOVEMENT AND PERFORMANCE.	
Outcomes and essential content	**Assessment options**

Apply concepts to authentic movement settings by
• combining elements of body, space, effort, and relationship with the performance of skills and skill combinations in small-sided practice tasks and games and dance and gymnastics environments; and
• using offensive and defensive strategies and tactics in small-sided practice tasks.
	Assess attainment by using answer keys, checklists, or rubrics to score students' levels of success.
	• Observation
	  ○ Correct performance of movement concepts with skills and combinations in games and dance and gymnastics environments
	  ○ Use of strategies and tactics in small-sided games
	• Evaluation of students' descriptions and explanations
	  ○ Movement concepts
	  ○ Application of concepts from strategies and tactics

STANDARD 3: DEMONSTRATE THE KNOWLEDGE AND SKILLS TO ACHIEVE AND MAINTAIN A HEALTH-ENHANCING LEVEL OF PHYSICAL ACTIVITY AND FITNESS.	
Outcomes and essential content	**Assessment options**

Use physical activity knowledge by charting and analyzing participation in physical activity outside of school for fitness benefit.
Use fitness knowledge by
• describing and applying the FITT guidelines to the components of health-related fitness,
• identifying the need for warm-up and cool-down in relationship to various physical activities,
• monitoring physiological indicators of moderate to vigorous physical activity (MVPA) and adjusting activity levels accordingly, and
• interpreting and understanding the significance of fitness test results and designing a fitness plan with help from the teacher.
	Assess attainment by using answer keys, checklists, or rubrics to score students' levels of knowledge about physical activity and fitness.
	Evaluate physical activity knowledge by documentation of regular participation in physical activity with logs such as Activitygram and Activity Log (Fitnessgram) and the Presidential Active Lifestyle Award materials from the President's Challenge youth fitness program.
	Evaluate fitness knowledge by
	• observation of safe and correct technique when performing activities for each component of fitness and
	• evaluation of students' ability to
	  ○ apply the FITT guidelines to the components of health-related fitness,
	  ○ describe the importance of warm-up and cool-down,
	  ○ monitor physiological indicators and adjust MVPA levels, and
	  ○ interpret Fitnessgram and President's Challenge test results and design a fitness plan.

STANDARD 4: EXHIBIT RESPONSIBLE PERSONAL AND SOCIAL BEHAVIOR THAT RESPECTS SELF AND OTHERS.	
Outcomes and essential content	**Assessment options**
Work independently, in pairs and small groups, and participate cooperatively in physical activities by <ul><li>identifying the purpose for and following activity-specific safe practices, rules, procedures, and etiquette;</li><li>working independently and productively for longer periods of time;</li><li>accepting responsibility for personal and interpersonal behavior in physical activity environments;</li><li>working cooperatively and involving others of all skill abilities in physical activities and group projects; and</li><li>respectfully listening and giving corrective feedback to peers.</li></ul>	Assess attainment by using answer keys, checklists, or rubrics to score students' levels of success. <ul><li>Observation of students<ul><li>Following safe practices, rules, procedures, and etiquette</li><li>Working independently and productively</li><li>Cooperating with others during peer feedback and goal-directed pursuits</li><li>Accepting rule infraction decisions positively</li><li>Assessing and accepting responsibility for own behavior problems without blaming others.</li></ul></li><li>Evaluation of student identification of the following:<ul><li>Safe practices, rules, procedures, and etiquette</li><li>Behaviors representing independent and productive work, cooperation, respect, and self-responsibility.</li></ul></li></ul>

STANDARD 5: RECOGNIZE THE VALUE OF PHYSICAL ACTIVITY FOR HEALTH, ENJOYMENT, CHALLENGE, SELF-EXPRESSION, AND/OR SOCIAL INTERACTION.	
Outcomes and essential content	**Assessment options**
Recognize the value of physical activity by <ul><li>attributing success and improvement to effort and practice,</li><li>choosing appropriate levels of challenge to develop success,</li><li>selecting and practicing skills that need improvement,</li><li>describing the social benefits gained from participation in physical activity,</li><li>explaining the health benefits and positive feelings associated with participation in physical activity,</li><li>positively participating with others,</li><li>analyzing physical activities for enjoyment and challenge, and</li><li>identifying the reasons for positive or negative responses to others.</li></ul>	Assess attainment by using answer keys, checklists, or rubrics to score students' levels of success. <ul><li>Observation of students<ul><li>Interacting positively with others</li><li>Choosing appropriate levels of challenge</li></ul></li><li>Evaluation of students in the following areas:<ul><li>Analysis of reasons for enjoying or not enjoying physical activities</li><li>Attribution of success and improvement to effort and practice</li><li>Selection and appropriate practice of skills for improvement</li><li>Explanations of the health benefits and positive feelings associated with participation in physical activity</li></ul></li></ul>

Based on SHAPE America 2014.

performances is to combine and apply both closed skills (as in dance and gymnastics) and open skills (as in games). The skill performance goal provides the basis for choosing instructional strategies from the Spectrum of Teaching Styles (see chapter 10). When the goal is to learn how to perform a specific skill or tactic, *reproduction* styles are often used—for example, an inclusion-style task card for performance of inverted balances or a practice-style task card for blocked practice of a give-and-go tactic.

On the other hand, when the goal is to create a new skill variation or new combination of closed skills, *production* styles are used to engage students in the design process. After the skill variation or combination is created, then reproduction styles are used to facilitate consistency in the learner's quality of performance of the closed skills. Similarly, when the goal is to figure out what tactics to use in open-skill, small-sided game play, production styles engage students in discovering when and how to effectively use the tactic. Reproduction styles are then used to engage students in random practice in order to use the tactic repetitively but under the different conditions of the small-sided game.

Since intermediate-level learners are becoming

more capable of determining correct and incorrect movement performance, the reciprocal and self-check styles are used more often. By fourth grade, students are capable of observing up to three movement cues or the execution of one tactic. In addition, they can be challenged by self-check questions to address the results of their choices about what to attend to and what movement response to use. For example, did one's choice of where to move in response to a defender's position help produce a shot on goal?

When designing learning experiences for grades 3 through 5, you can continue to use scaling of equipment and condition variables to provide affordances that allow learners to experience skill success (see chapter 6). By providing various equipment and environmental conditions, you can meet the unique needs of all children and deliver differentiated instruction. Equipment choices (e.g., size, length, width, and circumference) and various environmental conditions—differing, for example, in spatial (distance and trajectory) and temporal (speed) variables—should be offered to ensure that all children engage in purposeful learning and achieve success. The variable of relationship with others becomes more prominent in grades 3-5 as children are developmentally ready for

more complex interactions with others. The sample learning experiences presented in chapters 19-22 in games, dance, gymnastics, and fitness focus on individual, partner, and small-group learning. Station teaching provides the opportunity for greater interaction with others in movement contexts as well as for reflecting on the impact of positive and negative interactions on goal achievement.

PRACTICE AND FEEDBACK

The type of skill being practiced should inform your decisions about what type of practice and feedback to use. To structure practice for open skills (in game play), use blocked, serial, and random practice. For closed skills (in dance and gymnastics), use variable and constant practice. When teaching closed skills with children at the intermediate and advanced levels of skill learning, provide them with knowledge-of-performance descriptive (KPd) and prescriptive (KPp) feedback. Knowledge-of-results (KR) feedback is outcome based and used for outcome-based closed skills (e.g., "You made 4 out of 10 foul shots") and open skills (e.g., "you successfully outmaneuvered your opponent 3 out of 5 times"). For a review of practice and feedback design, see chapter 7.

Activities to Reinforce Personal and Social Responsibility

In the physical education setting, learners in grades 3 through 5 should demonstrate the following personal and social responsibility outcomes: persevering, accepting advice, cooperating interdependently, taking responsibility for a designated role, and accepting others. These behaviors help create a learning environment that is physically, emotionally, and socially safe, which in turn helps children establish a positive sense of self and others and enhances their learning. Therefore, we suggest having learners in grades 3 through 5 practice the behaviors associated with the grade-level values for personal and social responsibility *before* engaging them in movement activities addressing standards 1, 2, 3, and 5. Students' familiarity with these expected behaviors establishes the way that they are supposed to behave during physical education class. This approach sets the scene for decorum during all lessons and gives you the ability to reinforce, remind, and praise children's use of the personal and social responsibility behaviors, address behavior violations, and teach additional responsibility skills.

Table 18.3 illustrates the social contract that provides expected responsibility behaviors. Teachers often use team-building and cooperative physical education activities to engage students in learning and using behaviors of personal and social responsibility.

Table 18.3   Social Contract for Grades 3 Through 5

Learning outcomes	Behaviors	Response strategies
Persevere. Exhibit personal responsibility (SHAPE America, 2014, p.36).	Keep practicing to improve motor skills; don't give up! Seek opportunities to learn.	The student and teacher examine how the task or environment needs to be changed to be either more or less difficult.
Accept, implement, and respectfully give feedback (SHAPE America, 2014, p. 36).	Listen to teacher and peer feedback and try to use it to change behavior or improve motor skills. Provide approving and corrective feedback in a helpful way.	Hold a conference during which the student and teacher discuss the purpose of feedback, how to use it, and how to *accept* it positively; afterward, have the student write a journal entry. Hold a conference to discuss the purpose of feedback and how to *provide* it in a helpful way; afterward, have the student write a journal entry or engage in role playing to demonstrate appropriate feedback.
Cooperate interdependently. Work with others (SHAPE America, 2014, p. 36).	Show commitment to group as follows: • Using positive statements • Encouraging others • Working cooperatively • Demonstrating patience • Taking responsibility for one's role • Offering ideas • Accepting others' ideas	Student observes peers who are taking responsibility for their designated roles and describes how she or he could also exhibit these behaviors. Student completes a behavior ticket stating what he or she said that was not positive and what should have been said instead.
Exhibit application of rules, etiquette, and safety (SHAPE America, 2014, p. 36)	Adhere to etiquette and rules. Design appropriate etiquette and rules for created games. Apply safety principles in activity settings.	Say, "It looks like you are not adhering to rules." If the child acknowledges breaking the rules, say, "What should you be doing? . . . Let me see you do that." If the student does *not* admit to breaking rules, state the purpose of the rule and ask, "If you were to follow the rule, what would it look or sound like?" If the student provides a reasonable answer, have him or her commit to the behavior and rejoin the class. If not, state your expectations, ask if the student can comply, and say that you want to see her or him follow the rule. If the student continues to break rules, use a time-out with a focus question before allowing the student to rejoin the class.

The following examples of instructional activities are designed to elicit behaviors of personal and social responsibility and address national physical education standard 4 for children in grades 3 through 5. Each standard 4 activity includes a chart indicating what the positive and negative behaviors associated with the responsibility outcome look and sound like. Share the positive expectations with your students as goals for the activity; reinforce the behaviors through specific feedback and assess student performance of the behaviors through observation checklists and student reflection prompts. For additional resources, see the reference list at the end of the chapter.

CLEAN UP THE OIL SPILL

Learning Outcome

Cooperative interdependence: Work together to achieve a goal and praise others' success in movement performance (SHAPE America, 2014).

COOPERATIVE INTERDEPENDENCE LOOKS AND SOUNDS LIKE . . .	
Correct behavior 😊	**Incorrect behavior** ☹
Listening to and trying each other's ideas Encouraging the group to think of another way when an idea doesn't work Praising the group when we're making progress in solving a problem	Criticizing others' ideas and suggesting that they won't work Sitting back and providing little or no praise or encouragement, and few or no ideas, during the activity

Skill theme: Balance and locomotor skills

Movement concepts: space awareness (levels), relationship (over and under; on and off of)

Equipment: poly spots, hoops, carpet squares, ropes, scooters, task card indicating how equipment can be used, worksheet(s)

Directions: In this activity, the people represent oil polluting a body of water, which must be cleaned by removing the oil. To accomplish this cleaning, the oil (i.e., the participants) uses the equipment to travel across a specified space in specified ways. No oil—that is, no participant in the activity—is permitted to touch the floor; instead, the oil must stand on or be in the available equipment. The equipment can be reused and transported across the water. Successfully traveling across the space represents removing the oil from the polluted body of water. When the oil (i.e., participants) arrive on the shore, they complete a worksheet.

Feedback

Observe to see that students understand the criteria for solving the problem. Facilitate their efforts by providing ways for them to use equipment in order to cross the space without touching the floor.

Assessment

Standard 4: Use teacher observation (see rubric in figure 18.1).

Level 3: All participants offered verbal ideas about how to solve the problem; all group participants stayed physically active while solving the movement problem; participants used positive words of encouragement with each other; participants respected others' ideas.

Level 2: Most participants offered verbal ideas about how to solve the problem; most group participants stayed physically active while solving the movement problem; participants used some positive words of encouragement with each other; some participants ignored others' ideas.

Level 1: Participants experienced difficulty in sharing ideas about how to solve the problem; a few participants were not physically involved and stood off to the side.

Figure 18.1 Rubric for personal and social responsibility in oil spill activity.

BEACH-BALL HOOP

Learning Outcome

Cooperative interdependence (working together to achieve a goal)

COOPERATIVE INTERDEPENDENCE LOOKS AND SOUNDS LIKE . . .	
Correct behavior 🙂	**Incorrect behavior** 🙁
Moving the hoop to help teammates score	Moving hoops to prevent teammates from scoring
Aiming hits at playable heights for hoop holders and in playable directions for the receiver	Hitting without aiming purposefully
Praising and encouraging each other	Saying nothing, blaming, or ridiculing

Skill theme: striking with hands

Movement concepts: relationship (to hoop and partner)

Equipment: hoops; beach balls or junior volleyballs

Directions: This activity is performed by two pairs of players; one pair holds a hoop while the other pair (one on each side of the hoop) tries to volley a ball back and forth through the hoop. The hoop holders move to help the ball travel through the hoop. The volleyers can be permitted to hit the ball three times, then two, and then one in order to gradually add an element of challenge to the activity. A second challenge might include having players change roles (from hoop holder to volleyer or vice versa) without letting the ball touch the ground (Hastie, 2010, p. 153).

Feedback

Knowledge of Performance, descriptive (KPd): "I like how you are hustling to help the ball go through your hoop."

Assessment

Standard 4: Use a collective scorecard (figure 18.2).

Directions: Check a square for each point that your team earns during each round of play. One point is earned each time the ball goes through the hoop.

Round 1: three hits permitted before ball goes through hoop	❑❑❑❑❑❑❑❑❑❑❑❑❑❑ ❑❑❑❑❑❑❑❑❑❑❑❑❑❑
Round 2: two hits permitted before ball goes through hoop	❑❑❑❑❑❑❑❑❑❑❑❑❑❑ ❑❑❑❑❑❑❑❑❑❑❑❑❑❑
Round 3: one hit permitted before ball goes through hoop	❑❑❑❑❑❑❑❑❑❑❑❑❑❑ ❑❑❑❑❑❑❑❑❑❑❑❑❑❑

Collective score for all three rounds = _____

How did teammates work together to score?

Figure 18.2   Collective scorecard assessment for beach-ball hoop.

BASE SOCCER

Learning Outcome

Cooperative interdependence (working together to achieve a goal, encouraging group members)

COOPERATIVE INTERDEPENDENCE LOOKS AND SOUNDS LIKE . . .	
Correct behavior 🙂	**Incorrect behavior** 🙁
Adjusting one's body and speed in response to others in the group Making a playable pass to a teammate to keep the ball within the group's bounds Praising and encouraging others Honestly evaluating the team's adherence to rules	Tugging or pulling on the band Passing the ball recklessly and outside of the group boundary Inflating the score or awarding team points when the band is not taut

Skill theme: dribbling with feet

Movement concepts: relationship (inside of a stretched rope)

Equipment: one soccer ball and one long elastic ring of rope per group of four; six to eight bases positioned on the floor or field throughout general space. The elastic rope should be long enough for students to avoid contact while traveling as a group, but short enough to make continual passing important for goal attainment.

Directions: Four players stand inside a ring made by a wide elastic band or a long jump rope with the ends tied. The rope or band is placed around the players' waists, and the players may hold it with their hands. The challenge is for the group to work together to dribble and pass the soccer ball through general space and touch the ball to bases placed randomly on the field or gymnasium floor—all while keeping the elastic band taut around their waists (adapted from Orlick, 2006). The goal can be to touch a specified number of bases within a certain time limit.

Feedback

Encourage students to keep the rope or band taut and to award a point *only* when they dribble or pass the ball and touch a base with it completely taut.

Assessment

Standard 4: Use a T-chart for students to complete with specific group behaviors that demonstrate working together to achieve the game goal (figure 18.3)

🙂 Working together in base soccer...	
Looks like	Sounds like

Figure 18.3 T-chart assessment for base soccer.

COLLAGES

Learning Outcomes

Cooperative interdependence (offering ideas, accepting others' ideas), persevering

COOPERATIVE INTERDEPENDENCE LOOKS AND SOUNDS LIKE . . .	
Correct behavior 🙂	**Incorrect behavior** ☹
Offering balance ideas and accepting when one's idea is not used or doesn't quite work at that time Listening to and trying others' ideas Encouraging the group to stick with the task until completion	Sitting back and not offering ideas Getting upset when one's idea is not used Ignoring or ridiculing others' ideas

Skill theme: balancing on different body parts

Movement concepts: relationship (next to, over, and under others)

Equipment: one gymnastics mat per group of four of five students

Directions: The goal is to cooperate with peers to design a collage of static balances based on criteria provided by the teacher. Students follow the directions on the task card in figure 18.4, checking progress toward the goal. One member serves as the artistic director, who is responsible for making sure that the group meets the criteria in creating their collage.

Criteria for Collage

- Use different levels.
- Use negative space (e.g., "donut holes" or open space)
- Balances must connect physically.
- Use symmetry, asymmetry, or both.
- Use at least one inverted balance.

Completed?	Steps
	Each mover in your group must create a balance that can be held for at least five seconds.
	One mover should volunteer to begin and others should "add on" their balances.
	The artistic director checks the group balance against the criteria.
	When the collage is completed, the artistic director asks the teacher to take a photo.
	The group then views the picture and thinks of words to describe it; the recorder writes down the groups' ideas in the space below.

Figure 18.4   **Task card for designing a collage.**

Feedback

- "I see that everyone is offering balance ideas."
- "Remember to check your collage to see if it meets all criteria."

Assessment

Standard 4: Students use the assessment in figure 18.5 to rate their perceptions of their own and their group's ability to cooperate.

Describe your group's collage using three different words:

Self-Assessment

On a scale of 1 to 5, with 5 being the highest, how willing were you to accept your group members' ideas?

1	2	3	4	5
Not much		Somewhat		Very willing

Explain your rating: _____

Group-Assessment

How well did your group work together to complete the task?

1	2	3	4	5
Not at all		Somewhat		A lot

Explain your rating: _____

Figure 18.5 Designing a collage assessment for standard 4.

COOPERATIVE PARACHUTES

Learning Outcome

Cooperative interdependence (working together to achieve a goal)

COOPERATIVE INTERDEPENDENCE LOOKS AND SOUNDS LIKE . . .	
Correct behavior 🙂	Incorrect behavior 🙁
Working together with others to time the toss and catch of the parachute Cooperating by performing catchable tosses to other groups Praising and encouraging partner	Using too much or too little force when tossing Moving without regard to partner when moving to catch Ridiculing partner

Skill theme: tossing and catching with a mini parachute

Movement concepts: effort (creating and absorbing force), relationship (moving in relationship to others)

Equipment: one giant inflatable ball and a beach towel or mini parachute (6 feet, or 2 meters in diameter)

Directions: Groups of two or three practice using the towel or mini parachute to cooperatively toss and catch the ball. Different groups then cooperate to toss the ball back and forth. The activity can be made easier or more difficult by adjusting the distance, the size of the towel or parachute, or the height of a net to toss over.

Feedback

- "Your group is working together to time your toss into the air."
- "Make sure that you give together to absorb the force of the ball for a successful catch."

Assessment

Standard 4: Use the Cooperative Parachute Scorecard in figure 18.6 to record your highest number of consecutive passes from each round and answer the reflection prompt about group cooperation

Directions: Enter the highest number in the blank box for each round. Answer the reflection prompt.	
Round 1: What is the highest number of consecutive self-tosses and catches your group accomplished?	
Round 2: What is the highest number of consecutive catches you made between two groups?	
Round 3: What is the highest number of consecutive catches your groups made over the net?	
Reflection: Choose the results from one of the rounds and describe how you worked together to accomplish your highest score.	

Figure 18.6   Cooperative parachute scorecard.

TEAM WALKING

Learning Outcomes
Cooperative interdependence (working together to achieve a goal), perseverance

TEAM WALKING LOOKS AND SOUNDS LIKE . . .	
Correct behavior 🙂	**Incorrect behavior** 🙁
Providing verbal signals to coordinate the group's step pattern Moving in response to verbal signals Praising and encouraging group efforts	Paying no attention to verbal signals Moving independently Ridiculing others

Skill theme: dynamic balance

Movement concepts: space (direction, pathway, level), effort (speed), relationship (moving in unison with others)

Equipment: wooden walking planks with ropes attached for handholds

Directions: In groups of two to four, students move forward in unison on walking planks while using verbal signals to coordinate their step pattern. The challenge can be increased by adjusting the distance, pathway, speed, or incline or by having a group move in tandem with another group.

Feedback
"I am hearing verbal signals that are helping you move together as a team."

Assessment
Standard 4: What cues did your team use to help you move together in unison?

 Visit the web resource for learning activities, video clips, and review questions.

Chapter 19

Developmental Games

Key Concepts

- Defining developmental games
- Describing criteria for developmentally appropriate games
- Analyzing best practices in teaching games
- Describing game classifications and components
- Explaining how to structure student-designed games
- Implementing the combination and application task progressions to design learning experiences in game play

When asked, "What is a game?" physical education teacher candidates have given the following responses:

- "When two teams compete against each other."
- "A game is when you have offense and defense."
- "A game must have an object and equipment."
- "Games are activities that have winners and losers."

Though all of these responses are correct to a certain extent, we wish to expand on these definitions and describe developmental games as activities in which one or more persons engage in cooperative or competitive play, with or without an object, within a structure of rules and boundaries (Allison & Barrett, 2000). Similarly, Baumgarten & Langton (2006) define a game as "an activity involving one or more people, on the move, with or without an object, playing under an agreed upon set of rules, designed for self-testing, cooperative accomplishments or competitive outcomes" (p. 208).

This chapter provides progressive learning experiences for combination- and application-level movers in the four categories of game: target, striking and fielding, net or wall, and invasion. It also addresses the following topics: best practices for teaching games; the blueprint for tactical and skill learning goals used in designing assessments; variables for student-designed games; guidelines for the national physical education standards, as well as outcomes for learners in grades 3 through 5; and developmentally appropriate guidelines for designing instruction, practice, feedback, and assessment.

DEVELOPMENTALLY APPROPRIATE GAMES

In developmental physical education, games must be designed and modified to meet children's unique developmental needs across all domains of learning (i.e., motor, cognitive, and social). Figure 19.1 illustrates the fact that developmentally appropriate learning experiences in games are affected by movement concepts of body, space, effort, and relationship. As described in chapter 5 and reviewed in chapter 18, children in grades 3 through 5 are at the intermediate level of movement skill learning. At this level, they are more capable than before of timing their movements with objects and events and of adapting their movements to changing environments. They now combine mature-stage fundamental movement skills with the movement concepts of space, effort, and relationship to form specialized movement skills. They use these specialized skills to perform cooperative and competitive skills and to practice tactics in gamelike activities.

This chapter describes gamelike activities for each game form: target, striking and fielding, net or wall, and invasion. The combination-level skill progressions described here (see tables 19.8, 19.10, 19.12, and 19.14) are designed to help children combine skills into smooth sequences. The application-level skill progressions (see tables 19.9, 19.11, 19.13, 19.15) apply skills in cultural activities (i.e., modified sports). Both the combination and the application skill progressions provide affordances to learners by scaling equipment and conditions in the environment (see chapter 6). These developmentally appropriate skill progressions help children gradually become versatile game players who possess a repertoire of skills. This way of teaching games to children meets national guidelines for developmentally appropriate practice, which state

that "teachers select, design, sequence, and modify games to maximize specific learning, fitness/skill enhancement, and enjoyment" (National Association for Sport and Physical Education, 2009, p. 17).

The goals for addressing games in the developmental physical education curriculum include helping children to do the following:

Become skillful game players with versatile movement skills that they can adapt to various game situations

Learn to modify and design games

Understand tactical game play so that they can think quickly, anticipate, and make appropriate tactical decisions in game situations

Understand game structures (e.g., rules, boundaries, scoring systems)

Value game content and see game playing as a way to stay physically active for a lifetime

(adapted from Rovegno & Bandhauer, 2013 p. 273).

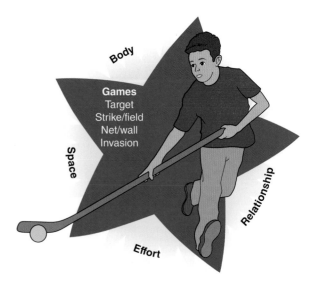

Figure 19.1 The Active Child: games.

BEST PRACTICES WHEN TEACHING GAMES

The tasks and environments created for game play must adhere to the following best practices.

- **Skill and tactical development:** Specialized skills used in cultural sport and game activities derive from fundamental skills developed in physical education in pre-K through grade 2. Specialized skills are learned in the context of small-sided practices and gamelike situations that include the tactics associated with smart play. "Game play includes not only the execution of motor skills but also components such as making decisions, supporting teammates who have the ball, marking or guarding opponents, covering teammates, adjusting position as play unfolds, and ensuring adequate court or field coverage by means of a base position" (Mitchell, Oslin, & Griffen, 2013, p. 6).

- **Maximum participation:** Children get better as a result of engaging in repetitive practice of skill and game tactics in gamelike contexts. As a result, it is inappropriate to use large-sided games (e.g., steal the bacon; kickball or softball; sideline soccer, basketball, or hockey) because they require that at any given time most children are waiting either for a turn or for an opportunity to participate (which may be rare, as when playing the outfield in kickball). In contrast, small-sided practices and games allow children to make as many attempts as necessary to become consistent at performing skills and reading and responding appropriately to tactical situations. Therefore, teachers need to provide opportunities for simultaneous play in the form of multiple groupings of one on one, two on one, and so on (up to three on three).

- **Inclusion:** Because elimination games put participants out of the action if they underperform, these games deprive less skilled players of the opportunity to improve their performance. Inclusion, on the other hand, requires teachers to provide children with multiple performance levels with the opportunity to engage repetitively in the skills and tactics used in small-sided games. Including children "at their level" may mean that games use different equipment, boundaries, or rules. Children are aware of performance differences among their peers. When sensitized to the idea that *fairness* in physical education class involves each child playing at his or her optimal level, children not only understand the need for diversity in playing conditions but also, when prompted, can come up with their own inclusion ideas. For example, inclusion might result in the following adjustments:

  - Some children receiving pitched balls and some using a batting tee; some using a shorter or wider bat or a shorter distance between bases

  - Using different boundaries on either side of the net, different distances from which to serve, or a different number of allowed bounces before a ball is returned

  - All participants receiving the game object before a goal is attempted; cool defense (farther away from the player with the game object) rather than warm defense (closer to the player)

- **Prosocial interaction:** Interactions that uplift, support, and encourage others should be promoted during game play. In this way, students learn to make catchable passes to teammates; pass among teammates; cooperate with others to reach a goal; and help others by giving appropriate feedback, encouraging them to keep trying, and uplifting them through praise. In contrast, activities should *avoid* games and situations that promote self-esteem at the expense of others (e.g., dodgeball), unmatched teams, and losing points or receiving a negative label for unsuccessful skill attempts (e.g., shooting games such as P-I-G, in which a player gets a letter with each missed shot and, after missing too many, is eliminated from play). Nor should participants tolerate antisocial behavior in the form of verbal or nonverbal putdowns or derisive comments. Instead, provide opportunities for students to engage in alternative behaviors and, when needed, conflict resolution.

GAME CLASSIFICATION

Classifying games based on common tactics allows physical educators to teach for transfer of gameplay tactics across categories of games and across games within a category. In competitive games, children use movement skills, skill combinations, and game tactics to vie toward a goal. In *noninvasive* competitive games, children compete in separate spaces, as in bowling and tennis. In *invasive* competitive games, they compete within the same space, as in soccer and basketball. Here are the major categories of competitive games.

- **Target:** This category includes noninvasive competitive games involving accuracy in which players perform independently by projecting objects toward a specific target. Examples include disc golf, bowling, and golf.

- **Striking and fielding:** In these noninvasive competitive games, students work independently to send an object into an opponent's territory in order to gain time to run bases and score. Meanwhile, opponents work together to move the object to the base that will halt the runner's progress and prevent scoring. As a result, baserunners and infielders are active at the bases simultaneously, usually one on one, as the fielder tries to tag the bag or runner, who tries at the same time to touch the bag first and avoid the tag. Examples include baseball, softball, cricket, and kickball.

- **Net or wall:** In these noninvasive competitive games, students remain within their team's boundaries and attack the opponent's space with objects while defending their own space against attack. Examples include the lead-up games of four square, pickleball, and Newcomb, as well as the games of volleyball, badminton, and tennis.

- **Invasion:** In these invasive competitive games, teammates and opponents occupy the same space as they simultaneously try to defend their territory and attack the opponent's goal. Offensive players try to maintain possession in order to advance the game object toward a goal and score. Defensive players try to defend space and opposing players in order to gain possession of the game object. Players' roles switch between offense and defense based on which team has possession of the game object.

This approach of teaching for transfer of tactical ability supports standards 1 and 2 by engaging children in demonstrating competency in skills and tactics related to movement performance (SHAPE America, 2014). Teaching for transfer has the virtues of economy and versatility. For example, students learn that striking a ball into an open space on the opponent's side of the court makes it more

difficult for the opponent to return the object and more likely that the offense will score. They also learn that this one tactic can be used over and over in many small-sided net games (e.g., four square, pickleball, tennis, badminton, and volleyball). The tactical approach also supports the learner's progression, within game categories, of combining skills and movement concepts (consistent level) with tactics that support teammates in offensive or defensive play (combination level) and finally with tactics that engage students in competing against each other (application level).

The tactical approach has been supported by a variety of research (Butler, 1997; Grehaigne, Wallian, & Godbout, 2005; Griffin, Brooker, & Patton, 2005; Rovegno, Nevett, Brock, & Babiarz, 2001). Findings have demonstrated that game lessons using a tactical approach (as compared with the traditional approach) resulted in increased student interest, involvement, understanding, creative input, and peer interaction. In addition, teachers provided more time for learning and practicing, increased the quantity and cognitive level of their questions, and focused on interventions and coaching rather than on officiating.

The four categories of competitive games addressed in the tactical games approach (Mitchell, Oslin, & Griffin, 2013) can be placed on a continuum ranging from easier to more difficult based on the tactical decisions that players make as they interact during game play (see table 19.1).

- Target games are the easiest because they involve only one tactical problem: accuracy. Children work on accuracy by setting up in an appropriate stance (base) and making good decisions about distance and direction (Mitchell, Oslin, & Griffin, 2013). In addition to target games (e.g., bowling, quoits), accuracy is a tactic that can be transferred into all other game categories, where it may be used not only to move game objects to teammates but also to serve and score. Aiming activities involving the variables of distance and direction are first addressed in the consistent-level progressions for many of the fundamental manipulative skills (e.g., throwing, kicking, striking to a target), and they remain critical in combination-level practice activities (e.g., throwing to a teammate on the move, receiving a pass, dribbling and kicking into the goal) and in application-level small-sided games (e.g., maintaining possession of the game object and scoring).

- Striking-and-fielding games come second in the progression because they build on returning to base (in this case, fielding position) and on using accuracy to throw to teammates (the tactic of supporting in fielding) and to send the game object to open spaces (in batting). Fielding also expands accuracy to include the element of quickness (in addition to distance and direction). In addition, fielding requires the child to decide where to throw the ball to get an out, who should field the ball, and who should back up the teammate going for the ball (the tactic of covering). This type of game also introduces new tactics involved in baserunning—for example, how many bases to try for on a struck ball and when to advance further after one gets on base.

- Net and wall games come third in the progression because they build on using accuracy to pass to teammates and accuracy to find open spaces in the territory of the defense (e.g., Newcomb, volleyball). Still, offense and defense remain separated in net games, and, though they are near each other in wall games, they still take turns hitting the ball and do not try to interfere with an opponent's shot. Initially, small-sided practice involves cooperative rallies to help players become consistent performers. Competitive play begins by sending game objects to open spaces, returning to a base position, and anticipating and moving to where the opponent will return the game object. In Newcomb and volleyball, players use the tactic of supporting to get into position to receive a pass from a teammate and use the tactic of covering to back up teammates going for the ball as it comes over the net. New tactics learned in net and wall games relate to placing shots to set up attacks by creating space in front of, behind, and to the sides of opponents.

- Invasion games are the most difficult because they require offense players to maintain possession of the game object and score in the opponent's territory while defensive players—who are in the same space—try to block or disrupt their efforts or take possession of the game object. When a change of possession does occur, the defense becomes the offense, and vice versa, thus requiring players to *adjust* their roles quickly. In addition, though shooting for a goal in an invasion game requires the same accuracy tactics (distance, direction, quickness through open spaces) used in less difficult game types, players in invasion games must also use tactics to outmaneuver defensive players. For example, they build on the tactic of sending a game object accurately to a teammate through open spaces by sending lead passes to teammates who fake, feint, and cut to open spaces in order to receive passes and score. In addition, in some invasion games, players can travel with the ball by dribbling, thus creating new tactics involving dribbling while protecting the ball and shooting or passing accurately off the dribble. Accordingly, defensive players must also use new tactics, including *guarding* (*marking*), pressuring, and goal keeping.

In addition to these four competitive game forms, children in grades 3 to 5 should also be engaged in student-designed games. These games involve a "process where students create, organize, implement, practice and refine their own games within certain limits presented by the teacher" (Hastie, 2010, p.3). When children design and modify their own games, they experiment with varying the components or structures of a game, including the equipment, rules, boundaries, scoring procedures, and tactics. The teacher's role is to "monitor task and environment constraints and intervene if they are not getting the movement responses they want children to learn" (Rovegno & Bandhauer, 2013, p. 305). Children must also adhere to all aspects of best practices for game instruction when they modify games or design their own. Children should begin by manipulating one or two variables after playing a teacher-designed game. The easiest variables for children to modify typically involve boundaries, equipment, and number of players because the ripple effect of changes across other categories is less.

Table 19.2 describes the variables that children can manipulate when designing tag, target, striking-and-fielding, and invasion games.

DESIGNING INSTRUCTION

The design of instruction for developmental games consistently addresses standards 1 and 2 by providing opportunities for students to become skilled and knowledgeable in game play and tactics. The content is derived from the task

Table 19.1 Learning Goal Blueprint for Tactical Decisions Across Game Forms

Game component	Target games	Striking-and-fielding games	Net and wall games	Invasion games
Base Position to which players return between skill tries	Starts in setup or stance position.	Returns to fielding position or base.	Returns to court position between shots or rallies.	Sets up in a position.
Decision making Ability to makes appropriate decisions (e.g., what to do with the ball) during a game	Makes decisions using distance and direction for accuracy.	Fielder: Decides where to move to receive or throw ball. Batter: Detects pitch and decides hit placement. Runner: Decides when to advance.	Positions body to hit to the most open area to set up an attack or score.	Makes appropriate decisions about passing, dribbling, and shooting.
Skill execution Efficient execution of selected skills	Demonstrates accuracy.	Fielder: Gets into position and accurately sends ball to receiver. Batter: Accurately hits ball to desired placement. Runner: Runs through or rounds bases.	Offense: Accurately sends shots to the most open area; varies the force and location of shots.	Offense: Shoots accurately when open, passes to open receivers, maintains possession, and fakes. Goalkeeper: Prevents scoring.
Supporting Movement into position to receive a pass from a teammate		Fielder: Moves into position to receive throws from teammates.	Volleyball player: Moves into position to receive passes from teammates.	Offensive player: Moves into position to receive passes from teammates.
Covering Action taken to back up a teammate making a challenge for the ball		Fielder: Backs up teammates fielding the ball.	Volleyball receiver: Backs up teammates as ball comes over net.	Defensive player: Moves into position to help or back up a teammate going for the ball.
Guarding (marking) Defensive maneuvering to deny the offense the ball or prevent it from scoring				Defensive player: Maneuvers to prevent scoring or block the offense and gain possession of the ball.
Adjusting Changing position to accommodate game flow			.	Adjusts from offense to defense.

Adapted from Hastie 2010.

progressions for each of the four game categories. This chapter provides a sampling of instructional activities for the content represented in the combination stage and the application stage of movement skill learning. The instructional activities provide a framework for designing lesson episodes; they do *not* necessarily represent a lesson episode per se, because children develop the capability to perform tactics with the skills by engaging in many attempts over time.

The rest of this section addresses the chain of decision making used to design instruction derived from motor-development and learning theory, the movement framework, standards-based physical education, assessment of student learning, and effective instruction practices. The categories addressed for each instructional activity include learning outcome, tactic, teaching style, task or game, enrichment, environment, practice, skill cues, feedback, and assessment.

Table 19.2   Variables for Designing Games

Game variable	Tag	Target	Striking-and-fielding	Net and wall	Invasion
Goal of game	• Getting to a specific target point • Number of tags in a time limit • Being the last one tagged • 1v1 tag: recording more tags than opponent within time limit	• Single target or multiple targets	• Use of implement or body to strike an object to an area • To field or catch an object (with or without an implement) and send it to an area	• Maintaining a cooperative rally • Hitting a game object over a net into opponent's zone so that opponent cannot return it	• Scoring by maintaining possession • Maintaining possession and scoring over an end line or into a goal
Environment	• Boundaries • Shape or size of playing area • Safety zones	• Stationary or moving target • Freestanding, hanging, or wall-mounted target • Size of target • Level of target • Distance or angle from target	• Boundaries • Pathways • Number and positioning of bases	• Dimensions of court and net height • Lines on court • Wall space used • Lines or targets on walls	• Boundaries (none, sidelines only, walled in, shape) • Court lines or zones • Type of goal (size, shape, location, number)
Rules	• How a player can be tagged • Whether tagged player is "frozen" • Whether players can be unfrozen (and how) • How long player can stay in a safety zone	• Collective or individual scoring • Scoring options: hitting target, hitting multiple targets, taking fewest turns to hit all targets, hitting most within time limit, hitting from farthest distance	• Scoring options: getting to a base or specific number of bases, hitting to an area or over a boundary line • How a player gets out: caught ball, specific number of failed attempts, getting tagged, getting run off of a designated pathway, batting out of designated area • Changing teams: after specific number of outs, after all or specified number of batters have a turn, after certain score	• Scoring options: collective, when opponent misses ball, when game object goes out of bounds • Ongoing scoring or only on serve • How game starts • What happens when game object goes out of bounds • Number of touches or bounces permitted • Game violations: out of bounds, hitting game object into net, serving to wrong area	• Whether moving with game object is allowed • Scoring: how many times players must touch game object before scoring, whether all players must touch it before scoring • How to start game: coin flip, jump ball, face-off, shoot-off • How to restart game after scoring: play goes on, other team gets ball, play begins from a starting line • What happens when game object goes out of bounds • How to get possession: after a score, interception, fumble, tackle or tag, rebound, violation, opponent out of turns

(continued)

369

Table 19.2 *(continued)*

Game variable	Tag	Target	Striking-and-fielding	Net and wall	Invasion
Equipment	• Object (if any) used to tag players	• Object used to hit target (e.g., beanbag, gator-skin ball, bowling ball)	• Type of ball • Type of striking implement (e.g., body, bat, stick)	• Type of object (e.g., foam ball, junior volleyball, tennis ball, ring, shuttlecock) • Type and size of striking imple-ment (e.g., racket, paddle) • Cones, ropes, nets	• Type of game object • Type of implement for moving game object
Number of players	• How many	• Single or teams	• Number on bat-ting team • Number in the field	• Singles or doubles • Teams of two to four	• Number per team
Players' roles	• Who tags • How many tag-gers	• To hit target	• Whether batter runs to a base(s) upon hitting • Positions taken by outfielders	• Positions on court	• Who can score • Who can move • Whether post players used • Whether goalies used • How to change play-ing positions
Skills	• Fast walking • Running • Scooter riding	• How to send object to target: overhand or underhand throw; kick; strike; bounce	• Striking • Fielding • Tagging • Running • Pitching • Covering base or area	• Serving • Striking with hands or arms • Receiving game object	• Bouncing • Passing or throwing • Kicking or dribbling with feet • Tackling • Receiving or catching • Long-handled stick for dribbling

The learning outcome reflects the skills and game tactics identified in the progression chart (e.g., maintain a rally or attack the goal). The tactic category listing describes how the tactic will be used (e.g., keep possession by moving forward to support passer).

Teaching style options are presented with an indication that the reproduction styles listed can provide opportunities for practice with feedback, whereas the production styles can be used to lead students to discover how, why, and when tactics are used. Multiple teaching styles can be used to engage students in learning. The choice of style, or order of styles (see the discussion of mobility ability in chapter 10), depends on the learning objectives of the lessons. For example, guided discovery can be used to help students discover how to set up an attack, the practice style can be used to help students practice skills (dribbling and passing), and the reciprocal style can be used to help students practice and reinforce the tactic by watching and giving feedback to a partner.

The task or game listing describes the relevant skills, player roles, rules, and scoring. Given these task or game elements, the environment listing includes choices for scaling the equipment and conditions to enable success for students of differing abilities—for example, different ball sizes, distances from the target, target heights, and playing area dimensions (see figures 6.1, 6.2, 6.3 in chapter 6). In addition, some tasks are followed by an enrichment category which suggests specific ways to challenge students who master the task by increasing difficulty.

The type of practice chosen should be based on the goal of the skill. For example, if the goal is to attain correct timing and technique (beginners or closed skills, e.g., foul shots), then the choice is constant practice in unvarying conditions. However, if the goal is to move in response to unpredictable settings (open skills), then the choice is variable practice with a progression of more predictable (blocked) to less predictable (random) conditions.

The skill cues listing describes the movements that a player must perform and the environmental conditions to which a player must attend. Closed-skill cues describe the movements of a skill (e.g., step with the opposite foot) that are used with beginners (e.g., kicking with the inside of the foot) and for closed skills (e.g., batting, serving, target games). Open-skill cues describe the environmental conditions to which the player must attend (e.g., where to look, what to look for) and how to move in response (e.g., point fingers up to catch ball arriving overhead) in dynamic net, invasion, or striking-and-fielding game play.

The level of movement skill learning and the goal of the skill (closed or open) determine the type of feedback used. Knowledge-of-performance (KP) feedback focusing on the *movement pattern* (skill cues) is most appropriate for beginning-stage learners who need to know how to correct the technique and timing of their movements. Knowledge-of-results (KR) feedback focuses on the outcome of movement performance (e.g., how high, how far, how long; shot intercepted, blocked, made). It is most appropriate for intermediate- and advanced-stage learners performing outcome-specific closed skills (as in serves, bowling, and golf) and open skills (as in interceptions, scoring, and successful passes).

The teacher's role is to augment the intrinsic KR feedback that students receive (e.g., knowing whether a shot went into the basket) by using KP feedback about *movement parameters* that address what they need to attend to in the environment (e.g., what to look for, where to look, timing, positioning) and how to respond more successfully (e.g., particular speed, force, direction, or body-part movement or placement). For example, after unsuccessful attempts at intercepting a ball coming over the net, a player might receive feedback about moving back to a central position on the court in order to be better prepared to move quickly to either side of the court.

When game skills and tactics are new to intermediate-level learners, use knowledge-of-performance descriptive feedback (KPd) (e.g., "your foot went over the line") and knowledge-of-performance prescriptive feedback (KPp) (e.g., "you need to stay between the offensive players rather than off to one side"). When students are refining skills as intermediate-level learners, use questions about the outcome of the skill (KR) or result of movement or parameters (KP) to encourage them to describe what they think happened and to try to come up with a solution. This approach is consistent with recommendations for giving intermediate-level learners less frequent feedback so that they become less dependent on outside sources of feedback.

Assessments give teachers and students information about the quality of learning. Standard 1 assessments focus on psychomotor performance and address either the process or the product of movements. If the goal of the skill is to use correct performance technique and timing, then process assessments usually take the form of observation checklists of movement cues. If the goal of the skill relates to the product of performance (e.g., how high, how far, blocks, accuracy), then quantitative measures of performance (product assessments) are used—for example, how many times out of 10, how many times in succession, or number of times that a particular tactic or skill was performed successfully or unsuccessfully in a game.

Assessments for standard 2 address cognitive aspects and represent the level of thinking that is developmentally appropriate for the learner. In grades 3 through 5, students are in the concrete stage of thought and can participate in most levels of thinking, as long as the question relates directly to what they are experiencing. Here are a few examples: "Describe why the defense should stay between the offensive player and the goal." "Diagram where on the court the ball should be thrown in order to set up an attack." "Compare the movement performance of a peer with the criteria and give feedback to help him or her improve." Figure 9.2 in chapter 9 provides examples of cognitive assessments reflecting the levels of thinking.

In game performance, standards 1 and 2 are often assessed simultaneously because psychomotor performance results from cognitive decision making. For instance, in a net game, a player might decide to send the ball deep into the opponent's court because the opponent is positioned close to the net.

Criteria from the learning goal blueprint (table 19.1) were used to design the summative rubrics for each of the game forms (see tables 19.3 through 19.6).

Table 19.3 Scoring Rubric for Target Games (Bowling and Golf)

Component	Proficient	Developing	Basic
Base	Consistently starts in a setup or stance position.	Sometimes starts in a setup or stance position.	Rarely starts in a setup or stance position.
Decision making	Consistently makes decisions using distance and direction for accuracy. • Where to step and roll or strike • Length of step and backswing	Sometimes makes decisions using distance and direction for accuracy.	Rarely makes decisions using distance and direction for accuracy.
Skill execution	Consistently demonstrates accuracy. • Steps and rolls or strikes in direction of target. • Creates enough force in length of step and backswing to cover distance to target. • Uses smooth, connected sequence of movements for approach and swing.	Sometimes demonstrates accuracy.	Rarely demonstrates accuracy.

Table 19.4 Scoring Rubric for Striking-and-Fielding Games (Baseball and Softball)

Component	Proficient	Developing	Basic
Base	• Fielder: Consistently starts in fielding position before each pitch. • Batter: Consistently starts with correct grip and stance. • Runner: Consistently returns to base.	• Fielder: Sometimes returns to fielding position before each pitch. • Batter: Sometimes uses correct grip and stance. • Runner: Sometimes returns to base.	• Fielder: Rarely returns to fielding position before each pitch. • Batter: Rarely uses correct grip and stance. • Runner: Rarely returns to base.
Decision making	• Fielder: Consistently decides where to move to receive and throw the ball. • Batter: Detects pitch and most often attempts appropriate hit placement. • Runner: Consistently runs to beat the throw and decides appropriately when to advance.	• Fielder: Sometimes hesitates or misjudges where to move to receive and throw the ball. • Batter: Detects pitch and sometimes attempts appropriate hit placement. • Runner: Sometimes runs to beat the throw; sometimes hesitates or misjudges when to advance.	• Fielder: Often hesitates or misjudges where to move to receive and throw the ball. • Batter: Sometimes swings early or late. • Runner: Sometimes runs to beat the throw; often hesitates or misjudges when to advance.
Skill execution	• Fielder: Consistently moves feet to the ball and catches it; uses smooth motion to throw with step and release toward target and enough force to reach it. • Batter: Consistently executes fast, horizontal swing; follows through in direction of placement; drops bat and runs. • Runner: Consistently uses appropriate footwork for running through or rounding bases.	• Fielder: Sometimes assumes ready position, moving feet to the ball and catching it; hesitates before throwing; inconsistently steps and releases toward target and generates enough force to reach it. • Batter: Sometimes contacts the ball and drops the bat; hesitates before running to base. • Runner: Sometimes uses appropriate footwork for running through or rounding bases.	• Fielder: Rarely assumes ready position, moves feet to the ball, and catches it; hesitates before throwing; inconsistently steps and releases toward target and generates enough force to reach it. • Batter: Rarely contacts the ball and drops the bat; hesitates before running to base. • Runner: Rarely uses appropriate footwork for running through or rounding bases.
Supporting	• Fielder: Consistently supports teammate with the ball by being in position to receive the throw.	• Fielder: Sometimes attempts to get into support position.	• Fielder: Rarely gets into support position.
Covering	• Fielder: Consistently backs up appropriate teammates who are fielding the ball.	• Fielder: Sometimes backs up teammates who are fielding the ball.	• Fielder: Rarely backs up teammates who are fielding the ball.

Table 19.5 Scoring Rubric for Net and Wall Games (Pickleball, Tennis, Volleyball)

Component	Proficient	Developing	Basic
Base	Consistently returns to court position between shots or rallies.	Sometimes returns to court position in between shots or rallies	Rarely returns to court position in between shots or rallies
Decision making	Consistently positions body to hit to the most open place in order to set up an attack or score a point (long and short shots; left, right, and mid court).	Sometimes positions body to hit to the most open place in order to set up an attack or score a point (long and short shots; left, right, and mid court).	Rarely positions body to hit to the most open place in order to set up an attack or score a point (long and short shots; left, right, and mid court).
Skill execution	Consistently sends shots to the most open area; varies the force and location of shots.	Sometimes sends shots to the most open area; varies the force and location of shots.	Rarely sends shots to the most open area; varies the force and location of shots.
Supporting	Volleyball: Consistently moves into position to receive passes from teammates to set up an attack and score.	Volleyball: Sometimes moves into position to receive passes from teammates to set up an attack and score.	Volleyball: Rarely moves into position to receive passes from teammates to set up an attack and score.
Covering	Volleyball receiver: Consistently backs up others as ball comes over net.	Volleyball receiver: Sometimes backs up others as ball comes over net.	Volleyball receiver: Rarely backs up others as ball comes over net.

Table 19.6 Scoring Rubric for Invasion Games (Team Handball, Soccer, Hockey, Basketball)

Component	Proficient	Developing	Basic
Base	Consistently sets up in position.	Sometimes sets up in position.	Rarely sets up in position.
Decision making	Consistently makes appropriate decisions about passing (and type of pass), dribbling, and shooting on goal. Goalkeeper: Consistently moves to right place to prevent scoring.	Sometimes makes appropriate decisions about passing (and type of pass), dribbling, and shooting on goal. Goalkeeper: Sometimes moves to right place to prevent scoring.	Rarely makes appropriate decisions about passing (and type of pass), dribbling, and shooting on goal. Goalkeeper: Rarely moves to right place to prevent scoring.
Skill execution	Offense: Consistently shoots on goal when open, passes to open receivers, and aptly uses fakes. Goalkeeper: Consistently prevents scoring (cuts down angle by moving toward offense and moves into position to block ball).	Offense: Sometimes shoots on goal when open, passes to open receivers, and uses fakes. Goalkeeper: Sometimes prevents scoring.	Offense: Rarely shoots on goal when open, passes to open receivers, and uses fakes. Goalkeeper: Rarely prevents scoring.
Supporting	Offense: Consistently moves into position to receive passes from teammates in order to maintain possession of ball and score.	Offense: Sometimes moves into position to receive passes from teammates in order to maintain possession of ball and score.	Offense: Rarely moves into position to receive passes from teammates in order to maintain possession of ball and score.
Guarding or marking	Defense: Consistently maneuvers to deny offense the ball or prevent scoring.	Defense: Sometimes maneuvers to deny offense the ball or prevent scoring.	Defense: Rarely maneuvers to deny offense the ball or prevent scoring.
Covering	Defense: Consistently backs up player making a challenge for the ball.	Defense: Sometimes backs up player making a challenge for the ball.	Defense: Rarely backs up player making a challenge for the ball.
Adjusting	Consistently changes from offense to defense when appropriate.	Sometimes changes from offense to defense when appropriate.	Is unsure of when to change from offense to defense.

Games can also serve as vehicles for developing fitness and personal and social responsibility and provide opportunities for challenge, enjoyment, and social interaction. When teachers incorporate objectives relating to these aspects of game play, they must also prepare assessments that match the intention of the relevant physical education standard.

- Standard 3: The most common component of fitness addressed through games is cardiorespiratory endurance. A sample assessment is provided later in this chapter and could be replicated in other game-learning experiences.

- Standard 4: Chapter 18 describes several learning activities that engage students in exhibiting personal and social responsibility through physical activity. During games, students should continue to respect and cooperate with others, follow rules, and appropriately receive and give feedback. To facilitate success in this area, teachers need to inform students that these behaviors of personal and social responsibility are expected every day; furthermore, teachers need to reinforce this expectation through reminders, prompts, praise, and feedback. The rubric presented in table 19.7 illustrates a way to assess personal and social responsibility throughout game-learning experiences.

- Standard 5: This standard asks children to recognize the value of physical activity. They can do so for themselves only through engaging in self-reflection about their own participation over time. To this end, figure 19.2 provides sample prompts to engage students in ongoing self-reflection. Teachers can use data collected from responses to these prompts early on to respond to students' needs and interests.

Table 19.7 Scoring Rubric for Personal and Social Responsibility (Grades 3-5)

Standard 4 behavior	Responsible	Developing	Irresponsible
Personal responsibility	Exhibits self-control. Works independently and safely without prompting from teacher. Engages in respectful interaction and conflict resolution with others. Accepts and uses feedback from teacher and peers. Demonstrates etiquette and follows rules.	Exhibits self-control. Works independently and safely with some prompting from teacher. Engages in respectful interaction with others. Accepts feedback from teacher and peers. Demonstrates etiquette and follows rules most of the time.	Denies personal responsibility by making excuses and blaming others. Has difficulty working independently; needs monitoring by teacher to stay on task. Engages in disrespectful interactions with others or ignores others. Disregards rules and etiquette.
Social responsibility	Works cooperatively with others. Accepts and involves others of different skill levels. Praises, encourages, and gives helpful feedback to others.	Needs occasional prompting from teacher to work cooperatively with others. Accepts others of different skill levels. Praises and encourages others. Gives feedback when prompted.	Cannot work productively with others.

A. Rate your *enjoyment* of participating in _____ [target, fielding-and-striking, net and wall, invasion] activities and tell why.

1 _____ 2 _____ 3 _____ 4 _____ 5

not enjoyable   enjoyable   very enjoyable

Reason:

B. Rate the *challenge* of participating in _____ (target, fielding-and-striking, net and wall, invasion) activities and tell why.

1 _____ 2 _____ 3 _____ 4 _____ 5

not challenging   challenging   very challenging

Reason:

C. Describe the positive social interactions (encouraging words or gestures, helping others, getting support from others, cooperation with teammates) that occurred when you were participating in _____ (target, fielding-and-striking, net and wall, invasion) activities.

Rubric

Proficient: The ratings in questions A and B match the reasons given, and the reasons are related to the activity. The description of social interactions is clearly related to the activity.

Developing: The ratings in questions A and B match the reasons given, and the reasons are somewhat related to the activity. The description of social interactions is somewhat related to the activity.

Beginning: There is a discrepancy between the ratings in questions A and B and the reasons given. The description of social interactions is minimal or consists of a one-word answer (e.g., "fun") without reference to the activity.

Figure 19.2   Standard 5: Self-report assessment.

Big Ideas

- Games are self-testing, cooperative, or competitive activities in which students combine fundamental movement skills with movement concepts in order to acquire specialized movement skills. Games involve one or more players, an agreed-upon set of rules, equipment, boundaries, and pursuit of an overall goal.

- Developmentally appropriate games address children's stage of motor development, level of motor skill learning, and cognitive and social development by modifying equipment, rules, boundaries, number of players, player roles, and the object of the game.

- Best practices for teaching games involve teaching movement skills and tactics, maximizing participation for all children, and promoting prosocial behavior.

- Competitive game classifications, based on the tactics used, include target games, striking-and-fielding games, net and wall games, and invasion games. As children learn the relevant tactics and skills, they become smarter game players. In addition, as children learn that similar tactics can be used across games and game categories, the resulting transfer of knowledge and skills speeds their learning.

- The process of teaching student-designed games gradually involves children in modifying games by manipulating game components; these experiences promote problem solving, group cooperation, and collaboration.

- Instructional activities provide a framework for designing lesson episodes. The content is derived from the task progressions for each of the four game categories, and this chapter provides a sampling of instructional activities for the content represented in the combination and application levels.

Target Games: Combination Level

Use the combination-level task progressions for target games in table 19.8 to guide your design of developmentally appropriate learning experiences. Examples of learning experiences from the progression appear below the table.

Table 19.8 Task Progressions for Target Games: Combination Level

SPECIALIZED	**Bowling**	Equipment: foam or rubber bowling balls Learning outcome: rolling for accuracy, distance, and direction Task and environment: • Use a three-step approach and adjust the length of the backswing to roll the ball through cones set at close to far distances. • Use a three-step approach and roll the ball from 15 to 20 feet (4.5 to 6 meters) between the 1-pin and the 2-pin (if right-handed) or the 1-pin and 3-pin (if left-handed) to knock down all three pins.
	Golf	Equipment: junior-size, polyurethane-head putter and iron-simulated golf clubs; foam balls, Wiffle balls (4- to 5-inch or 10- to 13-centimeter), no-bounce tennis balls Learning outcome: striking for distance and accuracy Task and environment: • Putt to different-sized targets at different distances. • Use a short swing to loft a ball over low obstacles. • Use a short swing to loft a ball over low obstacles toward a defined area or large target. • Sequence two strokes: loft and putt to target.

TARGET GAMES: COMBINATION LEVEL (BOWLING)

National Physical Education Standards
• Standard 1: Roll balls with mature form.
• Standard 2: Apply movement concepts to tactics in target games.

Learning Outcome
Rolling for accuracy, distance, and direction

Tactics
Approach, step, and release toward target; increase backswing to generate force for longer distances.

Teaching Styles
• Reproduction: all for practice with feedback
• Production: guided or convergent discovery to discover the relationship between accuracy and alignment of body parts with the target and the relationship between length of backswing and distance to target

Task: Children use a three-step approach and roll the ball at the wall through cones located about 3 to 6 feet (1 to 2 meters) apart at varying distances from a starting line: close (10 feet, or 3 meters), moderate (15 feet, or 4.5 meters), and far (20 feet, or 6 meters). Children must adjust the length of the backswing to match the distance that the ball must travel in order to hit the wall between the cones. One student rolls the ball from each distance, and the other student retrieves the ball and rolls it back. Students switch roles after two sets.

Environment: Each station has two students, two cones, and one ball (foam ball, small playground ball, softball, or rubber bowling ball). Use floor tape to designate three distances (red for close, yellow for moderate, and blue for far).

Practice: serial practice of two sets of one roll at each distance; repeated three times

Closed-skill cues:

- Assume starting position: balanced stance, body square with target, ball held in both hands at waist, and eyes focused on target.
- Step nondominant foot as ball is brought forward and down in front of body in two hands
- Step dominant foot and swing dominant arm back.
- Step nondominant foot toward target and swing dominant arm forward as knees bend to lower body for low release of ball toward target.

Feedback

- KPp: "Increase your knee bend to help you roll the ball along the floor."
- KPd: "The ball is being released too high."
- KPd: "Your nondominant foot is pointing toward the target—good job!"

Assessment

- Standard 1: Use a skill cue checklist.
- Standard 2: Use an open-ended question to help the student relate alignment to accuracy and backswing to generation of force (e.g., "What positions and movements help you roll the ball accurately?" "How does the backswing change in relation to the distance of the target?")

Learning Outcome

Rolling for accuracy, distance, and direction

Tactic

Complete three-step approach before reaching restraining line and release ball toward target.

Teaching Style

- Reproduction: all for practice with feedback

Task: Children start a three-step approach 6 to 8 feet (about 2 meters) behind a restraining line. They use footprint poly spots to mark the distance between steps that enables them to get a full backswing and release the ball from behind the restraining line through an open-ended box. The box measures 2 feet (0.6 meter) square and is placed 8 feet (about 2.5 meters) from the line toward a wall that is 15 to 20 feet (4.5 to 6 meters) away from the line. Partners take turns rolling and retrieving five sets of five balls.

Enrichment: Add a target of cones about 3 to 6 feet (1 to 2 meters) apart at the wall.

Environment: Each station has two students, one open-ended box, and one ball (foam ball, small playground ball, softball, or rubber bowling ball). Use floor tape to designate two distances (yellow for 15 feet, blue for 20 feet).

Practice: constant practice of three-step approach with full swing from behind the restraining line

Closed-skill cues:

- Assume starting position: balanced stance, body square with target, ball held in both hands, and eyes focused on target.
- Step nondominant foot with ball held in two hands at waist.
- Step dominant foot and swing arm back close to side.
- Step nondominant foot toward target and swing arm forward as knees bend to lower body for low release of ball toward opening in box.

Feedback

- KPp: "Start your three-step approach from the restraining line to see how far back from it you should initially stand."
- KPdp: "Your arm is swinging back away from your side. Keep it close so you can swing the pendulum and release in front of your body."

Assessment

- Standard 1: Use a skill cue checklist.
- Standard 2: Ask students, "What cues help you perform a smooth three-step approach?"

Learning Outcome

Rolling for accuracy, distance, and direction

Tactic

Complete three-step approach and release ball to roll toward pin.

Teaching Style

- Reproduction: all for practice with feedback

Task: Children complete a three-step approach behind a restraining line and roll the ball to knock down a pin at three distances: 8, 12, and 15 feet (about 2.5, 3.5, and 4.5 meters). Partners take two turns rolling at the pin at each distance, starting with the closest one. Retrievers roll the ball back and set up the pin. Rollers try to knock down each pin at least twice.

Enrichment: Increase the distance to 20 feet (6 meters).

Environment: Each station has two students, one plastic bowling pin, and one ball (foam ball, small playground ball, softball, or rubber bowling ball). Use floor tape to designate the three spots for the pin and the rolling line.

Practice: blocked practice (two rolls for each of three distances); repeated three times

Closed-skill cues:

- Assume starting position: balanced stance, body square with target, ball held in both hands, and eyes focused on target.
- Step nondominant foot with ball held in two hands at waist.
- Step dominant foot and swing arm back close to side while keeping eyes on target.
- Step nondominant foot toward target and swing arm forward as knees bend to lower body for low release of ball toward pin.

Feedback

KPp: "Release with your hand pointing toward the pin."

Assessment

- Standard 1: Use a skill cue checklist.
- Standard 2: Ask students, "How does the length of your pendulum swing change when the pin is close? Far? Why?"

TARGET GAMES: COMBINATION LEVEL (GOLF)

National Physical Education Standards
- Standard 1: Strike balls using mature form with long-handled implements.
- Standard 2: Apply movement concepts to tactics in target games.

Learning Outcome
Striking for distance and accuracy

Tactics
Align body and putter to putt toward target; slightly increase backswing to generate force for farther distances.

Teaching Styles
- Reproduction: all for practice with feedback
- Production: convergent discovery to discover relationship between size of pendulum swing and distance

Task: Children use a putting motion to strike a stationary ball to targets at distances of 3 to 15 feet (1 to 4.5 meters). They adjust the size of the pendulum swing to achieve different distances.

Enrichment: Use progressively smaller targets, such as flat archery-like targets or circular targets that mimic a golf hole.

Environment: Prepare an outdoor area or use indoor golf mats. Provide junior-size polyurethane putters and balls—either foam balls, Wiffle balls (4- to 5-inch or 10- to 13-centimeter), or no-bounce tennis balls. Students are organized within a circle, from which they putt toward outer rings marked on the grass or floor (figure 19.3). The blue ring signifies where students stand to putt toward red-, yellow-, and green-ring areas. Use poly-spot arrows to mark target lines.

Practice: blocked (five times to each target)

Closed-skill cues:

Preparation
- Use baseball batter's grip (dominant hand on bottom).
- Use square stance with feet shoulder-width apart, ball positioned in middle of stance and 10 to 12 inches (25 to 30 centimeters) in front, and knees slightly bent.
- Determine target line and adjust stance (i.e., feet) to line up with target.
- Keep blade square to target line.

Execution
- Keep head down and eyes over ball.
- Contact directly behind the ball to make it travel on the ground.
- Use a pendulum swing, keeping club low to ground, with short backswing.

Follow-Through
- Follow through toward target line.

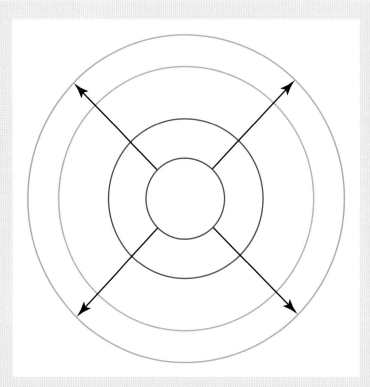

Figure 19.3 Putting circle setup.

Feedback

- KPd: "You kept your head down during your swing."
- KRp: "Shorten your pendulum backswing in order to keep the ball within the target area."
- KP: "How did you change your pendulum swing to reach the closest and farthest distances?"

Assessment

- Standard 1: Use an observation checklist of skill cues.
- Standard 2: Ask students, "What helped you keep the ball moving along the target line?" Answer: Releasing in line with the target line.

Learning Outcome

Striking for distance and accuracy

Tactics

Align body and club head to strike toward target; loft ball by using short swing and striking under ball with club head.

Teaching Style

- Reproduction: practice style with a partner

Task: Children use a short swing with the club head striking under the ball to loft it over a low obstacle toward a defined area or large target.

Environment: Students are partnered at a hitting line marked along the width of the gym three-quarters distance from the opposite wall. The observing partner is positioned diagonally against a wall behind the hitting partner. The hitters are positioned 3 feet (1 meter) apart from each other as they hit toward a wall. Each hitter has 10 balls. Cones with ropes create low obstacles to hit over and are placed 5 feet (1.5 meters) from the hitting line. Provide the hitters with junior-size polyurethane irons and appropriate balls: foam balls, 4- to 5-inch (10- to 13-centimeter) Wiffle balls, or no-bounce tennis balls).

Practice: constant

Closed-skill cues for short-swing iron shot:

Preparation

- Use baseball batter's grip with dominant hand on bottom.
- Use square stance with ball positioned in middle of stance and 10 to 12 inches (25 to 30 centimeters) in front.
- Make a Y with arms and club (Fronske, 1997, p. 118).
- Line up ball and club head with target.

Execution

- Initiate backswing with shoulders, keeping club low to ground.
- Use slow backswing, taking weight on back leg.
- Limit backswing, swinging club so hands are chest high.
- Keep nondominant arm straight during backswing.
- Keep head down and eyes on ball.
- Contact ball below its center to make it travel upward.
- Swing arms forward to hit through ball.

Follow-Through

- Follow through low toward target.

Feedback

- KPdp: "You hit in the middle of ball. Try to hit under the ball in order to loft it."
- KP: "What allowed you to loft the ball?" Answer: Hitting under the ball.

Assessment

Standard 2: Use the golf scorecard in figure 19.4 to score partner skill in lofting the ball over the rope.

Directions: Observe your partner during three sets of 10 hits.

Place a check mark in a square when your partner lofts the ball over the rope.

Performer:	Skill: lofting ball over rope									
Number of observations	1	2	3	4	5	6	7	8	9	10
Set 1	❏	❏	❏	❏	❏	❏	❏	❏	❏	❏
Set 2	❏	❏	❏	❏	❏	❏	❏	❏	❏	❏
Set 3	❏	❏	❏	❏	❏	❏	❏	❏	❏	❏

Figure 19.4   Golf scorecard assessment.

Learning Outcome

Striking for distance and accuracy

Tactics

Sequence two strokes by lofting and putting toward target; use appropriate backswing for distance from target.

Teaching Style

- Reproduction: practice with feedback

Task: In partner groups, students play a simulated golf hole using iron shot to reach the "green" (i.e., dotted arc), then putt to a poly-spot target. Students use golf hitting rules (i.e., taking turns hitting iron shots and putts).

Environment: Set up a golf "hole" with a designated starting point so that students use a lofted iron shot and a putt. Ideally, the activity is conducted in an outdoor space. Large circular areas (indicated by poly spots) serve as the golf holes, and a putt is successful when the ball rolls over the poly spot (see figure 19.5 for setup).

Practice: Block practice

Closed-skill cues:

See previous cues for putting and short swing iron shot.

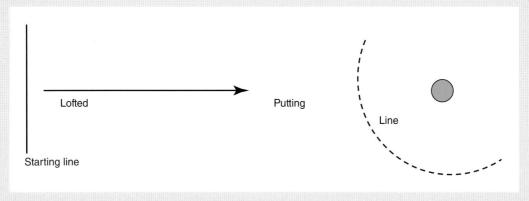

Figure 19.5   Setup for lofting and putting.

Feedback

- KP: "How could you impart more force or get more loft with your iron shot to get the ball closer to the putting area?"
- KR: "How did you line up the ball in order to hit over the poly spot?"

Assessment

- Standard 1: Use a golf scorecard.
- Standard 2: Ask students, "What's the difference between the way you move your body to loft a ball and to putt?" Answer: Adjust contact point on ball and size of swing.

Use the application-level task progressions for target games in Table 19.9 to guide your design of developmentally appropriate learning experiences. Examples of learning experiences from the progression appear below the table.

Target Games: Application Level

TARGET GAMES: APPLICATION LEVEL (BOWLING)

National Physical Education Standards

Table 19.9   Task Progressions for Target Games: Application Level

SPECIALIZED	**Bowling**	Equipment: foam or rubber bowling balls and pins Learning outcome: rolling for accuracy, distance, and direction Task and environment: • Adjust intermediate targets and starting position for accuracy and direction.
	Golf	Equipment: junior-size polyurethane-head putter and iron-simulated golf clubs; foam ball, 4- to 5-inch (10- to 13-centimeter) Wiffle balls, or no-bounce tennis balls Learning outcome: striking for distance and accuracy Task and environment: • Use a full swing to strike balls to varying distances. • Use a full swing to strike balls to varying distances and avoid simulated water hazards and sand traps. • Sequence three or four strokes to play a hole: full swing, short swing, and putt. • Play a mini golf course, selecting appropriate clubs and striking for distance and accuracy.

- Standard 1: Roll balls accurately using mature form.
- Standard 2: Apply movement concepts to tactics in target games.

Learning Outcome

Rolling for accuracy, distance, and direction

Tactics

Adjust starting position, intermediate target, and target line to hit the 1-2 or 1-3 pocket and knock down all three pins.

Teaching Styles

- Reproduction: all for practice with feedback
- Production: Use guided discovery to have students determine where to stand in order to start the approach when aiming for the pocket. Ask the following questions (Mitchell, Oslin, & Griffin, 2003, p. 137):

Q. (Pointing to the three-pin set-up) Will someone show me the best place to hit the pins so that they all fall down?

A. In the 1-2 or 1-3 pocket.

Q. When you had just one pin, you rolled right down the middle. Where do you roll the ball to hit between the 1-pin and 2-pin?

A. From the right side of the lane.

Q. If you want to roll the ball down the right side, where do you stand?

A. On the right side of the lane.

Task: Children play a game of three-pin, in which three pins are set up in a triangle 15 to 20 feet (4.5 to 6 meters) away. The roller aims to knock down all three pins, the retriever sets up pins, and the students switch roles after three turns.

Preparation: Partners take turns rolling the ball a few times to find the place that is to the right of center and lined up with the 1-2 pocket (or, for left-handed students, to the left of center and lined up with the 1-3 pocket). They mark their spot with footprint poly spots. Partners then look at the target line from the footprint through the pocket to determine the intermediate target (dot) to aim for. Partners then take turns rolling the ball a few times to find the intermediate target that helps them hit the pocket and place a star sticker on it.

Environment: Each station has two students, three plastic bowling pins set in a triangle at a wall, and one ball (foam ball, small playground ball, softball, or rubber bowling ball). Use floor tape to designate two distances (yellow for 15 feet, blue for 20 feet). Provide footprint poly spots and star stickers.

Practice: blocked practice

Closed-skill cues:

- Assume starting position: balanced stance, body square with target, ball held in both hands at waist, and eyes focused on target.
- Step nondominant foot as ball is brought forward and down in front of body in two hands at waist.
- Step dominant foot and swing dominant arm back close to side while keeping eyes on target.
- Step nondominant foot toward target and swing dominant arm forward as knees bend to lower body for low release of ball toward 1-2 or 1-3 pocket.

Feedback

KPp: "Keep your eyes on the intermediate target."

Assessment

- Standard 1: Use a skill cue checklist.
- Standard 2: Ask students, "How should you adjust your starting point and intermediate target when trying to aim for the 1-2 as opposed to the 1-3 pocket?"

TARGET GAMES: APPLICATION LEVEL (GOLF)

National Physical Education Standards
- Standard 1: Strike balls accurately using mature form with long-handled implements.
- Standard 2: Apply movement concepts to tactics in target games.

Learning Outcome

Striking for distance

Tactics

Use full backswing and swing through ball to strike to long distances.

Teaching Style
- Reproduction: all for practice with feedback

Task: Students hit toward long-distance targets using a full-swing iron shot.

Environment: If outdoors, use a driving-range setup; if indoors, have students hit to a wall. Mark distances with tall colored cones. All students begin on a hitting line with 10 balls each. Signal students when to retrieve balls. Provide each student with a junior-size polyurethane fairway wood.

Practice: blocked practice

Closed-skill cues for full-swing wood shot:

Preparation

- Use baseball batter's grip with dominant hand on bottom.
- Use square stance with ball positioned in middle of stance and 10 to 12 inches (25 to 30 centimeters) in front. Make a Y with arms and club (Fronske, 1997, p. 118).
- Line up ball and club head with target.

Execution

- Initiate backswing with shoulders, keeping club low to ground.
- Use slow backswing, taking weight on back leg.
- Use full swing, lifting hands to shoulder height; club goes behind head.
- Nondominant arm stays straight during backswing.
- Keep head down and eyes on ball.
- Contact ball below its center to make it travel upward.
- Swing arms forward to hit through ball.

Follow-Through

- Belly button faces hole.
- Swing club high.

Feedback

- KPd: "You started your swing low to the ground and took a full swing above your shoulder—good job!"
- KPp: "You topped the ball because you looked up too soon to see where it was going. Keep your head down and watch the club hit the ball."
- KR: "What did you do to achieve hitting at greater distances?" Response: "I took a larger backswing and swung through the ball."

Assessment

- Standard 1: Use an observation checklist of skill cues.
- Standard 2: Ask students, "How does your swing differ between an iron shot and a fairway wood shot?" Answer: Fairway wood shot uses a larger backswing.

Learning Outcome

Striking for distance and accuracy

Tactic

Align body with target to strike balls accurately.

Teaching Style

- Reproduction: practice with feedback

Task: Students lay a golf club on the ground, angling it toward the open space to which they want to hit the ball. Students then line up their body by adjusting their stance to line up with the golf club. Students hit four balls into a zone to avoid simulated hazards on the simulated golf course. On your direction, students move to a new zone. Have students retrieve balls after hitting in three different zones.

Environment: Arrange an outdoor setting with simulated water hazards and sand traps created with cones and ropes (figure 19.6). Set up six zones, each with four or five students per zone. Provide 12 balls for each student.

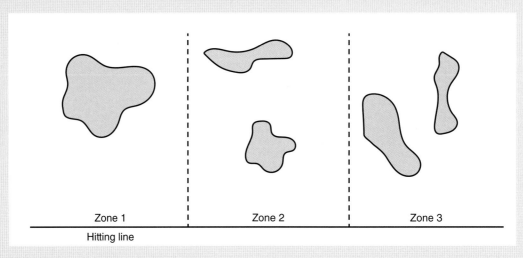

Zone 1   Zone 2   Zone 3

Hitting line

Figure 19.6 Setup for hazards and traps.

Practice: blocked

Closed-skill cues for setting up:
- Use baseball batter's grip with dominant hand on bottom.
- Adjust stance to line body up in direction of hit.

Feedback
- KPdp: "You adjusted your stance by lining up your feet in the direction of your hit."
- KR: "What did you do to avoid the hazards?"

Assessment
- Standard 1: Use the golf hazard scorecard in figure 19.7 to choose the stance that will send the ball between the hazards.
- Standard 2: Provide a picture of two hazards and a hitting line. Students must choose from among three stances the one that will send the ball between the two hazards.

Directions: Check the box if you avoided the hazards in the zone.

Performer:	Set 1				Set 2			
Number of observations	1	2	3	4	1	2	3	4
Zone 1	❏	❏	❏	❏	❏	❏	❏	❏
Zone 2	❏	❏	❏	❏	❏	❏	❏	❏
Zone 3	❏	❏	❏	❏	❏	❏	❏	❏
Zone 4	❏	❏	❏	❏	❏	❏	❏	❏
Zone 5	❏	❏	❏	❏	❏	❏	❏	❏
Zone 6	❏	❏	❏	❏	❏	❏	❏	❏

Figure 19.7   Golf hazards scorecard.

Learning Outcome

Striking for distance and accuracy

Tactics

Sequence three or four strokes (long swing, short swing, and putt) toward target. Align body with target and use appropriate backswing for distance from target.

Teaching Style

- Reproduction: all for practice with feedback

Task: Students use full-swing, short-swing, and putting strokes to play simulated golf-course holes. Students keep score by recording the number of strokes used for each hole.

Environment: In an outdoor setting, set up six holes with hazards in varying places. Use cones and ropes for hazards, poly spots or small flat archery-type targets for holes, poles and flags to denote each hole, small cones to mark starting line, and long ropes to create a circle for a simulated green.

Practice: random

Closed-skill cues: See preceding cues for short swing, full swing, and putting.

Feedback

KP: "How did you decide where to hit the ball to get to the 'green'?"

Assessment

- Standard 1: Use a scorecard to record number of strokes per hole.
- Standard 2: Review scorecard for accurate score keeping

Striking and Fielding Games: Combination Level

Use the combination-level task progressions for striking and fielding games in table 19.10 to guide your design of developmentally appropriate learning experiences. Examples of learning experiences from the progression appear below the table.

Table 19.10 Task Progressions for Striking-and-Fielding Games: Combination Level

SPECIALIZED · Throwing, catching, and batting	Equipment: yarn balls or Wiffle balls of various sizes; Wiffle bats of various widths and lengths
	Learning outcome: throwing and catching with reasonable accuracy in small-sided practice tasks (SHAPE America, 2014)
	Task and Environment
	• Move to catch balls thrown to the left and right along the ground and high in the air.
	• Move to catch balls thrown with variations in trajectory, level, and distance.
	• Combine fielding balls (thrown along ground and at chest height from different directions) and tagging a base.
	• Combine moving to field balls (thrown or batted with variation in direction and trajectory) with quick throws to a teammate (who tags a base).
	Learning outcome: combining batting and traveling skills in small-sided practice tasks (SHAPE America, 2014)
	• Bat ball with force (from tee, self-toss, or pitched ball) into outfield.
	• Roll, throw, kick, or bat ball (from tee, soft toss, or self-toss) to open space and run through first base.
	Learning outcome: applying movement concepts to offensive and defensive tactics in small-sided practice tasks (SHAPE America, 2014)
	• Roll, throw, kick, or bat ball (from tee, soft toss, or self-toss) to second base, then run through first base before defense fields the ball to the first base player (who tags the base).
	• Roll, throw, kick, or bat a ground ball (from tee, soft toss, or self-toss) between first base and second base, then run to first base to beat the tag on first base; right-field player backs up second-base player, who fields ball and sends to first-base player, who tags first base.

STRIKING AND FIELDING GAMES: COMBINATION LEVEL

National Physical Education Standards

- Standard 1: Combine skills in small-sided striking-and-fielding practice tasks.
- Standard 2: Apply movement concepts to tactics in striking-and-fielding practice tasks.

Learning Outcome

Throwing and catching with reasonable accuracy in small-sided practice tasks (SHAPE America, 2014)

Tactic (Defense)

Prevent scoring by fielding accurately.

Teaching Style

- Reproduction: all for practice with feedback

Task: Students move to catch balls thrown to the left and right; specifically, they field ground and fly balls thrown by a partner to the left and right from 15 to 20 feet (4.5 to 6 meters). The fielder varies the number of steps taken to the left or right (one to four side steps) based on where the feeder throws the ball.

Environment: Two students work within a general space large enough for them to be 15 to 20 feet (4.5 to 6 meters) apart and at least 10 feet (3 meters) away from another pair. Students use their choice of a 4-inch (10-centimeter) playground ball, gator-skin ball, or Wiffle softball. Poly spots mark the number of steps to the left and right (and provide a visual aid for the thrower).

Practice: blocked (if needed) and random

Open-skill cues:

Moving to Field

- Watch flight of ball to determine how far and where to move and how to position hands for catch.

Fielding a Grounder

- Position feet shoulder-width apart and bend at knees with slight bend at waist.
- Keep eyes on ball.
- Slide to the side (step, together, step along ground).
- Extend hands close to ground with pinkies together; keep elbows inside knees.
- Catch ball between feet in front of body with one knee bent and positioned low to ground to back up catch with hands.

Fielding a Fly Ball

- Position feet shoulder-width apart with weight forward on balls of feet.
- Move to position body underneath apex of ball flight; reach to sky with thumbs together and fingers extended.
- Keep eyes on ball into hands; catch with two hands.
- Bend elbows and bring ball into body to absorb force.

Feedback

- KPdp: "You are bending at your waist instead of bending at your knees."
- KR: "Why do you think you did not catch the ball?" Prompt if answer is unknown (e.g., "Was it because of your hand position or that you did not get behind the ball?").

Assessment

- Standard 1: Use a skill-cue checklist.
- Standard 1: Tally successful catches to left and right.
- Standard 2: Use skill cues to describe what student could do differently to catch ball.

Learning Outcome

Combining batting and traveling skills in small-sided practice tasks (SHAPE America, 2014)

Tactic (Offense)

Score.

Teaching Style

- Reproduction: all for practice with feedback

Task: Children bat a ball with force into the outfield (i.e., beyond the line marked with rope or polyspots that intersects first and third bases). Each of four players takes turns batting four Wiffle softballs off a tee or from a soft toss or underhand pitch. The other players are positioned in the outfield (beyond the line). A ball missed or dropped by fielders gives the batter a point. A ball that is caught in the air or does not make it over the line results in no score. Balls are returned to the pitcher or batter. Players rotate in sequence from batter to left field, center field, and right field (Gorecki, 2004).

Environment: See diagram in figure 19.8. Students choose length of Wiffle bat and from where/how ball is delivered (tee, toss, pitch). The angle of the V lines can be changed to give an advantage or disadvantage to the batter or fielders. The distance of the line from home plate can also be changed to accommodate the way in which the ball is delivered (batters using a tee may need the line closer).

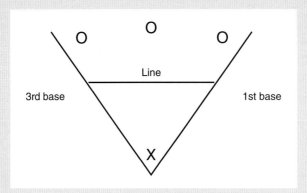

Figure 19.8 Setup for batting into the outfield.

Practice: random

Open-skill cues:

Batting

- Point side toward field and point foot toward target.
- Wind up with bat behind shoulders and elbows up.
- Keep eyes on ball.
- Unwind forcefully, shifting weight to front foot and "squashing the bug" with back foot.
- Swing fast to make contact under or at center of ball.

Moving to Field

- Watch flight and apex of ball to determine how far and where to move and how to position hands for catch.

Feedback

- KP: "Keep the bat level and swing through the ball."
- KP: "What did you do to cause the ball to go over the line and between the fielders?"

Assessment

- Standard 1: Use a skill-cue checklist.
- Standard 1: Tally successful hits over the line.
- Standard 2: Create three diagrams of a field. On each diagram, at home plate, draw a foot that is positioned either slightly toward 1st base, toward 2nd base, or slightly toward 3rd base. On each diagram, have students draw an arrow representing the part of the field to which the ball will be hit based on the position of the batter's lead foot.

Learning Outcome

Throwing and catching with reasonable accuracy in small-sided practice tasks (SHAPE America, 2014)

Tactic (Defense)

Prevent scoring by fielding accurately.

Teaching Style

- Reproduction: all for practice with feedback

Task: Children combine catching and immediately throwing to a base player. In a triangle formation, a receiver-thrower catches balls thrown on the ground and at chest height by a feeder and immediately throws the ball in one smooth motion to the base player, who repeats the catch-and-throw action back to the feeder.

Practice: blocked when type of throw is known, random when type is unknown

Environment: Three students stand in a triangle formation each next to one of three poly spots about 15 to 20 feet (4.5 to 6 meters) apart and choose a 4-inch (10-centimeter) playground ball, gator-skin ball, or Wiffle softball. The poly spots can be moved if necessary to afford success.

Open-skill cues:

Moving to Field

- Watch flight and apex of ball to determine how far and where to move and how to position hands for catch

Fielding a Grounder

- Position feet shoulder-width apart and bend at knees with slight bend at waist.
- Keep eyes on ball.
- Slide to side (step, together, step along ground).
- Extend hands close to ground with pinkies together; keep elbows inside knees.
- Catch ball between feet in front of body with one knee bent and positioned low to ground to back up catch with hands.

Fielding Ball Thrown at Chest Height

- Position feet shoulder-width apart with weight forward on balls of feet.
- Move to position in front of ball and reach toward ball with palms facing and fingers extended.
- Keep eyes on ball into hands and catch with two hands.
- Bend elbows and bring ball into body to absorb force.

Smooth Transition From Catch to Throw

- Continue bending elbows in absorption of catch to move into wind-up action of throw.
- Step and release ball toward intended target.

Feedback

- KPp: "Use a rocking or pendulum movement to smoothly transition from absorbing the catch to winding up for the throw."
- KP: "What did you do to make catchable throws to the receiver?"

Assessment

- Standard 1: Use a skill-cue checklist.
- Standard 1: Tally successful catch-and-throw rounds.
- Standard 2: Use skill cues to describe how the student performed smooth catch-and-throw transitions.

Learning Outcome

Throwing and catching with reasonable accuracy in small-sided practice tasks (SHAPE America, 2014)

Tactic (Defense)

Prevent scoring by fielding accurately.

Teaching Style

- Reproduction: all for practice with feedback

Task: Students combine catching with immediately touching a base and throwing to a base player (Rovegno & Bandhauer, 2013). In a diamond formation with corners marked by four poly spots, students catch a ball and in one smooth motion touch the base and throw. The action starts by going clockwise direction (from home to third to second to first) and then goes counterclockwise.

Environment: Four students stand in a diamond formation with corners marked by four poly spots about 15 to 20 feet (4.5 to 6 meters) apart (or as needed for success) and choose a 4-inch (10-centimeter) playground ball, gator-skin ball, or Wiffle softball. Two outfielders are positioned to move into a backup position behind the fielder receiving the ball. Outfielders throw the ball to the base player for whom they retrieved the ball. Students rotate from catcher to third base to left field to second base to right field to first base to catcher.

Practice: blocked (direction of throws known)

Open-skill cues:

Moving to Field

- Watch flight and apex of ball to determine how far and where to move and how to position hands for catch.

Smooth Transition From Catch to Throw

- Continue bending elbows in absorption of catch to move into wind-up action of throw.
- Step and release ball toward intended target.

Touching Base

- Catch ball, step on base with throwing-side foot, step toward target with opposite foot, and throw.
- When fielding balls coming from outside the baseline and to nondominant side, step on base and spin with throwing-side foot before planting opposite foot in direction of throw.

Feedback

- KPp: "When catching a ball coming to your nondominant side, turn before you throw."
- KP: "How does your footwork affect your ability to make a catchable throw?"

Assessment

- Standard 1: Use a skill-cue checklist.
- Standard 1: Tally successful sequences of catching and throwing between receivers.
- Standard 2: Describe changes in footwork for throwing clockwise and counterclockwise and for catching balls on the dominant and nondominant sides.

Learning Outcome

Applying movement concepts to offensive and defensive tactics in small-sided practice tasks (SHAPE America, 2014)

Tactics

On offense, run to first base to beat throw; on defense, prevent scoring by fielding ball to first base ahead of runner.

Teaching Style

- Reproduction: all for practice with feedback

Task: Children run to beat the throw and field to get the runner out. In a 2v2 format, offensive players take turns rolling, throwing, kicking, or batting a ball (from a tee, soft toss, or self-toss) to second base, then running through the first base before the defense fields the ball to the first-base player, who tags first base. The goal is for the offense to score three runs (by running through first base before the ball gets there) before the defense gets three outs. Offense and defense switch roles after three runs or three outs, whichever comes first. Have students change players on teams after two rounds. (The waiting offensive player can back up first base to retrieve overthrows.)

Environment: Set up half of a baseball infield: home, first base, and second base (see figure 19.9). Provide a choice of balls for rolling, throwing, and kicking. Provide a soft 4-inch (10-centimeter) ball for batting, along with a tee and an appropriately sized bat.

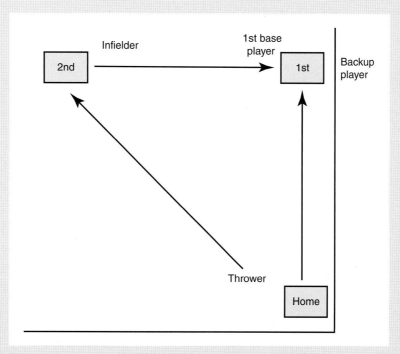

Figure 19.9 Setup for 2v2 gamelike activity.

Practice: random
Closed-skill cues:

Running to First Base
- Make smooth, quick transition from throwing, kicking, or batting into step with dominant foot toward first base.
- Run quickly in straight line toward first base.
- Touch base and slow down after touch.

Open-skill cues:

Fielding at Second Base
- Make smooth transition from recovery of catch to wind-up of throw.
- Step toward first base and throw to target made by hands of first-base player.

First-Base Player
- Take position between first and second base (quarter of way toward second).
- When ball goes to second base, move quickly to place left foot on inside edge of first base.
- Make large target with both hands and watch ball into hands.

Feedback

- KPp (running): "Keep your feet in line with first base as you are running."
- KP (fielding at second base): "What needs to change so you can get the ball to first base more quickly?"
- KP (first-base player): "Your foot came off of first base when you were catching. What do you need to do to keep it on the base?"

Assessment

- Standard 1: Use a scorecard for each round and a skill-cue checklist.
- Standard 2: Ask students, "What enabled your team to prevent the runner from scoring?" Answer: Second-base player fielded ball and quickly and accurately threw ball to first-base player, who provided good target for throw and quickly tagged base.

Striking and Fielding Games: Application Level

Use the application-level task progressions for striking and fielding games in table 19.11 to guide your design of developmentally appropriate learning experiences. Examples of learning experiences from the progression appear below the table.

Table 19.11   Task Progression for Striking-and-Fielding Games: Application Level

SPECIALIZED	Throwing, catching, and batting	Equipment: Wiffle balls of various sizes, Wiffle bats of various widths and lengths Learning outcome: applying the concepts of direction and force to strike an object with a bat (SHAPE America, 2014, p. 32) **Task and Environment** • Bat ball for accuracy (from tee, self-toss, or pitch) to left, center, and right fields. Learning outcome: applying basic offensive and defensive tactics in small-sided practice tasks for striking and fielding • 3v3: cutting the lead runner ○ Begin with a runner on first and get an out at second. ○ Begin with runners on first and second and get an out at third. • 4v4: defending space, tagging base, and advancing runner ○ Offense: bat an infield hit; seek scoring opportunities on second, third, or home base ○ Defense: fielders at first, second, third, and shortstop; prevent runners from advancing and scoring

STRIKING AND FIELDING GAMES: APPLICATION LEVEL

National Physical Education Standards

- Standard 1: Combine skills with reasonable accuracy in small-sided striking-and-fielding practice tasks.
- Standard 2: Apply offensive and defensive tactics in striking-and-fielding practice tasks.

Learning Outcome

Applying concepts of direction and force to strike a ball with a bat (SHAPE America, 2014, p. 32)

Tactics

Offense hits ball to open space to get on base; defense fields ball to base ahead of runner to get force-out.

Teaching Style

- Reproduction: all for practice with feedback

Task: Offense bats ball for accuracy to left field. Defense fields to get the runner out. This is a 2v2 infield game. Offense bats a ground ball to the left side of the infield and runs to first to beat the throw. Defense fields the ball and tries to get the force-out at first. A run is scored when the runner is safe at first base. Offense and defense switch roles after three outs or three runs, whichever comes first (Mitchell, Oslin, & Griffin, 2003).

Environment: Provide three bases (home, first, and second); one Wiffle softball to hit from a tee, soft toss, or pitch; and one appropriately sized bat.

Practice: blocked

Closed-skill cues:

Batting

- Align stance with tee and contact zone.
- Eye infield target (left side of infield).
- Wind up with bat behind shoulders and elbows up.
- Keep eyes on ball.
- Swing fast and down toward ground.

Open-skill cues:

Fielding Grounders and Throwing Ball Ahead of Runner

- Second-base player moves toward ball, stays low, scoops up ball, and immediately throws to first base.
- First-base player moves into position with foot on bag, makes big target with hands, and receives throw from second-base player.

Feedback

- KP (batter): "What cues will help you hit to the infield target?" Answer: Align stance, focus, and swing down toward the ground.
- KP (fielder): "How did you keep the offense from scoring?"

Assessment

- Standard 1: For batting, use a skill-cue checklist; for fielding and scoring, have students use a scorecard for each round.
- Standard 2: Ask students, "What skill cues help you hit to left field?"

Learning Outcome

Applying concepts of direction and force to strike a ball with a bat (SHAPE America, 2014, p. 32)

Tactics

Offense hits ball to open space to get on base; defense fields ball to base ahead of runner to get force-out.

Teaching Style

- Reproduction: all for practice with feedback

Task: Offense bats the ball for accuracy to right field. Defense fields to get the runner out. This is a 2v2 infield game with the goal of creating a force-out situation at third base. Offense bats ground ball to right side of infield (toward 1st base) and runs directly to third base (does not go to first or second) to beat the force-out throw to third base. Defense fields the ball and tries to get the force-out at third base. A run is scored when the runner is safe at third. Offense and defense switch roles after three outs or three runs, whichever comes first (Mitchell, Oslin, & Griffin, 2003).

Environment: Provide three bases (home, first, and third); one Wiffle softball to hit from a tee, soft toss, or pitch; and one appropriately sized bat.

Practice: blocked

Closed-skill cues:

Batting

- Align stance with tee and contact zone.
- Eye infield target (right side of infield).
- Wind up with bat behind shoulders and elbows up.
- Keep eyes on ball.
- Swing fast and down toward ground.

Open-skill cues:

Fielding Grounders and Throwing Ball Ahead of Runner

- First-base player moves toward ball, stays low, scoops up ball, and immediately throws to third base.
- Third-base player moves into position with foot on bag, makes big target with hands, and receives throw from first-base player.

Feedback

- KP (batter): "What cues will help you hit to the infield target?" Answer: Align stance, focus, and swing down toward the ground.
- KP (fielder): "How did you keep the offense from scoring?"

Assessment

- Standard 1: For batting, use a skill-cue checklist; for fielding and scoring, have students use a scorecard for each round.
- Standard 2: Ask students, "What skill cues help you hit to right field?"

Learning Outcome

Applying basic offensive and defensive tactics in small-sided practice tasks for striking and fielding

Tactics

Defense fields ball to second base ahead of runner to get force-out. Offense hits ball to left side of infield to advance runner to second base.

Teaching Style

- Reproduction: all for practice with feedback

Task: Defense cuts the lead runner at second base on a ball hit to left field. This is a 3v3 infield game.

- Offense: Start with offensive player 1 as a runner on first base. Offensive player 2 throws, kicks, or bats a ground ball to the left side of the infield. Player 1 runs to second to beat the throw while player 2 runs to first. (Replace the runner on first to start each play.) Player 3 is the first-base coach. A run is scored when the runner advances safely to second base.

- Defense: Third-base player or shortstop fields the ball and throws to the second-base player, who tags the base ahead of the runner. Infield players call for the ball and cover for each other. A run is scored when the runner advances safely to second base. Offense and defense switch roles after three outs or three runs, whichever comes first; in addition, fielder positions are rotated on each team's return to the field (Mitchell, Oslin, & Griffin, 2003).

Environment: Provide four bases; a choice of balls for rolling, throwing, and kicking; and a soft 4-inch (10-centimeter) ball for batting, along with a batting tee and an appropriately sized bat.

Practice: blocked

Closed-skill cues:

Advancing the Runner

- Hit to left side of infield to advance runner to second base.
- Align stance with tee and contact zone.
- Sight infield target.
- Wind up with bat behind shoulders and elbows up.
- Keep eyes on ball.
- Swing fast and down toward ground.

Runner

- Get into crouch with weight on front foot.
- Run quickly.
- To stop on second base, begin preparing about two steps before the base by leaning back and putting heel down ahead of toe. One foot must remain on the base and one may go over the base.

Open-skill cues:

Fielding Ball Ahead of Runner

- Either field ball and tag base ahead of runner or move into position with foot on bag to receive throw from fielder.

Covering

- Move into position behind player who calls for ball and be prepared to catch ball. If teammate misses ball, field it and throw to second base.

Feedback

- KP (batter): "What cues will help you hit to the infield target?" Answer: Align stance, focus, step, hit, and follow through toward target.
- KP (runner): "What cues help you stop on second base?"
- KR (fielder): "How did you decide who should field the ball and who should cover?" Answer: Person closest to path of ball calls for and fields; other player covers.

Assessment

- Standard 1: Use fielding performance checklist 1 (figure 19.10); tally score of each round, indicating runs and outs.
- Standard 2: Ask students, "What helped your team get the runner out at second?" Answer: Called for ball, covered for each other, made accurate throws to second-base player (who tagged base), and fielded cleanly.

Coding: Observe players for two-minute intervals. Each time the player performs correctly, place a check mark in the square; when the player performs incorrectly, place an X in the square.

Student	Skill: Fields ball cleanly.			Skill: Throws accurately to second base.			Skill: Covers (backs up fielder).		
	Observation			Observation			Observation		
	1 2 3 4 5 6 7			1 2 3 4 5 6 7			1 2 3 4 5 6 7		
	❑ ❑ ❑ ❑ ❑ ❑ ❑			❑ ❑ ❑ ❑ ❑ ❑ ❑			❑ ❑ ❑ ❑ ❑ ❑ ❑		
	❑ ❑ ❑ ❑ ❑ ❑ ❑			❑ ❑ ❑ ❑ ❑ ❑ ❑			❑ ❑ ❑ ❑ ❑ ❑ ❑		
	❑ ❑ ❑ ❑ ❑ ❑ ❑			❑ ❑ ❑ ❑ ❑ ❑ ❑			❑ ❑ ❑ ❑ ❑ ❑ ❑		
Percentage (sum of check marks ÷ sum of all tallies)	_____%			_____%			_____%		

Figure 19.10 Fielding performance checklist 1.

Learning Outcome

Applying basic offensive and defensive tactics in small-sided practice tasks for striking and fielding

Tactics

Defense fields ball to second base ahead of runner to get force-out. Offense hits ball to left side of infield to advance runner to second base.

Teaching Style

- Reproduction: all for practice with feedback

Task: Defense cuts the lead runner at second base on a ball hit to right field. This is a 3v3 infield game.

- Offense: Start with offense player 1 as a runner on first base. Offense player 2 throws, kicks, or bats a ground ball to the right side of the infield. Player 1 runs to second to beat the throw while player 2 runs to first. (Replace the runner on first to start each play.) Player 3 is the first-base coach. A run is scored when the runner advances safely to second base.

- Defense: Second-base player fields the ball and flips or throws it to the shortstop, who places a foot on second base and catches the ball ahead of the runner. First-base player backs up second-base player. Offense and defense switch roles after three outs or three runs, whichever comes first; in addition, fielder positions are rotated on each team's return to the field (Mitchell, Oslin, & Griffin, 2003).

Environment: Provide four bases; a choice of balls for rolling, throwing, and kicking; and a soft 4-inch (10-centimeter) ball for batting, along with a batting tee and an appropriately sized bat.

Practice: blocked

Closed-skill cues:

Advancing the Runner

- Hit to right side of infield to advance runner to second base.
- Align stance with tee and contact zone.
- Sight infield target.
- Wind up with bat behind shoulders and elbows up.
- Keep eyes on ball.
- Swing fast and down toward ground.

Runner

- Get into crouch with weight on front foot.
- Run quickly.
- To stop on second base, begin preparing about two steps before the base by leaning back and putting heel down ahead of toe. One foot must remain on the base and one may go over the base.

Open-skill cues:

- Field the ball cleanly and flip or throw to shortstop.
- Shortstop moves quickly into position, puts foot on edge of bag, makes good target, and watches ball into hands.
- First-base player covers for second-base player.

Feedback

- KP (batter): "What cues will help you hit to the infield target?" Answer: Align stance, focus, step, hit, and follow through toward target.
- KP (runner): "What cues help you stop on second base?"
- KR (fielder): "How did the fielders support each other to make the out at second base?"

Assessment

- Standard 1: Use fielding performance checklist 2 (figure 19.11); tally score of each round, indicating runs and outs.
- Standard 2: Ask students, "What helped your team get the runner out at second?" Answer: Called for ball, covered for each other, made accurate throws to second-base player (who tagged base), and fielded cleanly.

Coding: Observe players for two-minute intervals. Each time the player performs correctly, place a check mark in the square; when the player performs incorrectly, place an X in the square.

Student	Skill: Shortstop covers second and gets the out.	Skill: Makes accurate flip or throw to second base.	Skill: Covers (backs up fielder).
	Observation 1 2 3 4 5 6 7	Observation 1 2 3 4 5 6 7	Observation 1 2 3 4 5 6 7
	❑ ❑ ❑ ❑ ❑ ❑ ❑	❑ ❑ ❑ ❑ ❑ ❑ ❑	❑ ❑ ❑ ❑ ❑ ❑ ❑
	❑ ❑ ❑ ❑ ❑ ❑ ❑	❑ ❑ ❑ ❑ ❑ ❑ ❑	❑ ❑ ❑ ❑ ❑ ❑ ❑
	❑ ❑ ❑ ❑ ❑ ❑ ❑	❑ ❑ ❑ ❑ ❑ ❑ ❑	❑ ❑ ❑ ❑ ❑ ❑ ❑
Percentage (sum of check marks ÷ sum of all tallies)	_____%	_____%	_____%

Figure 19.11   Fielding performance checklist 2.

Learning Outcome

Applying basic offensive and defensive tactics in small-sided practice tasks for striking and fielding

Tactics

Defense fields ball to third base ahead of runner to get force-out. Offense hits ball to infield to advance runner to third base.

Teaching Style

- Reproduction: all for practice with feedback

Task: Defense cuts the lead runner at third. This is a 4v4 infield game.

- Offense: Start with runners on first and second bases. Throw, kick, or bat a ground ball into the infield, whereupon the player on second runs to third, the player on first runs to second, and the batter runs to first. The fourth offense player coaches first base. (Replace runners on first and second to start each play.) A run is scored when the runner advances safely to third base.
- Defense: Players field the ball and throw to third base. If the third-base player fields the ball, the shortstop covers third base. Offense and defense switch roles after three outs or three runs, whichever comes first; in addition, fielder positions are rotated on each team's return to field (Mitchell, Oslin, & Griffin, 2003).

Environment: Provide four bases; choice of balls for rolling, throwing, and kicking; and a soft 4-inch (10-centimeter) ball for batting, along with a batting tee and an appropriately sized bat.

Practice: random

Closed-skill cues:

Advancing the Runner

- Hit to part of field that gives second-base runner the most time to advance to third base.
- Align stance with tee and contact zone.
- Sight infield target.
- Wind up with bat behind shoulders and elbows up.
- Keep eyes on ball.
- Swing fast and down toward ground.

Runner

- Get into crouch with weight on front foot.
- Run quickly.
- To stop on second or third base, being preparing about two steps before the base by leaning back and putting heel down ahead of toe. One foot must remain on the base and one may go over the base.

Open-skill cues:

- Field ball cleanly and throw to third base.
- If third-base player fields ball, shortstop covers third (moves quickly into position with foot on edge of bag, makes good target, and watches ball into hands).

Feedback

- KP (runner): "What cues help you stop on second or third base?"
- KR (fielder): "How did the fielders support each other to get the out at third base?"

Assessment

- Standard 1: Use fielding performance checklist 3 (figure 19.12); tally score of each round, indicating runs and outs.
- Standard 2: Ask students, "What helped your team get the runner out at second?" Answer: Called for ball, covered for each other, made accurate throws to second-base player (who tagged base), and fielded cleanly.

Coding: Observe players for two-minute intervals. Each time the player performs correctly, place a check mark in the square; when the player performs incorrectly, place an X in the square.

Student	Skill: Makes accurate throw to third base.			Skill: Cleanly fields ball.			Skill: Covers (backs up fielder).		
	Observation			Observation			Observation		
	1 2 3 4 5 6 7			1 2 3 4 5 6 7			1 2 3 4 5 6 7		
	❑ ❑ ❑ ❑ ❑ ❑ ❑			❑ ❑ ❑ ❑ ❑ ❑ ❑			❑ ❑ ❑ ❑ ❑ ❑ ❑		
	❑ ❑ ❑ ❑ ❑ ❑ ❑			❑ ❑ ❑ ❑ ❑ ❑ ❑			❑ ❑ ❑ ❑ ❑ ❑ ❑		
	❑ ❑ ❑ ❑ ❑ ❑ ❑			❑ ❑ ❑ ❑ ❑ ❑ ❑			❑ ❑ ❑ ❑ ❑ ❑ ❑		
Percentage (sum of check marks ÷ sum of all tallies)	_____%			_____%			_____%		

Figure 19.12   Fielding performance checklist 3.

Learning Outcome

Applying basic offensive and defensive tactics in small-sided practice tasks for striking and fielding

Tactics

Offense hits ball to space that helps runner advance. Defense fields ball to base ahead of runner to get force-out.

Teaching Styles

- Reproduction: all for practice with feedback
- Production: guided or convergent discovery to discover best place to hit ball to advance runner

Directions to teacher: Use these or similar Guided Discovery Questions to help students discover what to do in each situation. Discovering the answers will prepare them to implement the decisions in the small-sided game played after they answer the questions.

Q: Where do you hit the ball if there are no outs and there is no runner on first?

A: To the left side of the infield because that is farther from the path of the runner.

Q: Where do you hit the ball if there is a runner on first?

A: To the right side of the infield (behind the runner) to allow the runner to get to second base.

Q: Why is it important to get the runner to second base?

A: To give the runner a better chance of scoring on the next hit.

Q: Where do you hit the ball if there are runners on first and second?

A: To the right side of the infield (behind the runner) to allow runners to get to second and third base.

Q: Why is it important to get the runner to third base?

A: To give the runner a better chance of scoring on the next hit.

(Adapted from Mitchell, Oslin, & Griffin, 2003, p. 104)

Task: Offense tries to score by hitting to get on base and advance the runner. Defense fields to get the runner out. This is a 4v4 infield game.

- Offense: Start with a runner on first base. Throw, kick, or bat a ground ball to the infield, then run to first to beat the throw. (Replace runner on first to start each play.) A run is scored when a runner advances to second, third, or home.
- Defense: Field the ball to a base ahead of the runner to get the runner out. Fielders are positioned at first, second, and third bases and at shortstop. Offense and defense switch roles after three outs or three runs, whichever comes first (Mitchell, Oslin, & Griffin, 2003).

Environment: Provide four bases; choice of balls for rolling, throwing, and kicking; and a soft 4-inch (10-centimeter) coated foam ball or Wiffle ball, along with a batting tee and an appropriately sized bat.

Practice: random

Closed-skill cues:

Advancing the Runner

- Hit to any part of infield to advance runner.
- Align stance with tee and contact zone.
- Sight infield target.
- Step, hit, and follow through toward target.

Open-skill cues:

Fielding Ball Ahead of Runner

- Field ball and tag base ahead of runner.
- Move into position with foot on bag to receive throw from fielder.
- Cover for fielder closest to or calling for ball.

Feedback

- KP (batter): "What cues will help you hit to the infield target?" Answer: Align stance, focus, step, hit, and follow through toward the target.
- KR (fielder): "To what base do you field the ball?" Answer: The base with the best chance for the force-out.

Assessment

- Standard 1: Use defensive and offensive performance assessments (figures 19.13 and 19.14); tally score of each round, indicating runs and outs.
- Standard 2: Have students diagram where to hit the ball in order to advance the runner on first and explain why. Student responses should show a line between first and second base because the fielder will be trying to get the runner out at first.

Coding: Observe players for two-minute intervals. Each time the player performs correctly, place a check mark in the square; when the player performs incorrectly, place an X in the square.

Student	Decision: Fields ball to base for force-out.			Skill: Fields ball cleanly.			Base: Starts in correct position		
	Observation 1 2 3 4 5 6 7			Observation 1 2 3 4 5 6 7			Observation 1 2 3 4 5 6 7		
	❑ ❑ ❑ ❑ ❑ ❑ ❑			❑ ❑ ❑ ❑ ❑ ❑ ❑			❑ ❑ ❑ ❑ ❑ ❑ ❑		
	❑ ❑ ❑ ❑ ❑ ❑ ❑			❑ ❑ ❑ ❑ ❑ ❑ ❑			❑ ❑ ❑ ❑ ❑ ❑ ❑		
	❑ ❑ ❑ ❑ ❑ ❑ ❑			❑ ❑ ❑ ❑ ❑ ❑ ❑			❑ ❑ ❑ ❑ ❑ ❑ ❑		
Percentage (sum of check marks ÷ sum of all tallies)	_____%			_____%			_____%		

Figure 19.13   Defensive performance assessment.

Coding: Observe players for two-minute intervals. Each time the player performs correctly, place a check mark in the square; when the player performs incorrectly, place an X in the square.

Student	Decision: Bats (sends) ball to space farthest from lead base runner.			Batting: Bats ball cleanly.			Baserunning: Starts in correct position and runs through (first or home) or stops on bag (second or third).		
	Observation 1 2 3 4 5 6 7			Observation 1 2 3 4 5 6 7			Observation 1 2 3 4 5 6 7		
	❑ ❑ ❑ ❑ ❑ ❑ ❑			❑ ❑ ❑ ❑ ❑ ❑ ❑			❑ ❑ ❑ ❑ ❑ ❑ ❑		
	❑ ❑ ❑ ❑ ❑ ❑ ❑			❑ ❑ ❑ ❑ ❑ ❑ ❑			❑ ❑ ❑ ❑ ❑ ❑ ❑		
	❑ ❑ ❑ ❑ ❑ ❑ ❑			❑ ❑ ❑ ❑ ❑ ❑ ❑			❑ ❑ ❑ ❑ ❑ ❑ ❑		
Percentage (sum of check marks ÷ sum of all tallies)	_____%			_____%			_____%		

Figure 19.14   Offensive performance assessment.

Net and Wall Games: Combination Level

Use the combination-level task progressions for net and wall games in table 19.12 to guide your design of developmentally appropriate learning experiences. Examples of learning experiences from the progression appear below the table.

Table 19.12 Task Progression for Net and Wall Games: Combination Level

SPECIALIZED — Striking with hands and rackets	Equipment: short nets or ropes suspended on cones; balloon-bladder balls and trainer volleyballs; short-handled rackets, large shuttlecocks, foam tennis balls Learning outcome: maintaining a rally in small-sided practice tasks Task and environment: • Perform a cooperative partner rally by striking a balloon up (with no net, over a line, with a net). • Perform a one-bounce cooperative rally with player-chosen ball (to a wall, over a line, over a low net). • Underhand throw and move to catch • Striking with hand(s) • Striking with racket • Maintain a rally with self against a wall. Learning outcome: combining skills and basic tactics in small-sided net or wall practice tasks (SHAPE America, 2014, p. 33) Task and environment: • Set up an attack and defend space. • 1v1: tossing over low net to open space, moving to catch, and returning to base position • 1v1: striking a ball tossed underhand by opponent on other side of net back to a court area (deep, short, or to the side) away from opponent, who moves into position to catch the ball • 1v2: striking a ball tossed underhand by an opponent to a teammate, who strikes the ball back to a court area (deep, short, or to the side) away from the opponent, who moves to catch it.

NET AND WALL GAMES: COMBINATION LEVEL

National Physical Education Standards

- Standard 1: Strike an object consecutively with a partner in cooperative and competitive settings.
- Standards 1 and 2: Combine skills and basic tactics in small-sided practice tasks for net and wall games.

Learning Outcome

Maintaining a rally in small-sided practice tasks

Tactic

Maintain a rally by sending game object in direction of partner.

Teaching Style

- Reproduction: all for practice with feedback

Task (game): Students make an underhand throw and move to catch. They stand on opposite sides of the net. Players start by throwing the ball underhand over a low net or line so that a partner can catch the ball after it bounces on their side of the court. Players must return the ball across the line or net from where they catch it. Partners keep track of how many consecutive bounce-catches they can make to each other.

Enrichment:

- Strike the ball over the net with an open hand from a self-bounce toward a partner, who catches it.
- Strike the ball over the net with a racket from a self-bounce toward a partner, who catches it.
- Strike the ball with hands or forearms after a self-toss (no bounce) toward a partner, who catches it.

Environment: Use poly spots to create a grid in which to play (size appropriate for the age and ability level of the group). A badminton net can be used if it is set at a low level so that the bottom of the net touches the ground; alternatively, use a line on the floor to represent a net. Equipment includes short-handled rackets and 6- to 7-inch (15- to 18-centimeter) playground balls, balloon balls, trainer volleyballs, and foam tennis balls.

Practice: random

Open-skill cues:

Moving to Catch

- Slide sideways, backpedal, or run to move toward ball.
- Square body, reach with hands toward ball, and grasp it.

Throwing Underhand

- Grasp ball with one hand on top and one hand on bottom.
- Swing arms low alongside and behind body for wind-up.
- Step toward partner and swing arms forward, releasing ball high to bounce in front of partner.

Striking Ball Over Net With Open Hand From Bounce to Self

- Point side to target.
- Assume forward-backward open stance with front foot pointed toward target.
- Extend nonstriking arm diagonally across and in front of body.
- Swing striking arm back and drop ball.
- Swing arm and shift weight forward as ball is contacted with open hand in line with target.

Striking Ball Over Net With Racket From Bounce to Self

- Point side to target; "shake hands" with racket (create a V with thumb and index finger).
- Assume forward-backward open stance with front foot pointed toward target.
- Extend nonstriking arm diagonally across and in front of body.
- Swing racket back and drop ball.
- Swing racket arm and shift weight forward as ball is contacted with racket face (sweet spot) in line with target.

Striking Ball With Hands or Forearms After Self-Toss (No Bounce)

- Point chest toward target; assume side-to-side stance with one foot slightly forward and pointed toward target.
- Bend knees slightly and toss ball up about head height.
- Grasp both hands together with thumbs on top and forearms extended to make a "flat table."
- Contact ball with forearms toward target and extend knees while slightly lifting arms.

Feedback

- KPd: "You moved quickly and got your body square with the ball."
- KPdp: "You locked your knees. To get more power, try to bend and extend your legs while striking with your forearms."
- KP: "What did you and your partner do to keep your rally going? Answer: Stepped and bounced ball toward partner; moved to get body in line with ball to catch.

Assessment

- Standard 1: Use an observation checklist of skill cues.
- Standard 2: On the handout, check the cues you use to have a cooperative rally with your partner.

    _____ Receiver moves to get behind and aligned with the ball.

    _____ Receiver waits for ball to bounce on his or her side of court before moving to ball.

    _____ Thrower or striker aims for open court.

    _____ Thrower or striker aims for partner.

Learning Outcome

Combining skills and basic tactics in small-sided practice tasks.

Tactics

Defend space by moving to catch or strike and returning to base position (in middle of court about two-thirds of way back from net). Set up attack by sending ball to open space.

Teaching Style

- Reproduction: all for practice with feedback

Task: Students attack and defend space in a 1v1 format. One player underhand-tosses over a low net to an open space and scores a point if the partner on the other side of the net is unable to catch the ball after one bounce. Partner must return the ball over the net from where it is caught and return to base position to prepare to move for the next catch.

Enrichment:

- Strike the ball over the net with an open hand from a self-bounce toward a partner, who catches it.
- Strike the ball over the net with a racket from a self-bounce toward a partner, who catches it.
- Strike the ball with hands or forearms after a self-toss (no bounce) toward a partner, who catches it.

Environment: Use poly spots to create a grid in which to play (size appropriate for age and ability level of the group). A badminton net can be used if it is set at a low level so that the bottom of the net touches the ground; alternatively, use a line on the floor to represent a net. Equipment includes short-handled rackets and 6- to 7-inch (15- to 18-centimeter) playground balls, balloon balls, trainer volleyballs, and foam tennis balls.

Practice: random

Open-skill cues:

Throwing to Open Space

- Line body up with open space to the side, front, or back of opponent's position on court.
- Step and release ball to open space.

Returning to Base

- Slide sideways, backpedal, or run forward to return to base position.

Moving to Catch

- Slide sideways, backpedal, or run to move toward ball.
- Square body, reach with hands toward ball, and grasp it.

Feedback

- KPp: "In order to get back to base position, you must move quickly."
- KPd: "Sliding sideways allowed you to catch balls that came to your left or right."
- KP: "How do you move your feet to catch balls that come to your left or right?" Answer: Slide sideways.

Assessment

- Standard 1: Have students use a checklist for open-skill cues; use a scorecard tracking the number of throws to open space in which the opponent does not catch the ball.
- Standard 2: Ask students, "Why do you return to base position after throwing the ball to open space?" Answer: To be in a good court position to move to catch the next ball.

Learning Outcome

Combining skills and basic tactics in small-sided practice tasks

Tactics

Defend space by moving to catch or strike and returning to base position (in middle of court about two-thirds of way back from net). Set up attack by sending ball to open space.

Teaching Style

- Reproduction: all for practice with feedback

Task: Students attack to side, short, and deep in a game-like 1v1 format. Player A tosses ball underhand to player B, who strikes ball (with open hand, short-handled racket, or forearms) back to one of the four open-space court areas (to side, short, or deep) away from player A, who moves to catch the ball. Player B returns to base position. Players switch after five tosses. A point is scored when player B hits back to an open court space so that player A does not catch the ball.

Environment: See setup in figure 19.15.

Practice: random

Closed-skill cues:

Underhand Toss to Opponent's Forehand Side

- Step and toss so ball bounces in front of opponent's open hand or racket on forehand side.

Open-skill cues:

Forehand Striking to Open Space

- Point side to target and put hand or racket in "back and down" position.
- Swing hand or racket from low to high while stepping with opposite foot.
- Follow through toward one of four open-space court areas.

Moving to Catch

- Slide sideways, backpedal, or run to move toward ball.
- Square body and reach with hands toward ball.

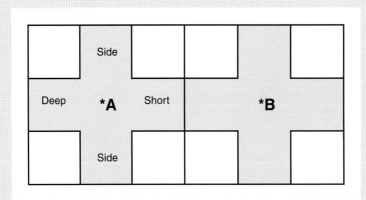

Figure 19.15   Setup for 1v1 attacking to side, short, and deep.

Feedback

- KPd: "You stepped and hit the ball toward one of the four open court areas—good job!"
- KP: "How should you move your feet to get to a ball going deep?" Answer: Quickly turn and move feet toward baseline, while keeping eyes on ball.

Assessment

- Standard 1: Use a scorecard, putting a check mark in each court area to which the ball was sent. Box the check mark if the opponent did not catch the ball.
- Standard 2: On the handout, check the two skill cues that help you to strike the ball into one of the four court areas:

    _____ Step with foot on same side as striking arm toward an open court area.

    _____ Step with opposite foot toward an open court area.

    _____ Follow through toward an open court area.

    _____ Follow through toward opponent.

Learning Outcome

Combining skills and basic tactics in small-sided practice tasks

Tactics

Defend space by moving to catch or strike and returning to base position (in middle of court about two-thirds of the way back from net). Set up attack by sending ball to an open space.

Teaching Style

- Reproduction: all for practice with feedback

Task: Students attack and defend space in a game-like 1v2 format. Player A (defense) tosses ball to player B (offense), who catches it in the air or after one bounce and then tosses it high to player C (offense). Player C strikes the ball back to an open court area away from player A, who moves to try to catch it.

Enrichment:

- Bump a tossed ball (received in the air or on one bounce) high in the air to a teammate, who strikes the ball back to an open court area.

Environment: See figure 19.16.

Practice: random

Closed-skill cues:

Underhand Toss From Player A to Player B

- Step and release ball high over low net toward player B.

Underhand Toss From Player B to Player C

- Step and release ball high toward player C.

Open-skill cues:

- Look for open court area.
- Move to get under ball.
- Position body toward open court.
- Bend knees.
- Extend knees and strike ball upward toward open court.

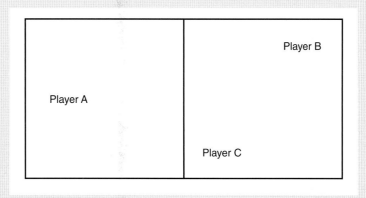

Figure 19.16   Setup for 1v2 attacking and defending space.

Feedback

- KPd: "You moved quickly to get under the ball and hit it to an open court area away from player A."
- KP: "When did you decide which open court area you wanted to hit the ball to?"

Assessment

- Standard 1: Use a scorecard of successful tosses from player B to player C and of successful hits from player C to an open court area.
- Standard 2: On the court diagram (see figure 19.16 above), draw an arrow where player C should decide to hit the ball based on the court position of player A (i.e., away from player A).

Net and Wall Games: Application Level

Use the application-level task progressions for net and wall games in table 19.13 to guide your design of developmentally appropriate learning experiences. Examples of learning experiences from the progression appear below the table.

Table 19.13 Task Progression for Net and Wall Games: Application Level

SPECIALIZED — Striking with hands and rackets	Equipment: nets; trainer volleyballs; short-handled rackets and junior tennis rackets; foam tennis balls and shuttlecocks Learning outcome: maintaining a rally in small-sided practice tasks **Task and Environment** • Maintain a rally with a partner against a wall or over a low net and move back into base position between rallies. • Perform a cooperative rally with the hands, with two players on each side, over a low to higher net. Learning outcome: applying basic offensive and defensive tactics in small-sided practice tasks for net and wall games (SHAPE America, 2014, p. 33) **Task and Environment (Setting Up Attack and Defending Space)** • One-bounce competitive rally against wall • One bounce competitive rally, returning to base position to defend own space: Opponent tosses or strikes ball underhand to a court area away from the player (deep, short, or to side). Player moves to catch the ball, strike with hand(s), or strike with a racket or paddle. **Task and Environment: Setting Up Attack, Defending Space, Winning the Point** • 1v1: Serve into designated areas in opponent's court with player moving to return ball. • Play four square using tactics. • 3v3: Receive a served ball and send it to a teammate, who attempts to score. • Small-sided games with tactics: Cover (volleyball), return to base, set up attack, hit to open court on opponent's side, and win a point.

NET AND WALL GAMES: APPLICATION LEVEL

National Physical Education Standard
- Standard 1: Strike an object consecutively with a partner in cooperative and competitive settings.
- Standard 2: Apply basic offensive and defensive tactics in small-sided practice tasks for net and wall games (SHAPE America, 2014, p. 33).

Learning Outcome

Applying basic offensive and defensive tactics in small-sided practice tasks

Tactics

Set up an attack by moving opponent around court. Defend space by moving to intercept object and returning to base position between hits.

Teaching Styles
- Reproduction: all for practice with feedback
- Production: Guided discovery or convergent discovery to enable students to discover setting up an attack by moving opposing player to the front, back, or sides of the court

Task: Students engage in a 1v1 one-bounce competitive rally (Mitchell, Oslin, & Griffin, 2013).

- Thrower tosses underhand over a low net or rope to an open space and returns to base position.

- Receiver moves to catch the ball after one bounce and throws it back from where the ball was caught over the net to an open space (deep, short, or to side).
- Rally is restarted if ball is missed, goes out of bounds, bounces twice on opponent's side, or bounces once on thrower's side.

Enrichment:

- Strike with hand (two square).
- Strike with racket.

Environment: low net or rope suspended from cones or poles; foam tennis ball or trainer volleyball; poly spots to mark square area (i.e., court)

Practice: random

Open-skill cues:

- Thrower: Choose an open court space where opponent is not positioned and throw ball to make opponent move; quickly return to home base position (feet shoulder-width apart with weight on balls of feet).
- Receiver: Start in home-base position in order to move quickly behind ball to catch it; make a quick decision about where to throw ball to make opponent move, then return to home base position.

Feedback

- KP (thrower): "What helped you to keep your opponent from catching the ball?" "Where are the open spaces on the court to which you can throw?" "If you make your opponent move back to catch the ball, where should your next throw be aimed?" "If you make your opponent move to the left to catch the ball, where should your next throw be aimed?"
- KP (receiver): "How does returning to the home-base position help you prepare to make the next catch?"

Assessment

- Standard 1: Use a performance checklist for setting up an attack (figure 19.17).
- Standard 2: On the diagram in the handout showing the opponent's court position, place an X where your throw should land to set up an attack. (Answer: in front court if opponent is in back; in back court if opponent is in front.)

Coding: Observe players for two-minute intervals. Each time the player performs correctly, place a check mark in the square; when the player performs incorrectly, place an X in the square.

	Decision Chooses shots that set up attack (long or short; left or right).	Skill Makes accurate in-bound throw.	Base Returns to base position to defend space.
Student	Observation 1 2 3 4 5 6 7	Observation 1 2 3 4 5 6 7	Observation 1 2 3 4 5 6 7
	❑ ❑ ❑ ❑ ❑ ❑ ❑	❑ ❑ ❑ ❑ ❑ ❑ ❑	❑ ❑ ❑ ❑ ❑ ❑ ❑
	❑ ❑ ❑ ❑ ❑ ❑ ❑	❑ ❑ ❑ ❑ ❑ ❑ ❑	❑ ❑ ❑ ❑ ❑ ❑ ❑
	❑ ❑ ❑ ❑ ❑ ❑ ❑	❑ ❑ ❑ ❑ ❑ ❑ ❑	❑ ❑ ❑ ❑ ❑ ❑ ❑
Percentage (sum of check marks ÷ sum of all tallies)	_____%	_____%	_____%

Figure 19.17 Performance checklist for setting up an attack.

Learning Outcome

Applying basic offensive and defensive tactics in small-sided practice tasks

Tactics

Set up an attack by moving opponent around court; defend space by moving to intercept object and returning to base position between hits.

Teaching Styles

- Reproduction: all for practice with feedback

Task: Students serve into an open space in a 1v1 format. Specifically, they serve over the net to open space away from the opponent; the receiver returns the ball and play stops. Opponents switch roles after three sets of three different serves. One point is scored for each serve placed accurately in the intended part of the grid.

- Tennis or pickleball: Use a forehand stroke to serve the ball from one or no bounce.
- Volleyball: Use an underhand serve deep into the service area.

Enrichment: Use a half-tennis serve (see skill cues).

Environment: Divide space into grids with progressive service lines (different distances from net). Provide short-handled and pickleball rackets, junior-size volleyballs, Wiffle balls, and foam tennis balls.

Practice: blocked (serving three times each to back left corner, back right corner, and center of grid space)

Closed-skill cues:

Pickleball Serve

- Assume a forward-backward open stance with forward foot aligned with target.
- Swing paddle back.
- Drop ball.
- Swing paddle underhand toward target and shift weight forward.
- Follow through toward target.

Underhand Volleyball Serve

- Preparation
  - Assume a forward-backward open stance.
  - Put weight on back foot and point front foot toward target.
  - Hold ball in nondominant hand diagonally across body just below waist.
  - Position hitting arm with palm up and hand either open or making a fist.
  - Swing hitting arm straight back behind hip.
- Execution
  - Swing striking arm forward to hit ball out of hand as weight is shifted forward.
  - Make contact on lower third of ball.
- Follow-Through
  - Follow through toward target (Fronske & Wilson, 2002).

Half Tennis Serve

- Assume a forward-backward stance.
- Put weight on back foot.
- Point side to net.
- Prepare racket in back-scratch position.

- Toss ball up.
- Extend racket arm and contact ball in sweet spot of racket face.
- Shift weight forward on front foot.
- Follow through across body.

Feedback

- KPp: "Do not toss the ball up; serve (out of your hand [volleyball] or from a dropped ball [pickleball or tennis]).
- KP: "What body parts did you position toward your target to be accurate?"

Assessment

Standard 1: Use an observation checklist of skill cues; use a tally sheet for accuracy.

Standard 2: Ask students, "What skill cues helped you to be accurate?"

Learning Outcome

Applying basic offensive and defensive tactics in small-sided practice tasks

Tactics

Set up an attack by moving opponent around court; defend space by moving to intercept object and returning to base position between hits.

Teaching Style

- Reproduction: all for practice with feedback

Task: Students serve and return the ball to open court space (see figure 19.18) in a 3v3 volleyball format. Serve the ball to an opponent, who sends the ball to a teammate, who in turn returns the ball over the net. Players start in base position (triad), and the back right player begins play with a toss serve over the net from a chosen service line. The back-court receiver calls "mine" and sends the ball to the front-court teammate, who then sends the ball to open space on the other side of the net. The player not playing the ball (on the receiving team) turns toward the player receiving the ball to watch him or her hit the ball. The serving team moves to catch the returned ball. Each server delivers three serves, after which the teams swap roles and each team rotates player positions from right back to left back to net. The serving team scores when the serve is not returned. The receiving team scores when the serving team does not catch the return. Keep ball in play using the method appropriate for player's skill levels:

- Throw and catch with no bounce
- Two contact hits (bump or set)
- One contact hit (bump or set)

Enrichment: Play on and use regular volleyball scoring.

Environment: Mark off four court areas with floor tape. Each court has three service lines, a low net, and a front court area.

Practice: random

Open-skill cues:

- Server: Throw ball to an open back court space to make opponent move.
- Back court receiver: Start in assigned court position in order to move quickly behind ball, call "mine," receive ball, line up body toward front-court player, and send ball to that player.
- Front-court player: Receive ball, line up body toward open court space, and send ball to that space.
- Bump or forearm pass: See forearm pass in first combination-level activity.

Overhead Set

- Preparation
  - Move under ball and get square with target.
  - Make triangular window with hands.
  - Bend knees and elbows slightly.
- Execution
  - Extend knees and elbows.
  - Use finger pads to contact ball above hairline.
  - Push vertically through ball toward target.

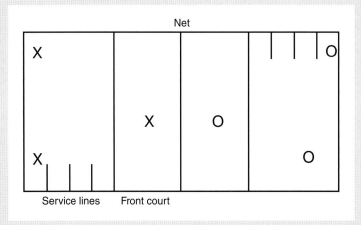

Figure 19.18 Setup for serving and returning ball to open court space.

Feedback

- KPd: "You lined up your body toward an open court space, which helped you score."
- KPp: "You need to line up and square your body with the front-court player so that you accurately send the ball to them."
- KP: "How did your team work together to score?"

Assessment

- Standard 1: Use success tallies.
  - Server: unreturned serves
  - Back-court receiver: sending ball to front-court player
  - Front-court player: scoring
- Standard 2: Ask students, "What did you do to score?"

Learning Outcome

Applying basic offensive and defensive tactics in small-sided practice tasks

Tactics

Return to base (midpoint of baseline), read the shot, hit to open court (deep, short, or to side away from opponent), and win the point.

Teaching Styles

- Reproduction: all for practice with feedback
- Production: guided discovery to discover shot placement to win the point

Directions to Teacher: Use these or similar Guided Discovery Questions to help students discover what to do in each situation. Discovering the answers will prepare them to implement the decisions in the small-sided game played after they answer the questions.

Guided discovery questions (Mitchell, Oslin, & Griffin, 2003, p. 75):

Q. What spaces are on the court for you to hit the ball to?

A. Front and back.

Q. Where should you try to make your opponent move?

A. Back. Try to get the ball to bounce close to the baseline.

Q. Why?

A. It's harder to return the ball from a deep position.

Q. When you get your opponent to move back, where is the space now?

A. In the front.

Q. So to make it hard for your opponent, where should you hit the ball next?

A. To the front.

Q. What type of shot can you use?

A. Volley.

Task: Students vie to win the point in 1v1 pickleball. They start play with a serve (forehand, half tennis serve, or pickleball underhand) from the chosen service line and return serve by hitting to an open court and moving back to base position. The try to win a point by moving the opponent around the court with deep, short, and wide shots.

Enrichment: Engage in skill practice by hitting forehands, backhands, and volleys either from a partner toss or soft hit or against a wall.

Environment: Set up small (half) courts with a low net (cones and rope) for three-minute games between opponents.

Practice: random

Open-skill cues:

Overall

- Look at opponent's body and racket position to read direction of hit. Select shot, move to get behind ball, hit to open court space, and return to base position.

Forehand or Backhand

- Move and get behind ball.
- Assume ready position: knees bent, square to net, racket held chest high, both elbows bent at sides, weight on balls of feet.
- Pivot feet and turn shoulders to take racket back.
- Swing racket horizontally from slightly low to high trajectory.

- Contact ball in middle of racket face out in front of forward foot as weight is shifted forward.
- Follow through toward target.

Volley

- Move and get behind the ball.
- Assume a ready position.
- Position side to net by turning shoulders and pivoting feet to prepare racket high by shoulder.
- Racket stays in front of front shoulder.
- Keep a firm wrist and grip; punch ball.

Feedback

- KPd: "When the opponent hits to your forehand side, you are reading the direction of the hit well."
- KPp: "After you hit deep and move your opponent, your next shot should be short."
- KR: "What cues from your opponent help you know where to move and what shot to perform?"

Assessment

- Standard 1: Use the performance checklist for setting up an attack (figure 19.19).
- Standard 2: Prompt students to take the role of a coach and provide their player with two tips for deciding how to return the ball to win a point.

Coding: Observe players for two-minute intervals. Each time the player performs correctly, place a check mark in the square; when the player performs incorrectly, place an X in the square.

	Decision Reads hit and moves to correct court position.	**Skill** Chooses shots that set up attack (deep, short, wide)..	**Base** Accurately executes stroke.
Student	Observation 1 2 3 4 5 6 7	Observation 1 2 3 4 5 6 7	Observation 1 2 3 4 5 6 7
	❏ ❏ ❏ ❏ ❏ ❏ ❏	❏ ❏ ❏ ❏ ❏ ❏ ❏	❏ ❏ ❏ ❏ ❏ ❏ ❏
	❏ ❏ ❏ ❏ ❏ ❏ ❏	❏ ❏ ❏ ❏ ❏ ❏ ❏	❏ ❏ ❏ ❏ ❏ ❏ ❏
	❏ ❏ ❏ ❏ ❏ ❏ ❏	❏ ❏ ❏ ❏ ❏ ❏ ❏	❏ ❏ ❏ ❏ ❏ ❏ ❏
Percentage (sum of check marks ÷ sum of all tallies)	_____%	_____%	_____%

Figure 19.19 Performance checklist for setting up an attack.

Invasion Games: Combination Level

Use the combination-level task progressions for invasion games in table 19.14 to guide your design of developmentally appropriate learning experiences. Examples of learning experiences from the progression appear below the table.

Table 19.14   Task Progression for Invasion Games: Combination Level

<table>
<tr><td rowspan="2" style="writing-mode: vertical-rl">SPECIALIZED</td><td rowspan="2" style="writing-mode: vertical-rl">Dribbling, passing, and receiving</td><td>

Equipment: flag belts and flags; #4 and #5 soccer balls, junior-size basketballs, hand-balls, and gator-skin balls; floor hockey sticks and pillow polo sticks; plastic pucks

Learning outcome: applying offensive and defensive tactics in chasing and fleeing activities (SHAPE America, 2014, p. 33)

Task and environment:
- Use boundaries and bases tactically (Revegno & Bandhauer, 2013, p. 313).
- Offense stays away from boundaries and moves to bases to avoid the defense.
- Defense constrains the offense by guarding the bases and scoring zones.

Using Goals
- Offense uses jab steps, picks, and decoys to support teammates in
- 1v2, 2v2, 3v2, and3v3 play.
- Defense uses player-to-player guarding tactics to prevent scoring (marking opponent, staying between opponent and goal, stealing the flag).

Learning outcome: combining movement concepts with skills in small-sided practice tasks (SHAPE America, 2014)

Task and Environment (Keeping Possession)
- Vary pathway, direction, and speed of dribble to avoid obstacles.
- Combine dribbling with faking to avoid stationary obstacles.
- Control and protect the ball while dribbling and evading others who are also dribbling.
- Passing and dribbling cooperatively with teammates while moving within a general area (general space).
- Passing and dribbling cooperatively with teammates moving down a field or court toward a goal.

Learning outcome: combining basic offensive and defensive tactics in small-sided practice tasks (SHAPE America, 2014)

Task and Environment (Keeping Possession and Marking Opponent)
- Dribbling 1v1 within a bounded area (grid)
  - Offense: Keep possession.
  - Defense: Mark opponent to gain possession of ball.

Task and Environment (Keeping Possession and Denying Space)
- Dribbling 1v1 toward a goal
- Offense: Keep possession.
- Defense: Mark opponent to deny space.

</td></tr>
</table>

INVASION GAMES: COMBINATION LEVEL

National Physical Education Standards

- Standard 1: Combine skills in dynamic, small-sided practice tasks (SHAPE America, 2014).
- Standard 2: Combine skills and basic tactics in small-sided invasion practice tasks.

Learning Outcome

Combining offensive and defensive tactics in chasing and fleeing activities (SHAPE America, 2014, p. 33)

Tactics

Offense avoids defender; defense constrains offense and guards base.

Teaching Style

- Reproduction: all for practice with feedback

Task: Students use boundaries and bases tactically in a 3v3 tag game. Use the setup in figure 19.20 to create scoring and safety zones for 3v3 tag. Offensive players wear two flags; if both flags are stolen, the player goes to the team hoop and gets another flag. Play begins and ends on teacher's command (whistle). An offensive player may stay in a safety zone for five seconds but then must resume play. The offense's goal is to keep its flags; the defense's goal is to the steal flags. When a flag is stolen, it is placed in the defense's hoop.

- Offense attempts to stay away from the corners of the playing space.
- Defense attempts to corner offensive players to steal flags.

Enrichment: Add a scoring zone measuring 3 by 3 feet (1 by 1 meter). If an offensive player enters the scoring zone with one flag on, the offense earns a point; if an offensive player enters with two flags on, the offense earns two points.

Environment: Define a rectangular space (e.g., gymnasium divided into four zones). Create two or three bases or safety zones designated by floor tape, poly spots, or domes (if playing outdoors on grass).

Practice: random

Open-skill cues:

Offense

- Faking: Move head and shoulders or use a jab step in one direction, then move in opposite direction.
- Jab step: Step to right or left of defender, then pivot or turn away from defender.
- Block or pick: One offensive player uses body by standing close to an offensive teammate, thus creating a block or pick; this maneuver protects the teammate by preventing the defense from taking his or her flag.

Defense

- Vary body position (moving high, low, right, left) so that actions are not predictable.
- Fake by moving head and shoulders or using jab step to pretend to move toward one offensive player, then move instead toward different offensive player.
- Try to deny space and "push" offense into a corner of the rectangular space.

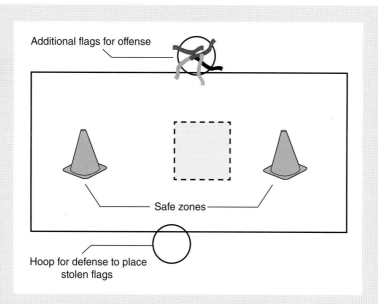

Figure 19.20   Setup for 3v3 tag game focused on tactical use of boundaries and bases.

Feedback

- KPd (offense): "Good job faking toward the right and quickly moving left!"
- KPd (defense): "Way to deny space for the offensive player by moving them into a corner of the playing space."
- KPp (offense): "When you jab-step to the right with your right foot, quickly move toward the left of the defense with your left foot."
- KPp (defense): "Move toward different players so that the offense is not expecting you to take their flag."
- KP (offense): "What did you do to avoid the defense?"
- KP (defense): "What did you do to steal the flag?"

Assessment

- Standard 1: Use the summative checklists in figure 19.21 and figure 19.22 to observe and rate students' use of offensive and defensive movements during 3v3 tag. These can also be adapted as formative assessments by making partner task/assessment cards when using the reciprocal teaching style.
- Standard 2: Use figure 19.23 to provide students the opportunity to reflect on how they moved to avoid the defense.

Check the column that corresponds to the offensive player's movement.

Student	Faked to get away.			Blocked for a teammate.			Used jab steps.		
	Often	Sometimes	Not yet	Often	Sometimes	Not yet	Often	Sometimes	Not yet

Figure 19.21   Checklist for offensive movement in 3v3 tag.

Check the column that corresponds to the defensive player's movement.

Student	Cornered an offensive player.			Used different body positions.			Used fakes.		
	Often	Sometimes	Not yet	Often	Sometimes	Not yet	Often	Sometimes	Not yet

Figure 19.22   Checklist for defensive movement in 3v3 tag.

Name:_____

Check which movements help you get away from the defensive players.

_____ Spinning around in a circle

_____ Pretending to go in one direction but going in a different direction

_____ Standing in place but changing body position by moving high, then low, and then from side to side

Figure 19.23   Self-assessment for 3v3 tag.

Learning Outcome

Combining offensive and defensive tactics in chasing and fleeing activities (SHAPE America, 2014, p. 33)

Tactics

Offense avoids defenders; defense constrains offense and guards base.

Teaching Style

- Reproduction: all for practice with feedback

Task: This is a 2v1, 2v2, or 3v3 tag game focused on offensive and defensive movement. Play begins and ends on the teacher's command (whistle). Offensive players wear two flags with the goal of keeping at least one flag and running over the end line to score (1 point if wearing one flag, 2 points if wearing two flags). The defense's goal is to steal flags; when a flag is stolen, it is placed in the defense's hoop. Students wear heart-rate monitors (or watches) and check heart rate periodically during play (see assessment).

Rules for 2v1

- When both of the offensive player's flags are stolen, play stops, and the defensive player changes roles with one of the offensive players.
- One point is earned for crossing the end line while wearing at least one flag.
- Stolen flags can be placed in a hoop or bin positioned along the sideline.

Rules for 2v2 and 3v3

- If an offensive player has both flags stolen, he or she remains in the game as long as a teammate still has a flag.
- Play stops when all offensive players have had both flags stolen, or when the teacher blows the whistle.

Environment: Use figure 19.24 to create a rectangular playing space that measures 20 by 20 feet (6 by 6 meters); use cones to mark the scoring zone.

Practice: random

Open-skill cues:

Offense

- Faking: Move head and shoulders or jab-step in one direction, then move in opposite direction.
- Jab step: Step to right or left of defender, then pivot or turn away from defender.
- Block or pick: One offensive player uses body by standing close to a teammate, thus creating a block or pick. This maneuver protects the teammate by preventing defense from taking his or her flag.

Defense

- Vary body position (moving high, low, right, left) so that actions are not predictable.
- Fake by moving head and shoulders or using a jab step to pretend to move toward one offensive player, but instead move toward different offensive player.
- Try to deny space and prevent offense from moving forward toward end line.

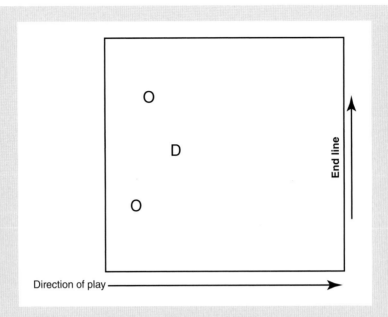

Figure 19.24 Setup for tag game focused on offensive and defensive movement.

Feedback

- KPd: "You set a pick for your teammate so the defense could not steal their flag—great job!"
- KPp: "Try to stay between the end line and your offensive opponent; don't run behind the opponent."
- KP: "What helped you to evade your defender and run across the end line?"

Assessment

- Standard 1: Use the checklist in figure 19.25 to code student offensive movement performance in tag games. This can also be adapted as a formative assessment by making partner task/assessment cards when using the reciprocal teaching style.
- Standard 3: Provide each student with a heart rate assessment card, pictured in figure 19.26, to record their heart rate at chosen times during the tag game and reflect on the effect of vigorous activity on their heart rate.

Coding: Observe players for two-minute intervals. Each time the player demonstrates the skill or scores, place a check mark in the appropriate square.

Set a pick for a teammate.	Used a jab step to change direction.	Scored.
Observation	Observation	Observation
1 2 3 4 5 6 7	1 2 3 4 5 6 7	1 2 3 4 5 6 7
❏ ❏ ❏ ❏ ❏ ❏ ❏	❏ ❏ ❏ ❏ ❏ ❏ ❏	❏ ❏ ❏ ❏ ❏ ❏ ❏
❏ ❏ ❏ ❏ ❏ ❏ ❏	❏ ❏ ❏ ❏ ❏ ❏ ❏	❏ ❏ ❏ ❏ ❏ ❏ ❏
❏ ❏ ❏ ❏ ❏ ❏ ❏	❏ ❏ ❏ ❏ ❏ ❏ ❏	❏ ❏ ❏ ❏ ❏ ❏ ❏
_____%	_____%	_____%

Figure 19.25 Checklist for offensive movement in tag game.

Name: _____

Directions: Check your pulse/heart rate monitoring device during your tag game when the teacher stops play. Walk to your learning-team area, get your heart-rate card, and check the column that represents your heart rate.

	Vigorous 151–180 beats per minute	Moderate 105–150 beats per minute	Below <105 beats per minute
Heart rate 1			
Heart rate 2			
Heart rate 3			
Debrief: Why did your heart rate change—or not change—during the game of tag?			

Figure 19.26 Heart rate self-assessment for tag game.

Learning Outcome

Combining movement concepts with skills in small-sided practice tasks (SHAPE America, 2014, p. 33)

Tactic

Keep possession and avoid others.

Teaching Style

- Reproduction: all for practice with feedback

Task: Students avoid obstacles; specifically, they dribble along varied pathways while changing speed and avoiding stationary obstacles.

Enrichment:

- Avoid moving obstacles. Defensive players are positioned throughout the playing area and are permitted to play "cold defense" (i.e., take one step toward offensive player but not steal the ball).
- Combine dribbling with a fake to avoid stationary obstacles.

Environment: If outdoors, create rectangular playing areas that measure 15 by 15 feet (4.5 by 4.5 meters). If indoors, divide the gymnasium into four zones. Use cones as stationary obstacles. In each playing area, six to eight players use soccer balls, basketballs, or floor hockey pucks (and sticks). If using defense, players act as stationary obstacles and play "cold defense." They are positioned at least 4 feet (about 1.25 meters) apart.

Practice: random

Open-skill cues:

Avoiding Obstacles

- Make quick directional changes (use zigzag pathways) when approaching a stationary obstacle.
- In soccer, use different parts of foot to manipulate ball in order to change directions quickly.
- In hockey, use different parts of stick face to push puck in direction away from obstacle.
- In basketball, use outside hand to dribble to keep ball away from stationary obstacle. Protect ball with nondribbling hand by extending it toward obstacle while keeping your body between obstacle and ball.
- In basketball, use a crossover dribble (left to right hand or right to left hand) to avoid obstacles.

Faking With Dribbling

- In soccer, push ball slightly to one direction with outside of foot, then quickly use inside of foot to dribble ball in opposite direction.
- In basketball, step in one direction with same foot as dribbling hand, then quickly step diagonally with opposite foot to avoid obstacle.

Feedback

- KPd: "You used both sides of your feet to quickly move the ball along a zigzag pathway while avoiding the cone."
- KP: "You did a great job executing the crossover dribble by quickly dribbling the ball from your left hand to your right hand."
- KPp: "Remember to protect the basketball with your nondribbling hand by extending it toward the obstacle and keeping your body between the obstacle and the ball."

Assessment

Standard 1: Use the checklist in figure 19.27 to code student use of skill/tactic cues when avoiding obstacles while dribbling. This can also be adapted as a formative assessment by making partner task/assessment cards when using the reciprocal teaching style.

Coding: Observe players for two-minute intervals. Each time the player performs correctly, place a check mark in the square; when the player performs incorrectly, place an X in the square.

Student	Used outside and inside of foot to quickly change direction.		Used crossover dribble to change direction.		Protected ball by keeping body between obstacle and ball.	
	Observation 1 2 3 4 5 6 7		Observation 1 2 3 4 5 6 7		Observation 1 2 3 4 5 6 7	
	❑ ❑ ❑ ❑ ❑ ❑ ❑		❑ ❑ ❑ ❑ ❑ ❑ ❑		❑ ❑ ❑ ❑ ❑ ❑ ❑	
	❑ ❑ ❑ ❑ ❑ ❑ ❑		❑ ❑ ❑ ❑ ❑ ❑ ❑		❑ ❑ ❑ ❑ ❑ ❑ ❑	
	❑ ❑ ❑ ❑ ❑ ❑ ❑		❑ ❑ ❑ ❑ ❑ ❑ ❑		❑ ❑ ❑ ❑ ❑ ❑ ❑	

Figure 19.27 Avoiding obstacles checklist.

Learning Outcome

Combining movement concepts with skills in small-sided practice tasks (SHAPE America, 2014, p. 33)

Tactic

Keep possession by using width, depth, and support.

Teaching Style

- Guided discovery to discover that keeping possession is accomplished by using a triangular formation of three players in order to create width, depth, and support

Environment: Players are organized into groups of three. Each group creates a triangular formation with the players about 10 feet (3 meters) apart. Groups are spread out in the general playing area. Groups must be organized so that they move across the width of the field or court. Half of the triangles (group A) line up on one sideline, and the other half (group B) line up on the other side of the area. Group A moves across the space; when it reaches the other side, group B moves across. The groups continue this back-and-forth pattern in which each group watches the other play in preparation to answer the teacher's questions.

Task: Students work to keep possession and discover width, depth, and support. They practice triangle passing in general space with the following progression of tasks, which can be described to students as indicated in the quoted remarks.

1. "Your task is to move and change positions with the other players in your triangle so that you maintain the triangular formation at all times. Your group should stay in your general playing area; you are not traveling across the field (or court). Whenever I blow the whistle, you should immediately freeze and check to see if your team is still in the triangular formation." **Feedback (KP):** "Why do you think it is important to maintain a triangular formation?" At this point, the teacher does not provide a final answer. The teacher does comment on what he or she observed in the groups. For example, "I saw some of you running in a triangular circle. I saw some of you cutting in between other players. Think about how a team moves during a game as you participate in the next series of tasks."

2. "Now try to change your triangular formation, but your movement should not be predictable. What do you need to do to be less predictable?" Answer: Cut between teammates rather than running in a circle (see figure 19.28). **Feedback (KP):** "I saw several of you cutting between other teammates. Let's look at the whiteboard diagram (figure 19.28) to see how this helped you be less predictable. Once you cut through, what did you have to do with your body to maintain your triangle and see your teammates?" Answer: Turn or pivot around so that your body again faces teammates.

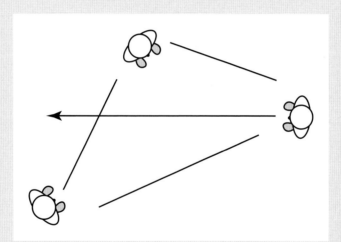

Figure 19.28 Cutting between teammates in triangle formation.

3. "Now, try to move and change positions with the other players in your triangle. The challenge now is to never lose total sight of any of your teammates. In other words, try to keep them in your eyesight." **Feedback (KP):** "What locomotor skills did you need to use this time in order to maintain your ability to move and see the other players in your triangle?" The teacher should then comment by confirming or asking a re-direct question or correcting players' responses (e.g., "Yes, backpedal, slide sideways, run forward . . .")

4. "Should you move the same speed when you are changing positions? [Student answers no.] You are correct. The answer is no, because that would make your movement more predictable, and you do not want to be predictable. So, let's add speed changes as you change positions in your triangular formation." **Feedback (KP):** "So, now let's discuss why we have been trying to maintain this triangular formation. What does this formation accomplish?" Teacher accepts and summarizes players' responses and concludes by saying, "Yes, it creates what we call width, depth, and support. These are three very important tactics that help you maintain space. When you have another teammate to support who is either behind you or to the side of you, you can maintain possession of the game object."

5. The teacher now adds a game object, such as a beanbag, gator-skin ball, soccer ball, basketball, or hockey puck (and stick). The teacher explains, "Now you are going to toss a

beanbag [or other game object] while continuing to change playing positions and maintain the triangular formation. When you have the game object, you cannot travel through space. Please continue to stay in your general playing area." **Feedback (KP):** "What challenges did you encounter when the game object was added to play? How did you send the game object to the other players on your team? Where did you need to aim when sending the game object?"

Enrichment: "Without a game object, you are now going to try to travel across space while keeping the triangular formation."

Practice: random

Open-skill cues:

Maintaining Space and Changing Position in Triangle

- Use running, sliding sideways, and backpedaling.
- Change speed of movement.
- Look for position of teammates.
- Cut between two teammates.
- Try to maintain width or adequate space from teammates.

Feedback

KP: "What were the new challenges you encountered when traveling and trying to maintain your triangular formation?" Possible responses: maintaining control of the game object, not moving too fast.

Assessment

- Standard 1: Use figure 19.29 as an individual checklist for students to indicate how they maintained space in the triangle formation.
- Standard 2: Use figure 19.30 to assess student knowledge of tactics that help keep possession of the game object.

Name:_____

Put a check mark by the movement tasks that you were able to do successfully.

_____ Use a variety of locomotor skills.

_____ Change speed.

_____ Quickly cut through other players.

_____ Keep my eye on my teammates.

Figure 19.29 Checklist for maintaining space in triangle formation.

Name:_____

List three tactics that help you keep possession of the game object when you maintain a triangular formation with your teammates:

1. _____

2. _____

3. _____

Figure 19.30 Self-assessment for triangle tactics.

Learning Outcome

Combining movement concepts with skills in small-sided practice tasks (SHAPE America, 2014, p. 33)

Tactic

Keep possession.

Teaching Style

- Reproduction: all for practice with feedback

Task: Students try to keep possession by moving forward to support the passer. Three offensive teammates pass the ball in a dynamic triangle to advance toward a goal line. Player A with possession remains stationary, passes forward toward teammate (B), and quickly moves forward in the direction of the goal line. The teammate (B) receives the pass and quickly passes forward to another teammate (C), who receives the pass and quickly passes to the first teammate (A).

Enrichment: Have the last pass in the sequence caught in the end zone over the goal line for a score.

Environment: Define lanes that are 8 feet (about 2.5 meters) wide across the width of a court. Provide foam handballs, basketballs, or soccer balls.

Practice: random

Open-skill cues:

- Passer: Remain stationary and make short, quick, accurate passes forward to receiver's hands.
- Receiver: Move forward quickly, keep eyes on passer, make a target with hands, receive ball, turn or pivot, and look for and quickly pass forward to next receiver.

Chest Pass

- Preparation
  - Hold ball on sides.
  - Hold ball at chest level.
  - Flex elbows.
- Execution
  - Step toward target.
  - Extend arms.
  - Release at chest level of target player.
- Follow-Through
  - Pronate hands on release.

Bounce Pass

- Preparation
  - Hold ball on sides.
  - Hold ball at chest level.
  - Flex elbows.
- Execution
  - Step into pass.
  - Push ball down toward floor on an angle.
  - Extend arms.
  - Position pass to land halfway between self and receiver.
- Follow-Through
  - Pronate hands on release.

Inside-of-Foot Soccer Pass

- Preparation
  - Push ball slightly ahead of body.
  - Draw leg back by bending at knee.
  - Hold arms out for balance.
- Execution
  - Swing toward middle of ball from knee on down.
  - Contact ball with big toe area of inside of foot.
  - Keep head down.
- Follow-Through
  - Use low follow-through (below waist) toward target.

Receiving in Soccer

- Present trapping surface to ball.
- Cushion ball (drawing body part back as ball is received).

Push Pass

- Assume hockey stance: form triangle with feet and stick, bend knees slightly, and hold stick flat on floor.
- Position nondominant hand on top of stick.
- Position dominant hand halfway down stick.
- Puck starts at heel of blade.
- Blade sweeps puck forward with cupping motion.
- See target, then puck, then pass.
- Roll wrists toward target.

(Fronske & Wilson, 2002, p.120)

Receiving in Hockey

- Assume hockey stance.
- Reach toward oncoming puck.
- Watch puck into blade.
- Absorb puck by pulling blade back to the back foot.

Feedback

- KP (passer): "What did you do to make a quick and accurate pass?" Answer: Looked at receiver, stepped, and released two-handed pass toward receiver's hands.
- KP (receiver): "How did you decide where to move to support the passer?" Answer: Moved forward, turned, squared off, and reached toward passer with hands.

Assessment

- Standard 1: Product assessment – Use a checklist or a count to document the number of successful passes after a reception and the number of successful moves into position to receive a pass. Create a ratio to determine levels of success (proficient=75%+, developing=50-74%, basic=up to 49%).
- Standard 2: Ask students, "What must teammates do to support the passer?" Answer: Move forward quickly, keep eyes on passer, and make target with hands (or with body to receive with feet).

Learning Outcome

Combining basic offensive and defensive tactics in small-sided practice tasks (SHAPE America, 2014)

Tactic

Offense keeps possession; defense marks opponent to gain possession.

Teaching Style

- Reproduction: all for practice with feedback

Task: Students try to keep or gain possession in a 1v1 game within a bounded area (i.e., grid). Offense tries to keep possession, while defense tries to gain possession.

Environment: Create multiple bounded areas measuring 15 by 15 feet (4.5 by 4.5 meters) as marked by domes, cones, or poly spots. Provide soccer balls, basketballs, pucks, and hockey sticks.

Enrichment: Each pair plays 1v1 toward a goal marked by two cones positioned 20 feet (6 meters) apart. Each player tries to score by touching the game object to his or her cone (i.e., goal); one player scores at cone A and the other player at cone B.

Practice: random

Open-skill cues:

Keeping Possession (Offense)

- For soccer, move ball with inside and outside of feet and pull it back with sole of foot to quickly change direction and speed.
- For basketball, bounce ball while changing speed, pathway, and direction.
- For hockey, move puck with face of stick along different pathways, directions, and speeds to avoid defender.

Gaining Possession (Defense)

- For soccer, use inside of foot to push ball away from offensive player's foot or use sole of foot to pull ball back and away from opponent.
- For basketball, use hands to tap ball away from offensive player, gain control, and dribble away.
- For hockey, use stick face to intercept puck.
- For soccer, basketball, and hockey, use body fakes to outwit offense (i.e., make defender think you are going to move in one direction but then move in a different direction).

Feedback

- KPd: "Way to tackle the ball and gain control."
- KPd: "You tapped the basketball away from your opponent without touching their body—good job!"
- KPp: "Be a bit patient and wait for the puck to leave your opponent's stick before you try to gain control of it."

Assessment

Standard 1: Use the peer observation in figure 19.31 to assess offense ability to maintain possession of game object within a grid. Use the peer observation in figure 19.32 to assess offense ability to maintain possession of game object while traveling down the field/court toward the goal.

Partner up with another pair. One group acts as observers while the other group acts as performers by playing 1v1 within the grid. The offense tries to keep possession of the game object; during this two-minute observation, if the defense gains possession, the game object is given back to the offensive player. Offensive and defensive players switch roles and observers watch the same player they originally watched. Then players and observers switch roles.

Defense Performer 1: **Defense Observer 1:**	**Offense Performer 1:** **Offense Observer 1:**
Put a check mark in a box for each time the defender gains possession of the game object during your two-minute observation.	Put a check mark in a box for each time the defender gains possession of the game object during your two-minute observation.
1 2 3 4 5 6 7 8 9 10 ❑ ❑ ❑ ❑ ❑ ❑ ❑ ❑ ❑ ❑	1 2 3 4 5 6 7 8 9 10 ❑ ❑ ❑ ❑ ❑ ❑ ❑ ❑ ❑ ❑
Defense Performer 2: **Defense Observer 2:**	**Offense Performer 2:** **Offense Observer 2:**
Put a check mark in a box for each time the defender gains possession of the game object during your two-minute observation.	Put a check mark in a box for each time the defender gains possession of the game object during your two-minute observation.
1 2 3 4 5 6 7 8 9 10 ❑ ❑ ❑ ❑ ❑ ❑ ❑ ❑ ❑ ❑	1 2 3 4 5 6 7 8 9 10 ❑ ❑ ❑ ❑ ❑ ❑ ❑ ❑ ❑ ❑

Figure 19.31 Peer observation for 1v1 within grid.

Partner up with another pair. One group acts as observers while the other group acts as performers. After your two-minute observation, switch roles.

Performer: _____ **Observer:** _____	**Performer:** _____ **Observer:** _____
Put a check mark in a box for each time the defender gains possession of the game object during your two-minute observation.	Put a check mark in a box for each time the defender gains possession of the game object during your two-minute observation.
1 2 3 4 5 6 7 8 9 10 ❑ ❑ ❑ ❑ ❑ ❑ ❑ ❑ ❑ ❑	1 2 3 4 5 6 7 8 9 10 ❑ ❑ ❑ ❑ ❑ ❑ ❑ ❑ ❑ ❑
Performer: _____ **Observer:** _____	**Performer:** _____ **Observer:** _____
Put a check mark in a box for each time the defender gains possession of the game object during your two-minute observation.	Put a check mark in a box for each time the defender gains possession of the game object during your two-minute observation.
1 2 3 4 5 6 7 8 9 10 ❑ ❑ ❑ ❑ ❑ ❑ ❑ ❑ ❑ ❑	1 2 3 4 5 6 7 8 9 10 ❑ ❑ ❑ ❑ ❑ ❑ ❑ ❑ ❑ ❑

Figure 19.32 Peer observation for 1v1 toward goal.

Learning Outcome

Combining basic offensive and defensive tactics in small-sided practice tasks (SHAPE America, 2014)

Tactics

Offense penetrates and attacks the goal. Defense guards player staying between ball and target.

Teaching Style

- Reproduction: all for practice with feedback

Task: Students score, prevent scoring, and restart play in a 2v1 game of basketball or team handball. From a position about 8 feet (2.5 meters) away from a wall target, the offensive player with the ball passes to his or her teammate, who is positioned in a passing lane. Offensive players cannot dribble, and they should make three passes before shooting to the wall target. The wider blue wall target area is worth 1 point; the narrower target area is worth 2 points. If a shot misses and the ball is rebounded by the shooting team, then offensive play continues from the position of the rebound. If a shot is made, or if the defender rebounds a missed shot or intercepts a pass, then the defender switches to offense and an offensive player switches to defense. When playing 2v2 or 3v3, if the defensive team recovers a rebound or intercepts a pass, then the ball must be cleared to the top of the playing area (i.e., the starting line) before beginning the offensive possession. After a successful shot (throw or set shot), the opposing team takes over the ball at the starting line.

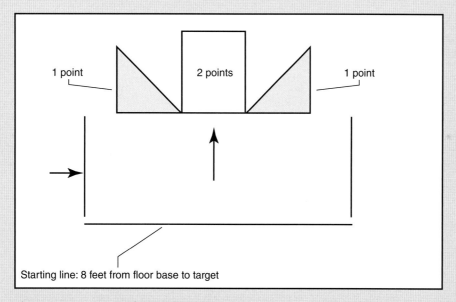

Figure 19.33 Setup for scoring, preventing scoring, and restarting play.

Enrichment: Play 2v2 or 3v3. The type of defense can also be changed.

- Cold defense: staying a body's length away, not stealing the ball, pressuring the player with the ball
- Warm defense: staying an arm's length away, stealing the ball on a pass, applying low-pressure defense
- Hot defense: applying full pressure (but no body contact), stealing the ball at any time (Stevens & Collier, 2001, p. 18)

Environment: Use setup in figure 19.33. Provide a wall target (see Stevens & Collier, 2001, p. 17) and a starting line for starting and restarting play.

Practice: random

Open-skill cues:

Offense

- On-the-ball player: Use bounce, chest, and overhead passes; use jab step to conceal which way pass will go.
- Off-the-ball player: Move into passing lane to receive pass, thus reducing likelihood of interception. Move into open space that is not behind defender.
- Give-and-go: After passing ball, passer moves toward sideline to get open.
- Set shot:
  - Preparation
    - Position feet square to basket and balance with knees slightly bent.
    - Hold shooting hand up as if balancing a waiter's tray.
    - Nonshooting hand faces side of ball with only fingers touching ball.
    - Line up arm, eye, and hand with basket; focus 2 inches (5 centimeters) above target.
  - Execution
    - Extend elbows and knees.
    - Ball rolls off of fingers.
    - Shoot ball in an arced pathway.
- Follow-Through
  - Use a gooseneck finish.

(Fronske & Wilson, 2002)

- Defense
  - Defend player with possession of ball.
  - Try to force offense to make lateral passes and prevent offense from advancing close to target area; position self between ball and target.
- Player-to-Player Defense: Warm Defense
  - Defend player with possession of ball
  - Bend knees and put weight on balls of feet.
  - Position hands in front of body: one under or mirroring ball, one in passing lane.

(Fronske & Wilson, 2002, p. 114)

Feedback

- KPd (offense): "I like how you use a jab step to fake out the defense and pass to your teammate."
- KPd (defense): "You did a great job of staying between the player with the ball and the wall target."
- KPp (offense): "Try not to move behind the defensive player. It makes it difficult for your teammate to pass to you."
- KP (offense): "What did you do to get open to shoot at the wall target?"

Assessment

Standard 1: Use the checklist in figure 19.34 to observe, record, and report your partner's offense and defense performances.

Two observers watch 2v1 play during a two-minute time period; one observer watches the offense and the other watches the defense.

Offensive players: _____

Defensive player: _____

Put a check mark in a box each time the offense makes a successful pass.

1	2	3	4	5	6	7	8	9	10
❏	❏	❏	❏	❏	❏	❏	❏	❏	❏

Put a check mark in a box each time the defense intercepts a pass.

1	2	3	4	5	6	7	8	9	10
❏	❏	❏	❏	❏	❏	❏	❏	❏	❏

Figure 19.34 Peer observation checklist for passing and intercepting.

Invasion Games: Application Level

Use the application-level task progressions for invasion games in table 19.15 to guide your design of developmentally appropriate learning experiences. Examples of learning experiences from the progression appear below the table.

Table 19.15   Task Progression for Invasion Games: Application Level

SPECIALIZED	Dribbling, passing, and receiving	Equipment: #4 and #5 soccer balls, junior-size basektballs, plastic floor-hockey sticks, plastic pucks
		
		Learning outcome: applying offensive and defensive tactics in chasing and fleeing activities (SHAPE America, 2014, p. 33)
		
		Task and Environment:
		• Moving to open space (six to eight players sharing space)
		• Moving with variations in direction, speed, and pathway
		• Moving and coming to a "slam stop" (i.e., taking off from one foot and landing on both feet)
		• Moving, coming to a slam stop, and pivoting
		• Playing 1v1 tag (trying to touch side of opponent's knee)
		
		Learning outcome: applying basic offensive and defensive tactics in small-sided invasion practice tasks (SHAPE America, 2014, p. 33)
		
		Task and environment: Offense keeps possession, penetrates, and attacks the goal; defense defends space, opponent, and goal and takes the ball.
		• Shooting on and defending the target
		  ◦ Offense: Shoot on target while being defended in 2v1 and 2v2 invasion game.
		  ◦ Defense: Defend the target in 2v1 and 2v2 invasion game.
		• Keep-away: 3v1 grid game and 3v2 and 3v3 keep-away
		  ◦ Offense passes, receives, dribbles, and fakes to maintain possession of game object in 3v1 grid game; 3v2 and 3v3 keep away games.
		  ◦ Defense defends the opponent in order to deny space and intercepts or steals the game object.
		• Penetrating and attacking: offense/defense passing and receiving game:
		  ◦ Offense passes and receives in small-sided games (2v2, 3v3) while using the tactics of maintaining possession, penetrating the defense, and attacking the goal (team handball, ultimate).
		  ◦ Defense defends or marks space or an opponent to pressure the offense in order to intercept or steal the game object.
		• Penetrating and attacking: offense dribble, pass receive practice: Offense dribbles, passes, and receives with the goal of scoring by passing to a teammate over an end line (3v3 or 4v4 with stationary post players).
		• Penetrating and attacking: offense/defense small-sided invasion game:
		  ◦ Offense tries to maintain possession, penetrate, and attack the goal by using dribbling, passing, receiving, and shooting in small-sided games.
		  ◦ Defense defends opponent to prevent scoring or to intercept the ball in a 2v2 or 3v3 invasion game.

INVASION GAMES: APPLICATION LEVEL

National Physical Education Standards

- Standard 1: Combine skills with reasonable accuracy in dynamic, small-sided practice tasks.
- Standard 2: Apply basic offensive and defensive tactics in small-sided invasion practice tasks.

(SHAPE America, 2014, p. 33)

Learning Outcome

Applying offensive and defensive tactics in chasing and fleeing activities (SHAPE America, 2014, p. 33)

Tactics

On offense, move to open space while avoiding others; on defense, mark offensive opponent.

Teaching Style

- Reproduction: all for practice with feedback

Task: Students work to perform effective offensive or defensive movement within a grid. Six to eight players each have their own space within a 10'-15' square grid. Movement starts and stops on the teacher's whistle (e.g., one blow to start, two to stop). The following offensive tasks are presented:

- Moving quickly to open spaces
- Moving in different directions and changing speed and pathway
- Coming to a "slam stop" (taking off of one foot and landing on both feet with a low center of gravity)
- Coming to a slam stop and pivoting to change direction sharply

Environment: Create 10-15'square grids marked by poly spots or cones.

Practice: random

Feedback

- KPd: "You performed a very controlled and quick slam stop and then pivoted without touching another player—great job!"
- KPp: "Look for open spaces to move toward and make your movements a bit smaller and quicker."

Learning Outcome

Applying offensive and defensive tactics in chasing and fleeing activities (SHAPE America, 2014, p. 33)

Tactics

On offense, move to open space while avoiding others; on defense, mark offensive opponent.

Teaching Style

- Reproduction: all for practice with feedback

Task: Students practice defensive movement in a 1v1 format within a grid. They try to touch the side of the opponent's knee, which requires changing body position (high and low), moving from side to side, and watching the opponent's torso to determine where he or she is going to move.

Environment: Create 10-15' square grids marked by poly spots or cones. Assign three student pairs to each grid.

Practice: random

Open-skill cues:

Offense

- Change speed with body control.
- Make quick, controlled movements with slam stops (taking off of one foot and landing on two feet).
- Change direction with a pivot on the balls of the feet.
- Use varied locomotor skills (e.g., running, sliding sideways, backpedaling).
- Avoid others in the grid.

Defense

- Use a slight knee bend for quick changes in direction.
- Keep hands free at sides with elbows bent and palms up.
- Keep eye on opponent's torso to anticipate direction in which she or he will move.
- Use slight tap to touch side of opponent's knee.

Feedback

- KPdp: "Your knees are locked. In order to change direction quickly, you need to keep them bent."
- KP (offense): "What allowed you to avoid the defense?"
- KP (defense): "What helped you anticipate where the offense was going?"

Assessment

Standard 1: Use the observation checklist in figure 19.35 to assess the student's offensive movements and the observation checklist in figure 19.36 to assess the student's defensive movements. This can also be adapted as a formative assessment by making partner task/assessment cards when using the reciprocal teaching style.

Check the column that represents the student's performance for each type of movement.

Student	USED VARIED LOCOMOTOR SKILLS.			CHANGED SPEED.			EXECUTED SLAM STOPS AND PIVOTS.		
	Often	Sometimes	Not yet	Often	Sometimes	Not yet	Often	Sometimes	Not yet

Figure 19.35 Teacher observation checklist for offensive movement in a grid.

Check the column that represents the student's performance for each type of movement.

Student	WATCHED TORSO AND MOVED IN SAME DIREC- TION AS OFFENSE.			MOVED QUICKLY FROM SIDE TO SIDE.			TOUCHED PARTNER'S KNEE.		
	Often	Sometimes	Not yet	Often	Sometimes	Not yet	Often	Sometimes	Not yet

Figure 19.36   Teacher observation checklist for defensive partner tag in a grid.

Learning Outcome

Applying offensive and defensive tactics in small-sided invasion practice tasks (SHAPE America, 2014, p. 33)

Tactics

On offense, use faking, passing, and the give-and-go; on defense, deny space and intercept passes.

Teaching styles

- Reproduction: all for practice with feedback
- Production: convergent discovery (Ask students, "Where do you position yourself to make it difficult for offensive players to pass the ball? To receive the ball?")

Task: Students try to gain or keep possession in a 3v1 game. Two students (D and O in figure 19.37) play one-on-one within the 10'-15' square grid while two others act as "posts" (P in the figure). The two post players collaborate with the offensive player, thus creating the 3v1 format. The goal is for the offensive player in the grid to receive a pass from one of the post players located outside of the grid's end line. Once a score (five total passes to post player) is made, or the defensive player obtains the ball, the players rotate to switch roles from post (near offense) to offense, from offense to defense, from defense to post (near defense) to post near defense to post near offense. One minute on either offense or defense provides quite a workout! The post players may not pass to each other, and the offensive player in the grid can pass to the same post player no more than twice in a row. The game can be played using a beanbag, gator-skin ball, basketball, soccer ball, or hockey puck and stick.

Enrichment:

- Add limited dribbling.
- Expand grid to 20 feet (6 meters) square.

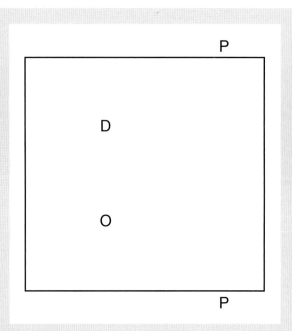

Figure 19.37 Setup for 3v1 game for keeping and gaining possession.

Environment: 10'-15'square grid marked with cones or polyspots
Practice: random
Open-skill cues:

Give-and-Go

- Make quick, short passes to post players.
- After passing, move quickly on an angle to open space in order to receive return pass from post player.

Jab Step and Pivot

- Jab toward left side of defender with right foot (or vice versa).
- Pivot away from defender on left foot (or vice versa).

Juke Step

- Step with one foot.
- Then quickly step on opposite foot and travel in opposite direction.

Feedback

- KPd (offense): "Way to move quickly after you passed to a post player. You were able to get open to receive a pass back—good job!"
- KPp (offense): "You can perform a jab step and then pivot away from the defensive player in order to get open."
- KP (offense): "What did you do in order to evade your defensive player inside of the grid?"

Assessment

- Standard 1: Use the self-check assessment in figure 19.38 for students to check the movement skills and tactics they were able to successfully perform.
- Standard 2: Use the questions in figure 19.39 to assess student's tactical knowledge for the 3v1 grid game.

Name: _____

Check the movement skills and tactics you were able to do successfully:

_____ Jab and pivot to evade defender.

_____ Give and go moving to open space.

_____ Receive return passes from post player.

Figure 19.38   Self-check assessment for 3v1 grid game.

Name:_____

Directions: Write the correct letter in the blank space provided.

1. _____ What does a give-and-go help you do?

  a. defend another player

  b. fake out the defense

  c. move to open space to receive another pass

2. _____ Which of the following contributes to good defense?

  a. changing body position between high and low

  b. chasing behind the offensive player

  c. staying far away from the offensive player

Figure 19.39   Tactical knowledge assessment for 3v1 grid game.

Learning Outcome

Applying offensive and defensive tactics in small-sided invasion practice tasks (SHAPE America, 2014, p. 33)

Tactics

On offense, use faking, passing, give-and-go and limited dribble; on defense, deny space and intercept passes.

Teaching Styles

- Reproduction: all for practice with feedback
- Production: convergent discovery (Ask students, "How do you make it difficult for defensive players to intercept the ball? How do you make it easier for your teammates to pass you the ball?")

Task: Play 3v2 keep-away inside a 20' square grid area. The offense's goal is to make seven consecutive passes, at least two of which must be sent to the post player standing in the center of the grid. If the defensive team intercepts the ball or puck before seven consecutive passes are made, play continues with the defense becoming the offense. If the offense achieves seven consecutive passes, play stops, and the ball or puck is given to the defense. Offense can use limited dribble to move a short distance to get into position to pass to a teammate. Refer to figure 19.40 for player setup in relation to the grid.

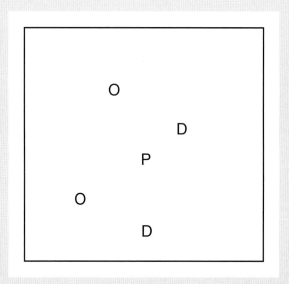

Figure 19.40 Setup for 3v2 keep-away game inside a grid area.

Practice: random

Open-skill cues:

- See the cues in the prior task for the give-and-go and the jab and juke steps.

Limited Dribble

- Use dribble to move ball away from defender.
- Use dribble to move to open space in order to pass to teammate.

Basketball Dribble and Pass

- Use yo-yo action with finger pads on ball.
- Protect ball with nondribbling hand.
- Keep eyes up to look for opportunity to pass.
- See defenders but don't focus on them.
- Control dribble and pull ball into chest with hands to protect the ball when ending the dribble.
- Step and pass toward target.

Soccer Dribble and Pass

- Maintain dribble.
- Push ball slightly ahead of body.
- Run to ball and plant nonkicking foot slightly behind and to side of ball and pointed toward target.
- Use inside of foot (big toe area) to execute pass toward target.

Hockey Dribble and Pass

- Assume a hockey stance.
- Keep blade flat on floor 2 or 3 feet (0.6 to 0.9 meters) in front of feet.
- Alternate pushing puck forward with opposite sides of stick face.
- Use blade to cup puck.
- Pass as stick blade comes into forward position toward target.

Feedback

- KPd (offense): "You kept your head up while dribbling. This helped you dribble and move to open space."
- KPd (defense): "You kept close (within an arm's length) to the player you were guarding and kept her from passing to a teammate."
- KPp (offense): "You chose a pass that was easily intercepted by the defense. You need to use a bounce pass when you are being closely guarded."
- KP (offense): "What did you do in order to evade your defender inside of the grid?"

Learning Outcome

Applying offensive and defensive tactics in small-sided invasion practice tasks (SHAPE America, 2014, p. 33)

Tactics

Offense uses faking, passing, and give-and-go: defense denies space and intercepts passes.

Teaching Styles

- Reproduction: all for practice with feedback
- Production: convergent discovery (Ask students, "Where do you position yourself to make it difficult for offensive players to *pass* the ball? Difficult for them to *receive* the ball?")

Task: Students try to defend space and keep possession in a 2v1 or 3v3 game of keep-away (team handball or basketball). Offense players move to get open and use short, quick passes to maintain possession of the ball. The defense stays between a receiver and the player with the ball and pressures the player with the ball by moving closer (arm's distance).

Environment: Use cones to mark boundaries (about one-fourth of the gym per group). Provide foam team-handball balls or junior sized basketballs.

Practice: random

Open-skill cues:

Defense

- Assume a ready stance: feet staggered, weight toward balls of feet, and knees slightly bent.
- Guard receiver as follows:
  - Stay between receiver and passer, with one side to each to maintain view of both.
  - Move to get body in front of ball to intercept.
- Guarding passer as follows:
  - Pressure passer by moving closer (arm's distance), spreading arms wide, and glancing at hips to detect direction of upcoming throw.
  - Move hands toward ball to block.

Feedback

KP (defense): Ask students, "In what position do you need to keep your body so you can quickly move in any direction? Where did you focus your attention when you were successful at intercepting the ball? When you were unsuccessful?"

Assessment

- Standard 1: Use the product assessment of defensive performance (figure 19.41).
- Standard 2: Prompt students to take the role of a coach and provide their player with two tips for intercepting passes. (For the answer, see the description of skill cues for defense.)

Coding: Observe players for two-minute intervals. Each time the player performs correctly, place a check mark in the square; when the player performs incorrectly, place an X in the square.

Student	Decision Moves to get between passer and receiver.										Skill Blocks or intercepts ball.									
	Observation										Observation									
	1	2	3	4	5	6	7	8	9	10	1	2	3	4	5	6	7	8	9	10
	❑	❑	❑	❑	❑	❑	❑	❑	❑	❑	❑	❑	❑	❑	❑	❑	❑	❑	❑	❑
	❑	❑	❑	❑	❑	❑	❑	❑	❑	❑	❑	❑	❑	❑	❑	❑	❑	❑	❑	❑
	❑	❑	❑	❑	❑	❑	❑	❑	❑	❑	❑	❑	❑	❑	❑	❑	❑	❑	❑	❑
Percent (sum of check marks ÷ sum of all tallies)	_____%										_____%									

Figure 19.41   Product assessment of defensive performance for keep-away game.

Learning Outcome

Applying offensive and defensive tactics in small-sided invasion practice tasks (SHAPE America, 2014, p. 33)

Tactics

Offense uses faking, passing, and the give-and-go; defense denies space and tries to intercept passes.

Teaching Styles

- Reproduction: all for practice with feedback
- Production: convergent discovery (Ask students, "What helps you to quickly decide where to shoot the ball to avoid the goalie?")

Task: Students attack the goal in a 2v1 game (team handball, soccer, or floor hockey). From a position opposite and 20 feet (6 meters) away from a goal, the shooter passes (using a one-handed overhand or underhand throw, an inside-of-foot pass, or a push pass) to a teammate positioned to one side and closer to the goal. The shooter then runs toward the goal, noting the position of the goalie and open space, receives a pass back from the teammate, and *quickly* shoots the ball into the goal, avoiding the stationary goalie. The sequence is repeated with the shooter receiving a pass from the other side of the goal.

Enrichment: Position the goalie in different places in front of the goal to change the shot placement.

Environment: Place cones 6 to 8 feet (about 1.75 to 2.5 meters) apart in front of a wall. Provide foam team-handball balls, pillow-polo ball and sticks, or foam soccer balls.

Practice: blocked

Open-skill cues:

- Shooter: Pass and move quickly toward goal.
- Receive pass, step toward open space between goalie and side of goal, and quickly shoot.
- Teammate: Make smooth transition from receiving by stepping toward and passing to spot where shooter will be for return pass.

Feedback

KP (shooter): "What did you look for before you took the shot?" Answer: Open space between the goalie and the side of the goal.

Assessment

- Standard 1: Compare accuracy records for three sets of three trials each.
- Standard 2: Ask students, "What environmental cues did you attend to in order to make an accurate shot on goal?" Answer: Open spaces surrounding the goalie.

Learning Outcome

Applying offensive and defensive tactics in small-sided invasion practice tasks (SHAPE America, 2014, p. 33)

Tactics

Goalkeeper moves to cut down the shooting angle; offense quickly and accurately shoots on goal.

Teaching Styles

- Reproduction: all for practice with feedback
- Production: convergent discovery (Ask students, "Where does the goalie move to cut down the shooting angle?")

Task: Students cut down the angle in a 3v1 game (team handball, soccer, or hockey). Offensive players spread out, remain at least 15 feet (4.5 meters) from the goal, pass the ball at least three times, and take a shot on the goal. The goalkeeper slides his or her feet in the direction of the player with the ball and moves toward the shooter to cut down the shooting angle.

Enrichment: Offense uses fakes for direction of shot.

Environment: Place cones 6 to 10 feet (about 1.75 to 3 meters) apart. Provide foam team-handball balls, foam soccer balls, or plastic pucks and floor-hockey sticks.

Practice: random (order of shooters unknown)

Open-skill cues:

- Offense: Pass quickly and accurately to teammates.
- Shooter: Receive pass, fake and step toward open space, and quickly shoot.
- Goalkeeper: Slide in direction of player with ball, move quickly toward player who squares off and steps toward goal, and keep eye on and align body behind ball to intercept (by using body, hands, stick, or feet).

Feedback

KP (goalkeeper): "How did you make it difficult for the offense to score?" Answer: Aligned with the shooter and moved toward the ball.

Assessment

- Standard 1: Record the number of goalkeeping receptions out of 10 attempts.
- Standard 2: Create three diagrams each with a goal keeper positioned in the middle and slightly outside the goal. Vary the placement of the shooter in each diagram with instructions for students to show where the goalkeeper should move to prevent the player with the ball from scoring, and explain why. (Answer: In line with and toward player to cut down the shot angle).

Learning Outcome

Applying offensive and defensive tactics in small-sided invasion practice tasks (SHAPE America, 2014, p. 33)

Tactics

Offense uses quick throws and fakes and moves forward to support passer. Defense makes it difficult for offense to pass and score by staying between passer and receiver or goal and by reaching toward ball to intercept or block.

Teaching Styles

- Reproduction: all for practice with feedback
- Production: convergent discovery (Ask students, Offense: "How do you pass the ball to make it difficult for the defense to intercept?" Defense: "Where do you position yourself to make it difficult for offensive players to *pass* the ball? Difficult for them to *receive* the ball?")

Task: Students work to penetrate, attack, and defend. This is a 3v3 game with two post players in which the offense tries to get the game object over the end line between the cones (see figure 19.42). One player on each team acts as a stationary post player. Goals are scored by passing to a teammate over an end line between the cones. Post players are restricted to a circular area 4 or 5 feet (1.25 to 1.5 meters) in diameter; the circles can be made with poly spots. Post players pass back to teammates, and the teacher regularly switches out the student playing the post position. The defense uses warm defense (arm's length away and allowed to steal the ball) when guarding a passer and stays between the passer and potential receivers. A goal or turnover restarts play at the end line of the team that was scored on or won the ball. Rules of the game include but need be limited to the following:

- All players, including the post player, must receive a pass before a goal can be scored.
- Players cannot run when in possession of the game object.

Enrichment

- Add limited dribbling to the 3v3 game.
- Play 3v3 without post players (i.e., all players can move freely).
- Play 4v4 with a stationary post player on each team.

Environment: Use the setup in figure 19.42 to create four courts for the 3v3 game. Use poly spots to mark circles for the post players. Use cones to create the end-line goals. One team wears pinnies.

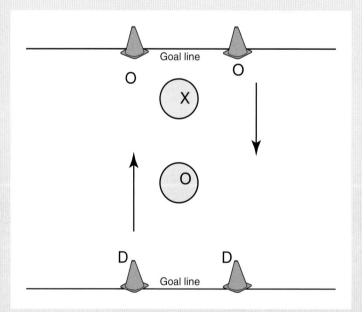

Figure 19.42   Setup for 3v3 game of penetrate, attack, and defend.

Practice: random

Open-skill cues:

Offense

- Provide good support by moving forward quickly into open space toward the goal after passing. Make quick, accurate pass to open player.

Defense

- Stay between receiver and passer, with one side to each to maintain view of both.
- Move to get body in front of ball to intercept.
- Pressure passer by moving closer (arm's distance), spreading arms wide, and glancing at hips to detect direction of upcoming throw.
- Move hands toward ball to block.

Feedback

- KP (offense): "What tactics enabled your team to penetrate the defense and pass over the end line?"
- KP (defense): "What tactics enabled your team to intercept or block passes?"

Assessment

- Standard 1: Use the product assessment to determine an observational rating of offensive and defensive decision-making and skill execution (figure 19.43).
- Standard 2: Prompt students to take the role of a coach and give offensive players two tips for providing good support for their teammates. For the answer, see the description of skill cues.

Scoring Key

3 = effective performance

2 = somewhat effective performance

1 = ineffective performance

Components and Criteria

Decision making: using appropriate passes to open teammates

Skill execution: making accurate passes

Support: moving into position to receive passes

Guarding and marking: moving into position and intercepting or blocking passes

Coding

Observe a player for 2-5 minutes and assign a rating of 3, 2, or 1 (described above) to represent the quality of performance in the components observed.

Name	Decision making	Skill execution	Support	Guarding or marking
Average				

Figure 19.43   Product assessment of offensive and defensive game play.

Learning Outcome

Applying offensive and defensive tactics in small-sided invasion practice tasks (SHAPE America, 2014, p. 33)

Tactics

Offense tries to move into position to score; defense tries to prevent scoring and gain possession.

Teaching Styles

- Reproduction: all for practice with feedback
- Production: convergent discovery (Ask students, Offense: "How do you decide when to take the shot on goal?" Defense: "What did you do to intercept the ball? As the goalie, how did you prevent scoring?")

Task: Students work to keep possession, penetrate, attack, and defend in a game of 3v3. Offense shoots to the goal (basketball) or against the goalie (floor hockey, soccer, and handball). Defense stays between offensive players and goal to block shots and gain possession of the ball.

- Possession: After a shot in basketball, rebound and play on. After an interception by the goalie in soccer or hockey, the goalie puts the ball or puck back into play. After an interception by a defensive player on the field or court, play continues.
- Game object out of bounds: Restart play with a throw-in or push pass from the sideline.
- After a goal: The team that does not score puts the ball in play from behind the half-court or half-field line.

Environment: Use the width of a gymnasium court or a small field (20 by 25 yards, or 18 by 23 meters). Goals depend on game object used (basketball hoop, floor-hockey goal, cones or portable soccer goal, end line for ultimate).

Practice: random

Open-skill cues:

Scoring Decisions

- If open (cold or no defense between you and goal), take shot.
- Shoot on angle away from goalie.

Goalkeeping

- Slide in direction of player with ball.
- Move quickly toward player who squares off and steps toward goal.
- Keep eye on and align body behind ball to intercept (by using body, hands, stick, or feet).

Basketball: Scoring

- Use one or two-handed set shot (see previous activity for skill cues).

Basketball: Prevent Scoring

- Guard offensive players (see previous activity for skill cues).

Basketball: Gain Possession

- Blocking Out
  - Get in front of opponent.
  - Use wide stance.
  - Keep elbows out and palms wide.
  - Push buttocks back toward opponent to create stable wall between opponent and ball.

- Rebounding
  - Block out, then attack basket.
  - Cover side of basket opposite the shot.
  - Jump, reach, and pull ball into stomach area to protect it.
  - Pivot to find open teammate to pass to or dribble out of congested playing area.

Floor Hockey

- Forehand Wrist Shot
  - Bottom hand on stick should slide 2 or 3 inches (5 to 7.5 centimeters) down stick.
  - Assume hockey stance.
  - Bend knees more than for a pass.
  - Drive off of back leg (load back leg by putting full weight on it).
  - Use fast sweeping motion with stick.
  - Roll wrist over and point blade at target.

(Fronske & Wilson, 2002, p. 122)

Soccer Instep

- Head is down and chest is over ball
- Pull kicking leg back and point instep of foot toward target.
- Position nonkicking foot alongside ball with toes pointing at target.
- Contact ball in middle with shoelaces and with ankle locked and toes pointed down.
- Hold arms out for balance.
- Follow through toward target.

(Fronske & Wilson, 2002)

Soccer Throw-In

- Assume a forward-backward stance.
- Face the field and use both hands with elbows bent.
- Start behind the head.
- Throw over the head.
- Shift weight forward as both feet stay behind sideline or touchline.
- Both feet stay on ground.
- Snap arms down for short throw and up for long throw.

(Fronske & Wilson, 2002, p. 180)

Feedback

- KPdp: Provide feedback based on skill cues.
- KP: "What did you do to gain possession of the game object?" "What did you do to score?" "As a goalie, what did you do to prevent scoring?"

Assessment

- Standard 1: Use the assessments in figures 19.44 and 19.45 to code decision-making and skill execution.
- Standard 2: Ask students the following questions:

Any invasion game: "As a coach, what two tips would you give players to help them score?" Answer: see description of skill cues.

Basketball: "As a coach, what two tips would you give players to help them rebound?"

Soccer or hockey: "As a coach, what two tips would you give the goalies to help them anticipate shots?"

Coding: Observe players for two-minute intervals. Each time the player performs correctly, place a check mark in the appropriate box.

Student	Decisions Shoots when open. Shoots on angle away from goalie. Observation 1 2 3 4 5 6	Skill Makes accurate shots. Observation 1 2 3 4 5 6	Skill ✔ Gets in position for rebound. + Gets rebound. Observation 1 2 3 4 5 6
	❏ ❏ ❏ ❏ ❏ ❏	❏ ❏ ❏ ❏ ❏ ❏	❏ ❏ ❏ ❏ ❏ ❏
	❏ ❏ ❏ ❏ ❏ ❏	❏ ❏ ❏ ❏ ❏ ❏	❏ ❏ ❏ ❏ ❏ ❏
	❏ ❏ ❏ ❏ ❏ ❏	❏ ❏ ❏ ❏ ❏ ❏	❏ ❏ ❏ ❏ ❏ ❏

Figure 19.44 Standard 1 offense checklist.

Coding: Observe players for two-minute intervals. Each time the player performs correctly, place a check mark in the appropriate box.

Student	Decisions Goalie moves to correct position to intercept. Player covers correct side of basket for rebound. Observation 1 2 3 4 5 6	Skill Goalie intercepts game object. ✔ Player gets in position for rebound. + Gets rebound. Observation 1 2 3 4 5 6	Guarding or marking ✔ Stays between offense and goal. + Gains possession of game object. Observation 1 2 3 4 5 6
	❏ ❏ ❏ ❏ ❏ ❏	❏ ❏ ❏ ❏ ❏ ❏	❏ ❏ ❏ ❏ ❏ ❏
	❏ ❏ ❏ ❏ ❏ ❏	❏ ❏ ❏ ❏ ❏ ❏	❏ ❏ ❏ ❏ ❏ ❏
	❏ ❏ ❏ ❏ ❏ ❏	❏ ❏ ❏ ❏ ❏ ❏	❏ ❏ ❏ ❏ ❏ ❏

Figure 19.45 Standard 1 defense checklist.

▶ Visit the web resource for learning activities, video clips, and review questions.

Chapter 20

Developmental Dance

Key Concepts

- Defining developmental dance and justifying its role in the elementary physical education program
- Describing the outcomes of educational dance
- Describing the main genres of dance and the content of dance as an expressive movement form
- Defining the fundamentals of rhythm
- Describing how reproduction and production teaching styles are used to teach dance
- Teaching standards-based learning experiences with aligned assessments in dance

Dance is . . .

- an art form that communicates and expresses an idea or feeling;
- a form of social interaction;
- a representation of cultural traditions, values, and beliefs;
- a lens into a period of history;
- a form of recreation;
- a form of entertainment;
- a form of competition;
- a form of religious expression; and
- a form of therapy or exercise (National Association for Sport and Physical Education & National Dance Association [NASPE &NDA], 2007, p. 8).

To put it more prosaically, dance is an **expressive movement form** that may communicate an idea, reflect a particular aspect of a culture, or evolve from the desire for individuals to move together in community or share a celebration (Cone & Cone, 2005). Unlike games and gymnastics, dance offers children an opportunity to use their movement repertoire (i.e., movement skills and concepts) to express themselves in a unique fashion. Games and gymnastics are **functional movement forms** in which movement skills and concepts are used to accomplish specific objectives, such as kicking a ball into a goal or performing a forward roll. Dance, on the other hand, is a movement form that enables participants to express themselves. As a result, a well-balanced elementary physical education program offers children varied opportunities to express themselves through both creative dance and structured dance (i.e., folk, square, and social dance forms). When dancing, a child uses her or his body as an instrument of self-expression and communication in much the same way that a painter uses line, color, shape, and texture to express ideas on canvas.

The preceding description of dance focuses on its purposes, but what are its characteristics? Murray (1975) defined dance as "movement put into rhythmic and spatial form, a succession of movements which starts, proceeds, and finishes" (p. 7). Boswell, Cossey, and Oliver (1998) described dancing as "moving one's body in a skillful, rhythmically coordinated, and expressive manner" (p. 4).

In addition, in developmental dance, children do more than simply replicate dances taught to them by a teacher. They not only learn the content of dance—that is, the elements of the movement framework (body, space, effort, and relationship awareness)—but also the process of dance. This process involves teaching children the following elements:

- How to describe their movements by noting elements of the movement framework
- How to use these elements to vary their movements
- How to recognize dance as an art form that uses the elements of movement as tools to express and communicate an idea or feeling
- Terminology specific to particular forms and styles of dance
- Understanding of dance as a means of improving one's physical fitness
- Knowledge of choreographic structures

Thus developmental dance provides a "means through which children develop, express, and communicate their life experiences" (Cone & Cone, 2005, p. 5).

MOVEMENT FRAMEWORK FOR DEVELOPMENTAL DANCE

The Active Child illustration (figure 20.1) depicts the fact that the movement concepts of body, space, effort, and relationship affect developmentally appropriate learning experiences in the various types of dance: lyric-directed, cultural, social, and creative. The specific relationships between these dance forms and the movement concepts are described in the learning goal blueprint presented in table 20.1.

Developmental dance provides the children in grades 3 through 5 with progressive movement experiences based on their unique psychomotor, cognitive, and social attributes. As described in chapter 5 and reviewed in chapter 18, children in grades 3 through 5 are at the intermediate level of movement skill learning. At this level, they have gained a better kinesthetic feel for the position of their body parts and the timing of their movements. This sense is especially useful as they build on the stability and locomotor skills developed in kindergarten through grade 2 to learn form-based,

Figure 20.1   The Active Child: dance.

ment concepts, combine skills in sequences, and perform skills and sequences with partners and in small groups. The combination skill progressions (table 20.6) challenge students to apply rhythmic fundamentals to step sequences, use movement concepts to modify locomotor and stability skills, learn simple dance formations, and begin to create dances with teacher guidance. In the application skill progressions (table 20.8) students refine rhythm by adding accent and focus, begin to isolate their use of various body parts, engage in more complex dance formations, expand their ability to create dances, and participate in partner dances. Dance activities highlighting these skill progressions are provided later in this chapter.

closed-skill dance steps and movement sequences involved in combination and application progressions.

In developmental dance, students increase the difficulty of skills, vary skills using the move-

THE ROLE OF DANCE IN PHYSICAL EDUCATION

Physical educators should teach the *whole* child—that is, the thinking, feeling, and moving child. Dance addresses all three of these domains of learning in an essential fashion by fostering children's ability to express their ideas and thoughts through

Table 20.1   Learning Goal Blueprint for Specialized Skill Performance in Developmental Dance (Grades 3 Through 5)

Content	Body	Space	Effort	Relationships
Lyric-directed dance	Intentionally uses body actions and shapes in unison, opposition, and sequence as directed by lyrics with correct technique.	As designated by lyrics, correctly performs dance steps while changing direction, level, pathway, or range of movement.	Performs dance actions to the tempo of the music.	Maintains relationships with others as designated by dance lyrics.
Cultural dance	Intentionally uses body actions and shapes in unison, opposition, and designated dance sequence with correct performance technique while expressing the desired meaning.	Correctly performs changes of direction, level, pathway, or range of movement in accordance with dance steps.	Performs dance actions to the tempo of the music. Intentionally uses force for correct performance technique while expressing the desired meaning.	Uses props, formations, roles, and positions as designated by the dance.
Creative dance	Intentionally uses body actions and shapes in unison, opposition, and sequence with correct performance technique while expressing the desired meaning.	Performs dance movements by varying direction, level, pathway, or range of movement while expressing the desired meaning.	Performs dance actions using appropriate tempo, force (strong, medium, or light), and flow (bound or free) to express the desired meaning.	Uses props, positions (e.g., in front of, alongside, behind, above), roles, and groupings to express the desired meaning.
Social dance	Intentionally uses body actions and shapes in unison, opposition, and sequence with correct performance technique.	Correctly performs dance steps while changing direction, level, pathway, or range of movement.	Performs dance actions to the tempo of the music.	Performs dance using correct positions and roles of leading and following.

movement. Indeed, the intent of dance differs from that of games and gymnastics: "Whereas the movements in games and gymnastics are functional and are concerned with mastery of objects, implements, and apparatus, the movements in dance focus more on communicating the inner feelings of the learner" (Baumgarten & Langton, 2006, p. 406). Children need to have the opportunity to develop their movement competence in both functional and expressive ways. Several years ago, a wonderful educator, Margie Hanson, put it this way:

> Movement is fundamental to life; dance is movement. Dance as art, dance as movement, and dance as a means to communication and expression has a unique contribution to the developing child because it encompasses all the domains of learning. . . . The arts are part of our world. Children [who are] denied experiences in the arts are denied a comprehensive basic education to prepare them for a full and rewarding life. (1979, p. 42)

Framing the question a bit differently, Cone & Cone (2005, p. 9) advocate including dance in physical education because children need to do the following three things:

- Express and communicate their ideas, feelings, and understandings
- Know and understand themselves and their world
- Develop their movement abilities

Children can do all three of these things in well-crafted dance instruction. Specifically, they can express and communicate their ideas, feelings, and understandings in physical education lessons that give them opportunities to replicate, modify, or create dance movements and sequences. They are also encouraged to communicate when collaborating with others and sharing ideas to create a dance. At the same time, children increase their knowledge and understanding of both themselves and the world by participating in dances from various cultures and ethnicities; in addition, they enhance their skills of perception and concentration when they observe and critique each other's dances. Finally, children develop their movement abilities in dance by advancing their grasp of the components of physical fitness and expanding their vocabulary for movement skills and concepts.

Beyond all of these benefits, dance is also "one of the most viable of the program areas for integrating classroom curriculum with movement. Almost any classroom subject—language arts, history, math, music . . . and/or science" (Baumgarten & Langton, 2006, p. 407) can be reinforced through the various forms of dance.

OUTCOMES OF DEVELOPMENTAL DANCE

Each dance form, or genre, has unique learning outcomes. In lyric-directed dance, the words of a song designate the type and sequence of movements for a specific dance. Students dance while the song is played and coordinate their movements to the tempo of the music and the words of the song. Examples include square dances and many songs found in children's music. The outcomes of lyric-directed dance include the following:

- Increasing children's ability to listen and follow verbal directions
- Helping children learn new movement sequences
- Teaching children to perform dances independently by following directions voiced in the song
- Developing children's collaborative skills as they learn and perform a dance with others

The dance form of cultural dance represents the values, beliefs, traditions, and ways of living of a culture as expressed through the movements, rhythms, and formations of dance. The outcomes of cultural dance include the following:

- Helping children gain an understanding of how movements, rhythms, and formations reflect various cultures' traditions, beliefs, and values
- Developing children's respect for a variety of cultures and for each culture's way of living
- Helping children learn to perform movements, rhythms, and formations from a variety of cultures
- Increasing children's movement skills, rhythmic responses, memory, directionality, sequencing, and spatial awareness
- Developing children's cooperative skills
- Learning and experiencing the fact that dance is an enjoyable, sociable, lifelong form of physical activity

Social dance emphasizes using dance as a way to experience the joy of moving with others. Social dances exist within cultural and historical contexts and represent one of the ways in which people share, celebrate, and experience life as a community. Outcomes of social dance include the following:

- Gaining the social skills to cooperate with different partners and members of a group
- Developing the ability to remember sequences of movement
- Developing the ability to accurately reproduce movement patterns
- Increasing respect for others by accepting them as partners or as part of a group
- Learning dances that can be applied in social settings outside of the school environment

In creative dance, children generate, vary, and manipulate movements by using the elements of dance to express and communicate an idea, concept, or feeling. Students use guided discovery and the improvisation process to explore and select movements. They may then arrange these movements into a sequence and structure in order to compose a dance. The outcomes of creative dance include the following:

- Acquiring knowledge about different movements that can be used to express and communicate an idea, concept, or feeling
- Developing critical and creative thinking skills used to discover multiple solutions to a task

- Expanding movement abilities, skills, and types of movements
- Creating new movements, movement sequences, and complete dances
- Learning to use movement as a means of expression and communication
- Developing collaborative skills

These outcomes of developmental dance address both the national content standards for physical education (SHAPE America, 2014) and the national content standards for dance (National Dance Association [NDA], 1994). Both sets of standards are highlighted in table 20.2. Let's now consider how dance specifically addresses each of the national content standards in physical education.

- **Standard 1:** The physically literate individual demonstrates competency in a variety of motor skills and movement patterns. Dance is a means for students to acquire basic locomotor and non-locomotor skills. Students may create or perform choreographed dances and movement sequences that combine locomotor and nonlocomotor skills. Young students need many different types of dance experiences in order to expand their ability to move with efficiency and control.

- **Standard 2:** The physically literate individual applies knowledge of concepts, principles, strategies, and tactics related to movement performance. The concepts relating to body awareness and movement (including time, space, force, flow, and relationship) are the essential elements that

Table 20.2 Comparison of National Physical Education Standards and National Dance Standards

National standards for physical education (SHAPE America, 2014)	National Standards for Dance Education (NDA, 1994)
Standard 1: The physically literate individual demonstrates competency in a variety of motor skills and movement patterns.	Standard 1: Identifying and demonstrating movement elements and skills in performing dance
Standard 2: The physically literate individual applies knowledge of concepts, principles, strategies, and tactics related to movement performance.	Standard 2: Understanding choreographic principles, processes, and structures
Standard 3: The physically literate individual demonstrates the knowledge and skills to achieve and maintain a health-enhancing level of physical activity and fitness.	Standard 3: Understanding dance as a way to create and communicate meaning
Standard 4: The physically literate individual exhibits responsible personal and social behavior that respects self and others.	Standard 4: Applying and demonstrating critical and creative thinking skills in dance
Standard 5: The physically literate individual recognizes the value of physical activity for health, enjoyment, challenge, self-expression, and/or social interaction.	Standard 5: Demonstrating and understanding dance in various cultures and historical periods
	Standard 6: Making connections between dance and healthful living
	Standard 7: Making connections between dance and other disciplines

describe dance movements; these same elements are applicable, of course, to movements used in a variety of physical activities. Through dance experiences, students manipulate these elements to create movements, add personal expression to movement, and analyze and describe movement. Students apply such concepts as weight transfer, balance, and form when learning and creating dances that express ideas, cultural traditions, or social relationships. Successful learning and performance of dance movements requires repetitive practice, critical observation, and the ability to use feedback to improve motor performance.

• **Standard 3:** The physically literate individual demonstrates the knowledge and skills to achieve and maintain a health-enhancing level of physical activity and fitness. Regular physical activity in the school environment is essential for effective learning; however, the ultimate goal is to provide students with the skills and self-confidence to pursue an *ongoing* active lifestyle. In accordance with this goal, dance education teaches students the skills they need in order to engage in dances at social and cultural events and therefore is important for their future participation in dance. Young students enjoy the opportunity to move to music, to have fun dancing with others, and to create new movements. Dance experiences that respect students' individuality, culture, and social nature motivate them to participate in dance in a variety of settings outside of school. Successful acquisition and performance of dance movements requires students to draw on the components of health-related fitness. Specifically, many dances include repetition of movement sequences that challenge strength, cardiorespiratory endurance, and flexibility. Dance lessons also contribute to fitness by emphasizing active engagement in creating, learning, and practicing. For example, numerous repetitions of dances that include skipping, running steps, hops, and jumps help students maintain a heart rate in the target zone.

• **Standard 4:** The physically literate individual exhibits responsible personal and social behavior that respects self and others. Dance is a social activity. In the school environment, students dance as individuals, as partners, and as members of small or large groups. Whether they are creating a dance about clouds with a partner or learning a line dance with the whole class, students experience differences and similarities in how people think, feel, and move. Similarly, when students

participate in cultural dances, they gain appreciation for the various ways in which people use dance to express heritage, celebratory events, traditions, and beliefs. This understanding is best acquired through the active learning of rhythms, steps, gestures, and dance formations from various cultures.

• **Standard 5:** The physically literate individual recognizes the value of physical activity for health, enjoyment, challenge, self-expression, and/or social interaction. This standard addresses a vital reason for including dance in the physical education curriculum. By creating dances, students learn to transform ordinary movements into movements that express their personal meanings, understandings, and connections to others. They also learn to respect the creative and artistic voices in themselves and in others as they develop their movement skills. The smiles of students who collaborate to create a new dance and share it with their peers indicate feelings of joy and accomplishment. As a result, students develop self-esteem in facing challenges, cooperating with others, and discovering dance as a way of knowing themselves.

Based on Cone and Cone 2012; NASPE 2007.

RHYTHMIC FUNDAMENTALS AND THE ELEMENTS OF RHYTHM

Rhythmic fundamentals lay the foundation for all dance forms (i.e., lyric directed, cultural, social, and creative). These fundamentals involve the elements of rhythm—namely underlying beat, rhythmic pattern, tempo, accent, and intensity—and each of them can be addressed through movement. When teaching children about the elements of rhythm, you can use percussive instruments (e.g., drum, Maori sticks), prerecorded music, or live music to supply the musical phrasing. In fact, children themselves may provide the musical accompaniment by means of vocal sounds, body percussion, or homemade rhythm instruments.

Using movement as a way to help children develop the elements of rhythm reinforces their development of fundamental movement skills and fosters their understanding of and feel for rhythm. This point also carries broader significance because all coordinated, purposeful movement requires an element of rhythm; as a result, practice in rhythmic fundamentals and in singing rhythms reinforces children's development of coordinated movement. Through practice with certain fundamental movements, children begin to understand the structural

Tinikling sticks *(a)* and jump bands *(b)*.

elements of rhythm and become able to express this understanding through coordinated, purposeful movement.

Let's now take a closer look at each of the elements of rhythm. **Underlying beat** is the steady, continuous sound in any rhythmical sequence. Teachers can promote listening and responding to the underlying beat by having children move to the beat of a drum or tambourine with appropriate locomotor step sequences, such as the following:

- Step-touch, step-touch (to right and left)
- Step to side, step together, step to side (to right and left)
- Step to side, step behind, step to side (i.e., grapevine; to right and left)

Children can also begin to grasp an understanding of underlying beat by jumping rope to the beat of music, bouncing balls to the beat, or using a homemade rhythm instrument to keep time with the beat.

A **rhythmic pattern** is a group of beats related to the underlying beat, which can be either even or uneven. Children can develop and express an understanding of rhythmic pattern by walking, running, hopping, or jumping to an even beat; by skipping, sliding, or galloping to an uneven beat; and by using tinikling sticks or jump bands (see photos).

Tempo is the speed of the movement, music, or rhythmic accompaniment. Children can increase their understanding of tempo by responding to speed changes in the beat of a drum with various locomotor and stability movements, by performing animal walks at various speeds, by bouncing a ball at various speeds, and by jumping rope to different tempos.

Accent is the emphasis given to any one beat; the accented note is usually the first beat of the measure. Children can develop a keener awareness of accent by listening to music and clapping on the accented beat; moving about the room with

The elements of rhythm are found in all forms of coordinated movement. These two teachers lead a class in urban **folk dance**, which emphasizes rhythmic stepping patterns, tempo changes, and accent.

the appropriate rhythmic pattern and changing direction or level on each accented beat; clapping on every beat *except* for the accented one; and varying their response to the accented beat with a specific locomotor, stability, or manipulative movement. Accent adds a dynamic quality to a movement by emphasizing a specific count with a specific movement. A movement itself can become an accent when it is made larger, sharper, or more pronounced. For example, the first beat of a measure might be accented by changing level, direction, or the movement of a specific body part.

Intensity is the quality of music in terms of its loudness or softness. Children can develop understanding of intensity by altering their movements for different intensities, changing their level, changing the amount of force they use to move, bouncing a ball with appropriate amounts of force, or dribbling a ball as softly as possible and then as loudly as possible.

DANCE AND THE SPECTRUM OF TEACHING STYLES

Both the reproduction and production clusters of the Spectrum of Teaching Styles are valuable when teaching lyric-directed, cultural, social, and creative dance. In the reproduction cluster, the command style is quite useful when teaching the specific steps of any genre of dance. It is critical to provide several demonstrations for children to observe and then replicate in synchrony with the teacher or other demonstrator. When using the

command style, students are often organized in staggered lines. In this case, the front row of students should be periodically changed out, or the teacher's location should be periodically shifted, so that all students have the opportunity to be in front of the class. The practice style can then be used to provide students with ample time to practice the steps without following a model.

In addition, when teaching a sequence of steps, an "add-on" method is often used. In this method, children learn step 1 and step 2 in isolation, then "add on" by performing them one after the other. They then learn step 3 in isolation and add that step, and so on. A combination of command and practice styles can be used throughout the add-on method. Once students have learned a step or sequence of steps, the reciprocal-style or peer teaching is beneficial; for example, peers can observe each other to see if the steps are performed in the correct order and to the tempo of the music.

Self-check can also be used by creating a task card with a list of steps taught during a specific lesson. During the lesson, or at its conclusion, students might check off how well they met the criteria for creating a dance sequence—for example, including two different shapes on different body parts. Similarly, you might provide an inclusion task card with steps of varying levels of difficulty. Students could then self-select the steps to incorporate into a dance sequence.

When using styles in the production cluster, such as guided or divergent discovery, teachers need to provide instructional stimuli, such as descriptive images, props, music, instruments, ideas, and events. Such stimuli help students create their own movement responses. For example, props such as body sox and large, colored elastic bands that stretch the height of a child's body can be used to prompt children's discovery of making different shapes at different levels and on different body parts. The following section describes a progressive approach to stimulating creative movement.

DEVELOPMENTAL PROGRESSION FOR TEACHING CREATIVE DANCE

Creative dance can be challenging for a physical educator to teach if she or he does not have substantial experience as a mover in creative dance. To help you understand how to view and teach creative dance from a developmental perspective, we focus here on progressive levels of dance. Children in your classes will have varying levels of experience with dance. To accommodate this heterogeneity, Nichols (1991) provides a developmental or progressive approach to teaching children creative movement. Specifically, Nichols uses four levels to describe both the characteristics of children and the teaching methodology best suited for teaching children at a specific level. The predominant teaching style for the four levels is divergent discovery; in addition, if students in your class are on different levels of dance, divergent discovery tasks can be provided in an inclusion format.

Level I dance is a teacher-dependent experience with the emphasis on awareness, exploration, and discovery. At this level, lessons foster creativity through single-movement challenges in which the teacher provides the stimulus for movement, whether verbally or through music or visuals. The teacher must provide appropriately timed cues that are simple and specific, such as action words, which are descriptive verbs that can be translated easily into movement responses. Examples include *wiggle*, *float*, *plop*, and *shrivel*. Action words can also be connected by movement transitions, as in the following sample sequences: "wiggle, turn, wiggle" and "wiggle, turn, plop."

Level II dance is a teacher–student interdependent experience. Here, the teacher gives students a movement problem (i.e., a combination of movement tasks) to solve and offers guidance and feedback as needed. The movement problem should stimulate divergent thinking and provide children with time to create several physical responses.

Level II movement tasks involve combined dance elements and are more comprehensive than level I tasks. For these experiences, students are organized into partner groups. The teacher might combine dance elements by asking the partners to do the following:

1. Create a connecting shape (element = body awareness: shapes).
2. Move out of the shape and travel along a curved pathway away from a partner (element = space: pathways).
3. Travel back to the partner and re-create the connected shape.

Level III dance is teacher initiated and student directed. The teacher provides the stimulus but leaves the development up to the students. Level III places more emphasis on form and the development of selected ideas; it also challenges students to perform what they have practiced. Students must have a good grasp of the dance elements and their components—for example, space (direction, level, range, pathways, general space, and personal space)—in order to succeed at exploring and developing their ideas. Here is a sample movement challenge for level III: "Working with your partner, create a short dance that has three dependent and connecting shapes, as well as an action-word transition between shapes." In level III learning experiences, students should create dances that have a beginning, a middle, and an end. The teacher's role is to support, clarify, and offer aesthetic suggestions.

Level IV dance, the highest level in the developmental dance progression, is student initiated and student directed. At this level, students generate and develop their own ideas. To facilitate this work, the teacher must establish a nonthreatening, noncompetitive environment that fosters creative work. As students work, the teacher's role is to provide guidance and feedback as needed. Level IV demands a mature willingness and ability to commit to working on a dance for an extended period of time. This level can be reached by intermediate-grade students who have experienced creative dance throughout their elementary physical education program.

This progressive approach to teaching creative dance considers children's developmental status, taking into account both their experience and their knowledge of the ingredients or concepts of dance. Children are more likely to be motivated and successful as they discover the joy of creating their own dances.

In a physical education curriculum that fosters creative dance from kindergarten through grade 5, children can achieve level IV in grades 3 through 5. However, they must have the developmental experiences provided by the teacher in levels I through III.

DESIGNING INSTRUCTION FOR DEVELOPMENTAL DANCE

The design of instruction for educational dance consistently addresses standards 1 and 2 by providing opportunities for students to become skilled and knowledgeable in dance steps and sequences. The content is derived from the combination and application stages of movement skill learning shown in the choreographic theme progression charts (see tables 20.6 and 20.8). The choreographic theme progressions—for example, the combination-level theme of "step sequences moving forward and back"—can be implemented with any of the four genres of dance: lyric-directed, cultural, social, or creative. The instructional activities for a given theme provide a framework for designing lesson episodes; they do *not* necessarily represent one lesson episode per se, because children develop the capability to perform dance steps and sequences by engaging in many attempts over time.

The rest of this section addresses the chain of decision making used to design instruction derived from motor-development and learning theory, the movement framework, standards-based physical education, assessment of student learning, and effective instructional practices. The categories for each instructional activity include learning outcome, teaching style, task, environment, practice, skill cues, feedback, enrichment, and assessment.

Let's now take a closer look at the categories. The learning outcome reflects the dance steps and sequences identified in the choreographic theme progression chart. The choice of teaching style is then determined based on the objectives of the lesson and the form of dance being taught. Next, the task listing indicates the relevant skills, movement concepts, and progressions. Given these task elements, the environment listing includes choices for scaling the conditions (see figures 6.2 and 6.3) to fit the performers by adjusting variables of space, time, and relationship. The type of practice chosen should be based on the goal of the skill. For example, if the goal is to perform steps and sequences

to a rhythmical beat and tempo, the best choice is constant practice under invariant conditions. However, if the goal is to discover alternate ways of performing or combining body actions, then variable practice is used with an emphasis on exploring new approaches by blending movement skills and concepts. The skill cues listing describes the specific sequence or timing of movements for performance of either a single skill or combined skills.

Feedback is determined by the stage of learning, the goal of the skill (closed or open), and the teaching style. Knowledge-of-performance (KP) feedback focuses on skill cues. It is most appropriate for beginning-stage learners who need to know how to correct the technique and timing of their movements and for intermediate-stage learners who are refining their performance of closed-skill (dance) sequences. With beginning-level learners, teachers employs direct descriptive (d) feedback (e.g., "Your step was performed right on the beat of the music!") and prescriptive (p) feedback (e.g., "Make your steps smaller so you can keep up with the tempo of the music") to help students succeed. With intermediate-level students who are refining skills, teachers use questions to encourage them to describe what they think happened and to come up with a solution. This approach is consistent with recommendations for giving intermediate-level learners less frequent feedback so that they become less dependent on outside sources of feedback. Here is an example: "What could you do to add more emphasis on that set of eight counts?"

Assessments give teachers and students information about the quality of learning. Standard 1 assessments focus on psychomotor performance and address either the process or the product of movements. In dance, process assessments are used most often, because the goal of the skill is correct technique and timing. Specifically, teachers are encouraged to use formative assessment such as observation checklists of movement cues for skills, variations, combinations, and partner work. The summative assessment rubrics for developmental dance presented in tables 20.3 and 20.4 were derived from the learning goal blueprint (table 20.1). Once a dance has been learned or created, these rubrics can be used to determine student performance and progress in key aspects of developmental dance.

Assessments for standard 2 are cognitive and represent the level of thinking that is developmentally appropriate for the learner. In grades 3 through 5,

Table 20.3 Scoring Rubric for Developmental Dance (Lyric Directed, Cultural, and Social)

	1 Developing	2 Proficient	3 Advanced
Performance of steps	Single steps can be performed to the underlying beat (rhythm) of music or accompaniment, directional changes are not performed on the correct count or beat, and the student has difficulty in synchronizing steps with others.	Two or three steps can be performed rhythmically in a coordinated sequence, directional changes are performed on the correct count most of the time, and steps can be synchronized with others.	Four or more steps can be performed rhythmically in a coordinated fashion, multiple direction changes are performed on correct counts, and steps can be synchronized with others.
Upper-body action	Simple arm positions can be coordinated with a single step.	Arm actions can be performed in unison with both sides of the body in two- and three-step sequences.	Body parts (e.g., shoulders, head) can be combined with arm actions, and arm actions can be isolated to the right or left side.
Accent	No accent on body parts or steps can be performed.	Accents can be performed on a designated count with upper- or lower-body movements.	Accents can be performed on multiple counts with upper- and lower-body movements.
Focus	Focus is straight ahead and sometimes down.	Focus is varied (straight ahead and to side).	Focus is varied on different body parts to accentuate the dance style.

Table 20.4 Scoring Assessment Rubric for Developmental Dance (Creative)

	1 Developing	2 Proficient	3 Advanced
Movement creativity	Student can create a movement based on the lesson theme or construct after seeing a teacher example.	Student can create two or three movements based on the lesson theme and one or two elements (from space, effort, and relationship) to create variety.	Student can create four or more movements based on the lesson theme or construct and can use multiple elements (from space, effort, and relationship) to vary movements.
Choreographic variables	Student cannot integrate choreographic variables.	Student can integrate entrances and exits and one change of formation.	Student can integrate entrances, exits, stillness, canon, and two or three formation changes.
Accent	No accent on body parts or steps can be performed.	Accents can be performed on a count with upper- or lower-body movements.	Accents can be performed on multiple counts with upper- and lower-body movements.
Focus	Focus is straight ahead and sometimes down.	Focus is varied (straight ahead and to side).	Focus is varied on different body parts to accentuate the intent of the dance or movement.

students are in the concrete stage of thought and can participate in most levels of thinking, as long as the question relates directly to what they are experiencing, as in the following examples: "Describe how the movements should be combined to achieve a smooth, flowing sequence." "Compare the movement performance of a peer with the criteria and give feedback to help her improve." In chapter 9, table 9.1 provides examples of cognitive assessments that reflect the levels of thinking and the state standards for language and literacy.

Dance can also serve as a vehicle for addressing standards 3, 4, and 5 by helping children develop fitness and personal and social responsibility and by providing them with opportunities to experience challenge, enjoyment, and social interaction. When teachers incorporate objectives that address these standards in dance learning activities, they must also design assessments that match the intention of the relevant standard.

- Standard 3: The most common component of fitness addressed through dance is cardiorespiratory endurance. Increases in this fitness component can be documented throughout dance lessons by having students monitor their heart rate and level of perceived exertion (see chapter 22)

- Standard 4: Chapter 18 describes several learning activities that engage students in exhibiting personal and social responsibility through physical activity. During dance instruction, students should continue to respect and cooperate with others, follow directions, and appropriately receive and give feedback. To facilitate success in this area, teachers need to inform students that these behaviors of personal and social responsibility are expected every day; furthermore, teachers need to reinforce this expectation through reminders, prompts, praise, and feedback. The rubric presented in table 20.5 illustrates a way to assess personal and social responsibility throughout learning experiences in dance.

- Standard 5: This standard asks children to recognize the value of physical activity. They can

do so for themselves only through engaging in self-reflection about their own participation over time. To this end, figure 20.2 provides sample prompts to engage students in ongoing self-reflection. Teachers can use data collected early on from responses to these prompts to respond to students' needs and interests. The rubric for figure 20.2 is as follows:

Rubric

- Proficient: The ratings in questions A and B match the reasons given, and the reasons are related to the activity. The description of social interaction is clearly related to the activity.

- Developing: The ratings in questions A and B match the reasons given, and the reasons are somewhat related to the activity. The description of social interaction is somewhat related to the activity.

- Beginning: There is a discrepancy between the ratings in questions A and B and the reasons given. The description of social interactions is minimal or consists of a one-word answer (e.g., "fun") without reference to the activity.

Table 20.5   Scoring Rubric for Personal and Social Responsibility

Standard 4 behavior	Responsible	Developing	Irresponsible
Personal responsibility	Exhibits self-control. Works independently and safely without prompting from teacher. Engages in respectful interaction and conflict resolution with others. Accepts and uses feedback from teacher and peers. Demonstrates etiquette and follows rules.	Exhibits self-control. Works independently and safely with some prompting from teacher. Engages in respectful interaction with others. Accepts feedback from teacher and peers. Demonstrates etiquette and follows rules most of the time.	Denies personal responsibility by making excuses and blaming others. Has difficulty with working independently; needs monitoring by teacher to stay on task. Engages in disrespectful interactions with others or ignores others. Disregards rules and etiquette.
Social responsibility	Works cooperatively with others. Accepts and involves others of different skill levels. Praises, encourages, and gives helpful feedback to others.	Needs occasional prompting from teacher to work cooperatively with others. Accepts others of different skill levels. Praises and encourages others; gives feedback when prompted.	Cannot work productively with others.

A. Rate your *enjoyment* of participating in _____ (the tinikling dance lesson) and tell why.

1 _____ 2 _____ 3 _____ 4 _____ 5

not enjoyable   enjoyable   very enjoyable

Reason:

B. Rate the *challenge* of participating in _____ (the tinikling dance lesson) and tell why.

1 _____ 2 _____ 3 _____ 4 _____ 5

not challenging   challenging   very challenging

Reason:

C. Describe the positive social interactions (encouraging words or gestures, helping others, support from others, cooperation with teammates) that occurred when you were participating in _____ (e.g., creating a dance about referee signals).

Figure 20.2   Standard 5: self-report assessment.

Big Ideas

- Developmental dance is based on children's level of movement skill learning, motor development, and cognitive and social characteristics.

- The four main forms of dance are lyric-directed, cultural, social, and creative.

- The outcomes of including dance in physical education include, but are not limited to, the following: developing social skills; gaining the ability to express an idea through movement; learning about diverse cultures; learning to use the elements of body, space, effort, and relationship to vary movement; and learning to coordinate and sequence steps.

- Rhythmic fundamentals include accent, tempo, intensity, rhythmic pattern, and underlying beat.

- Effective dance instruction uses the reproduction and the production teaching styles (from the Spectrum of Teaching Styles).

- Designing instruction involves identifying the learning outcome, **choreographic theme**, and teaching style; describing the task and environment; and choosing the type of practice, feedback, and assessment.

- Assessments for standards 1 through 5 can be conducted in dance learning experiences.

Learning Experiences for Developmental Dance: Combination Level

Use the combination-level task progressions for dance in table 20.6 to guide your design of developmentally appropriate learning experiences. Examples of learning experiences from the progression appear below the table.

Table 20.6 Task Progressions for Developmental Dance: Combination Level

Skills	

Transfer of weight
• Traveling
• Flight
• Balance
• Step-like
	Learning outcome: rhythmically combining skills and movement concepts in short dances.
	Choreographic themes:
	• Discovering rhythm
	   • Underlying beat
	   • Rhythmic pattern
	   • Tempo
	• Traveling at high, medium, and low levels
	• Shaping at high, medium, and low levels
	• Changing levels while traveling
	• Combining time and weight: sudden and strong, sudden and light, sustained and strong, sustained and light
	• Traveling on curved pathways
	• Using a variety of gestures (especially with upper body) while traveling and while in personal space
	• Using both sides of body in developing movement phrases
	• Using step sequences that move forward and back
	• Using step sequences that move side to side
	• Using step sequences with simple, symmetrical upper-body movements
	• Doing dances that face one wall or two walls
	• Use choreographic themes provided by, and variables manipulated by, the teacher
	• Doing dances of short duration with partners and small groups

LEARNING EXPERIENCES FOR DEVELOPMENTAL DANCE: COMBINATION LEVEL

National Physical Education Standards
- National Standard 1: Rhythmically perform dances.
- National Standard 2: Apply movement concepts in dance.
- National Standard 3: Apply fitness knowledge.

Learning outcome: rhythmically combining skills and movement concepts in short dances

Choreographic theme: discovering rhythm—underlying beat, rhythmic pattern, and tempo

Teaching style: reproduction (command, practice)

Dance genre: cultural

Task: Children learn basic tinikling steps, first without sticks and then with sticks. When using tinikling sticks, children hit the sticks on the ground two times and then hit the sticks together in the air two times to several musical selections. After each round of tinikling, students can use an InstaPulse wand or other method to monitor heart rate and then use the heart rate chart to determine whether they are engaged in moderate or vigorous physical activity. The basic step is as follows (in personal space, with no sticks):

- Step 1: For counts 1 and 2, hop on right (outside of the tinikling pole) foot two times (hop, hop).

- Step 2: For counts 3 and 4, leap or step onto left foot and then onto right foot while moving to the left (step, step).
- Step 3: For counts 5 and 6, hop on left foot two times (outside foot).
- Repeat moving toward the right.

Enrichment:
- Do the basic step with tinikling sticks.
- Jump on two feet outside of the sticks and on two feet inside of the sticks.
- Mirror a partner while doing the basic step or a jump step.
- Explore the origin of the dance (Philippines).
- Increase the tempo of the music.

Environment: Provide enough tinikling sticks for each group of four students to have its own. Mats can be placed on the floor under the sticks to reduce the noise. Children should all face in the same direction. Video sources are readily available online.

Practice: constant

Closed-skill cues: Use verbal cues to describe what children should do (e.g., "hop, hop; step, step; hop, hop"), then use counting cues.

Feedback

Provide feedback about underlying beat by clapping out the rhythm for children and providing the verbal skill cues.

Assessments

- Standard 1: Use checklist for tinikling basic steps (table 20.7).
- Standard 2: Have students complete a dance terminology formative assessment (figure 20.3).
- Standard 3: Have students use a formative heart rate assessment (figure 20.4).

Table 20.7 Checklist for Tinikling Basic Steps

Name:	Consistent	Sometimes	Not yet developed
Can sequence two sets of the basic step in personal space.			
Can sequence more than two sets of the basic step in personal space.			
Can sequence two sets of the basic step with tinikling sticks.			
Can sequence more than two sets of the basic step with tinikling sticks.			

Name:_____

True or false: Underlying beat is the steady continuous sound in any rhythmical sequence.

True or false: Tempo is the speed of movement.

Figure 20.3 Assessment of dance term knowledge.

Name:

Directions: Check the intensity of your heart rate after each round of dancing. Then put a check mark in the column that represents your heart rate.

	Vigorous 151–180 beats per minute	**Moderate** 105–150 beats per minute	**Below** <105 beats per minute
Heart rate 1			
Heart rate 2			
Heart rate 3			
Debrief: Why did your heart rate change (or *not* change) during the tinikling dance?			

Figure 20.4 Tinikling Intensity Check: How Hard Is Your Heart Working?

National Physical Education Standard

- National Standard 1: Rhythmically perform dances.

Learning outcome: rhythmically combining skills and movement concepts in short dances.

Choreographic theme: discovering rhythm (underlying beat, rhythmic pattern, tempo, upper-body movement in personal space)

Teaching styles: reproduction (command, practice) and production (divergent discovery)

Dance genre: creative gestures

Task: Students create gestures and perform them to music.

- **Step 1:** Create gestures. The teacher defines *gesture,* asks students for examples of common gestures, and then asks students to create new gestures using upper-body parts. To stimulate students' thinking, the teacher models a gesture to represent his or her first name, after which children do the same with their names. The children perform the movement while the teacher plays a drum for eight beats at a moderate tempo. Children repeat their gesture for several eight-count beat phrases, thus creating a pattern. The children can now be engaged in practice-style learning.

- **Step 2:** Add music. Children now perform their upper-body movement to the eight-count beat of a selected piece of popular music.

- **Step 3:** Use peer teaching. Organize children into groups of three or four, in which they teach each other their gestures or upper-body movements. The children then sequence the three or four gestures while the teacher beats a drum for eight moderate-tempo counts. Music is then added.

Environment: In steps 1 and 2, children are spread out individually in general space; in step 3, they are organized into groups.

Practice: variable (when creating gestures), then constant

Closed-skill cue: Maintain the eight-count beat with the upper-body movement.

Feedback

- KPd: "Good job making your gesture last for the entire eight counts!"
- KPp: "Try to slow your gesture down a little and make it move for the entire eight beats!"

Assessment

- Standard 1: The rubric shown in figure 20.5 can be used to assess the children's gesture dance.

Name:	Consistent	Sometimes	Not yet developed
One gesture could be performed repeatedly to an eight-count beat.			
Can sequence three gestures to the beat of the music.			

Figure 20.5 Checklist for creating and performing gestures.

National Physical Education Standard

- National Standard 1: Rhythmically perform dances.

Learning outcome: rhythmically combining skills and movement concepts in short dances

Choreographic theme: using shapes at high, medium, and low levels

Teaching style: reproduction (practice)

Dance genre: creative

Task: Students create shapes based on verbal prompts from the teacher, on shapes as expressed in sport photos, or shapes expressed in other artwork.

Verbal Prompts

- Can you make a tall narrow shape on your feet?
- Can you make a tall narrow shape *not* using your feet to stand on?
- Can you make a twisted shape at a medium level?
- Can you make a low, wide shape?
- Can you make a medium-level bent shape?
- Can you make a high-level round shape?
- Can you make an inverted shape—that is, with your head below one foot only?

Photo Prompts

You can find interesting shapes (usually sport action shots) from the Internet, newspaper sports sections, or magazines. Have children make the shapes depicted in the photos you choose. Or you might have children use three different photos and sequence them, holding each shape for 8 counts.

Enrichment: Work with a partner to make shapes that contrast with each other. One partner makes a shape, and then the other partner tries to make the opposite of that shape.

Environment: Children are spread out in the general space.

Practice: variable, then constant

Closed-skill cues:

- Are shapes at designated level?
  - High—as tall as child or higher
  - Medium—around waist level
  - Low—below waist level and close to ground

Feedback

- KPd: "Your high shape is very extended and taller than your height—good job!"
- KPp: "Keep your shapes controlled and still by tightening your muscles."

Assessment

- Standard 1: Use the shape checklist (figure 20.6).

Name: _____

	Narrow	Twisted	Round	Bent	Wide	Inverted
High						
Medium						
Low						

Figure 20.6 Shape checklist.

National Physical Education Standards

- National Standard 1: Rhythmically perform dances.
- National Standard 2: Apply movement concepts in dance.

Learning outcome: rhythmically combining skills and movement concepts in short dances

Choreographic theme: traveling at high, medium, and low levels

Teaching styles: reproduction (command, practice) and production (divergent)

Genre: creative

Task: Children use a variety of locomotor skills to travel at high, medium, and low levels. Initially, the teacher can model and have children replicate the movement skills; later, children can improvise to imagery prompts from the teacher.

High-Level Options

- Running and leaping from one foot to another
- Running and jumping vertically into the air
- Moving on tiptoe while stretching arms vertically into the air and possibly adding twists and turning actions

Medium-Level Options

- Traveling while bending over, as if being blown over by the wind
- Traveling on hands and feet with bottom high
- Traveling while stepping and kicking with legs and extending arms out in coordination with legs

Low-Level Options

- A low level break-dance movement: weight on one hand, other arm stretched up vertically, kick legs out to side
- Rolling actions
- Turning in a squat position

Imagery prompts:

High Level

- Can you soar into the air like an airplane?
- Spring off an imagery springboard and see how high you can get!

Medium Level

- You are moving through a cave.
- You are trying to move through your house so no one sees you through the windows.

Low Level

- You are in a house filled with smoke and must move fast and low to escape.
- You are moving through a tunnel.

Environment: Children are spread out into general space.

Practice: variable, constant

Closed-skill cues: Give cues consistent with moving at the various levels.

Feedback

- KPd: "You are really getting your arms stretched out into the high space!"
- KPp: "Be sure you move as close to the ground as possible when moving at a low level!"

Assessments

- Standard 1: Use a teacher checklist addressing students' ability to move at each level.

National Physical Education Standard

- National Standard 1: Rhythmically perform dances.

Learning outcome: rhythmically combining skills and movement concepts in short dances

Choreographic theme: changing levels while traveling

Teaching styles: reproduction (practice) and production (divergent discovery)

Dance genre: creative

Task: Students sequence three modes of traveling as demonstrated by the teacher or as chosen from a grab bag of locomotor skills. Students perform each locomotor skill at a different level. Here are some sample sequences:

- Jump high into the air, crawl low on hands and feet, and spin at a medium level while traveling.
- Creep at a low level, step and kick at a medium level, and skip at a high level.
- Slide sideways at a high level, leap at a medium level, and roll at a low level.

Enrichment

- Have children create their own movements at varying levels as they travel through space.
- Add changing direction one time during the sequence.
- Add moving along pathways (e.g., curved, straight, diagonal).

Environment: Students are in general space; if desired, they can work with a partner by moving alongside the partner. The teacher selects different types of music and uses selection with different tempos and time signatures (e.g., 3/4 or 4/4), thus changing the number of beats per measure.

Practice: variable, then constant

Closed-skill cues: Give cues consistent with moving at the various levels and using different locomotor skills, changing direction one time and traveling along two different pathways.

Feedback

- KPd: "I could see all three levels clearly as you traveled through space."
- KPp: "How can you make your medium-level traveling different from your high-level traveling?"

Assessments

- Standard 1: The rubric shown in figure 20.7 can be used to assess children's performance of locomotor skills at different levels.

Name:	Consistent	Sometimes	Not yet developed
Can travel and transition from one level to another with good body control.			
Can travel to the beat of the music.			

Figure 20.7 Assessment for sequencing locomotor movements at different levels.

National Physical Education Standard

- National Standard 1: Rhythmically perform dances.

Learning outcome: rhythmically combining skills and movement concepts in short dances

Choreographic theme: combinations of time and weight: sudden and strong, sudden and light, sustained and strong, sustained and light

Teaching styles: reproduction (command, practice) and production (guided discovery)

Dance genre: creative

Task: Students respond to the stimulus of vocabulary words to create movements using any part of the body. Movements can be stationary or traveling and can be performed at any level. The teacher can initially demonstrate different movements for the action words, then verbally guide students by asking them to use different body parts at different levels while either stationary or traveling. Here are some vocabulary words to consider:

Sudden and Strong

- Pow
- Zap
- Crash
- Boom
- Thump
- Bang

Sudden and Light

- Flick
- Dab
- Tap
- Brush
- Dash

Sustained and Strong

- Push
- Pull
- Drag
- Strain

Sustained and Light

- Float
- Drift

- Glide
- Soar

Enrichment: Individual movements can be put into a movement "sentence," such as pow, flick, glide.

Environment: Students are positioned in general space.

Practice: variable

Closed-skill cues: Use cues consistent with the effort action being demonstrated.

Feedback

- KPd: "Your leg kick was very quick, direct, and strong."
- KPp: "Try to make your movement a bit lighter, like a cloud floating in the sky."

Assessments

- Standard 1: The rubric shown in figure 20.8 can be used to assess children's use of different efforts (i.e., time and weight)

Student	CAN CREATE MOVEMENTS THAT ARE . . .							
	Sudden and strong		Sudden and light		Sustained and strong		Sustained and light	
	Yes	No	Yes	No	Yes	No	Yes	No

Figure 20.8   Assessment for vocabulary and movement.

National Physical Education Standards

- National Standard 1: Rhythmically perform dances.
- National Standard 2: Apply movement concepts in dance.

Learning outcome: rhythmically combining skills and movement concepts in short dances

Choreographic theme: step sequences moving forward and back and moving side to side

Teaching style: reproduction (practice)

Dance genre: social

Task: Children perform a line dance called "Crazy Cow Kids!" Children replicate four sets of eight-count step sequences demonstrated by the teacher. Each sequence is taught separately, after which the add-on strategy is used to put together sequences.

Sequence 1: Step-Touch

- Part A: counts 1 and 2
  - Step to right with right foot, then touch ball of left foot to floor next to right foot.
- Part B: counts 3 and 4
  - Step to left with left foot, then touch ball of right foot to floor next to left foot.
- Part C: counts 5 and 6
  - Repeat part A.
- Part D: counts 7 and 8
  - Repeat part B.

Sequence 2: Forward and Back

- Part A: counts 1 through 4
  - Walk forward, beginning with right foot (right, left, right), and touch ball of left foot to floor next to right foot.
- Part B: counts 5 through 8
  - Walk backward, beginning with left foot (left, right, left), and touch ball of right foot to floor next to left foot.

Sequence 3

- Put sequences 1 and 2 together for a total of 16 counts.

Sequence 4: Kick and Cross

- Part A: counts 1 through 4
  - Step on right foot; kick left foot low and forward; cross left foot in front of right ankle, leading with heel; and kick left foot out low and forward.
- Part B: counts 5 through 8
  - Step-touch, beginning with left step and right step-touch, followed by right step and left step-touch
- Part C: counts 1 through 4
  - Step on left foot; kick right foot low and forward; cross right foot in front of left ankle, leading with heel; and kick right foot out low and forward.
- Part D: counts 5 through 8
  - Step-touch, beginning with right step and left step-touch, followed by left step and right step-touch

Sequence 5: Put sequences 1, 2, and 4 together for a total of 32 counts.

Environment: Children should be organized in staggered lines, and either the front line or the teacher's position should be changed frequently to allow the teacher to view all students.

Practice: reproduction (command, practice)

Feedback

KPdp: "When you do your kick and cross movement lead the crossing action with the heel of your foot."

Assessments

- Standard 1: The rubric shown in figure 20.9 can be used to assess children's ability to perform steps to the beat of the music.

	Performed consistently to the beat of the music.	Sometimes performed to the beat of the music.	Cannot yet perform the step to the beat of the music.
Step-touch sequence			
Forward-and-back sequence			
Kick-and-cross sequence			

Figure 20.9 Checklist for step sequences.

National Physical Education Standards

- National Standard 1: Rhythmically perform dances.
- National Standard 2: Apply movement concepts in dance.

Learning outcome: rhythmically combining skills and movement concepts in short dances

Choreographic theme: dances that face one wall or two walls

Teaching style: reproduction (command, practice)

Dance genre: cultural

Task: Students dance a leprechaun jig, adapted from NASPE (2007), with musical accompaniment of "Dance Above the Rainbow" from Michael Flatley's *Feet of Flames* (Hardiman, 1998) or other Irish music in 4/4 time. Before teaching this dance, teachers can excite students by showing them videos of boys and girls performing Irish step dancing. If any students in the class take Irish step-dance lessons, they can be invited to perform if they so choose. The teacher can then describe the music, steps, and body positions used in this form of dance and discuss why it involves keeping the arms down at the sides and moving only the lower body. Originally, people would use the doors to their houses as a hard surface on which to dance and as such there was not enough room to move their arms in coordination with their feet. Additionally, keeping the arms still and down to the sides of one's body brings more attention to the footwork of the dance.

Adapted from the SHAPE America - PIPEline *Dance over the rainbow.* Copyright 2007.

Progression 1: Stamping

- Stamp right foot and kick it out, then take three steps in place (right, left, right) with pacing of quick, quick, slow.
- Stamp left foot and kick it out, then take three steps in place (left, right, left) with pacing of quick, quick, slow.
- Teaching cues: Have students begin by simply clapping out the pacing (quick, quick, slow) to become familiar with the rhythm, then add the feet.

Progression 2: Grapevine Step Variation

- Step right foot to right, step left foot behind right, and take three steps in place (right, left, right).
- Step left foot to left, step right foot behind left, and take three steps in place (left, right, left).
- Teaching cues: This is a shortened grapevine step (side, behind).

Progression 3: Combining Progressions 1 and 2

- Add music and perform progressions 1 and 2; repeat several times.

Progression 4: Walking

This progression changes the dance to face the second wall. If the intricacy of the turn and the three steps (right, left, right) are too difficult, simply have students walk forward for two steps on counts 1 and 2 and then turn to face the opposite wall to the beat on counts 3 and 4.

- Walk forward two steps (right, left), then take three steps to turn to the right halfway (right, left, right).
- Walk forward two steps (left, right), then take three steps in place but do not turn (left, right, left).

Progression 5: Combining Progressions 1 Through 4

- Add music and perform progressions 1 through 4; repeat several times.

Progression 6: Pointing

- Point right foot forward, point right foot to side, and take three steps in place (right, left, right).
- Point left foot forward, point left foot to side, and take three steps in place (left, right, left).
- Repeat dance again, this time turning right halfway back to face front of room.

Progression 7: Combining all progressions

- Add all progressions together; this may take more than one physical education class period.

Enrichment: Have students make up their own eight-count Irish step-dance sequences.

Environment: Students should be organized into staggered lines so that all students can see the teacher's demonstration and leading. The front line should be changed frequently throughout the lesson so that different children are in the front of the class during the dance performance. This provides recognition to a variety of children during the activity.

Practice: constant

Closed-skill cues: Provide descriptive verbal cues while students are learning the steps. Here is an example for progression 1: "Stomp, kick; right, left, right; stomp, kick; left, right, left."

Feedback

- KPd: "You are performing your steps to the tempo of the music. They are quick and clean! Good job!"
- KPp: "You need to make your movements a bit smaller so you can perform them quicker and move to the tempo of the music."

Assessments

- Standard 1: The assessment shown in figure 20.10 can be used to evaluate students' performance of the four main dance steps.

Proficient (P): The step is performed consistently to the tempo of the music and with proper technique.

Developing (D): The step is sometimes performed to the tempo of the music and with proper technique.

Not yet developed (ND): The step is not consistently performed with correct technique to the tempo of the music.

Student	Stamp	Grapevine	Walk and turn	Point	All four steps in sequence	
					Yes	No

Figure 20.10 Rubric for leprechaun jig.

National Physical Education Standards

- National Standard 1: Rhythmically perform dances.
- National Standard 2: Apply movement concepts in dance.

Learning outcome: rhythmically combining skills and movement concepts in short dances

Choreographic theme: themes provided and variables manipulated by teacher

Teaching styles: reproduction (practice) and production (guided discovery)

Dance genre: creative

Task: Referees dance too! This creative dance activity uses referee signals (see figure 20.11 for examples) as the stimulus for creating dance movements. The teacher can provide photos of signals, model signals, or organize students in small groups to come up with three or four signals.

Figure 20.11 Referee signals.

- Progression 1: Perform first referee signal for two sets of 8 counts (total of 16 counts).
- Progression 2: Perform same referee signal at different level for two sets of 8 counts.
- Progression 3: Perform same referee signal while turning in personal space for two sets of 8 counts.
- Progression 4: Put all three progressions together in a sequence.

Use the add-on method to integrate new referee signals. You can prompt students to vary the signals by asking them to perform the signals in the following ways:

- In slow motion
- As big as possible
- Mirroring a partner
- While supporting the body in different balanced positions
- On different levels

Environment: Students can work independently or in small groups.

Practice: variable practice to create the dance, then constant practice

Closed-skill cues:

- Cues should be consistent with the emphasized element of the movement framework. For example, if the student is trying to mirror a partner, then both performers should be in unison. Tempo and rhythm can also be cued. The teacher should verbally count out the two sets of eight counts to help students perform their signal for the eight-count measure.

Feedback

- KPd: "You are making your signal last for the entire two sets of 8 counts. Great job!"
- KPp: "How can you make your referee signal go slow in motion and last for 24 counts of music?"

Assessment

- Standard 1: The assessment shown in figure 20.12 can be used to evaluate students' ability to perform the referee signals.

Directions: Indicate whether the student is able to do the following.

Student	Perform one referee signal for two sets of eight counts.	Vary one referee signal and perform to tempo of music.	Connect three referee signals and perform to tempo of music.

Figure 20.12   Checklist for referee dance.

Learning Experiences for Developmental Dance: Application Level

Use the application-level task progressions for dance in table 20.8 to guide your design of developmentally appropriate learning experiences. Examples of learning experiences from the progression appear after the table.

Table 20.8   Task Progressions for Developmental Dance: Application Level

Skills	
Transfer of weight • Traveling • Flight • Balance • Step-like	Learning outcome: rhythmically performing more complex combinations and choreographing short dances **Choreographic themes:** • Refining rhythm • Varying directional combinations • Accents and focus • Greater isolation and variation of body parts • Dances that face three or four walls • Choreographic themes and variables guided by teachers • Partner and group relationships: meeting and parting, together and apart, contrasting and alternating • Student-choreographed dances of longer duration with small groups • Social dancing with partners

LEARNING EXPERIENCES FOR DEVELOPMENTAL DANCE: APPLICATION LEVEL

National Physical Education Standards

- National Standard 1: Rhythmically perform dances.
- National Standard 2: Apply movement concepts and choreograph dances.

Learning outcome: rhythmically performing more complex combinations and choreographing short dances

Choreographic theme: rhythm and accent

Teaching style: reproduction (command)

Task: The teacher demonstrates a series of combinations of locomotor and stability skills focused on rhythm and accent. To build students' vocabulary the teacher should also define what rhythm and accent are. This could be written for students' reference on a whiteboard. A sample assessment is provided in Figure 20.14. Here are two examples:

Sequence 1

- Step-hop (counts 1 and 2)
  - Step on left foot and lift right knee.
- Step-hop (counts 3 and 4)
  - Step on right foot and lift left knee.
- Run (counts 5 and 6)
  - Left, right.
- Leap (count 7 and 8)
  - Leap off of left foot and onto right foot.
- Accent on Leap
  - Step out of leap onto left foot to begin the sequence again onto right foot (no count "and").
  - Repeat entire sequence.

Sequence 2

- Counts 1 through 3
  - Do three-step turn (right, left, right), turning 360 degrees.
- Count 4
  - Stretch arms out on high right diagonal.
  - Accent is on the stretch during count 4.
- Repeat to left.

Environment: Students are organized into dance-team lines that move across general space when cued.

Practice: constant

Closed-skill cues: Perform actions on correct counts. Teacher can cue steps with a drum beat, verbal cue, or music.

Feedback

- KPd: "You are skipping on counts 1-2 and 3-4—good job!"
- KPp: "For the leap on counts 7 and 8, you need to take off from your right foot and land on your left foot."

Assessments

- Standard 1: Use assessment shown in figure 20.13 to evaluate students' performance of the dance steps; specifically rhythm and accent.
- Standard 2: Have students define related dance terminology and describe a sample 8-count movement sequence.

Advanced (A): Performs sequence consistently to correct rhythm and always puts accent on the correct count.

Proficient (P): Performs sequence consistently to correct rhythm and sometimes puts accent on the correct count.

Developing (D): Performs sequence rhythm inconsistently and does not use an accent.

Student	A	P	D

Figure 20.13   Rubric for performing sequences with correct rhythm and accent.

Name:_____ **Date:**_____

1. Define *rhythm* in a brief sentence.

_____

_____

2. Define *accent* in a brief sentence.

_____

_____

3. Describe an 8-count locomotor sequence that is performed twice in a row (for a total of 16 counts). Underline the accented movements.

Figure 20.14   Assessment for vocabulary building.

National Physical Education Standard

- National Standard 1: Rhythmically perform dances.

Learning outcome: rhythmically performing more complex combinations and choreographing short dances

Choreographic themes:

- Varying directional combinations
- Accents and focus
- Greater isolation and variation of body parts
- Dances that face three or four walls

Teaching styles: reproduction (command) and production (divergent discovery)

Dance genre: social (hip-hop)

Task: The teacher leads the class in performing a movement sequence of hip-hop steps.

Sequence 1: Forward Walk (8 Counts)

- Counts 1 through 4
  - Walk forward two steps (counts 1 and 2; right/left), jump on both feet (count 3), then shift right foot to heel only (on count 4) and simultaneously scoop arms forward and outward at chest level with fists clenched.
- Counts 5 through 8
  - Repeat steps used in counts 1 through 4, but start with the left foot, and on count 8 shift left foot to heel only.

Sequence 2: Grapevine (8 Counts)

- Counts 1 through 4
  - Grapevine to right (step to right with right foot, behind with left foot, and to side with right foot, then touch ball of left foot next to right foot).
- Counts 5 through 8
  - Jump off of both feet, cross right foot over left foot, and spin 360 degrees to the left.
  - Bend knees and spin down to low and back up to high.
- Accent: Comes on count 5 with the jump and crossing of feet.

Sequence 3: Box Step (8 Counts)

- Note: This step uses a quarter turn; thus students face all four walls.
- Counts 1 and 2
  - Leading with right side, step to right and slide left foot to right foot; make a quarter turn during stepping action.
  - Accent: Comes on count 1 with lead right foot; arm action can be performed in unison with the side step by reaching arms out to sides.
- Counts 3 and 4
  - Leading with left side, step to left and slide right foot to right foot; make a quarter turn during stepping action.
  - Accent: Comes on count 3 with lead left foot.
- Counts 5 and 6
  - Leading with right side, step to right and slide left foot to right foot; make a quarter turn during the stepping action.
  - Accent: Comes on count 5 with lead right foot.
- Counts 7 and 8
  - Leading with left side, step to left and slide right foot to right foot; make a quarter turn.
  - Accent: Comes on count 7 with lead left foot.

Sequence 4: Shoulder Shrug (8 Counts)

- Counts 1 and 4
  - In shoulder-width stance, lunge to right and shrug right shoulder on count 1, lunge to left and shrug left shoulder on count 2, and then shrug right shoulder two times, on counts 3 and 4.
  - Accent: Comes on counts 1 and 3 with larger and sharper shoulder shrug.

- Counts 5 and 8
  - Repeat sequence of counts 1 through 4.
  - Accent: Comes on counts 5 and 7 with larger and sharper shoulder shrug.

Environment: Students should be organized in staggered lines so that all students can see the teacher. The front line should be changed frequently by the teacher. Each line can perform as a dance team.

Practice: constant (add-on strategy)

Feedback

- KPdp: "Try to jump off of two feet and quickly place your heel down on the walk-forward sequence."
- KPp: "Lunge a little farther to each side and raise your shoulder shrug higher."

Assessment

Standard 1: Use the assessment shown in figure 20.15 to evaluate students' performance of the hip-hop dance sequence.

Advanced (A): Student can perform all four sequences with all accents on appropriate count.

Proficient (P): Student can perform three sequences with most accents on appropriate count.

Developing (D): Student can perform two sequences with a few accents on appropriate count.

Not yet developed (NYD): Student can perform sequences but cannot perform accented movements.

Student	A	P	D	NYD

Figure 20.15 Scoring rubric for assessment of dance sequence.

National Physical Education Standards

- National Standard 1: Rhythmically perform dances.
- National Standard 2: Apply movement concepts and choreograph dances.
- National Standard 4: Use personal and social responsibility while engaged in dance.

Learning outcome: rhythmically performing more complex combinations and choreographing short dances

Choreographic theme: refining rhythm and choreographic themes and variables guided by the teacher

Teaching styles: reproduction (command and practice) and production (divergent discovery)

Dance genres: creative and cultural (sasa)

Sasa dance.

Task: This sample dance activity can be introduced after the teacher has already taught the sasa, a Samoan dance (see following sample Samoan dance sequences), and after children have studied Samoan culture (e.g., food and dress), geography, and religious practices. Students can then be asked to create three 8-count phrases of movement reflecting Samoan culture. Each 8-count phrase must be performed twice in a row for a total of 16 counts. The teacher circulates, assists students with their ideas, and helps them perform their creations to the tempo of the selected drumming music. After students create their phrases, they practice to the music. The teacher should introduce the sasa with factual information such as the following:

- The sasa is an energetic, rhythmic dance from the South Pacific islands of Samoa. Most of the dance takes place on the floor in a cross-legged position. Dancers clap their hands and use other rhythmic gestures to depict activities in everyday life such as rowing a boat, cracking a coconut, or pounding poi. Each dance is different, and gestures can be put together in any order. Dancers also use their voices in the Sasa and energetically shout Samoan words such as "Talofa" which is the Samoan greeting meaning "Hello!"

Here is a sample sasa.

Set 1 (16 Beats)

- Begin by sitting cross-legged in evenly spaced rows and columns about 3 feet (1 meter) apart.
- Keep knees bouncing throughout the dance.
- Counts 1 through 4: Clap hands four times with flat palms, which creates a higher-pitched sound (referred to as *Pati*).
- Counts 5 through 8: Clap hands four times with cupped palms, which creates a lower-pitched sound (referred to as *Po*).
- Repeat the 8-count sequence to make a total of 16 counts.

Set 2 (16 Beats)

- Count 1: Perform *Pati* high (forehead level).
- Count 2: Perform *Po* low (in front of tummy).
- Count 3: Flick both hands up to just above head level.
- Count 4: Slap thighs.
- Repeat this 4-count sequence three more times to make a total of 16 counts.

Set 3 (16 Beats)

- Count 1: Flick wrists about 12 inches (30 centimeters) in front of face, ending with palms facing away from face.
- Count 2: Slap ground at left diagonal.
- Count 3: Flick wrists in front of face again.
- Count 4: Slap ground at right diagonal.
- Count 5: Flick wrists in front of face again.
- Count 6: Slap ground in front.
- Count 7: Do *Pati*.
- Count 8: Do *Po*.
- Repeat this 8-count sequence to make a total of 16 counts.

Set 4 (16 Beats)

- Counts 1 and 2: Move right arm straight out to right and shake twice as if shaking someone's hand in the air. Left hand touches side of head with left elbow out to left.
- Counts 3 and 4: Reverse in-the-air handshake by going to left—left arm out to left side doing two shakes while right hand touches side of head.
- Counts 5, 6: Do in-the-air handshake with right arm straight in front of face while left hand returns to side of head.
- Count 7: Clap both hands straight out in front of face and shout *Talofa!* ("hello" in Samoan).
- Count 8: Hold.
- Repeat this 8-count sequence to make a total of 16 counts. On count 7 the second time through, shout "Samoa!"

Environment: Students are in pairs or small groups, and they organize themselves into a straight line. For music, use "Mother Tongue" from *The Serpent's Egg* (Dead Can Dance, 1988) or "Sinnerman" from *Verve Remixed 2* (Housecat & Simone, 2003).

Practice: constant

Closed-skill cues:

- Make movements sharp.
- Perform movements to tempo of music.
- Connect each movement to next one without hesitation.

Feedback

- KPd: "Your movements look like you are spearing a fish. Great! How many counts does the spearing action last?"
- KPp: "Try to make your movements a bit smaller, faster, and up to the tempo of the music."

Assessments

- Standard 1: Figure 20.16 is a self-assessment for performing the sasa.
- Standard 2: The assessment shown in figure 20.17 can be used to evaluate students' understanding of cultural terminology.
- Standard 4: Use the partner/small group assessment in figure 20.18 to assess group interaction.

Name: _____

Date: _____

Class period: _____

Please assess yourself with respect to the following criteria.

When the teacher was leading the dance, I was able keep up with the movements and tempo.

Yes _____ Sometimes _____ No _____

I can perform ____ (number of) sets of the sasa on my own without the teacher leading the dance.

Figure 20.16   Sasa self-assessment.

1. What is the climate like in Samoa?

_____ Usually cold   _____ Tropical all year   _____ Seasonal

2. What does the word *sasa* mean?

Answer: _____

3. The movements in the sasa are about _____ life.

Figure 20.17   Sasa knowledge assessment.

Student	Student contributed own ideas when creating the three movement phrases.		Student accepted others' ideas.		Student encouraged others in group.	
	Yes	No	Yes	No	Yes	No

Figure 20.18   Checklist for group interaction.

National Physical Education Standards

- National Standard 1: Rhythmically perform dances.
- National Standard 4: Use personal and social responsibility while engaged in dance.

Learning outcome: rhythmically performing more complex combinations and choreographing short dances

Choreographic theme: partner and group relationships (meeting and parting; contrasting movements)

Teaching styles: reproduction (command, practice)

Dance genre: creative **country-and-western** (barn and circle dance)

Task: Students use previously learned barn and circle dance movements but modify them to meet the following criteria.

- The dance includes meeting and parting of all dancers two times.
- The dance uses a canon approach, in which dancers begin on different counts; for example, partner A moves on counts 1 through 4, and partner B begins on count 5.
- The dance uses contrasting movements, such as the following:
  - Some dancers moving forward while others move backward
  - Inside circle and outside circle moving in opposite directions
  - Alternation of movements (e.g., doing one step or movement, then another step or movement, then repeating)

Circle Dance Steps and Formations

1. Do-si-do: Partner A and partner B pass each other with right shoulder to right shoulder, move around each other back to back, and return to original position.
2. Grapevine step: Step to right, step left foot behind right foot, step to right, and touch left ball of foot next to right foot (and reverse to left).
3. Shuffle step: Step, together, step (alternating lead foot).
4. Heel-toe step: Place heel of right foot on floor in front of body, cross left foot, and place toe of right foot on floor; can reverse with left after performing the shuffle step. (Can add heel-toe plus shuffle step.)
5. Circle to right and left by sliding sideways. Dancers can join hands to form a circle or circle with hands on their waist.
6. Star right and left: Dancers put right hands in middle of circle and walk clockwise; reverse, with left hand in circle. Off hand can be placed on waist.
7. Elbow swing: Hook right (or left) elbows with partner and turn once around.
8. Arch: One partner group forms an arch for others to duck under.
9. Allemande left and right: Partners A and B face each other, grasp forehands (or hands), turn each other around, and then go back to original position. Dancers can pull away from each to take advantage of centrifugal force (Pittman, Waller, & Dark, 2009).
10. Baskethold grasp: Each dancer puts right hand into the center, and they all face left, one behind the other, and put the right hand on the wrist (or over the shoulder) of the next person in front.

Environment: Students are organized in a circle of 8 to 10 dancers and organized into pairs; facing each other. One person is partner A, and one is partner B. Fiddle music can be used.

Practice: constant

Closed-skill cues:

- Make meeting and parting clearly observable.
- Canon: Move every two or four counts.
- Make contrasting movements evident.

Suggested resource: Laufman, D., & Laufman J. (2009). *Traditional barn dances with calls and fiddling.* Champaign, IL: Human Kinetics.

Feedback

- KPd: "Your meeting and parting with the entire group was performed right to the beat of the music—good job!"
- KPp: "When you use canon movement, everyone should count out loud so you know who moves when and movements are performed right on the beat."

Assessments

- Standard 1: Use the assessment shown in figure 20.19 to evaluate students' ability to perform the circle dance.
- Standard 4: Figure 20.20 assesses criteria related to cooperation in the circle dance.

Student	Used meeting and parting twice.		Used canon.		Used contrasting steps and formations.	
	Yes	No	Yes	No	Yes	No

Figure 20.19   Checklist for circle dance criteria.

Student	Cooperated with partner.		Used encouraging words.	
	Yes	No	Yes	No

Figure 20.20   Checklist for circle dance cooperation.

National Physical Education Standards

- National Standard 1: Rhythmically perform dances.
- National Standard 2: Apply movement concepts and choreograph dances.

Learning outcome: rhythmically performing more complex combinations and choreographing short dances

Choreographic theme: student-choreographed dances of longer duration with small groups

Teaching styles: production (divergent)

Dance genre: creative

Task: After studying a topic in the classroom, students create a dance based on that area of study. For example, if students have studied environmental concerns (e.g., amount of plastic trash thrown away annually), they might create a dance using props (e.g., plastic bottles) and conveying a message about environmental waste. As discussed earlier, level III creative dances are teacher initiated and student directed. Therefore, the teacher provides guidelines as follows:

- Use plastic bottles and bags as props in your dance.
- Incorporate locomotor, manipulative, and stability skills.
- Vary skills by using elements of the following (see movement content in chapter 5):
  - Space (level, direction, pathway)
  - Effort (percussive, loose, sustained, quick)
  - Relationship (mirroring, matching, meeting and parting, following and leading, under and over)

- Use an entrance and an exit.
- Use unison movement phrases; however, at some point, dancers must not all be moving at the same time.
- Include one change of formation (e.g., straight line, staggered line, circle, diagonal line).

Environment: Students are organized into groups of three to five dancers and positioned throughout the gymnasium area.

Practice: variable practice to create the dance, then constant practice

Closed-skill cues: Base cues on the guidelines just discussed.

- Were dancers in unison at some point during the dance?
- Did the dance include a clear entrance and a clear exit?
- Did the dance include a clear formation change?

Feedback

- KPd: "I saw three dancers moving and one dancer balancing. That fulfilled the requirement of having one dancer still. Good job!"
- KPp: "Your unison movement phrase needs everyone's arm action to be at the same level."

Assessment

- Standards 1 and 2: Use the group choreography assessment (figure 20.21).

Advanced: Props were used in three ways to convey meaning. The dance used the following elements: unison, stillness, change in level, direction, pathway, following and leading, meeting and parting, and mirroring. The dance included one change of formation, as well as an effective entrance and an effective exit.

Proficient: Props were used in two ways to convey meaning. The dance used the following elements: unison, change in direction, pathway, and meeting and parting. The dance included one change of formation, as well as an effective entrance and exit.

Developing: Props were used in one way to convey meaning. The dance included the following elements: unison, change in direction, and pathway.

Group member	Developing	Proficient	Advanced

Figure 20.21 Group choreography assessment.

National Physical Education Standard

- National Standard 1: Rhythmically perform dances.

Learning outcome: rhythmically performing more complex combinations and choreographing short dances

Choreographic theme: social dancing with partners

Teaching style: reproduction (command, practice, and inclusion)

Dance genre: social (swing)

Task: Before learning this dance, students should do some research or receive background information about the dance from the teacher. Here is the background: The dance made its first appearance in the 1920s. After Charles A. Lindbergh flew from New York to Paris in 1926, the dance became known as the Lindbergh Hop, a name that was later shortened to the Lindy Hop and then simply to the Lindy. The origins of the dance are unclear, but the music is 4/4, or cut time, and the dance form evolved under the African American influences of jazz in the 1930s. The dance is syncopated, and shoulder movements add to the swinging feeling. At times, the dance has taken many free and acrobatic forms, often including crouches, jumps, and swiveling feet. In recent years, it has evolved into a smoother and more graceful form.

Single-step rhythm:	Slow (1-2), slow (3-4), quick (5), quick (6)
1, 2 3, 4 5 6	
Single step:	Step, step, rock step

Progression 1: Single Step

- Directions are for the lead; follower's part is opposite.
  - Side, side, side, side
  - Slow, slow, quick, quick
  - Left, right, left, right

Progression 2: Rock Step

- Leaders left foot back, followers with right foot back.
  - Back, forward, back, forward
  - Slow, slow, quick, quick

Progression 3: Basic Step

- Students are in staggered lines facing the front. Leaders are on the left, and followers are on the right. Leaders always begin with the left foot, and followers always begin with the right foot. After the basic step is taught, the two groups face each other and practice.
  - Side, side, back-forward (rock step)
  - Slow, slow, quick, quick
  - Left, right, left, right

Progression 4 Hand-Hold Position

- After students learn this part, they face each other in a formation of two lines of partners with each pair in two-hand position (holding both hands with partner).
- Leaders frequently rotate clockwise to a new partner.
- For doggy-paw hands, leader has palms up with thumbs on top, and followers have palms down.
- Practice the basic step to music, then switch partners.
- During the rock step, partners should not have limp or "noodle" arms; some countertension is useful in leading and following.

Progression 5: Arch Underturn

- Students form two lines of facing partners.
- Leaders frequently rotate clockwise to a new partner.
- After two basic steps, the leader raises his or her left hand and the follower's right hand. The follower moves under the arch toward the left diagonal side of the leader on counts 1 and 2 (right on 1 and 2, slow, slow), pivot 180 degrees, left on 3 and 4, slow, slow). At the same time, the leader walks forward, changing places with the follower (left on 1 and 2, pivot 180 degrees, right on 3 and 4). The two finish facing each other again with a rock step (5 and 6).

Closed-skill cues:

- Perform steps on correct counts.
- Make complete weight shift from foot to foot.

Feedback

- KPd: "You are using countertension during your rock step and keeping your arms firm—good job!"
- KPp: "When you perform the rock step, you are not transferring weight onto your forward foot. Actually *step* onto your forward foot."

Assessment

Standard 1: Use the assessment shown in figure 20.22 to evaluate students' performance of the swing dance steps.

Student	Completes basic step facing partner with no handhold.		Completes basic step facing partner with double handhold.		Completes basic step facing partner with double handhold and does arch underturn.	
	Yes	No	Yes	No	Yes	No

Figure 20.22 Swing dance checklist.

 Visit the web resource for learning activities, video clips, and review questions.

Chapter 21

Developmental Gymnastics

Key Concepts

- Describing the difference between traditional and developmental gymnastics

- Describing best practices in teaching gymnastics

- Discussing the relationship between stage of motor development, level of movement skill learning, and standards-based instruction in designing gymnastics learning experiences for children in grades 3 through 5

- Implementing combination and application task progressions for developmental gymnastics

When students are asked to describe gymnastics, they typically either refer to Olympians performing somersaults and twists in difficult routines or describe how reluctant they themselves are to tumble, vault, or move on a beam or parallel bars. Common retorts include "I'm too big," "I'm not flexible," and "I'm scared." These responses are usually aimed at a competitive or traditional view of gymnastics as a prescribed set of skills that are performed in routines on special apparatus (e.g., vault, rings) and judged for adherence to a set of performance standards.

In response to this resistance, teachers have turned to *educational* gymnastics as a developmentally appropriate way to engage students in gymnastics actions without the constraints of the single-standard skills performed on regulation equipment imposed by competitive gymnastics. In educational gymnastics, the body actions of balance, rolling, step-like actions (e.g., cartwheels), and flight (e.g. jumping) are combined with the movement concepts (body, space, effort, and relationship) to engage students in a wide array of body management skills and movement sequences (Nilges, 1999). *Developmental* gymnastics, in turn, adheres to the tenets of educational gymnastics—that is, combining gymnastics actions with movement concepts—*and* provides a progression of developmentally appropriate learning experiences that use a variety of small and large equipment scaled to the body dimensions of elementary-school children.

MOVEMENT FRAMEWORK FOR DEVELOPMENTAL GYMNASTICS

The Active Child illustration (figure 21.1) depicts the developmental gymnastics movement-framework categories, which include gymnastics actions (balance, rolling, step-like action, and flight) and the movement concepts (body, space, effort, and relationship). The framework is used to determine how actions and concepts can be combined to vary skills and design sequences. Teachers and students can each experiment with endless blends—both within and between the gymnastics actions and the movement concepts—to provide a range of challenges and novelty in skill performance in the gymnastics environment.

For instance, think about the possible blends of movement-concept categories with the gymnastics action of static balance, as depicted in table 21.1. Balances can be created and performed using one or more of the movement concept variables of body or space. For example, balance 1 might involve finding ways to balance on two hands and one foot with the front, back, or side facing the floor and with different positioning of the nonsupport leg. Balance 2 might involve balancing on one's seat in different shapes and trying different arm positions. Students could then perform balances created by blending the movement concepts of body and shape, as in the following examples:

- In relationship to equipment
  - Balance 1: with support foot on low equipment and hands on floor or different piece of equipment
  - Balance 2: on top of, beside, or under different pieces of equipment

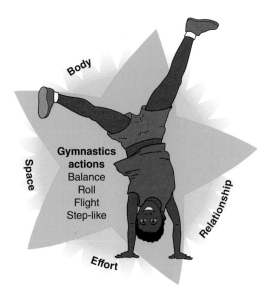

Figure 21.1 The Active Child: gymnastics.

- In relationship to others
  - Balance 1: with nonsupport foot touching partner's
  - Balance 2: facing, back to back, or side to side
- In relationship to equipment *and* others
- Combining balances into sequences with other gymnastics actions on mats (e.g., balance 1 to balance 2 to backward roll; forward roll to balance 2 to balance 1) and apparatus

As described in chapter 5 and reviewed in chapter 18, children in grades 3 through 5 are at the intermediate level of movement skill learning. At this level, they have gained a better kinesthetic feel for the position of their body parts and the timing of their movements. This sense is especially useful

Table 21.1 Blending Static Balance With Movement Concepts

Body	Space	Relationship with equipment	Relationship with others	Effort
Support parts Nonsupport parts Shape	Level (high, medium, low)	On Under Beside	Noncontact (beside, face to face, back to front, matching, mirroring) Counterbalance Countertension Support	Smooth sequences that connect balances with other balances, rolls, flight, and step-like actions Combining skills using different speeds

as they build on the stability and locomotor skills (developed in kindergarten through grade 2) to learn the form-based, closed-skill gymnastics actions and movement sequences involved in combination and application progressions. In developmental gymnastics, students increase the difficulty of skills, vary skills using the movement concepts, combine skills in sequences, and perform skills and sequences with partners. These four areas—skills, variations, combinations, and partners—form the categories for the developmental gymnastics learning goal blueprint (see table 21.2)

The *combination-level* skill progressions increase the difficulty of balancing and step-like actions through inverted movements (e.g., headstands, cartwheels); challenge students to combine movements in short, smooth movement sequences on mats and apparatus; and work with partners in countertension and counterbalancing. The *application-level* skill progressions include more difficult inverted combinations (e.g., handstand roll, roundoff roll), vaults, sequencing of movements into routines on mats and apparatus, and work with partner supports. Both the combination and the application skill progressions provide affordances through the scaling of equipment and conditions to fit the performers (see chapter 6). These developmentally appropriate skill progressions gradually help children gain the body management skills to perform gymnastics actions and develop muscular strength, endurance, and flexibility.

The inclusion of gymnastics in the developmental physical education curriculum helps children achieve the following goals:

- Becoming skilled and versatile movers in the gymnastics environment
- Using the movement framework to create gymnastics skills and sequences
- Increasing their movement confidence and personal safety by developing the ability to manage their body weight
- Increasing their core and upper-body muscular strength and endurance, and their total-body joint flexibility
- Using movement skill criteria to understand correct performance and help others improve skills
- Understanding how to practice closed skills
- Working cooperatively with others to perform and create partner and small-group balances and gymnastics sequences

BEST PRACTICES WHEN TEACHING GYMNASTICS

The tasks and environments created for developmental gymnastics must adhere to the following best practices.

- **Skill development:** The specialized skills used in the gymnastics actions of balance, rolling, step-like actions, and flight derive from fundamental stability and locomotor skills developed in pre-K through grade 2. Students should be capable of performing the consistent-level skills before starting the combination-level progressions.

Table 21.2 Learning Goal Blueprint for Developmental Gymnastics

Content	Skills	Variations	Combinations	Partners
Balance **Rolling** **Step-like actions** **Flight**	Intentionally uses body actions for correct performance technique on mats and equipment.	Performs and creates variations of gymnastics actions on mats and equipment using movement concepts. Body: Varies symmetrical or asymmetrical shapes by curling, stretching, and twisting either during or to get into or come out of actions; varies position of nonsupport body parts. Space: Varies level, range, direction, and pathway during actions or for transition between actions. Effort: Varies speed and force during actions or for transition between actions.	Combines three or four gymnastics actions on mats and equipment using variations as transitions. Combines and sequences skills on mats and equipment with few hesitations.	Coordinates movements with partner on mats and equipment for counterbalance, countertension, and support. Coordinates combinations of skills in relation to partner on mats and equipment to meet and part; to move next to; and in roles of leading, following, and matching.

Specialized skill progressions take into account the need for learning skills on mats before performing them on equipment, starting from wider bases of support before narrowing the base, starting with equipment for balancing that is wider and lower, using slopes to raise the center of balance for ease in getting the hips over the head in rolling and step-like actions, and combining skills in short sequences before taking on longer routines.

• **Safe and effective practice conditions.** Children get better as a result of engaging in gymnastics skill and sequence practice repetitively under the right conditions. The goal of gymnastics is consistent performance of smoothly combined sequences of skills under predictable (closed) conditions. Closed-skill practice conditions require many repetitions to gain the kinesthetic feel for skills and skill combinations to perform them consistently. Even though repetition under the same conditions is necessary to gain and improve gymnastics skills, practice must be distributed (short numbers of repetitions with breaks) for safety. A loss of balance could easily lead to falls from too many repetitions of rolling skills (dizziness) and too many repetitions of step-like actions (upper body muscle fatigue). Skill and sequence practice opportunities should include breaks either in the form of short recovery periods or engaging students in skills using alternate muscle groups.

• **Maximizing participation and inclusion:** It can be a challenge to provide opportunities for all students to be actively involved in gymnastics. Given their concerns about safety, teachers often have students waiting in line for turns as the teacher monitors one student or a few students performing single-standard skills or taking turns at stations with one piece of equipment. The solution is to include all students in distributed practice conditions by planning multitask and station environments infused with skill progressions that offer students *choices* based on their level of ability. Thus, at any given time, students may be learning new skills, improving skills, varying skills, or combining skills. Stations based on these practice options enable teachers to concentrate or distribute their time and attention according to learners' needs. For instance, a teacher might choose to spend more time monitoring students who have rotated to the "new skill" station while the rest of the class works on refining skills, varying skills, or combining skills at other stations.

• **Prosocial interactions:** Teachers provide opportunities to reinforce prosocial interactions by having students help each other improve skill performance and perform gymnastics actions together as partners and in small groups. Teachers who use the reciprocal style of teaching engage students in using skill criteria to observe and provide helpful feedback to classmates. Thus this style provides benefits both for prosocial behavior and for maximizing participation and safe practice. The performing classmate gets helpful feedback that supports or improves his performance, and the observer uses criteria to help the performer while reinforcing the skill criteria for herself and receiving a distributed practice break. This approach also maximizes participation because all students are involved in either skill performance or active observation. During partner and small-group performance of gymnastics skills, students learn to present ideas, listen to each other's ideas, and work together to choose skills that meet the learning goal—for example, performing a counterbalance with a total of only three body parts touching the floor. Teachers monitor and provide feedback about prosocial behaviors observed in the partner and small-group work; when needed, they also engage students in alternative behaviors and conflict resolution (see chapter 12).

DESIGNING INSTRUCTION FOR DEVELOPMENTAL GYMNASTICS

The design of instruction for developmental gymnastics consistently addresses national physical education standards 1 and 2 (SHAPE America, 2014) by providing opportunities for students to become skilled and knowledgeable in gymnastics actions and sequences. The content is derived from the combination- and application-level task progression charts presented in tables 21.5 and 21.6. The instructional activities presented in this chapter for each level provide a framework for designing lesson episodes; they do *not* necessarily represent one lesson episode per se, because children develop the capability to perform gymnastics actions and sequences by engaging in many attempts over time.

The rest of this section addresses the chain of decision making used to design instruction derived from motor-development and learning theory, the movement framework, standards-based physical education, assessment of student learning, and effective instructional practice. The categories for each instructional activity include learning outcome, teaching style, task, enrichment, environment, practice, skill cues, feedback, and assessment.

Let's take a closer look at the categories. The learning outcome reflects the gymnastics actions and sequences identified in the progression chart. Teaching style options are presented with an indication that the reproduction styles listed can provide opportunities for practice with feedback, whereas the production styles can be used to lead students to discover biomechanical concepts and multiple ways of performing and combining gymnastics actions into sequences. The choice of style, or the order of styles (see the discussion of mobility ability in chapter 10), depends on the learning objectives of the lessons. For example, divergent discovery can be used to help students discover a variety of balances, the practice style can be used to help students practice the balances, and the reciprocal style can be used to help students practice and reinforce correct technique by watching and giving feedback to a partner.

The task describes the relevant skills, movement concepts, and progressions. Given these task elements, the environment includes choices for scaling the equipment and conditions to enable success for differing abilities—for instance, different heights and widths of equipment (figure 6.1, 6.2, and 6.3 in chapter 6). The type of practice is determined by the goal of the skill. For example, if the goal is to attain correct timing and technique (beginners, closed skills), then the choice is constant practice under unvarying conditions. However, if the goal is to discover alternate ways of performing or combining gymnastics actions, then variable practice is used with an emphasis on exploring new ways to blend gymnastics actions and movement concepts. The skill cues describe the sequence or timing of movements for performance of single or combined skills.

The goal of the skill (closed or open) and the stage of learning determine the type of feedback used. Since gymnastics are closed skills, knowledge-of-performance (KP) feedback is most appropriate because it focuses on skill cues. KP feedback is used for beginning-stage learners who need to know how to correct the technique and timing of their movements and for intermediate-stage learners who are refining their performance of closed-

skill gymnastics actions and sequences. When students are beginning-level learners, use knowledge of performance descriptive feedback (KPd) (e.g., "Your roll was bumpy") and knowledge of performance prescriptive feedback (KPp) (e.g., "You need to keep your chin tucked, knees to chest, and back rounded for a smooth roll") to help them perform skills with appropriate mechanics. When students are refining skills as intermediate-level learners, use questions to encourage them to describe what they think happened and to try to come up with a solution. This approach is consistent with recommendations for giving intermediate-level learners less frequent feedback so that they become less dependent on outside sources of feedback.

Assessments give teachers and students information about the quality of learning. Standard 1 assessments focus on psychomotor performance and address either the process or the product of movements. In gymnastics, process assessments are used most often, because the goal of the skill is correct technique and timing. Specifically, teachers use observation checklists of movement cues for skills, variations, combinations, and partner work. The summative assessment rubric developmental gymnastics presented in table 21.3 was derived from the learning goal blueprint (table 21.2). The rubric can be used to determine student performance and progress in key aspects of developmental gymnastics.

Assessments for standard 2 are cognitive and represent the level of thinking that is developmentally appropriate for the learner. In grades 3 through 5, students are in the concrete stage of thought and can participate in most levels of thinking, as long as the question relates directly to what they are experiencing, as in the following examples: "Describe how the movements should be combined to achieve a smooth, flowing sequence." "Compare the movement performance of a peer with the criteria and give feedback to help her improve." In chapter 9, table 9.2 provides examples of cognitive assessments that reflect the levels of thinking.

Gymnastics can also serve as a vehicle for addressing standards 3, 4, and 5 by helping children develop fitness and personal and social responsibility and by providing them with opportunities to experience challenge, enjoyment, and social interaction. When teachers incorporate objectives that address these standards in gymnastics learning activities, they must also design assessments that match the intention of the relevant standard.

Table 21.3 Scoring Rubric for Developmental Gymnastics

	1 Developing	2 Proficient	3 Advanced
Gymnastics skills: balance, rolling, step-like actions, flight	Sometimes coordinated	Coordinated Intentional use of body actions for correct technique	Effortless
Complexity of variation	Limited to one or two variables (e.g., shape, level, speed)	Use of a few variables from two movement concepts: Body—varying symmetrical or asymmetrical shapes by curling, stretching, and twisting either during or to get into or come out of; varying position of nonsupport body parts Space—varying level, range, direction, and pathway during actions or for transition between actions Effort—varying speed and force during actions or for transition between actions	Using multiple variables from among three movement concepts
Combination	Combinations somewhat choppy; decrease in skill quality	Combining and sequencing gymnastics actions with few hesitations	Smooth and flowing combinations and sequences
Complexity of combination	Combining two skills	Combining three or four gymnastics actions on mats and equipment using variations for transition	Combining more than four actions using variations to modify skills and for transition
Partner work	Inconsistent coordination of movements with partner; decrease in skill quality	Coordination of movements with partner on mats and equipment for counterbalances, countertensions, and supports Coordination of skill combinations in relation to partner on mats and equipment to meet and part; move next to; and in roles of leading, following, and matching	Synchronization with partner of movements on mats and equipment

• **Standard 3:** The most common components of fitness addressed through gymnastics are muscular strength and endurance, and flexibility. Increases in these fitness components can be tracked throughout gymnastics lessons by having students document changes in their capabilities (e.g., increase in strength from being able to perform a scissor-kick handstand to being able to hold a handstand with one's feet against a wall).

• **Standard 4:** Chapter 18 describes several learning activities that engage students in exhibiting personal and social responsibility through physical activity. During gymnastics instruction, students should continue to respect and cooperate with others, follow directions, and appropriately receive and give feedback. To facilitate success in this area, teachers need to inform students that these behaviors of personal and social responsibility are expected every day; furthermore, teachers need to reinforce this expectation through reminders, prompts, praise, and feedback. The rubric presented in table 21.4 illustrates a way to assess personal and social responsibility throughout learning experiences in gymnastics.

• **Standard 5:** This standard asks children to recognize the value of physical activity. They can do so for themselves only through engaging in self-reflection about their own participation over time. To this end, figure 21.2 provides sample prompts to engage students in ongoing self-reflection. Teachers can use data collected early on from responses to these prompts to respond to students' needs and interests.

Table 21.4 Rubric for Personal and Social Responsibility

Standard 4 behavior	Responsible	Developing	Irresponsible
Personal responsibility	Exhibits self-control. Works independently and safely without prompting from teacher. Engages in respectful interaction and conflict resolution with others. Accepts and uses feedback from teacher and peers. Demonstrates etiquette and follows rules.	Exhibits self-control. Works independently and safely with some prompting from teacher. Engages in respectful interaction with others. Accepts feedback from teacher and peers. Demonstrates etiquette and follows rules most of the time.	Denies personal responsibility by making excuses and blaming others. Has difficulty with working independently; needs monitoring by teacher to stay on task. Engages in disrespectful interactions with others or ignores others. Disregards rules and etiquette.
Social responsibility	Works cooperatively with others. Accepts and involves others of different skill levels. Praises, encourages, and gives helpful feedback to others.	Needs occasional prompting from teacher to work cooperatively with others. Accepts others of different skill levels. Praises and encourages others; gives feedback when prompted.	Cannot work productively with others.

A. Rate your *enjoyment* of participating in _____ [balance, rolling, flight, step-like, combination] activities and tell why.

1 _____ 2 _____ 3 _____ 4 _____ 5
not enjoyable   enjoyable   very enjoyable

Reason:

B. Rate the *challenge* of participating in _____ [balance, rolling, flight, step-like, combination] activities and tell why.

1 _____ 2 _____ 3 _____ 4 _____ 5
not challenging   challenging   very challenging

Reason:

C. Describe the positive and negative social interactions (encouraging or discouraging words or gestures, being or not being helped by others, helping others, support or lack of support from others, cooperation or lack of cooperation with others) that occurred when you were participating in _____ (balance, rolling, flight, step-like, combination) activities.

Rubric

Proficient: The ratings in questions A and B match the reasons given, and the reasons are related to the activity. The description of social interaction is clearly related to the activity.

Developing: The ratings in questions A and B match the reasons given, and the reasons are somewhat related to the activity. The description of social interaction is somewhat related to the activity.

Beginning: There is a discrepancy between the ratings in questions A and B and the reasons given. The description of social interactions is minimal or consists of a one-word answer (e.g., "fun") without reference to the activity.

Figure 21.2 Standard 5: self-report assessment.

Big Ideas

- Developmental gymnastics combines the gymnastics actions of balance, rolling, step-like actions, and flight with the movement concepts of body, space, effort, and relationship in a progression of developmentally appropriate learning experiences in an environment that provides equipment and conditions scaled to fit the performers.

- Best practices for teaching gymnastics involve using progressions, based on student need, from the consistent (K-2), combination, and application levels of learning; maximizing participation and including all children in safe and effective practice; and promoting prosocial interactions.

- The movement framework for developmental gymnastics is used to determine how actions and concepts can be combined in order to vary skills and design sequences.

- The design of instruction for developmental gymnastics uses concepts from motor development, motor skill learning, the movement framework, and standards-based instruction.

Combination-Level Task Progressions

Instructional task progressions for the combination level in grades 3 through 5 (table 21.5) are based on the consistent-level progressions for K-2 stability skills (tables 16.2, 16.3 and 16.4) and locomotor skills (tables 15.2 and 15.3). Students should be able to perform the consistent-level skills in a gymnastics action category (e.g., balance, rolling) before starting the combination-level progressions; refer to the prerequisite skills indicated with the combination-level learning tasks presented in this chapter.

Table 21.5 Task Progressions for Gymnastics: Combination Level

	Gymnastics actions	

SPECIALIZED SKILLS	**Balance** **Rolling** **Flight** **Step-like**	Equipment: boxes, benches, trapezoids, beams, foam shapes, vaulting board, hoops, ropes, tires
		
		 Learning outcome: performing, varying, and combining gymnastics actions
		 • Balance
		    • Balancing in upright positions
		    • Combining balances
		    • Balancing and turning
		    • Dynamic balancing
		    • Balancing in inverted positions
		    • Balancing with partner relationships of countertension and counterbalance
		 • Rolling
		 • Combining rolls, balances, and locomotor skills
		 • Rolling in relationship to equipment
		 • Flight
		    • Flight with changes in direction
		    • Combining flight with changes in direction and rolling
		    • Flight in relationship to equipment
		 • Step-like
		    • Cartwheels
		    • Vaulting over equipment

BALANCE

Learning Outcomes

- Standards 1 and 2: Combine skills and perform variations by using gymnastics actions and movement concepts.
- Standard 4: Work cooperatively with others.

Teaching Styles

- Production: divergent to create variety
- Reproduction: practice, reciprocal, and inclusion to choose and practice skills and combinations

BALANCING IN UPRIGHT POSITIONS

Prerequisite skills: stability (chapter 16)—balancing on different bases, shapes, and levels

Task: Students perform static gymnastics balances on mats. Instruct them to "Keep the center of balance over the base of support, the trunk tight, the head and chest up, and the eyes focused forward." The task sheet is used to check off balances held for three seconds and to vary balances by changing the position of free body parts.

Straddle stand: Spread the legs wide, raise the arms out to the sides, and bend forward at the waist until the trunk is parallel to the floor. Keep the chest and head up.

Knee–foot balance: Balance on one knee with the other leg bent in front and its foot on the floor. Keep the trunk upright and the arms raised.

One leg balance: Balance on one foot with other leg bent at knee.

Variation of one leg balance: Stork stand balance on one foot with the trunk upright, the free foot touching the inside of the opposite knee, and the arms out to the sides.

L-stand: Balance on one foot with the trunk upright and raise the free leg straight up in front of the body.

Side balance: Stand on one foot with the other leg raised out to the side, one arm raised by the ear, and the other arm raised at shoulder height.

Knee scale: Balance on one knee and two hands with the chest and head raised.

Side knee scale: Balance on one knee and the same-side hand. The side should face the floor. Raise the opposite leg and stretch the free arm by the ear.

Front scale: Balance on one foot with free leg and head and chest raised.

V-seat: Balance on the seat, pike the hips, and raise straight legs with the hands on the mat by the hips. Then try it with the arms raised.

Enrichment: Perform static balances on different pieces of low equipment.

Environment: Provide mats for practicing balances; for the enrichment, provide low benches, beams, folded panel mats, and trapezoids. Provide balance cards or a poster with pictures of static balances at one or more stations. Provide task sheets so that students can note the balances that they are able to hold for three seconds, describe or illustrate how they varied free body parts, and list pieces of equipment on which they could perform static balances.

Practice: variable when trying different balances, constant when practicing chosen balances

Closed-skill cues:

- Keep center of balance over base of support.
- Keep trunk tight.
- Keep head and chest raised.
- Focus eyes forward.

Feedback

- KPp: "To help yourself balance, keep your chest and head up as you lean forward from the waist in the T-scale."
- KPp: "How can you use your arms to help you stay balanced when you have one foot as your base of support?"

Assessments

Standards 1 and 2: Use the students' task cards to spot-check balances they indicated they could hold for three seconds and the variations they reported.

COMBINING BALANCES

Prerequisite skills: stability (chapter 16)—adding one balance to another

Task: Students practice performing combinations of balances and hold each balance in the sequence for a count of three. Students are instructed to "Keep a tight core to smoothly move the center of balance over the base of support for the next balance. Make connections smooth and fluid with no hesitation, wobbling, or loss of balance." Students can select "gymnastics" balances or other balances that they know or create. Possible connecting movements include rising or sinking to change level, stretching, curling or twisting to change shape, turning to face a new direction, changing speed, and transferring weight to different body parts. Here are some sample challenges:

- Level: Combine three balances, each at a different level. Start at the high level and sink smoothly to connect to the medium level and then to the low level. Then reverse the sequence and rise smoothly from the low level to the medium level and then to the high level. Repeat the sequence using a turn to connect two of the balances.
- Shape: Combine five balances of different shapes at the low and medium levels. Smoothly combine the balances by using the actions of stretching, curling, and twisting. Repeat the sequence using a change of speed when connecting two of the balances.
- Weight transfer: Combine four balances, each with a different combination of body parts as a base. Combine the balances by means of turns, speed changes, and the actions of stretching, curling, and twisting.

Environment: Provides mats and task cards presenting different challenges. Students can design and work on sequences and have a partner use the reciprocal style to "check out" their combinations. To provide different options for creating balance combinations, balance illustrations and movement concept cards can be chosen either purposefully or at random.

Practice: variable when creating balance combinations, constant when practicing chosen combinations

Closed-skill cues:
- Combining Balances
  - Hold balances for three seconds (keep center of balance over base of support).
  - Keep core tight.
  - Connect balances with shift of weight or body position to move or keep center of balance over new base.
  - Make smooth, fluid connections with no hesitation or loss of balance.

Enrichment: Combine balances in relationship to equipment: onto, on top of, beside, and under.

Feedback

KPd: "You created a smooth connection by opening the curl from your low balance right through the stretch of your high balance. Nice work."

KPp: "To prevent wobbling, tighten your core as you sink into your last balance."

Assessments

Standards 1 and 2: Students rate their partner's performance by completing the reciprocal-style card for balance combination in figure 21.3.

Directions: Place an X somewhere along the line to show how the partner performs.

My partner _____ [name] is able to combine balances as follows:

Holding balances for three seconds

_____

always   often   sometimes

Smoothly connecting balances (no hesitations, wobbles, stops, or falls)

_____

always   often   sometimes

Figure 21.3   Reciprocal-style card for balance combination.

BALANCING AND TURNING

Prerequisite skills: stability (chapter 16)—balances on different bases, shapes, and levels

Task: Students perform turns from balances on different body parts. For steady turns, they work to keep the center of balance over the base; depending on the chosen base, some turns require a pivot, some a wind-up, and some a push. Students use the card for creating turns (figure 21.4) to explore designing turns by varying the body part(s) on which the turn is performed in combination with the movement concepts of body, space, and effort.

Supporting body part(s) used for turn	Body variations	Space variations	Effort variations
2 feet 1 foot Knee(s) Bottom Hip Back Belly	Placement of nonsupport parts Shape (curling, stretching, piking, wide, narrow) Use of parts to initiate or stop rotation	Revolution (quarter, half, full) Level (high, medium, low)	Speed (slow, moderate, fast)

Figure 21.4   Card for creating turns.

Environment: Provide floor and mats. Provide cards, or post or project a chart, with pictures and words of different body parts and variables. Provide blank charts on which students can record the combinations they use; they can also draw or take a picture or video of their turns using technology provided by the teacher.

Practice: variable when creating turns, constant when practicing chosen turns

Closed-skill cues:

General

- Determine revolutions to do and which wall to face at end of turn.
- Keep center of balance over base.

Pivot Turn

- Stand with one foot in front of other and weight on balls of feet.
- Turn in direction of back foot.

Crossover Turn

- Stand with one foot next to other and weight on balls of feet.
- Cross one foot in front of or behind other.
- Perform pivot turn in direction of back foot.

Swing Turn

- Stand with one foot in front of other and weight on balls of feet.
- Swing straight back leg forward.
- At height of swing, look and perform half turn on ball of, and in direction of, support foot.

Pivot turn.

Crossover turn.

Swing turn: beginning *(a)* and end *(b)*.

Wind-Up Turn

- Standing on both feet with weight on one foot, wind up trunk and arms in direction opposite of turn.
- Shift weight and center of balance over turning foot.
- Quickly move head and unwind body toward ending wall.
- Step onto free foot to end turn.

Wind-up turn: beginning *(a)* and end *(b)*.

Push Turn

- Start on trunk (bottom, hip, back, belly).
- Place hands on floor and push off in direction opposite of turn.
- Quickly move hands close to body during turn.
- Use hands or open arms wide to end turn.

Feedback

- KPp: "Quickly move your head and look for a spot on the wall that you'll be facing."
- KPp: "Where should your center of balance be in that turn?"

Assessments

- Standards 1 and 2: Perform (or provide a photo or video of performance of) a selection of turns on different body parts. For each turn, do the following:
    - Tell how you used the movement concept variables.
    - Describe how you could create a new variation for your turn.

DYNAMIC BALANCE

Prerequisite skills: stability (chapter 16)—adding locomotor and balance skills; locomotor skills (chapter 15) adding traveling and flight skills

Task: Students perform dynamic "gymnastics" movements on mats, then along floor lines, folded panel mats, benches, and low beams. Students are instructed to, "Keep the center of balance over the moving base of support, the trunk tight, the head and chest up, and the eyes focused forward." Students use inclusion-style task sheets to check off the dynamic balances performed on mats and along equipment. Use the divergent production style to prompt students to vary dynamic balances by changing the position of free body parts, the level of the body, the direction of travel, and the speed of movements.

- Locomotor skills: Walk, gallop, slide, skip continuously for 8 to 12 feet (about 2.5 to 3.5 meters).
- Grapevine: Travel sideward, alternately crossing one foot in front of and then behind the other, continuously for 8 to 12 feet (about 2.5 to 3.5 meters).
- Jump with two feet to two feet three times in a row.
- Jump with one foot to two feet three times in a row.
- Hop three times in a row.
- Perform a leap.
- Perform a pivot turn from upright and squat positions; look toward the end of the beam with the arms out to the sides.
- Perform a crossover turn.
- Perform a swing turn.

Perform combinations of dynamic and static "gymnastics" skills on mats, then along floor lines, folded panel mats, benches, and low beams. Use the end position of the first move as the beginning position of the next skill to make combinations flow (no hesitations or stops). Try the following types of combination:

- Locomotor skills
- Grapevine to pivot turn
- Locomotor skills and jumps, hops, and leaps
- Locomotor skills and turns
- Jumps, hop, leap, and turns
- All of these, from or into a variety of static "gymnastics" balances

Environment: Provide mats, folded panel mats, a low bench, and a low beam. Set up multiple stations with multiple skills.

Practice: variable practice of various dynamic skills and combinations, constant practice of chosen dynamic skills and combinations

Closed-skill cues:

Dynamic Balance

- Keep center of balance over moving base of support.
- Keep trunk tight.
- Keep head and chest up.
- Generally focus eyes forward; for turns, look toward new direction.

Dynamic and Static Balance Combinations

- Use end position of first move as beginning position of next skill to perform skills with flow (no stops or hesitations).
- Use cues given earlier for dynamic and static balances and turns.

Assessments

- Standards 1 and 2: Perform (or provide a photo or video of performance of) a selection of the following:
  - Dynamic balances on equipment
  - Dynamic balances on equipment with variations (and description of how movement concepts were used to vary movements)
  - Dynamic and static balance combinations (and description of how flowing combinations were created)

BALANCING IN INVERTED POSITIONS

Prerequisite skills: modified headstand and mule kick

Task: Students perform the following tasks.

- **Tripod:** Form a triangle with the head (hairline on mat) and hands, walk the hips up over the triangle, and place the knees on the backs of the upper arms. Hold for three seconds, then come down one leg at a time. Hint: To make the triangle the right size, kneel on the mat and place the forearms on the mat with the fingers of both hands crossed over each other. Replace the crossed fingers with the hairline and look back to replace each elbow with the same side hand.

- **Headstand:** From a tripod position, open the hips to shift the weight over the center of the triangle and straighten the legs, moving the feet toward the ceiling and keeping the core tight. For an alternate method, perform the triangle in front of a low box or beam, place one foot on the beam, and swing the free leg up over the triangle as the other foot pushes off of the beam and the legs are brought together overhead. A spotter may stand to the side and hold the performer's calf. Caution: If overbalancing, tuck the head quickly and roll.

Tripod.   Headstand.

• **Scissor-kick handstand:** Start in a forward-backward standing position with the arms raised overhead, the weight on the back foot, and the front leg raised. Step onto the front foot, place the hands on the mat shoulder-width apart, lock the elbows, swing the back leg up, and push off of the front leg as the weight is shifted over the shoulders. As the push-off leg reaches height, the swing leg is coming back down for the landing. Get as close to 90 degrees as possible. A chart on the wall can be used to determine body angle (e.g., 45, 67, or 90 degrees).

Environment: Provide mats and a low bench or low beam. Students work in groups of four: partners using reciprocal style and, if necessary, two spotters for the headstand.

Practice: constant practice for balance positions; distributed practice for few repetitions with short breaks or practice of other, noninverted skills

Scissor-kick handstand.

Closed-skill cues:

Tripod

• Make triangle with head and hands.
• Walk hips over triangle.
• Position knees on backs of upper arms.

Headstand

• Make triangle with head and hands.
• Assume tripod position.
• Straighten legs toward ceiling.

Scissor-Kick Handstand

• Start in standing position with arms raised.
• Step forward and place hands on mat.
• Scissor-kick extended legs up and down.
• Try to get body beyond 45-degree angle (close to 90 degrees, with shoulders over hands).

Feedback

• KPp: "To keep your head and body aligned, focus your eyes on your fingers when performing the scissor kick handstand."
• KPp: "Where were your hips positioned so you could successfully extend your legs during the headstand?" [Over the head.]

Assessments

Standard 1: Use an evaluation checklist of skill cues.

Standard 3: Use the time line of ability to perform a scissor-kick handstand to 90 degrees (figure 21.5).

Name:				
	<45°	**45° to 67°**	**>67°**	**90°**
Date				

Figure 21.5 Time line for scissor-kick handstand.

BALANCING WITH PARTNER RELATIONSHIPS OF COUNTERTENSION AND COUNTERBALANCE

Prerequisite skills: stability (chapter 16)—nonsupport partner balances

Task: Students perform countertension and counterbalances with partners; change partners often, noting what needs to be done to balance with someone of similar or different weight. Both of these types of balance are performed with the center of balance outside the partners' bodies; therefore, the partners depend on each other to remain balanced and avoid falling. On a signal, performers recover from the balance by bringing their bodies back to the starting position. Partners try the listed balances and then use the card for creating balances (figure 21.6) to design their own. They work together by listening, sharing, and choosing from among both partners' ideas. Here are instructions for the balances.

- Countertension balances (partners leaning away from each other)
  - Facing: Stand facing each other with toes touching and hold hands with elbows bent. While keeping trunk tight, straighten elbows and lean away from each other.
  - Side: Stand side to side with outside edges of inside feet touching and hold inside hands. While keeping trunk tight, straighten elbows and lean away from each other. Position outside leg to keep foot off of ground.
- Counterbalances (partners leaning into each other)
  - Facing: Stand facing each other, one arm's length apart. Raise straight arms in front of body to shoulder height. Place palms together, keep trunk tight, and slowly bend elbows, bringing upper body close to partner's and side of face next to side of partner's face.
  - Back: Stand back to back with upper back touching partner's upper back. While keeping trunk tight, slowly walk feet forward until weight is supported not only by feet but also by position of partners' backs together.

Body variations	Space variations	Relationship variations
Body parts touching	Level of each partner	Face to face, side, or back
Placement of free body parts		Side to side or back
Shapes of bodies		Back to back

Figure 21.6   Card for creating counterbalance and countertension.

Environment: Provide mats, as well as cards (or a large chart posted or projected on the wall) with pictures and words denoting different body parts and movement-concept variables. Provide blank charts for students to record the variables they chose for their balances; they can also make drawings or take a picture or video of their countertension and counterbalancing with technology provided by the teacher.

Practice: variable when creating balances, constant when practicing chosen balances

Closed-skill cues:

Countertension Balance

- Lean away from partner.
- Center of balance is between partners.
- Keep trunk tight.

Countertension balance.

Counterbalance

- Lean toward partner.
- Center of balance is between partners.
- Keep trunk tight.

Working Cooperatively With Others

- Listen to others.
- Share with others.
- Choose movements from among both partners' ideas.

Counterbalance.

Assessments

Standards 1, 2, and 4: Perform (or provide a photo or video of performance of) a selection of partner countertensions and counterbalances. For each partner balance, do the following:

- Indicate the type of balance and describe how you used the movement concept variables.
- Describe how you worked together to create balances.
- Describe how you could create a new variation for one of your balances.

ROLLS

Learning Outcome

Standards 1 and 2: Combine actions, balances, and weight transfers with movement concepts to perform gymnastics sequences.

Teaching Styles

- Production: divergent to create variety
- Reproduction: practice, reciprocal, and inclusion to choose and practice skill combinations

COMBINING ROLLS, BALANCES, AND LOCOMOTOR SKILLS

Prerequisite skills: stability (chapter 16)—rolling, adding rolls and balances, adding locomotor skills and rolls, and adding locomotor skills and balances

Tasks: Students perform the following tasks.

1. Practice combining traveling, rolling, and balancing skills. Hold each balance in the sequence for a count of three. Keep a tight core to smoothly move the center of balance beyond the base of support in order to start a travel or rolling skill or to stop momentum from a travel or roll in order to connect to a balance. Make connections smooth and fluid, with no hesitation, wobbling, or loss of balance. Inclusion style can be used by giving students the choice to perform smaller segments of a combination. Here are some sample combinations:

   - Forward roll, walkout, front scale
   - Walk to front scale, forward roll to walk
   - Skip, stork stand, step into forward roll
   - Stork stand, step into forward roll, skip to stork stand
   - Slide, side balance, pivot, backward roll
   - Pivot to backward roll, side balance to pivot, slide to side balance to pivot
   - Backward roll, straddle balance, forward roll, gallop
   - Forward roll to gallop, straddle balance to forward roll to gallop, backward roll to straddle

2. Design combinations from the card for creating combinations (figure 21.7). Combine actions and connecting movements that keep movements flowing; use the end of one movement as the beginning of the next movement. Use the inclusion style to give students the choice of combining either two or three skills with different connections.

ACTIONS		
Locomotor	**Roll**	**Balance**
Walking	Sideward	2 feet
Galloping	Forward	1 foot
Skipping	Backward	Feet and hands
Sliding		Bottom
Grapevine		Hands and knee
		"Gymnastics" balances
CONCEPTS FOR CONNECTING ACTIONS		
Body	**Space**	**Effort**
Curl	Direction change (turns)	Speed change
Stretch	Level change (rising, sinking)	
Twist		

Figure 21.7 Card for creating combinations.

Environment: Provide mats. Provide cards (or a large chart projected or posted on a wall) with pictures and words denoting different actions and concepts. Provide blank charts for students to record the actions and concepts they choose for their combinations; they can also use drawings or symbols or videos of their combinations with technology provided by the teacher.

Practice: variable when creating skill combinations, constant when practicing chosen combinations

Closed-skill cues:

- Flowing combinations: End of one movement becomes beginning of next movement.
- Balance to roll: From balance position with center of balance over base of support, move center of balance beyond base of support to shift weight to hands (forward) or lower spine (backward) and start roll. If starting from high balance, hips and legs must bend to get hands or spine close to mat for safe roll.
- Roll to balance: As weight is transferred to upper and middle of spine, push forcefully with hands and position legs and feet to accept weight at end of roll (e.g., straddle, together, one foot in front of the other).
- Locomotor connections: Keep center of balance over moving base; position center of balance just beyond base to transfer weight to body parts for roll or to stop motion and keep center of balance over new balance skill.

Feedback

- KPp: "For fluent motion, combine movements that travel in the same direction."
- KPd: "What should you do to adjust your center of balance to make a smooth connection between your locomotor skills and your roll?"

Assessments

- Standards 1 and 2: Use the completed charts on which students recorded the actions and concepts they chose for their combinations, as well as their drawings, symbols, or videos of their combinations. Ask students, "How did you position your center of balance to keep your movements flowing?"

ROLLING IN RELATIONSHIP TO EQUIPMENT

Prerequisite skills: stability (chapter 16)—rolling, adding jumps and rolls

Task: Students roll along, off of, and onto equipment that is placed on or next to floor mats. Here are specific instructions:

- Perform forward and backward rolls along the tops of trapezoids, folded panel mats, and wedge mats.
- Perform a forward roll off of a folded panel mat, trapezoid, or low bench. Start from a crouch on shins or feet and place hands on floor mat. Tuck head and roll. For safety: always come off of equipment by performing the roll along the floor mat. Do *not* roll forward off of equipment causing the back to hyperextend on the edge of the equipment.
- Perform a backward roll off of a folded panel mat, trapezoid, or low bench. Crouch and roll along and toward the end of the surface. Use the push-off phase of the roll to push the body up and off of the equipment in order to land on the feet on the floor mat.
- Perform a forward roll onto a folded panel mat or trapezoid. Place and keep the hands on the end of the surface. Jump, raising the hips and taking weight on the arms. Tuck head and roll forward along the surface. Run into the jump or use a vaulting board to get the hips high.

Environment: Provide folded panel mats, trapezoids, and low benches, as well as floor mats on which to end the rolls.

Practice: constant, distributed practice

Closed-skill cues:

Forward Roll

- Crouch, raise hips, tuck chin, push off with feet, and roll on rounded back to stand.
  - Off of: Crouch on equipment with hands on floor mat. Tuck and roll.
  - Onto: Stand at end of surface with hands on top. Jump to raise hips above head. Tuck and roll.

Backward Roll

- Crouch with chin tucked, overbalance, and roll back on rounded back. As hands contact mat, push up forcefully, extend hips, and land on feet.
- Off of: Roll backward along surface so hands and head arrive at end of surface. Push forcefully up to raise hips above head and land on feet on floor mat.

Assessment

Standard 1: Use an observation checklist of cues.

FLIGHT

Learning Outcome

- Standards 1 and 2: Combine flight with gymnastics actions and movement concepts to perform a sequence with and without equipment (SHAPE America, 2014).
- Standards 1 and 2: Combine skills and perform variations by using gymnastics actions and movement concepts.

Teaching Styles

- Production: divergent to create variety
- Reproduction: practice, reciprocal, and inclusion to practice chosen skills and combinations

FLIGHT WITH CHANGES IN DIRECTION

Prerequisite skills: locomotor (chapter 15)—flight (jumping; jumping with different body shapes)

Task: Students perform jumps from two feet to two feet and from one foot to two feet with different degrees of turn during flight. Teacher instructs students to "Determine revolutions and the wall to face at the end of the jump turn. To turn quickly, start with a jump straight up and a fast movement of the head to look over the shoulder in the direction of the turn. Stop the head when facing the chosen wall; the body will follow the head. Keep the trunk tight and land on two feet with a slight knee bend to absorb force." Tasks in progression series 2 and 3 can be used for an inclusion-style episode so that students can choose the level that is appropriate for them.

Progression Series 1: Over Small Equipment

- Standing on the floor, practice turning your head quickly to look over your shoulder.
- Half turn: With your partner standing behind you, jump up from two feet, quickly move your head to see your partner, and land on two feet. Your partner should see your face before seeing the front of your body. If not, you're moving your body and head as one unit.
- Practice jumps with quarter and half turns over poly spots, over ropes, and into and out of hoops; turn your head quickly to see the wall before your body faces the wall.

Progression Series 2: Off of Low Equipment

- Stand on a low bench, beam, or trapezoid with your back to the direction you will be facing when you land. Take off from two feet and perform a pencil jump with a half turn. Land on two feet, keeping your head and trunk erect and bending your knees to absorb force.
- Stand on a low bench, beam, or trapezoid facing the opposite wall you will face on landing. Take off from two feet and perform a pencil jump with a half turn. Land on two feet keeping your head and trunk erect and walk backward quickly to take up backward momentum, if necessary.
- Take off from both positions above (with back to the wall you will be facing on landing or facing the wall opposite the wall you will face on landing), moving head quickly to look for and land on poly spots or in hoops placed next to low equipment.
- Take off from the most confident position above (with back to the wall you will be facing on landing or facing the wall opposite the wall you will face on landing) and try a full turn. Move your head quickly, wrap your arms close to your trunk, and look for the wall you started out facing. Land on two feet, keeping your head and trunk erect, and bend your knees to absorb force.

Progression Series 3: From a Run Off of Low Equipment

- No turn: From a run, take off with one foot from a low bench or beam and jump straight up. Land on two feet, bending your knees to absorb force.
- No turn: From a run, take off with one foot from a low bench or beam and jump straight up. At the height of the jump, take and release the shape from a seat kicker, tuck, or star jump. Land on two feet, bending your knees to absorb force.
- Half turn: From a run, take off with one foot from a low bench or beam and jump straight up. At the height of the jump, look quickly over your shoulder to see the opposite wall. Land on two feet, bending your knees to absorb force. If necessary, walk backward quickly to absorb up backward momentum.

Environment: For series 1, scatter poly spots, ropes, and hoops for students to move over. For series 2, provide low benches, beams, and trapezoids for students to take off from and mats for them to land on. For series 3, provide low benches and beams for students to take off from and mats for them to land on.

Practice: Use variable practice for trying different jumps in progression series, constant for practicing chosen jumps. Distribute practice to provide breaks in order to prevent muscle fatigue.

Closed-skill cues:

Jump With a Turn

- Determine revolutions and which wall to face at end of jump turn.
- Keep trunk tight.
- Swing arms up and jump straight up.
- Quickly look over shoulder in direction of turn and spot wall.
- Land on two feet with slight knee bend to absorb force.

Feedback

- KPp: "Remember to jump up and then quickly look over your shoulder so you can turn at the height of your jump."
- KPp: "Swing your arms up by your ears to help give you more height."

Assessment

- Standard 1: Use an evaluation checklist of skill cues.

COMBINING FLIGHT AND ROLLING

Prerequisite skills: stability (chapter 16)—adding jumps and rolls

Task: Students perform jumps before and after rolls and to connect rolls. Teacher instructs students to "Use the crouch position at the end of the roll as the take-off position for the jump; conversely, perform a yielding landing from the jump to start the roll from a crouch." Tasks in the progression series can be used for an inclusion-style episode so that students can choose the level that is appropriate for them. The progression is as follows:

- Pencil jump with half turn into forward roll
- Pencil jump with half turn into backward roll
- Forward roll into pencil jump with half turn
- Backward roll into pencil jump with half turn
- Forward roll, pencil jump with half turn into backward roll
- Backward roll, pencil jump with half turn into forward roll

Environment: Provide mats and inclusion-style task cards.

Practice: Use variable practice for trying different jumps in progression series and constant practice for practicing chosen jumps. Distribute practice to provide breaks in order to prevent dizziness and muscle fatigue.

Closed-skill cues:

- Jump with half turn (see cues given earlier).
- Roll to jump: Use crouch from end of roll as starting position for jump.
- Jump to roll: Perform yielding landing from jump as crouch to start roll.

Feedback

- KPd: "After your roll, you stood up and then performed your jump." Followed by:
- KPp: "What must you do to smoothly connect your roll and jump?"

Assessment

Standards 1 and 2: Use an inclusion-style criteria sheet (figure 21.8).

Name _____

Directions:

- Put a check mark by the level that you think you can perform with practice.
- Try it!
- If too easy or too hard, put an X by your new choice.
- Practice three times, then self-assess with critical elements.
- Repeat as often as necessary to reach goal.

Level	Self-assessment	Set 1	Set 2	Set 3	Set 4
1. Jump with half turn to roll	Half turn				
2. Roll to jump with half turn	End of jump as start of roll				
3. Roll, jump with half turn, roll	End of roll as start of jump				

Figure 21.8 Inclusion-style criteria sheet.

Task: Students perform jumps off of low equipment into yielding landings and roll; specifically, they land the jump on two feet and immediately crouch and roll. Students can use task cards with a list of challenges to perform and, when ready, ask a classmate or the teacher to check their performance.

- Perform jumps from both feet to both feet off of low equipment from a standing position.
- Into a forward roll
- Half turn, landing, forward roll
- Seat kicker, landing, forward roll
- Tuck jump, landing, forward roll
- Star jump, landing, forward roll
- Half turn into backward roll
- One-foot takeoff on a run from low equipment, landing on two feet

Environment: Spread out low benches, beams, and trapezoids with landing mats for multiple students to try the different challenges.

Practice: Use variable practice for trying different jumps and constant practice for practicing chosen jumps. Distribute practice to provide breaks in order to prevent muscle fatigue.

Closed-skill cues:

- Yielding landing flows into roll.
- Complete half turn in air.
- Take shape quickly at height of jump and release it to land with feet together, then crouch and roll.

Feedback

- KPp: "Swing your arms up by your ears to help keep your trunk erect when you take off and perform shapes and turns in the air."

Assessments

- Standard 1: Use an observation checklist of skill cues.
- Standard 2: Describe how to perform movements to create flowing sequences of jumps with turns, jumps to rolls, and jumps with turns to rolls.

FLIGHT IN RELATIONSHIP TO EQUIPMENT

Prerequisite skills: locomotor (chapter 15)—flight; stability (chapter 16)—rolls, adding jumps and rolls

Task: Students move through the obstacle courses by performing jumps and leaps over low equipment, jumping onto equipment, and jumping off of equipment (*no* leaping off of equipment as it is unsafe to land on one foot from a height). They design combinations of skills along each obstacle course by using the choice card for skill combination (figure 21.9). All rolls must be performed from a two-foot landing. Students practice connecting skills to make movements flow without hesitations and stops.

Flight	Rolls	Body and space	Relationship to equipment
2 feet to 2 feet 1 foot to 2 feet Leap	Forward Backward	Half turn in air Shapes in air • Pencil • Seat kicker • Star	Over Onto Off of

Name _____

Record your obstacle course skill combinations:

1. _____   _____   _____   _____

2. _____   _____   _____   _____

Figure 21.9   Choice card for skill combination.

Environment: Provide low benches, beams, trapezoids, folded panel mats, vaulting boards, landing mats, ropes, and hoops. Sequence equipment to elicit different combinations of skills. Students can adjust the distance between pieces of equipment to accommodate their chosen movements.

> Obstacle course 1: vaulting board and landing mat; two hoops; low bench and landing mat
>
> Obstacle course 2: Panel mat, trapezoid, and landing mat; two ropes in V shape
>
> Obstacle course 3: Low beam and landing mat; trapezoid, hoop on landing mat
>
> Obstacle course 4: vaulting board, panel mat, suspended slanted rope over landing mat

Practice: variable when trying different skill combinations, constant when practicing for flow in chosen combinations

Closed-skill cues:

- Flow: End of one movement becomes beginning of next movement.

Assessments

- Standard 1: Use an observation checklist for flow.
- Standard 2: Ask students, "What should you do to achieve flow in your skill combinations?"

WHEELS

Learning Outcome
- Standards 1 and 2: Perform wheeling actions varied by movement concepts.
- Standard 3: Chart and analyze changes in strength.

Teaching Style
- Reproduction: practice, reciprocal, and inclusion to practice cartwheels

CARTWHEEL

Prerequisite skills: stability (chapter 16)—wheels

Task: Students start in a standing position with one foot in front of the other, the weight on the back foot, and the arms raised overhead. They then perform a cartwheel using a hand-hand-foot-foot pattern with the legs passing overhead. The inclusion style can be used by allowing students to find the environment that helps them perform the cartwheel pattern and get the feet over the head.

Environment:
- Cartwheel down an incline created by a folded panel mat with a wedge mat against the end.
- Cartwheel off the end of a folded panel mat with hands on mat and feet stepping onto floor.
- Cartwheel over an inclined rope.
- Cartwheel over two parallel ropes, placing the first hand between the ropes.
- Cartwheel over two ropes shaped in a V. Place your hands on the opposite side of the V from where you're standing and at the farthest possible distance (created by the V) that you can create enough force to cartwheel over.
- Cartwheel placing the hands and feet along a curved line.
- Cartwheel placing the hands and feet along the straight line.
- Cartwheel up an incline formed by a wedge mat pressed up against a folded panel mat.

Practice: Use constant practice of skills, increasing the number of repetitions as strength develops. Vary practice among types of skill.

Closed-skill cues:
- Hand, hand, foot, foot, straight legs in V above head.
- Start in standing position with arms raised above head and one foot in front of the other.
- As weight is taken onto first hand, swing back leg up and push off with front leg.
- As weight comes off of first hand, swing leg lands.
- Push off with second hand, raise trunk, and step down on second leg.

Cartwheel: beginning *(a)*, action *(b, c)*, recovery *(d)*.

Assessments

- Standard 1: Use an observation checklist of cues.
- Standard 3: Use the cartwheel time line (figure 21.10).

	Down an incline or off the end of a panel mat	Along a curved line	Along a straight line	Up an incline
Date				

Figure 21.10   Cartwheel time line.

VAULTS

Learning Outcome

- Standards 1 and 2: Perform vaulting actions varied by movement concepts.

Teaching Style

- Reproduction: practice, reciprocal, and inclusion to practice vaults

VAULTING FROM A VAULTING BOARD OVER EQUIPMENT

Prerequisite skills: stability (chapter 16)—vaults

Task: Students approach a vaulting board from a run and take off with two feet using a "punch" action.

- Tuck front vault: Place the hands on top of surface with the fingers pointing toward end and the elbows straight. Raise the hips and tuck the knees to vault sideways over the surface. Land with side to the surface.
- Piked front vault: Place the hands on top of the surface with the fingers pointing toward the end and the elbows straight. Raise the hips with the legs in pike to vault sideways over the surface. Land with side to surface.
- Flank vault: Place the hands on top of the surface with the fingers pointing forward and the elbows straight. Raise the hips and straight legs out to the side, keeping the side (flank) facing the surface. Remove the inside hand to let the body pass over the surface. Land with the back to the surface.
- Squat vault: Place the hands shoulder-width apart on the surface with the fingers pointing forward and the elbows straight. Tuck the knees to the chest, push off from the hands, and land with the back to the surface. If necessary, proceed with a squat onto the surface.

Environment: Place a vaulting board in front of a vaulting surface made from stacked panel mats or stacked trapezoids.

Practice: Use constant practice of skills, increasing the number of repetitions as strength develops. Vary practice among the types of skill.

Closed-skill cues:

All Vaults

- Approach vaulting board from a run.
- Take off with one foot and bring feet together low in air.
- Punch off of board with balls of both feet.

Front Vaults

- Position elbows straight and fingers pointed toward end of surface.
- Raise hips.
- Front of body passes over surface (tuck or pike position).
- Land on two feet with side to surface.

Flank Vault

- Position elbows straight and fingers pointed forward.
- Raise hips and legs out to side (flank to surface).
- Remove inside hand.
- Land on two feet with back to surface.

Flank vault: preparation *(a)*, action *(b)*, recovery *(c)*.

Squat Vault

- Position elbows straight and fingers pointed forward.
- Raise hips and tuck body between arms.
- Push off with hands and keep head up.
- Land on two feet with back to surface.

Feedback

- KPp: "Punch the vaulting board hard to help you raise your hips high."
- KPp: "Keep your head and chest up to make a more balanced landing."

Squat vault.

Assessment

Standard 1: Use an observation checklist of cues.

Application-Level Task Progressions

Instructional task progressions for the application level in grades 3 through 5 (table 21.6) are based on the combination-level progressions. Students should be able to perform the combination-level skills in a gymnastics action category (e.g., balance, rolling) before starting the application-level progressions; refer to the prerequisite skills provided with the application-level learning tasks.

Table 21.6 Task Progressions for Gymnastics: Application Level

Gymnastics actions	
Balance **Rolling** **Flight** **Step-like**	Equipment: boxes, benches, trapezoids, beams, foam shapes, vaulting board, hoops, ropes, tires

	Learning outcome: performing, varying, and combining gymnastics actions into sequences
	 • Inverted balances and roll combinations
	 • Balancing with partner relationship of support
	 • Flight in symmetrical and asymmetrical shapes
	 • Wheeling
	 • Vaulting over equipment
	 • Sequencing rolls, flights, balances, and step-like actions
	     ○ On mats
	     ○ In relationship to equipment
	     ○ In relationship to others and equipment

SPECIALIZED SKILLS

BALANCE

Learning Outcome

- Standards 1 and 2: Perform, vary, and combine gymnastics actions in gymnastics sequences.
- Standard 4: Work cooperatively with others.

Teaching Style

- Reproduction: practice, reciprocal, and inclusion to practice cartwheels

INVERTED BALANCES AND ROLL COMBINATIONS

Prerequisite skills: combination-level balancing in inverted positions and rolling in relationship to equipment

Task: Students perform a handstand and variations.

1. Start in standing position with the arms raised, step forward, place the palms on the mat with the fingers spread, and kick the legs up above the head one after the other. Keep the trunk tight (pull in the abs) and align the shoulders over the hands, the hips over the shoulders, the heels over the head, and the head with the shoulders. Focus the eyes on the fingertips. Work in groups of four—either two performing and two spotting or one performing, one spotting, and two observing (using the handstand checklist in figure 21.11).

   - Perform a handstand from walking up a wall; start crouched with the back to the wall and the hands about 2 feet (0.6 meter) from the wall.
   - Perform a handstand from kicking up against a wall; start by facing the wall and placing the hands about 1 foot (0.3 meter) from the wall.

- Perform a handstand with two spotters and then with one spotter; spotters are positioned on either side, grasping the lower leg just below the knee to stabilize the performer.
- Continue to use a spotter until performer can consistently do the handstand and safely recover.
- Practice holding handstands for at least three seconds and coming back down with one leg after the other.
- When in a handstand, move the legs into different positions: knees bent, straddle, split with legs straight or bent. (Tell the spotter where the legs will be moved.)

2. Perform a handstand forward roll. From a handstand, keep the trunk tight and slightly overbalance. Bend the elbows, tuck the head, and flex the hips. Roll along the rounded back to a stand. (Use spotters to stop the performer in the handstand position, before starting the roll.)

3. Perform a backward extension roll from equipment. Start a backward roll from a crouch, rolling along and toward the end of a folded panel mat or trapezoid. As the hands forcefully push off of the surface, the hips extend and the straight legs are pushed up into the air. The legs are brought down, and the feet land on the floor mat. To work on getting closer to a handstand, try to extend the body over a rope suspended at different heights close to the end of the folded panel mat or trapezoid.

Environment: Locate a handstand station near a wall with mats. Groups of four can take turns spotting, performing, and giving feedback.

Practice: Use constant, distributed practice to help students get a "feel" for inverted balances; increase the number of repetitions as strength develops.

Closed-skill cues:

Handstand

- Step forward and place palms on mat with fingers spread.
- Kick legs up above head one after the other.
- Keep trunk tight (pull in abs).
- Align shoulders over hands, hips over shoulders, heels over head, and head in line with shoulders.
- Focus eyes on fingertips.

Handstand Forward Roll

- From handstand, keep trunk tight and slightly overbalance.
- Bend elbows, tuck head, and flex hips.
- Roll along rounded back to stand.

Handstand.

Handstand forward roll: preparation *(a)*, action *(b)*, recovery *(c)*.

Back Extension Roll From Equipment

- Roll backward toward end of folded panel mat or trapezoid.
- As hands push forcefully, extend hips and raise legs toward ceiling.
- Lower legs to land on feet.

Back extension roll from equipment: preparation *(a)*, action *(b)*, recovery *(c)*.

Feedback

- KPp (handstand): "Pull in your abdomen and look down at your hands to avoid arching your back."
- KPdp (handstand forward roll): "You are tucking your head too soon and coming straight down on your shoulders. Remember to overbalance slightly, bend your elbows, and then tuck your head."

Assessment

Standards 1, 2, and 4: Use an observation checklist of handstand skill cues and spotting cues (figure 21.11).

Name _____

Handstand skill cues	Yes	Needs work.	Spotting cues	Yes	Needs work.
Puts palms on mat, spreads fingers, and focuses eyes on fingertips.			Stands to side.		
Kicks legs above head one after the other.			Grabs calf just below knee on way up.		
Keeps trunk tight.			Uses spotting actions to aid (stabilize) performer.		
Aligns shoulders over hands, hips over shoulders, heels over head, and head in line with shoulders.			Encourages performer.		

Figure 21.11 Peer assessment for handstand skill and spotting.

PARTNER SUPPORT BALANCES

Prerequisite skills: combination-level balancing with partner relationships of countertension and counterbalance

Task: Students perform partner support balances (Ward, 1997) with someone close to the same weight and size. They support the partner's lower body weight—*not* all of the partner's weight. Both partners must keep a tight core and lock elbows once in the support position. The base partner is in a standing position, or on hands and knees, or lying on the back (either with the knees bent or with the legs extended). The top partner is in a push-up position with the hands on the mat and the feet supported by the base partner. Each partner balance *starts*, however, with the base partner in position and the top person in a push-up position with the legs *on either side of the base* and close to the partner's body part that will support the weight in the balance position. The top partner moves one leg at a time onto the base partner or into the base partner's hands. The support balance is held for 5 to 10 seconds. The top partner then brings down one leg at a time to end the support, and the partners switch positions. Partners should talk to one another about the timing of actions and the placement of body parts. Once they are in the support position, they should count together, encourage each other, and then celebrate!

Enrichment: Try balances with the top partner in a reverse push-up position (i.e., with bottom facing the floor).

Environment: Provide mats. If the top partner is unable to hold self up in a push-up position, the base partners can support more of the top partner's weight by holding and supporting the thighs, just above the knees. Students can practice the top position by using a folded panel mat as the base partner.

Practice: Use variable practice when trying new balances. Use constant, distributed practice to become consistent and to increase the length of time for which support positions are held as strength develops.

Closed-skill cues:

- Communicate with partner.
- Keep core tight.
- Lock elbows when in the support position.
- Go into and come out of partner support one leg at a time.

Feedback

KPp: "Let your partner know when you're ready for her or him to take your weight."

Assessment

Standards 1 and 4: Use an observation checklist of skill cues and interactions.

FLIGHT

Learning Outcome

- Standards 1 and 2: Perform, vary, and combine gymnastics actions in gymnastics sequences.

Teaching Styles

- Reproduction: practice, reciprocal, and inclusion for repetition
- Production: divergent for creating flight shapes

FLIGHT IN SYMMETRICAL AND ASYMMETRICAL SHAPES

Prerequisite skills: combination-level flight

Task: Students perform jumps into symmetrical shapes and asymmetrical shapes off of low equipment and from vaulting boards onto floor mats. Symmetrical shapes are created when both sides of the body match (e.g., tuck jump, star jump); in asymmetrical shapes, the sides of the body move into different positions (e.g., one arm raised, other arm out to side; one knee bent, one leg straight). Teacher instructs students "Whenever a shape is performed in the air, form the shape quickly at the height of the jump, release it, and quickly bring the legs together to land with the feet together. If necessary, crouch and roll to absorb momentum."

Symmetrical Shapes

- Straddle jump: Take off with two feet. At the height of the jump, flex the hips and straddle the legs (spread the legs apart). Extend the hips and bring the feet together. Land on both feet and bend the knees to absorb force.
- Pike jump: Take off from two feet. At the height of the jump, flex the hips and raise straight legs together. Extend the hips and bring the legs down together. Land on both feet and bend the knees to absorb force.
- Create symmetrical shapes by varying arm and leg position and making sure that both sides of the body move in the same way at the same time.

Asymmetrical Shapes

- L-arms pencil jump: Take off from two feet. At the height of the jump, raise one arm up and the other out to the side. Land on both feet and bend the knees to absorb force.
- 4 jump: Take off from two feet. At the height of the jump, bring the inside of one foot to the other knee. Raise the arms out to the sides. Extend the hips and bring the legs down together. Land on both feet and bend the knees to absorb force.
- Stag jump: Take off from two feet. At the height of the jump, bring the inside of one foot to the other knee and raise one arm up and the other out to the side. Extend the hips and bring the legs down together. Land on both feet and bend the knees to absorb force.
- Create asymmetrical shapes by varying arm and leg position and making sure that the limbs on either side of the body move to different positions.

Perform jumps into symmetrical shapes and asymmetrical shapes on the floor mat from a standing position or preceded by a few steps or a short run. Perform a yielding landing by going into a forward or backward roll.

Environment: Set up one or more stations with folded panel mats, trapezoids, benches, and vaulting boards to take off from onto floor mats.

Practice: variable practice when trying different jumps; constant, distributed practice to become consistent, with an increasing number of repetitions as strength develops

Closed-skill cues:

Flight Into Symmetrical Shape

- Use forceful leg spring and upward arm thrust to gain height.
- Keep head and chest up throughout jump to remain in balance.
- At height of jump, quickly take shape with both sides of body matching.
- Release shape and bring legs together to land on both feet.
- To absorb force, bend knees (or bend knees and roll).

Flight into symmetrical shape.

Flight Into Asymmetrical Shape

- Use forceful leg spring and upward arm thrust to gain height.
- Keep head and chest up throughout jump to remain in balance.
- At height of jump, quickly take shape with each side of body in a different position.
- Release shape and bring legs together to land on both feet.
- To absorb force, bend knees (or bend knees and roll).

Feedback

- KPp: "To gain more height, thrust your arms up at takeoff."
- KPp: "For safe landings, quickly release shape and bring your legs together to land on both feet."

Assessments

- Standard 1: Use an observation checklist of skill cues.
- Standard 2: Ask students, "How would you explain to a new classmate the timing for taking shape during a jump? How would you explain the difference between a symmetrical shape and an asymmetrical shape?"

Flight into asymmetrical shape.

WHEELS

Learning Outcome

- Standards 1 and 2: Perform, vary, and combine gymnastics actions in gymnastics sequences.

Teaching Style

- Reproduction (practice, reciprocal, and inclusion)

ROUND-OFF

Prerequisite skills: combination-level cartwheels

Task: Students perform a round-off. This move starts out like a cartwheel, but the legs are then brought together and a quarter turn is performed in the inverted position, followed by a landing on two feet with the legs together. A round-off is an important connecting movement for advanced gymnastics skills, such as back handsprings. Students can work in pairs or groups of three to help each other with the turn.

- From a surface: To give students more time to perform the new turn and the leg action, they can perform the round-off off of folded panel mats and land on floor mats. If necessary, spotters can stand to the same side as the performer's first arm down and place their hands on the performer's thighs to help with the quarter turn.
- Along the floor: Students can precede the step into the round-off with a crow hop (i.e., a step-hop raising the knee of the free leg) to add momentum. They use a strong push from the shoulders during the quarter turn to land on both feet with the head and chest up.

Environment: Create a station with folded panel mats and floor mats.

Practice: Use constant, distributed practice and increase the number of repetitions as strength and timing develop.

Closed-skill cues:

- Crow-hop on leg opposite of first arm down.
- Start cartwheel action (hand, hand).
- Bring legs together at top of inverted position.
- Perform quick quarter turn of hips and push from shoulders.
- Land on both feet with legs together.

Roundoff: preparation *(a)*, action *(b, c)*, recovery *(d)*.

Feedback

- KPp: "Connect the crow hop to the beginning of the round-off with a quick swing overhead of your free leg and a strong push with your other leg."
- KPp: "Perform a quick quarter turn as soon as your legs come together in the inverted position."

Assessment

Standard 1: Use an observation checklist of skill cues.

VAULTS

Learning Outcome

- Standards 1 and 2: Perform, vary, and combine gymnastics actions in gymnastics sequences.

Teaching Style

- Reproduction (practice, reciprocal, and inclusion for repetition)

VAULTING OVER EQUIPMENT

Prerequisite skills: combination-level vaults

Task: Vaults in the application level are more difficult as a result of body position, amplitude, or variations.

1. Approach the vaulting board from a run and take off with two feet using a "punch" action.
   - High front vault: Place the hands on top of the surface with the fingers pointing toward the end and the elbows straight. Raise the hips and forcefully open into the pike position, thrusting the feet toward the ceiling (handstand position). Flex at the hips to pike down and land with the side to the surface.
   - Straddle vault: Place the hands shoulder-width apart on the surface with the fingers pointing forward and the elbows straight. Raise the hips and straddle the legs. Push off from the hands and land with the back to the surface. If necessary, precede with straddle onto surface.

2. Vary vaults by adding a change of direction before landing. Look quickly and face in the direction of the intended landing. Try quarter and half rotations when in the air, at the height of the push-off from the surface before landing:

- Front vault
- Flank vault
- Squat vault
- Straddle vault

3. Vary vaults by adding a roll, or a turn and a roll, after landing on the feet. Keep the head and chest up while landing before starting the roll away from the vault equipment. Try forward rolls, backward rolls, and turns into rolls after the following:

- Front vault
- Flank vault
- Squat vault
- Straddle vault

Environment: Place a vaulting board in front of a vaulting surface made from stacked panel mats or stacked trapezoids. Provide floor mats for landing.

Practice: Use constant practice of vaults with an increasing number of repetitions as strength develops. Vary practice among types of vault and types of variation.

Closed-skill cues:

For All Vaults

- Approach vaulting board from a run.
- Take off with one foot and bring feet together low in air.
- Punch off of board with balls of both feet.

High Front Vault

- Position elbows straight and fingers pointed toward end of surface.
- Raise hips and forcefully open pike position, thrusting feet toward ceiling.
- Body passes over surface in handstand position.
- Flex at hips to pike down and land on both feet with side to surface.

Straddle Vault

- Place hands shoulder-width apart on surface with fingers pointing forward and elbows straight.
- Raise hips and straddle legs.
- Push off from hands and bring legs together.
- Land with back to surface.

Straddle vault: preparation *(a)*, action *(b)*, recovery *(c)*.

Adding Quarter or Half Turn at End of Vault

- Add turn at height of push-off from vaulting surface
- Look quickly and face direction of intended landing.

Adding Roll, or Turn and Roll, After Landing

- Keep head and chest up while landing.
- Bend knees into yielding landing and roll away from vault surface.
- If landing with side to vault surface, perform quarter turn into roll.

Feedback

KPp (straddle): "Push off from the surface as your hips reach the highest point to be able to land with your head and chest up."

Assessment

Standard 1: Use an observation checklist of skill cues.

SEQUENCES

Learning Outcome

- Standards 1 and 2: Perform, vary, and combine gymnastics actions in gymnastics sequences.
- Standard 4: Work cooperatively with others.

Teaching Styles

- Reproduction: practice, reciprocal, inclusion for repetition of sequences
- Production: divergent discovery for creating sequences

PERFORMING GYMNASTICS SEQUENCES

Prerequisite skills: combination level—combining balances; combining rolls, balances, and locomotor skills; combining flight and rolls

Introduction: Gymnastics sequences can be designed by the teacher or by students. Teachers can designate the specific order in which to combine gymnastics actions and concepts or give students the choice of the order for the chosen movements. Students can select skills from gymnastics-action and movement-concept cards and then decide the order; alternatively, they can design sequences of their own. The purpose of a gymnastics sequence is to connect movements into smooth and flowing sequences without hesitations, wobbles, or stops. Sequences can be varied by making changes in the following aspects:

- Order of skills
- Difficulty of skills
- How skills are connected
- How equipment is used
- Relationship to a partner

From the following options, choose a sequence that you think you can perform with few hesitations and no stops. Perform your sequence for a partner and get feedback about how well you performed. Next, work with your partner to change both of your sequences by choosing from the following:

- Changing the order or difficulty of a skill
- Adding a turn or change of speed between two skills

- Using a folded panel mat, hoop, or trapezoid in the sequence
- Performing in unison with your partner

Here are some sample sequences:

- Sequence 1: grapevine to pivot turn, forward roll to headstand to knee–foot balance
- Sequence 2: forward roll, front scale, handstand scissor kick, backward roll, knee scale
- Sequence 3: cartwheel, backward roll to straddle stand, forward roll, slide to side balance

Work with a partner to create sequences using the task card in figure 21.12. Use connections and at least three categories of gymnastics action to create a sequence of six skills performed in relationship to your partner in one of the following ways:

- Leading and following one another
- Being next to each other
- Meeting with and parting from each other

Connections	Gymnastics actions
Changes in the following: • Shape • Level • Direction • Pathway • Speed	Rolls: forward, backward
	Balances: gymnastics upright balances
	Inverted balances: shoulder stand, tripod, headstand, handstand, handstand scissor kick, handstand to forward roll
	Flight: leap; jumps (half turn, pencil, seat kicker, tuck, star, straddle, pike, stag)
	Turns: pivot, crossover, swing, wind-up, push
	Wheels: cartwheel, roundoff
	Vaults: front, flank, squat, straddle

Figure 21.12 Task card for creating sequences.

1. Create and perform sequences in relationship to equipment. Use gymnastics actions and connections to try different ways to do the following:
   - Mounting (getting onto) equipment: from a roll or from a jump
   - Moving along equipment: locomotor, rolling, flight, or step-like actions
   - Balancing on equipment: upright balances, turns, inverted balances
   - Dismounting (getting off of) equipment: jumps, rolls, step-like actions
2. Create tracks of gymnastics equipment and mats. Perform sequences of gymnastics actions and connections through the tracks. Here are some examples:
   - Floor mat, folded panel mat, wedge, floor mat, vaulting board, trapezoid, floor mat
   - Wedge mat, floor mat, beam, trapezoid, floor mat
   - Vaulting board, trapezoid, folded panel mat, two stacked and folded panel mats, floor mat, beam, floor mat

Environment: Set up multiple stations with appropriately placed mats and low equipment (e.g., trapezoids, folded panel mats, benches, beams).

Practice: variable when trying new skills and variations, constant when practicing for a smooth and flowing sequence

Closed-skill cues:

Sequences

- Use ending movement or position of first skill as beginning action or position of next skill.
- Keep core tight.
- Use good technique.
- Make rolls compact.
- Keep balances steady.
- Take and release flight shapes and turns at height of jump.
- Perform wheels with legs above head.
- Perform vaults over equipment with compact positions and landings.

Feedback

- KPp: "Connect actions that promote flow rather than create breaks."
- KPd: "How did you decide which movements to connect?"

Assessment

Standards 1 and 2: Use an observation checklist of skill cues, including all parts indicated in the task description.

 Visit the web resource for learning activities, video clips, and review questions.

Chapter 22

Fitness Education for Grades 3 Through 5

Debra Ballinger

Key Concepts

- Describing developmentally appropriate applications of the FITT guidelines and principles of exercise for children in grades 3 through 5

- Describing best practices in fitness education

- Selecting and using fitness assessments to teach and plan for developmentally appropriate fitness education

- Identifying fitness education programs for youth in grades 3 through 5 that meet SHAPE America guidelines and national mandates for comprehensive school wellness

- Identifying technology for enhancing physical activity and fitness among children in grades 3 through 5

- Selecting fitness education learning experiences that meet national standards for K-12 physical education

Developmental physical education helps children acquire the fundamental and specialized movement skills that give them the movement repertoire to engage in a physically active lifestyle. By the time children enter grade 3, they have the physical capacity to acquire specialized movement skills specific to the components of physical fitness. Therefore, this chapter focuses on understanding and implementing national physical education standard 3: "The physically literate individual demonstrates the knowledge and skills to achieve and maintain a health-enhancing level of physical activity and fitness" (SHAPE America, 2014, p. 12). The intent of this standard is to help children establish patterns of regular participation in physical activity and acquire the knowledge and skills to achieve and maintain physical fitness. Thus standard 3 serves two purposes by encouraging both daily physical activity and physical fitness. To help you achieve these purposes, this chapter details fitness guidelines and best practices, current fitness education programs, and standards-based fitness learning experiences.

FITT GUIDELINES

Guidelines for fitness programming are commonly referred to as the FITT (frequency, intensity, time, and type) guidelines or principles. Children and their parents need to fully understand these guidelines and how following them can benefit a child's overall health and well-being.

Let's take a closer look at each FITT element. *Frequency* refers simply to how often an activity occurs—that is, how many days per week a child performs a specific type of activity. *Intensity* refers to the level of stress placed on the body as a whole or on a particular body system during activity—in practical terms, how hard an activity feels. Intensity is typically assessed either by monitoring physiological indexes (e.g., heart rate, breathing rate) or by the determining the amount of perceived exertion needed to complete an activity. Whereas K-2 children have difficulty with pacing themselves and monitoring their intensity of activity, children in grades 3 through 5 are generally ready to discern differences in activity intensity, which therefore becomes a major focus of fitness education for this age group.

Methods of monitoring and assessing intensity are addressed more completely in the technology section of this chapter. For now, here is a brief summary of how intensity can be measured for activities focused on cardiorespiratory effect, strength building, and flexibility. For cardiorespiratory intensity, the typical assessment strategy is to monitor heart rate. Specifically, children should be taught that moderate physical activity refers to an intensity equal to brisk walking and that it can be performed for a relatively long time without fatigue. In contrast, vigorous physical activity expends more energy—that is, it is performed at a higher intensity—than brisk walking. For strength training, intensity is typically measured in terms the amount of weight lifted. For flexibility, intensity relates to the amount of discomfort felt as an individual stretches or attempts to increase the range of motion of a joint. In all three areas, the goal is

for children to be able to recognize the differences between light, moderate, and vigorous activity and to adjust the intensity to meet the recommended daily guidelines.

The *time* of activity refers to the length or duration of an activity session or bout. Children should achieve a cumulative daily total of at least 60 minutes of moderate to vigorous physical activity (MVPA) in order to maintain a health-enhancing level of fitness. Recent research has demonstrated that the 60 minutes can be accumulated through multiple activity bouts (each lasting 15 minutes or longer) spread throughout the day (Physical Activity Guidelines for All Americans Midcourse Report, 2012, Chapter 2, p. 2). For example, the accumulated time of 60 minutes might be reached by doing 30 minutes of MVPA in physical education class, one 15-minute bout during morning recess, and another 15-minute bout during afternoon recess. Unfortunately, however, children seldom achieve 15 minutes of MVPA in a 15-minute recess, which makes it critical for teachers to encourage classroom teachers, as well as parents and caregivers, to provide children with opportunities for physical activity outside of school. In fact, recent research has shown that parental influence and an atmosphere of activity in the home are critical factors in reversing the trends of sedentary living and obesity (Ostbye et al., 2013).

The last item in the FITT guidelines is the *type* of activity. Physical educators play a major role in providing children with a variety of activities. They also offer new and exciting activities that not only help children achieve their targeted intensity levels but also afford opportunities for challenge and success.

EXERCISE PRINCIPLES

Whereas the FITT guidelines provide general parameters for creating a fitness program, the exercise principles affect how activities lead to increases in fitness and health. This section provides a summary of the following exercise principles:

uniqueness, progression and overload, specificity, regularity, and reversibility.

As children in grades 3 through 5 recognize, different activity choices bring out different competencies, both between and within individuals. Similarly, the principles of exercise and conditioning affect each child independently from his or her peers. This differentiation between individuals is commonly referred to as the **principle of uniqueness**. For many children, the most important lesson they learn may be that each of them is unique and responds to training in their own way, at their own rate, and with their own results.

Just as children at this level quickly recognize that their peers are talented and skilled at different sports and activities, they also quickly learn that the *lack* of talent can result in teasing or being left out when teams or groups are formed. Teaching them about the principle of uniqueness helps them understand that some children will have a lifelong battle with obesity, whereas others will remain slender regardless of the foods they eat. Similarly, some children anticipate the path of an oncoming ball more readily than others, thus leading to a higher batting average. Some show signs of muscular strength quickly, whereas others may work for months and never attain the same muscular definition. In the midst of these differences, children should be encouraged to develop their own unique strengths, and this process can begin with selecting different types of activity in physical education in grades 3 through 5.

The principle of progression and overload refers to the fact that physiological enhancements in strength and physical conditioning take place only if the system is stressed beyond its normal levels of functioning. In other words, children in elementary school need to learn that gains in strength and endurance require working beyond what is easy. They need to apply overload of time or weight to their training regimen in order to see regular increases. They also need to learn that too much overload results in injury or failure. Therefore, teachers should guide children in creating a progression that is optimally challenging and help them learn to set progressive goals, monitor their progress, and revise their plan as goals are met. Goal setting matters not only for the purpose of progression and overload but also as a skill critical to healthy living throughout the lifespan.

The principle of specificity refers to the fact that changes in any body system or segment occur only if that specific area of the body is targeted or overloaded. Teachers can demonstrate the principle of specificity by having students compare grip strength or skill based on a child's dominant side versus the child's nondominant side; the dominant side is typically stronger due to regular use and activity. The principle of specificity is also emphasized by new fitness assessments for hip and shoulder flexibility. As teachers use these assessments (discussed later), they can point out that each joint and body part is specific. Therefore, in order to increase a joint's range of motion, a person must stretch or actively overload that specific joint.

The **principles of regularity** and **reversibility** relate to the popular saying "use it or lose it." Children need to be taught that when a person stops being active, any gains that he or she had made in fitness and weight management will be reversed and may even decline (perhaps at a faster rate than that of the original gains). Again, each individual responds differently to inactivity, but, in general, failure to engage in regular exercise leads to rapid declines in strength, endurance, and flexibility.

Table 22.1 highlights and provides examples of the principles of training, as well as the FITT guidelines.

SKILL-RELATED FITNESS DEVELOPMENT

Skill-related fitness is critical to successful performance of recreational sport and lifetime physical activities. Students need to develop basic skills and concepts common to all movement forms in order to become self-sufficient in health-related fitness activities (Ayers & Sariscsany, 2011, p. 157). Teachers also need to help children understand the relationship between skill-related concepts and growth and development. The teacher's focus should be on defining both health-related and skill-related fitness and explaining how each can be improved. To reiterate, when teaching health-related fitness, the emphasis should be placed on students' work toward obtaining and maintaining a healthful level of aerobic (cardiorespiratory) fitness, muscular fitness (strength and endurance), flexibility (joint range of motion), and body composition (which is influenced by both physical activity and nutrition).

Skill-related fitness comprises multiple factors influenced heavily by both genetics and practice:

Table 22.1 FITT Guidelines and Principles of Training

Guidelines and principles	Definition and example(s)
F = frequency	How often (days per week) an activity occurs Example: daily physical activity
I = intensity	Level of stress placed on the body or on a body system—light, moderate, or vigorous for heart rate; amount of resistance for strength training; amount of stress or pull for stretching Example: Walking fast vs. a jog vs. a sprint
T = time	Amount of time (minutes) per exercise or activity session or bout Example: 60 minutes of physical activity accumulated in a day
T = type	Activity selected to achieve a goal Examples: brisk walking, running, strength training, stretching
Principle of uniqueness (individuality)	Each individual is unique and responds uniquely to training (individual differences theory). Example: Each child has a specific body type, bone structure, and pattern of activity and, therefore, will respond to exercise differently.
Principle of overload	Positive change requires working the system beyond what is normal for it. Examples: adding two minutes per day to a walking session, adding 2.5 lb to the barbell lifted, reaching half an inch farther during the sit-and-reach test
Principle of progression	Overload must be increased gradually in order to be safe and effective. Example: Beginning with using only body weight for lunges, then adding 1 lb weight, then 3 lb weights
Principle of specificity	Changes in any body system or segment occur only if that specific area is targeted or overloaded (note: does not apply to fat reduction). Examples: Doing arm curls does not increase strength in the legs. Flexibility (range of motion) in the right hip may differ from that in the left hip.
Principle of regularity	Physical activity must be done regularly to avoid reduction in strength, endurance, and flexibility and to minimize the risk of injury (use it or lose it!). Example: Running for 30 continuous minutes or three 10 minute bouts during one day, a minimum of 4-5 times per week
Principle of reversibility	Gains achieved through training are lost through inactivity (this principle is often combined with the principle of regularity). Example: If you can run 1 mile in 10 minutes and then you stop running for two weeks, it is likely you will not be able to achieve running 1 mile in 10 minutes due to lack of cardiovascular exercise.

agility, balance, coordination, power, reaction time, and speed. Balance, power, and speed require muscular strength and endurance. Teaching children about this connection helps them understand the importance of health-related fitness and motivates them to engage in exercises and activities that increase muscle fitness.

BEST PRACTICES FOR FITNESS EDUCATION

The fact that children's bodies are not merely smaller versions of adult bodies has been recognized for some time. Still, many teachers try to apply to children the same training principles and FITT guidelines that they themselves use for conditioning. Best practice dictates a different approach to applying the FITT guidelines to children. Just as K-2 children cannot accurately pace their cardiorespiratory intensity, and require many breaks in activity, children in grades 3 through 5 also differ from adults in their ability to pace themselves or engage in long-term MVPA. As with sport skills, fitness skills and test items must be taught with careful attention to both content knowledge and movement forms. Activities must be developed with an eye toward promoting physical activity, enjoyment, and safety in a progression from simplest to more complex. The Physical Activity Pyramid for Kids (Corbin et al., 2010; Corbin & Le Masurier, 2014; Ayers & Sariscsany, 2011) was developed to depict how the FITT guidelines apply to activity types and levels of child development (see figure 22.1).

The National Association for Sport and Physical Education (Ayers and Sariscsany, 2011) has developed specific recommendations for applying the FITT guidelines to children (5 to 12 years old) and adolescents (11 years and older). The recommendations are presented in figure 22.2.

Best practice calls for teachers to help students gain knowledge about how fitness is acquired by using the FITT guidelines and the principles of training. The selection of activities should be guided by a conceptual framework that provides information not only about how to perform activities but also (and even more important) about why the movements are important to each student's health and wellness (National Association for Sport

and Physical Education [NASPE], 2012). In other words, a comprehensive conceptual framework for health-related fitness education provides students with the information they need in order to understand terms and value fitness for a lifetime.

To put it more bluntly, teachers need to teach students to take personal responsibility for their health and fitness, and this process requires turning over that responsibility—and the choice of activities—to students as soon as they are ready to handle it. The major focus here should be on self-assessment, goal setting using personal results, and motivational strategies that take into account the needs and interests of the individual student (Ayers & Sariscsany, 2011; NASPE, 2012).

Fitness education should precede fitness assessment. In order to help children realize that fitness matters for a lifetime, teachers should deemphasize test scores (outcomes) and teach *why* each test is used, what fitness component is being assessed through the test, and how the test results should be used (process) to facilitate personal goal setting

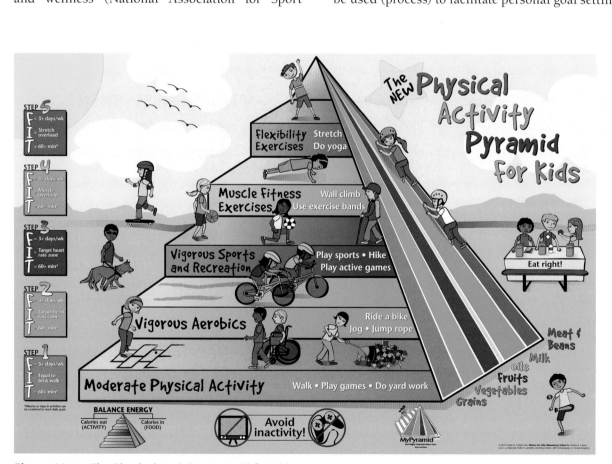

Figure 22.1   The Physical Activity Pyramid for Kids.

Reprinted, by permission, from G.C. Le Masurier, C.B. Corbin, M. Greiner, and D.D. Lambdin, 2010, *Fitness for life*, 5th ed. (Champaign, IL: Human Kinetics), 12. Source: Charles Corbin.

Guideline	Children (age 5–12)	Adolescents (age 11+)
Frequency	Developmentally appropriate physical activity on all or most days of the week Several daily bouts of physical activity lasting 15 minutes or more	Daily or nearly every day Three or more sessions per week
Intensity	Mixture of moderate and vigorous intermittent activity	Moderate to vigorous activity: 12 to 16 on Borg Rating of Perceived Exertion (RPE) Scale
Time	At least 60 minutes, and up to several hours, of accumulated activity time per week Up to 50 percent of total time involving bouts of 15 minutes or more	30 to 60 minutes of daily activity 20 minutes or more in a single session
Type	Variety of activities Activities from first three levels of the activity pyramid (figure 22.1) Continuous activity not expected for most children Muscular strength exercise limited to one focused exercise per muscle (or muscle group) per session	Games, sport work, transportation, recreation, physical education, planned exercise, community activities Brisk walking, jogging, stair climbing, basketball, racket sports, soccer, dance, lap swimming, skating, lawn mowing, cycling Muscular strength exercise limited to one focused exercise per muscle (or muscle group) per session until about age 16

Figure 22.2   Application of FITT Guidelines to Children and Adolescents

and improvements in health. Test scores should never be used for grading purposes in physical education. Instead, they should be interpreted with privacy and with explanations about what the results mean for the future health and well-being of the child. Results should be shared with parents and caregivers with the same considerations for privacy and education.

Children should be given multiple opportunities to learn and practice the tests before results are recorded. This approach ensures the reliability and validity of the results; that is, it produces results that reflect a child's true physiological strengths and limitations rather than any uncertainty about the most efficient technique for performing the activity. Providing multiple opportunities also reduces anxiety, which can lead to reduced motivation and poorer performance. It is also a good idea to teach only one or two tests at a time and to teach the appropriate technique while discussing the purpose of the test item and its relationship to health-related fitness. The rest of the lesson can involve enjoyable activities chosen specifically to reinforce and apply the relevant concepts and fitness components, thus enhancing children's learning. Programs such as Physical Best (SHAPE America.org) provide a myriad of activities that teach concepts while engaging children in activities designed for full inclusion, enjoyment, reduced competition, and skill practice.

FITNESS ASSESSMENT

The President's Council on Fitness, Sports, and Nutrition (PCFSN) developed the Presidential Youth Fitness Program (PYFP) as a three-tiered effort to address fitness education, fitness assessment, and motivational recognition. The program "places emphasis on the value of living a physically active and fit life—in school and beyond" (Presidential Youth Fitness Program, 2013a). In 2012, PCFSN and PYFP adopted the Fitnessgram assessments (Cooper Institute, 2010) as the national fitness test in the United States based on years of research into fitness development and best practices. This section focuses on the specific Fitnessgram assessments recommended by PCFSN (www.fitness.gov) and SHAPE America to assess the health-related fitness of children in grades 3 through 5.

The history of the assessments and the specific protocols are available online (Presidential Youth Fitness Program, 2015). The first section of the Presidential Youth Fitness Program provides an overview of Fitnessgram test administration and each of the specific tests. The subsequent sections provide guidelines for test interpretation, appropriate use of assessment results, and uses of fitness data. The final sections provide information related to the promotion of physical activity, including the benefits of activity, current statistics about youth activity, and strategies for improving the quality of physical education. The promotional strategies include the Presidential Active Lifestyle Award (PALA) program, which is designed to help children and families meet national guidelines for physical activity and nutrition. Teachers are encouraged to use the free program resources, including monitoring worksheets and awards, as well as an interactive website accessible free of charge. Figure 22.3 depicts a sample PALA activity and nutrition log.

The Fitnessgram assessments measure and report on indexes linked to health rather than skill performance. Test results are given in the form of scores relative to a range of scores—the Healthy Fitness Zone (HFZ)—that are linked to criteria for each health-related fitness component: cardiorespiratory endurance, muscular strength and endurance, flexibility, and body composition and nutrition. Depending on their scores, children are provided with feedback encouraging them to maintain their fitness levels by staying active or to improve by choosing from a variety of physical activities aligned with specific areas reflected in the tests. Research such as that from the Iowa State University Department of Kinesiology (n.d.) has linked scores in the HFZ to healthier living and reduced risk of diseases associated with sedentary living. Teachers can become trained to use the Fitnessgram assessments by accessing program resources through the websites of the Presidential Youth Fitness Program, the Cooper Institute, Fitnessgram, and SHAPE America's Physical Best training program (www.shapeamerica.org).

The Fitnessgram test comprises recommended, alternative, and optional assessments in each area of health-related fitness. Standards have been established for children from ages 5 through 17; however, testing for kindergarten through grade 3 is recommended for educational purposes only. Fourth graders should be introduced to the tests in a manner that emphasizes form and self- and partner assessment, and formal recording and reporting of results should begin in grade 5 or at age 10 (Cooper Institute, 2010). For teachers of elementary children (grades 3 through 5), best practice suggests gradually introducing the tests to students in grade 3, one test at a time. The emphasis should be on the purpose of the test, appropriate technique, the FITT guidelines corresponding to improving scores, the training principles that affect results, and the creation of an environment that provides positive feedback and encouragement (NASPE, 2009, 2012).

In grades 4 and 5, tests should be administered regularly, and students should enter their own scores. Self- and peer assessment are encouraged so that children understand correct technique, how to correct their technique, and critical elements of each test. Ideally, children should be able to print out their reports privately and should be encouraged to share them with family members. The scores should be reported and interpreted in terms of areas of strength (i.e., in the HFZ or better), areas for improvement, and the setting of personal goals based on test performance (NASPE, 2009, 2012). Teachers should provide multiple opportunities for assessment through the year and across years, in keeping with the fact that the *National Standards and Grade-Level Outcomes for K-12 Physical Education* (SHAPE America, 2014) encourage not only achievement but also maintenance of health-enhancing fitness.

As alluded to earlier, Fitnessgram includes recommended, alternative, and optional tests for each health-related fitness component. For cardiorespiratory endurance, the recommended test is the Progressive Aerobic Cardiovascular Endurance Run (PACER), which is the default aerobic-capacity test in the Fitnessgram software (Cooper Institute, 2010). For children in kindergarten through grade 3, the PACER is recommended because students are likely to have a positive experience with it and because it helps them learn the skill of pacing (Cooper Institute, 2010, p. 29). The objective of the test is for the child to run as long as she or he can continue covering the 20-meter distance within the given amount of time (the cadence gets faster with each successive minute).

When the PACER test is first introduced, the teacher should stress the fact that the pace increases gradually, thus aligning the assessment with the principle of progression. The test can also be aligned with the principle of overload by encouraging students to try to exceed their previous number of laps; this process also introduces them to the concept and skill of goal setting. The optional cardiorespiratory tests include a 15-meter PACER, which can be used for teaching children in smaller spaces or for children who are younger or

The Active Lifestyle Activity Log

Participant Name _____   Date Started _____

Group ID _____   Age _____   Date Completed _____

Week 1

Day	Physical Activities	# of Minutes or Pedometer Steps
Mon		
Tues		
Wed		
Thurs		
Fri		
Sat		
Sun		

Healthy Eating—Select a goal for this week

Participant Signature	Date

Week 2

Day	Physical Activities	# of Minutes or Pedometer Steps
Mon		
Tues		
Wed		
Thurs		
Fri		
Sat		
Sun		

Healthy Eating—Circle and continue with last week's goal, and add a new goal

Participant Signature	Date

Week 3

Day	Physical Activities	# of Minutes or Pedometer Steps
Mon		
Tues		
Wed		
Thurs		
Fri		
Sat		
Sun		

Healthy Eating—Circle and continue with previous goals, and add a new goal

Participant Signature	Date

Week 4

Day	Physical Activities	# of Minutes or Pedometer Steps
Mon		
Tues		
Wed		
Thurs		
Fri		
Sat		
Sun		

Healthy Eating—Circle and continue with previous goals, and add a new goal

Participant Signature	Date

Week 5

Day	Physical Activities	# of Minutes or Pedometer Steps
Mon		
Tues		
Wed		
Thurs		
Fri		
Sat		
Sun		

Healthy Eating—Circle and continue with previous goals, and add a new goal

Participant Signature	Date

Week 6

Day	Physical Activities	# of Minutes or Pedometer Steps
Mon		
Tues		
Wed		
Thurs		
Fri		
Sat		
Sun		

Healthy Eating—Circle and continue with previous goals, and add a new goal

Participant Signature	Date

Key to Healthy Eating

- I made half my plate fruits and vegetables
- At least half of the grains that I ate were whole grains
- I chose fat-free or low fat (1%) milk, yogurt, or cheese
- I drank water instead of sugary drinks
- I chose lean sources of protein
- I compared sodium in foods like soup and frozen meals and chose foods with less sodium
- I ate seafood   I ate smaller portions

Verification

I certify that I met the requirements of the Presidential Active Lifestyle Award.

- ☐ I was physically active for at least 5 days each week and I met my healthy eating goals.
- ☐ I have performed my healthy eating and physical activities for at least 6 weeks.

Participant Signature _____

Supervising Adult's Signature (if applicable) _____

Note: Submit this paper log to your teacher or group administrator, or keep for your own records. Please do not submit to the President's Challenge office. See inside back cover for award ordering information.

Figure 22.3 PALA activity and nutrition log.

Reprinted from The Presidents Challenge. Available: https://www.presidentschallenge.org/tools-resources/docs/PALA_log.pdf

Curl-up test *(a)* and push-up test *(b)*.

need more encouragement. Another alternative, a 1-mile (1.6-kilometer) run, is designed for students who enjoy running and are highly motivated. For students of age 13 or older, there is also a walking test, but it has not been validated sufficiently for younger students (Cooper Institute, 2010).

Fitnessgram also includes recommended and optional tests for the components of muscular strength, endurance, and flexibility. When introducing each test, the teacher should carefully explain the part(s) of the body isolated by the test. This information reinforces the **principle of specificity**. Beyond that, as indicated earlier, the grade 3 experience should focus attention on proper form. Teaching the technique involves explaining that changes in form or technique result in recruitment or use of difference muscles and body parts, thus rendering the results less valid as indicators of strength, endurance, or flexibility in the targeted regions. Finally, these tests are designed to be monitored by a peer, which not only reinforces concepts and form but also aids in teaching personal and social responsibility.

Recommended strength and endurance tests include the following: the curl-up test for abdominal strength and endurance; the trunk extensor test for strength and flexibility of the back, abdominal muscles, hamstrings, and back extensors (which are critical to maintenance of posture and lower-back health); and the 90-degree push-up for upper-body strength and endurance (Cooper Institute, 2010, p. 49). Alternatives to these tests include the modified pull-up test, the flexed-arm hang,

and (for users of the 6.0 version of the software) the pull-up test. Protocols, HFZ grade-level standards, and teaching suggestions can be found in the Fitnessgram test manual and in the Presidential Youth Fitness Program instructions.

Because flexibility is not a common problem among younger students, the flexibility tests are considered optional for students in grades 3 through 5. Even so, teachers are advised to help students learn about the importance of flexibility for injury prevention as they age, and the tests can serve as invaluable tools for teaching students about the principle of specificity and the concept of range of motion. The two optional flexibility tests included in Fitnessgram are the back-saver sit and reach and the shoulder stretch (Cooper Institute, 2010, pp. 57–59). The back-saver sit and reach assesses each leg and hip joint independently, thus reinforcing the principle of specificity. It gets harder for children to reach the HFZ on this test as they progress through their school years, and especially as they enter their adolescent growth spurt. Therefore, teaching beginning as early as third grade about what the health-related fitness components are and practicing and assessing each component helps children understand more about their own fitness development.

The shoulder stretch requires no equipment and only limited space, and it is ideal for teaching the concept of specificity because it often shows that the shoulder joints differ in a given individual. It also provides a great motivational tool if students learn it and then use it to test their parents or

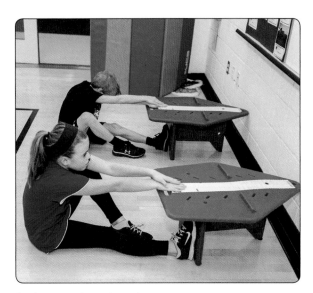

Back-saver sit and reach.

caregivers at home. Quite often, a family member cannot touch the fingertips on one or both sides, whereas the younger child is successful. Not only does this motivate children, but also it encourages family members to regularly assess and monitor flexibility at home.

The final component of health-related fitness assessment consists of tests of body composition and nutrition. In the past, body composition was discussed independently from nutrition in the Physical Best materials, but today many references tie them together. This linkage has been made partly because the two concepts are intertwined in the management of body weight and composition and partly because it is more comfortable for teachers and practitioners to talk about them as an integral aspect of health. Assessment of body composition in both field-based and educational settings is not only time consuming but also difficult to approach with children and their families. Although the current obesity epidemic has catapulted the topic to the top of the health-risk list for children, the assessment process remains a concern for most teachers.

Body composition is expressed as the amount of lean body tissue (i.e., bone, muscle, organ, and body fluid, including water) and fat that makes up one's body weight. In 2010, Fitnessgram released new body composition standards for boys and girls that identify the recommended percentage of body fat and body mass index (BMI) for good health and for reducing one's risk for diseases associated with obesity. The new standards describe risk in the fol-

lowing relative terms: very lean, Healthy Fitness Zone, some risk, and high risk. This newer classification may help teachers talk with children and parents about body composition and its importance in the overall context of the health-related fitness scores from the tests. As with the other Fitnessgram assessments, teachers should teach the concepts, encourage students to self-assess and self-monitor their body composition, help students set appropriate personal goals, and share results privately and with concern for the self-concept of the children.

The recommended assessment for body composition in Fitnessgram is the two-site skinfold measurement using calipers; the alternative assessments accounted for in the software involve height and weight measurements. The results of the measurements are entered directly into the software as raw scores, and the resulting report indicates the child's body composition. This is a more sensitive and private means of measuring body composition than those that report a percentage of fat directly from a scale or a bio-impedance instrument. Keep assessments private and the results confidential. Discuss generally with the class what the risk factors and columns mean with respect to health and fitness. Share the message that body composition is an integral component of health-related fitness and that it is directly affected by physical activity.

Teachers are encouraged to get trained in using Fitnessgram, as well as Physical Best and Fitness for Life (both of which are described later in this chapter). Physical Best workshops and online PYFP training, both available through SHAPE America, focus on health-related fitness concepts and assessments designed for school-age children and youth.

Since children need not only achieve and maintain a health-enhancing level of fitness but also participate regularly in physical activities, teachers must provide them with tools and instruction specifically related to physical activity participation. To that end, Fitnessgram provides activity questions, a sample of which can be seen at the bottom of the sample Fitnessgram report presented in figure 22.4. Teachers often fail to use these critical tools for helping students learn about the importance of regular physical activity and for assessing the FITT appropriateness of students' participation in physical activity.

To summarize, the purpose of health-related fitness testing for children in grades 3 through 5 is to teach them the knowledge and skills they need in

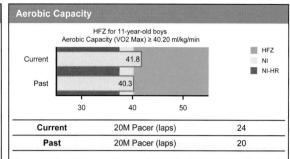

FitnessGram Student Report

FITNESSGRAM®

Student (ID:829202044)

Grade:	5 (Age: 11)	
Teacher:	Jogger, Jane	
School:	Cooper Elementary	
District:	Cooper District	
Report Date:	10/29/2015	

	Past	Current
Test Date:	11/3/2015	5/1/2016
Height:	5' 6"	5' 6"
Weight	125 lbs	124 lbs

Aerobic Capacity

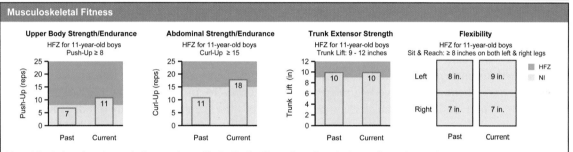

Current	20M Pacer (laps)	24
Past	20M Pacer (laps)	20

Congratulations! Your aerobic capacity is in the Healthy Fitness Zone and you are physically active most days. To maintain health and fitness, continue to participate in physical activities for at least 60 minutes each day. Keep your Body Mass Index (BMI) in the Healthy Fitness Zone.

Musculoskeletal Fitness

Your abdominal, trunk, and upper-body strength are all in the Healthy Fitness Zone. To maintain your fitness, be sure that your strength-training activities include exercises for all of these areas. Strength activities should be done at least 3 days per week.
In addition to aerobic and muscle-strengthening activities, it is important to perform stretching exercises to maintain or improve flexibility and some weight-bearing activity (e.g. running, hopping, jumping or dancing) to ensure good bone health at least 3 days per week.

Body Composition

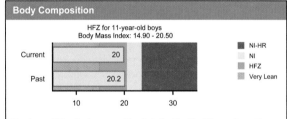

Good news! Your body composition is in the Healthy Fitness Zone. To maintain this healthy level of body composition, remember to:
-Be active for at least 60 minutes every day.
-Limit screen time to less than 2 hours a day.
-Make healthy food choices including fresh fruits and vegetables.
-Limit fried foods, foods with added sugars and sugary drinks.

Physical Activity

Reported Activity/Past 7 Days	Days	Goal
Aerobic activity for a total of 60 minutes or more	7	7
Muscle strengthening activity	3	3
Bone strengthening activity	2	3

To be healthy and fit, it is important to do some physical activity for a total of 60 minutes or more daily. Aerobic exercise is good for your heart and body composition. Muscular and bone-strengthening exercises are good for your muscles and joints.Congratulations! You are doing aerobic activity most or all days and muscular-strengthening exercises. Add some bone-strengthening exercises to improve your overall fitness.

HFZ: Healthy Fitness Zone; NI: Needs Improvement; NI-HR: Needs Improvement - Health Risk

 Cooper Institute·
WELL INTO THE FUTURE.

FitnessGram.net

 A PROGRAM OF **Play60** THE NFL MOVEMENT FOR AN ACTIVE GENERATION

Figure 22.4 Sample Fitnessgram printout.

Reprinted, by permission, from The Cooper Institute 2016.

order to achieve and maintain a health-enhancing level of physical activity and fitness. As identified by NASPE (2012), the focus should be on teaching best practices for physical fitness assessment (including self-assessment) and analysis; using the results to set goals and create a fitness improvement plan; encouraging students to work to improve in the various fitness components; teaching strategies for self-monitoring and adjusting plans; and providing a strategy whereby students can achieve their goals (see figure 22.5 for a sample goal-setting worksheet). Fitness testing is used not for sheer recording of results and outcomes but as part of the process of teaching concepts; as a result, test outcomes are used to begin the process of setting individual goals for lifetime activity.

Fitnessgram includes a section called Activitygram, which asks students to log their activity behaviors by time, type, and intensity for at least two school days and one nonschool day. Teachers are encouraged to incorporate activity monitoring and concepts of behavior change beginning at about grade 4. When students examine their own activity by time of day, they can see areas where

they spend the most time in sedentary or active tasks. This information can help them and their parents find time for physical activities that lead to healthier living.

The Activity Log allows teachers to view students' activity logs and allows students to monitor their physical activity by logging steps and activity time accumulated on each day of the month. It is designed to interface with pedometers (steps) and activity monitors (time) and can be used to create interclass or group challenges that motivate children to work collectively or independently to increase their daily activity. Thus it is an excellent tool for teaching children about individual goal setting, self-monitoring of goals, and collective goal setting (Cooper Institute, 2010).

FITNESS EDUCATION PROGRAMS

Several user-friendly, researched-based curricular supplements are available for physical education teachers to infuse into their existing programs. Typically, such programs are not designed as stand-alone fitness education curricula but as tasks or ac-

---

Name _____ Date _____

Use the following questions to help you set a goal that you want to achieve. Show your completed worksheet to your teacher or a family member who can encourage you in reaching your goal.

1. *What?* Goal setting can help us understand our limits and feel satisfied with our accomplishments. Goals can be our wishes or even our dreams for the future. What would you like to achieve or do in the next month? (e.g., "I'd like to be stronger in my upper arms.") Write your "what" here: _____

_____

2. *Why?* Goals motivate us to action and give us control. When we accomplish them, we feel a sense of satisfaction. (e.g., ask yourself why being stronger would be good or important to you.) Write why the goal is important and how you will feel when you reach it. _____

_____

3. *When?* When will you start working toward your goal, and when do you think you will reach the goal? (Hint: Give yourself a couple of weeks. Getting stronger takes practice and work over time. Let your teacher or another adult help you set a realistic timeline.)

Put a start date here: _____ Put a finish date here: _____

4. *How?* Write two or three actions that you can take to help you reach your goal. Make them personal by using "I will" statements. (Here is an example: "I will do 20 push-ups every day for one month.")

Action 1: I will _____

Action 2: I will _____

5. Feelings of accomplishment: When I reach my goal, I will feel good because . . . _____

_____

Figure 22.5   Goal-setting worksheet.

Reprinted, by permission, from SHAPE America, 2011, *Physical best activity guide: Elementary level,* 3rd ed. (Champaign, IL: Human Kinetics), 20.

tivities that can be integrated into a comprehensive quality physical education program. This section provides an overview of two such programs: Fitness for Life and Physical Best.

The Fitness for Life elementary school program (Corbin et al., 2010) was developed to provide a schoolwide wellness program tied into guidelines for healthy eating, such as MyPlate (U.S. Department of Agriculture, n.d.), as well as the Physical Best and Fitnessgram assessments. The Fitness for Life program involves classroom teachers, physical education teachers, health educators, wellness coordinators, cafeteria staff, and school communities.

The Physical Best program focuses on age-appropriate activities that give all participants an equal opportunity to play, make friends, improve social skills, and enhance their fitness. Physical Best activities are aligned with the Fitnessgram and Presidential Youth Fitness Program assessments and provide enjoyable activities as they reinforce FITT guidelines and principles of exercise. The Physical Best program offers two major resources for teaching concepts and infusing fitness education into the regular physical education curriculum: the *Physical Best Activity Guide: Elementary Level* (NASPE, 2011) and *The Physical Best Teacher's Guide: Physical Education for Lifelong Fitness* (Ayers & Sariscsany, 2011).

ENHANCING PHYSICAL ACTIVITY AND FITNESS WITH TECHNOLOGY

Technology continues to evolve in all areas of life, including the monitoring of physical activity and the teaching of physical education. New apps abound for teaching, coaching, assessment, data management, information sharing, skill demonstrations and feedback, and tracking of physiological indicators of activity intensity. In addition, the web gives teachers access to vast amounts of information—some reliable and some less so—and teachers need to continuously update their technology knowledge and skills. With respect to fitness education, teachers are finding that technology can be motivational and advantageous in helping students individualize and personalize their activity goals.

Pedometers, although not new technology, have been used widely in the past two decades and are likely found in the equipment inventory of most quality physical education programs. Inexpensive and easy to use, pedometers have been incorpo-

rated into the Fitnessgram, Fitness for Life, and **Physical Best** program materials for monitoring of activity in terms of both time (minutes active) and steps taken. Using the FITT guidelines, teachers can encourage students to use pedometers to increase their activity level by taking more steps or accumulating more active minutes. When students are challenged in this way to take more steps in a set period of time—for example, during a physical education class—a teacher is using technology to increase intensity. Similarly, when using pedometers with entire classes, a teacher can point out the **principle of individuality** by comparing the number of steps taken by different students to cover the same distance. Students who are taller and have a longer stride length will report fewer steps per 100 yards walked than will shorter students who have shorter stride lengths.

Discussions about such activities lead students into critical thinking about the importance of individualized goals and personal fitness. Children in grades 3 through 5 can readily see these individual differences and therefore gain understanding of the principles involved in creating personal plans. Self-improvement goals, such as taking 500 more steps per day, can lead to success; therefore, they can serve as motivational tools to help children increase their physical activity without focusing on specific exercises. For example, to earn the Presidential Youth Fitness Program's PALA award, girls must log at least 11,000 steps per day—and boys must log at least 13,000 steps per day—on five days per week for six weeks (Presidential Youth Fitness Program, 2013b).

As technology continues to evolve, monitors are becoming less cumbersome and less invasive. For example, activity monitors now often combine pedometer technology with physiological indicators of heart rate (pulse rate) and even respiratory rate. In another example, as a precursor to middle school education, children can use heart rate monitors with grab bars that provide immediate feedback about activity intensity (i.e., heart rate). Children can then compare their intensity (i.e., heart rate) with levels of intensity (i.e., moderate or vigorous) associated with their heart rate and aligned with their age provided on charts. When children are learning to monitor their pulse, concurrent use of heart-rate monitors enhances the validity of pulse recordings and helps children learn to associate pulse rate with the cardiorespiratory system.

Once children understand the relationship of intensity to heart rate, they can also be taught how to use the rating of perceived exertion (RPE) and become better able to pace their activity in order to perform longer aerobic bouts. Teachers are encouraged to use both pedometers and heart-rate monitors during class and during fitness testing (e.g., PACER). The children's OMNI RPE scale (Lagally, 2013) is designed for ages 8 through 15 and provides both pictures and words to help children indicate how hard they feel they are working on an intensity scale of 0 to 10. The OMNI RPE verbal descriptors for children are as follows:

0 = not tired at all

1 or 2 = a little tired

3 or 4 = getting more tired

5 or 6 = tired

7 or 8 = really tired

9 or 10 = very, very tired

A sample OMNI child scale appears in figure 22.6 (Lagally, 2013, p. 36).

Heart rate monitors can help children learn to use and refine their RPE ratings by equating feelings of effort and tiredness with activity at the moderate or vigorous heart-rate levels. However, heart rate is *not* the recommended method of monitoring activity intensity for children. Instead, the preferred method is to tie recommendations for MVPA to the levels in the Physical Activity Pyramid through either the OMNI scale or the "talk and sing method." As Ayers and Sariscsany (2011, p. 78) put it, if children can talk but not sing, then intensity is appropriate. If, on the other hand, they are too out of breath to talk, then the intensity is too high; if they can still sing, then the intensity is too low.

The assessment of body composition also relies on various forms of technology, including bioimpedance measurement devices and the use of scales and body mass index (BMI) formulas to estimate percentage of body fat or lean body mass based on height and weight. BMI formulas are available on various websites, including those sponsored by PYFP and MyPlate. Fitnessgram software provides the option to use either BMI or skinfold caliper assessments.

For children in primary and intermediate grades, Fitnessgram encourages teachers to use calf and triceps skinfold measurements because those sites are less invasive (Cooper Institute, 2010), but the software also allows for data from other sources that calculate percent body fat. The resulting report provides feedback in terms of four categories: Healthy Fitness Zone, needs improvement (some risk), needs improvement (high risk), and very lean. Regardless of the method or technology applied, the goal should be to teach children about

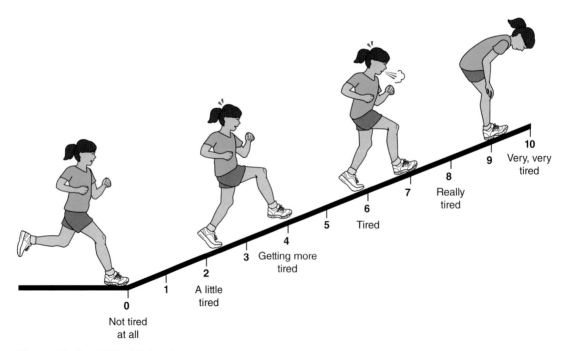

Figure 22.6 OMNI child scale.

"Using ratings of perceived exertion in physical education," K. Lagally, *JOPERD,* 84(5): 35-39, reprinted by permission of SHAPE America.

the relationship between healthy body composition and regular physical activity while downplaying the use of weight or body composition assessments. More specifically, Fitnessgram encourages teachers to focus on attaining and maintaining appropriate body composition by participating in regular aerobic physical activity that contributes to lean body mass and endurance, as well as eating a diet that provides healthy and balanced nutrition.

Various apps are now available for managing fitness data, BMI, height and weight, dietary intake, and other health indexes. Teachers are encouraged to explore the apps with children and share them with parents to extend physical education outside of school and into the home. For example, Fitnessgram recently released an app for iPhone and Android smartphone users. The app can be used to score input in either synchronous or asynchronous mode; for teachers, it facilitates quick input without the presence of a personal computer or other larger device.

Physical educators strive to provide students with the knowledge and skills to become fit and to identify and participate in health-enhancing physical activities with their families, friends, and fellow community members. To enhance students' participation in physical activity outside of school, teachers provide homework assignments that encourage students to participate in a variety of movement experiences. Through the use of physical activity logs, students can record and reflect on their physical activity choices and learn to identify a range of enjoyable health-enhancing physical activities. Teachers can create their own logs by using tables and spreadsheets; however, we recommend using Fitnessgram, Activitygram, and Activity Log as the basis of monitoring and comparing in-school and out-of-school activity levels. Another easy way to teach students about the importance of participating in physical activity outside of physical education class is to help them create a personal or family account on the websites Let's Move! Active Schools (www.letsmoveschools.org) and the Presidential Youth Fitness Program (www.shapeamerica.org).

To use technology appropriately in fitness education, consider the following suggestions:

- Keep it simple and user friendly.
- Use technology as a *tool* to teach concepts and reinforce learning.
- Use technology to help set and monitor goals for personal fitness.

- Recognize that online resources may or may not be valid for fitness assessment or education.
- Wean students off of technology as a primary indicator of intensity so that they become more aware of their personal *physiological* responses to activity.

DESIGNING INSTRUCTION

To plan developmentally appropriate fitness activities, teachers must first use the concept of individuality. Students in grades 3 through 5 experience greater success and enjoyment in movement when teachers create fitness stations that offer a variety of challenges using task progressions based on the FITT guidelines. Each set of station tasks should offer choice activities centered on a particular theme, fitness concept, or body part. Ideally, stations are arranged to alternate muscular strength and endurance work, aerobic endurance work, flexibility work, and critical thinking combined with personal goal setting.

For warm-up and cool-down activities, teachers are encouraged to use prerecorded music to help with managing tempo and intensity of movement. Warm-ups should be accomplished through engaging activities that incorporate the large muscle groups, get the heart pumping at a moderate level of intensity, and stimulate blood flow to the extremities. Though station work is recommended for individual fitness development, teachers should use group activities for warm-ups and cool-downs. Each of these three segments should incorporate self-checks or assessments of physiological indicators of intensity (e.g., OMNI scale, breathing) and time (e.g., steps, activity time, number of repetitions).

Each of the following learning experiences addresses the essential content (see figure 22.7) of national physical education standard 3 for K-12 physical education (SHAPE America, 2014). The intent of Standard 3 is the establishment of patterns of regular participation in physical activity and acquiring the knowledge and skills to achieve and maintain physical fitness. The following activities are aligned with Standard 3 and also include formative assessments that are differentiated for varying fitness levels. Warm-up and cool-down activities are designed for whole-group participation, whereas stations provide students with opportunities to develop each fitness component at their own level.

FITNESS CONCEPTS

Standard 3: "The physically literate individual demonstrates the knowledge and skills to achieve and maintain a health-enhancing level of physical activity and fitness" (SHAPE America, 2014a, p. 12). The intent of this standard is establishment of patterns of regular participation in physical activity and acquiring the knowledge and skills to achieve and maintain physical fitness (NASPE, 2004).

Standard 3 (grades 3–5)

Essential content	Measurement of success
Uses physical activity knowledge by • charting and analyzing participation in physical activity outside of school for fitness benefit. Uses fitness knowledge by • describing and applying FITT* guidelines to the components of health-related fitness, • identifying the need for warm-up and cool-down in relationship to various physical activities, • monitoring physiological indicators of moderate to vigorous physical activity and adjusting activity levels accordingly, and • interpreting and understanding the significance of fitness test results and designing a fitness plan with help from the teacher.	Assess attainment by using answer keys, checklists, or rubrics to score students' levels of success in terms of knowledge about physical activity and fitness. Evaluate physical activity knowledge by documentation of • regular participation in physical activity with logs such as Activitygram and Activity Log (Fitnessgram) and • Presidential Active Lifestyle Award materials from the President's Challenge youth fitness program. Evaluate fitness knowledge by observation of • safe and correct technique when performing activities for each component of fitness. Evaluate students' ability to • apply FITT guidelines to the components of health-related fitness, • describe the importance of warming up and cooling down, • monitor physiological indicators and adjust moderate to vigorous activity levels, and • interpret test results from Fitnessgram or the President's Challenge and design a fitness plan.

Instruction engages children in learning the essential content and successfully demonstrating attainment.

*FITT guidelines: frequency (how often), intensity (how hard), time (how long), and type (mode of activity/exercise) are used to improve performance with each of the components of fitness.

Figure 22.7 Alignment chart for standard 3, grades 3-5.

GRADES 3 TO 5 FITNESS LEARNING EXPERIENCES

National Physical Education Standard 3

Essential content: describing and applying the FITT guidelines to the components of health-related fitness

Learning outcome: applying the intensity guideline to the development of muscular strength and endurance

Teaching styles: reproduction for practice at own level (inclusion, practice, reciprocal, self-check), production for discovering fitness guideline applications to fitness components (guided discovery, convergent discovery)

Activity: Four stations each represent a way to increase intensity for muscular strength and endurance. Heart rate monitoring is used to assess differences in intensity level at each station.

- Station 1: Increasing Intensity Through Distance. Jump back and forth 10 consecutive times from both feet to both feet at each color across the width of a V taped on the floor (see figure 22.8 for setup). On the intensity task card, record heart rate at each color, then put a check mark by the distance that increased exercise intensity the most. Rest for 60 seconds after jumping at each color.

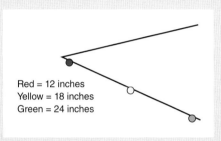

Red = 12 inches
Yellow = 18 inches
Green = 24 inches

Figure 22.8 Setup for jumping with varying intensity.

- Station 2: Increasing Intensity Through Gravity. Perform 10 consecutive sit-ups on each incline, downhill, flat, or uphill surface. On the intensity task card, record heart rate at each surface and put a check mark by the one that increased exercise intensity the most. Rest for 60 seconds after each surface.

- Station 3: Increasing Intensity Through Repetition. Perform 20, then 30, and then 40 repetitions of forward rope jumping in personal space. On the intensity task card, record heart rate after each set of jumps and put a check mark by the number that increased your exercise intensity the most. Rest for 60 seconds after each set.

- Station 4: Increasing Intensity Through Height. Perform the basic step (stepping up on top of the aerobic step with the right foot, then with the left foot, then step down onto the floor with the right foot and then with the left foot) for one minute at the set cadence at each of three step levels. Level 1 is on the floor (march in place), level 2 is one aerobic step in height, and level 3 is two aerobics steps in height. On the intensity task card, record heart rate after each step level and put a check mark by the height that increased exercise intensity the most. Rest for 60 seconds after each step level.

Environment: four stations in each quarter of the gymnasium with enough equipment for five to seven students per station

Practice: constant

Closed-skill cues:

Station 1: Jumping

- Use quick touch-and-go jumps.

Station 2: Sit-Ups

- Bend knees.
- Use full range of motion (all the way up).
- Put hands across chest.

Station 3: Rope Jumping

- Use two-foot to two-foot jumps.
- Use hands to turn rope with small circles at sides.

Station 4: Stepping

- Step up on ball of foot in middle portion of step (not on edge of step).
- Maintain cadence while alternating feet (up-up, down-down).

Feedback

KPp = Knowledge of Performance prescriptive
KPd = Knowledge of Performance descriptive
KRp = Knowledge of Results prescriptive
KRd = Knowledge of Results descriptive

- KR: "How are the different intensity levels affecting your heart rate?"
- KPd: "You are keeping the cadence while stepping—good job!"
- KPp: "Use the ball of the foot rather than a flat foot when stepping."

Assessment

Standard 2 (figure 22.9) and 3 (figure 22.10): Students assess each activity to determine what variable was used to increase intensity.

Name: _____

Directions: Record your heart rate after each exercise trial, then answer the question about that station.

Station 1: Jumping
Trial 1 _____ Trial 2 _____ Trial 3 _____
What changed to increase intensity at this station?

Station 2: Sit-ups
Trial 1 _____ Trial 2 _____ Trial 3 _____
What changed to increase intensity at this station?

Station 3: Rope Jumping
Trial 1 _____ Trial 2 _____ Trial 3 _____
What changed to increase intensity at this station?

Station 4: Stepping
Trial 1 _____ Trial 2 _____ Trial 3 _____
What changed to increase intensity at this station?

Choose one of the following activities. Explain how to change the intensity level while performing the activity.

Bike riding
Jumping jacks
Push-ups

Figure 22.9   Exercise intensity task card.

Name: _____

Directions: Check your watch during your tag game when the teacher stops play. Walk to your learning-team area, get your heart rate card, and put a check mark in the column that represents your heart rate.

	Vigorous 151–180 beats per minute	Moderate 105–150 beats per minute	Low <105 beats per minute
Heart rate 1			
Heart rate 2			
Heart rate 3			

Figure 22.10   Heart rate assessment.

National Standard 3

Essential content: monitoring daily MVPA (and adjusting activity levels accordingly)

Learning outcome: identifying personal activities; labeling as light, moderate, or vigorous; and comparing with national recommendations for 60 minutes of daily MVPA

Teaching style: practice and inclusion (student's choice of activities)

Activity: Students learn about Activitygram (for homework or an in-class critical thinking station).

Environment: Hang the Physical Activity Pyramid for Kids in the gym or classroom. Students work independently or with a partner in the classroom or gym. Provide each student with one pencil and one copy of the Activitygram worksheet from either the Fitness for Life or the Physical Best program.

Content cues: Review activities on each pyramid level. Define moderate physical activity as equal to brisk walking and vigorous physical activity as activity during which one is unable to talk.

Feedback

- Use Activitygram feedback and printouts. Ask students to think about how many minutes of MVPA they accumulated and whether or not they met the national goal of 60 minutes of daily MVPA.

Assessment

- Learning outcome check: After the activity, ask the students if they met the daily recommendation of 60 minutes; if not, ask how they could increase their personal activity. Collect the Activitygram worksheets and review with the class some of the activities listed by students (maintain anonymity). Ask students whether the activities are correctly identified as light, moderate, or vigorous and whether they are assigned to the correct level of the activity pyramid.

- Self-assessment (preferred): Have students use their worksheets to enter data into the Activitygram software. They can self-assess because the program will not allow them to enter the activity in the wrong level of the activity pyramid. Have students print out their Activitygrams and take them home for parental review.

WARM-UPS

National Standard 3

Essential content: identifying the need for a warm-up

Learning outcome: identifying that the purpose of a warm-up is to get the heart pumping blood to all parts of the body through continuous total body movement

Teaching style: practice

"CUPID SHUFFLE" DANCE

In a group, all students dance at the same time. Students can either perform a dance taught previously or perform their own continuous movements in self-space.

Environment: For music, use the song "Cupid Shuffle" by Cupid. Students are spread out in general space.

WALK, SKIP, HOP, JUMP, GALLOP, AND CHECK

Students spread around the gym in general space. They use locomotor skills as directed by the teacher to move clockwise around the perimeter at a moderate pace while taking turns to answer questions such as the following:

- What does frequency (F) mean? (how often, times per week)
- What is the intensity (I) of this current activity? (moderate)
- How long should we perform a warm-up activity? (for three to five minutes)
- How many minutes of activity is needed daily for good health? (60)
- What does MVPA mean? (moderate to vigorous physical activity)
- Teacher choice: Create questions aligned with the content of the next lesson to come.

Environment: Use moderate-tempo music. Students spread out in general space and, to avoid injury, move clockwise around the perimeter of the gym or outdoor activity area.

HOOP HOPPING AND JUMPING

When the music starts, children are asked to jump into and out of their hoops. Use different challenges, such as the following:

- "Jump into and out of your hoop sideways."
- "Jump into and out of your hoop forward and backward."
- "Hop on one foot inside your hoop."
- "Hop on one foot around your hoop clockwise (or counterclockwise)."

Then challenge students in personal space to try hooping—specifically, keeping the hoop moving in a circular pattern for 30 seconds, one minute, or two minutes. Next, challenge students in open space to roll their hoops and chase after them. Once they catch the hoops, challenge them to roll the hoops and run through them (this last part may be done best outdoors).

Environment: Use moderate-tempo music. Students are spread out in general space, each standing inside a hula hoop. Use music to manage two-minute intervals of activity with a rest between episodes. (Alternatively, this activity can be done with jump ropes, creating shapes on the floor to jump into and out of. In this case, rather than chasing hoops, students can be challenged to jump over their ropes using two feet, skipping, or leaping activities.)

Feedback

- KR:
  - Ask children to notice their hearts beating faster.
  - Ask children if they feel their muscles and skin getting warmer.

- Ask if they are breathing faster.
- Ask how long they were able to hoop without stopping.
- Ask how long a warm-up activity should be (three to five minutes).
- KPp: "Use your arms to swing from low to high to help you build energy or momentum for jumping and hopping."

FOUR CORNERS

Children perform different locomotor skills to travel from one cone to the next in a series of four cones. Children are divided into four groups (red, blue, green, and yellow). On the teacher's cue, each group begins at a specified cone and performs its designated locomotor skill (see sample posters in figure 22.11). When they reach the second cone, they change to the locomotor skill indicated for their group color on the poster. Once the members of a group reach their home cone (the one at which they started), they continue traveling, but now they switch to the next color (e.g., red now performs blue, blue performs green, green performs yellow, and yellow performs red). This pattern is followed until all groups have performed all 16 locomotor skills.

Environment: Place a cone in each corner of the gymnasium or movement area. Each cone has a poster listing four locomotor skills, each of which is written in a different color (corresponding with the four group colors). This activity can be accompanied by music.

Feedback

Provide skill cues specific to each locomotor skill and observe children's use of space as they travel around the area. In addition, direct students' attention as follows:

- Ask them to notice their heart beating faster.
- Ask if they feel their muscles and skin getting warmer.
- Ask if they are breathing faster.

| 1. Skip forward
2. Move on hands and feet
3. Run and jump from one to two feet
4. Jog forward along a zigzag pathway | 1. Gallop forward
2. Move in a low level
3. Move sideways in a twisted shape
4. Walk backward slowly | 1. Jump forward
2. Move on two hands and one foot
3. Hop forward
4. Slide, right side leading |

Figure 22.11   Sample posters for four corners.

FITNESS BINGO

This is a great activity for helping kids work cooperatively. With a partner, students picks up a die and a card (see sample in figure 22.12). One partner rolls the die and chooses a fitness activity with the number that comes up. After the child performs the activity, the partner follows and does the same. This pattern continues until they have completed one row of activity. The number of rolls with the die and exercises performed depends on the challenge level you choose for the students; you can also specify horizontal or vertical.

Environment: Place bingo cards in three or four locations for easy distribution upon entering the gymnasium (e.g., in hoops at the front of the gymnasium). Provide pencils in small bins beside the hoops.

Feedback: Provide skill-cue feedback addressing performance technique for the exercises included on the bingo card. Ask students the following questions:

- "Which exercises elevated your heart rate the most?"
- "Why do you think this was the case?"

Fitness Bingo

B Cardio	I Upper	N Lower	G Ab	O Flex
1 Jump rope 30 ×	1 Modified push-ups 10 ×	1 Wall sit Count to 30	1 Side crunches 20 per side	1 Rest 30 seconds
2 Jog 2 laps	2 Shake teacher's hand	2 Leg extensions 15 ×	2 Ab rolls 20 ×	2 Sit and reach Count to 30
3 Get a drink	3 *Marching pushups Count to 30	3 Calf raises Count to 30	3 Hold the hover 30 seconds	3 Quad stretch Count to 30
4 Shuttle run 4 × AB	*Beanbag Hockey One person scores 10 goals	4 Rest	4 2 count curls 2 up 2 down	4 Biceps stretch 30 seconds each
5 Line jumps across and back 2 ×	5 Biceps curls w/ Dynaband 15 × each side	5 Squats 15 ×	5 Reverse curls 20 ×	5 Triceps stretch 30 seconds each

Figure 22.12   Fitness bingo card.

Based on Francesca Zavacky, Charlottesville, VA: 1995 NASPE Southern District Middle School Teacher.

CATCH THE LEADER

Position students in lines of six to eight spread out along the periphery of the gymnasium. Each group starts to jog as a pack, and the last student in line sprints to the front of the line to become the leader. This pattern continues until the original leader is back in front. Each group adjusts its general speed to the ability of the slowest jogger.

Environment: gymnasium or outdoor space of similar size; music (optional)

TOPSY-TURVY

Divide the class into two groups that start the activity on opposite sides of the gym or activity area. One group is assigned to knock down cones and the other half is assigned to stand cones upright. On the starting cue (music, teacher command, or whistle), students run to cones to either knock them over or stand them back up. Students cannot stand still or remain near a cone that was just touched; they must keep moving. After three minutes, stop and count cones. Then have the two teams swap roles so that they each take on the opposite challenge—knocking down or standing up.

Environment: Use a gymnasium or outdoor space of equivalent size. Arrange 20 cones about 10 feet (3 meters) apart from each other and scattered throughout the activity area. This activity can be accompanied by music (when the music starts, children move; when it stops, they freeze).

Feedback

- KR: "Why does continuous movement for three to five minutes help your body warm up?"
- KR: "How does _____ qualify as a warm-up activity?"

Assessments

Standards 2 and 3: Use a learning goal check.

- After the activity, ask students how they know that their bodies are ready and warm. (Answer: The heart is beating faster, and the breathing is faster.)
- Ask students to describe to a hypothetical new student what must be done to warm up the body before engaging in moderate to vigorous physical activity. (Answer: Use continuous total body movement for three to five minutes to get the heart pumping blood to all parts of the body.)

HEALTH-RELATED FITNESS COMPONENT LEARNING EXPERIENCES

National Standard 3

Essential content: describing and applying the FITT guidelines to the components of health-related fitness

Learning outcome: selecting a challenging intensity and identifying the type of activity

Teaching styles: reproduction for practice at own level—inclusion (student choice), practice (student choice of same activity in effort to increase personal goal), reciprocal (working with a partner), self-check (keeping a personal log and using a pedometer)

Activity: Set up the 15 stations described in figure 22.13. Organize students in groups of three to five and assign each to begin at an aerobic station. Allow children to choose the activity level at each station. Select moderate-tempo music prerecorded to accompany three minutes of activity, allow for a 30-second interval, and then accompany another three minutes of movement.

At the conclusion of the entire activity, children should work in their assigned groups to address reflection questions provided on a handout (figure 22.14). After all groups have recorded their answers, debrief with the entire class.

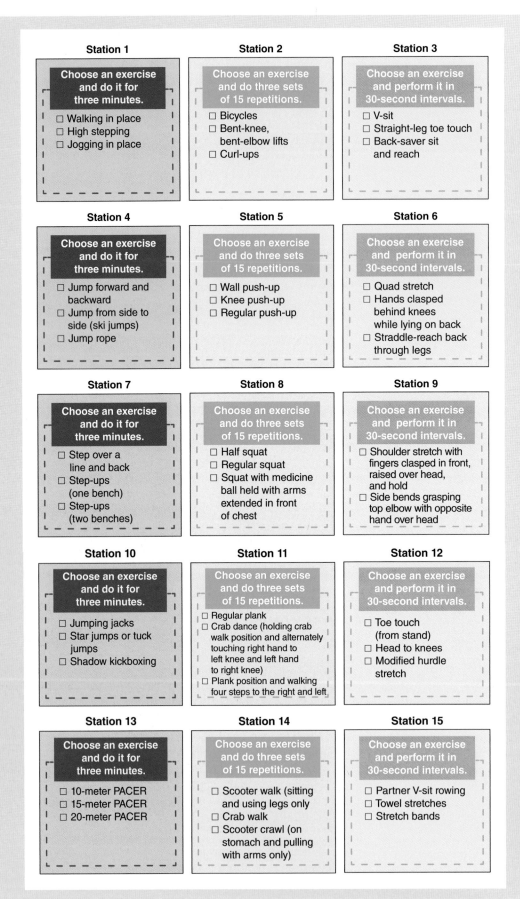

Figure 22.13 Station posters.

1. What type of exercise is performed at the purple stations?

Answer:

2. What type of exercise is performed at the green stations?

Answer:

3. What type of exercise is performed at the gold stations?

Answer:

4. What FITT guideline is varied by the choices provided at each station?

Answer:

5. If you did the 15 stations workout two times one week and then three times the next week, which guideline did you vary?

Answer:

6. If you did three sets of each exercise for 30 seconds one week, three sets for 45 seconds the next week, and three sets for 60 seconds the third week, which FITT guidelines did you vary?

Answer:

Figure 22.14   Reflection questions.

Environment: Select moderate-tempo music prerecorded to accompany two or three minutes of activity, allow for a 30-second interval, and then accompany another three minutes of movement. At stations with floor activity, provide yoga mats or small gymnastics mats. Provide pencils in a can at each station. I didn't write this chapter and am not sure what the intent was, so let's omit the record sheet direction.. All students start at one of the five *aerobic* stations (remind them never to stretch cold muscles). Encourage students to select the challenge with which they feel most comfortable; it if turns out to be too easy, they can move on to the next most difficult activity. For each activity, provide both a picture and a description.

Enrichment: Substitute student-created activities.

Performance cues: See exercise glossary.

Intensity cues: speed, body position in relation to gravity, distance, height, range of motion, OMNI level

Type cues:

- **Flexibility:** Hold how long? Which joint?
- **Muscular strength and endurance:** Which muscles? Which body part is being overloaded?
- **Aerobic:** OMNI level? Are you breathing hard? Can you still talk?

Feedback

- KR: "What variable did you use to increase your intensity?"
- KR: "What type of exercise are you doing, and how do you know?"

COOL-DOWNS

National Standard 3

Essential content: identifying the need for a cool-down

Learning outcome: identifying that the purpose of a cool-down is to gradually return the heart to its resting rate and prevent pooling of blood in large muscle groups after exercise, thus preventing discomfort

Teaching style: practice and inclusion (when selecting activities)

Activity note: Because most activities designed for flexibility enhancement can also be used as excellent cool-down activities, several flexibility activities are presented here. For worksheets, assessments, pictures, and other ancillaries related to flexibility and cool-down activities, consult the *Physical Best Activity Guide: Elementary Level* (NASPE, 2011) and the *Fitness for Life: Elementary school physical education lesson plans* (Corbin et al., 2010).

YOGA ANIMAL POSES

Gather all students in a circle on the floor, facing the center and sitting on mats. Ask for volunteers to lead poses, which students hold for 10 to 15 seconds. During the pose, students focus on creating the pose, breathing in to a count of five, and exhaling to a count of five. Before moving into another pose, ask students where they feel the stretch. Here are some possible poses (adapted from Pizer, 2015):

- **Cat-to-cow stretch:** On hands and knees, while maintaining an angle of about 90 degrees of hip and knee bend, slowly arch the back, with the head arched backward and the lower back stretching (cat). Then slowly reverse the arch to form a rounded back, extending the middle back higher than the hips (cow). Move to cat stretch to a slow count of five, hold the position for a count of five, and return to the starting position to a count of five. Then move to cow position using the same cadence.

- **Downward-facing dog:** Stand with the legs straight, the arms extended over the head, and the back straight. Bend at the waist, reaching to touch the hands to the floor and extending forward to feel a stretch in the back and shoulders. During the movement, "keep your weight mostly in your legs, your butt high, and your heels reaching toward the floor. Bending your knees a little or a lot is an accepted modification for people with tight hamstrings" (Pizer, 2015).

Downward-facing dog.

- **Bending star:** Stand erect with the legs wider than the shoulders and make a straight line from the top of the head through the back and bottom. Stretch the arms wide to the sides to make a star. Then slowly bend sideways at the waist to the right, sliding the right arm down toward the right leg to a count of five. Hold for five counts, then slowly return to the star position. Repeat slowly to the left side.

- **Inchworm:** While side-lying on a mat, curl into a tight ball with the arms bringing the knees tightly to the chest and with the head and neck bent toward the knees to form a "frightened inchworm." Hold this position tightly for 8 to 10 seconds, then slowly relax the curl and return to a straight side-lying position (as in toothpick pose). Hold the extended position for 8 to 10 seconds. Perform the same sequence while lying on the opposite side. Alternate from curled to extended three times slowly, with one repetition on the right side, one on the left side, one on the right side, one on the left side, and so on.

- **Toothpick:** Stand tall, making a straight line from the top of the head through the back, the bottom, the knees, and the heels. Rise onto the toes and lift the arms to reach over the head for a count of five, then return to the heels on a count of five.

- **Lunge/warrior:** Step forward with the right leg, with the toes pointing forward and the knee bent at 90 degrees. Try to align the right thigh parallel with the floor while the trunk remains aligned (with the spine erect and straight). Slide the left leg backward with the toes pointing to the left. Reach the arms straight overhead. Be sure to keep the hips facing forward and parallel with the shoulders. The stretch is felt in the upper and inner thigh. Hold for 10 counts, then exchange leg positions (left leg forward, right leg back).

- **Alternative warrior:** Hold a lunge position. When right leg is forward, right arm extends forward parallel to the ground. Left arm is extended backward, parallel to the ground. Hold for 15 seconds and then switch to the opposite side.

Alternative warrior.

- **Caterpillar:** Start in plank position (push-up position). While keeping the knees straight, slowly (to a count of eight) walk the feet toward the hands, letting the head move to a position between the outstretched arms and ending in the downward dog position (described earlier). Hold for eight counts, then walk the arms forward (alternating right and left) to a count of eight, thus returning to the plank position (see also NASPE, 2011, p. 154, for pictures).

Environment: Select quiet, slow music prerecorded to accompany five minutes of activity. Arrange yoga or small gymnastics mats like a pinwheel, with one mat in the middle. Allow volunteer students to lead an animal yoga pose and hold it for 10 seconds. Provide each student with a personal record sheet to ensure that each major muscle group is stretched. For each activity, provide pictures and descriptions. See NASPE (2011, activity 5.4, intermediate yoga poses) for signs and assessments.

SPORTS IN SLOW-MO

Cut out action pictures of athletes from magazines or newspapers for a variety of popular sports. Mount them on index cards and scatter them around the room or on cones. While playing slow music (prerecorded with 60-second intervals), have students circulate clockwise from cone to cone. Students start by standing with their feet together, then move through the range of motion depicted in the action picture to the count of 10. Do this five times.

TOWEL/HAMSTRING STRETCHING

- Sit on a mat or on the floor with the legs in a V position, stretching wide, and grasp a towel with one hand at each end. Bend toward the right leg, placing the middle of the towel around the bottom or arch of the foot. Gently pull, keeping the knee straight, and draw the chest toward the knee to a count of five. Hold for five counts, then return to the seated starting position. Repeat with the left leg. Alternate legs and stretch each leg three times. Inhale to start; exhale to hold the position.

- Repeat the preceding sequence with the legs straight ahead and together. Loop the towel over the arches of both feet and pull the chest gently toward both knees. Remember to breathe. Move slowly and hold the stretch.

- Repeat as before, with the legs straight, but from an erect standing position. Bend only at the waist.

- For the next variation of stretching with a towel grasp one end of the towel from a standing or seated position with one hand and let the other end drape down the back. With the free hand, reach low and behind the back to grasp the free end of the towel. Gently and gradually pull the upper arm and shoulder backward to stretch the front of the shoulder joint. Repeat with the opposite side.

- While standing, grasp each end of the towel with the arms at the sides and the towel extended in front of the waist. Slowly, to a count of eight, rotate the arms forward and upward, extending them over the head and as far back as is comfortable. Return to the starting position.

- Then perform the exercise with the towel extended behind the buttocks. Slowly rotate backward and upward, then return to the starting position.

FLEXIBILITY CACHING

Patterned after geocaching, this activity uses task cards for flexibility activities addressing each part of the body. Turn the cards upside down inside different-colored hoops in a pattern around the gym or activity area. Students must walk in order, following directional cues (e.g., arrows, words, diagrams) posted on a map and do the task shown when they get to each hoop.

Feedback

- KR: "What is the purpose of a cool-down?" (Answer: It returns the heart rate slowly to resting level and prevents the pooling of blood and exercise by-products in the muscles and extremities.)
- KR: "As you stretch, the blood is returning to your center, removing lactic acid from your muscles, and gradually cooling them to normal temperatures."
- KR: "Flexibility exercises are good cool-down activities."
- KRp: "Never exercise at high intensity without slowly cooling down."
- KPp: "Inhale slowly and exhale completely."
- KPp: "Feel the stretch as you extend; feel relaxation as you exhale."
- KPp: "With each stretch, and each breath, feel more relaxation."
- KPp: "Move slowly and extend completely."

DESIGNING A FITNESS PLAN

National Standards 2 and 3

Use the following steps to teach children how to design a personal fitness plan.

1. **Assess current fitness level.** Each child and his or her caregivers must be taught that planning a personal program begins with determining one's current fitness and activity levels. Any of the previously discussed tools can help start this process for students: Fitnessgram, Activitygram, Activity Log, and the Presidential Youth Fitness Program (which offers an online spreadsheet at www.presidentialyouthfitnessprogram.org/resources/index.shtml).

2. **Compare fitness level with standards.** The next step is to post the HFZ standards for children to read and use in evaluating their results. The standards can be downloaded from the Cooper Institute's website.

3. **Create simple goals.** For children, numerical goals are easy to understand. A good starting point is to choose activities taught in physical education class; another good option is to use Fitnessgram test items. The tables below provide some guidelines for progressions and activities. Remember, however, that the best plan is individualized so that children have choices.

4. **Create deadlines.** Regardless of the activities chosen, each chart or log must specify dates for reassessment.

5. **Evaluate progress regularly.** Provide students with time each week to reassess and incorporate their results into their goals and plans.

FITNESS TESTING

Essential content: interpreting and understanding the significance of physical activity log results; designing a fitness plan with help from the teacher; identifying and regularly participating in health-enhancing physical activity (e.g., after school, in community programs)

Learning outcome: identifying that the purpose of physical activity assessment is to provide information for designing a personal activity plan that maintains or increases one's activity level at 60 minutes or more of daily MVPA

Teaching style: inclusion (each child's plan is based on the child's baseline level of fitness)

Administer any physical activity assessment from Fitnessgram or one like the example shown in figure 22.15. Have students log their activity for at least one week, either as an in-class activity or as homework.

Name: _____ Date started:_____

Age _____ Grade:_____ Class: _____ Date completed: _____

Week 1 Day (date)	Physical activity (minutes) Examples: walking (15), bike riding (20), shooting hoops (10)	Minutes (goal = 60 MVPA)	Steps (goal = 15,000)	Goal met? (circle Y or N)
Monday ( )		M _____ V _____		Y N
Tuesday ( )		M _____ V _____		Y N
Wednesday ( )		M _____ V _____		Y N
Thursday ( )		M _____ V _____		Y N
Friday ( )		M _____ V _____		Y N
Saturday ( )		M _____ V _____		Y N
Sunday ( )		M _____ V _____		Y N

On how many days did you meet your goal? (Circle one.) 1 2 3 4 5 6 7

❏ I was physically active for at least 5 days per week.

Supervising adult's signature: _____

Note: Submit this paper log to your teacher and keep a copy for your own records. You can use this log to enter your Activitygram or Activity Log when near a computer.

Figure 22.15 Activity log.

Activity: Have a class discussion of ways to find time to be active, such as wear a pedometer daily. Here are some more examples:

- When watching TV, take a commercial activity break; for example, do curl-ups, run in place, or walk around the house during every commercial.
- Before school, take a walk.
- While waiting in line for the school bus, jog in place.
- Ask a friend or parent to play catch with a flying disc.
- Walk to the bus stop rather than riding in a car.
- Be active on the playground during recess.
- Before every meal, take a walk or run.
- If playing video games, choose an activity game, such Wii Fit.
- Before sitting down to do homework, take a bike ride.
- Invite a friend over to shoot some hoops, play a game of catch, play tag, or do an activity of your choice.
- Get up 15 minutes earlier and do exercise!
- Ask your parent or caregiver to park far away from your destination and walk the rest of the way.
- Take the stairs (down is easier to begin with, then also up) if you live in an apartment or when you go shopping.
- Join a school activity club or team.
- Ask your teacher if you can jog or move next to your desk when you are finished with your seat work.
- Dance, step, or jog in place while your teacher takes attendance.
- Phone or text a friend and agree to be activity partners.
- When doing homework, take an activity break every 15 minutes.
- Offer to help adults with housework or yardwork.
- Offer to teach a brother or sister how to throw a ball or flying disc.

Create goals based on where you are starting. For example, if you have been doing activity for 30 minutes, try increasing the time by 5 or 10 minutes per day until you reach 60 minutes.

Log your information every day before dinner. If you haven't reached your goal, do something active after dinner.

Feedback
- KR: "Did you meet your goal?"
- KP: "Just get active."
- KP: "Whatever you play, get 60 minutes a day."

ASSESSING FITNESS TEST RESULTS

Essential content: interpreting and understanding the significance of fitness test results; designing a fitness plan with help from the teacher

Learning outcome: identifying that the purpose of fitness assessment is to provide information for designing a personal fitness plan

Teaching style: inclusion (each child's plan based on his or her fitness starting point)

Activity: Administer the Fitnessgram, enter the data into the software, and help students print out their own results. Based on the printed feedback, encourage each student to select activities taught in class or included in the Physical Activity Pyramid for Kids to create a personal fitness plan (see Figure 22.16) that meets their needs. To get started, use or modify this table.

Students then may complete a goal-setting worksheet such as the one shown in figure 22.17. For each fitness component assessed by Fitnessgram, students select one or two activities done in physical education class. They then write a target (goal) in either repetitions or minutes for next class, next week, and next month. Remind students that *time* refers to number of repetitions for muscular strength and muscular endurance activities, to number of minutes (or pedometer steps) for aerobic activities, and to number of seconds for flexibility activities.

Environment: When providing Fitnessgram test results, each student's score is best discussed privately or in a parent–teacher–student conference. Explain that the results are meant to serve as a starting point for creating a personal program and that improvement takes weeks—and commitment.

Feedback

- KR: "Fitness assessment and results are personal and individual, unique to each of you. Your plan will be personal and based on your own test results."

- KP: "Do your best to get your best results when taking the tests."

Name:_____ Pre-test date:_____

Self-assessment date:_____ Post-test date:_____

Directions: In the "Starting number" column, enter your "pre-test" score. Examples are given throughout the chart to help you. For week 1, add 1 lap to your pretest score. This sample student would have a week 1 goal of 11 laps. For week 2 you would add 2 laps to the week 1 goal of 11 laps, and so on.

Fitnessgram test	Starting number	Week 1 goal	Week 2 goal	Week 3 goal	Week 4 goal	Suggested weekly increase in time or intensity	Suggested weekly frequency
PACER (helps with body composition)	10 laps	_____ +1 lap	_____ +2 laps	_____ +3 laps	_____ +4 laps	1 to 2 laps per week	Practice daily (5 times per week).
Curl-up	10 curl-ups	_____ +2	_____ +2	_____ +2	_____ +2	2 or 3 reps	Practice every other day.
Push-up	2 push-ups	_____ +1	_____ +1	_____ +1	_____ +1	1 or 2 reps	Practice every other day.
Back-saver sit and reach	1 (R), 2 (L)	_____ +.5	_____ +.5	_____ +.5	_____ +.5	0.5 in (1.25 cm), holding position for 5 sec.	Perform 3 times twice per day on each leg.
Shoulder stretch	Yes (R), no (L)	_____ +.25	_____ +.25	_____ +.25	_____ +.25	0.25 in (0.6 cm), using towel and holding for 5 sec.	Perform 3 times twice per day on each arm.
Body composition	Some risk	Eat breakfast.	Cut back sugar snacks.	Eat 5 to 9 fruits and vegetables.		Monitor diet with MyPlate tracker; get 60 minutes of MVPA.	Daily

Figure 22.16   Personalized plan worksheet.

Name: _____ Date: _____

Goal #	Activity type	Time this class	Time next class	Time next week	Time next month
1	Aerobic activity: Circle one or choose your own with the teacher's help. Walking Running Jumping rope Step-ups Choice:	Try +1 minute. My goal:	Try +2 minutes. My goal:	Try +3 or more minutes. My goal:	Try + 4 or more minutes. My goal:
2	Muscular strength and endurance: Circle one. Arms (push-ups) Abs/trunk (curl-ups) Legs (squats) Choice:	Reps: My goal: _____	Reps: My goal: _____	Reps: My goal: _____	Reps: My goal: _____
3	Flexibility joint: Circle one or list others. Shoulder Back Trunk Other:	Seconds or distance My goal:	Seconds or distance My goal:	Seconds or distance My goal:	Seconds or distance My goal:

Figure 22.17 Goal-setting worksheet.

Feedback

- KR (for younger students): "Circle the goals that you achieved."
- KR: "Why do you think you achieved (or didn't achieve) your goal?"
- KR: "If you met your goals, consider revising them to make them a little harder."
- KP: "Commit to fit—it takes time."

USING TEST RESULTS TO DESIGN A PLAN

Essential content: designing a physical activity plan with help from the teacher

Learning outcome: identifying that the purpose of physical activity assessment is to provide information for designing a personal activity plan (e.g., for activity after school or in community programs) that allows the child to maintain or increase activity in order to meet the recommended goal of at least 60 minutes of daily MVPA

Environment: Arrange a variety of physical activity stations, each with three levels of difficulty, around the gym. At each station, provide cut-out or clip-art pictures of moderate and vigorous activities (or use resources from Physical Best, Fitness for Life, or the President's Challenge). Have each student spend about three minutes at each station, trying each of the activities. Then give each student a handout (figure 22.18) to use in determining her or his preferred activity type and intensity level.

Name: _____ Date: _____

Directions: Visit each station and try each activity. Put a check mark in the column that matches the difficulty (intensity) of the activity for you. After selecting an activity that has an intensity level that is just right for you, perform however many reps of that activity you can in one minute and write that number in the "Reps" column.

Station #	Activity	Too hard	Too easy	Just right	Reps (#)
1	A. Brisk walking				
1	B. Running				
1	C. Jumping in and out of hoops				
2	A. Climbing wall				
2	B. Pull-ups on bar				
2	C. Modified Pull-up				
3	A. Scooter walking				
3	B. Squat thrusts				
3	C. Jumping rope				
4	A. Curl-ups				
4	B. V-sit				
4	C. Supine bicycle (knee to elbow)				
5	A.				
5	B.				
5	C.				

Figure 22.18   Worksheet for determining preferred activity type and intensity level.

Feedback

- KR (for younger students): "Circle the activities that were 'just right' for you."
- KR: "Put those activities and the number you did for each on your personal plan."
- KR: "These can be your goals."
- KR: "Try doing one more 'repetition (rep)' of each activity tomorrow."
- KR: "Adding one more rep each day or every other day is called 'progression' and is important for increasing your strength and endurance in your personal plan."

Big Ideas

- Children's fitness is best developed by being physically active, both at home and during school hours. Teachers need to help children understand that the biggest changes in fitness are achieved through regular physical activity; they must also teach the specific fitness benefits of regular physical activity.

- Best practice for teaching the components of health-related fitness to intermediate-grade children involves teaching them to self-assess and self-monitor the FITT of their physical activity—that is, the frequency, intensity, time, and type.

- The best use of fitness testing results is for developing a personalized plan; test result should not be used for grading purposes.

- Children and their parents need to fully understand both the FITT guidelines and the exercise principles (overload, progression, specificity, regularity, uniqueness, and reversibility). They also need to understand how adherence to the guidelines and principles affects the child's overall health and well-being.

- The FITT guidelines should be applied as follows: Frequency (F) is determined in number of days per week and should be daily. Intensity (I) refers to how hard one exercises and should be moderate to vigorous, with at least one-quarter of the child's daily 60 minutes (time, or T) being at the vigorous level. The type (T) of activity should be varied and should be determined by the interests and abilities of the child. It should also should include both aerobic and flexibility activities on a daily basis and muscular strength and muscular endurance activities addressing each body area at least every other day.

- Children's beliefs about the importance of physical activity are strongly influenced by getting parents and other caregivers involved in their physical activity assessments, monitoring efforts, and activity choices.

- Before grade 5 or so, physical activity intensity is best assessed by using children's own ratings and feelings about how hard they are working (e.g., breathing rate, children's OMNI scale). At about grade 4 or grade 5, teachers can begin introducing children to heart rate monitoring for assessing their activity intensity.

- Many user-friendly, state-of-the-art fitness education programs are available for working with children in grades 3 through 5 in ways that meet national guidelines and national mandates for comprehensive school wellness. Teachers should help children explore the programs and teach them ways to monitor their physical activity and nutritional intake. Introducing children to healthy uses of technology and gaming can help motivate them to become and remain active.

- Teachers are strongly encouraged to teach about fitness by using a variety of enjoyable movement activities, including dance, lead-up games, team sports, and individual and lifetime activities. Fitness education should be integrated into each day—not taught as a separate unit—and teaching children to monitor FITT and fitness development should be part of every physical education class and activity. To accomplish this goal, teachers merely need to regularly stop activities and then ask children questions about how each activity contributes to their personal fitness.

Exercise Glossary

Aerobic Bench Step-Up

What: activity to increase leg endurance and aerobic conditioning by incrementally increasing vertical stepping and gravity resistance

Starting position: standing erect, toes next to aerobic bench or stair, arms bent about 90 degrees at elbow

Action: Step onto bench or stair with right (or left) foot, followed by opposite foot, in an "up, up, down, down" stepping motion. Be sure arms move in opposition to legs on each step.

Cadence: "up, up, down, down" in an even rhythmic pattern; best done to moderate or vigorous music with a strong beat

Bent-Knee to Elbow Lift

What: activity to increase abdominal muscular strength and muscular endurance using gravity as resistance

Starting position: supine lying, knees bent 90 degrees, lower legs parallel to floor, head touching mat, arms clasped behind head, weight on back and shoulders

Action: Touch elbows to opposite knees during bicycle motion as trunk rotates and upper body is lifted slightly off of mat. Touch each knee, lie back down, and rest for two counts. Repeat.

Cadence: two elbow-to-knee touches every second with two-second rest between touches (right, left, down, relax); for more advanced option, no rest period (just right and left rotation between elbows and knees)

Bicycle

What: test to measure abdominal muscular strength and muscular endurance using gravity as resistance

Starting position: supine lying, knees bent, feet in air, head touching mat, arms clasped behind head, weight on back and shoulders

Action: Keep arms behind head and legs completely off of floor while rotating as if riding a bicycle.

Cadence: two or more complete leg rotations every second

Crab Walk

What: test to measure muscular strength and endurance in the upper body, arms, and shoulders using gravity as resistance

Starting position: supine position (chest facing ceiling), knees bent, feet flat on ground, head looking toward knees, hands at sides and even with shoulders

Action: Pushing with arms, lift bottom and back off of floor. Support weight on legs and straight arms (with fingers pointing toward head) with 90-degree knee bend and 90-degree angle between trunk and arms (like a table, with stomach facing ceiling). Walk with a four-point support (hand, hand, foot, foot).

Cadence: either hand, hand, foot, foot or right hand, right foot, left hand, left foot.

Curl-Up

What: Fitnessgram-recommended test to measure abdominal muscular strength and muscular endurance using gravity as resistance

Starting position: supine lying, knees bent, feet flat, head touching mat, arms straight by sides, measuring strip placed where fingertips touch

Action: Keep arms straight during curl. Reach to opposite side of measuring strip (3-inch, or 7.5-centimeter) during abdominal curling motion. Keep heels in contact with floor.

Cadence: once every three seconds according to the "up" and "down" commands on Fitnessgram CD

Head to Knee

What: activity for flexibility in the trunk, lower back, and hamstrings

Starting position: sitting with legs straight at 90-degree angle to back

Action: Keep arms straight while reaching forward to grasp ankles. Slowly bring chest and head to legs and hold stretch. Keep knees straight.

Cadence: slow stretch, holding for five to eight seconds, then returning for five seconds to sitting position; breathing out when reaching toward knees, breathing in when returning to sitting position

High Stepping

What: activity to enhance aerobic endurance (more vigorous than walking, less vigorous than jogging)

Starting position: body erect, elbows bent at 90 degrees

Action: Perform high walking (marching) in place by lifting knees to waist level with arms moving in opposition to legs and maintaining 90-degree bend.

Cadence: two steps every second or faster to evenly paced music

Jumping Jack

What: full-body exercise using large muscle groups

Starting position: straight standing, arms at sides, straight back, legs together (toothpick position)

Action: Spring open to position, feet shoulder-width apart, while simultaneously moving arms laterally to 180 degrees and aligned with shoulders (star position). Return to toothpick and repeat.

Cadence: Alternate between open and closed positions (star and toothpick) at an even tempo.

Knee Push (Modified Push-Up)

What: modified push-up to increase muscular strength and endurance in the upper body and shoulders using gravity as resistance

Starting position: Support weight on knees and hands with fingers spread and hands positioned shoulder-width apart directly under shoulders. Keep body straight from head to knees with head looking at floor.

Action: Bend arms to 90 degrees at lower position. Maintain rigid plank (straight body position) and 50-degree knee bend.

Cadence: one every three seconds to "up" and "down" commands for 90-degree push-up on Fitnessgram CD

Push-Up (90-Degree Push-Up)

What: Fitnessgram-recommended test to measure upper-body muscular strength and endurance using gravity as resistance

Starting position: plank position; weight supported on toes and hands with fingers spread and hands positioned shoulder-width apart directly under shoulders; body straight and head looking at floor

Action: Bend arms to 90 degrees at lower position. Maintain rigid plank (straight body position) throughout.

Cadence: one every three seconds to "up" and "down" commands on Fitnessgram CD

Scooter Walk

What: lateral (side-to-side) jumping with knees flexed and feet together; aerobic activity with higher intensity than jumping in place; an alternative to jumping rope

Starting position: sitting on scooter with knees flexed, feet flat on the floor, arms at sides (or holding onto scooter—but clear of wheels for finger safety), elbows flexed at 45-degree angle, head and eyes forward

Action: Move feet in opposition to each other to pull scooter forward. Push away with alternating feet to move backward. If unable to move when using feet separately, use feet (heels) simultaneously to push or pull. If necessary, use arms in opposition to help generate force.

Cadence: self-paced alternation of left and right

Ski Jump

What: lateral (side to side) jumps, with knees flexed and feet together; aerobic activity with higher intensity than jumping in place; alternative to jumping rope

Starting position: standing (on one side of a line or rope), knees flexed, feet together, arms at sides with elbows at 45-degree angle, head and eyes forward

Action: Jump with both feet together across line or rope. Land with feet together, flexing knees and ankles to absorb force. Use arms to generate force and propel self upward with jump.

Cadence: back and forth every second to a count of "left, right, left . . ."

Squat

What: activity to increase leg strength and endurance by bending knees to 90 degrees and straightening them, slowly, either with or without weight

Starting position: standing erect with feet shoulder-width apart, arms straight out (forward or to sides) and holding weights, head and eyes forward

Action: Bend both knees together, lowering body to maximum of 90 degrees of knee flexion. Keep back and head position erect and eyes forward.

Cadence: down and up to count of "down, 2, 3" and "up, 2, 3, hold"

Toe Touch

What: activity to promote back and trunk flexibility

Starting position: erect (toothpick position) with arms straight at sides

Action: Bend at waist with arms straight to touch floor just in front of toes. Return to start position.

Cadence: For flexibility, hold toe-touch position for five seconds.

Trunk Lift

What: Fitnessgram-recommended test to measure trunk strength and flexibility using gravity as resistant force

Starting position: prone lying (flat on stomach) with body straight, head looking at mark placed on floor, arms straight by sides, hands under thighs.

Action: Raise upper body by arching back while keeping thighs and feet on ground.

Cadence: Lift torso from waist only to arched position and hold for about five seconds. Keep eyes on mark on floor.

V-Sit

What: activity to increase muscular strength and endurance, abdominal and lower back region

Starting position: sitting on floor, back straight, legs straight forward and together, toes pointed away, arms straight at sides, head erect and forward looking

Action: Lift legs together, maintaining straight knees, while reaching arms forward toward toes to create a V between hand and leg position with waist as fulcrum (bending) joint. Hold balance for count of five. Return to sitting position. Gradually increase balance time.

Cadence: one every eight seconds (five-second hold, three-second recovery and relaxation)

V-Sit and Reach

What: flexibility activity for inner thighs, hamstrings, and lower back

Starting position: sitting on floor, back straight, legs straight forward spread at 60-degree angle to form a V on floor, arms straight, head erect and forward looking

Action: Reach arms slowly forward between legs as far as possible. Hold for count of five. Return to sitting position. Gradually reach farther forward.

Cadence: one every eight seconds (five-second hold, three-second recovery and relaxation)

Wall Push-Up (Modified Push-Up Reducing Gravity Resistance)

What: activity to increase upper-body muscular strength and endurance by using gravity as resistance; simulated push-up with hands against wall and feet about two feet (0.6 meter) away from wall to reduce force of gravity

Starting position: plank position; weight supported on toes and hands with fingers spread and hands positioned shoulder-width apart on wall at height lower than shoulders; toes walked backward from wall about 2 feet (0.6 meter) or more; back and legs straight; head looking at wall

Action: Bend arms to 90 degrees at inward position. Maintain rigid plank (straight body position) throughout.

Cadence: one every three seconds to "up" and "down" commands on Fitnessgram CD.

 Visit the web resource for learning activities, video clips, and review questions.

PART
VI

Professional Development

Chapter 23

Developmental Physical Education Curriculum

Key Concepts

- Describing the relationships among the six steps in developing a physical education curriculum

- Designing block plans from sample yearly outcomes

- Providing a rationale and description for a comprehensive school physical activity program

The physical education curriculum is an integral part of the total elementary school program. As such, it incorporates a broad series of movement experiences that enable children to acquire the knowledge, skills, and dispositions to become physically active individuals. When a physical education curriculum is planned, taught, and assessed according to standards and grounded in children's developmental levels, it is not a frill or a mere appendage to the overall school curriculum. Rather, it is an academic program in its own right, and one that is a positive force in the education of the total child.

In this book, you have explored theoretical foundations pertaining to learners (chapters 2 through 4), the content of physical education (chapters 5 through 7), and standards-based instruction (chapters 8 through 12). You have also learned about designing learning experiences that put theory into practice for children from ages 3 through 10 (chapters 13 through 22). With that foundation in place, this chapter provides a step-by-step approach to designing and implementing a developmental standards-based curriculum.

Contemporary curriculum design is often guided by national and state standards. The *National Standards and Grade-Level Outcomes for K-12 Physical Education* (SHAPE America, 2014), which were recently published in a new format and have been adopted or adapted by many states, represent the knowledge, skills, and dispositions that are important for achieving a physically active life.

STEPS IN CURRICULUM PLANNING

Curriculum design protocols are similar regardless of content area. Here is a six-step approach to the process:

1. Establish a value base for the program.
2. Develop a conceptual framework.
3. Determine program goals.
4. Design the program.
5. Establish program assessment procedures.
6. Implement the program.

These six steps have been used for many years, both in education and in business and industry, and they are a commonly accepted way of doing what has come to be known as strategic planning. The process of strategic planning is simply a means of organizing a new program and putting it into action. Each step is discussed in the following subsections.

Establishing a Value Base

A necessary first step in all curricular planning is to establish the value base on which the curriculum is built. Your value statement represents your beliefs and rationale about the purpose and goals of physical education for children. Chapter 1 noted a suggestion by the Institute of Medicine of the National Academies to the U.S. Department of Education designating physical education as a core subject since "physical education in school is the only sure opportunity for all school-aged children to access health-enhancing physical activity and the only school subject area that provides education to ensure that students develop knowledge, skill, and motivation to engage in health-enhancing physical activity for life" (Institute of Medicine Report of the National Academies, 2013, p. 2). When we value physical education as a way to help children achieve and maintain a healthy life, we substantially engage the goals of physical education:

> The goal of physical education is to develop physically literate individuals who have the knowledge, skills and confidence to enjoy a lifetime of healthful physical activity. (AAH-PERD, 2013b)

A physically literate individual

- has learned skills necessary to perform a variety of physical activities,
- knows the implications and benefits of involvement in various types of physical activity,
- participates regularly in physical activity,
- is physically fit, and
- values physical activity and its contributions to healthful living.

Developing a Conceptual Framework

Any curriculum should be undergirded by a conceptual framework—that is, by essential concepts on which the curriculum is purposefully based. The conceptual framework provides the necessary link between the program design and your values and goals; as such, it clarifies, defines, and classifies the terms and concepts used in the curriculum. In a developmental physical education curriculum, the conceptual framework is composed of categories in child development, movement content and learning environment, and standards-based physical education. Figure 23.1 outlines the conceptual framework for the developmental physical education curriculum presented in this text.

Determining Program Goals

Once you have determined the value base of your curriculum and the conceptual framework that will govern its structure, you can determine the goals for the program. As you know from chapter 8, the national standards for K-12 physical education (SHAPE America, 2014) are based on the developmental needs of children; specifically, the standards take into account the phases and stages of motor development; the levels and stages of movement skill learning; children's cognitive, fitness, and affective development; and the movement framework. As a result, the standards can be used to guide the goal-setting process for a developmental physical education curriculum. The exit goals for elementary physical education describe the behaviors that grade 5 students should exhibit on the path to becoming physically literate. Here they are:

1. Demonstrates competence in fundamental motor skills and selected combinations of skills.
2. Uses basic movement concepts in dance, gymnastics, and small-sided practice tasks.
3. Identifies basic health-related fitness (HRF) concepts.

The Learner

Phases and stages of motor development

- Fundamental phase—initial stage, emerging-elementary stage, and mature stage
- Specialized phase—transition stage, application stage, and lifelong utilization stage

Levels and stages of movement skill learning

- Immature beginner
- Beginning level (cognitive stage)
- Intermediate level (associative stage)
- Advanced level (autonomous stage)

Cognitive and affective development

- Cognitive—sensorimotor, preoperational, concrete, and formal operation
- Affective—solitary, parallel, associative, cooperative, and competitive play

Health-related fitness development

- Cardiorespiratory
- Muscular strength and endurance
- Flexibility
- Body composition

Movement Content and Learning Environment

Active Child movement framework

- Fundamental skills—locomotor, stability, manipulative
- Specialized skills—developmental games, dance, and gymnastics
- Movement concepts—body, space, effort, relationship

Environment variables and affordances

- Equipment (size, height, weight, distance, etc.)
- Conditions (space, time, force, relationships)

Task

- Movement skills (critical elements, biomechanical principles, types)
- Task progression (preconsistent, consistent, combination, application)
- Task design (practice and feedback)

Standards-Based Physical Education

National standards for K-12 physical education (SHAPE America, 2014)

1. Demonstrates competency in a variety of motor skills and movement patterns.
2. Applies knowledge of concepts, principles, strategies, and tactics related to movement performance.
3. Demonstrates the knowledge and skills to achieve and maintain a health-enhancing level of physical activity and fitness.
4. Exhibits responsible personal and social behavior that respects self and others.
5. Recognizes the value of physical activity for health, enjoyment, challenge, self-expression, and/or social interaction.

Standards-based assessment

- Psychomotor, cognitive, fitness and affective (process and product)
- Diagnostic, formative, and summative methods, and scoring tools

Instruction

- Developmentally appropriate movement activities, environments and practice
- Teaching Strategies
  - Reproduction styles (command, practice, reciprocal, self-check, inclusion)
  - Production styles (guided discovery, convergent discovery, divergent discovery)

Figure 23.1 Conceptual Framework for Developmental Physical Education

4. Exhibits acceptance of self and others in physical activities.

5. Identifies the benefits of a physically active lifestyle.

As you apply the standards to your program, you will need to decide which goals are emphasized, which goals are achievable or need to be modified, whether you have additional goals (Rink, 2009), and what summative assessments you will use to measure how well students have achieved the goals (see chapter 9 for summative assessments).

In determining the emphasis for each goal (standard), teachers can use their knowledge of children's development in all domains. For instance, pre-K children are at the inconsistent level of fundamental movement skill development, whereas K-2 children are at the consistent level. The fundamental movement skills form the foundation for the movement activities in which children participate and serve as the vehicle for physical literacy and physical activity. Therefore, the primary emphasis for pre-K and K-2 children is to gain the fundamental skills (standard 1) and use movement concepts (standard 2). In turn, through appropriately designed movement experiences, children develop the mature movement patterns that lead to movement skill competence and the ability to gain the health benefits of regular participation in moderate to vigorous physical activity (standard 3). In addition, as children participate with others in the movement environment, they need structured opportunities to gain positive social interaction skills (standard 4) and recognize

the value of physical activity for both enjoyment and challenge (standard 5).

With all of this in mind, figure 23.2 illustrates the emphasis that could be given to each standard as a result of the developmental needs of pre-K and K-2 children. The shift from 5 percent to 10 percent emphasis on standard 3 in grades 1 and 2 reflects children's greater ability to be moderately to vigorously active as a result of gaining more maturity in movement skill performance.

In contrast, children in grades 3 through 5 have progressed to the combination and application levels of specialized movement skill development. Although some children remain at the combination level through grade 5, some others advance to the application level as early as grade 4 due to variation in children's rates of physical development and opportunities to participate in organized physical activities (e.g., youth sport) outside of the school physical education program. More generally, grades 3 through 5 constitute a time of transition from fundamental to specialized skills (standard 1), from movement concepts to tactics and strategies (standard 2), from simple cooperation to teamwork and competition (standard 4), and from valuing physical activity for enjoyment and challenge to also valuing it for health and social interaction (standard 5). In addition, by grade 4, children's systems have matured enough that they can begin applying the FITT guidelines in order to gain health-related fitness (standard 3). Figure 23.2 illustrates the emphasis that could be given to each standard as a result of the developmental needs of children in grades 3 through 5.

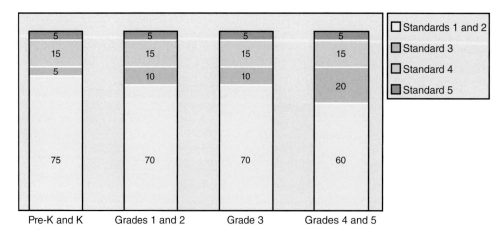

Figure 23.2 Emphasis for each standard in pre-K through grade 5.

Designing the Program

Once you have established the goals for the program and the extent to which each will be emphasized, your next step is to select and sequence the outcomes or objectives that will lead students to attain the exit goals. This process is often referred to as creating a "scope-and-sequence chart." An additional consideration involves the conditions under which the program is to be implemented.

The term **program scope** refers to the breadth and range of the program's content throughout the academic year; specifically, the scope for a particular grade level is the variety of skill and concept units covered during the year at that grade level. A curriculum must have sufficient scope in order to be effective. It should be broad enough to encompass multiple outcomes, skills, and activities for a variety of ability levels. Table 23.1 shows the movement content areas for the program scope in developmental physical education for pre-K through grade 5. The content areas from the preconsistent

and consistent skill progressions serve as the vehicles for addressing the standards in pre-K through grade 2. Content areas from the combination and application skill progressions—and from health-related fitness—serve as the vehicles for addressing the standards in grades 3 through 5.

The term **program sequence** refers to progression in terms of the *year-to-year* ordering of skills taught in the curriculum. The national grade-level outcomes for physical education (SHAPE America, 2014) suggest developmentally appropriate outcomes for each standard for each grade level. The outcomes serve as benchmarks that can guide districts and teachers as they sequence physical education content, assessments, instruction, and learning experiences for K-12 learners. Table 23.2 illustrates the sequencing of K-5 grade-level outcomes for a standard 1 skill and a standard 4 skill. As you can see, the outcomes increase in difficulty, thus representing a progression from kindergarten through grade 5 in both psychomotor and affective development.

Table 23.1 Movement Content Areas for Developmental Physical Education

	Locomotor	Stability	Manipulative
Pre-K through grade 2	Traveling: running, galloping, hopping, sliding, and skipping through general space; to rhythms; to chase, flee, and dodge; and to engage in moderate and vigorous physical activity	Balancing: on different bases; on equipment; with others; adding balance and travel skills	Sending away objects: rolling, throwing, kicking, volleying, and striking (with bat, paddle, and polo stick) to targets and cooperatively with others
	Flight: jumping and leaping through general space, to rhythms, and in relation to equipment; adding traveling and flight skills	Step-like actions: animal walks, wheels, vaults; using body as resistance for building muscular strength	Gaining possession of objects: catching objects sent from others in cooperative relationships
		Rolling: sideward, forward, backward; adding rolling to traveling, balance, and flight skills	Maintaining possession of objects: bouncing and dribbling through general space
	Dance	Gymnastics	Games	Fitness
---	---	---	---	---
Grades 3 through 5	Combining traveling, flight, balance, and step-like actions in rhythmic combinations:	Combining and sequencing gymnastics actions on mats and equipment:	Combining skills and tactics for small-sided practice:	Engaging actively in physical activity in and out of physical education class
	Lyric-directed dance	Balances	Target games	Health-related fitness components (HRF)
	Cultural dance	Rolls	Striking-and-fielding games	Monitoring HRF
	Creative dance	Step-like actions	Net and wall games	Adjusting with FITT
	Social dance	Flight	Invasion games	Fitness testing
				Fitness planning

LIVERPOOL JOHN MOORES UNIVERSITY
LEARNING SERVICES

Figure 23.3 presents a sample scope-and-sequence chart. When completed, it provides a general view of the outcomes throughout the school year (scope) for each grade level (sequence) and reflects a broad range of activities. For instance, each block could represent a four-week unit that included a total of 12 lessons (if the physical education class met three days per week).

In the developmental curriculum, the scope-and-sequence chart serves as the point of contact between the program's goals and outcomes and its content objectives and learning activities. From the chart, teachers derive the yearly **units of instruction** to reach the goals (standards) and outcomes for each grade level. Consider the following sample units of instruction for grade 2:

Personal and Social Responsibility

- Cooperate with others during small-group activities.
- Apply rules and use equipment safely.
- Independently persist in personal and small-group activities.

Locomotor Skills

- Achieve mature stage in traveling and flight skills.
- Combine traveling and flight skills.
- Use chasing, fleeing, and dodging in competitive relationships.
- Use locomotor skills as a way to engage in moderate and vigorous activity.

Table 23.2 Sample Sequence of K-5 Outcomes

	K	1	2	3	4	5
Standard 1: dribbling with feet	Taps a ball forward with inside of foot.	Dribbles ball forward with inside of foot while walking in general space.	Dribbles with feet in general space with control of ball and body.	Dribbles at slow to moderate jogging speed.	Dribbles while increasing and decreasing speed.	Combines dribbling with other skills in one-on-one practice tasks.
Standard 4: working with others	Shares equipment and space with others.	Works independently in small and large groups.	Works independently with partners.	Works cooperatively with others.	Accepts players of all skill levels into physical activity.	Accepts, recognizes, and actively involves others with higher and lower skill abilities in physical activities.

(SHAPE America, 2014)

Sequence---------Grades	WEEKS								
	1–4	5–8	9–12	13–16	17–20	21–24	25–28	29–32	33–36
Pre-K									
K									
1									
2									
3									
4									
5									
------------------------------ Scope ------------------------------									

Figure 23.3 Scope-and-sequence chart

Stability Skills

- Add balances and traveling skills in relationship to equipment.
- Add a roll to a balance and/or flight skill.
- Perform lead-ups to wheels and vaults.
- Use body as resistance to build upper-body strength.

Manipulative Skills

- Approach mature stage in throwing and catching.
- Send objects away to stationary and moving targets of varied height, distance, and direction.
- Maintain possession of objects while moving continuously along different pathways, in different directions, and while avoiding obstacles.

In pre-K through grade 2, students are in the process of developing fundamental skills. As a result, teachers often revisit units throughout the school year to provide ongoing practice rather than segregating a unit into just one part of the school year. In grades 3 through 5, students are in the process of refining and combining skills for participation in fitness and cultural physical activities. Therefore, teachers often segregate physical activity content units (e.g., games, dance, gymnastics) and provide ongoing practice in fitness and affective skills throughout the year. Here are sample units for grade 5:

Personal and Social Responsibility

- Accept and involve others in group work.
- Persevere to improve performance.
- Accept feedback.
- Work cooperatively with others.

Developmental Games

- Target: Roll and strike for accuracy, distance, and direction.
- Striking and fielding: Bat with force and accuracy; cut the lead runner.
- Net and wall: Maintain a rally, set up an attack, and defend space.
- Invasion: Keep possession, defend space, and win the ball in small-sided games.

Developmental Dance

- In different dance genres, refine rhythm, add multiple direction changes, include accent and focus, and use greater isolation and variation of body parts.

Developmental Gymnastics

- Perform, vary, and combine gymnastic actions into sequences.

Developmental Fitness

- Interpret Fitnessgram test results.
- Apply the FITT guidelines to the components of health-related fitness.
- Design a fitness plan with help from the teacher.

Objectives describe the specific behaviors that students will use to reach outcomes. Measurable objectives are tangible; they indicate behaviors or products of behavior that can be seen or heard. All of the following objectives describe specific behaviors that students could use to reach the standard 1 outcome of combining skills in small-sided practice tasks.

- Students will combine throwing and receiving of lead passes to advance the ball.
- Students will combine moving to receive a batted ball and throwing to first base.
- Students will combine dribbling and passing to advance the ball.
- Students will combine moving to receive a serve and returning the ball to an open space in the opponent's court.

All of these behaviors are measurable—that is, they can be observed and rated using a checklist or rubric. Districts and teachers need to customize the objectives for outcomes in order to provide the appropriate path for their students to use in reaching the standards.

The breadth and depth of a program's scope and sequence are affected by the program operating conditions in which the curriculum is implemented. Conditions include the following:

- Number of days per week that children have physical education
- Average number of students per class
- Indoor and outdoor facilities
- Equipment (amount, variety, and developmental appropriateness)

Certainly, districts that provide physical education on only one day per week are much more limited in the goals they can reach than are districts that provide physical education every day. Therefore, advocating for daily physical education is an important undertaking when looking at the value of physical education for helping children develop physical activity patterns that lead to health. Table 23.3 illustrates a yearlong block of units and content areas for a school that provides physical education three days per week (adapted from Rink, 2009).

For any physical education curriculum to provide real value for children, educators must achieve congruence between scope, sequence, and the conditions in which the program is implemented. This congruence helps ensure that children engage in activities reflecting standards and physical education content (scope) that are developmentally appropriate (sequence) and that match the conditions in which the program is implemented.

Establishing Program Assessment Procedures

Program assessment, the fifth step in planning the curriculum, is the primary means of determining whether or not the goals and outcomes of the curriculum have been achieved. Assessment serves as a basis for determining the strong and weak points of your program and helps you target areas for cur-

ricular revision. A standards-based curriculum is rich in potential assessment data when teachers choose and administer summative assessments that show student progress toward achieving the outcomes and report the results on standards-based report cards (see figure 9.26).

Program assessment is conducted through a process known as **data aggregation**, which involves combining data to give you a picture of the achievement of a whole group. The process starts with aggregating data from each class (e.g., all standards-based report card results for Ms. Thompson's second-grade class) and builds to aggregating data for all classes in each grade level (e.g., all second-grade classes). Ultimately, data from each grade level can be compared to provide a picture of how well all students in K-2 and grades 3 through 5 are progressing in achieving all aspects of each of the five physical education standards.

Data aggregation can provide valuable information. For example, table 23.4 presents results from data aggregation for manipulative skill outcomes in grade 2. The chart shows the percentage of students who accomplished the proficient level of performance in each manipulative skill outcome (1.11, 1.12, and so on) in each of a school's four second-grade classes (A, B, C, D); it also presents an ag-

Table 23.3 Yearlong Block of Units for Grade 5

Weeks	Number of lessons	Unit and content
1–3	9	Personal and social responsibility: team building
4–6	9	Target games: striking for accuracy, distance, and direction (golf)
7–9	9	Fitness: applying FITT guidelines to HRF
10–13	12	Developmental gymnastics: sequences on floor and apparatus
14–16	9	Net and wall games: maintaining a rally, setting up an attack, and defending space (volleyball)
17–19	9	Fitness: interpreting Fitnessgram and designing a plan
20–23	12	Invasion games: keeping possession, defending space, and winning the ball in small-sided games (basketball, floor hockey)
24–26	9	Dance: refining rhythm, adding multiple direction changes, including accent and focus, and using greater isolation and variation of body parts (social and creative dance)
27 and 28	6	Net and wall games: maintaining a rally, setting up an attack, and defending space (pickleball)
29–31	9	Invasion games: keeping possession, defending space, and winning the ball or object in small-sided games (soccer, ultimate)
32–34	9	Striking-and-fielding games: batting with force and accuracy and cutting the lead runner (softball)
35 and 36	6	Fitness testing and summative assessment make-up

gregated average percentage for each outcome. Consider the following questions: How might a physical education teacher use the data from the table to describe the program's effect on students' learning of manipulative skills? If the developmentally appropriate expectation were that most students (80 percent) would achieve the proficient level in manipulative skill outcomes for grade 2 by the end of the school year, how would you interpret the results from the table shown in figure 23.4 regarding skill development? Here are some more specific questions to aid your analysis:

- In which skills did 80 percent or more of the students demonstrate proficiency?

- In which skills did less than 80 percent of the students demonstrate proficiency?

- What does the physical education teacher need to examine in order to determine why less than 80 percent of students were proficient in some skills?

- How can the physical education teacher use the data collected at the end of this year to plan for teaching these students in grade 3? To revise how to teach manipulative skills next year in grade 2?

Implementing the Program

The sixth and final step in the curricular process is to implement the program. Implementation is the critical transition between program planning (the big picture) and planning the units and the lessons that will actualize the program. Implementation is where you flesh out the number of lessons per unit, the measurable objectives and assessments, and the learning tasks addressed through lesson plans. Often, teachers map out the progression of lessons for a unit by preparing a block plan, which consists of the sequence of unit objectives, assessments, and learning activities. Figure 23.4 presents a sample grade 5 block plan for the outcome of applying the FITT guidelines to the components of health-related fitness.

In summary, a careful reading of these six planning steps should alert you to the extent and scope of planning that goes into the curricular process. The key point to remember is that each step relates directly to the preceding one, thus making curriculum building a sequential, orderly process.

COMPREHENSIVE SCHOOL PHYSICAL ACTIVITY PROGRAM

A physical education teacher is frequently responsible for coordinating and collaborating with faculty, staff, and parents to provide a comprehensive school physical activity program (CSPAP). This type of program is a systemic approach by which schools use all opportunities for school-based physical activity to develop physically educated students who participate in the nationally recommended 60-plus minutes of physical activity each day and who develop the knowledge, skills, and confidence to be physically active for a lifetime (AAHPERD, 2013a). A CSPAP is characterized by the following five components:

- Physical education

- Physical activity during the school day

- Physical activity before and after school

- Staff involvement

- Family and community engagement (AAHPERD, 2013a)

Table 23.4 Outcomes Data for Manipulative Skill in Grade 2 (Percentage Proficient)

Grade 2 class	1.9 Throwing	1.11 Catching	1.12 Bouncing	1.13 Kicking	1.14 Volleying	1.16 Striking
A	85	70	75	80	80	65
B	80	75	80	85	75	60
C	85	80	85	90	80	55
D	90	80	90	90	85	70
Range	80–90	70–80	75–90	80–90	75–85	55–70
Average	85	76	83	86	80	62.5
Goal	80					

Block 1 (one lesson)	Block 2 (two lessons)	Block 3 (one lesson)
Unit objective: Apply the FITT guidelines to the components of health-related fitness. Diagnostic assessment: Demonstrate how to use each FITT guideline with the sample cardiorespiratory-endurance (CRE), flexibility, and muscular strength activities. Fitness activities: stations for each HRF component using FITT terms to identify how to perform (e.g., how many times, how long, to what extent)	Block 2 objective: Apply the FITT guidelines to cardiorespiratory endurance. Formative assessment: • Identify FITT guidelines used at each CRE station. • Choose a CRE activity to do outside of school and tell how to apply the type and frequency guidelines. Fitness activities: • CRE stations (inclusion style) • Flexibility and muscular strength routine (command style)	Block 3 objective: Apply the FITT guidelines to flexibility. Formative assessment: • Identify FITT guidelines used at each flexibility station. • Choose flexibility activities to do outside of school and tell how to apply the intensity and frequency guidelines. Fitness activities: • Flexibility stations (inclusion style) • CRE and muscular strength routine (practice style)
Block 4 (two lessons)	**Block 5 (two lessons)**	**Block 6 (one lesson)**
Block 4 objective: Apply the FITT guidelines to muscular strength. Formative assessment: • Identify FITT guidelines used at each muscular strength station. • Choose a muscular strength activity to do outside of school and tell how to apply the intensity and duration guidelines. Fitness activities: • Muscular strength stations (inclusion style) • CRE and flexibility routine (practice style)	Block 5 objective: Apply the FITT guidelines to a component of health-related fitness. Formative assessment: Cooperate with a small group to design, perform, and share a station that applies all the FITT guidelines to a chosen component of HRF. Fitness activities: Equipment and resources available for small groups to create a station (divergent discovery style)	Block 6 objective: Apply the FITT Guidelines to HRF components. Summative assessment: • Demonstrate how to use each FITT guideline with chosen CRE, flexibility, and muscular strength activities. • Choose one personal HRF test result and describe how to apply the FITT guidelines. Fitness activities: CRE, flexibility, and muscular strength station

Figure 23.4 Block plan for grade 5

This section of the chapter highlights four school-based physical activity opportunities that extend the school physical education curriculum: recess, daily fitness programs, intramural programs, and special programs. Each can make positive contributions to various aspects of children's development, but none should be viewed as a substitute or replacement for a quality instructional program in physical education. These opportunities are summarized in table 23.5.

Recess

Recess is a North American tradition that is practiced in some form by just about every elementary school on the continent. The recess period typically takes the form of a midmorning or midafternoon break from the normal classroom routine.

Recess usually lasts from 10 to 20 minutes and is held outdoors whenever possible.

"Recess provides children with discretionary time to engage in physical activity that helps them develop healthy bodies and enjoyment of movement. It also allows children the opportunity to practice life skills, such as cooperation, turn taking, rule following, sharing, communication, negotiation, problem solving, and conflict resolution. Furthermore, participation in physical activity may improve attention, focus, behavior, and learning in the classroom" (National Association for Sport and Physical Education, 2006, p. 1).

There is enough empirical evidence to warrant continuation of quality recess programs (NASPE, 2006). The success of a recess program depends in part on the available facilities, whether indoors or outdoors. They should be free of safety hazards

Table 23.5 Elementary Physical Activity Opportunities

During the day	Before and after school
• Start the day with a schoolwide morning activity via classroom media. • Provide opportunities for daily walks. • Participate in low-organized, teacher-led games or rhythmic experiences. • Engage in brief (3- to 5-minute) active transitional activities between classroom tasks. • Integrate movement into academic content. • Provide daily recess for at least 20 minutes. • Host schoolwide special events (e.g., walking programs, field days, fundraisers with a physical activity component).	• Walking or biking to school • Intramural sports (upper elementary) • Physical activity clubs • Youth sports • Traditional daycare and after-school programs • Informal recreation or play on school grounds

(AAHPERD, 2013a).

and should be checked regularly for unsafe conditions, which must be eliminated.

An outdoor recess area should provide ample space for primary-grade children to play separately from older children. When possible, the play area should contain hanging and climbing apparatuses; ideally, they also include large grassy and asphalt areas for a variety of activities. To help stimulate purposeful, vigorous activity, provide markings for line and circle games (e.g., hopscotch, four square). Similarly, an indoor facility, whether a gymnasium or a multipurpose room, should be set up to allow for free choice and encourage vigorous activity.

The second key to a successful recess program involves availability of equipment. There should be enough equipment (e.g., balls, flying discs, ropes) so that all who want to play may do so. In many schools, classroom teachers keep a "fun box" containing equipment to be used for recess. Children check out the equipment and are responsible for returning it to the box at the end of their recess period.

The third key to a successful recess is supervision. One teacher is assigned to supervise no more than two classes at one time. Use the following guidelines to adequately supervise recess:

- The supervisor can see all children at all times.
- There is ample space and equipment for meaningful activity.
- The children are given instruction in appropriate playground activities.

The physical education teacher can play an important role in helping make recess both worthwhile to children and easier for classroom teachers to supervise. For example, the physical education teacher can share with recess supervisors the importance of helping children use carryover skills from the instructional program, such as including others in game play and resolving conflicts respectfully. It is also helpful to ensure that the supervising teacher knows the basic rules of several appropriate games and has access to the proper equipment to help children get started. Finally, establishing a behavior code for play on the playground or in the gymnasium helps reduce problems and maximize the educational potential of recess.

Daily Fitness Programs

Because of the sedentary nature of contemporary society, many children do not get a sufficient amount of regular, vigorous physical activity. In addition, the instructional physical education program generally does not have the time or daily regularity to positively influence children's fitness levels to a significant degree. In response to these facts, as well as recent research (Kahn, et al., 2002; Trudeau, et al., 2005; Kreimler, et al., 2011; van Sluijs et al., 2007) linking vigorous physical activity to human wellness, many educators have advocated adding daily fitness activities to the total school curriculum. As a result, in recent years, many school districts in the United States and Canada have introduced daily fitness programs.

These programs frequently replace a recess period or take place during the first or last 20 minutes of the school day. They serve as an addition to the instructional physical education program and often involve the entire student body, faculty, and staff. The possibilities are varied. For example, hallways may be used for stationary jogging or aerobic exercise to music. A gymnasium or multipurpose room may serve as a station for rope-jumping activities, and a classroom may be used for flexibility and vigorous strength- and endurance-building exercises. The sessions can be led by students and teachers who have been trained as fitness leaders. Daily fitness programs strive for total, active involvement for the entire time that has been set aside. People perform at their individual level of ability and are encouraged to do their best.

As the physical education teacher, you may be responsible for the daily fitness program. If no such program exists at your school, it is your responsibility to develop a solid rationale to convince the administration, faculty, and students of the need for it. Once they are convinced, you will need to train teachers and students as fitness leaders. It is also important to keep interest in the program high by varying types of activities, giving choices, setting school-wide goals, and demonstrating improved levels of fitness.

Intramural Programs

The intramural sports program is a logical extension of a quality physical education program, but it should never be a substitute for physical education. Intramurals are physical activity programs conducted between groups of students within the same school. They generally take place before school, during the noon hour, or after school. An intramural program should include all students who desire to participate, regardless of their skill level. In elementary school, intramurals are special-interest programs for boys and girls who want to use the skills they have learned in the physical education class. An intramural program places greater emphasis on playing the game than on instruction, though there is often an instructional component relating to rules and the application of strategies.

The physical education teacher is frequently responsible for conducting a varied intramural program throughout the school year. Activities may be seasonal and may last four to six weeks. Popular intramural activities with elementary students include dance (urban folk dance or stepping), step aerobics, in-line skating, rope jumping, biking, and a variety of team sports (e.g., floor hockey). Players may be grouped into teams in a variety of ways. Regardless of the procedure used, the teacher's primary consideration should be to equalize the teams; all players should have a nearly equal chance to play and contribute to a team's success. Remember, the emphasis in an intramural program should be on skill application and fun in a wholesome recreational setting.

For an intramural program to succeed, participants should all be provided with written policies regarding parental approval, eligibility, first aid, medical care, and any awards that will be given. The program should be evaluated regularly in relation to its stated goals and objectives. Because participation is voluntary, the number of participants is often a good barometer of the program's success in terms of student interest.

Special Programs

A physical education teacher is often asked to conduct various special programs. In contrast to extended curricular activities, special programs typically last anywhere from less than an hour to a full day; however, whether they are long or short, they usually involve extensive planning and preparation. Special activities may include field days, family activity events, fundraisers (e.g., Jump Rope for Heart, Hoops for Heart), and physical education showcases.

A field day focuses on a variety of activities and is generally held within a single school, usually near the end of the school year; track-and-field days are popular in many elementary schools. Field day is usually held during school hours, and all children from each class compete against other classes. Other exciting options include cooperative field days and interdisciplinary field days. Cooperative field days focus on team-building activities and focus on themes such as trust, cooperation, and interdependence. Themes for an interdisciplinary field day might focus on recycling, multicultural awareness, cultural games, or "a year of science" (with each station featuring a different science concept, such as angular momentum or friction).

Family activity events help families see physical activity as a focus for spending time together. Physical educators can collaborate with parent groups and staff members to sponsor fun runs, hikes, cultural dance events, orienteering, and other recreational pursuits.

The Jump Rope for Heart and Hoops for Heart programs, both sponsored by the American Heart Association (AHA) and SHAPE America, engage children in community service learning. The goal of the programs are to teach children the following:

- The importance of developing heart-healthy habits
- Being physically active can be fun
- Raising funds to support research and education helps save lives in their community and

across the country (American Heart Association, 2013b)

In schools, these programs are conducted by physical education teachers, who prompt students to get sponsors and prepare for the event by practicing their rope-jumping and basketball-shooting skills. Events can be scheduled during physical education class, during the lunch period, or before or after school. As part of the programs, students can help their school earn gift certificates for free physical education equipment (AHA, 2013a).

Many experienced physical education teachers promote their programs with an annual **physical education showcase**. The showcase may be held after school, during the early evening hours, or on a weekend. The goal of the showcase is to give children an opportunity to demonstrate what they have learned in physical education class. Here are some guidelines for mounting a successful showcase:

- Involve all grades and every child in the show.
- Keep the program short; forty-five minutes to one hour should be sufficient.
- Select activities that are part of the regular physical education program.

- Select activities that can be easily learned and performed by all.
- Do not use physical education class time for extended practices.
- Provide the audience with a printed program that outlines the sequence of performances and the objectives they achieve.
- Use scarves, sashes, or hats as simple costumes to enhance the general appearance of a performance.
- Use appropriate musical accompaniment whenever possible to add to the general effect.
- Use props such as parachutes, streamers, and hoops to enhance the performance.
- Publicize the showcase.
- Enlist the help of classroom teachers for supervision on the night of the performance.

A comprehensive school physical activity program provides several opportunities for students to reach the physical activity goal of at least 60 minutes per day. In addition, the extended program supports students and staff in developing a daily physical activity habit that supports them in leading a healthy and active lifestyle.

Big Ideas

- Each of the six steps for designing a curriculum builds on the previous step.
- The cornerstone of a developmental conceptual framework is the value of physical education as a way to ensure that students develop the knowledge, skill, and motivation to engage in health-enhancing physical activity for life.
- The developmental conceptual framework is reflected in the national K-12 physical education standards and K-5 grade-level outcomes, which are used to design the scope and sequence of an elementary physical education program.
- Program assessment helps verify that the unit and lesson plans in the program's scope and sequence have prepared students to reach the grade-level outcomes; if outcomes are not met, the assessment also helps teachers make adjustments in the program.
- Block plans provide the structure to flesh out measurable objectives, assessments, and learning activities for unit and lesson plans that help children reach grade-level outcomes.
- A comprehensive school physical activity program provides opportunities for all school staff to become physically active and for children to apply what they have learned in physical education class to leading a healthy and active life (Centers for Disease Control and Prevention, 2013).

 Visit the web resource for learning activities, video clips, and review questions.

Chapter 24

Professionalism, Leadership, and Advocacy

Key Concepts

- Describing the importance of ongoing professional development
- Explaining the benefits of state, district, and national professional membership
- Describing how to collaborate with others to develop a comprehensive school physical activity program
- Describing ways to market and inform others about your physical education program

The standards-based lessons that you prepare, the developmentally appropriate practices that you employ, and the assessments that you administer to determine the effect of your teaching on students' learning are of paramount importance. However, in order to stay current with new developments in quality physical education, you will also need to become involved in professional organizations and participate in ongoing professional development. In addition, you will need to garner support for your program through a variety of advocacy efforts. This chapter explores ways in which you can continue your learning and serve as an effective advocate for quality developmental physical education.

PROFESSIONAL STANDARDS

The national physical education teacher education (PETE) standards are currently being revised by the Society of Health and Physical Educators (SHAPE America; formerly the American Alliance for Health, Physical Education, Recreation and Dance, or AAHPERD). The PETE standards describe the knowledge, skills, and dispositions that beginning teachers of physical education should possess when they enter the teaching ranks. The standards serve as the basis for both teacher certification and program development for the preparation of physical education teachers. Standard 6 of the PETE standards (SHAPE America, 2009) addresses professionalism and leadership and provides the following expectations for physical educators:

6.1 Maintain currency with developments, trends, and support research in the profession and broader society.

6.2 Provide leadership and support collaboration with significant constituents (e.g., classroom teachers, school staff, school administrators, parents, community organizations).

6.3 Contribute to the promotion and social marketing of quality physical education programming and additional physical activity programming for all students throughout the day.

6.4 Participate in activities that target advocacy and policy development change.

6.5 Demonstrate behaviors of a reflective professional.

Let's now use these guidelines as focal points for examining professionalism and leadership in some depth.

Staying Current

The wide array of professional developmental opportunities ranges from school in-service days to professional workshops to graduate school programs. All of these options are important avenues for gaining the knowledge and skills that you need in order to remain current and grow as an educator. For example, a master's degree can help you become a full-fledged professional who is able to lead curriculum design, administer physical education programs, conduct research, and publish in

the field. Workshops, on the other hand, typically provide practical experiences related to the discipline (e.g., adventure-based education and tactical approaches for teaching games) and address specific educational topics (e.g., anti-bullying and brain-based learning strategies). Such workshops are offered regularly by state, district, and national professional associations.

Webinars and podcasts provide direct access to engagement with the latest trends in education and the physical education profession. They are offered on a variety of pre-K through grade 12 physical education topics by SHAPE America and its affiliated state associations. Yet another avenue for staying current can be found in online communities. For example, SHAPE America members can connect via Exchange, an online communication forum. Another online community is PHYSEDagogy.com, which offers online "summits" featuring presentations by K-12 physical education teachers on a variety of topics; all of the presentations are archived on YouTube. PHEAmerica.org is yet another online vehicle for pre-K through grade12 teachers to stay abreast of current research and trends in the profession.

In addition, all physical educators should be active members of their national, district, and state professional associations. Membership in a state AHPERD or state SHAPE, such as PSAHPERD or Oregon SHAPE, is separate; thus, each state has their own membership fee structure. If you are a member of a state association, you are not automatically a member of the national association. Membership in our national association, SHAPE America (see www.shapeamerica.org/about/membership) also includes membership in the district in which you reside. For example, if you teach in Pennsylvania you would be a member of the SHAPE America Eastern District. Active membership keeps you abreast of workshops and webinar offerings. It also gives you the opportunity to present at conferences; publish in professional journals; and collaborate with colleagues in areas such as research, curriculum development, and legislative policy. You may also choose to become even more involved by serving on a committee or holding an office on a state, district, or national board.

At the national level, you can stay abreast of all current trends in the field. Membership in SHAPE America provides you with access to a full spectrum of elementary physical education resources to help you continue your learning and excel in your career. To find out more about the benefits of membership, visit www.shapeamerica.org/about/membership/. SHAPE America publishes many important resources, such as the *Journal of Physical Education, Recreation and Dance* (JOPERD) and *Strategies* (see www.shapeamerica.org/publications/journals).

Collaboration and Leadership

Physical activity is vital to children's well-being in multiple ways. For example, a plethora of research has demonstrated its relationship to academic achievement, and it can also help address the increase in childhood obesity (Phillips, James, & Castelli, 2015; Mullender-Wijnsma et al., 2016). Given this importance—and being mindful of the *Physical Activity Guidelines for Americans* (U.S. Department of Health and Human Services, 2008)—physical educators must not only provide physical education classes but also help coordinate and deliver before- and after-school physical activity programs, as well as physical activity breaks throughout the school day. Collectively, all physical activity opportunities provided at school can be part of what is now referred to as a comprehensive school physical activity program. One such program is Let's Move! Active Schools (see chapter 1), which empowers school champions (physical education teachers, classroom teachers, principals, administrators, and parents) to create active environments that enable all students to get moving and reach their full potential.

The Physical Activity Leader (PAL) Learning System is a "cutting-edge, all-inclusive professional development resource within the *Let's Move!* Active Schools framework" (SHAPE America, 2016). The Physical Activity Leader (PAL) initiative is designed to develop and support individuals to champion efforts in their local school or district to ensure 60 minutes a day of physical activity for all school-age youth. The 12-month **PAL learning system** is an action-focused initiative resulting in skilled individuals who can initiate tailored plans of action in their respective school settings.

The PAL Learning System begins with a one-day in-person leadership workshop. PALs leave with:

- The formula and tools for making sustainable change and shifting the culture of physical education and physical activity in their community.
- Data to clearly communicate and make the case for a Comprehensive School Physical Activity Program (CSPAP).
- Leadership skills to engage colleagues and the community in support of implementing 60 minutes a day of physical activity for school-aged youth.
- A personalized implementation and action plan.
- The ability to demonstrate the effectiveness of site-selected CSPAP components. (SHAPE America, 2016)

Meg Greiner, the 2005 NASPE National Elementary Physical Education Teacher of the Year, is an example of a teacher who models being a school champion and leader of physical activity. Meg conducts a before-school activity program called "Team Time," during which children engaged in teacher-led aerobic activities.

Collaboration can easily be accomplished by working with classroom teachers to integrate physical activity throughout the school day. For example, physical educators can work with classroom teachers to design and implement "brain breaks," and brain-break activities can also be posted on school websites. Here are three websites that provide brain-break ideas:

Action for Healthy Kids: www.action-forhealthykids.org/tools-for-schools/1252-brain-breaks-instant-recess-and-energizers.

Austin (Texas) Independent School District: http://curriculum.austinisd.org/pe_health/resources/BrainBreaks/index.html.

Educational Materials Center of Central Michigan University: http://emc.cmich.edu/EMC_Orchard/brain-breaks.

Collaboration can also involve working with physical education colleagues across a school district to provide a sequential K-12 curriculum aligned with physical education standards. Ongoing program assessment and data analysis across all levels assures that you and your colleagues make informed decisions about K-12 curriculum revisions. As an elementary physical educator, you can play a critical role in this process because the elementary physical education curriculum lays the foundation for standards-based programs in middle school and high school.

Promotion of Quality Developmental Physical Education

It is important to inform your colleagues, administrators, and parents about the scope of your program

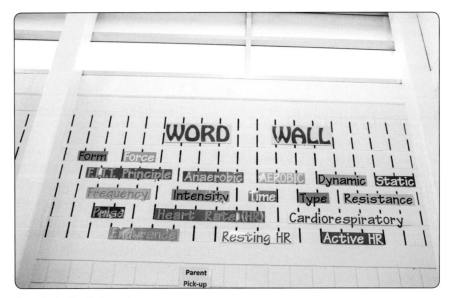

Sample bulletin board.

and its relevance to children's health and development. In this regard, your job is to help others understand that physical education, like other disciplines, is an academic subject with national standards. These constituents also need to understand how the national standards and grade-level outcomes for physical education (SHAPE America, 2014a) affect the development of the whole child. To provide credibility to your program, communicate the conceptual framework (see chapter 23) and how you are implementing it on a daily basis.

The work of promoting a physical education program involves many "layers." It may begin with the design of your gymnasium environment. Is the physical education setting stimulating? Does it convey what you do in physical education? One layer in the process involves putting up bulletin boards that feature photos of classroom learning activities, posters depicting healthy messages, and information about community events that foster physical activity. A sample bulletin board is shown in the photo.

Another layer might consist of an electronic monthly newsletter about the physical education program. A newsletter can provide an excellent means for informing students, faculty, parents, and administrators about your program. Your newsletter might provide the following kinds of information:

- The philosophy of the physical education program
- Current and future curricular activities
- Physical education homework
- Links to national position papers
- Physical activity opportunities for families
- Physical education schedules
- Introductions of new teachers
- Community events promoting physical activity

School websites offer another "layer" for social marketing and promotion of your physical education program. A school website can inform your colleagues, school administrators, and parents about the physical education curriculum, special school events designed to promote physical activity, and classroom teachers who conduct brain breaks with their students.

Yet another layer involves community events that provide opportunities to promote your physical education program. For example, one of our colleagues participated in a community autumn parade. The physical educator even had a float featuring students engaged in physical activities—a very novel approach!

Advocacy and Policy Change

Every state AHPERD or SHAPE, as well as the national association, targets advocacy and policy change. The need is urgent: "The time for advocacy on behalf of all physical education students across this great country is now, and the voice needed is yours and mine. Without the involvement of educators and the critical information we can provide, it will always be others who will shape the education policy agenda" (Psimopoulos, 2013, p. 45). To facilitate action, SHAPE America offers an advocacy-oriented web page featuring several resources, including the 2016 *Shape of the Nation Report* (SHAPE America, American Heart Association, & Voices for Healthy Kids, 2016), various tools for advocacy (e.g., position paper on physical education as an academic subject), a listing of advocacy events, and information about legislative and policy initiatives.

SHAPE America also spearheads SPEAK Out! Day, an annual event wherein professionals meet at the organization's headquarters to engage is a day-long workshop that educates them about current bills and federal policies affecting physical education. Participants then go to Capitol Hill and visit their elected representatives in the U.S. House and U.S. Senate to discuss these issues and garner their support.

Important legislation is also targeted by SHAPE America. SHAPE America was intricately involved in advocating for the Every Student Succeeds Act, passed in December, 2015. In March of 2016, SHAPE America members lobbied on Capitol Hill encouraging senators and congressmen to support full authorization of the Every Student Succeeds Act (www.shapeamerica.org/advocacy/essa.cfm/). School health and physical education are now identified as part of a student's "well-rounded" education. Ongoing advocacy efforts can be accessed at www.shapeamerica.org/advocacy.

Big Ideas

- Ongoing professional development is imperative; it expands your knowledge base and helps you become an educational leader who can provide a quality physical education program based on current research and best practices.

- Membership in professional organizations helps you remain current, network with other professionals, and give back to the profession by presenting at conventions and serving on committees or boards.

- Collaboration with your colleagues, administrators, and parents is key to the development of a comprehensive school physical activity program that enables children to meet national physical activity guidelines.

- Efforts to communicate about and market the physical education program can take various forms—for example, displaying student products (e.g., formative assessment, entry/exit tickets, poster projects, and participation in physical activity) on bulletin boards, publishing newsletters, and maintaining a physical education web page.

 Visit the web resource for learning activities, video clips, and review questions.

Appendix A
Stages of Fundamental Movement Skills

LOCOMOTOR SKILLS

Traveling

Running:

	I. Running	
A Initial stage	1. Short, limited leg swing 2. Stiff, uneven stride 3. No observable flight phase 4. Incomplete extension of support leg 5. Stiff, short swing with varying degrees of elbow flexion 6. Arms tend to swing outward horizontally 7. Swinging leg rotates outward from hips 8. Swinging foot toes outward 9. Wide base of support	
B Elementary stage	1. Increase in length of stride, arm swing, and speed 2. Limited but observable flight phase 3. More complete extension of support leg at takeoff 4. Arm swing increases 5. Horizontal arm swing reduced on back swing 6. Swinging foot crosses midline at height of recovery to rear	
C Mature stage	1. Stride length at maximum; stride speed fast 2. Definite flight phase 3. Complete extension of support leg 4. Recovery thigh parallel to ground 5. Arms swing vertically in opposition to legs 6. Arms bent at approximate right angles 7. Minimal rotary action at recovery leg and foot	

II. Developmental difficulties
A. Inhibited or exaggerated arm swing   B. Arms crossing the midline of the body   C. Improper foot placement   D. Exaggerated forward trunk lean   E. Arms flopping at the sides or held out for balance   F. Twisting of the trunk   G. Poor rhythmical action   H. Landing flat-footed   I. Flipping the foot or lower leg in or out

Initial

Elementary

Mature

Galloping and Sliding:

I. Galloping and sliding	
A *Initial stage*	1. Arrhythmical at fast pace 2. Trailing leg often fails to remain behind and often contacts surface in front of lead leg 3. Forty-five degree flexion of trailing leg during flight phase 4. Contact in a heel-toe combination 5. Arms of little use in balance or force production
B *Elementary stage*	1. Moderate tempo 2. Appears choppy and stiff 3. Trailing leg may lead during flight but lands adjacent to or behind lead leg 4. Exaggerated vertical lift 5. Feet contact in a heel-toe, or toe-toe, combination 6. Heel-toe contact combination 7. Arms not needed for balance; may be used for other purposes
C *Mature stage*	1. Moderate tempo 2. Smooth, rhythmical action 3. Trailing leg lands adjacent to or behind lead leg 4. Both legs flexed at 45-degree angles during flight 5. Low flight pattern 6. Heel-toe contact combination 7. Arms not needed for balance; may be used for other purpose

II. Developmental difficulties

A. Choppy movements
B. Keeping legs too straight
C. Exaggerated forward trunk lean
D. Overstepping with trailing leg
E. Too much elevation on hop
F. Inability to perform both forward and backward
G. Inability to lead with non-dominant foot
H. Inability to perform to both left and right
I. Undue concentration on task

Initial

Elementary

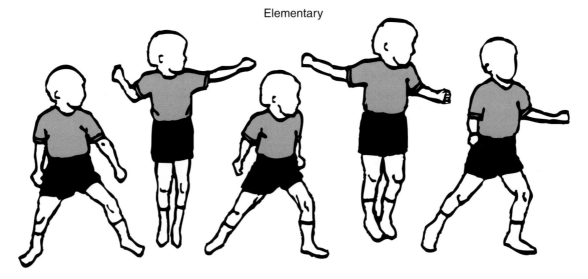

Mature

Skipping:

I. Skipping		
A Initial stage	1. One-footed skip 2. Deliberate step-hop action 3. Double hop or step sometimes occurs 4. Exaggerated stepping action 5. Arms of little use 6. Action appears segmented	
B Elementary stage	1. Step and hop coordinated effectively 2. Rhythmical use of arms to aid momentum 3. Exaggerated vertical lift on hop 4. Flat-footed landing	
C Mature stage	1. Rhythmical weight transfer throughout 2. Rhythmical use of arms (reduced during time of weight transfer) 3. Low vertical lift on hop 4. Toe-first landing	

II. Developmental difficulties
A. Segmented stepping and hopping action B. Poor rhythmical alteration C. Inability to use both sides of body D. Landing flat-footed E. Exaggerated, inhibited, or unilateral arm movements F. Inability to move in a straight line G. Inability to skip backward and to side

Initial

Elementary

Mature

Dodging:

I. Dodging		
A Initial stage	1. Segmented movements 2. Body appears stiff 3. Minimal knee bend 4. Weight is on one foot 5. Feet generally cross 6. No deception	
B Elementary stage	1. Movements coordinated but with little deception 2. Performs better to one side than to the other 3. Too much vertical lift 4. Feet occasionally cross 5. Little spring in movement 6. Sometimes outsmarts self and becomes confused	
C Mature stage	1. Knees bent, slight trunk lean forward (ready position) 2. Fluid directional changes 3. Performs equally well in all directions 4. Head and shoulder fake 5. Good lateral movement	

II. Developmental difficulties		
A. Inability to shift body weight in a fluid manner in direction of dodge B. Slow change of direction C. Crossing of feet D. Hesitation E. Too much vertical lift F. Total-body lead G. Inability to perform several dodging actions in rapid succession H. Monitoring of body I. Rigid posture		

Initial

Elementary

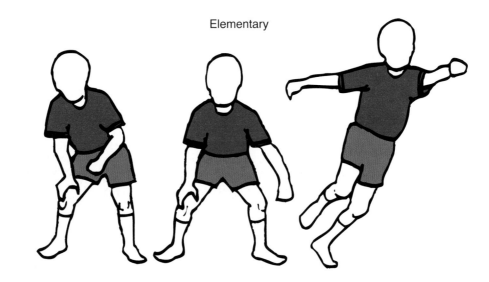

Mature

Flight

Horizontal Jump:

	I. Horizontal jumping	
A Initial stage	1. Limited swing; arms do not initiate jumping action 2. During flight, arms move sideward-downward or rearward-upward to maintain balance 3. Trunk moves in vertical direction; little emphasis on length of jump 4. Preparatory crouch inconsistent in terms of leg flexion 5. Difficulty in using both feet 6. Limited extension of the ankles, knees, and hips at takeoff 7. Body weight falls backward at landing	
B Elementary stage	1. Arms initiate jumping action 2. Arms remain toward front of body during preparatory crouch 3. Arms move out to side to maintain balance during flight 4. Preparatory crouch deeper and more consistent 5. Knee and hip extension more complete at takeoff 6. Hips flexed during flight; thighs held in flexed position	
C Mature stage	1. Arms move high and to the rear during preparatory crouch 2. During takeoff, arms swing forward with force and reach high 3. Arms held high throughout jumping action 4. Trunk propelled at approximately 45-degree angle 5. Major emphasis on horizontal distance 6. Preparatory crouch deep, consistent 7. Complete extension of ankles, knees, and hips at takeoff 8. Thighs held parallel to ground during flight; lower leg lands vertically 9. Body weight forward at landing	

II. Developmental difficulties

A. Improper use of arms (that is, failure to use arms opposite the propelling leg in a down-up-down swing as leg flexes, extends, and flexes again)
B. Twisting or jerking of body
C. Inability to perform either a one-foot or a two-foot takeoff
D. Poor preliminary crouch
E. Restricted movement of arms or legs
F. Poor angle of takeoff
G. Failure to extend fully on takeoff
H. Failure to extend legs forward on landing
I. Falling backward on landing

Initial

Elementary

Mature

Leaping:

I. Leaping		
A Initial stage	1. Child appears confused in attempts 2. Inability to push off and gain distance and elevation 3. Each attempt looks like another running step 4. Inconsistent use of takeoff leg 5. Arms ineffective	
B Elementary stage	1. Appears to be thinking through the action 2. Attempt looks like an elongated run 3. Little elevation above support surface 4. Little forward trunk lean 5. Stiff appearance in trunk 6. Incomplete extension of legs during flight 7. Arms used for balance, not as an aid in force production	
C Mature stage	1. Relaxed rhythmical action 2. Forceful extension of takeoff leg 3. Good summation of horizontal and vertical forces 4. Definite forward trunk lean 5. Definite arm opposition 6. Full extension of legs during flight	

II. Developmental difficulties
A. Failure to use arms in opposition to legs B. Inability to perform one-foot takeoff and land on opposite foot C. Restricted movements of arms or legs D. Lack of spring and elevation in push-off E. Landing flat-footed F. Exaggerated or inhibited body lean G. Failure to stretch and reach with legs

Initial

Elementary

Mature

Hopping:

I. Hopping		
A Initial stage	1. Non-supporting leg flexed 90 degrees or less 2. Non-supporting thigh roughly parallel to contact surface 3. Body upright 4. Arms flexed at elbows and held slightly to side 5. Little height or distance generated in single hop 6. Balance lost easily 7. Limited to one or two hops	
B Elementary stage	1. Non-supporting leg flexed 2. Non-supporting thigh at 45-degree angle to contact surface 3. Slight forward lean, with trunk flexed at hip 4. Non-supporting thigh flexed and extended at hip to produce greater force 5. Force absorbed on landing by flexing at hip and by supporting knee 6. Arms move up and down vigorously and bilaterally 7. Balance poorly controlled 8. Generally limited in number of consecutive hops that can be performed	
C Mature stage	1. Non-supporting leg flexed at 90 degrees or less 2. Non-supporting thigh lifts with vertical thrust of supporting foot 3. Greater body lean 4. Rhythmical action of non-supporting leg (pendulum swing aiding in force production) 5. Arms move together in rhythmical lifting as the supporting foot leaves the contact surface 6. Arms not needed for balance but used for greater force production	

II. Developmental difficulties		

A. Hopping flat-footed
B. Exaggerated movement of arms
C. Exaggerated movement of non-supporting leg
D. Exaggerated forward lean
E. Inability to maintain balance for five or more consecutive hops
F. Lack of rhythmical fluidity of movement
G. Inability to hop effectively on both left and right foot
H. Inability to alternate hopping feet in a smooth, continuous manner
I. Tying one arm to side of body

Initial

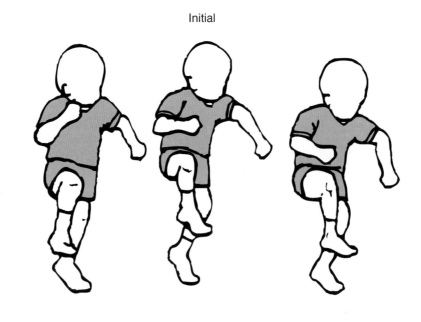

Elementary

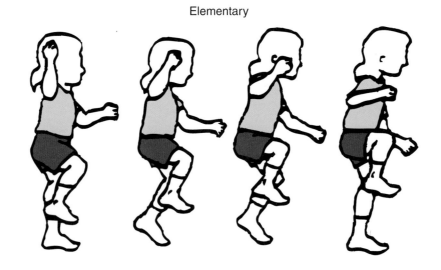

Mature

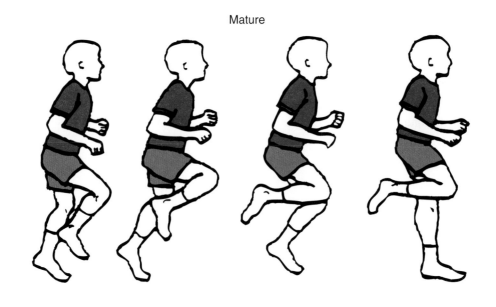

STABILITY SKILLS

Static

One-foot balance:

I. One-foot balance	
A Initial stage	1. Raises nonsupporting leg several inches so that thigh is nearly parallel with contact surface 2. Is either in or out of balance (no in-between) 3. Overcompensates ("windmill" arms) 4. Inconsistent leg preference 5. Balances with outside support 6. Only momentary balance without support 7. Eyes directed at feet
B Elementary stage	1. May lift nonsupporting leg to a tied-in position on support leg 2. Cannot balance with eyes closed 3. Uses arms for balance but may tie one arm to side of body 4. Performs better on dominant leg
C Mature stage	1. Can balance with eyes closed 2. Uses arms and trunk as needed to maintain balance 3. Lifts nonsupporting leg 4. Focuses on external object while balancing 5. Changes to nondominant leg without loss of balance

II. Developmental difficulties

A. Tying one arm to side
B. No compensating movements
C. Inappropriate compensation of arms
D. Inability to use either leg
E. Inability to vary body position with control
F. Inability to balance while holding objects
G. Visual monitoring of support leg
H. Overdependence on outside support

Initial

Elementary

Mature

Dynamic

Forward roll:

	I. **Body rolling**		
A Initial stage	1. Head contacts surface 2. Body curled in loose "C" position 3. Inability to coordinate use of arms 4. Cannot get over backward or sideways 5. Uncurls to "L" position after rolling forward		
B Elementary stage	1. After rolling forward, actions appear segmented 2. Head leads action instead of inhibiting it 3. Top of head still touches surface 4. Body curled in tight "C" position at onset of roll 5. Uncurls at completion of roll to "L" position 6. Hands and arms aid rolling action somewhat but supply little push-off 7. Can perform only one roll at a time		
C Mature stage	1. Head leads action 2. Back of head touches surface very lightly 3. Body remains in tight "C" throughout 4. Arms aid in force production 5. Momentum returns child to starting position 6. Can perform consecutive rolls in control		

II. Developmental difficulties

A. Head forcefully touching surface
B. Failure to curl body tightly
C. Inability to push off with arms
D. Pushing off with one arm
E. Failure to remain in tucked position
F. Inability to perform consecutive rolls
G. Feeling dizzy
H. Failure to roll in a straight line
I. Lack of sufficient momentum to complete one revolution

Initial

Elementary

Mature

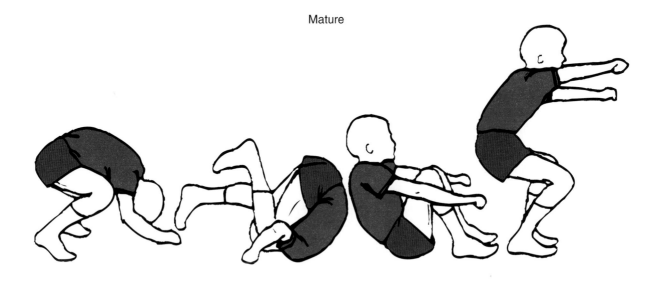

MANIPULATIVE SKILLS

Sending Away

Kicking:

I. Kicking	
A Initial stage	1. Movements are restricted during kicking action 2. Trunk remains erect 3. Arms are used to maintain balance 4. Movement of kicking leg is limited in backswing 5. Forward swing is short: there is little follow-through 6. Child kicks "at" ball rather than kicking it squarely and following through 7. A pushing rather than striking action is predominant
B Elementary stage	1. Preparatory backswing is centered at the knee 2. Kicking leg tends to remain bent throughout the kick 3. Follow-through is limited to forward movement of the knee 4. One or more deliberate steps are taken toward the ball
C Mature stage	1. Arms swing in opposition to each other during kicking action 2. Trunk bends at waist during follow-through 3. Movement of kicking leg is initiated at the hip 4. Support leg bends slightly on contact 5. Length of leg swing increases 6. Follow-through is high; support foot rises to toes or leaves surface entirely 7. Approach to the ball is from either a run or leap
II. Developmental difficulties	
	A. Restricted or absent backswing B. Failure to step forward with non-kicking leg C. Tendency to lose balance D. Inability to kick with either foot E. Inability to alter speed of kicked ball F. Jabbing at ball without follow-through G. Poor opposition of arms and legs H. Failure to use a summation of forces by the body to contribute to force of the kick I. Failure to contact ball squarely or missing it completely (eyes not focused on ball) J. Failure to get adequate distance (lack of follow-through and force production)

Initial

Elementary

Mature

Striking:

I. Striking		
A Initial stage		1. Motion is from back to front 2. Feet are stationary 3. Trunk faces direction of tossed ball 4. Elbow(s) fully flexed 5. No trunk rotation 6. Force comes from extension of flexed joints in a downward plane
B Elementary stage		1. Trunk turned to side in anticipation of tossed ball 2. Weight shifts to forward foot prior to ball contact 3. Combined trunk and hip rotation 4. Elbow(s) flexed at less acute angle 5. Force comes from extension of flexed joints; trunk rotation and forward movement are in an oblique plane
C Mature stage		1. Trunk turns to side in anticipation of tossed ball 2. Weight shifts to back foot 3. Hips rotate 4. Transfer of weight is in a contralateral pattern 5. Weight shift to forward foot occurs while object is still moving backward 6. Striking occurs in a long, full arc in a horizontal pattern 7. Weight shifts to forward foot at contact
II. Developmental difficulties		

A. Failure to focus on and track the ball
B. Improper grip
C. Failure to turn side of the body in direction of intended flight
D. Inability to sequence movements in rapid succession in a coordinated manner
E. Poor backswing
F. "Chopping" swing

Initial

Elementary

Mature

Throwing:

I. Throwing	
A Initial stage	1. Action is mainly from elbow 2. Elbow of throwing arm remains in front of body; action resembles a push 3. Fingers spread at release 4. Follow-through is forward and downward 5. Trunk remains perpendicular to target 6. Little rotary action during throw 7. Body weight shifts slightly rearward to maintain balance 8. Feet remain stationary 9. There is often purposeless shifting of feet during preparation for throw
B Elementary stage	1. In preparation, arm is swung upward, sideward, and backward to a position of elbow flexion 2. Ball is held behind head 3. Arm is swung forward, high over shoulder 4. Trunk flexes forward with forward motion of arm 5. Shoulders rotate toward throwing side 6. Trunk flexes forward with forward motion of arm 7. Definite forward shift of body weight 8. Steps forward with leg on same side as throwing arm
C Mature stage	1. Arm is swung backward in preparation 2. Opposite elbow is raised for balance as a preparatory action in the throwing arm 3. Throwing elbow moves forward horizontally as it extends 4. Forearm rotates and thumb points downward 5. Trunk markedly rotates to throwing side during preparatory action 6. Throwing shoulder drops slightly 7. Definite rotation through hips, legs, spine, and shoulders during throw 8. Weight during preparatory movement is on rear foot 9. As weight is shifted, there is a step with opposite foot

II. Developmental difficulties

A. Forward movement of foot on same side as throwing arm
B. Inhibited back swing
C. Failure to rotate hips as throwing arm is brought forward
D. Failure to step out on leg opposite the throwing arm
E. Poor rhythmical coordination of arm movement with body movement
F. Inability to release ball at desired trajectory
G. Loss of balance while throwing
H. Upward rotation of arm

Initial

Elementary

Mature

Ball rolling:

I. Ball rolling	
A Initial stage	1. Straddle stance 2. Ball is held with hands on the sides, with palms facing each other 3. Acute bend at waist, with backward pendulum motion of arms 4. Eyes monitor ball 5. Forward arm swing and trunk lift with release of ball
B Elementary stage	1. Stride stance 2. Ball held with one hand on bottom and the other on top 3. Backward arm swing without weight transfer to the rear 4. Limited knee bend 5. Forward swing with limited follow-through 6. Ball released between knee and waist level 7. Eyes alternately monitor target and ball
C Mature stage	1. Stride stance 2. Ball held in hand corresponding to trailing leg 3. Slight hip rotation and trunk lean forward 4. Pronounced knee bend 5. Forward swing with weight transference from rear to forward foot 6. Release at knee level or below 7. Eyes are on target throughout

II. Developmental difficulties

A. Failure to transfer body weight to rear foot during initial part of action
B. Failure to place controlling hand directly under ball
C. Releasing the ball above waist level
D. Failure to release ball from a virtual pendular motion, causing it to veer to one side
E. Lack of follow-through, resulting in a weak roll
F. Swinging the arms too far backward or out from the body
G. Failure to keep eye on target
H. Failure to step forward with foot opposite hand that holds ball
I. Inability to bring ball to side of the body

Initial

Elementary

Mature

Receiving

Catching:

I. Catching	
A Initial stage	1. There is often an avoidance reaction of turning the face away or protecting the face with arms (avoidance reaction is learned and therefore may not be present) 2. Arms are extended and held in front of the body 3. Body movement is limited until contact 4. Catch resembles a scooping action 5. Use of body to trap ball 6. Palms are held upward 7. Fingers are extended and held tense 8. Hands are not utilized in catching action
B Elementary stage	1. Avoidance reaction is limited to eyes closing at contact with ball 2. Elbows are held at sides with an approximately 90-degree bend 3. Since initial attempt at contact with child's hand is often unsuccessful, arms trap the ball 4. Hands are held in opposition to each other; thumbs are held upward 5. At contact, the hands attempt to squeeze ball in a poorly timed and uneven motion
C Mature stage	1. No avoidance reaction 2. Eyes follow ball into hands 3. Arms are held relaxed at sides, and forearms are held in front of body 4. Arms give on contact to absorb force of the ball 5. Arms adjust to flight of ball 6. Thumbs are held in opposition to each other 7. Hands grasp ball in a well-timed, simultaneous motion 8. Fingers grasp more effectively

II. Developmental difficulties
A. Failure to maintain control of object B. Failure to "give" with the catch C. Keeping fingers rigid and straight in the direction of object D. Failure to adjust hand position to the height and trajectory of object E. Inability to vary the catching pattern for objects of different weight and force F. Taking eyes off object G. Closing the eyes H. Inability to focus on or track the ball I. Improper stance, causing loss of balance when catching a fast-moving object J. Closing hands either too early or too late K. Failure to keep body in line with the ball

Initial

Elementary

Mature

Trapping:

I. Trapping/Collecting		
A Initial stage	1. Trunk remains rigid 2. No "give" with ball as it makes contact 3. Inability to absorb force of the ball 4. Difficulty getting in line with object	
B Elementary stage	1. Poor visual tracking 2. "Gives" with the ball, but movements are poorly timed and sequenced 3. Can trap a rolled ball with relative ease but cannot trap a tossed ball 4. Appears uncertain of what body part to use 5. Movements lack fluidity	
C Mature stage	1. Tracks ball throughout 2. "Gives" with body upon contact 3. Can trap both rolled and tossed balls 4. Can trap balls approaching at a moderate velocity 5. Moves with ease to intercept ball	

II. Developmental difficulties

A. Failure to position body directly in path of ball
B. Failure to keep eyes fixed on ball
C. Failure to "give" as ball contacts body part
D. Failure to angle an aerial ball
E. Causing body to meet ball instead of letting ball meet body
F. Inability to maintain body balance when trapping in unusual or awkward positions

Initial

Elementary

Mature

Maintaining Possession

Bouncing:

I. Ball bouncing	
A Initial stage	1. Ball held with both hands 2. Hands placed on sides of ball, with palms facing each other 3. Downward thrusting action with both arms 4. Ball contacts surface close to body, may contact foot 5. Great variation in height of bounce 6. Repeated bounce and catch pattern
B Elementary stage	1. Ball held with both hands, one on top and the other near the bottom 2. Slight forward lean, with ball brought to chest level to begin the action 3. Downward thrust with top hand and arm 4. Force of downward thrust inconsistent 5. Hand slaps at ball for subsequent bounces 6. Wrist flexes and extends and palm of hand contacts ball on each bounce 7. Visually monitors ball 8. Limited control of ball while dribbling
C Mature stage	1. Feet placed in narrow strike position, with foot opposite dribbling hand forward 2. Slight forward trunk lean 3. Ball held waist high 4. Ball pushed toward ground, with follow-through of arm, wrist, and fingers 5. Controlled force of downward thrust 6. Repeated contact and pushing action initiated from fingertips 7. Visual monitoring unnecessary 8. Controlled directional dribbling
II. Developmental difficulties	
	A. Slapping at ball instead of pushing it downward B. Inconsistent force applied to downward thrust C. Failure to focus on and track ball efficiently D. Inability to dribble with both hands E. Inability to dribble without visually monitoring ball F. Insufficient follow-through G. Inability to move about under control while dribbling

Initial

Elementary

Mature

Appendix B

Fundamental Movement Skill Assessment Rubrics

TRAVELING SKILLS

Traveling: Running Rubric for Mature and Versatile Performance

Rating	Body	Space	Effort	Relationship
Advanced	Mature performance (as described in the "Consistent mature performance" box below) Runs greater distances with consistent mature performance.	Stride covers more space. Can run along zigzag pathways.	Can accelerate when running.	Can run alongside others.
Proficient	Consistent mature performance Arms and legs are rhythmically coordinated. *Main action:* Alternately pushes off of balls of feet with complete extension of support leg; stride length is at a maximum with trail-leg heel close to buttocks; exhibits definite flight phase; arms swing in opposition and are bent at right angle.	Can cover maximum forward distance with running stride. Can run along varied pathways (curvy, straight, diagonal).	Can vary speed from slow to fast.	Can run around objects and others. Can follow and lead while running.
Developing	Inconsistent mature performance Arms and legs are somewhat rhythmically coordinated. *Main action:* Exhibits limited but observable flight phase; exhibits incomplete extension of support leg; arm swing in opposition is of limited range; sometimes one foot crosses midline of body.	Can cover moderate forward distance with stride. Can run on straight pathways.	Runs at a slow or medium speed.	Can run around objects and others.
Beginning	Emerging-elementary performance Arms and legs are not rhythmically coordinated (stride is uneven). *Main action:* No flight phase is observable; exhibits incomplete extension of support leg; arms swing outward horizontally; arm swing is stiff and short; sometimes one foot crosses midline of body; base of support is wide.	Covers short distance with running stride. Can run forward.		

Traveling: Galloping and Sliding Rubric for Mature and Versatile Performance

Rating	Body	Space	Effort	Relationship
Advanced	Mature performance (as described in the "Consistent mature performance" box below) Can gallop/slide with either foot leading.	Can gallop/slide with increased flight phase thus gaining more height. Gallops/slides along zigzag pathways.	Can purposely vary amount of force exerted when performing small- and large-range galloping/sliding.	Can gallop/slide using a ribbon stick. Can gallop/slide in unison with others or small group.
Proficient	Consistent mature performance Galloping/sliding is rhythmically coordinated; can gallop/slide with right foot as lead foot three or more times in sequence and left foot as lead foot three or more times in sequence. *Main action:* Uses a step-close-step pattern (forward for gallop, sideward for slide). Gallop—Uses step-together with trail leg touching heel of lead foot; push-off of trail foot is forceful enough to achieve flight phase with feet; arms swing forward in coordination with legs to achieve distance and height. Slide—Side of body leads action; uses step-together with trail leg touching inside of lead foot; push-off of trail foot is forceful enough to achieve flight phase with feet; arms stay extended out to side.	Gallops/slides along straight and curved pathways.	Gallops/slides to an external beat or music.	Gallops/slides around objects. Gallops alongside a partner. Slides while mirroring a partner.
Developing	Inconsistent mature performance Gallops/slides are somewhat rhythmically coordinated; galloping/sliding in a sequence is inconsistent. *Main action:* Gallop—Trail leg sometimes moves beyond heel of lead leg; arms swing forward inconsistently to achieve forward distance and height. Slide—Trail leg does meet or come together with lead foot; feet stay shoulder-width apart.	Gallops/slides along a straight pathway.	Gallops/slides inconsistently to an external beat or music.	Gallops/slides around objects.
Beginning	Emerging-elementary performance Gallops/slides are not rhythmically coordinated; cannot gallop on either leg; cannot slide leading with either side; gallops/slides are not sequenced. *Main action:* Gallop—Trail leg moves beyond heel of lead leg; there is no forward arm swing. Slide—There is no flight phase; steps sideways with feet wide apart.	Gallops/slides forward and covers short distance.		

Traveling: Skipping Rubric for Mature and Versatile Performance

Rating	Body	Space	Effort	Relationship
Advanced	Mature performance (as described in the "Consistent mature performance" box below) Can skip with varied arm action; can skip and turn; can combine skipping with other traveling skills.	Can skip forward and backward.	Can skip to an external rhythm and change tempo.	Can skip in unison with others.
Proficient	Consistent mature performance *Main action:* Skipping is rhythmically coordinated with step-hop, step-hop pattern and alternating feet; exhibits low vertical lift on hop from balls of feet; uses arms rhythmically in opposition to legs.	Skips along straight and curved pathways.	Skips to an external beat or music.	Skips around objects. Skips alongside a partner.
Developing	Inconsistent mature performance *Main action:* Step and hop are coordinated; uses arms rhythmically; exaggerates vertical lift on hop; uses flat-footed landing.	Skips along a straight pathway.	Skips inconsistently to an external beat or music.	Skips around objects.
Beginning	Emerging-elementary performance *Main action:* Cannot sequence two step-hops; uses step-hop on one foot to step on opposite foot; pattern continues; uses no arm action and usually wings out to side.	Skips forward and covers short distance.		

FLIGHT SKILLS

Flight: Jumping Rubric for Mature and Versatile Performance

Rating	Body	Space	Effort	Relationship
Advanced	Mature performance (as described in the "Consistent mature performance" box below) Moves body quickly into and out of symmetrical and asymmetrical (twisted) shapes.	Jumps over high levels and wide distances and performs at least a half change of direction in the air.	Makes smooth, effortless transitions between three or more traveling and flight skills.	Makes smooth transitions between combinations of flight skills in low obstacle courses and with others.
Proficient	Consistent mature performance Jumps in a coordinated, rhythmical pattern. *Preparation:* Takeoff crouch and arm position are appropriate for height and distance of jump (two feet to two feet or one foot to two feet). *Main action:* Uses quick extension of legs and arms. *Recovery:* Lands on balls of feet with appropriate crouch to absorb height and distance of jump. Moves body into and out of symmetrical shapes (round, narrow, wide) at height of flight movement and recovers to land on two feet.	Achieves jumps to high, medium, and low levels. Jumps forward across wide, moderate, and short distances. Performs small sideward and backward jumps.	Consistently jumps rhythmically to beats and music. Makes smooth transitions between combinations of jumps with other flight or traveling skills (e.g., run and jump, gallop to jump, jump to jump).	Uses flight skills to move adeptly over, into, out of, onto, and off of low equipment. With others, adeptly uses flight to move in front of, next to and behind, and in roles of leading, following, mirroring, and matching.
Developing	Inconsistent mature performance Jumps are somewhat coordinated. *Preparation:* Takeoff crouch and arm position are somewhat appropriate for height and distance of jump (two feet to two feet or one foot to two feet). *Main action:* Extends legs and arms. *Recovery:* Lands on balls of feet, sometimes flat-footed; uses moderate to appropriate crouch to absorb height and distance of jump. Timing of movement into symmetrical shapes is inconsistent (may start to take shape early or late and may release shape late).	Varies jumps with moderate changes in level and distance.	Times some jumps to beats and music. Combines jumps with other flight or traveling skills with some hesitation (e.g., run and jump, gallop to jump, jump to jump).	Uses flight skills to move over, into, and out of lines, hoops, or ropes on the floor. Can jump off of (not onto) low equipment. Uses flight to move in front of, next to, and behind others; may have trouble keeping up with others.
Beginning	Emerging-elementary performance Performs preparation, main action, and/or recovery with moderate degrees of flexion and/or extension; timing is somewhat coordinated.	Level and distance are seldom varied.	Performs inconsistently in rhythmically timing jumps. Combinations of jumps and other traveling skills are hesitant, stiff, or off balance.	Can jump off of (not onto) low equipment. Is inconsistent in achieving flight to move over, into, and out of lines, hoops, or ropes on the floor and when moving in front of, next to, or behind others; has trouble keeping up with others.

Flight: Hopping Rubric for Mature and Versatile Performance

Rating	Body	Space	Effort	Relationship
Advanced	Mature performance (as described in the "Consistent mature performance" box below) Can hop on either foot.	Can change direction of hop.	Can hop to an external rhythm.	Can hop in unison with a partner. Can hop while using a ribbon stick.
Proficient	Consistent mature performance Hopping is rhythmically coordinated. *Main action:* Takes off and lands on same foot; take-off leg is fully extended; nonsupporting thigh lifts with vertical thrust; arms pump up together as supporting foot pushes off ground; body leans forward into hop; lands with slight knee bend to absorb force.	Hops at a medium level. Can hop and cover forward distance. Can hop along varied pathways.	Smoothly connects three or more hops.	Can hop around objects, alongside a partner, and in and out of a hula hoop.
Developing	Inconsistent mature performance Hops are somewhat rhythmically coordinated. *Main action:* Takes off and lands on same foot; take-off leg has moderate extension; nonsupporting thigh is partially raised; arms swing from back to front in partial range of motion; landing is flat-footed.	Hops at a low level. Hop covers short-range forward distance.	Combines two hops.	Can hop around objects.
Beginning	Emerging-elementary performance Hops are not rhythmically coordinated. *Main action:* Little height or distance is generated in single hop; balance is lost easily; arms are held out to sides and do not pump; body is upright; lands on one foot and sometimes on two feet.	Hop does not cover forward distance and is at a low level.		

Flight: Leaping Rubric for Mature and Versatile Performance

Rating	Body	Space	Effort	Relationship
Advanced	Mature performance (as described in the "Consistent mature performance" box below) Can leap with either leg forward and demonstrate mature performance.	Can perform leap with full extension of legs and arms.	Can leap to an external rhythm (run, run, run, leap, and repeat).	Can leap in unison with a partner.
Proficient	Consistent mature performance Leaps in a coordinated, rhythmical pattern. *Preparation:* Exhibits forceful extension from take-off foot. *Main action:* Legs are fully extended; arms are stretched out for balance and in opposition to legs; achieves full extension of legs during flight; uses forward trunk lean. *Recovery:* Lands on ball of one foot; bends knee slightly to absorb force; can recover and step out of leap into standing position.	Leaps at medium levels covering forward distance.	Uses smooth transitions between running and leaping. Can leap to an external beat on occasion.	Can leap over medium-high objects.
Developing	Inconsistent mature performance Leaps are somewhat rhythmically coordinated. *Preparation:* Produces limited force on takeoff. *Main action:* Legs are extended but not fully; some bend in legs is evident. *Recovery:* Lands on one foot; recovery is not consistent; cannot step out of leap.	Leaps at low levels, covering moderate forward distance.	Transition between running and leaping is not consistently smooth.	Can leap over low objects (one foot [0.3 meter] off the ground).
Beginning	Emerging-elementary performance Leaps are not rhythmically coordinated and resemble an exaggerated run. *Preparation:* Takeoff from one foot is inconsistent; little force is produced. *Main action:* Legs are bent. *Recovery:* Lands on one foot and sometimes two feet.			Can leap over a jump rope or foam noodle on floor.

MANIPULATIVE SKILLS

Manipulative Skill: Rolling

Rating	Body	Space	Effort	Relationship
Advanced	Consistent mature performance (as described in the box below)	Controls direction toward target or partner.	Uses appropriate force for distance of target or partner.	Can roll toward a partner or target.
Proficient	• Uses forward/backward stride stance. • Holds ball in hand corresponding to back leg. • Uses slight hip rotation and forward trunk lean. • Uses pronounced knee bend. • Uses forward swing with weight transfer from rear to forward foot. • Releases ball at or below knee level. • Keeps eyes on target throughout.	Controls direction of ball.	Can vary force.	Can roll toward large stationary target.
Developing	• Uses stride stance. • Holds ball with one hand on bottom of ball and one on top. • Uses backward arm swing without weight transfer to rear foot. • Uses limited knee bend. • Forward swing has limited follow-through. • Releases ball between knee and waist level. • Eyes alternately monitor target and ball.	Cannot control direction and trajectory.		
Beginning	• Uses straddle stance. • Holds ball with hands on sides with palms facing each other. • Exhibits acute bend at waist and backward pendulum motion of arms. • Eyes monitor ball. • Uses forward arm swing and trunk lift with release of ball.			

Manipulative Skill: Overhand Throw

Rating	Body	Space	Effort	Relationship
Advanced	Mature performance (as described in the box below)	Throws to moving targets at high, medium, and low levels.	Can generate appropriate force for medium and far distances to moving targets.	Can throw to moving partner.
Proficient	Preparation • Positions side toward target. • Holds ball in both hands at waist level and off center toward throwing side. Execution • Winds up, bringing throwing arm back behind head with elbow bent at 90-degree angle (L shape). • Steps toward target on opposite foot. • Rotates chest and hips toward target as throwing arm is extended toward target. Follow-through • Throwing arm follows through across body.	Throws to stationary targets at high, medium, and low levels.	Can generate appropriate force to reach medium distance to stationary targets.	Can throw to stationary partner.
Developing	Preparation • Positions side to target. • Holds ball in both hands at waist level and off center toward throwing side. Execution • Wind-up is limited, and arm is not drawn back behind head. • Steps toward target on opposite foot. • Uses some rotation of hips and chest as throwing arm is extended toward target. Follow-through • Sometimes follows through across body.	Throws to medium-level targets.	Force is generated inconsistently.	Can throw to large stationary targets.
Beginning	Preparation • Chest faces target. • Holds ball in both hands at waist level. Execution: • Wind-up is limited. • Elbow leads throwing action. • Steps with same foot as throwing arm or takes no step. Follow-through • Does not follow through.	Cannot throw consistently to a specified level. Throws downward toward low targets.	Generates little force.	Throws to wall as target.

Manipulative Skill: Kicking

Rating	Body	Space	Effort	Relationship
Advanced	Mature performance (as described in the box below) Can consistently loft ball or kick it low.	Kicks to medium and far distances to targets of varying size.	Can generate appropriate force for required distance.	Can consistently kick to specified area.
Proficient	Preparation • Eyes focus on ball. • Uses two- or three-step approach with last step on nonkicking foot. • Nonkicking foot is placed beside and slightly behind ball. Execution • Leg action is from knee down. • Contacts ball with shoelaces. • Contacts middle of ball for low kick (trunk leans forward). • Contacts bottom of ball for lofted kick (trunk leans backward). Follow-through • Leg extends toward target at low level.	Kicks to medium distance and large targets.	Can generate medium force with approach.	Can kick to specified large area on occasion.
Developing	Preparation • Eyes focus on ball. • Nonkicking foot is placed beside and slightly behind ball with no approach. Execution • Leg action is from knee down. • Contacts ball with shoelaces. • Cannot control level of kick by foot placement on ball. Follow-through • Leg extends toward target at low level.	Kicks to close distance and large targets.	Can generate medium force.	Cannot kick to specified target area.
Beginning	Preparation • No approach is used. • Needs markers on floor for placement of nonkicking foot. Execution • Kicks from hip rather than knee-on-down action. Follow-through • Follow-through is high and not consistently toward target.	Can kick to close distances; direction of kick is unpredictable.	Generates little force.	Can kick only to very large area.

Manipulative Skill: Catching

Rating	Body	Space	Effort	Relationship
Advanced	Consistent mature performance (as described in the box below)	Can catch any size of ball from low, horizontal, or high trajectory.	Can absorb force when catching ball coming fast.	Can position body to get behind or square with oncoming ball from any distance and speed.
Proficient	Preparation • Reaches out for ball with hands. • Keeps thumbs together for above-head catch. • Keeps pinkies together for below-waist catch. • Moves to get behind oncoming ball or anticipates ball position. • Keeps eyes on ball. • Catches with hands only. Recovery • Gives with body. • Pulls ball into body.	Can catch medium-size ball from horizontal trajectory.	Can absorb force when catching ball coming at medium speed.	Can position body to get behind or square with oncoming ball from medium distance and medium speed.
Developing	Preparation • Reaches out for ball with hands. Execution • Does not position with thumbs or pinkies for height of catch. • Sometimes anticipates oncoming ball and moves to get behind ball. • Keeps eyes on ball. • Uses body (chest) and hands to catch ball. Recovery • Inconsistently gives in upon catching ball.	Can catch large ball from medium distance.	Can catch large ball coming at slow speed.	Sometimes positions or adjusts body to get behind ball.
Beginning	Preparation • Does not reach for oncoming ball. Execution • Uses chest and forearms to catch ball. Recovery • Does not absorb force by giving in with arms and body.	Inconsistently catches large ball from short distance.	Can catch large ball coming at slow speed.	Cannot position body in relation to oncoming ball.

Manipulative Skill: Dribbling With Hands

Rating	Body	Space	Effort	Relationship
Advanced	Consistent mature performance (as described in the box below)	Can dribble in any direction and along any pathway.	Can vary speed on demand.	Can dribble around moving obstacles.
Proficient	• Uses finger pads to push ball down. • Keeps ball in front and slightly to side of body (to right if bouncing with right hand, to left if bouncing with left hand). • Keeps elbow of bouncing arm flexed. • Keeps wrist firm. • Bounces ball waist high. • Keeps chest and head up.	Can dribble along varied pathways.	Can dribble consistently at slow and medium speeds, thus varying force.	Can dribble with control around stationary obstacles.
Developing	• Uses finger pads to push ball down but slaps ball with palm on occasion. • Ball position is not consistent. • Bounces ball waist high most of time. • Head is not up consistently.	Can dribble in straight pathway and in open general space.	Cannot vary speed consistently; generates little force.	Can dribble around stationary obstacles with some control.
Beginning	• Uses palm of hand. • Ball is bounced low and sometimes too high. • Focus is on ball.	Can bounce in open general space.	Force is not controlled at will.	Cannot dribble around obstacles.

Manipulative Skill: Volleying

Rating	Body	Space	Effort	Relationship
Advanced	Consistent mature performance (as described in the box below)	Controls direction and trajectory toward target or partner.	Uses appropriate force for distance of target or partner.	Can volley toward partner from toss.
Proficient	• Gets under ball. • Contacts ball with finger pads. • Extends legs and arms. • Wrists remain stiff. • Arms reach vertically to follow through.	Controls direction and trajectory of ball.	Can vary force.	Can volley toward large stationary target.
Developing	• Gets under ball. • Slaps at ball. • Achieves little lift with legs. • Wrists flex, and ball often travels backward.	Unable to control direction and trajectory.		
Beginning	• Does not judge path of ball or balloon. • Does not get under ball or balloon. • Slaps at ball or balloon from behind. • Does not contact ball with both hands simultaneously.			

Manipulative Skill: Striking With Bat

Rating	Body	Space	Effort	Relationship
Advanced	Consistent mature performance (as described in the box below)	Can strike to any direction or level with consistency.	Can generate appropriate force for distance.	Can strike to specific base area for strategic purposes.
Proficient	Preparation • Uses dominant hand on top of grip. • Prepares bat over back shoulder and behind ear. • Front elbow is level with shoulder. • Uses side-to-side stance. • Side points toward pitcher or tee. • Weight is on back foot. • Keeps eye on ball. Execution • Swing is level. • Shifts weight forward during swing. Follow-through • Follows through across body.	Can strike with some consistency to specific direction and at specific level.	Can generate some force.	Can strike to specific base area on occasion.
Developing	Preparation • Uses dominant hand on top of grip. • Prepares bat over back shoulder and behind ear. • Uses side-to-side stance. • Side points toward pitcher or tee. • Weight distribution is not consistently on back foot. Execution • Swing is level with some consistency. • Shifts weight forward during swing on occasion. Follow-through • Follows through across body on occasion.	Direction of strike is unpredictable.	Generates little force.	Cannot strike in relationship to bases or players on base.
Beginning	Preparation • Either hand is placed on top. • Holds bat in front of shoulder. • Stance has chest toward tee. Execution • Swing is not level; goes either high to low or low to high. Follow-through • No follow-through is used.	Direction of strike is unpredictable.	Generates little force.	Exhibits no relationship awareness.

Glossary

A

accent—Emphasis given to a musical beat, usually the first beat of each measure.

accordion principle—Rule of practice for shaping social behavior in which time is given to or taken away from student participation based on their level of successful self-direction.

Active Child—Visual representation of the relationship between movement content and movement concepts.

Activitygram (The Cooper Institute, 2010)—A program for recording the regularity and modification of intensity of participation in physical activity.

advanced level—Third and final level of the process of learning a new movement skill, in which the learner refines performance and individualizes the task; also referred to as *fine-tuning level*.

advocacy—Process of informing others of the benefits of our profession.

affective learning goal—Learning goal focused on personal and social responsibility and on the ability to identify with the benefits of physical activity.

affordance—Factor in the requirements of a task, the biology of an individual, or the conditions of a learning environment that tends to promote or encourage developmental change.

age-appropriate instruction—Inclusion of learning experiences in the physical education experience based on chronological age or grade level.

aggressive behavior—Teacher or student behavior that may be, among other things, nagging, accusative, argumentative, and bullying.

agility—A skill-related fitness component, the ability to change the direction of the entire body quickly and with accuracy while moving from one point to another.

alignment—Process of using the focus of essential content as the focus for instruction and for assessment.

alignment charts—Charts detailing the association between essential content, assessments, and instruction for each of the national standards for physical education for pre-school, grades K-2 and grades 3-5.

application stage—The fourth level of a progression in developmental physical education, typically for grade 3-5 children at the intermediate level of learning characterized by combining movement patterns or phrases in cultural activity settings (game, sport, dance, etc).

Appropriate Instructional Practice Guidelines for Elementary School Physical Education—Document published by the National Association for Sport and Physical Education (now SHAPE America) to establish developmentally appropriate guidelines for physical education instruction of young children with respect to learning environment, instructional strategies, curriculum, assessment, and professionalism.

assertive behavior—Teacher or student behavior that is, among other things, respectful, persistent, honest, and straightforward.

assessment—Way of determining student knowledge, skill, physical capacity or behavior either before a unit of instruction (see *diagnostic assessment*), during a unit (see *formative assessment*), or at the end of a unit (see *summative assessment*).

asthma—Chronic inflammation of the airways, sometimes induced by prolonged intense exercise, that prevents oxygen from getting to the lungs and causes respiratory conditions such as chest tightness, coughing, wheezing, and shortness of breath.

ataxic CP—Form of cerebral palsy characterized by very poor balance and coordination and resulting in movements that are slow, deliberate, and wobbly.

athetoid CP—Form of cerebral palsy characterized by movement that is involuntary, jerky, uncoordinated, random, and almost constant.

attention-deficit/hyperactivity disorder (ADHD)—Condition associated with three main behavioral issues: hyperactivity, difficulty with paying attention, and impulsivity.

augmented feedback—Information about learner performance coming from a source outside the learner (teacher, peer, etc.).

authentic assessment—Contextually relevant means of evaluating student progress in the cognitive, affective, and motor domains; sometimes referred to as *alternative assessment*.

autism spectrum disorder—Social communication disorder involving limitations in empathy and social interaction that range from mild to severe; not to be confused with intellectual disability or with emotional and behavioral disorders.

B

backward design—The process of designing standards-based learning by starting at the end, identifying the goal or outcome, then developing the assessments to measure goal/outcome attainment and, lastly, developing the instruction and activities.

balance—A skill-related fitness component, the ability to maintain one's equilibrium in relation to gravity both in static postures and in dynamic activities.

balancing—Gymnastic skill theme including static and dynamic stability skills

beginner level—First level of learning a new movement skill, in which the learner gains general awareness of task requirements, explores various movement possibilities, and discovers efficient ways of performing; also referred to as *novice level*.

bioimpedance measurement devices—Devices that estimate percentage of body fat or lean body mass.

biomechanical principles—Universal laws of physics that apply to all movement on earth.

block plan—A strategy for mapping lesson progressions in a unit of instruction; generally contains aligned objectives, learning activities, and assessment strategies.

body actions—A category of movement from the movement concept of body awareness involving curling, bending, stretching, twisting, turning.

body awareness—Three-component learning process involving knowledge of body parts, what they can do, and how to make them move.

body composition—Lean body mass in proportion to fat body mass; the amount of lean body tissue (bone, muscle, organ, and body fluid) and fat tissue that makes up body weight.

body rolling—Fundamental stability skill and gymnastic skill theme in which the body moves through space around its own axis while momentarily inverted, as in a forward or backward roll; sometimes referred to as *rolling*.

body shapes—A category of movement from the movement concept of body awareness involving forming the body into straight or round, angular or bent, wide or narrow, twisted, symmetrical or asymmetrical shapes.

bouncing with hands—Sequentially imparting force downward to and receiving force upward from an object while stationary or on the move.

Brockport Physical Fitness Test—Unique health-related criterion-referenced fitness test for children of ages 10 to 17 years with various disabilities.

C

cardiorespiratory endurance—The ability to continue a vigorous activity that places demands on the heart, lungs, and vascular system for an extended period of time without undue fatigue.

center of gravity—In a geometric shape, the exact center of the object; in the human body, which is asymmetrical, a point that changes constantly when the body is in motion and that always moves in the direction of the body's movement or of the additional weight. One's center of gravity falls in the middle of one's base of support.

cerebral palsy—Nonprogressive, permanent *neuromuscular limitation* caused by damage to the motor area of the cortex and, depending on type and severity, resulting in paralysis, weakness, tremor, or uncoordinated movement.

childhood obesity—See *obesity*.

choreographic theme—Choreographic themes are ideas based on topics such as the environment, an event, a prop, or an age-related academic topic such as robots. Themes are developed using the movement concepts of body, space, effort, and relationship awareness.

classroom management—Process of organizing students for learning by means of class protocol and rules for good behavior.

closed skill—Movement skill performed in a predictable and stable environment with the goal of consistency.

cognitive assessment—Process requiring the learner to first think about a concept and then demonstrate that it has been learned.

cognitive learning goal—What students need to *know* in order to understand and enhance their acquisition and performance of skill learning.

combination level—The third level of a progression in developmental physical education, typically for grade 3-5 children at the intermediate level of learning characterized by combining skills into coordinated and controlled movement patterns or phrases.

command style—Reproduction teaching style in which the teacher makes all decisions about what is to be performed and how and when it is to be done and the learner practices the "correct" performance.

Common Core State Standards—Language and math standards designed to homogenize grade-level learning targets across the Unites States.

communication disorder—Condition related to auditory processing or speech and language that ranges from complete inability to use speech and language to stuttering or misarticulation of words.

competitive game—Children vie to achieve a goal through the use of movement skills, skill combinations, and game tactics.

conceptual framework—Essential concepts, theories, and research findings that form the basis for the developmental physical education curriculum.

concrete operational stage—Jean Piaget's third stage of cognitive development, which occurs during the elementary school years and is characterized by curiosity, exploration, experimentation, and self-discovery of new cognitive structures, usually through games, play, and general physical activity.

conflict resolution—Specific problem-solving technique in which two disagreeing students engage in dialogue that involves information gathering, clarification, identification, brainstorming, agreement, and closure.

consistent level—The second level of a progression in developmental physical education, typically for K-2 children at the beginning level of learning new movement skills.

constant practice—Practice approach that is useful at the beginning level of learning a new movement skill and involves multiple repetitions of a skill using the same movement characteristics.

constraint—Factor in either the nature of a movement task, an individual's biology, or the conditions of the learning environment that has the potential to impede development.

content standards for physical education—The five national standards for physical education that focus on what students should know, be able to do and be like as physically literate individuals.

contextual interference—Variation of practice schedules of open skills in one of three ways (blocked, serial, and random mental practice) in order to improve performance and aid transfer and retention of a skill.

convergent discovery style—Production teaching style in which students solve task-related problems assigned by the teacher without guiding clues and the teacher provides feedback without giving the solution for "correct" performance.

cooperative game—Involves partner and small-group activities that promote personal and social responsibility emphasizing group interaction, positive socialization, and working together.

coordination—A skill-related fitness component, the ability to integrate separate motor systems with varying sensory modalities into efficient movement, as in dribbling a ball.

counterbalancing—Process of keeping two individuals in balance by moving their weight and force inward, or toward one another.

countertension—Process of keeping two individuals in balance by moving their weight and force away from one another.

country-and-western dance—Form of folk dance reflecting early settler culture and including activities such as line dances and square dances.

creative dance—Form of rhythmic movement permitting expression and interpretation of ideas, emotions, and feelings.

criterion referenced—Student performance is compared to a rating based on level of achievement rather than, for example, a norm.

critical thinking—Process of comparing ideas, making deductions, generating alternative responses, analyzing situations, and synthesizing information.

cultural dance—Dance activities that express the values, beliefs, traditions, and ways of living that characterize a culture.

cultural norm—Standard of behavior expected of all members of a society regardless of their status or perceived role.

D

daily fitness program—Specific time set aside daily, in addition to the physical education program, in which the entire school (including students, faculty, and staff) engages in a variety of planned fitness activities.

data aggregation—Collection and collation of information on a class-by-class or grade-by-grade basis that yields an overall picture of the entire group.

depth perception—Process by which one sees three-dimensionally through the use of monocular and binocular depth cues and judges distance of others or objects from oneself.

descriptive feedback—Feedback, in the form of either knowledge of performance (KPd) or knowledge of results (KRd), that describes the learner's performance ("You kept your feet together").

development—Continuous process of change, both positive and negative, throughout the life cycle from conception to death.

developmental dance—Developmentally appropriate movement activities in which children use their bodies as instruments of communication and creative expression.

developmental game—Activity in which participants engage in developmentally appropriate cooperative or competitive play, with or without an object in the structure of rules and boundaries.

developmental gymnastics—Self-testing activity in which participants engage in developmentally appropriate gymnastic actions of rolls, balances, flight and step-like actions, varied by the movement concepts, on mats and body-scaled equipment, alone or with others; sometimes referred to as *educational gymnastics* and not to be confused with the sport of competitive gymnastics.

developmental physical education—Physical education program that emphasizes the acquisition of movement skills and increased physical competence based on the developmental level of the learner (i.e., individual appropriateness) and on characteristics of the group (i.e., age-group appropriateness).

diabetes—Inability of the body either to produce insulin (type 1 diabetes) or to properly use it (type 2 diabetes).

diagnostic assessment—Assessment made prior to unit of instruction to help the teacher understand what students already know and can do.

Dietary Guidelines for Americans—Authoritative advice published by the U.S. Department of Agriculture about consuming fewer calories, making informed food choices, and being physically active in order to attain and maintain a healthy weight, reduce the risk of chronic disease, and promote overall health.

differentiated instruction—Use of instructional tasks modified to address all students' developmental needs.

directionality—Ability to recognize spatial concepts in relation to the environment including *left*, *right*, *up*, *down*, *in*, *out*, *among*, *behind*, and *between*.

direction of movement—Category of movement from the movement concept of space awareness involving moving through space from one point to another such as forward or backward, right or left, up or down, and into or out of.

discipline—Process of enabling students to use time effectively in order to meet learning objectives, without hindering other students' attempts to do the same, by helping them learn to make good choices and take responsibility for their choices.

divergent discovery style—Production teaching style in which the teacher decides lesson content and structures movement problems and the learner explores and discovers a variety of movement solutions.

dribbling with feet—Imparting force from the feet to a ball so that it moves along the ground.

dynamic balance—ability to maintain one's equilibrium while the body is in motion, as in walking on a balance beam. As the body moves through space, the center of gravity to constantly shifts over the new base.

E

educational gymnastics—See *developmental gymnastics*.

effort awareness—Awareness of how the body moves in terms of the amount of force applied and the timing and flow of movement.

egocentric—Seeing oneself as the center of the universe and being unable to view the world with objectivity; typical of young children.

element of rhythm—One of the five rhythmic fundamentals, which are underlying beat, tempo, accent, intensity, and rhythmic pattern; also referred to as *rhythmic element*.

emerging elementary stage—Second stage in the fundamental movement phase of motor development, which depends partly on growth and maturation and largely on opportunities for practice, encouragement, high-quality instruction, and during which major elements of the movement task begin to become more coordinated and controlled even as some elements are missing or are performed awkwardly.

encouraging others—Giving positive support to others and celebrating their successes.

enduring understanding—The major intent of each standard that distinguishes it from all other standards.

essential content—What students need to know, perform, and behave like in order to achieve the enduring understanding of a standard.

essential question—Prompts beginning with words such as *what, where, how, when, why,* and *who* to guide detailed exploration of the knowledge, skills, and dispositions that make up the essential content of standards.

explicit learning—Motor skill learning that takes place through active instruction and conscious attempts to improve a particular movement skill.

expressive movement form—Dance that enables an individual, couple, or group to communicate an idea, thought, or emotion.

F

faded feedback—Feedback by an instructor that occurs after several trials and then occurs less and less frequently.

family activity event—Special school-related event bringing parents and children together in physical activities that promote positive family bonds and health enhancement.

feedback—Information that performers receive about their movement responses with the purpose of influencing their rate of learning and level of performance.

field day—Informal, all-school event that involves a variety of fun physical activities and is usually held near the end of the school year.

figure–ground perception—Ability to separate an object of regard (whether visual, auditory, tactical, kinesthetic, or gustatory) from its background.

fine tuning level—See *advanced level.*

fitness education—Process by which learners become fit, informed, and eager movers.

Fitnessgram—Physical fitness testing program designed to accurately and easily assess the components of health-related fitness in individuals and groups from grade 4 through the college years.

fitness learning goal—Focus chosen to help a learner attain and maintain physical capacity and regular participation.

FITT guidelines—Acronym that stands for frequency, intensity, time (duration), and type of exercise and is closely associated with the principles of overload, specificity, and progression.

flexibility—Ability of various joints of the body to move through their full range of potential motion.

flexible feature—Aspect of a generalized motor program or schema that is affected by the specific goals and environmental context features of the movement task.

flight gymnastic skills—Transfer of weight from feet to hands to feet with a flight phase between takeoff and landing as in vaulting or springing

flight locomotor skills—Locomotor skills that involve takeoff, flight, and landing phases (e.g., jumping, leaping, hopping).

flow of movement—A category of movement from the movement concept of effort awareness involving continuity of movement.

folk dance activity—Structured dance activity drawing on cultures around the world.

force of movement—A category of movement from the movement concept of effort awareness involving the strength or power with which a movement is performed.

formal operational stage—Stage of cognitive development, described by Jean Piaget and beginning around age 10, in which the child becomes able to think and reason in more abstract terms, think about the future, and set goals.

formative assessment—Assessment of student progress conducted during a unit of instruction in order to help the teacher understand the student's progress (or lack thereof) and make adjustments in order to maximize learning potential.

functional movement form—Set of movement skills used to accomplish specific objectives in which the product of the action is deemed important (e.g., making a basket in basketball, performing a cartwheel in gymnastics).

fundamental movement phase—Period, typically ranging from age 2 to age 6, during which children learn a wide variety of basic locomotor, manipulative, and stability movement skills. There are three stages of development–initial, emerging-elementary, and mature–within the fundamental movement phase.

fundamental movement skill themes—Movement content topics (locomotor, manipulative, and stability movement skills) from which developmentally appropriate activities are designed for children ages 2-6.

G

generalized motor program—Consistent schema formed in the performance of a movement task that accounts for both specific, stable features and variable, flexible features.

general space—A category of movement from the movement concept of space awareness involving the total space available for one to move through in a room, gymnasium, or playground.

grade-level student outcomes—Specific objectives for students at each K-12 grade level derived from each of the content standards.

guided discovery style—Production teaching style in which the teacher guides learners in the process of discovering a predetermined concept by answering a sequence of teacher-designed questions.

H

health-related fitness—The aspect of physical fitness composed of muscular strength, muscular endurance, cardiorespiratory endurance, joint flexibility, and body composition.

Healthy fitness zone—A rating of body composition related to healthy percentages of fat to lean body mass.

heart rate monitor—Digital device attached to the body to monitor one's heart rate in situations ranging from resting to vigorous activity.

Hoops for Heart—See *Jump Rope for Heart.*

I

immature beginner level—Level of learning for preschool children in the initial stage and the early part of the emerging-elementary stage of fundamental motor development when movements are constrained by perception, body proportion, neuromuscular immaturity, and limited ranges of motion.

implicit learning—Motor skill learning that takes place through play or other incidental activity without the learner being consciously aware of it.

inclusion—Process of integrating children who have a disability into the regular classroom and physical education program.

inclusion style—Reproduction teaching style in which the teacher provides multiple levels of performance for the same task. Students self-assess and choose a challenging level based on individual ability.

industry versus inferiority—Erikson's stage of psychosocial development, during ages 6-12, when children are learning to relate to others and begin to develop a sense of pride in their accomplishments and abilities.

Individualized Education Program (IEP)—Key component of the Individuals with Disabilities Education Act, which mandates that all U.S. children (aged 3 to 21 years) diagnosed with disability be offered educational experiences in the "least restrictive environment" as determined by a personalized evaluation of their present level of functioning.

Individualized Family Service Plan (IFSP)—Early intervention program that serves very young children (birth to 3 years) with disability by taking an interdisciplinary approach to supports and services in order to prevent further developmental delay and help very young children achieve age-level developmental stages before entering school.

individually appropriate—Geared to a learner's phase of motor development and his or her level and stage of movement skill learning.

Individual Transition Plan (ITP)—Planned program that focuses on education, training, and employment objectives in order to facilitate the transition into the postsecondary world by individuals who have a disability and are 16 to 21 years old.

initial stage—First stage in the fundamental movement phase of motor development, during which the individual makes the first observable and purposeful (albeit uncoordinated and often incomplete) attempts to perform a particular movement task.

intellectual disability—Significant limitation, originating before age 18, in age-appropriate intellectual function and adaptive behavior; also referred to as *cognitive disability*.

intensity—In exercise, the level of stress placed on the body or on a body system during activity; how *difficult* an activity feels (see *activity intensity*). In dance, the loudness or softness of the movement or music; how *loud* it sounds.

intensity scale—Tool for shaping social behavior in which a 10-point scale is posted on a gymnasium wall to help students assess their individual level of effort and their willingness to participate in class activities for the day.

intermediate level—Second level of learning a new movement skill, in which the learner begins to combine and apply movement skills in more complex movement forms; also referred to as *practice level*.

intermittent feedback—Feedback by an instructor after every few trials.

intramurals—Competitive sport programs conducted before, during, or after school between groups of students from the same school.

intrinsic feedback—Information about performance that comes from the performer's senses (vision, hearing, touch, etc.).

invasion games—A category of games with tactical interactions including keeping possession of the ball, penetrating the defense, attacking the goal, defending space, and defending the goal.

isometric strength—Ability of a muscle or group of muscles to maintain a contracted state for several seconds.

isotonic strength—Ability of a muscle or group of muscles to alternately shorten and lengthen repetitively.

J

Jump Rope for Heart—Physical activity program, sponsored by the American Heart Association (AHA) and SHAPE America, that promotes development of heart-healthy habits, fun through physical activity, and fundraising for the AHA.

K

kinesthetic perception—The movement sense, which provides information about the position of the body and body parts in the environment, and where the body is moving.

knowledge of performance (KP)—Feedback to the performer about the process or movement pattern of the performance; it includes information about the location, speed, direction, placement, or coordination of body parts or actions.

knowledge of results (KR)—Feedback to the performer about the outcome or end result of movement performance (points scored, shot percentage, etc.).

L

laterality—Internal "feel" for direction that enables one to know left from right and top from bottom without giving conscious attention to the task.

later childhood—Period in developing children that spans ages 7 through 11 years.

learning disability—Restriction in the ability to read, write, think, speak, spell, or perform math operations due *not* to visual, auditory, or motor disability, or to intellectual disability, but due instead to inability to fully use the basic psychological processes involved in speaking or writing.

learning goal blueprint—A chart that illustrates the relationship between a movement content category and the movement concepts.

Let's Move! Active Schools (LMAS)—National initiative begun by First Lady Michelle Obama focused on empowering "school champions" to create active environments that enable students to get moving and reach their full potential.

level of movement—A category of movement from the movement concept of space awareness involving where the body moves, as in a high, medium, or low level.

levels of thinking—Six-step classification scheme developed by Benjamin Bloom in 1959 that has stood the test of time and gained universal acceptance among educators as a progressive hierarchy of learning: knowledge, comprehension, application, analysis, synthesis, and evaluation.

lifelong utilization stage—Third stage in the specialized movement skill phase, in which the individual selects a small set of physical activities to pursue for fun, fitness, and perhaps competition during the adult years.

locomotor skill—Movement skills that move the body through space from one place to another, horizontally or vertically, on the limbs as in walking, running, jumping, and skipping.

low socioeconomic status—Living in a household at or below the poverty level, which is generally measured by eligibility for assistance from the federal lunch program.

lyric-directed dance—Dance activity that uses the words of a song to indicate movements and their proper sequence.

M

maintaining possession—Gross body movement in which force is intermittently imparted to an object to travel with it through space as in dribbling; or to travel with an object by holding it as in carrying a ball.

manipulative skill—Gross body movement in which force is imparted to or received from an object such as throwing, catching, dribbling.

mature stage—Third stage in the fundamental movement phase, which depends on maturation as well as opportunities for practice, encouragement, and high-quality instruction, and is characterized by motor control, movement coordination, and complete integration of all components of a particular fundamental movement skill; sometimes referred to as *proficient stage*.

mental practice—Use of visualization and mental rehearsal in order to improve performance.

method of assessment—The vehicle for students to demonstrate the knowledge, skill or disposition they have learned (e.g., a quiz, skill demonstration, journal entry).

mild intellectual disability—Intellectual disability requiring occasional and limited support in daily functioning.

mobility ability—In a teaching sense, the ability to incorporate multiple teaching styles into a lesson based on the varying needs of learners.

motion perception—Ability to detect the location, direction, and speed of an object in motion.

motor development—Progressive change in movement behavior throughout the life cycle, brought about by interaction between the requirements of movement tasks, individual biology, and learning environment conditions.

motor learning—Relatively permanent change in motor behavior brought about by practice and experience.

movement concept—Four kinds of awareness about how the body moves including body, space, effort, and relationship awareness. Originally described by Rudolph Laban.

movement content—Core of the movement framework categorizing movements as stability, locomotor, or manipulative.

movement framework—A structure that illustrates the relationships among the content and concepts of movement.

multiple tasks, multiple stations—Teaching technique in which advanced learners move from station to station in order to practice various movement tasks.

multiple tasks, single station—Teaching technique in which many different tasks are performed either in the learner's personal space or in space shared with a partner.

muscular endurance—Ability to exert force against an external object for several repetitions without fatigue.

muscular strength—Ability to exert maximum force against an external object.

myelin—Fatty substance surrounding neurons that increases from infancy through early childhood, thus resulting in more efficient transmission of nerve impulses.

MyPlate—Graphic depiction of recommended portion sizes in each food group; published by the U.S. Department of Agriculture.

N

national physical education teacher education (PETE) standards—Performance indicators established by the Society of Health and Physical Educators to provide the basis for quality physical education programs.

net or wall games—A category of games with tactical interactions including maintaining a rally, setting up an attack, winning a point, defending space and initiating play.

norm—Standard of performance derived statistically from population sampling.

novice level—See *beginner level*.

O

obesity—In childhood, body-fat content at the 95th percentile or above as measured by body mass index (BMI) for age.

objectives—Observable and measurable behaviors that students use to reach outcomes.

OMNI scale—See *rating of perceived exertion*.

open skill—Movement skill performed in an unpredictable environment.

overfatness—A condition of having more than a healthy percentage of body fat.

P

PAL learning system—An action-focused initiative resulting in skilled individuals who can initiate tailored plans of action in their respective school settings for a Comprehensive School Physical Activity Program (CSPAP).

paraprofessionals—Individuals who provide instructional support to teachers in the form of one-on-one tutoring, assisting with classroom management, providing instructional assistance, and conducting parental involvement activities, all under the direct supervision of a highly qualified teacher.

pathway of movement—A category of movement from the movement concept of space awareness involving the course followed along the ground when moving through space (e.g., straight, curved, or zigzag pathway).

pedometer—Relatively inexpensive and easy-to-use personal device that makes a digital record of one's amount of physical activity (i.e., amount of steps taken) over a specified time period and is often used in fitness education programs.

peer assessment—Assessment technique in which, using specific criteria, students learn how to critique one another's movement in terms of both process and product.

perceived competence—Aspect of self-esteem involving evaluation of one's own competence in comparison with that of others.

perception—Knowledge or interpretation brought about by a process of combining incoming sensory information (visual, auditory, tactile, kinesthetic, olfactory, gustatory) with information already stored in the brain and leading to a modified response pattern.

perceptual–motor learning—Interaction of perceptual and motor processes through movement experiences resulting in improved spatial and temporal integration.

performance stage—First stage in the advanced or fine-tuning level of learning a new movement skill, in which the learner further refines the elements of the task by working for greater precision and using the skill in various sport settings.

performer scaling—See *scaling.*

personal responsibility—Process by which a learner takes ultimate responsibility for her or his own welfare.

personal space—A category of movement from the movement concept of space awareness involving the area immediately surrounding one's body, usually as far as one can reach.

Physical Activity Guidelines for Americans—Guidelines put forth by the U.S. Department of Health and Human Services recommending that children and adolescents (aged 6 to 17 years) do one hour or more of moderate to vigorous physical activity every day in order to accrue substantial health benefits.

physical activity guidelines for children—Recommendations from NASPE (now SHAPE America) for how often and how long children should engage in moderate to vigorous physical activity.

Physical Best—Comprehensive program for teaching health-related fitness concepts that offers activity guides for the elementary and secondary levels.

physical disability—In students, any physical condition that interferes with one's educational performance, including disability resulting from disease, congenital factors, or other causes.

physical education showcase—Special event, often held yearly, in which classes and grade levels throughout a school provide an entertaining and positive overview of the physical education program.

physical fitness—In a general sense, the ability to perform daily tasks without fatigue and to have sufficient energy reserves to participate in additional physical activities and meet emergency needs; in a specific sense, a set of personal attributes related to the ability to perform physical activity, one's genetic makeup, and adequate nutrition.

physical growth—Generally, structural increase in size; in childhood, steady increase in height, weight, muscle mass, and often fat mass.

physically literate person—As defined by SHAPE America, a person who "has learned the skills necessary to participate in a variety of physical activities; knows the implications and the benefits of involvement in various types of physical activities; participates regularly in physical activity; is physically fit; [and] values physical activity and its contributions to a healthy lifestyle."

physical practice—Progressive repetition of movements with the intent of improving performance.

poly spot—Colorful, rubberized plastic shape often used on gymnasium floors and playground surfaces to indicate specific locations in a lesson or play environment.

power—A skill-related fitness component, the ability to perform a maximal effort in the shortest time possible (striking, throwing a ball for distance).

practice—See *movement skill practice.*

practice level—See *intermediate level.*

practice style—Reproduction teaching style that is similar to the command style insofar as the teacher controls the content but in which the learner has some opportunity for individualized pacing within given boundaries.

preconsistent level—The first level of a progression in developmental physical education typically for preschool children at the beginning or novice level of learning new movement skills.

preoperational stage—Jean Piaget's second stage of cognitive development, which occurs during early childhood, is characterized by egocentric thinking in the formation of cognitive structures, and is facilitated through movement.

prescriptive feedback—Instructional feedback, in the form of either knowledge of performance (KPp) or knowledge of results (KRp), that provides the learner with cues for improved performance.

principle of individuality—Each person improves in fitness at his or her own rate.

principle of overload—In order to enhance strength or endurance, a muscle must do more work than it is accustomed to doing, either by increasing the load of the work or by decreasing the time in which the work is done.

principle of progression—Strength and endurance increase over time in response to the individual's threshold of training and target zone.

principle of regularity—Regular engagement in moderate to vigorous physical activity is essential in order to maintain or increase fitness.

principle of reversibility—Failure to remain active results in measurable decline in one's fitness.

principle of specificity—A specific muscle that is overloaded by increased load or by decreased time for the same load increases in strength, endurance, or both.

principle of uniqueness—See *principle of individuality.*

process assessment—Observational approach to movement skill assessment that emphasizes the qualitative aspects of movement, including mechanics, form, and style.

product assessment—Quantitative approach to motor assessment concerned with the end result of movement in terms of such things as how far, how fast, how high, and how many.

production cluster—Series of teaching styles (including guided, convergent, and divergent discovery) requiring the learner to use critical thinking processes that facilitate the discovery of concepts and the development of alternative concepts.

proficient stage—See *mature stage.*

program assessment—Continuous process that uses both objective and subjective means to evaluate a curriculum's strong and weak points, thereby leading to curricular revisions and improvement.

program operating conditions—Location-specific environment in which a physical education program is conducted, including such elements as time of year, climate and weather conditions, number of times and minutes per week, available facilities and equipment, and class size.

program scope—In curriculum construction, the breadth or range of program content during one school year.

program sequence—In curriculum construction, the timing and depth of the program in terms of year-to-year progression.

psychomotor learning goals—For young children, mature patterns of various fundamental movement skills, which enable them to progress to more complex skills that provide the tools for a lifetime of active living.

R

range of movement—A category of movement from the movement concept of space awareness involving the extent to which the body can reach from a fixed point on the supporting surface.

rating of perceived exertion—Verbal descriptor of felt exertion on a 10-point scale in which 1 indicates "not tired at all" and 10 indicates "very, very tired"; sometimes referred to as *OMNI scale.*

reaction time—A skill-related fitness component, the amount of time elapsed between onset of a stimulus (e.g., "Go") and the first movement of the body, as in the quickness off the blocks in swimming or running.

receiving—Gross body movement in which force is received from an object as in catching and trapping.

recess—Defined period of time (usually 10 to 20 minutes in the midmorning, midafternoon, or both) in which elementary school children take a break from regular learning activities to engage (preferably outdoors) in unstructured free play.

reciprocal style—Reproduction teaching style in which students work in pairs, one as the performer and the other as the observer. The observer uses criteria designed by the teacher to provide feedback to the performer. The teacher provides feedback to the observer about their assessment of the peer.

reframing—Skill of understanding and rephrasing a potential disciplinary situation through the lens of personal and social responsibility in order to facilitate the best chance for a positive outcome.

relationship awareness—In movement settings, a movement concept about the ability to move effectively with objects or other people.

relationships of body parts to each other—A category of movement from the movement concept of body awareness involving placing body parts in relation to each other by leading, above or below, supporting or nonsupporting, isolated, moving or still, unison, opposition or sequenced.

reproduction cluster—Series of teaching styles (including command, practice, reciprocal, self-check, and inclusion) requiring the learner to use lower-order thinking processes that involve memory, recall, identification, and sorting.

rhythm—Regulated flow of energy that is organized in both duration and intensity, results in balance and harmony, and involves repetition of regular groupings of sights, sounds, or movements.

rhythmic element—See *element of rhythm.*

rhythmic fundamentals—Awareness of and ability to respond to the five elements of rhythm (underlying beat, tempo, accent, intensity, rhythmic pattern).

rhythmic pattern—Group of beats related to the underlying beat.

roles and groupings—A category of movement from the movement concept of relationship awareness involving relating to others in parallel, cooperative, or competitive interactions on their own, with a partner, in a group, or between groups by leading, following, avoiding contact, or meeting and parting.

S

scaling—Adjusting the learning environment, in terms of either performance task requirements or equipment modifications, in order to elicit specific movement skills and movement concepts from the learner.

schema—Set of rules stored in the brain that one develops in learning a new movement pattern.

schema theory—Theoretical framework, proposed by Schmidt in 1975 and now widely accepted, that describes the manner in which one develops schemata as part of the process of learning new motor skills.

scope and sequence chart—In curriculum construction, a large chart outlining program scope (breadth) and program sequence (depth) both for a given school year and from year to year.

scoring tools - the instrument containing the criteria used to evaluate student learning/performance (e.g., observation checklist, rubric, answer key).

self-assessment—Assessment of oneself that helps meet the goal of learning how to learn.

self-check style—Reproduction teaching style which promotes self-reliance by shifting to the performer the post-impact decisions of assessing their own performance using criteria provided by the teacher.

self-concept—Value-free understanding of one's physical, social, and cognitive abilities.

self-confidence—Aspect of self-concept that involves an inner belief in one's ability to accomplish a given task.

self-control—Self-initiated and self-regulated behavior that respects the rights and feelings of others; in a movement context, maintenance of standards of acceptable behavior in a competitive situation.

self-esteem—Description of self, rooted in what one thinks about oneself, and is affected by what an individual values. For example, if one values physical ability, then their self-esteem (i.e., high- or low-) depends on their proficiency in the psychomotor domain.

self-worth—See *self-esteem*.

sending away—Gross body movement in which force is imparted to an object to send it away from the body as in throwing, kicking, striking, and volleying.

sensorimotor stage—Jean Piaget's first stage of cognitive learning, which occurs during infancy and toddlerhood and during which the child's motor activities and perceptual abilities are brought together into a tenuous whole to form cognitive structures.

Shape of the Nation Report—Regular report, published by SHAPE America and first released in 1997, that addresses the status of physical education in U.S. public schools.

single task, multiple stations—Teaching technique that uses multiple stations, each of which addresses one task but offers various equipment and condition choices to fit varying levels of student ability.

single task, single station—Teaching technique in which all learners practice the same movement skill with equipment and condition choices embedded in the activity.

skill cue—Description of a movement that a player must perform or an environmental conditions to which a player must attend.

skill development—Single most important part of a daily developmental physical education lesson, which is contained in the body of the lesson and emphasizes new skill learning.

skill-related fitness—Aspect of physical fitness composed of the following: body balance, movement coordination, movement speed, agility, and power; sometimes referred to as *motor fitness* or *performance-related fitness*.

skill theme—One of the organizing centers around which a developmental physical education curriculum is built. Themes come from *movement content* or *movement concept* categories.

social contract—An agreement between teacher and students about the values, rules, and consequences for classroom behavior.

social dance—Partner or group dance that reflects the mores of a particular culture at the time of its popularity.

social responsibility—Process by which learners take on a greater role in being sensitive and responsive to the needs and well-being of others.

Society of Health and Physical Educators (SHAPE America)—Primary U.S. professional organization for physical educators and publisher of national standards for physical education teacher education (PETE); formerly known as the American Alliance for Health, Physical Education, Recreation and Dance (AAHPERD).

space awareness—Knowledge of where the body moves in terms of level, direction, pathway, and range; not to be confused with *spatial awareness*.

spastic CP—Form of cerebral palsy characterized by limited voluntary control of movement due to muscle hypertonia.

spatial positioning—A category of movement from the movement concept of relationship awareness involving moving over and under, in and out, on and off, along, around, through, near and far, in front of, behind, and alongside objects and others.

specialized movement activity themes—Movement activity content topics (games, dance, gymnastics) from which developmentally appropriate activities are designed for children in grades 3-5.

specialized movement phase—Time period, typically beginning around age 7, when individuals begin to combine and apply a variety of fundamental movement skills into more complex patterns of movement for use in sport, dance, and other activities.

Spectrum of Teaching Styles—A continuum of teaching styles based on decision-making, first identified by Muska Mosston.

speed—Ability to move from one point to another in the shortest time possible, as in the 50-meter dash.

sport court—Teacher-appointed group of students who discuss an issue and devise an acceptable solution for the entire class.

stability skill—The most basic of the three categories of movement (locomotor skill and manipulative skill being the other two), which involves the ability to sense a shift in the relationship of body parts that alters one's balance and to adjust rapidly and accurately through appropriate compensating movements.

stability skill theme—Skill themes that engage children in both static and dynamic body-control activities such as balance, rolling and step-like actions.

stabilizing—Reducing anger, avoiding power struggles, and lowering the noise that can increase hostility to the point where interventions cannot work.

stable feature—Aspect of a generalized motor program or schema that involves the mechanics of the movement itself.

static balance—Any posture (upright or inverted) in which the center of gravity remains stationary and the line of gravity falls within the base of support.

step-like actions—Transfer of weight from feet to hands or from hands to feet.

striking and fielding games—A category of games with tactical interactions including accuracy, batting, base running, fielding, and support.

summative assessment—Assessment of student learning and comprehension at the end of a unit of instruction.

T

tactic—Manner in which a progression of skill combinations is to be applied in order to maximize efficiency and success.

tactical approach—Approach that emphasizes improving movement skills through game instruction by stressing the *why* and *when* of using a particular skill in a game situation; sometimes referred to as *games-for-understanding approach*.

talking bench—Technique for resolving issues of respect between students in which two students go to a designated place (e.g., a bench) to discuss a problem and then report back to the teacher about how they resolved it.

target games—A category of games with tactical interactions including direction and distance.

task—See *movement task.*

task card—Written verbal or visual description of a skill or movement activity to be performed.

teaching personal and social responsibility (TPSR)—Self-awareness model for positive discipline, developed by Don Hellison, that highlights the importance of creating opportunities for children to reflect on their personal behavior and developing strategies for learning to care for others.

teaching style—The delineation of who (teacher or student) makes which decisions about what and when for a teaching-learning transaction.

teamwork—Work performed with others in a cooperative manner.

tempo—Speed of movement, music, or accompaniment.

time-out—Discipline technique that involves sending a disruptive student to an easy-to-monitor, safe, and neutral place for a period of time before she or he is permitted to reenter the learning activity.

timing of movement—A category of movement from the movement concept of effort awareness involving the speed at which a movement occurs.

transition stage—First stage in the specialized movement phase, during which children attempt to apply their movement skills to a wide variety of game, sport, and dance activities.

traumatic brain injury—Primary cause of mental retardation, characterized by damage (before, during, or after birth) to the central nervous system.

traveling locomotor skill—Continuous locomotor skill that has a brief flight phase and takes the body from place to place (e.g., walking, running, galloping, sliding, skipping).

U

underlying beat—Steady, continuous sound of any rhythmical sequence.

unit of instruction—Preplanned time frame for focusing on a particular area of emphasis in the curriculum that may be revisited from time to time in an attempt to gain skill mastery.

unit plan—Subset of a yearly plan that engages an instructional theme as well as the national standards for physical education.

Universal Design for Learning (UDL)—Framework that guides the development of curriculum and instruction to accommodate individual learning differences.

unpacking standards—Process of delving into the meaning of a standard to extract the meaning of terms and the critical or essential content.

V

value statement—First step in curriculum and program building, which involves developing a list of critically important indicators of curriculum or program success to form a value statement that provides the framework for a mission statement.

variable practice—Practice of a skill in a wide variety of conditions in order to increase fluidity and adaptability.

visual acuity—Ability to clearly distinguish visual detail.

visual perception—Process of integrating sensory information received on the retina with information stored in the visual cortex in order to make sense of what one sees.

References

Preface

Institute of Medicine of the National Academies. (2013). *Educating the student body: Taking physical activity and physical education to school*. www.iom.edu/Reports/2013/Educating-the-Student-Body-Taking-Physical-Activity-and-Physical-Education-to-School.aspx.

Mosston, M., & Ashworth, S. (2008). *Teaching physical education* (6th ed.; 1st online version). www.spectrumofteachingstyles.org.

National Association for Sport and Physical Education (NASPE) & American Heart Association (AHA). (2012). *Shape of the nation report: Status of physical education in the USA*. Reston, VA: American Alliance for Health, Physical Education, Recreation and Dance.

SHAPE America. (2014). *National standards and grade-level outcomes for K-12 physical education*. Champaign, IL: Human Kinetics.

Chapter 1

Centers for Disease Control and Prevention (CDC). (2000). *School health index for physical activity and healthy eating: A self-assessment and planning guide for elementary school*. Atlanta: U.S. Department of Health and Human Services. www.cdc.gov/HealthyYouth/shi/pdf/Elementary.pdf.

Centers for Disease Control and Prevention (CDC). (2010, July). *The association between school-based physical activity, including physical education, and academic performance*. U.S. Department of Health and Human Services. www.cdc.gov/healthyyouth/health_and_academics/pdf/pa-pe_paper.pdf.

Centers for Disease Control and Prevention (CDC). (2015). Comprehensive school physical activity program (CSPAP). www.cdc.gov/healthyschools/physicalactivity/cspap.htm.

Ericcson, I. (2008). Motor skills, attention, and academic achievements: An intervention study in school years 1–3. *British Educational Research Journal, 34*(3), 301–303.

Fudge, M.L. (2013). *Congresswoman Fudge introduces the PHYSICAL Act* (Press release). http://fudge.house.gov/latest-news/congresswoman-fudge-introduces-the-physical-act1/.

Gallahue, D.L., Ozmun, J.C., & Goodway, J.D. (2012). *Understanding motor development: Infants, children, adolescents, adults* (7th ed.). New York: McGraw-Hill.

Haywood, K.M., & Getchell, N. (2014). *Life span motor development* (6th ed.). Champaign, IL: Human Kinetics.

Institute of Medicine of the National Academies. (2013). *Educating the student body: Taking physical activity and physical education to school*. www.iom.edu/Reports/2013/Educating-the-Student-Body-Taking-Physical-Activity-and-Physical-Education-to-School.aspx.

Let's Move! (n.d.). *About Let's Move: America's move to raise a healthier generation of kids*. www.letsmove.gov/about.

National Association for Sport and Physical Education (NASPE). (2004). *Moving into the future: National standards for physical education* (2nd ed.). Oxon Hill, MD: American Alliance for Health, Physical Education, Recreation and Dance.

National Association for Sport and Physical Education (NASPE). (2007). *Position statement: What constitutes a highly qualified physical education teacher*. Reston, VA: American Alliance for Health, Physical Education, Recreation and Dance.

National Association for Sport and Physical Education (NASPE). (2009). *Appropriate instructional practice guidelines for elementary school physical education*. Reston, VA: American Alliance for Health, Physical Education, Recreation and Dance.

National Association for Sport and Physical Education (NASPE) & American Heart Association (AHA). (2010). *Shape of the nation report—Status of physical education in the USA*. www.heart.org/idc/groups/heart-public/@wcm/@adv/documents/downloadable/ucm_308261.pdf.

National Association for Sport and Physical Education (NASPE) & American Heart Association (AHA). (2012). *Shape of the nation report: Status of physical education in the USA*. Reston, VA: American Alliance for Health, Physical Education, Recreation and Dance.

Ogden, C.L., Carroll, M.D., Kit, B.K., & Flegal, K.M. (2012). Prevalence of obesity and trends in body mass index among US children and adolescents, 1999-2010. *JAMA, 307*(5):483-490.

Payne, G., & Issacs, D. (2008). *Human motor development: A lifespan approach* (7th ed.). London: Mayfield.

SHAPE America. (2014). *National standards and grade-level outcomes for K-12 physical education* Champaign, IL: Human Kinetics.

SHAPE America, American Heart Association, and Voices for Healthy Kids. (2016). *Shape of the nation report—Status of physical education in the USA*. http://www.shapeamerica.org/advocacy/son/2016/upload/Shape-of-the-Nation-2016_web.pdf.

U.S. Department of Health and Human Services. (2008). *Physical activity guidelines for Americans*. www.health.gov/paguidelines/guidelines/default.aspx.

Chapter 2

Bryan, J., Osendarp, S., Hughes, D., Calvaresi, E., Baghurst, K., & van Klinken, J. (2004). Nutrients for cognitive development in school-aged children. *Nutrition Reviews, 62*(8), 295–306.

Centers for Disease Control and Prevention (2013). *Comprehensive school physical activity programs: a guide for schools*. Atlanta, GA: U.S. Department of Health and Human Services. www.cdc.gov/healthyyouth/physicalactivity/pdf/13_242620-A_CSPAP_SchoolPhysActivityPrograms_Final_508_12192013.pdf

Conrad, B. (n.d.). *Media Statistics - Children's Use of TV, Internet, and Video Games.* www.techaddiction.ca/media-statistics.html.

Cooper Institute. (2010). *Fitnessgram & Activitygram test administration manual* (updated 4th ed.). Champaign, IL: Human Kinetics.

Corbin, C. (2010). Fitness for Life Physical Activity Pyramid for kids [Poster]. Champaign, IL: Human Kinetics.

Corbin, C.B., Welk, G., Corbin, W.R., & Welk, K. (2008). *Concepts of fitness and wellness: A comprehensive lifestyle approach* (7th ed.). New York: McGraw-Hill.

Fogelholm, M., Nuutinen, O., Pasanen, M., Myohanen, E., & Saatela, T. (1999). Parent-child relationship of physical activity patterns and obesity. *International Journal of Obesity and Related Metabolic Disorders: Journal of the International Association for the Study of Obesity, 23*(12), 1262–1268.

Fox, M., & Cole, N. (2004). *Nutrition and health characteristics of low-income populations: Volume III—School-age children.* U.S. Department of Agriculture, E-FAN-04-014-3.

Gallahue, D.L., Ozmun, J.C., & Goodway, J.D. (2012). *Understanding motor development: Infants, children, adolescents, adults* (7th ed.). New York: McGraw-Hill.

Gillaspy, R. *The American diet: characteristics, food habits & guidelines.* http://study.com/academy/lesson/the-american-diet-characteristics-food-habits-guidelines.html.

Ginsburg, K.R. (2007). The importance of play in promoting healthy child development and maintaining strong parent–child bonds. *American Academy of Pediatrics, 119*(1), 182-191.

Gleave, J. & Cole-Hamilton, I. (2012). *A world without play—a literature review.* Play England www.playengland.org.uk/media/371031/a-world-without-play-literature-review-2012.pdf.

González, C., Nazaret, G., Navarro, V., Cairós, M., Quirce, C., Toledo, P., & Marrero-Gordillo, N. (February, 2016). Learning healthy lifestyles through active videogames, motor games and the gamification of educational activities. *Computers in Human Behavior, 55*, 529-551.

Graham, G., Holt/Hale, S., & Parker, M. (2013). *Children moving* (9th ed.). New York: McGraw-Hill.

Kouli, O., Rokka, S., Mavridis, G., & Derri, V. (2009). The effect of an aerobic program on health-related fitness and intrinsic motivation in elementary school pupils. *Studies in Physical Culture & Tourism 2009, 16* (3), 301-306.

Let's Move! Active Schools. (n.d.). *Let's Move! America's move to raise a healthier generation of kids.* www.letsmoveschools.org.

National Association for Sport and Physical Education (NASPE). (2009a). *Active start: A statement of physical activity guidelines for children from birth to age 5* (2nd ed.). Reston, VA: American Alliance for Health, Physical Education, Recreation and Dance.

National Association for Sport and Physical Education (NASPE). (2009b). *Appropriate instructional practice guidelines for elementary school physical education.* Reston, VA: American Alliance for Health, Physical Education, Recreation and Dance.

National Association for Sport and Physical Education (NASPE). (2009c). *Appropriate practices in movement programs for children ages 3-5* (3rd ed.). Reston, VA: American Alliance for Health, Physical Education, Recreation and Dance.

National Association for Sport and Physical Education (NASPE). (2010). *Appropriate uses of fitness measurement.* Reston, VA: SHAPE America.

National Physical Activity Plan Alliance. (2014). The 2014 United States Report Card on Physical Activity for Children and Youth. www.physicalactivityplan.org/reportcard/NationalReportCard_longform_final%20for%20web.pdf.

SHAPE America. (2014). *National standards and grade-level outcomes for K-12 physical education.* Champaign, IL: Human Kinetics. www.shapeamerica.org/prodev/lmas.cfm

Strand, B., & Mauch, L. (2008). *Assessing and improving fitness in elementary physical education* (2nd ed.). Reston, VA: National Association for Sport and Physical Education.

U.S. Department of Agriculture. (2015). *2015-2020 Dietary guidelines for Americans.* http://health.gov/dietaryguidelines/2015/guidelines.

U.S. Department of Agriculture. (n.d.). *ChooseMyPlate.* www.choosemyplate.gov.

U.S. Department of Health and Human Services (HHS). (2008). *Physical activity guidelines for Americans.* www.health.gov/paguidelines/guidelines/default.aspx.

Vadivello, M., Zhu, L., & Quatromoni, P. (2009). Diet and physical activity patterns of school-aged children. *Journal of the American Dietetic Association, 109*(1), 145–151.

Chapter 3

Alvarez, J.M. (2012). Self-concept. *Child Development Reference,* 7. http://social.jrank.org/pages/554/Self-Concept.html.

Haibach, P., Reid, G., & Collier, D. (2011). *Motor learning and development.* Champaign, IL: Human Kinetics.

Hellison, D. (2011). *Teaching personal and social responsibility through physical activity* (3rd ed.). Champaign, IL: Human Kinetics.

Kruger, H., & Kruger, J. (1989). The Preschool Teacher's Guide to Movement Education. Baltimore, MD: Gerstung Publications.

Mercier, R., & Hutchinson, G. (2003). Social psychology. In B. Mohnsen (Ed.), *Concepts and principles of physical education: What every student needs to know* (2nd ed.; pp. 245-307). Reston, VA: National Association for Sport and Physical Education.

Midura, D., & Glover, D. (1999). *The competition–cooperation link: Games for developing respectful competitors.* Champaign, IL: Human Kinetics.

National Association for Sport and Physical Education (NASPE). (2004). *Moving into the future: National standards for physical education.* (2nd ed.). Oxon Hill, MD: American Alliance for Health, Physical Education, Recreation and Dance.

Nichols, B. (1994). *Moving and learning: The elementary school physical education experience* (3rd ed.). Boston: Mosby.

Piaget, J. (1954). *The construction of reality in children.* New York: International Universities Press.

Shaffer, D.R. (1999). Developmental Psychology: Childhood and Adolescence. Pacific Grove, CA: Brooks/Cole Publisher.

SHAPE America. (2014). *National standards and grade-level outcomes for K-12 physical education.* Champaign, IL: Human Kinetics.

Chapter 4

Coker, C. (2004). *Motor learning and control for practitioners.* New York: McGraw-Hill.

Fairbrother, J. (2010). *Fundamentals of motor behavior.* Champaign, IL: Human Kinetics.

Fitts, P., & Possner, M. (1967). *Human performance.* Belmont, CA: Brooks/Cole.

Gallahue, D.L., Ozmun, J.C., & Goodway, J.D. (2012). *Understanding motor development: Infants, children, adolescents, and adults* (7th ed.). New York: McGraw-Hill.

Gentile, A.M. (1972). A working model of skill acquisition with application to teaching. *Quest, 17,* 3-23.

Gentile, A.M. (2000). Skill acquisition: Action, movement and neuromotor processes. In J.H. Carr & R.B. Shepherd (Eds.), *Movement Science: Foundations for physical therapy in rehabilitation* (2nd ed., p. 111-187). Rockville, MD: Aspen.

Haibach, P., Reid, G., & Collier, D. (2011). *Motor learning and development.* Champaign, IL: Human Kinetics.

Haywood, K.M., & Getchell, N. (2014). *Life span motor development* (6th ed.). Champaign, IL: Human Kinetics.

Newell, K.M. (1984). Physical constraints to development of motor skills. In J. Thomas (Ed.), *Motor development during preschool and elementary years* (pp. 105–120). Minneapolis, MN: Burgess.

Payne, V.G., & Isaacs, L. (2008). *Human motor development: A lifespan approach.* (7th ed.). Boston: McGraw Hill.

Piaget, J. (1952). *The origins of intelligence in children.* New York: International Universities Press.

Schmidt, R.A. (1975). A schema theory of discrete motor skill learning. *Psychological Review, 82,* 225-260.

Chapter 5

Allison, P.C., & Barrett, K.R. (2000). *Constructing children's physical education experiences: Understanding the content for teaching.* Needham Heights, MA: Allyn & Bacon.

Baumgarten, S., & Langton, T. (2006). *Elementary physical education: Building a solid movement foundation.* Champaign, IL: Stipes.

Glover, D., & Midura, D. (1992). *Team building through physical challenges.* Champaign, IL: Human Kinetics.

Graham, G., Holt/Hale, S., & Parker, M. (2012). *Children moving* (9th ed.). Boston: McGraw-Hill.

Langton, T. (2007). Applying Laban's movement framework in elementary physical education. *Journal of Physical Education, Recreation and Dance, 78*(1), 17–24.

Midura, D., & Glover, D. (1995). *More teambuilding challenges.* Champaign, IL: Human Kinetics.

Midura, D., & Glover, D. (1999). *The competition–cooperation link: Games for developing respectful competitors.* Champaign, IL: Human Kinetics.

Mitchell, S., Oslin, J., & Griffin, L. (2013). *Teaching sport concepts and skills: A tactical games approach for ages 7 to 18* (3rd ed.). Champaign, IL: Human Kinetics.

Nichols, B. (1994). Moving and learning: The elementary school physical education experience. (3rd ed.). St. Louis: Mosby.

Orlick, T. (2006). Cooperative games and sports: Joyful activities for everyone. (2nd ed.). Champaign, IL: Human Kinetics.

Werner, P., & Almond, L. (1990). Models of games education. *JOPERD, 61*(4), 23–27.

Chapter 6

Coker, C. (2004). *Motor learning and control for practitioners.* New York: McGraw-Hill.

Griffey, D., & Housner, L. (2007). *Designing effective instructional tasks for physical education and sports.* Champaign, IL: Human Kinetics.

Mitchell, S., Oslin, J., & Griffen, L. (2013). *Teaching sport concepts and skills: A tactical games approach for ages 7-18.* Champaign, IL: Human Kinetics.

Payne, V.G., & Isaacs, L. (2008). *Human motor development: A lifespan approach.* (7th edition). Boston: McGraw Hill.

Werner, P., & Almond, L. (1990). Models of games education. *Journal of physical education, recreation and dance, 61*(4), 23-27.

Chapter 7

Coker, C. (2004). *Motor learning and control for practitioners.* New York: McGraw-Hill.

Fairbrother, J. (2010). *Fundamentals of motor behavior.* Champaign, IL: Human Kinetics.

Griffey, D., & Housner, L. (2007). *Designing effective instructional tasks for physical education and sports.* Champaign, IL: Human Kinetics.

Haibach, P., Reid, G., & Collier, D. (2011). *Motor learning and development.* Champaign, IL: Human Kinetics.

Rovegno, I., & Bandhauer, D. (2013). *Student assessment and lesson plan workbook: Elementary physical education.* Burlington, MA: Jones and Bartlett Learning.

Young, D., LaCourse, M., & Husak, W. (2000). *A practical guide to motor learning* (2nd ed.). Peosta, IA: Bowers.

Chapter 8

Council of Chief State School Officers (CCSSO) and National Governor's Association Center for Best Practices (NGACBP). (2010). *Common Core State Standards Initiative: Preparing America's students for college and career.* www.corestandards.org.

Covey, S. (2004). *The seven habits of highly effective people.* New York: Simon & Schuster.

Lund, J., & Tannehill, D. (2010). *Standards-based physical education curriculum development* (2nd ed.). Boston: Jones and Bartlett.

National Association for Sport and Physical Education (NASPE). (1995). *Moving into the future: National standards for physical education.* St. Louis: Mosby.

National Association for Sport and Physical Education (NASPE). (2004). *Moving into the future: National standards for physical education* (2nd ed.). Reston, VA: Author.

National Association for Sport and Physical Education (NASPE). (2009a). *Active start: A statement of physical activity guidelines for children from birth to age 5.* Reston, VA: NASPE.

National Association for Sport and Physical Education (NASPE). (2009b). *Appropriate practices in movement programs for children ages 3-5.* Reston, VA: NASPE.

National Association for Sport and Physical Education (NASPE). (2010a). *Opportunity to learn: Guidelines for elementary school physical education* (3rd ed.). Champaign, IL: Human Kinetics.

National Association for Sport and Physical Education (NASPE). (2010b). *Opportunity to learn: Guidelines for high school physical education* (3rd ed.). Champaign, IL: Human Kinetics.

National Association for Sport and Physical Education (NASPE). (2010c). *Opportunity to learn: Guidelines for middle school physical education* (3rd ed.). Champaign, IL: Human Kinetics.

National Association for Sport and Physical Education. (2004). *Physical activity for children: A statement of guidelines for children ages 5-12* (2nd ed.). Reston, VA: Author

SHAPE America. (2014a). *National standards and grade-level outcomes for K-12 physical education.* Champaign, IL: Human Kinetics.

SHAPE America. (2014b). *Scope and Sequence for K-12 physical education* [Brochure]. Champaign, IL: Human Kinetics.

Wiggins, G., & McTighe, J. (1998). *Understanding by design.* Alexandria, VA: Association for Supervision and Curriculum Development.

Chapter 9

Aguilar, E. (2012, March 27). *Beyond student engagement: Achieving a state of flow.* Edutopia. www.edutopia.org/blog/student-engagement-elena-aguilar.

Andrade, H. (2007, December/2008, January). Self-assessment through rubrics. *Educational Leadership, 65*(4), 60–63.

Black, P.J., & William, D. (1998). Inside the Black Box: Raising standards through classroom assessment. *Phi Delta Kappan, 80,* 139-48.

Bloom, B.S., et al. (1956). *Taxonomy of educational objectives, Handbook I: Cognitive Domain.* NY: McKay.

Fox, C. (2012). How teachers can use PE metrics for grading. *Journal of Physical Education, Recreation and Dance, 83*(5), 16–22.

Gallahue, D., & Cleland Donnelly, F. (2003). *Developmental physical education for all children.* (4th ed.). Champaign, IL: Human Kinetics.

Giles-Brown, L. (2006). *Physical education assessment toolkit.* Champaign, IL: Human Kinetics.

Heritage, M. (2010). *Formative assessment and next-generation assessment systems: Are we losing an opportunity?* Washington, DC: Council of Chief State School Officers.

Lambert, L. (2007). *Standards-based assessment of student learning: A comprehensive approach* (2nd ed.). Reston, VA: National Association for Sport and Physical Education.

Lujan, M. (2008). *Critical thinking educator wheel.* www.MentoringMinds.com/critical-thinking-wheel.html.

Marzano, J., & Heflebower, T. (2011). Grades that show what students know. *Educational Leadership, 69*(3), 34–39.

McManus, S. (2008). *Attributes of effective formative assessment.* Washington, DC: Council of Chief State School Officers.

Melagrano, V. (2007). Grading and report cards for standards-based physical education. *Journal of Physical Education, Recreation and Dance, 78*(6), 45–53.

Moss, C., & Brookhart, S. (2009). *Advancing formative assessment in every classroom: A guide for instructional leaders.* Alexandria, VA: ASCD.

Moss, C., & Brookhart, S. (2012). *Learning targets: Helping students aim for understanding in today's lesson.* Alexandria, VA: ASCD.

National Association for Sport and Physical Education. (2004). *Moving into the future: National standards for physical education* (2nd ed.). Reston, VA: Author.

National Association for Sport and Physical Education. (2010). *PE metrics: Assessing national standards 1–6 in elementary school.* Reston, VA: Author.

National Association for Sport and Physical Education. (2011a). *Physical best activity guide: Elementary level* (3rd ed.). Champaign, IL: Human Kinetics.

National Association for Sport and Physical Education. (2011b). *Physical education for lifelong fitness: The Physical Best teacher's guide* (3rd ed.). Champaign, IL: Human Kinetics.

O'Connor, K., & Wormeli, R. (2011). Reporting student learning. *Educational Leadership, 69*(3), 40–44.

Pollock, J. (2007). *Improving student learning one teacher at a time.* Alexandria, VA: Association of Supervision and Curriculum Development.

SHAPE America. (2014). *National standards and grade-level outcomes for K-12 physical education.* Champaign, IL: Human Kinetics.

The Cooper Institute. (2010). *Fitnessgram and Activitygram: Test Administration Manual.* (M. Meredith and G. Welk, Editors). Champaign, IL: Human Kinetics.

Ulrich, D.A. (2000). *Test of gross motor development.* PRO-ED, 5341 Industrial Blvd., Austin, TX 78735 (512-892-3142).

Virgilio, S. (1997). *Fitness education for children: A team approach.* Champaign, IL: Human Kinetics.

Winnick, J., & Short, F. (2014). *The Brockport Physical Fitness Test Manual* (2nd ed.). Champaign, IL: Human Kinetics.

Chapter 10

Bergman, J., & Sams, A. (2012). *Flip your classroom.* Washington, DC: International Society for Technology in Education; and Alexandria, VA: Association for Supervision and Curriculum Development.

Cothran, D.K., Kulinna, P.H., & Ward, E., (2000). Students' experiences with and perceptions of Mosston's teaching styles. *Journal of Research and Development in Education, 33*(5), 93–102 www.spectrumofteachingstyles.org/library-resources-c.php.

Hasty, D. (1997). *The impact of British National Curriculum Physical Education on teachers' use of teaching styles.* Unpublished doctoral dissertation, University of Alabama, Tuscaloosa.

Hertz, M. (2012). The flipped classroom: Pros and Cons. *Edutopia.* www.edutopia.org/blog/flipped-classroom-pro-and-con-mary-beth-hertz.

Kulinna, P.H., Cothran, D.J., & Zhu, W. (2000). *Teachers' experience with and perception of Mosston's Spectrum: How do* they compare with students? Paper presented at the annual meeting of the American Educational Research Association, New Orleans, LA.

Lund, J., & Tannehill, D. (2010). *Standards-based physical education curriculum development* (2nd ed.). Boston: Jones and Bartlett.

Moss, C., & Brookhart, S. (2012). *Learning targets: Helping students aim for understanding in today's lesson.* Alexandria, VA: ASCD.

Mosston, M. (1966). *Teaching physical education.* Columbus, OH: Charles E. Merrill Books, Inc.

Mosston, M., & Ashworth, S. (2008). *Teaching physical education* (6th ed.; 1st online version). www.spectrumofteachingstyles.org.

National Center on Universal Design for Learning. (2014). *Universal design for learning guidelines 1.0.* www.udlcenter.org/aboutudl/udlguidelines_theorypractice.

Rose, D., & Meyer, A. (2002). *Teaching every student in the digital age: Universal design for learning.* Alexandria, VA: ASCD.

SHAPE America. (2014). *National standards and grade-level outcomes for K-12 physical education.* Champaign, IL: Human Kinetics.

Vatterott, C. (2011). Making homework central to learning. *Educational Leadership, 69*(3), 60–64.

Wiggins, G., & McTighe, J. (1998). *Understanding by design.* Alexandria, VA: Association for Supervision and Curriculum Development.

Chapter 11

Ambrose, M.W. (1996). Do you cheat girls? *Learning, 25,* 72–75.

American Association on Intellectual and Developmental Disabilities (AAIDD). (2010). *Intellectual disabilities: Definition, classifications, and systems of support,* p. 10. (11th ed.). Annapolis Junction, MD: Author.

American Psychiatric Association. (2000). *Diagnostic and statistical manual of mental disorders* (4th ed.). Washington, DC: Author.

Bloom, B., Cohen, R.A., & Freeman, G. (2012). Summary health statistics for U.S. children: National health interview survey, 2011. *Vital and Health Statistics, 10*(254).

Bouchard, D., & Tetreault, S. (2000). The motor development of sighted children and children with moderate low vision aged 8-13. *Journal of Visual Impairment & Blindness, 94,* 564-573.

Brown, S., Brown, D., & Hussey, K. (1996). Promote equality in the classroom. *Strategies: A Journal for Physical and Sport Educators, 9*(6), 1922.

Centers for Disease Control and Prevention (CDC). Prevalence of Autism Spectrum Disorders–Autism and Developmental Disabilities Monitoring Network, United States, 2012. *Morbidity and Mortal Weekly Report (MMWR), 61*(3).

Centers for Disease Control and Prevention. (2013). *Tracking and research on cerebral palsy.* www.cdc.gov/ncbddd/cp/research.html.

Chepyator-Thomson, J.R., & Ennis, C. (1997). Reproduction and resistance to the culture of femininity and masculinity in secondary physical education. *Research Quarterly for Exercise and Sport, 68*(1), 89–99.

Child and Adolescent Health Measurement Initiative. (2007). National survey of children's health, 2007. Data Resource Center for Child and Adolescent Health. www.childhealthdata.org/learn/NSCH

Davis, K.L. (2003). Teaching for gender equity in physical education: A review of literature. *Women in Sport and Physical Activity Journal, 12*(2), 55–81.

Davis, R., & Davis, T. (1994). Inclusion and the least restrictive environments. *Teaching Elementary Physical Education, 5*(5), 1, 4–5.

Diette, G.B., Markson, L., Skinner, E.A., Nguyen, T.T., Algatt-Bergstrom, P., & Wu, A.W. (2000). Nocturnal asthma in children affects school attendance, school performance, and parents' work attendance. *Archives of Pediatrics and Adolescent Medicine, 154,* 923–928.

Dowling, C. (2001). *The frailty myth: Redefining the physical potential of women and girls.* New York: Random House.

Dunbar, R.R., & O'Sullivan, M.M. (1986). Effects of intervention on differential treatment of boys and girls in elementary physical education lessons. *Journal of Teaching Physical Education, 5,* 166–175.

Elbaum, B., & Vaughn, S. (2001). School-based interventions to enhance the self-concept of students with learning disabilities: A meta-analysis. *The Elementary School Journal, 101*(3), 303–329.

Ellis, M.K., Lieberman, L. J., & Dummer, G. (2013). Parent influences on physical activity participation and physical fitness of deaf children. *Journal of Deaf Studies and Deaf Education, 9*(2), 270-281.

Ellis, M.K., Lieberman, L. J., Fittipauldi-Wert, J., & Dummer, G. (2005). Health-related physical fitness of deaf children: How do they measure up? *Palaestra, 21*(3), 36-43.

Ellis, M.K., Lieberman, L.J., & LeRoux, D. (2010). Using differentiated instruction in physical education. *Palaestra, 24*(4), 19–23.

Erickson, W., Lee, C., & von Schrader, S. (2013). Disability statistics from the 2011 American Community Survey (ACS). Ithaca, NY: Cornell University Employment & Disability Institute (EDI). www.disabilitystatistics.org.

Friend, M., & Bursuck, W.D. (2011). *Including students with special needs: A practical guide for classroom teachers* (6th ed.). New York: Pearson.

Gheysen, F., Loots, G., & Van Waelvelde, H. (2008). Motor development of deaf children with and without cochlear implants. *Journal of Deaf Studies and Deaf Education, 13*(2), 215-224.

Gregory, G.H., & Chapman, C. (2007). *Differential instructional strategies.* Thousand Oaks, CA: Corwin Press.

Griffiths, L.J., Parsons, T.J., & Hill, A.J. (2010). Self-esteem and quality of life in obese children and adolescents: A systematic review. *International Journal of Pediatric Obesity, 5*(4), 282–304.

Gunter, P.L., Coutinho, M.J., & Cade, T. (2002). Classroom factors linked with academic gains among students with emotional and behavioral problems. *Preventing School Failure, 46*(3), 126–133.

Hall, T., Strangman, N., & Meyer, A. (2009). Differentiated instruction and implications for UDL implementation. Wakefield, MA: National Center on Accessing the General Curriculum.

Halpern, D.F. (2006). Assessing gender gaps in learning and academic achievement. In P.A. Alexander & P.H. Winnie (Eds.), *Handbook of educational psychology.* Mahwah, NJ: Erlbaum.

Hansen, S., Walker, J., & Flom, B. (1995). *Growing smart: What's working for girls in school.* Washington, DC: AAUW Educational Foundation.

Hartman, E., Houwen, S., & Visscher, C. (2011). Motor skill performance and sports participation in deaf elementary school children. *Adapted Physical Activity Quarterly, 28,* 132-145.

Heward, W.L. (2006). *Exceptional children: An introduction to special education.* New York: Pearson.

Hilton, C.L., Zhang, Y., White, M.R., Klohr, C.L., & Constantino, J. (2012). Motor impairment in sibling pairs concordant and discordant for autism spectrum disorders. *Autism: The International Journal of Research and Practice, 9*(2), 139–156.

Hyde, J.S. (2005). The gender similarities hypothesis. *American Psychologist, 60*(6), 581–592.

Janssen, I., Craig, W.M., Boyce, W.F., & Pickett, W. (2004). Associations between overweight and obesity with bullying behaviors in school-aged children. *Pediatrics, 113,* 1187–1194.

Kamps, D., Kravits, T., Stolze, J., & Swaggart, B. (1999). Prevention strategies for at-risk students and students with EBD in urban elementary schools. *Journal of Emotional and Behavioral Disorders, 7*(3), 178–189.

Kamps, D., Wendland, M., & Culpepper, M. (2006). Functional assessment as a tool for designing interventions for students with behavioral risks in general education classrooms. *Behavioral Disorders, 31,*12S-U3.

Kauffman, J. (2001). *Characteristics of emotional and behavioral disorders of children and youth.* (7th ed.). Upper Saddle River, NJ: Merrill Prentice Hall.

Kim, Y. S., Leventhal, B. L., Koh, Y. J., Fombonne, E., Laska, E., Lim, E. C., Cheon, K. A., Kim, S. J., Kim, Y. K., Lee, H., Song, D. H., & Grinker, R. R. (2011). Prevalence of autism spectrum disorders in a total population sample. *American Journal of Psychiatry, 168*(9), 904-912.

Klassen, A.F., Miller, A., & Fine, S. (2004). Health-related quality of life in children and adolescents who have a diagnosis of attention-deficit/hyperactivity disorder. *Pediatrics, 114*(5), e541–e547.

Kollipara, S., & Warren-Boulton, E. (2004). Diabetes and physical activity in schools. *School Nurse News, 21*(3), 12–16.

Kolotkin, R.L., Crosby, R.D., & Williams, G.R. (2002). Health-related quality of life varies among obese subgroups. *Obesity Research, 10,* 748–756.

Lieberman, L. J., & McHugh, E. (2001). Health-related fitness of children who are visually impaired. *Journal of Visual Impairments & Blindness, 95,* 272-287.

Lock, R.S., Minarik, L.T., & Omata, J. (1999). Gender and the problem of diversity: Action research in physical education. *Quest, 51*(4), 393–407.

MacDonald, D. (1990). The relationship between the sex composition of physical education classes and teacher–pupil verbal interaction. *Journal of Teaching Physical Education, 9,* 152–163.

Mellon, N. K., Niparko, J. K., Rathmann, C., Mathur, G., Humphries, T., Napoli, D. J., Handley, T., Scambler, S., & Lantos, J. D. (2015). Should all Deaf children learn sign language? *Pediatrics, 136*(1), 170-176.

Nakamura, T. (1997). Quantitative analysis of gait in the visually impaired. *Disability Rehabilitation, 19*(5), 194-197.

Napper-Owen, G.E., Kovar, S.K., Ermler, K.L., & Mehrhof, J.H. (1999). Curricula equity in required ninth-grade physical education. *Journal of Teaching in Physical Education, 19,* 2–21.

National Center for Education Statistics (NCES). (2012). *Digest of education statistics, 2011* (NCES 2012-001). Washington, DC: U.S. Department of Education.

National Eye Institute. (2013). *Low vision & blindness.* https://nei.nih.gov/health.

Oaksford, L. & Jones, L. (2001). Differentiated instruction abstract. Tallahassee, FL: Leon County Schools.

Ormrod, J.E. (2010). *Educational psychology: Developing learners.* (7th ed.). Upper Saddle River, NJ: Pearson-Prentice Hall.

Owens, R.E., Metz, D.E., & Farinella, K.A. (2010). Introduction to communication disorders: A lifespan evidence-based perspective (4th ed.). Boston: Allyn & Bacon.

Pellegrino, L. (2007). Cerebral palsy. In M.L. Batshaw, L. Pellegrino, & N.J. Roizen (Eds.), *Children with disabilities* (6th ed.) pp. 387-408. Baltimore, MD: Brookes Publishing.

Penney, D. (2002). *Gender and physical education: Contemporary issues and future directions.* London: Routledge.

Rajendran, V., & Roy, F.G. (2011). An overview of motor skill performance and balance in hearing impaired children. *Journal of Pediatrics, 37,* 33.

Rink, J. (2005). Physical activity for young adults. *Journal of Physical Education, Recreation and Dance, 76*(8), 18.

Rosenbaum, P. (2003). *Cerebral palsy: What parents and doctors want to know.* BMJ, *326*(7396), 970-974.

Sadker, D., & Zittleman, K. (2009). *Still failing at fairness.* New York: Scribner's.

Sass-Lehrer, M., & Bodner-Johnson, B. (1989). Public Law 99-457: A new challenge to early intervention. *American Annals of the Deaf, 134*(2), 71–77.

Shaffer, D., Fisher, P., Dulcan, M.K., Davies, M., Piacentini, J., Schwab-Stone, M.E., et al. (1996). The NIMH Diagnostic Interview Schedule for Children Version 2.3 (DISC-2.3): Description, acceptability, prevalence rates, and performance in the MECA Study. Methods for the Epidemiology of Child and Adolescents Mental Disorders Study. *Journal of the American Academy of Child and Adolescent Psychiatry, 35,* 865–877.

Sigal, R.J., Kenny, G.P., Wasserman, D.H., & Castaneda-Sceppa, C. (2004). Physical activity/exercise and type 2 diabetes, technical review, American Diabetic Association. *Diabetes Care, 27*(10), 2518-2539.

Skaggs, S., & Hopper, C. (1996). Individuals with visual impairments: A review of psychomotor behavior. *Adapted Physical Activity Quarterly, 13,* 16-26.

Thousand, J.S., Villa, R.A., & Nevin, A.I. (2007). *Differentiating instruction: Collaborative planning and teaching of universally designed learning.* Thousand Oaks, CA: Corwin Press.

Tomlinson, C.A. (2001). *How to differentiate instruction in mixed ability classrooms* (2nd ed.). Alexandria, VA: ASCD.

U.S. Census Bureau. (2012). Statistical Abstract of the U.S. Current population reports, PPL-148, P-20. Author.

U.S. Department of Education. (1998). *Federal Register,* 34 CFR 300.8, July 1, 1998.U.S. Department of Education. (2006). Assistance to states for the education of children with disabilities and preschool grants for children with disabilities. *Federal Register, 71*(156), 46539-46845. (§300.8(c)(9).

U.S. Department of Education. (2013a). U.S. Department of Education Clarifies Schools' Obligation to Provide Equal Opportunity to Students with Disabilities to Participate in Extracurricular Athletics. http://www.ed.gov/news/press-releases/us-department-education-clarifies-schools-obligation-provide-equal-opportunity-students-disabilities-participate-extracurricular-athletics.

U.S. Department of Education. (2013b). Students with disabilities in extracurricular activities. http://www2.ed.gov/about/offices/list/ocr/letters/colleague-201301-504.pdf.

U.S. Office of Special Education Programs. (2001). *History: Twenty-five years of progress in educating children with disabilities through IDEA.* Washington, DC: Author.

Vetiska, J., Glaab, L., Perlman, K., & Daneman, D. (2000). School attendance of children with type 1 diabetes. *Diabetes Care, 23*, 1706–1707.

Wehby, J.H., Lane, K.L., & Falk, K.B. (2003). Academic instruction for students with emotional and behavioral disorders. *Journal of Emotional and Behavioral Disorders, 11*(4), 194–197.

Weiller, K.H., & Doyle, E.J. (2000). Teacher–student interaction: An exploration of gender differences in elementary physical education. *Journal of Physical Education, Recreation and Dance, 71*(3), 43–45.

Wellhousen, K., & Yin, Z. (1997). "Peter Pan isn't a girls' part:" An investigation of gender bias in a kindergarten classroom. *Women and Language, 20*(2), 35.

Zhang, J., & Griffin, A.J. (2007). Including children with autism in general physical education: Eight possible solutions. *Journal of Physical Education, Recreation and Dance, 78*(3), 33–37.

Zwierzchowska, A., Gawlik, K., & Grabara, M. (2008). Deaf and motor ability levels. *Biology of Sport, 25*(3), 263-274.

Chapter 12

Cruz, L., & Peterson, S. (2011). Teaching diverse students: How to avoid marginalizing difference. *JOPERD, 82*(6), 21–24.

Curwin, R., Mendler, A., & Mendler, B. (2008). *Discipline with dignity: New challenges, new solutions.* Alexandria, VA: Association for Supervision and Curriculum Development.

Evertson, C., Emmer, E., & Worsham, M. (2009). *Classroom management for elementary teachers* (7th ed.). Boston: Allyn & Bacon.

French, R., Silliman, L., & Henderson, H. (1990). Too much time out! *Strategies, 3*, 5–7.

Graham, G., Holt/Hale, S., & Parker, M. (2013). *Children moving: A reflective approach to teaching physical education.* New York: McGraw-Hill.

Harrison, L., Russell, R.L., & Burden, J. (2010). Physical education teachers' cultural competency. *Journal of Teaching in Physical Education, 29*(2): 184–196.

Hellison, D. (2011). *Teaching personal and social responsibility through physical activity* (3rd ed.). Champaign, IL: Human Kinetics.

Henderson, H.L., French, R., Fritsch, R., & Lerner, B. (2000). Time-out and overcorrection: A comparison of their application in physical education. *JOPERD, 72*(3), 31–35.

Jensen, E. (2009, 1ˢᵗ ed.). Teaching with Poverty in Mind. Alexandria, VA: ASCD.

Kahan, D. (2003). Religious boundaries in public school physical-activity settings. *JOPERD, 74*(1), 11–13.

Kerri, T. (2016). Homeless students and academic achievement. *Urban Education. 51*(2), 197-220.

Lavay, B., French, R., & Anderson, H.L. (1997). *Positive behavior management strategies for physical educators.* Champaign, IL: Human Kinetics.

Lavay, B., French, R., & Henderson, H.L. (2006). *Positive behavior management in physical activity settings* (3rd ed.). Champaign, IL: Human Kinetics.

Media Education Foundation. (2005). Media Violence: Facts and Statistics. http://www.mediaed.org/Handouts/Children-Media.pdf.

Molnar, A., & Linquist, B. (1990). *Changing problem behavior in schools.* San Francisco: Jossey-Bass.

Moone, T. (1997). Teaching students with respect. *Teaching Elementary Physical Education, 8*(5), 16–18.

National Association for Sport and Physical Education. (2009). *Appropriate instructional practice guidelines for elementary school physical education* (3rd ed.). Reston, VA: American Alliance for Health, Physical Education, Recreation and Dance.

Nelson, J. (2006). *Positive discipline.* New York: Ballantine.

Pastor, P. (2002). School discipline and the character of our schools. *Phi Delta Kappan, 83*, 658–661.

SHAPE America. (2014). *National standards and grade-level outcomes for K-12 physical education.* Champaign, IL: Human Kinetics.

Shidler, L. (2009, September). Teaching children what we want them to learn. *Young Children*, 88–91.

U.S. Federal Trade Commission (2000). Marketing of Violent Entertainment to Children. https://www.ftc.gov/news-events/press-releases/2000/09/ftc-releases-report-marketing-violent-entertainment-children.

Williams, P.A., Alley, R.D., & Henson, K.J. (1999). *Managing secondary classrooms.* Boston: Allyn & Bacon.

Wubbels, T., Brekelmans, M., van Tartwijk, J., & Admiral, W. (1999). Interpersonal relationships between teachers and students in the classroom. In H.C. Wasman & H.J. Walberg (Eds.). *New directions for teaching practice and research* (pp. 151-170). Berkeley, CA: McCutchan.

Chapter 13

Campbell-Towell, L., & Murray, J.S. (2016). "Walk the Lonesome Trail." *Cat paws: Songs for moving and playing.* Hal Leonard Corporation.

Logsdon B., Alleman, L.M., Straits, S.A Belka, D., & Clark, D. (1997). Physical Education Unit Plans for Grades 1-2-2nd Edition: Learning Experiences in Games, Gymnastics, and Dance. Champaign, IL: Human Kinetics.

National Association for Sport and Physical Education. (2009). *Active Start: A statement of physical activity guidelines for children from birth to age 5* (2nd ed.). Reston, VA: Author.

SHAPE America. (2014). *National standards and grade-level outcomes for K-12 physical education.* Champaign, IL: Human Kinetics.

Chapter 14

Orlick, T. (2006). *Cooperative games and sports: Joyful activities for everyone* (2nd ed.). Champaign, IL: Human Kinetics.

SHAPE America. (2014). *National standards and grade-level outcomes for K-12 physical education*. Champaign, IL: Human Kinetics.

Chapter 15

SHAPE America. (2014). *National standards and grade-level outcomes for K-12 physical education*. Champaign, IL: Human Kinetics.

Chapter 16

SHAPE America. (2014). *National standards and grade-level outcomes for K-12 physical education*. Champaign, IL: Human Kinetics.

Werner, P., & Rini, L. (1976). *Perceptual motor development* (Vol. 1). New York: Wiley.

Werner, P. (2004). *Teaching children gymnastics*. (2nd ed.). Champaign, IL: Human Kinetics.

Chapter 17

SHAPE America. (2014). *National standards and grade-level outcomes for K-12 physical education*. Champaign, IL: Human Kinetics.

Chapter 18

Demers, J. (2008). *Character-building activities: Teaching responsibility, interaction, and group dynamics*. Champaign, IL: Human Kinetics.

Glover, D., & Anderson, L. (2003). *Character education: 43 fitness activities for community building*. Champaign, IL: Human Kinetics.

Hastie, P. (2010). *Student-designed games: Strategies for promoting creativity, cooperation, and skill development*. Champaign, IL: Human Kinetics.

Hellison, D. (2011). *Teaching personal and social responsibility through physical activity* (3rd ed.). Champaign, IL: Human Kinetics.

Midura, D., & Glover, D. (2005). *Essentials of team building: Principles and practices*. Champaign, IL: Human Kinetics.

Orlick, T. (2006). *Cooperative games and sports: Joyful activities for everyone* (2nd ed.). Champaign, IL: Human Kinetics.

SHAPE America. (2014). *National standards and grade-level outcomes for K-12 physical education*. Champaign, IL: Human Kinetics.

Chapter 19

Allison, P., & Barrett, K. (2000). *Constructing children's physical education experiences*.

Boston: Allyn and Bacon.

Baumgarten, S., & Langton, T. (2006). *Elementary physical education: Building a solid movement foundation*. Champaign, IL: Stipes.

Butler, J. (1997). *Research comparing teaching games for understanding and technical games teaching*. EDA Conference presentation, Burlington, VT.

Fronske, H. (1997). *Teaching cues for sports skills*. Boston: Allyn & Bacon.

Fronske, H., & Wilson, R. (2002). *Teaching cues for basic sport skills for elementary and middle school students*. San Francisco: Cummings.

Gorecki, J. (2004). Over-the-line: An alternative striking/fielding game for understanding. *Teaching Elementary Physical Education, 15*(3), 21–24.

Grehaigne, J.F., Wallian, N., & Godbout, P. (2005). Tactical-decision learning model and students' practices. *Physical Education and Sport Pedagogy, 10*, 255–269.

Griffin, L., Brooker, R., & Patton, K. (2005). Working towards legitimacy: Two decades of teaching games for understanding. *Physical Education and Sport Pedagogy, 10*, 213–223.

Griffin, L., Mitchell, S., & Oslin, J. (1997). *Teaching sports concepts and skills: A tactical games approach*. Champaign, IL: Human Kinetics.

Hastie, P. (2010). *Student-designed games: Strategies for promoting creativity, cooperating, and skill development*. Champaign, IL: Human Kinetics.

Mitchell, S., Oslin, J., & Griffin, L. (2003). *Sport foundations for elementary physical education: A tactical games approach*. Champaign, IL: Human Kinetics.

Mitchell, S., Oslin, J., & Griffin, L. (2013). *Teaching sport concepts and skills: A tactical games approach for ages 7 to 18* (3rd ed.). Champaign, IL: Human Kinetics.

National Association for Sport and Physical Education. (2009). *Appropriate instructional practice guidelines for elementary school physical education* (3rd ed.). Reston, VA: SHAPE America.

Rovegno, I., & Bandhauer, D. (2013). *Elementary physical education curriculum and instruction*. Burlington, MA: Jones and Barlett.

Rovegno, I., Nevett, M., Brock, S., & Babiarz, M. (2001). Teaching and learning basic invasion game tactics in fourth grade: A descriptive study from situated and constraints theoretical perspectives. *Journal of Teaching in Physical Education, 20*, 370–388.

SHAPE America. (2014). *National standards and grade-level outcomes for K-12 physical education*. Champaign, IL: Human Kinetics.

Stevens, P., & Collier, C. (2001). Shooting hoops: WallTar as an alternative. *Teaching Elementary Physical Education, 12*(1), 17–19, 27.

Chapter 20

Baumgarten, S., & Langton, T. (2006). *Elementary physical education: Building a solid movement foundation*. Champaign, IL: Stipes.

Boswell, J., Cossey, J., & Oliver, L. (1998). *Creative dance in New Zealand primary schools: A handbook for teachers*. Masterson, NZ: Wairarapa Educational Resource Center.

Cone, T., & Cone, S. (2012) *Teaching children dance*. Champaign, IL: Human Kinetics.

Dead Can Dance. (1988). "Mother Tongue." On *The Serpent's Egg* [CD]. London: 4AD/WEA.

Hanson, M. (1979). The right of children to experiences in dance/movement/arts. *Journal of Physical Education, Recreation and Dance, 50*(7), 41–42.

Hardiman, R. (1998). Above the rainbow. On *Michael Flatley's Feet of Flame* [CD]. Unicorn Entertainments. London: Unicorn.

Housecat, F.D., & Simone, N. (2003). "Sinnerman." On *Verve Remixed2* [CD]. Santa Monica, CA: Verve.

Murray, R. (1975). *Dance in elementary education*. New York: Harper & Row.

National Association for Sport and Physical Education. (2007). PIPEline "Dance Over the Rainbow." Reston: Author.

National Association for Sport and Physical Education & National Dance Association. (2007). *Teaching dance in elementary physical education*. Reston, VA: Author.

National Dance Association. (1994). *National standards for dance education*. Reston, VA: Author.

Nichols, B. (1991). *Creative dance for the primary child: a progressive approach*. In Early Childhood Creative Arts: Proceedings of the International Early Childhood Creative Arts Conference. Reston, Virginia: National Dance Association, 1991. 144-59.

Pittman, A., Wallter, M., & Dark, C. (2009). *Dance a while: A handbook for folk, square, contra, and social dance*. San Francisco: Pearson Benjamin Cummings.

SHAPE America (2014). *National standards and grade-level outcomes for K-12 physical education* (3rd ed.). Champaign, IL: Human Kinetics.

Chapter 21

Gerstung, S. (1974). *10 original tumbling charts*. Baltimore, MD: Gerstung Inter-Sport.

Malmberg, E. (2003). *Kidnastics: A child-centered approach to teaching gymnastics*. Champaign, IL: Human Kinetics.

Nilges, L.M. (1999). Refining skill in educational gymnastics: Seeing quality through variety. *JOPERD 70*(3). 43-48.

SHAPE America. (2014). *National standards and grade-level outcomes for K-12 physical education*. Champaign, IL: Human Kinetics.

Ward, P. (1997). *Teaching tumbling*. Champaign, IL: Human Kinetics.

Werner, P. (1994). *Teaching children gymnastics: Becoming a master teacher*. Champaign, IL: Human Kinetics.

Chapter 22

Ayers, S., & Sariscsany, M.J. (2011). *The Physical Best teacher's guide: Physical education for lifelong fitness* (3rd ed.). Reston, VA: National Association for Sport and Physical Education.

Cooper Institute. (2010). *Fitnessgram & Activitygram test administration manual* (Updated 4th ed.). Champaign, IL: Human Kinetics.

Corbin, C.B., & Le Masurier, G.C. (2014). *Fitness for Life* (6th ed.). Champaign, IL: Human Kinetics.

Corbin, C.B., Le Masurier, G.C., Lambdin, D., & Greiner, M. (2010). *Fitness for Life: Elementary school guide for wellness coordinators*. Champaign, IL: Human Kinetics.

Iowa State University Department of Kinesiology (n.d.). *Summaries of Fitnessgram Research*. www.physicalactivitylab.org/fitnessgram-research.html

Lagally, K. (2013). Using ratings of perceived exertion in physical education. *Journal of Physical Education, Recreation and Dance, 84*(5), 35–39.

Le Masurier, G.C., Corbin, C.B., Greiner, M., & Lambdin, D. (2010). *Fitness for Life: Elementary school physical education lesson plans*. Champaign, IL: Human Kinetics.

Let's Move. (2013). www.letsmove.gov.

Let's Move, Active Schools. (2013). www.letsmoveschools.org/.

National Association for Sport and Physical Education (NASPE). (2009). *Appropriate instructional practice guidelines for elementary school physical education*. Reston, VA: Author.

National Association for Sport and Physical Education (NASPE). (2011). *Physical Best activity guide: Elementary level* (3rd ed.). Champaign, IL: Human Kinetics.

National Association for Sport and Physical Education (NASPE). (2012). *Instructional framework for fitness education*. Reston, VA: NASPE.

Ostbye, T., Malhotra, R., Stroo, M., Lovelady, C., Brouwer, R., Zucker, N., & Fuemmeler, B. (2013). The effect of the home environment on physical activity and dietary intake in preschool children. *International Journal of Obesity*. doi:10.1038/ijo.2013.76.

Physical Activity Guidelines for All Americans Midcourse Report. (2012). U.S. Department of Health and Human Services. http://health.gov/paguidelines/midcourse/pag-midcourse-report-final.pdf.

Pizer, A. (2015). Beginners' yoga pose library. *About Health*. http://yoga.about.com/od/yogaposes/a/beginnersposes.htm.

Presidential Youth Fitness Program. (2013a). About. www.presidentialyouthfitnessprogram.org/about/index.shtml.

Presidential Youth Fitness Program. (2013b). Physical educator resource guide. http://www.pyfp.org/doc/teacher-guide.pdf.

Presidential Youth Fitness Program. (2015). Assessment. www.presidentialyouthfitnessprogram.org/assessment/index.shtml.

SHAPE America. (2014). *National standards and grade-level outcomes for K-12 physical education*. Champaign, IL: Human Kinetics.

U.S. Department of Agriculture. (n.d.). ChooseMyPlate. www.choosemyplate.gov.

Chapter 23

American Alliance for Health, Physical Education, Recreation and Dance. (2013a). *Comprehensive school physical activity programs: Helping all students achieve 60 minutes of physical activity each day* [Position statement]. Reston, VA: Author.

American Alliance for Health, Physical Education, Recreation and Dance. (2013b). New PE standards and outcomes offer more guidance than ever before. *Momentum*. Reston, VA: AAHPERD.

American Heart Association. (2013a). Jump Rope for Heart. www.heart.org/HEARTORG/Giving/ForSchools/ForSchools_UCM_313648_SubHomePage.jsp.

American Heart Association. (2013b). Jump Rope for Heart and Hoops for Heart. http://www.heart.org/idc/groups/heart-public/@wcm/@fdr/documents/downloadable/ucm_457204.pdf.

Centers for Disease Control and Prevention. (2013). *Comprehensive School Physical Activity Programs: A Guide for Schools.* Atlanta, GA: U.S. Department of Health and Human Services.

Council of Chief State School Officers (CCSSO) and National Governors Association (NGA) Center for Best Practices. (2010). *Common Core State Standards Initiative.* www.corestandards.org/resources.

Institute of Medicine Report of the National Academies. (2013). *Educating the student body: Taking physical activity and physical education to school.* www.iom.edu/Reports/2013/Educating-the-Student-Body-Taking-Physical-Activity-and-Physical-Education-to-School.aspx.

Kahn, E.B., Ramsey, L.T., Brownson, R.C, et al. (2002). The effectiveness of interventions to increase physical activity: A systematic review. *American journal of preventive medicine* 35(2). 89-105.

Kreimler, S., Meyer, U., Martin, E., et al. (2011). Effect of school-based interventions on physical activity and fitness in children and adolescents: A review of reviews and systematic update. *British journal of sports medicine.* 45(11) 923-930.

National Association for Sport and Physical Education. (2006). *Recess for elementary school students* [Position statement]. Reston, VA: Author.

Rink, J. (2009). *Designing the physical education curriculum: Promoting active lifestyles.* Boston: McGraw-Hill.

SHAPE America. (2014). *National standards and grade-level outcomes for K-12 physical education.* Champaign, IL: Human Kinetics.

Trudeau, F., & Shephard, R.J. (2005). Contribution of school programmes to physical activity levels and attitudes in children and adults. *Sports medicine.* 35(2) p. 89–105.

van Sluijs E.M., McMinn A.M., & Griffin S.J. (2007). Effectiveness of interventions to promote physical activity in children and adolescents: systematic review of controlled trials. *British Medical Journal.* 335 (7622) 703.

Chapter 24

Mullender-Wijnsma, M., Hartman, E., deFreef, J., Bosker, R., Doolaard, S., & Visscher, C. (2015). Improving academic performance of school-age children by physical activity in the classroom: 1-year program evaluation, *The Journal of School Health.* 85(6), 365-371.

National Association for Sport and Physical Education & American Heart Association. (2012). *Shape of the nation report: Status of physical education in the USA.* Reston, VA: American Alliance for Health, Physical Education, Recreation and Dance.

Phillips, D., James, C., & Castelli, D. (2015). Effects of vigorous intensity physical activity on mathematics test performance. *Journal of Teaching in Physical Education,* 34(3), 346-362.

Psimopoulos, C. (2013). Winning the game of policy at the state and federal levels: First we need to know how to play. *Strategies,* 26(1), 45-46.

SHAPE America. (2009). *National Standards & Guidelines for Physical Education Teacher Education* (3rd ed.). Champaign, IL: Human Kinetics

SHAPE America. (2014a). *National standards and grade-level outcomes for K-12 physical education* (3rd ed.). Champaign, IL: Human Kinetics.

SHAPE America. (2014b). *Physical Activity Leader Learning System.* Reston, VA: Author.

SHAPE America. (2016). *Physical Activity Leader (PAL) Learning System & Training.* www.shapeamerica.org/prodev/workshops/lmas/.

SHAPE America, American Heart Association, & Voices for Healthy Kids. (2016). *Shape of the nation: status of physical education in the USA.* www.shapeamerica.org/advocacy/son/2016/upload/Shape-of-the-Nation-2016_web.pdf.

U.S. Department of Health and Human Services. (2008). *Physical activity guidelines for Americans.* www.health.gov/paguidelines/guidelines/default.aspx.

Index

Index

Note: The italicized *f* and *t* following page numbers refer to figures and tables, respectively.

About the Authors

Frances Cleland Donnelly, PED, is a professor in the department of kinesiology at West Chester University in West Chester, Pennsylvania. She served on the SHAPE America board of directors and has been president of the National Association for Sport and Physical Education and Pennsylvania State AHPERD (now SHAPE America).

Photo courtesy of Caroline Shorey.

Cleland Donnelly has numerous articles in refereed publications and chapters in books, as well as the previous edition of this book, to her credit. She has made many dozens of presentations at the international, national, district, and state levels. In 2014 she was inducted into the North American Society of HPERSD Professionals and has received numerous awards for teaching and service throughout her career.

David L. Gallahue, EdD, is professor emeritus and dean emeritus of the School of Public Health at Indiana University. For over 40 years he was active in the study of the applied aspects of the motor development and movement skill learning of young children and youths in physical activity and sport

Photo courtesy of Indiana University.

settings and is the author of numerous textbooks, book chapters, and journal articles. His work has been translated into Chinese, Farsi, Greek, Japanese, Portuguese, Spanish, and Turkish.

Gallahue has been a visiting professor, guest lecturer, and keynote speaker on more than 300 occasions at universities and at professional conferences in 23 countries. He is a past president of the National Association for Sport and Physical Education and a past chair of the Council on Physical Education for Children and the Motor Development Academy. He is an elected member of the NASPE Hall of Fame, the National Academy of Kinesiology, and the North American Society of HPERSD. He also received the Healthy American Fitness Award in recognition of his work with young children. Gallahue has been recognized nationally and internationally for scholarship and leadership focused on young children and has received honorary professorships at Beijing Sport University and Chengdu Sport University, both in China.

Suzanne S. Mueller, EdD, is professor emeritus in the physical education department at East Stroudsburg University, where she taught and administered graduate and undergraduate programs in physical education teacher education for more than three decades. She specialized in the application of stan-

Photo courtesy of Lifetouch Portrait Studios.

dards-based curriculum alignment and the spectrum of teaching styles, motor development and motor learning theory, and developmentally appropriate content and practices for programs and children in pre-K through elementary physical education.

Dr. Mueller has been a consultant for several university and school district faculty on standards-based alignment of their programs with state and national physical education standards. She has published articles and presented at national and international conferences and evaluated university and school programs for state and national accreditation.

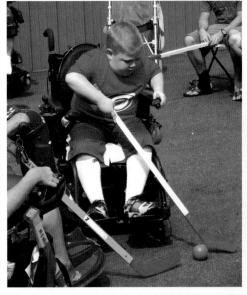

You'll find other outstanding
physical education resources at

www.HumanKinetics.com

In the U.S. call 1.800.747.4457
Australia. 08 8372 0999
Canada. 1.800.465.7301
Europe . . . .+44 (0) 113 255 5665
New Zealand 0800 222 062

HUMAN KINETICS
The Information Leader in Physical Activity
P.O. Box 5076 - Champaign, IL 61825-5076